Small Business Management

Portland Community College

Custom Edition

Justin G. Longenecker | J. William Petty
Leslie E. Palich | Frank Hoy

CENGAGE
Learning

Australia • Brazil • Japan • Korea • Mexico • Singapore • Spain • United Kingdom • United States

Small Business Management, Portland Community College, Custom Edition

Small Business Management: Launching and Growing Entrepreneurial Ventures, 17th Edition
Justin G. Longenecker | J. William Petty | Leslie E. Palich | Frank Hoy

© 2014, 2012 Cengage Learning. All rights reserved.

> For product information and technology assistance, contact us at
> **Cengage Learning Customer & Sales Support, 1-800-354-9706**
>
> For permission to use material from this text or product, submit all requests online at **cengage.com/permissions**
> Further permissions questions can be emailed to
> **permissionrequest@cengage.com**

This book contains select works from existing Cengage Learning resources and was produced by Cengage Learning Custom Solutions for collegiate use. As such, those adopting and/or contributing to this work are responsible for editorial content accuracy, continuity and completeness.

Compilation © 2015 Cengage Learning

ISBN: 9781305745889

WCN: 01-100-101

Cengage Learning
20 Channel Center Street
Boston, MA 02210
USA

Cengage Learning is a leading provider of customized learning solutions with office locations around the globe, including Singapore, the United Kingdom, Australia, Mexico, Brazil, and Japan. Locate your local office at: **www.international.cengage.com/region.**

Cengage Learning products are represented in Canada by Nelson Education, Ltd.

For your lifelong learning solutions, visit **www.cengage.com/custom.**

Visit our corporate website at **www.cengage.com.**

Brief Contents

Appendices A and B are available online. The online appendices can be accessed by going to www.CenageBrain.com and selecting the Longenecker text.

Appendix A   **Sample Business Plan**

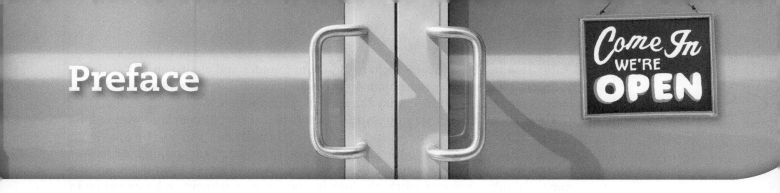

Preface

Welcome to the 17th edition of *Small Business Management: Launching and Growing Entrepreneurial Ventures*, which continues to be the leading textbook in the field of small business management. As its authors, we believe that the reason for its success is our decision to take on each new edition as though we were writing the book for the very first time. By doing so, we are certain that you will be provided with the best and most recent advice on running your business.

We completely agree with the age-old saying that you can't know a book by its cover. But you can learn a lot about a textbook and its success simply by knowing how many students have chosen to keep it rather than sell it back to a bookstore at the end of a semester. In the case of *Small Business Management*, a large number of students have made it a part of their permanent library. As one student explained, "*Small Business Management* is one of the few books from my college days that I have kept for future reference."

> *I didn't realize how hard it was to run a small business.*
>
> **Andrew Mason,**
> **former CEO of Groupon**
>
> Andrew Mason, the founder of Groupon, is featured in the case for Chapter 3. Even though Mason created the company, he was eventually fired by the board. He clearly had a creative idea but discovered too late that building and running a successful business require more than having a good idea—a concept, along with many others, that you will understand more fully after reading *Small Business Management: Launching & Growing Entrepreneurial Ventures*.

Why do so many consider the book to be a "keeper?" We believe that they find in its pages practical ways of thinking and acting that help them achieve their dream of starting and building successful enterprises. For example, readers have described how the chapters on finance helped them to understand financial statements and to make better decisions based on that information. Others have said that the business plan chapter, with the real-life examples it presents, provides an excellent guide for writing their own plans. Finally, many describe how the chapters on managing the business have kept them from making the kinds of mistakes that Andrew Mason (see sidebar above) and others have made.

Small Business Management lays out, in a step-by-step fashion the knowledge and insights needed to lead and manage a small business. Our aim is to provide instruction and guidance that will greatly improve your odds for success as you take your own entrepreneurial journey. In this edition, we present the best information available today about launching and growing small businesses. Furthermore, we offer examples throughout the text to demonstrate that there is not a single path to success. The goal is to help you to find one that will work best for you.

It is our hope that the information presented in this book—and in the ancillaries that accompany it—will support the varied goals of those seeking independent business careers, either directly or indirectly. Most of all, we encourage you to continue learning every day, building on the foundation provided by this text. This advice is supported by the words of Richard Branson, founder and chairman of the Virgin Group, which comprises more than 400 companies: "My biggest motivation? Just to keep challenging myself. Everyday I'm learning something new."

Throughout the text, we emphasize the importance of building relationships along the way. Managing a business is a team sport. As the owner, you will be the key to making the basket, reaching the goal line, crossing home plate, jumping the net (or whatever analogy you want to use)—but you cannot do it alone. Even if you are the company's only employee, working alone in your own apartment or basement or in your parents' garage, you still have relationships with and depend on others, including your family, a banker, a former professor, and/or a key customer or supplier. You must be effective in your relationships with other people, including those you don't control. The bottom line: You cannot accomplish anything of any real significance by yourself!

Follow Your Dreams

As you will see, *Small Business Management* is focused on teaching you the essential concepts and building skills that you will need to grow and manage a business successfully. It also focuses on a much broader concern—the pursuit of entrepreneurial dreams. Entrepreneurs build businesses to fulfill dreams—for themselves, their families, their employees, and their communities. Your journey will always be about more than the money. Entrepreneurs are individuals whose business lives have an impact on a wide range of people. For most, what they do matters.

Many students enroll in colleges and universities to gain qualifications that help them to get a job. In fact, most colleges spend the bulk of the curriculum teaching students how to work for someone else. But the best way to achieve your goals, no matter what your major is, may be through owning a business of your own. If so, why not make it something special, something that solves a problem, that makes life better for others, that builds wealth while at the same time providing a way for you to give back to your community and to nonprofit organizations that you believe in.

There are definite advantages to working initially for someone else. It may allow you to learn an industry, build relationships, and develop important skills for the future. But many individuals choose to start their own company early in life:

- Michael Dell started assembling computer parts and selling personal computers when he was a pre-med student at the University of Texas.
- Fred DeLuca opened a submarine sandwich shop when he was 17 years old to earn money to pay his tuition at the University of Bridgeport. Today, his company, SUBWAY, has more locations worldwide than any other franchise organization.
- Jeremy Hitchcock started Dyn, a global leader in software as a service (SaaS), when he was a management information systems major at Worcester Polytechnic Institute. (Chapter 16, "Pricing and Credit Decisions," and the case for the chapter present more information about this company.)

Our best wishes to you for a challenging and successful learning experience!

This list could go on for pages. We all know entrepreneurs and small business owners who will not be the next Bill Gates but who will build or already own small businesses that create value and make a difference in the community. These small companies are the heart and soul of our economy. We challenge you to give serious thought to joining them— and if you do, *dream big*. Follow a dream that you really care about, and enjoy a life that you truly want to live!

What's New?

A primary purpose of *Small Business Management* is to present current, relevant content in unique and interesting ways, drawing on an abundance of real-world examples to keep the reader totally engaged. Thus, the 17th edition of *Small Business Management* offers plenty that's new, including the following:

- A host of misconceptions about becoming a small business owner can cause you to give up your entrepreneurial dream. We have revised Chapter 1, "The Entrepreneurial Life," to help you better understand your motivations for starting a business and to avoid distorted concepts about what is required for you to be an effective business owner. Getting off on the right foot is critical to your success.

- Social entrepreneurship has become a major topic in entrepreneurial circles, both in practice and on college campuses. Recognizing this trend, Chapter 1 introduces some of the important issues when considering the launch of a socially oriented enterprise. We have also included examples of socially minded entrepreneurs, such as Amy George at BlueAvocado and Robert Hennessy at DashLocker.

- Prioritizing a small business owner's responsibilities to major stakeholders can be difficult. With that in mind, Chapter 2, "Integrity and Ethics: Foundations for Success in Small Business," now presents a framework (adapted from the writings of ethics and morality scholar Archie Carroll) for managing stakeholder considerations as a unified whole, which will help owners to determine how to balance stakeholder interests.

- We are thrilled to announce an optional course add-on from Business Plan Pro, the unquestioned leader in business planning software. Its new *LivePlan* has interactive features that guide you through the writing process in ways not previously available.

- We provide a new example of a complete business plan on the Longenecker website (www.cengagebrain.com) that was used successfully in raising capital from investors.

- Locating small businesses on the Internet continues to grow. Chapter 9, "The Location Plan," includes an expanded section on effective models of e-commerce and emerging options that can lead to new business opportunities for online entrepreneurs.

- In a previous edition, we improved the presentation of financial statements and the preparation of financial forecasts for small businesses (in Chapter 10, "Understanding a Firm's Financial Statements," and Chapter 11, "Forecasting Financial Requirements"). Our goal was to make the material more logical for the reader to follow. We have continued to build on this approach in the 17th edition in order to make the material even easier to grasp. Bill Petty, the co-author who wrote these chapters, invites any instructor using the text to contact him for suggestions or assistance in teaching these chapters. Just call him directly (254-710-2260) or e-mail him (bill_petty@ baylor.edu).

- Updated information on raising capital to grow a business, including best practices for raising money on the Internet (or what is called *crowdfunding*), is provided in Chapter 12, "A Firm's Sources of Financing." But stay tuned: New regulations are being prepared by the Securities and Exchange Commission that may significantly change how entrepreneurs can raise capital from the public.

- Because of the importance of establishing and improving relationships with customers, and the development of new and more sophisticated tools to make this more manageable, the sections on creating and using customer data in Chapter 14, "Building Customer Relationships," have been greatly expanded. These sections now offer more practical instruction on CRM methods that make sense for small businesses, regardless of the level of sophistication. Privacy issues related to the use of customers' personal data are also addressed in more detail.

- Small business owners are discovering that social media can offer cost-effective ways of getting their message out. They are also learning that more and more customers rely on social media to make buying decisions. With this in mind, Chapter 17, "Promotional Planning," has been rewritten to place far greater emphasis on social media marketing strategies.

- Legal regulations of human resource management practices continue to become more complicated. For this reason, Chapter 20, "Managing Human Resources," has been revised to provide helpful information for entrepreneurs who wish to hire employees, including updated descriptions of relevant employment laws, an outline of limitations that apply to interview questioning, and other issues related to compliance in hiring practices.

- The world of health care and insurance provided by small businesses is undergoing major changes. Chapter 23, "Managing Risk in the Small Business," has been revised to show you how to adjust to these changes.

- Updated Living the Dream features in each chapter capture entrepreneurs in action as they face the challenges of small business and entrepreneurship. The authors' personal conversations and correspondence with many of the entrepreneurs profiled add depth to these features and ensure accuracy.

- New cases have been added to the case section at the end of the text, including DashLocker, The Kollection, the Avedis Zildjian Company (the oldest family business in the United States), Hyper Wear, and Auntie Anne's Pretzels in China. These and other relevant cases provide opportunities for students to apply chapter concepts to entrepreneurial situations in a realistic and timely way. Because reaction to the video cases added in the 16th edition was so positive, we decided to retain them in this edition.

- In addition to the cases appearing in the book, many others, old and new, are available on the Longenecker website (www.cengagebrain.com).

Achieving Your Best

Small Business Management is organized to help students and future entrepreneurs achieve success in whatever field they choose. The wide spectrum of content, applications, cases, graphics, stories, and other details offered in *Small Business Management* has assisted many small business entrepreneurs in making their dreams come true. With a focus on learning, our features emphasize activities that capture student interest and guarantee practical knowledge, including the following:

- **In the Spotlight.** The chapter-opening "In the Spotlight" feature profiles an amazing collection of entrepreneurs, whose unique insights into how to start, run, and grow a business will help readers identify and explore the full range of issues facing today's business owners. More than half of the spotlights are video enriched, because nothing helps students master the lessons of small business and entrepreneurship as much as seeing those lessons put into practice.

- **Unique Support for Building a Business Plan.** The material in Part 3, "Developing the New Venture Business Plan," is integral to learning how to develop workable plans. Closely aligned with the approaches to planning that we present in the textbook, additional business plan templates can be found in *Small Business Management Online* (www.cengagebrain.com).

- **Integrated Learning System.** Our integrated learning system uses each chapter's learning objectives to give structure and coherence to the text content, study aids, and instructor's ancillaries, all of which are keyed to these objectives. The numbered objectives are introduced in the "Looking Ahead" section, and each is concisely addressed in the "Looking Back" section at the end of each chapter. The integrated learning system also simplifies lecture and test preparation. The lecture notes in the *Instructor's Manual* are grouped by learning objective and identify the PowerPoint® slides that relate to each objective. Questions in the *Test Bank* are grouped by objective as well. A correlation table at the beginning of each *Test Bank* chapter permits selection of questions that cover all objectives or that emphasize objectives considered most important by individual instructors.

- **You Make the Call.** "You Make the Call" sections at the end of each chapter are very popular with both students and instructors because they present realistic business situations that require the examination of key operating decisions. By having students take on the role of a small business owner, these exercises give them a leg up in addressing issues facing small businesses.

- **Living the Dream.** Practical examples from the world of small business and entrepreneurship carry both instructional and inspirational value. "Living the Dream" boxes appear at critical junctures throughout the chapters, refueling and refreshing chapter concepts with documented experiences of practicing entrepreneurs.

- **STARTUPS.** The "STARTUP" feature highlights useful entrepreneurial tools, actions, and resources for new businesses, as well as ways to transform the ventures. These boxes are interspersed throughout the chapters in appropriate settings.

- **Video Cases.** Actual interviews with small business owners and entrepreneurs bring together high-interest video segments and in-text case material. Case instruction augmented by video filmed on location in diverse businesses such as TWO MEN AND A TRUCK, PortionPac Chemicals, Cookies-N-Cream, *ReadyMade* Magazine, and other entrepreneurial success stories makes studying effective small business management all the more interesting.

- **Small Business & Entrepreneurship Resource Center (SBERC) Exercises.** Each chapter includes an exercise that directs the student to a current article in the Gale database about topics covered in the chapter.

Updated and Enhanced Supplements

All resources and ancillaries that accompany *Small Business Management,* 17th edition, have been created to support a variety of teaching methods, learning styles, and classroom situations.

- **Instructor's Manual.** Lecture notes in the *Instructor's Manual* are grouped by learning objective and tied to PowerPoint slides that relate to each objective. The manual also contains sources of audio/video and other instructional materials, answers to the "Discussion Questions," comments on "You Make the Call" situations, and teaching notes for the cases. This edition's *Instructor's Manual* has been revised by Patricia Worsham of Cal Poly Pomona. It is available on the text website (www.cengagebrain.com) and on the *Instructor's Resource* CD (IRCD).

- **Test Bank.** The *Test Bank* has been revised by Carol Heeter of Ivy Technical Community College. Questions in the *Test Bank* are grouped by learning objectives and include true/false, multiple-choice, and discussion questions. Metadata tags are attached to each question. The *Test Bank* in Word is available on the *Instructor's Resource* CD (IRCD).

- **ExamView® Testing Software.** ExamView contains all of the questions in the printed *Test Bank*. This easy-to-use test-creation software program is compatible with Microsoft Windows®. Instructors can add or edit questions, instructions, and answers. Questions may be chosen by previewing them on screen, selecting them randomly, or selecting them by number. Instructors can also create quizzes online, either on the Internet, a local area network (LAN), or a wide area network (WAN).

- **PowerPoint® for Instructors.** A complete PowerPoint package is available to aid in lecture presentation. The PowerPoint slides, revised by Charlie Cook of the University of West Alabama, are available on both the IRCD and the password-protected instructor's website.

- **Instructor's Resource CD.** Instructors can get quick access to all of these ancillaries from the easy-to-use *Instructor's Resource* CD (IRCD) that lets the user electronically review, edit, and copy what's needed. The IRCD contains the *Instructor's Manual, Test Bank* in Microsoft Word and in ExamView, PowerPoint slides, and business plan templates.

- **"Startup Stories" Videos.** Available online through CourseMate, CengageNow, and MindTap sites, 17 videos created for this text let you in on some very big ideas at work in a variety of innovative small businesses. Some of the small businesses covered include *ReadyMade* Magazine, TWO MEN AND A TRUCK, River Pools & Spas, and Graeter's Ice Cream, among many others. Use these videos to bring the real world into your classroom, and let your students learn from the experts.

- **Small Business & Entrepreneurship Resource Center.** The Small Business & Entrepreneurship Resource Center (SBERC) from Gale, a part of Cengage Learning and a leader in e-research for libraries and schools, can be accessed through CourseMate and directs students to 900,000 published full-text articles directly related to small business management. These articles are easily searchable by business topic, business type, and commonly asked how-to questions. This powerful resource also includes access to hundreds of sample business plans and the legal forms necessary to start a new venture in every state. Powered by InfoTrac, the how-to section provides direct access to the most popular topics and questions students have about starting and running a small business.

- **CengageNow.** This robust, online course management system gives you more control in less time and delivers better student outcomes. CengageNOW includes teaching and learning resources organized around lecturing, creating assignments, grading, quizzing, and tracking student progress and performance. Automatic grading and a gradebook option provide more control while saving you valuable time. A "Personalized Study" diagnostic tool empowers students to master concepts, prepare for exams, and become more involved in class.

- *LivePlan®.* Students can now learn how to use the award-winning, best-selling professional software *LivePlan* to create a business plan. This online resource provides all the essentials to create winning business plans, including step-by-step instructions for preparing each section of a plan. Ready-to-customize samples, advice, a detailed marketing analysis with links to demographic and marketing tools, and helpful financial tools make it easy to create a solid plan. Video and written tutorials from Palo Alto Software founder Tim Berry ensure that students fully understand how to maximize *LivePlan*'s dynamic tools

- *Write Experience.* Cengage Learning's Write Experience helps students write effectively without adding to instructor workload! Write Experience utilizes artificial intelligence to score student writing instantly and accurately. It also provides students with detailed revision goals and feedback on their writing to help them improve written communication and critical thinking skills. Write Experience is the first product designed and created specifically for the higher education market through an exclusive agreement with McCann Associates, a Vantage Learning Affiliated operating company, and also powered by e-Write IntelliMetric Within™.

- *MindTap.* MindTap is a fully online, highly personalized learning experience built upon Cengage Learning content. MindTap combines student learning tools—readings, multimedia, activities and assessments—into a singular Learning Path that guides students through their course. Instructors personalize the experience by customizing authoritative Cengage Learning content and learning tools, including the ability to add their own content in the Learning Path via apps that integrate into the MindTap framework seamlessly with Learning Management Systems.

Special Thanks and Acknowledgments

There are numerous individuals to whom we owe a debt of gratitude for their assistance in making this project a reality. In particular, we thank our friends—and we mean *good friends*—at Cengage Learning. We are especially indebted to Michele Rhoades, Jason Fremder, Julia Chase, Tim Bailey, and word master Jeanne Yost. Without them, this book would exist only in our heads! They are amazing when it comes to coordination and motivation, keeping us on track and moving forward. Besides all that, they let us have a little fun along the way. They are just wonderful people, and they take seriously their roles in making certain that *Small Business Management* continues its tradition of excellence.

Others who worked on various aspects of the book also deserve our thanks: our designer, Stacy Shirley; our marketing guru, Robin Lefevre; and media editors Courtney Bavaro and Sally Nieman. We also offer our thanks to Mary Abrahams, David Allen, Lauren Houser, Brett Harper, and Dallena Nguyen for their careful review of selected chapters, which means fewer errors for readers to encounter.

We also want to offer words of appreciation and acknowledgment to Wes Bailey, who was a contributing author of Chapter 23, "Managing Risk in the Small Business." Mr. Bailey is president of Bailey Insurance and Risk Management, Inc., in Waco,

Texas, and is well recognized as a leader in the industry. His assistance with the authorship of this chapter should assure readers that they are receiving timely and relevant information about risk management. And we thank Bradley Norris, a colleague and lecturer at Baylor University, for his suggestions regarding Chapter 21, "Managing Operations." Finally, we thank Brian Lovin at Baylor University for assisting us with our research and for his contribution to the writing of some of the cases.

A talented team of writers contributed an outstanding set of ancillary materials. Special thanks go to Carol Heeter of Ivy Tech Community College for her revision of the *Test Bank*, and to Patricia Worsham of Cal Poly Pomona for her preparation of the *Instructor's Manual*. We offer our thanks as well to Charlie Cook, of the University of West Alabama, who created the PowerPoint slides.

Finally, we offer heartfelt appreciation for the understanding and patient support of our wives—Donna, Dianna, and Patricia—during this process. Their faithful encouragement made the arduous task of bringing our best to this edition all the more manageable.

For their insightful comments and thoughtful suggestions, which helped to shape this edition, we are grateful to the following reviewers:

J. David Allen
Baylor University
Dr. Jeffrey Alstete
Iona College
David Ambrosini
Cabrillo College
Mark Andreasen
Northwest College
Kimberly Asonevich
Mount Aloysius College
Chandler Atkins
Adirondack Community College
Barrett Baebler
Webster University
Lee Baldwin
University of Mary Hardin-Baylor
Francis B. Ballard
Florida Community College
Andrea Balsamo
Consumnes River College
Hilton Barrett
Elizabeth City State University
Melissa Baucus
University of Louisville
Bill Bauer
Carroll University
Verona K. Beguin
Black Hills State University
Narendra C. Bhandari
Pace University
Greg Bier
Stephens College

Karl Binns
University of Maryland Eastern Shore
Karen Bishop
University of Louisville
Ross Blankenship
State Fair Community College
John Boos
Ohio Wesleyan University
Marvin Borgelt
University of Mary Hardin-Baylor
Steven Bradley
Austin Community College
Don B. Bradley III
University of Central Arkansas
Margaret Britt
Eastern Nazarene College
Mark Brosthoff
Indiana University
Penelope Stohn Brouwer
Mount Ida College
Rochelle R. Brunson
Alvin Community College
Kevin Chen
County College of Morris
Felipe Chia
Harrisburg Area Community College
Mike Cicero
Highline Community College
Edward G. Cole
St. Mary's University

Michael D. Cook
Hocking College
Roy A. Cook
Fort Lewis College
George R. Corbett
St. Thomas Aquinas College
Brad Cox
Midlands Technical College
Karen Cranford
Catawba College
George W. Crawford
Clayton College & State University
Bruce Davis
Weber State University
Helen Davis
Jefferson Community College
Terri Davis
Howard College
Bill Demory
Central Arizona College
Michael Deneen
Baker College
Sharon Dexler
Southeast Community College
Warren Dorau
Nicolet College
Max E. Douglas
Indiana State University
Bonnie Ann Dowd
Palomar College
Michael Drafke
College of Dupage

Franklin J. Elliot
Dine College
Franceen Fallett
Ventura College
R. Brian Fink
Danville Area Community College
Dennette Foy
Edison College
David W. Frantz
Purdue University
Janice S. Gates
Western Illinois University
Armand Gilinsky, Jr.
Sonoma State University
Darryl Goodman
Trident Technical College
William Grace
Missouri Valley College
William W. Graff
*Maharishi University
of Management*
Jack Griggs
Texas Heritage Bank
Mark Hagenbuch
*University of North Carolina,
Greensboro*
Carol Harvey
Assumption College
James R. Hindman
Northeastern University
Betty Hoge
Limestone College
Eddie Hufft
Alcorn State University
Sherrie Human
Xavier University
Ralph Jagodka
Mt. San Antonio College
Larry K. Johansen
Park University
Michael Judge
Hudson Valley Community College
Mary Beth Klinger
College of Southern Maryland
Charles W. Kulmann
Columbia College of Missouri
Rosemary Lafragola
University of Texas at El Paso
William Laing
Anderson College
Ann Langlois
Palm Beach Atlantic University

Rob K. Larson
Mayville State University
David E. Laurel
South Texas Community College
Alecia N. Lawrence
Williamsburg Technical College
Les Ledger
Central Texas College
Michael G. Levas
Carroll University
Richard M. Lewis
Lansing Community College
Thomas W. Lloyd
*Westmoreland County
Community College*
Elaine Madden
Anne Arundel Community College
Kristina Mazurak
Albertson College
James J. Mazza
Middlesex Community College
Lisa McConnell
Oklahoma State University
Richard McEuen
Crowley's Ridge College
Angela Mitchell
Wilmington College
Frank Mitchell
Limestone College
Douglas Moesel
University of Missouri-Columbia
Michael K. Mulford
*Des Moines Area Community
College*
Bernice M. Murphy
University of Maine at Machias
Eugene Muscat
University of San Francisco
John J. Nader
Grand Valley State University
Marc Newman
Hocking College
Charles "Randy" Nichols
Sullivan University
Robert D. Nixon
University of Louisville
Marcella M. Norwood
University of Houston
Mark Nygren
Brigham Young University-Idaho
Donalus A. Okhomina, Sr.
Jackson State University

Rosa L. Okpara
Albany State University
Timothy O'Leary
*Mount Wachusett Community
College*
Pamela Onedeck
*University of Pittsburgh at
Greensburg*
Dick Petitte
*SUNY Brockport & Monroe
Community College*
Claire Phillips
North Harris College
Dean Pielstick
Northern Arizona University
Mark S. Poulos
St. Edward's University
Julia Truitt Poynter
Transylvania University
Fred Pragasam
University of North Florida
Thomas Pressly
Penn State-Shenango
Mary Ellen Rosetti
*Hudson Valley Community
College*
June N. Roux
*Delaware Technical and
Community College*
Jaclyn Rundle
Central College
John K. Sands
Western Washington University
Craig Sarine
Lee University
Duane Schecter
Muskegon Community College
Joseph A. Schubert
*Delaware Technical and
Community College*
Matthew Semadeni
Texas A&M University
Marjorie Shapiro
Myers University
Sherry L. Shuler
American River College
Cindy Simerly
Lakeland Community College
James Sisk
Gaston College
Victoria L. Sitter
Milligan College

Bernard Skown
Stevens Institute of Technology
Kristin L. H. Slyter
Valley City State University
William E. Smith
Ferris State University
Bill Snider
Cuesta College
Roger Stanford
Chippewa Valley Technical College
George Starbuck
McMurry University
Phil Stetz
Stephen F. Austin State University
Johnny Stites
J&S Construction
Peter L. Stone
Spartanburg Technical College
John Streibich
Monroe Community College
Ram Subramanian
Montclair State University

James Swenson
*Minnesota State University
Moorhead*
Ruth Tarver
West Hills Community College
Paul B. Thacker
Macomb Community College
Darrell Thompson
Mountain View College
Melodie M. Toby
Kean University
Charles N. Toftoy
George Washington University
Charles Torti
Schreiner University
Gerald R. Turner
Limestone College
Barry L. Van Hook
Arizona State University
Brian Wahl
*North Shore Community
College*

Mike Wakefield
University of Southern California
Charles F. Warren
Salem State College
Bill Waxman
Edison Community College
Janet Wayne
Baker College
Charles Wellen
Fitchburg State College
Nat B. White, Jr.
South Piedmont Community College
Jim Whitlock
Brenau University
Ira Wilsker
Lamar Institute of Technology
Patricia A. Worsham
Cal Poly Pomona

To the Instructor

As a final word of appreciation, we express our sincere thanks to the many instructors who use our text in both academic and professional settings. Based on years of teaching and listening to other teachers and students, *Small Business Management* has been designed to meet the needs of its readers. And we continue to listen and make changes in the text. Please write or call us to offer suggestions to help us make the book even better for future readers. Our contact information is Bill Petty (254-710-2260, bill_petty@baylor.edu), Les Palich (254-710-6194, les_palich@baylor.edu), and Frank Hoy (508-831-4998, fhoy@wpi.edu). We would love to hear from you.

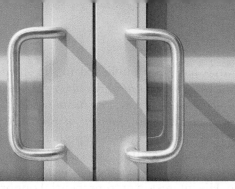

About the Authors

JUSTIN G. LONGENECKER Justin G. Longenecker's authorship of *Small Business Management* began with the first edition of this book. He authored a number of books and numerous articles in such journals as *Journal of Small Business Management, Academy of Management Review, Business Horizons,* and *Journal of Business Ethics.* He was active in several professional organizations and served as president of the International Council for Small Business. Dr. Longenecker grew up in a family business. After attending Central Christian College of Kansas for two years, he went on to earn his B.A. in political science from Seattle Pacific University, his M.B.A. from Ohio State University, and his Ph.D. from the University of Washington. He taught at Baylor University, where he was Emeritus Chavanne Professor of Christian Ethics in Business until his death in 2005.

J. WILLIAM PETTY J. William "Bill" Petty is Professor of Finance and the W. W. Caruth Chairholder in Entrepreneurship at Baylor University and the first Executive Director of the Baylor Angel Network. He holds a Ph.D. and an M.B.A. from the University of Texas at Austin and a B.S. from Abilene Christian University. He has taught at Virginia Tech University and Texas Tech University and served as dean of the business school at Abilene Christian University. He has taught entrepreneurship and small business courses in China, the Ukraine, Kazakhstan, Indonesia, Thailand, and Russia. Dr. Petty has been designated a Master Teacher at Baylor and was named the National Entrepreneurship Teacher of the Year in 2008 by the Acton Foundation for Excellence in Entrepreneurship. His research interests include acquisitions of privately held companies, shareholder value-based management, the financing of small and entrepreneurial firms, angel financing, and exit strategies for privately held firms. He has served as co-editor for the *Journal of Financial Research* and as editor of the *Journal of Entrepreneurial Finance.* He has published articles in a number of finance journals and is the co-author of a leading corporate finance textbook, *Foundations of Finance.* He is a co-author of *Value-Based Management in an Era of Corporate Social Responsibility* (Oxford University Press, 2010). Dr. Petty has worked as a consultant for oil and gas firms and consumer product companies. He also served as a subject-matter expert on a best-practices study by the American Productivity and Quality Center on the topic of shareholder value-based management. He was a member of a research team sponsored by the Australian Department of Industry to study the feasibility of establishing a public equity market for small- and medium-size enterprises in Australia. Finally, he serves as the audit chair for a publicly traded energy firm.

LESLIE E. PALICH Leslie E. "Les" Palich is Professor of Management and Entrepreneurship and the W.A. Mays Professor of Entrepreneurship at Baylor University, where he teaches courses in small business management, international entrepreneurship, strategic management, and international management to undergraduate and graduate students in the Hankamer School of Business. He is also Associate Director of the Entrepreneurship Studies program at Baylor. Dr. Palich holds a Ph.D. and an M.B.A. from Arizona State University and a B.A. from Manhattan Christian College.

His research has been published in the *Academy of Management Review, Strategic Management Journal, Entrepreneurship Theory & Practice, Journal of Business Venturing, Journal of International Business Studies, Journal of Management, Journal of Organizational Behavior, Journal of Small Business Management,* and several other periodicals. He has taught entrepreneurship and strategic management in a host of overseas settings, including Austria, Costa Rica, the Czech Republic, Germany, Italy, Switzerland, Cuba, France, the Netherlands, the United Kingdom, and the Dominican Republic. His interest in entrepreneurial opportunity and small business management dates back to his grade school years, when he set up a produce sales business to experiment with small business ownership. That early experience became a springboard for a number of other enterprises. Since that time, he has owned and operated domestic ventures in agribusiness, automobile sales, real estate development, and educational services, as well as an international import business. Dr. Palich currently owns and operates Lead Generation X, an Internet marketing firm that employs cutting-edge promotional methods to serve its clients and their customers.

FRANK HOY Frank Hoy is the Paul R. Beswick Professor of Innovation and Entrepreneurship in the School of Business at Worcester Polytechnic Institute. Dr. Hoy, who was previously director of the Centers for Entrepreneurial Development, Advancement, Research and Support at the University of Texas at El Paso (UTEP), also serves as director of the Collaborative for Entrepreneurship & Innovation (CEI), in WPI's nationally ranked entrepreneurship program in the School of Business. He joined the WPI faculty in August 2009. He holds a B.B.A. from the University of Texas at El Paso, an M.B.A. from the University of North Texas, and a Ph.D. in management from Texas A&M University. He spent 10 years as a faculty member in the Department of Management at the University of Georgia, where he founded and directed the Center for Business and Economic Studies, coordinated the entrepreneurship curriculum, and served as state director of the Georgia Small Business Development Center. In 1991, he returned to El Paso, Texas, to join UTEP as a professor of management and entrepreneurship and dean of the College of Business Administration. Dr. Hoy is a past president of the United States Association for Small Business and Entrepreneurship and past chair of the Entrepreneurship Division of the Academy of Management. He is president of the Family Enterprise Research Conference and a member of the global board of directors of STEP, the Successful Transgenerational Entrepreneurship Practices project. His research has appeared in the *Academy of Management Journal, Academy of Management Review, Journal of Business Venturing,* and *Family Business Review,* and he is a past editor of *Entrepreneurship Theory and Practice.*

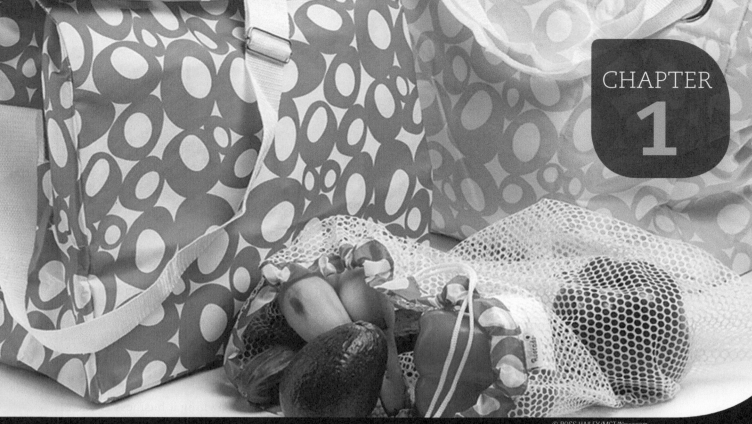

The Entrepreneurial Life

For three women in Austin, Texas, starting a business was more than personal ambition; it was about inviting millions to take simple steps to reduce their impact on the planet by making it easy to "do good and get it done." In 2008, those words became the mission statement of founders Melissa Nathan, Paige Davis, and Amy George, and BlueAvocado was born. Since its inception, the company has helped to upcycle 875, 000 plastic bottles into beautiful products that are keeping 70 million disposables out of landfills and oceans.

In 2008, San Francisco became the first city in the country to ban plastic bags, highlighting the environmental consequences of a disposable lifestyle. Retailers IKEA and Whole Foods led the retailer pack, banning plastic bags and offering rebates to customers. Sisters Nathan and Davis keyed in on this lifestyle transformation, developing the country's first reusable, multifunctional shopping kit to meet the needs of the American shopper.

In the SPOTLIGHT
BlueAvocado
www.blueavocado.com

After a failed prototype, the company honed its shoppingkit product offering, and by the end of 2008, it had secured its first orders from Whole Foods Southwest Region and HEB Grocers for a pilot program. These beginning efforts led to 8 regions and 180 Whole Foods stores adopting BlueAvocado's products. In March 2009, the company landed key placements at specialty grocery and flagship retailers like Nieman Marcus, Home Shopping Network, Amazon.com, and Drugstore.com.

By 2011, BlueAvocado had expanded its product portfolio to include lunch kits, washable Ziploc replacement bags, recycling bins, and eco-travel and eco-beauty items. In 2012, the company launched its green rewards iPhone app with Whole

OPEN LOOKING AHEAD

After studying this chapter, you should be able to...

1-1. Explain the importance of small business and entrepreneurship in our society.

1-2. Distinguish between the terms *small business* and *entrepreneurial opportunity*.

1-3. Explain the basic characteristics of entrepreneurs, and describe different kinds of entrepreneurship.

1-4. Discuss the importance of understanding your motivations and perceptions related to owning a small business.

1-5. Describe five potential competitive advantages of small entrepreneurial companies over large firms.

1-6. Explain the concept of an entrepreneurial legacy and its challenges.

Foods and the Whole Planet Foundation, rewarding shoppers who actively buy green with coupons that can be used or donated to the foundation. In Amy George's words,

Since day one, we have put an impact label on every single product that shows you the difference you make by reducing your ecological footprint. We also created a sustainability report in line with international standards, which may make us the earliest-stage, privately held company (possibly in the world) to do this. Our business is about impact, measuring what matters, and inspiring others by sharing the potential we have to create a better world if we look at our products and actions differently.

BlueAvocado represents a new kind of company whose long-term value will be measured not only by the return to its shareholders, but by its contribution to the lives of the people on its journey and the ability to preserve precious natural resources.

Source: Written by Amy George, CEO, BlueAvocado, October 15, 2012.

Having worked for four decades with both entrepreneurs and students who aspire to own companies, we have designed this book to prepare you for owning your own small business—one that may even grow over time to become a large firm. In addition, we will be drawing on the extensive experience of entrepreneurs who offer their advice and counsel on important issues. Understand that this book is not just about learning facts; rather, we want to prepare you to act on your dreams.

Let us say at the very beginning that we believe that owning a business is one of the most noble of all professions—*especially if done well*. No other life's work does more to help you learn and develop as a person, contribute to the success of a team, create value for customers, and make a significant difference in the community. While owning a business is generally about producing a product or service and selling it for a profit, you will find that the deepest rewards of entrepreneurship come from helping your employees grow, both professionally and personally, and offering goods or services that improve the lives of your customers. After all, what happens at work carries over into your personal life.[1]

The primary purpose of this chapter is to offer words of encouragement for anyone wanting to be a small business owner. We will begin the chapter by providing an overview of small business and entrepreneurship, along with stories of entrepreneurs who started and grew businesses. Then we will quickly get you started thinking about your motivations and perceptions related to owning a small business. Next, we will explain the ways small firms can be competitive, even against industry giants. Finally, we want you to think about building an entrepreneurial legacy that you can leave to those who follow in your footsteps.

The entrepreneurs and owners of small businesses are some of our greatest heroes. We believe that the words of Theodore Roosevelt, when he described "the man in the arena," apply perfectly to these individuals:

It is not the critic who counts; not the man who points out how the strong man stumbles, or where the doer of deeds could have done them better. The credit belongs to the man who is actually in the arena, whose face is marred by dust and sweat and blood; who strives valiantly; who errs, who comes short again and again, because there is not effort without error and shortcomings; but who does actually strive to do the deeds; who knows great enthusiasms, the great devotions, who spends himself in a worthy cause; who at the best knows in the end the triumph of high achievement, and who at the worst, if he fails, at least fails while daring greatly, so that his place shall never be with those cold and timid souls who neither know victory nor defeat.[2]

So, if you, like so many others who come from many different walks of life, want to have your own business, then read on. You are about to embark on a course of study that will prove invaluable in reaching your goal. Entrepreneurship can provide an exciting life and offer substantial personal rewards. We passionately contend that there is no finer calling.

1-1 SMALL SIZE BUT LARGE SIGNIFICANCE

Explain the importance of small business and entrepreneurship in our society.

If you have a serious interest in starting and operating your own business—now or in the future—you are not alone. Paul Reynolds, a leading researcher in the field, says that entrepreneurship is "on the scale of a lot of other major social phenomena."[3]

Within the United States, it is estimated that 12 million people are involved in some form of entrepreneurial venture, and that as many as half of all adults will be engaged in self-employment at some point during their working careers.[4] As shown graphically in Exhibit 1.1, the industries in which small businesses are more prevalent include services, construction, retail trade, health care, and hospitality (accommodations and food). To get a sense of the breadth and depth of the impact of small businesses on the economy overall, consider the following facts, as reported by the U.S. Small Business Administration:[5]

- As of 2009, there were almost 6 million businesses in the United States with employees. Of these businesses, 90 percent had fewer than 20 employees, and companies with fewer than 500 employees accounted for almost all the firms—99.7 percent.
- The companies with fewer than 500 employees hired almost 50 percent of all employees, accounted for 43 percent of all the salaries paid to employees, and in 2007, generated 38 percent of all business revenues.
- Small enterprises hire 43 percent of all high-tech employees (scientists, engineers, computer programmers, and others)
- From 1992 to 2010 when there were job increases in the economy, small businesses with fewer than 500 workers outperformed large firms in net job creation in about three out of four quarters.
- Many small companies have been going global, representing 97.3 percent of all exporters.
- For the 10 years ending in 2010, one of the most dramatic trends has been the increase in minority business owners, which is up 86 percent for both Hispanics and Asian Americans and 13 percent for blacks, as compared to only 5 percent for whites.
- The growth in self-employed individuals with college degrees, both baccalaureate and master's degrees, increased 32 percent from 2000 to 2010.

It's also interesting to note that about one-fourth of the 23.5 million military veterans in the United States are interested in starting or buying their own business.[6]

In a study sponsored by the Kauffman Foundation Research Series, Tim Kane talks about the role of startups in job creation:

The oft-quoted American sports slogan "Winning isn't everything. It's the only thing" could well be attributed to the economic importance of firm formation in creating jobs.... A relatively new data set from the U.S. government called Business Dynamics Statistics validates that U.S. startups classified as "less than one year old" create an average of 3 million new jobs annually. All other ages of firms, including … firms established two centuries ago, are net job destroyers, losing 1 million jobs net per year.[7]

Number of Firms with Fewer than 500 Employees by Industry (2009)

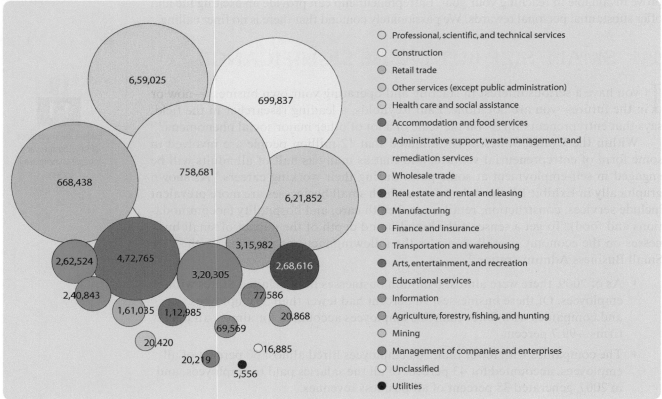

- ○ Professional, scientific, and technical services
- ○ Construction
- ◔ Retail trade
- ○ Other services (except public administration)
- ○ Health care and social assistance
- ◕ Accommodation and food services
- ● Administrative support, waste management, and remediation services
- ◔ Wholesale trade
- ● Real estate and rental and leasing
- ◑ Manufacturing
- ◔ Finance and insurance
- ○ Transportation and warehousing
- ◕ Arts, entertainment, and recreation
- ◔ Educational services
- ◔ Information
- ◑ Agriculture, forestry, fishing, and hunting
- ○ Mining
- ◑ Management of companies and enterprises
- ○ Unclassified
- ● Utilities

6,59,025

699,837

668,438

758,681

6,21,852

2,62,524

4,72,765

3,15,982

2,68,616

3,20,305

2,40,843

77,586

1,61,035

1,12,985

20,868

69,569

20,420

16,885

20,219

5,556

Source: "The Small Business Economy 2011," United States Government Printing Office, www.sba.gov/sites/default/files/SBE_2011_2.pdf.

Still, the most recent recession was a particularly difficult time for small businesses. The number of startups declined from 670,058 in 2006 to 597,074 in 2008, with bankruptcies increasing from 19,605 in 2006 to 60,837 in 2009.

In whatever way you choose to measure it, those individuals who start and lead small businesses are making a significant difference in the economy and in the quality of our lives. As we have already said, they are some of the heroes among us.

1-2 SMALL BUSINESS AND ENTREPRENEURIAL OPPORTUNITY: THE SAME OR DIFFERENT?

LO
1-2

Distinguish between the terms *small business* and *entrepreneurial opportunity*.

Let's take a more detailed look at the terms *small business* and *entrepreneurial opportunity* to gain a better understanding of what they represent. Both are at the heart of all that you will study in this book.

1-2a What Is a Small Business?

What does it mean to talk about "small business"? A neighborhood restaurant or bakery is clearly a small business, and Toyota is obviously not. But among small businesses, there is great degree of diversity in size, in organizational structure, and often in culture.

Many efforts have been made to define the term *small business,* using such criteria as number of employees, sales volume, and value of assets. But there is no generally accepted or universally agreed-on definition. Size standards are basically arbitrary, adopted to serve a particular purpose. For example, the U.S. Small Business Administration defines a small business as having fewer than 500 employees.[8] But in specific cases, the government may define a small business differently—such as one with fewer than 10 employees—in order to exempt a really small business from certain regulations if compliance would prove to be too costly, given its small size.

© Jose Antonio Revidiego Pavon/iStockphoto.com

In addition to size, small businesses differ drastically in their growth potential. The few businesses that have phenomenal prospects for growth are called **high-potential ventures**, or **gazelles**. Even within this group, there is variation in styles of operation and approaches to growth. Very few begin as high-tech startups—the kind that made Silicon Valley in California famous. In contrast to such high-potential ventures, **attractive small firms** offer substantial financial rewards for their owners. Income from these entrepreneurial ventures may grow into the millions or even tens of millions of dollars. They represent a major segment of small businesses—solid, healthy firms that can provide rewarding careers and create financial wealth for the owners.

The least profitable types of small businesses—including many service companies, such as pool cleaning businesses, dry cleaners, beauty shops, and appliance repair shops—provide modest returns to their owners. These are called **microbusinesses**, and their distinguishing feature is their limited ability to generate significant profits. Entrepreneurs who devote personal effort to such ventures receive a profit that essentially compensates them for their time. Many companies of this type are also called **lifestyle businesses** because they permit an owner to follow a desired lifestyle, even though they provide only modest financial returns. They employ fewer than 10 employees and make up the largest sector of the U.S. economy. Such enterprises usually do not attract investors and are financed with owner savings or money provided by friends and family.

Lifestyle businesses are not only important to the U.S. economy, but they have also become vital for many individuals in developing countries in Asia, South America, and Africa. In these countries, starting and running a small business can easily double or triple a family's income and make a significant difference in the quality of family members' lives. To help these individuals, some organizations are providing **microloans**, sometimes for only a few dollars, to allow them to buy inventory or do whatever else needs to be done to get started in business.

So, understanding a small business is dependent on our definition of *small* and the firm's growth potential. In this book, we will mostly be directing our attention to **small businesses** that meet the following criteria, at least in spirit:

1. Compared to the largest firms in the industry, the business is small; in most instances, the business has fewer than 100 employees.
2. Except for its marketing function, the business's operations are geographically localized.
3. Financing for the business is provided by no more than a few individuals.
4. The business may begin with a single individual, but it has the potential to become more than a "one-person show" and may eventually grow to be a mid-sized company or even a large firm.
5. The business must have growth potential, whether or not the owner chooses to capture that growth.

Obviously, some small firms will fail to meet all of these standards, but they are still of great interest to us. For example, a small executive search firm—a firm that

high-potential venture (gazelle)
A small firm that has great prospects for growth.

attractive small firm
A small firm that provides substantial profits to its owner.

microbusiness
A small firm that provides minimal profits to its owner.

lifestyle business
A microbusiness that permits the owner to follow a desired pattern of living.

microloans
Very small loans, often provided to entrepreneurs in developing countries.

small business
A business with growth potential that is small compared to large companies in an industry, has geographically localized operations, is financed by only a few individuals, and has a small management team.

helps corporate clients recruit high-level managers—may operate in many sections of the country and thereby fail to meet the second criterion. Nevertheless, the discussion of management concepts in this book is aimed primarily at the type of firm that fits the general pattern outlined by these criteria.

1-2b What Is an Entrepreneurial Opportunity, and Who Are the Entrepreneurs?

At its core, the entrepreneurial process begins with identifying an attractive entrepreneurial opportunity, which is more than merely having a good idea. Such opportunities make the enterprise economically attractive for the owners while offering customers a product or service that is so appealing that they are willing to pay their hard-earned money for it. In other words, an entrepreneur must find a way to create value for customers. An **entrepreneurial opportunity**, then, is an *economically attractive and timely opportunity* that creates value both for prospective customers and for the firm's owners. (You can look forward to Chapter 3 to learn how to identify good opportunities.)

So an **entrepreneur** is a person who relentlessly pursues an opportunity, in either a new or an existing enterprise, to create value while assuming both the risk and the reward for her or his efforts. Entrepreneurs generally think differently about resources than do employee-managers. While managers in large corporations so often think like administrators or bureaucrats—wanting larger budgets or more employees—entrepreneurs work to do more with less. They may try to use other people's resources, which is called **bootstrapping**. For example, an entrepreneur might resort to bartering or, in the early days of a business, work to create income from other sources to fund the business.

THREE SUCCESS STORIES Let's look at three ventures started by some present-day entrepreneurs who have successfully created value for customers and themselves alike.

Table Occasions (El Paso, TX).[9] Chia Stewart believes that the key ingredients of the success of Table Occasions are strong partnerships, hard work, and passionate creativity, as well as giving back and taking calculated risks. Stewart and Claudia Narvaez launched their table-decorating business in 2006 and have seen it blossom into the community's center for event-planning activity. The outcome has been that new related businesses have cropped up all around town to join in this new industry that Table Occasions carved out, resulting in economic development and opportunities for many. The company also sponsors numerous nonprofit organizations by providing services and products at free or deeply discounted rates. "We have to give back to the community that has given so much to us," says Stewart.

Stewart and Narvaez met in middle school, but their friendship has transformed into something much different in the business partnership that they formed. Much like a marriage, they have struggled through changes, managed complex situations, supported each other personally and professionally, and reaped the rewards of a successful company. They rely on the different strengths that each brings to the company, support each other's visions, and always act with the utmost integrity toward one another. "Without trust in each other, we would not have been able to come this far" claims Stewart. "Business is all about people, and we have to surround ourselves with people we can depend on, and who depend on us."

When Table Occasions started its operations, events were not a big deal in the community—at least not from an artistic perspective. But Stewart and Narvaez saw

entrepreneurial opportunity
An economically attractive and timely opportunity that creates value for interested buyers or end users.

entrepreneur
A person who relentlessly pursues an opportunity, in either a new or an existing business, to create value while assuming both the risk and the reward for his or her efforts.

bootstrapping
Doing more with less in terms of resources invested in a business, and, where possible, controlling the resources without owning them.

an unexploited niche that they could develop. They made event decorating a "must" in social and professional circles, to the point that skimping on decorations is now seen as showing a lack of dedication to the cause. This has solidified their customer base and redefined decorating expenses as "essential," which is why the recent recession has not weakened their sales and revenues.

The services that Table Occasions offers do not feature run-of-the mill table clothes. They are truly transformative. Stewart says, "We use products that, when coordinated with a wide range of event concepts, helps the planners pull off the perfect memorable and successful event—without overwhelming themselves in the process. Almost every event in town is now a virtual wonderland of visual treats for event-goers to enjoy and remember. It has truly made events magical."

Even as far as they have come, Stewart and Narvaez still engage in hard labor when it is needed. The buck stops with them, and they always make sure that a host is proud of the event. But as working mothers and wives, the hardest part of their work does not come from the physical labor, it comes from having to juggle their work and personal lives. Weekends away, early mornings, late nights, last-minute changes, and weather emergencies pull them away from their families. It's hard work … so hard it hurts!

These ingredients may seem simple, but successfully executing them is the real key. Stewart and Narvaez remain humbled by their success and are grateful for the support that comes from their families. "We had a dream and worked hard to make it come to life with the help of our support network," Stewart says. "We hope our story inspires others to dedicate their skills to spending every day doing what they love."

Blank Label (Boston, MA).[10] When Fan Bi was working his first professional job in London in 2006, he was introduced to the business world's dress code. Bi loved custom tailoring but understood that this luxury came at a price. He discovered the vast difference in experience between shopping by size for pre made clothes and shopping by style of fabric for customizable clothes.

"I used to buy dress shirts off the rack in Sydney," Bi says. "But this idea of going to a fabric market, being measured, being able to choose different fabrics … I thought, 'Wow, you know, this is a really different experience.'"

Then, during a vacation to Shanghai in the summer of 2008, where custom tailoring was provided at a far more competitive price, he asked the question "Can custom be affordable?"

Bi came up with the idea for affordable custom shirts during his study abroad program at Babson College. The faculty at Babson helped Bi hone his idea and recruit campus sales reps. One of these sales reps was Danny Wong, a student at nearby Bentley University. Unfortunately, the idea was met with a lack of interest from the college students. Also, the business was not scalable and lacked a clear supply chain.

But the pair did not give up. Bi partnered with Wong to bring the business online, where overhead expenses are lower and the potential market is large. At the beginning of 2010, they launched the Blank Label website.

"We want to be the destination where people can come and design their own apparel," Bi says. Online visitors can build a custom shirt by selecting fabric, color combination, and style of cuff, collar, placket, pocket, button, monogram, and even custom label—all for less than $100.

Since going online in 2010, the pair has seen their customer demographic shift toward business professionals who purchase six to ten dress shirts per year. They've gone from generating $345,000 in sales during their first year of business (2010) to over $1.1 million in 2011. By June 2012, Blank Label had sold 30,000 dress shirts. The web-savvy founders have managed almost the entire process remotely. "Thanks to the Internet," Bi says, "you can work with the best people in the world, not just the best people in your neighborhood."

As you might have guessed, Bi and Wong aren't content just being shirt makers. Wong hopes that Blank Label will emerge as a hub for everything "co-created," since it is supporting other co-creation companies as well. Companies are rapidly realizing that customers are hungry for more personalized products that are made specifically for them. As Wong explains, "While other companies were calling themselves *mass-customization* businesses, we rejected that old-world concept, redefining it as *co-creation* because it is a snappier term, it isn't an oxymoron, and it is new and interesting to consumers."

It will be interesting to see where Blank Label takes the custom business in the future. The company has already proved that it is a significant force in the co-creation world. Bi explains that it has been a challenge: "You have to take it one day at a time, but it has been worth it to wake up and be excited about my day job."

***Tender Greens (Pasadena, CA).*[11]** Erik Oberholtzer, Matt Lyman, and David Dressler met while working in the kitchen at a luxury beach resort in Southern California. Together, they envisioned a restaurant where they could follow their cooking passions and serve organic, farm-fresh, "slow food" dishes at affordable prices. Once the trio decided to join forces and launch an eatery, they took their time to carefully plan every aspect of the business before taking the plunge.

"It took probably two years from idea to opening," says Oberholtzer, chef and co-owner of Tender Greens, which opened in 2006 and now operates seven locations across California. Much of those two years involved fundraising and constantly revising the business plan.

"We would make revisions to our plan after every meeting with a potential investor, because sophisticated investors would ask questions we hadn't thought of, causing us to go back and refine the numbers," Oberholtzer says. "That process was really beneficial, because we went into the opening with a lot of focus ... knowing the culture we wanted to create, the brand we wanted to build, and the type of employers we wanted to be."

All that planning paid off. First-year profits were projected at $850,000, but the company ended up with $3 million. Last year, Tender Greens reported a 53 percent year-over-year sales increase from $10.9 million in 2010 to $16.7 million in 2011. The owners have plans to open three more locations in 2012; starting in 2013, the plan is to open four to five new stores per year.

Tender Greens offers a casual, walk-up dining environment, where guests can watch meats grilling and meals being prepared behind a glass partition as they walk through the line. The core menu consists of "big salads," "hot stuff" (a hot plate or sandwich), and soups. A few crowd favorites include the Southern fried chicken salad, the octopus salad, the Happy Vegan salad, and the mashed potatoes. Executive chefs at each restaurant also create their own specials that vary by location, change twice daily, and are made from scratch.

What really sets Tender Greens apart from other fast-casual eateries is the care taken in preparing the cuisine. The chefs cure the bacon in-house, make their own salami, craft handmade pastas, cure their own caviar, mix their own natural sodas, and work to support small farmers.

1-3 ENTREPRENEURIAL QUALITIES: NO BIG EGO REQUIRED

LO
1-3

Explain the basic characteristics of entrepreneurs, and describe different kinds of entrepreneurship.

People often ask, "Are entrepreneurs born or made?" That question has long been debated with little agreement. However, Stephen Spinelli and Robert Adams have nicely summarized research on entrepreneurial characteristics. The entrepreneurs they describe as having and exhibiting "desirable and acquirable attitudes and behaviors" fall under the following six descriptors:[12]

1. *Commitment and determination*—tenacious, decisive, and persistent in problem solving
2. *Leadership*—self-starters and team builders who focus on honesty in their business relationships
3. *Opportunity obsession*—aware of market and customer needs
4. *Tolerance of risk, ambiguity, and uncertainty*—risk takers, risk minimizers, and uncertainty tolerators
5. *Creativity, self-reliance, and adaptability*—open-minded, flexible, uncomfortable with the status quo, and quick learners
6. *Motivation to excel*—goal-oriented and aware of personal strengths and weaknesses

On the other side of the coin, there are some attitudes and behaviors that should be avoided at all cost. An almost certain way to fail as an entrepreneur, as many have learned by experience, is to do the following:

1. Overestimate what you can do
2. Lack an understanding of the market
3. Hire mediocre people
4. Fail to be a team player, which is usually the result of taking oneself too seriously
5. Be a domineering manager
6. Fail to share ownership in the business in an equitable way

For the most part, this list describes a leader without humility. Contrary to popular belief, humility is a quality that serves leaders well. Scott Cook is the founder and chief executive officer (CEO) of Intuit, a computer software company that helps millions of consumers and businesses manage their financing, with products such as Quicken, QuickBooks, TurboTax, QuickBase, and Payroll. Cook believes that humility is an essential trait for any entrepreneur:

> *The future belongs to humble leaders. Humble to let your people lead and be led by them. Humble to make the customer your boss. Humble to listen and listen intently. Humble to know that almost all of the best ideas come from others. Humble to admit you were wrong.*[13]

1-3a Founders versus Other Entrepreneurs

We typically think of "pure" entrepreneurs as being founders of new businesses that bring new or improved products or services to market. However, at some point after a new firm is established, it may be purchased or taken over by a second-generation family member or another individual who was managing the company. These "second-stage" entrepreneurs do not necessarily differ greatly from founding entrepreneurs in the way they manage their businesses. Sometimes, these well-established small firms

founder
An entrepreneur who brings a new firm into existence.

grow rapidly, and their orientation will be more akin to that of a founder than to that of a manager. Nevertheless, it is helpful to distinguish between entrepreneurs who start or substantially change companies and those who direct the continuing operations of established businesses. Ryan Gibson, a young entrepreneur in Waco, Texas, says he has come to understand that his passion and aptitude are for starting new companies, which he has successfully done on several occasions. However, when the business is up and running, he turns the operations over to his team. He knows he is not good at running a business on a day-to-day basis. Again, it comes back to understanding yourself—your motivations and personality—if you want your journey to be a good one in the long run.

1-3b Franchisees

Franchisees comprise yet another category of entrepreneurs. **Franchisees** differ from other business owners in the degree of their independence. Because of the guidance and constraints provided by contractual arrangements with franchising organizations, franchisees function as limited entrepreneurs. (Chapter 4 presents more information about franchisees.)

franchisee
An entrepreneur whose power is limited by a contractual relationship with a franchising organization.

1-3c Entrepreneurial Teams

Our discussion thus far has focused on entrepreneurs who function as individuals, each with his or her own firm. And this is frequently the case. However, entrepreneurial teams can be beneficial, if not essential, particularly in ventures of any substantial

Living the Dream

Bootstrapping Is at the Heart of Entrepreneurship

Erica Zidel spent two years holding down a day job while bootstrapping her new company on the side. During regular working hours, she served as a consultant. Then, in the evenings and on weekends, she committed her time and energy to her startup, Sitting Around, an online company that makes it easy for parents to find and coordinate babysitting in their neighborhoods. As a result, she has been able to self-fund her business, allowing Zidel and her business partner, Ted Tieken, to retain 100 percent ownership of the babysitting venture. Zidel says that until the business brings in enough money to pay an adequate salary, she will continue to balance her duties with her

© Courtesy of SittingAround

consulting work. When she hears someone say that in order to be a true entrepreneur, you must leave your day job, she is quick to respond:

A lot of people think that to be a successful entrepreneur, you need to be sleeping on an air mattress and working on your business 80 to 90 hours a week. But I think that definition of success is silly. I'm living proof that if you have a quality idea and you spend your time well and execute it well, you can wind up with something great.

Source: Michelle Goodman, "How to Bootstrap Your Business," *Entrepreneur*, December 2011, p. 90.

size. An **entrepreneurial team** consists of two or more individuals who combine their efforts to function in the capacity of entrepreneurs. In this way, the talents, skills, and resources of two or more entrepreneurs can be concentrated on one endeavour. This very important form of entrepreneurship is discussed at greater length in Chapter 8.

1-3d Social Entrepreneurs

The social issues affecting businesses are numerous and diverse. Businesses are expected—at different times and by various groups—to help solve social problems related to education, crime, poverty, and the environment. In fact, in the past anyone wanting to make a difference might think they would need to start a not-for-profit organization, whereas those aspiring to build financial wealth would have to launch a high-potential business. These days, it's not so black and white. More not-for-profits are being managed like businesses, and more traditional businesses have a social dimension, if not a key social mission. These expectations are converging into a form of venturing called **social entrepreneurship**, which is rapidly gaining momentum. Though the term has been defined in different ways, Harvard researchers suggest that *social entrepreneurship* refers to "entrepreneurial activity with an embedded social purpose."[14] In other words, a social entrepreneur is one who comes up with innovative solutions to society's most pressing needs, problems, and opportunities.

Becoming a social entrepreneur usually does not mean that one is no longer concerned with making money—rather, this is just one of an expanded set of goals. In fact, the outcomes of interest are sometimes referred to as the "triple bottom line," because they focus on people, profits, and the planet. Profits are essential since no enterprise can exist for long without them. But social entrepreneurs believe ventures should also be concerned with people and the environment. To get a feel for the wide range of enterprises that fall under the social entrepreneurship umbrella, consider that the demand by consumers for organic products has grown significantly during the past decade or so, according to the United States Department of Agriculture. But only 0.36 percent of U.S. farmland is certified organic. Recognizing this disconnect, Craig Wiehner co-founded Farmland LP, a startup private equity firm that acquires conventional farmland and converts it to organic. The idea, says Wiehner, is simple. Organically raised products provide higher profit margins, giving small farmers a competitive advantage, as well as earning good returns for environmentally minded investors.[15] Kevin Henry is the founder of Pangea Bottles, which makes and sells eco-friendly, BPA-free, stainless steel water bottles. For each bottle sold, Pangea gives a person in need clean water for four years by drilling water wells in developing countries. Henry says he started Pangea Bottles because he wanted to make a difference in people's lives without relying on charitable donations. He explains, "Social entrepreneurship was just beginning to take root across the country, and I had heard that around one billion people did not have access to clean water, so I wanted to find a way to help."[16]

Within the area of social entrepreneurship, the issue of environmentalism has become a key concern. In Chapter 2, we will discuss this issue, which is important to many small businesses.

1-3e Women Entrepreneurs

It is interesting to note that an increasing number of women are starting and growing profitable businesses in previously male-dominated industries, such construction, manufacturing, and computer services. However, despite their progress, there

entrepreneurial team
Two or more people who work together as entrepreneurs on one endeavor.

social entrepreneurship
Entrepreneurial activity whose goal is to find innovative solutions to social needs, problems, and opportunities.

still exists a gender gap. Only 36 percent of women-owned companies create jobs for others, compared to 44 percent for men. Also, only 1.8 percent of women firms have $1 million or more in revenues, while 6.3 percent of firms owned by men have revenues in excess of $1 million.[17] In the words of Sharon Hadary, the former director and founder of the Center for Women's Business:

> *Men tend to start businesses to be the "boss," and their aim is for their businesses to grow as big as possible. Women start businesses to be personally challenged and to integrate work and family and they want to stay at a size where they personally can oversee all aspects of the business.*[18]

However, in a recent study sponsored by the Ewing Marion Kauffman Foundation, Robb and Watson found no difference in firm performance between companies owned by women and those owned by men. There were no differences between the two groups in failure rates, in profitability, and in the returns earned relative to the risk being assumed. The findings indicate that women are just as effective as men when it comes to running profitable, wealth-creating businesses. Based on their findings, the authors offer a word of encouragement to women who aspire to start a business:

> *Women who are contemplating starting a new venture [should] not be discouraged from doing so by a false belief that new ventures initiated by women are less likely to succeed than those initiated by men.*[19]

1-3f Be a Small Business Owner Who Thinks and Acts Like an Entrepreneur

While they are not precisely the same, we will use the terms *small business owner* and *entrepreneur* interchangeably. After all, a business owner is fundamentally different from a salaried employee. The business owner takes risks not assumed by employees and is rewarded or punished financially based on the results he or she can achieve. But we recognize that many small business owners fail to think or act entrepreneurially—identifying and capturing new opportunities to grow the business are not objectives they care to pursue. The choice to grow or not to grow begins with the owner's personal preferences, which ideally should be aligned with his or her life objectives.

Many entrepreneurs have found **mentors** along the way, individuals who can offer guidance based on their experience in a given field. As you begin and continue on the entrepreneurial journey, you can make no better decision than to find mentors to guide you. These individuals can show you how to avoid mistakes. They want you to succeed and support your efforts. Most importantly, they will encourage you on those days when you want to throw in the towel.

What type of opportunity do you want to pursue? In answering this question, you should be intentional. Don't let your business endeavors develop by chance. Consider seeking opportunities that have growth potential and that challenge you to grow personally. You may start small, but we would encourage you to dream big. Think and act entrepreneurially. Ewing Marion Kauffman, the founder of Marion Labs, offers this encouragement to entrepreneurs and small business owners:

> *You should not choose to be a common company. It is your right to build an uncommon company if you can—to seek the opportunity to compete, to desire to take the calculated risks, to dream, to build—yes, even to fail or succeed.*[20]

mentor
A knowledgeable person who can offer guidance based on experience in a given field.

Living the Dream

My First Step

Jeff Sandefer, a highly successful entrepreneur, leading educator, and the founder of the Acton MBA in Entrepreneurship, tells a fun story and offers some words of encouragement to anyone wanting to be an entrepreneur.

My first step toward an entrepreneurial calling began with my burning desire for air conditioning.

As a teenager, my father wisely insisted that I work summers as a laborer in the oil fields, under an unrelenting West Texas sun. I hated what seemed like meaningless manual labor, the bullying and the boasting conversations about sex, drugs, and alcohol. But most of all I hated the relentless heat, which started at dawn and made even the wind feel like a blast furnace.

To me, heaven was the inside of an air-conditioned pickup truck, the spot reserved for a foreman, a spot no one was going to give to a teenage boy.

But as I went on with my sweaty work, longing to sit in that position of air-conditioned power, I began to notice things. First, I noticed that all the heavy equipment lying around wasn't needed for the light painting and clean-up work that occupied most of our time, but was nonetheless charged to customers. Then I noticed that my fellow

© John A Davis/Shutterstock.com

laborers, paid by the hour, had little incentive to do anything other than shirk work and wait for quitting time to come.

So I formed a plan to get into air conditioning. I partnered with my best friend and we convinced our high school football coaches to go to work for us. They contributed the use of their pickup trucks to haul painting equipment, and we agreed to pay them by the job, not the hour. They, in turn, hired their football players to work for them, and paid them the same way. My job became finding customers and overseeing the work. My partner handled the operations.

The hourly workers painted a large metal storage tank in three days. Our crews arrived at dawn, painted until dark, and could finish three tanks a day—a ninefold-productivity gain.

I was seventeen that summer, and my best friend and I made $100,000. More importantly, I got to spend most of my time in air conditioning.

You should know that Sandefer ultimately sold an energy investment firm that had several billion dollars in assets.

Source: Jeff Sandefer and Robert Sirico, *A Field Guide for the Hero's Journey* (Grand Rapids, Michigan: Acton Institute, 2012), p. 2.

1-4 YOUR MOTIVATIONS FOR OWNING A BUSINESS

Before you choose to enter the small business game, you need to think carefully about the person you want to be and how owning a business will help make you that person. In other words, you do not begin with the business. *You begin with you.* Jeff Sandefer, puts it this way: "[W]hen you embark upon a heroic journey—a life filled with meaning and purpose—the first step is to heed the admonition inscribed over the entrance to the Oracle of Delphi in ancient Greece: 'Know Thyself.' Search out who you are, and then you will be equipped to discover your heroic calling."[21]

LO 1-4

Discuss the importance of understanding your motivations and perceptions related to owning a small business.

Don't let anyone deceive you: Being an entrepreneur is extremely challenging. As one entrepreneur said, "You get sand kicked in your face all the time, and worse. It takes undying love and passion to keep going. If your mind is wandering to something else you'd rather do, go do that." There will be times when you will be discouraged, maybe even terrified. Some days, you will wish you had opted for the security (or at least the perception of security) of a regular job in an established company.

Understanding clearly why you want to own a small business and what motivates you is vital to eventually achieving fulfillment through your business. Founders who know what their core values are and what is important to them are more likely to create businesses that they find rewarding. According to Noam Wasserman, an associate professor at the Harvard Business School,

> *One of the key things about entrepreneurs is that they have far more potential to make decisions with both head and heart…. When you're taking the world on your shoulders, you have to ask yourself, why am I doing this? If you only listen to your head, the decisions you make at every fork in the road can drive you farther from your personal promised land.*[22]

You may decide to own a small business because of the influence of family members or friends who have their own businesses. Researchers at Case Western Reserve University's Weatherhead School of Management have found a strong connection between entrepreneurship and genetics. Also, the U.S. Census Bureau reports that half of all small business owners worked in their family's business before founding their own ventures.[23] In other words, they had the opportunity to observe the "entrepreneurial life" up close.

Starting a business may also provide an escape from an undesirable job situation. Some individuals become entrepreneurs after being laid off by an employer. Unemployed personnel with experience in professional, managerial, technical, and even relatively unskilled positions often contemplate the possibility of venturing out on their own. Those who started or acquired small businesses as a result of financial hardship or other severely negative conditions have appropriately been called **reluctant entrepreneurs**.

Individuals may also flee the bureaucratic environment of a corporation that seems stifling or oppressive to them. In a survey of 721 office workers, 42 percent had considered quitting their jobs over bureaucratic hassles.[24] Entrepreneurship often provides an attractive alternative for such individuals, who are sometimes called **corporate refugees**.

Michelle Lawton left the corporate world to do her own thing. She had done well as an executive with such firms as Procter & Gamble, Pepperidge Farm, Lavazza Coffee, and Remy Cointreau. She had also been compensated very well, at least until you consider the long hours she worked. She finally decided she had endured enough of the corporate world. "I was at a point in my life where I was looking for a real shift," Lawton says. She wanted to do something that she was really passionate about and that would allow her to pave her own way moving forward.

reluctant entrepreneur
A person who becomes an entrepreneur as a result of some severe hardship.

corporate refugee
A person who becomes an entrepreneur to escape an undesirable job situation.

As her own boss in food and beverage branding, Lawton was able to do things she never could do before, such as lunchtime yoga and Pilates classes. "It's something I can't quantify," explains Lawton. "I've never been healthier. What I'm not gaining in financial rewards, I've gained in personal well-being. It sounds like a cliché, but it's a trade-off."[25]

Being influenced by friends and family or simply wanting to make a change in your current situation is not a sufficient reason to start your own business. You need to understand the specific motivations that that will keep you going on the tough days.[26] Chris DeLeenheer, founder of Sunzer Consulting Group in Bangalore, India, describes his early days and what got him through the tough times:

> *In starting my company, it was really challenging. We knew no one, had no reputation in the region, and low initial start-up capital. At times there were long days with what felt like little return, but the journey has been a rich experience. Three things kept me going: a drive to win, determination not to give up, and the discipline to work on the right stuff.[27]*

The point is, it's vitally important that you know your own motivations before you get into the small business game.

1-4a Types of Entrepreneurial Motivations

The most common motivations for founding a business can be divided into four categories: personal fulfillment, personal satisfaction, independence, and financial rewards. These types of motivations, along with specific examples of each, are shown in Exhibit 1.2 and discussed in the following sections.

PERSONAL FULFILLMENT Owning a business should provide significant personal fulfillment. If it doesn't, then you should look elsewhere. All other motivations will not be enough in the really tough times—and the difficult times are sure to come.

If you want to get started on the right foot, we suggest that the core value for becoming an entrepreneur and owning your own business should be *to make the world a better place*. John Doerr, one of the most famous venture capitalists of all time, inspired the phrase "make meaning," suggesting that the most impactful and sustainable businesses are built on such a foundation.[28] Your first goal should be to create a product

EXHIBIT **1.2** Entrepreneurial Motivations

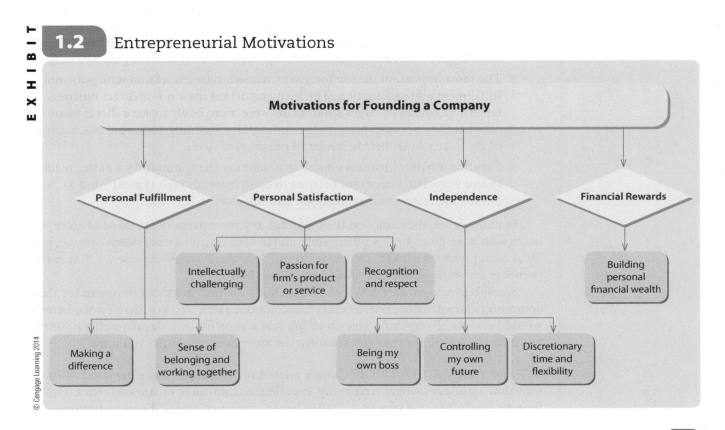

© Cengage Learning 2014

or service that improves life for others. Only when your company is about something more significant than yourself, will you have a sense that what you are doing is meaningful and well worth the effort. Apple co-founder Steve Jobs said it well:

> *The only way to be truly satisfied is to do what you believe is great work. And the only way to do great work is to love what you do. If you haven't found it yet, keep looking. Don't settle. As with all matters of the heart, you'll know when you find it.*

Also, it is through their businesses that entrepreneurs develop a sense of belonging. They come to understand that they can do nothing of significance by themselves. Only by working with others—hopefully, with people they enjoy—can entrepreneurs realize personal fulfillment.

Bill Waugh, the founder of Casa Bonita, a very successful chain of Mexican food restaurants that includes Taco Bueno, sought to make a difference by providing his company's resources to not-for-profit organizations. He says, "My company is my base for helping others."

When Nick Sarillo started his pizza business, his goal was to create a corporate culture unlike any he had seen. One part of his plan was to develop a strong relationship with the communities where he had restaurants. He wanted to "feel the community's pain, share its joy." The company hosts fundraisers every week and contributes 15 percent of its gross profits to charitable causes. And it sponsors benefits once or twice a year for families who are experiencing large medical bills. Christopher Adams, Sarillo's partner, believes that giving back to the community has an ancillary benefit for the business: "It reminds our team members how incredibly different we are from any other place they know."[29]

A survey by the National Federation of Independent Business found that[30]

- Ninety-one percent of small business owners contributed to their community through volunteering, in-kind contributions, and/or direct cash donations. About 41 percent contributed in all three ways. The estimated average value of contributions was $6,600 per small employer, for a total of roughly $40 billion.
- The most important reason for giving tended to be associated with personal fulfillment and satisfaction. The least important reason was direct business benefits. Owners of larger small firms were more likely to see a direct business benefit in contributing to the community, but they, too, were much more likely to attribute their behavior to personal reasons.
- Creating a better business climate and making the community a better place to live were also important reasons to contribute, though typically not as important as personal satisfaction and fulfillment.

In many cases, the names on the buildings at your university are those of entrepreneurs who have given back to their alma mater. One university president commented, "It is entrepreneurs who endow universities." It is the authors' experience that entrepreneurs are some of the most giving people we know.

Small business owners don't—and shouldn't—expect anything in return for their community stewardship. But, as Gary Deaton points out, "To say there's not a benefit would be naive. Everything you do in life has a positive or a negative effect. So the more things you do for the right reasons, the more positive results you'll see."[31]

PERSONAL SATISFACTION Closely related to fulfillment is the personal satisfaction that business owners frequently experience from their businesses. Rick Davis, founder and CEO of Davaco, a Dallas-based company, says, "There is nothing else

I would rather do. I love the challenges, working with others to see our dreams come true, and making a difference in the community. It is fun."[32]

In a Gallup Poll of over 100,000 working adults, researchers examined the relationship between work and happiness for different occupational groups. The researchers developed an overall index of contentment based on six criteria: emotional health, physical health, job satisfaction, healthy behaviors, access to basic needs, and self-reports on overall life quality. Business owners were found to outrank all other occupational groups in terms of overall contentment. For one thing, entrepreneurs feel rewarded in working with a particular product or service and being good at it. They find great satisfaction from being the best at what they do.

Entrepreneurs are energized from enjoyable associations within their businesses. There is a reward that comes from helping their people develop. Jack Griggs, president of Texas Heritage Banks Holding Company, believes that one of his primary roles is to help his employees become better at what they do. He takes great pride in the number of his people who have gone on to great careers, even if not at one of his banks. Also, because they share similar experiences, business owners enjoy friendships with other business owners, and they learn from one another. Finally, if they are visible within the community, small business owners can garner the respect of their community. So for many entrepreneurs, the personal satisfaction received from business is no small matter in their lives.

INDEPENDENCE One of the conclusions drawn from the Gallup Poll cited earlier was that it "reflects the importance of being free to choose the work you do and how you do it, the way you manage your time, and the way you respond to adversity."[33] John Howard, director of the National Institute for Occupational Safety and Health, says the survey "reaffirms my view that the more control you have over your work, the happier you are."[34] In other words, many people have a strong desire to make their own decisions, take risks, and reap the rewards.

© Rosamund Parkinson/Shutterstock.com

Business owners also have discretion about when they want to engage in nonbusiness activities. They have the freedom to decide when to work, when to be with family, and when to be engaged in community activities in ways that employees frequently cannot be.

Charlie Avallone agrees. Avallone was a technical writer in the investment field. Recognizing his boss had no plans to retire anytime soon, Avallone felt he was running out of options. So, he borrowed money on his house to cover health care and day-to-day living expenses and started his own consulting business. "It was very satisfying to leave my job and support myself and be able to think that I was my own boss," says Avallone.[35]

Of course, independence does not guarantee an easy life. Most entrepreneurs work very hard and for long hours. They must remember that the customer is, ultimately, the boss. But they do have the satisfaction of making their own decisions within the constraints required to build a successful business.

FINANCIAL REWARDS Contrary to what some people believe, there is nothing wrong with making money. As a general rule, when businesses are profitable, everyone benefits. Jobs are created, taxes are paid, and charities receive donations. Furthermore, like any other job or career, starting a business is a way to earn money and make ends meet. Of course, some entrepreneurs earn *lots* of money. In *The Millionaire Next Door*, Stanley and Danko note that self-employed people are four times more likely to be millionaires than are those who work for others.[36]

How much money should an entrepreneur expect to get in return for starting and running a business? Making a profit is certainly necessary for a firm's survival. Many entrepreneurs work night and day (literally, in some cases) just to generate enough profits to survive; others receive a modest income for their time and investment. From an economic perspective, however, the financial return of a business should compensate its owner not only for his or her investment of personal time (in the form of a salary equivalent) but also for any personal money invested in the business (in the form of cash distributed to the owner and the increased value of the business) and for the risk he or she is taking.

A significant number of entrepreneurs are, no doubt, highly motivated by the prospect of making money. While some entrepreneurs do become rich quickly, the majority do not. Therefore, a more reasonable goal would be to "get rich slowly." Wealth will most likely come, provided the business is economically viable and the owner has the patience and determination to make it happen. When it comes to making money, keep in mind the adage "Money is not a problem, but money without wisdom is a problem."

To conclude, only you can know why owning your own business is appealing *and* rewarding. Undoubtedly, there will not be just one motivation, but multiple ones—even one or more that we have not discussed. Whatever the reasons, it is wise to identify what truly motivates you to be an entrepreneur. It will help you understand what is important to you and give you guidance when making decisions. Clayton Christensen offers wise advice:

> *It is impossible to have a meaningful conversation about happiness without understanding what makes you tick. When we find ourselves stuck in unhappy careers—and even unhappy lives—it is often the result of a fundamental misunderstanding of what really motivates us.*[37]

1-4b Understanding Your Paradigm

So knowing your motivations is important to anyone interested in starting a business. But that is not enough. You also need to understand if your perceptions of what it takes to be successful in business are accurate. In *The 7 Habits of Highly Effective People*, Stephen Covey teaches that if we want to make important changes in our lives, we need to change from the *inside-out*. He says that having a positive attitude or working harder is not enough. Instead, we have to change how we fundamentally see a situation, or what he calls a **paradigm shift**.[38] So the question for someone wanting to found a business is, "What do you believe it will take for you to create a successful business?" Your answer to this question will depend largely on your past experiences, which have a significant influence on your paradigm, that being the way you see the situation.

In his book, *The E-Myth Revisited: Why Most Businesses Don't Work and What to Do About It*, Michael Gerber describes three paradigms, or what he calls *personalities*, that come into play when you are starting a business: the technician personality, the manager personality, and the entrepreneur personality. He contends that each of us exhibits these personalities to some varying degree, and successful business owners need a balance of all three. Let's briefly look at the three personalities, which are shown graphically in Exhibit 1.3. As you read about these personalities, consider how you would describe yourself.

THE TECHNICIAN PERSONALITY If you start an auto repair business because you love working on cars or a pie shop because your friends say you make the best pies they have ever eaten, you most likely have what Gerber calls a technician personality. The **technician personality** is a steady worker, experienced at *doing* what he

paradigm shift
A change in how we fundamentally see a situation.

technician personality
A personality that focuses on an already developed technical skill, wants to be left alone to get the job done, and is primarily concerned about the present.

1.3 Understanding Your Business Paradigm

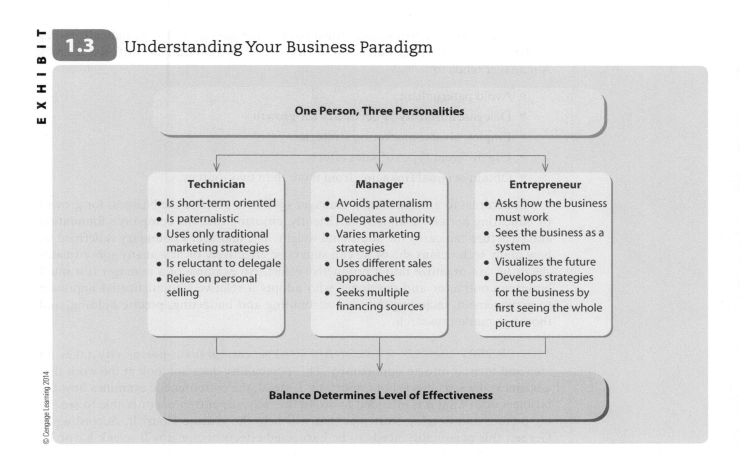

One Person, Three Personalities

Technician	Manager	Entrepreneur
• Is short-term oriented • Is paternalistic • Uses only traditional marketing strategies • Is reluctant to delegate • Relies on personal selling	• Avoids paternalism • Delegates authority • Varies marketing strategies • Uses different sales approaches • Seeks multiple financing sources	• Asks how the business must work • Sees the business as a system • Visualizes the future • Develops strategies for the business by first seeing the whole picture

Balance Determines Level of Effectiveness

or she knows best. The technician dislikes managing, wanting instead to be left alone to get the job done. He or she lives in the moment, without thinking of the future. To the technician, starting a business may be both a dream-come-true and a nightmare at the same time. The thought of no longer being managed and having total control over what gets done is exciting, but the need to be organized and think strategically is daunting.

A technician's approach to business decision making can be characterized as

- Paternalistic (he or she guides the businesses much as he or she might guide family members).
- Reluctant to delegate authority.
- Defining marketing strategy in terms of the traditional components of price, quality, and company reputation.
- Focusing on sales efforts that are primarily personal.
- Short-term oriented, with little planning for future growth or change.

The technician is prone to making a fatal assumption. According to Gerber, the technician thinks that "if you understand the technical work of a business, you understand the business that does that technical work… But the technical work of a business and a business that does that technical work are two totally different things!"[39]

THE MANAGER PERSONALITY An individual with a **manager personality** is pragmatic, assuming responsibility for the planning, order, and predictability of the business. In Gerber's words, "The manager is the part of us that goes to Sears and

manager personality
A personality that is pragmatic and likes order and planning operations.

buys stacking plastic boxes, takes them back to the garage, and systematically stores all the various mixed nuts, bolts, and screws in their own carefully identified drawer."[40] A manager tends to

- Avoid paternalism.
- Delegate authority as necessary for growth.
- Employ diverse marketing strategies.
- Use different types of sales efforts.
- Obtain original financing from more than two sources.

In contrast to a technician, a manager's job is to prepare the business for growth by educating herself or himself sufficiently, ensuring that the company's foundation and structure can carry the additional weight. The manager's boundary is defined by how many technicians she or he can supervise effectively or how many subordinates she or he can organize into a productive effort. An example of a manager is a small building contractor and developer who adopts a relatively sophisticated approach to management, including detailed accounting and budgeting, precise bidding, and thorough market research.

THE ENTREPRENEUR PERSONALITY The **entrepreneur personality** takes an idea and turns it into an opportunity. This personality does not look at the work that a business does, as this is not important. Instead, the entrepreneur examines how the business does what it is intended to do. In this way, the entrepreneur is able to see the big picture and develop strategies that will help the venture flourish. According to Gerber, this personality needs to be harnessed effectively, or it will wreak havoc by trying to pull the business in many directions at the same time.[41]

The entrepreneurial perspective tends to

- Ask the question: "How must the business work?"
- See the business as a system for producing outside results for the customer, and in so doing, produces profits.
- Start with a picture of a well-defined future, and then attempt to change the present to match the vision.
- Develop strategies for the business by first seeing the whole picture.

The entrepreneur looks at the business as the product. The commodity is not what is important; rather, it is the way the commodity is delivered. The entrepreneur surveys the world to identify an opportunity and then finds a solution to the problem. In this way, the business is tailored to meet the needs of the customer and not the needs of the business owner (as is the case with a technician-founded business).

We all have a bit of each of these personalities. However, for most of us, one personality dominates the others to the detriment of the business, *and the owner's personal life as well.* Thus, Gerber offers the following counsel:

> *Without all three of these personalities being given the opportunity, the freedom, the nourishment they each need to grow, your business cannot help but mirror your own lopsidedness…. And if they were equally balanced, we would be describing an incredibly competent individual. The entrepreneur would be free to forge ahead into new areas of interest; the manager would be solidifying the base of operations; and the technician would be doing his technical work. Each would derive satisfaction for the work he does best, serving the whole in the most productive way.*[42]

entrepreneur personality
A personality that focuses on the business as a whole and providing results for the customer.

So, if you don't understand who you are as a business owner, you may think that the business is the problem, when in reality you are the problem. You need to know your motivations for wanting to be a business owner and how your past experiences affect how you see the business. By first understanding yourself, you can potentially avoid a lot of disappointment and long-lasting problems.

1-5 THE COMPETITIVE EDGE OF ENTREPRENEURS

LO
1-5

Describe five potential competitive advantages of small entrepreneurial companies over large firms.

To maintain their position as a robust part of the total economy, small entrepreneurial companies must compete effectively with firms of all sizes, including large publicly owned companies.

How is it that small and entrepreneurial firms can hold their own and often gain an edge over successful, more powerful businesses? The answer lies in the ability of new and smaller firms to exploit opportunities. If a business can make its product or service cheaper, faster, and better, then it can be competitive. Small companies—if well managed—are just as able as larger firms to develop strategies that offer a competitive advantage.

In this section, we will take a look at some ways in which new firms can gain a competitive advantage. In Chapter 3, we'll elaborate on strategies for exploiting these potential advantages and capturing the business opportunities they make possible.

1-5a Customer Focus

Business opportunities exist for those who can produce products and services desired by customers. Small companies are particularly adept at competing when they commit to a strong customer focus. Good customer service can be provided by a business of any size. However, in many instances, small businesses have a greater potential than larger firms to achieve this goal. If properly managed, small entrepreneurial companies have the advantage of being able to serve customers directly and effectively, avoiding the layers of bureaucracy and corporate policies that tend to stifle employee initiative. In many cases, customers are personally acquainted with the entrepreneur and other key people in the small business.

Not all small enterprises manage to excel in customer service. After all, it's easier said than done. But many do make it happen. Having a small number of customers and having a close relationship with them makes customer service a powerful tool for entrepreneurial businesses. For further discussion of this subject, see Chapter 14.

© kurhan/Shutterstock.com

1-5b Quality Performance

There is no reason that a small business needs to take a back seat to larger firms when it comes to achieving quality in operations. We frequently talk to owners of small businesses whose operations not only equal the quality performance of larger firms, but in fact surpass the performance of the giants.

No finer example of quality performance can be found than MFI International in El Paso, Texas, owned by Cecilia Levine. A visitor to MFI can feel Levine's passion for quality. As a small business owner, she can insist on high levels of quality without experiencing the frustration of a large-company CEO who may have to push a quality philosophy through many layers of bureaucracy. She is convinced that a small business owner should have no fears about being able to compete when it comes to quality. It just needs to part of the business culture.

In general, quality is mostly independent of firm size. But if there is an advantage, it most often goes to the smaller business. As a small business owner, you should not accept anything less than the highest-quality performance. An uncompromising commitment to quality will move you a long way on the road to having a competitive advantage relative to other firms in your industry.

1-5c Integrity and Responsibility

In order to maintain a strong competitive advantage, it is essential that you add a solid reputation for honesty and dependability to good customer service and excellent product quality. In fact, the quickest way to lose a competitive advantage is to act without regard for others—or worse, to act dishonestly. We all respond positively to evidence of integrity because we all have, at times, been taken advantage of when buying a product or service.

Consistently operating with integrity can set a small business apart as being trustworthy at a time when stories of corporate greed and corruption abound. Above all else, the core values of the entrepreneur, as reflected in what she or he says and how she or he acts, determine the culture within a business. After all, others will do business with a company only when they feel that they can trust that company. Trust is the foundation of all relationships, including business relationships. Chapter 2 discusses the critical importance of integrity and its role in entrepreneurship.

1-5d Innovation

How the world is changing! When Bill Clinton was elected president in 1992, hardly anyone—with the exception of a small number of people in the government and academia—had e-mail. In his book *The World Is Flat*, Thomas Friedman describes the convergence of 10 forces that have "flattened" the world.[43] Friedman's contention that the world is flat means that anything can now be done from anywhere in the world. Individuals, not governments or large corporations, are driving the globalization that is happening all around us. Innovation, both in products or services and in competitive strategies, is within the reach of the small business in ways that were not thought possible a few years ago.

The SBA's Office of Advocacy has a history of funding research that documents the role, nature, and importance of innovation and technological breakthrough by small firms. Office of Advocacy research shows that small businesses outperform their larger counterparts in producing more patents per employee (a measure of innovation). Small firm patents also outperform those of larger firms along a number of measures, including growth, citation, and originality. Small "patenting firms" produce 16.5 times more patents per employee than large firms do, and these patents are twice as likely as those from large firms to be among the 1 percent most cited by others in their patent applications.[44] Most of the radical inventions of the last century, such as the computer and the pacemaker, came from small companies, not large ones. And this will not change.

Research departments of big businesses tend to focus on improving existing products. Creative ideas may be side-tracked because they are not related to existing product lines or because they are unusual. But preoccupation with an existing product can obscure the value of a new idea. In his book, *The Innovator's Dilemma*, Clayton Christensen documents how large established companies have missed major transformations in a number of industries—computers (mainframes to PCs), telephones (landline to mobile), photography (film to digital), stock markets (floor trading to online trading), and many others.[45]

When discussing the role of entrepreneurs in innovation, Amar Bhide, a noted business researcher at Columbia University, describes how entrepreneurs are good at developing others' ideas. Bhide advises us not to equate innovation with technological breakthroughs and scientists in white coats, because few small businesses can afford the luxury of spending large amounts of money on research and development. Instead, he contends that entrepreneurs are better able to take inventions or innovations developed elsewhere and put them into use, which requires marketing, sales, and organization.[46] In Bhide's opinion, these latter activities are just as innovative as creating something in a science lab. The mere fact that a small business is not "high tech" should not be taken to mean that it is not innovative; it may be just the opposite.

Access to technology has also helped smaller firms compete. Mike Whaling, president of 30 Lines, a social media marketing company, explains, "It starts to level the playing field. It gives small businesses the opportunity to put themselves out there and really compete with larger companies."[47] Sophisticated computer software, once accessible only to large businesses, is now available at prices small companies can afford. In fact, the Web is full of free tools to help entrepreneurs start, run, and grow their businesses.

As an example of using existing technology to innovate, consider the current trend among many small businesses to take advantage of "location-based social networking." Restaurants, retailers, and other types of small businesses are signing up for services provided by such companies as Facebook and Foursquare that allow consumers equipped with smartphones to "check-in" and broadcast their current store location to their entire social network. This type of viral marketing is an inexpensive and easy way for small businesses to get their names out in the marketplace in real time and engage other consumers who might be perusing their social networks. While these small businesses did not create this technology, they are clearly being innovative in using it.

1-5e Niche Markets

Almost all small businesses try to shield themselves from competition by targeting a specific group of customers who have an identifiable but very narrow range of product or service interests and comprise what is called a **niche market**. The niche might consist of a uniquely specialized product or service, or it might be a focus on serving a particular geographical area.

An article in *The Wall Street Journal* highlighted the re-emergence of small specialty shops in the United States by writing somewhat humorously about Tom Hanks and Meg Ryan as stars in a sequel to the 1998 hit movie "You've Got Mail." Tom's mega-bookstore chain Fox & Sons has to file for bankruptcy because the Internet has taken away much of his large-volume discount business. At the same time, an opportunity develops for the re-emergence of a local store to better serve those consumers who prefer not to spend their time searching for books online. Tom and Meg find themselves investing their savings to re-open Meg's old neighborhood bookstore to take advantage of this niche market.[48] This entertaining example is only one of many illustrating why the future looks bright for those who are willing to put in the necessary work to follow their dream. In reality, numerous small businesses are uniquely positioned to capture niche markets.

niche market
A specific group of customers with an identifiable but narrow range of product or service interests.

Successful entrepreneurs are not overly concerned about their ability to compete with their larger counterparts. With few exceptions, large corporations are bureaucracies, with bureaucrats as managers. As already pointed out, their R&D methods focus on the status quo. In addition, large companies have difficulty creating effective incentives for employees so that they will think entrepreneurially. There is considerable evidence that most workers in today's huge corporations are simply not engaged in their work. Many, like Jim Halpert from the popular TV show "The Office," would declare, "This is just a job…. If this were my career, I'd have to throw myself in front of a train."[49] The bottom line is that small companies with an entrepreneurial culture can compete and compete well.

1-6 BUILDING AN ENTREPRENEURIAL LEGACY

An entrepreneur builds a business, a life, and a legacy day by day, starting with the initial launch and proceeding through the months and years of operations that follow. A person exiting an entrepreneurial venture has completed the business part of his or her legacy—it must be constructed during the life of the enterprise itself. Therefore, an entrepreneur needs to keep the end in mind, while making innumerable operating decisions. By selecting the proper values and wisely balancing their application, an entrepreneur can make a satisfying exit, leaving a positive and substantial legacy to heirs, employees, the community, and the broader society.

When an entrepreneur comes to the point in time to exit the business usually by selling or passing it on to the next generation, his or her business achievements become history. Reflecting on their lives and businesses, many entrepreneurs come face to face with questions such as these: Was it a good journey? What kind of meaning does it hold for me now? Can I feel good about it? What are my disappointments? How did I make a difference?

In anticipating this time of looking back, an entrepreneur should think in terms of a legacy. A legacy consists of those things passed on or left behind. In a narrow sense, it describes material possessions bequeathed to one's heirs. In a broader sense, it refers to everything that one leaves behind—material items, good or bad family relationships, and a record of integrity or greed, of contribution or exploitation. An **entrepreneurial legacy** includes both tangible items and intangible qualities passed on not only to heirs but also to the broader society. You can appreciate, then, the seriousness with which the entrepreneur needs to consider the kind of legacy he or she is building.

It is easy for entrepreneurs to get caught up in activities, working harder and harder to keep up with the busy pace of life. Ultimately, such entrepreneurs may find their business accomplishments overshadowed by the neglect or sacrifice of something more important to them. It's possible to score points in the wrong game or win battles in the wrong war.

Ed Bonneau revolutionized the distribution of sunglasses in the United States and eventually dominated that market with his highly successful business. While growing the firm, Bonneau purchased Pennsylvania Optical (with its patents and contracts with Walmart and Kmart) and industry giant Foster Grant (with its patents and manufacturing divisions). Then, Bonneau sold the business and walked away from it all. From a business standpoint, his was a huge entrepreneurial success story. However, in a comment on how he'd like to be remembered, Bonneau downplayed his financial wealth:

I would hope that they knew something else besides that I once ran the biggest sunglass company in the world. That's not the number one thing that I'd want to be

entrepreneurial legacy
Material assets and intangible qualities passed on to both heirs and society.

known for. It's okay, but I'd much rather have that final assessment made by my kids and have them say, "He was a terrific dad." I never wanted to sacrifice my family or my church for my business. [50]

And Bonneau's advice to younger entrepreneurs follows a similar theme:

Take your faith and your family with you when you go into business, and keep that balance in your life. Because when you get to be 60 years old and you look back over your life, if all you have is the biggest sunglass company in the world and a pot full of money in the bank … it won't be enough. Your life is going to be hollow, and you can't go back and redo it. [51]

© Maksym Bondarchuk/Shutterstock.com

When he was an MBA student, Ty Findley talked about his father, Steven Findley, who founded and was CEO of Titan Dynamics. Ty explains, "His legacy as an entrepreneur was not limited to building a company. He also wanted to make a difference through his family and community involvement. Dad managed to balance operating his business with raising and supporting a family of eight children." Steven says, "It means a lot to know that my children have always felt loved by their father, and that they are growing into individuals who will hopefully have a positive impact on the world."[52]

In entrepreneurial terms, what constitutes a worthy legacy? One issue is the nature of the endeavor itself. For most entrepreneurs looking back on their careers, *fulfillment* requires that their businesses have been constructive or positive in their impact. The late Bernard Rapaport, a highly successful, principled, and generous entrepreneur, stressed the importance of the means a person takes to achieve a given end. "Whatever it is you want to achieve," he said, "*how* you achieve it is more important than if you achieve it." Reflecting on his life and legacy at the age of 93, he said, "What do I want to do? I want to save the world."[53]

Such idealism can guide an entrepreneur into many endeavors that are useful to our economic system and even society, either during their business life—or afterwards. For example, after he sold his business, J. O. Stewart, who lived in El Paso, Texas, launched a new firm whose primary objective was to provide good, low-cost housing to families in Mexico who could not otherwise afford it. His motivation for this venture was personal concern for the needs of low-income families.

It is the authors' deepest hope that your journey in owning your own business and being an entrepreneur—if you should choose to take that step—will be a richly rewarding experience, not only financially but also in the other important facets of your life. Above all, we hope that your legacy will bring both satisfaction *and* fulfillment for you and the important people in your life.

1-7 WHERE TO FROM HERE?

An airplane pilot not only controls the plane during take-off but also flies it and lands it. Similarly, entrepreneurs not only launch firms but also "fly" them; that is, they manage their firm's subsequent operation. In this book, you will find a discussion of the entire entrepreneurial process. It begins in the remainder of Part 1 (Chapter 2) with an examination of the fundamental values of the entrepreneur. Parts 2 and 3 look at a firm's basic strategy, the various types of entrepreneurial ventures, and the initial planning that is required for business startups. Parts 4 through 6 deal with the marketing and management of a growing business, including its human resources, operations, and finances.

1-1. Explain the importance of small business and entrepreneurship in our society.

- Owning a business is one of the most noble of all professions.
- Within the United States, it is estimated that 12 million people are involved in some form of entrepreneurial venture. Also, as many as half of all adults will be engaged in self-employment at some point during their working careers.
- There were almost 6 million businesses in the United States with employees in 2009. Of these companies, 90 percent had fewer than 20 employees and companies with fewer than 500 employees accounted for almost all the firms—99.7 percent.
- The companies with fewer than 500 employees hired almost 50 percent of all employees, accounted for 43 percent of all the salaries paid to employees, and in 2007, generated 38 percent of all business revenues. They also hired 43 percent of high-tech employees.
- Small firms accounted for 97.3 percent of all exporters
- Industries in which small businesses are more prevalent include services, construction, retail trade, health care, and hospitality.

1-2. Distinguish between the terms *small business* and *entrepreneurial opportunity*, and provide examples.

- Definitions of *small business* are arbitrary, but we focus on firms that are small compared to the largest firms in the industry, have mostly localized operations, are financed by a small number of individuals, and have growth potential.
- An entrepreneurial opportunity is an *economically attractive and timely opportunity* that creates value both for prospective customers and for the firm's owners. Entrepreneurs relentlessly pursue an opportunity, in either a new or an existing enterprise, to create value while assuming both the risk and the reward for his or her efforts. They generally think differently about resources than do employee-managers. They even try to use other people's resources, which is called bootstrapping.

- Table Occasions, Blank Label, and Tender Greens are examples of highly successful startups in different industries with different types of owners.

1-3. Explain the basic characteristics of entrepreneurs, and describe the different types of entrepreneurship.

- Research suggests that there are desirable and undesirable qualities of entrepreneurs.
- "Pure" entrepreneurs are often considered founders of new businesses that bring new or improved products or services to market
- Second-generation owner-managers and franchisees comprise yet another category of entrepreneurs.
- An entrepreneurial team consists of two or more individuals who combine their efforts to function in the capacity of entrepreneurs.
- The social issues affecting businesses are numerous and diverse. Businesses are expected—at different times and by various groups—to help solve social problems related to education, crime, poverty, and the environment.
- Social entrepreneurship refers to "entrepreneurial activity with an embedded social purpose."
- An increasing number of women are starting and growing profitable businesses in previously male-dominated industries. Despite their progress, there still exists a gender gap. A study found no difference in firm performance between women-owned and men-owned companies.

1-4. Discuss the importance of understanding your motivations and perceptions related to owning a small business.

- Understanding clearly why you want to own a small business and what motivates you are vital to eventually achieving fulfillment through your business.
- Friends and family who own or have owned businesses can be influential in your decision to start a business.
- Entrepreneurship often provides an attractive alternative for individuals fleeing from undesirable job situations.
- One of the primary reasons for becoming an entrepreneur is to make the world a better place (make meaning). Others include personal satisfaction, personal fulfillment (contributing to one's community), independence, and financial rewards.
- Three personalities come into play when you are starting a business: the technician personality, the manager personality, and the entrepreneur personality.
- The technician personality is a steady worker, experienced at *doing* what he or she knows best. The technician dislikes managing, wanting instead to be left alone to get the job done. Also, the technician lives in the moment, without thinking of the future.

- An individual with a manager personality is pragmatic, assuming responsibility for the planning, order, and predictability of the business.

- The entrepreneur personality takes an idea and turns it into an opportunity. This personality examines how the business does what it is intended to do.

1-5. Describe five potential competitive advantages of small entrepreneurial companies over large firms.

- *Customer focus*: Small business owners have an opportunity to know their customers well and to focus on meeting their needs.

- *Quality performance*: By emphasizing quality in products and services, small firms can build a competitive advantage.

- *Integrity and responsibility*: Independent business owners can build an internal culture based on integrity and responsibility that is reflected in relationships both inside and outside the firm. Such a culture helps strengthen the firm's position in a competitive environment.

- *Innovation*: Many small firms have demonstrated a superior talent for finding innovative products and developing better ways of doing business.

- *Niche markets*: Small firms that find a distinct market segment of some type can gain an advantage in the marketplace.

1-6. Explain the concept of an entrepreneurial legacy and its challenges.

- An entrepreneur's legacy includes not only money and material possessions but also such nonmaterial things as personal relationships and values.

- Part of the legacy is the company's contribution to the community.

- A worthy legacy includes a good balance of values and principles important to the entrepreneur.

- Building a legacy is an ongoing process that begins with the launch of the firm and continues throughout its operating life.

Key Terms

attractive small firm p. 5	founder p. 9	niche market p. 23
bootstrapping p. 6	franchisee p. 10	paradigm shift p. 18
corporate refugee p. 14	high-potential venture (gazelle) p. 5	reluctant entrepreneur p. 14
entrepreneur p. 6	lifestyle business p. 5	small business p. 5
entrepreneur personality p. 20	manager personality p. 19	social entrepreneurship p. 11
entrepreneurial legacy p. 24	mentor p. 12	technician personality p. 18
entrepreneurial opportunity p. 6	microbusiness p. 5	
entrepreneurial team p. 11	microloans p. 5	

Discussion Questions

1. The three stories discussed at the beginning of the chapter are to some extent exceptions to the rule in the amount of success the entrepreneurs experienced. What, then, is their significance in illustrating entrepreneurial opportunity? Are these stories misleading?

2. What is meant by the term *entrepreneur*?

3. Consider an entrepreneur you know personally. What was the most significant reason that she or he decided to follow an independent business career? If you don't already know the reason, discuss it with that person.

4. What do you believe would be the two most desirable and the two most undesirable qualities of an entrepreneur?

5. The motivators/rewards of profit, independence, and personal satisfaction and fulfilment are reasons that individuals enter entrepreneurial careers. What problems might be anticipated if an entrepreneur became obsessed with one of these rewards—for example, if she or he had an excessive desire to accumulate wealth, operate independently, or achieve a particular lifestyle?

6. How do different personality traits affect an entrepreneur's effectiveness in running a small business?

7. What do you believe is the advantage of having an entrepreneurial team when starting a business?

8. Explain how customer focus and innovation can be special strengths of small businesses.

9. Explain the concept of an entrepreneurial legacy.

10. Explain the following statement: "One can climb the ladder to success only to discover it is leaning against the wrong wall."

Situation 1

In the following statement, a business owner attempts to explain and justify his preference for slow growth in his business.

I limit my growth pace and make every effort to service my present customers in the manner they deserve. I have some peer pressure to do otherwise by following the advice of experts—that is, to take on partners and debt to facilitate rapid growth in sales and market share. When tempted by such thoughts, I think about what I might gain. Perhaps I could make more money, but I would also expect a lot more problems. Also, I think it might interfere somewhat with my family relationships, which are very important to me.

Question 1 Should this venture be regarded as entrepreneurial? Is the owner a true entrepreneur?

Question 2 Do you agree with the philosophy expressed here? Is the owner really doing what is best for his family?

Question 3 What kinds of problems is this owner trying to avoid?

Situation 2

You are a senior manager of strategy and business development at American Express, and have no plans to start your own company. You have just been given the opportunity to become the director of business development and marketing at a startup company. You believe the opportunity would build nicely on your experience at American Express. You have become excited about the opportunity. After all, you would be a position to make things happen, but you recently read an article that advised middle managers not to be too quick to leave a bigger company where they are gaining experience and moving up in the ranks.

Question 1 What information would you want to help make your decision?

Question 2 What would keep you from joining the startup company?

Question 3 How does the timing in your career affect your decision?

Question 4 Why might you accept the offer?

Question 5 What terms would you want to negotiate if you are inclined to take the offer?

Situation 3

Bear Bills, Inc., was started in 2008 by three Baylor University alumni in their early 20s as a solution to a problem every college student faces—paying utilities! The company's name originated from the university's mascot, the Baylor Bears. The business helps students pay their utility bills without all the hassles of having to collect from each roommate and getting a check to the utility company. Bear Bills pays the bills each month and splits the amount based on each student's prorated portion. The utility companies like the arrangement and are willing to give Bear Bills a commission for increasing their market share. The apartment houses where the students live like the deal because the utilities remain in the renters' names and the management receives a referral fee from Bear Bills. Of course, the students sign up because they do not have to bug a roommate to pay their share of the bill. And Bear Bills makes money.

The first year, Bear Bills signed up over 2,000 college students at the university. The second year, it incorporated as Simple Bills, Inc., and went to other college campuses, doubling its customer base to over 4,000.

At this point, the concept is proven, but the owners have a decision to make. They can raise money from investors and grow the company faster to capture market share, but that will mean they will have to give up some of their ownership in the company. Alternatively, they can continue to bootstrap the business to conserve ownership percentage but cannot grow as rapidly. In other words, they would limit the growth of the business to what can be financed from the cash flows currently being generated from operations.

Question 1 What do you like and not like about the Simple Bills concept?

Question 2 Would you recommend raising funds from outside investors and growing faster or continuing to bootstrap the operations to conserve ownership? Why?

Question 3 What strategy would you suggest for growing the business, assuming new investors are brought in?

Question 4 If you choose to raise funds, whom might you seek as investors?

Situation 4

Bracken Arnhart, the founder and CEO of WSR Tool Services, Inc., has basically immersed himself for the past 10 years in growing his business, and has been unquestionably successful in doing so. When he started the company, there were only three employees. Today, he has over 100 employees, and he has achieved more than he even had hoped for in terms of financial rewards.

To realize the goals he set out for the business, Arnhart knows it has been at some cost to his personal and family life. He explains that he always tries to be at home when his children get up in the morning and is there to help tuck them into bed at night. The rest of the time, he is focused on the business. In discussing his life–work balance, he says,

> Living a balanced life is generally more accepted by society than sacrificing much of one's time to pursue one thing in particular. However, I would argue that to truly do something great, one must give an inordinate amount of time and hard work to see it come to pass.
>
> There are the people that are just not ok with the fact that there are only 24 hours in a day. However, unable to alter this fact of life, they are bent on wringing the most out of those 24 hours, and doing it eight days a week, 53 weeks out of the year, only slowing down when they die (and even then, still going at about half-pace). They welcome angels such as caffeine, and curse crutches such as food and sleep. I would probably fall into this category.
>
> I would say that I have exchanged work-life balance for building a business. I am told that I'm pretty hard to get ahold of, and even when I do have "free time," my mind is still fully engaged with my business. I am passionate about what I am doing and wouldn't want to be doing anything else. I'll admit that I may miss meals, social events, and really anything that could distract me from my goal, and I am generally ok with it.
>
> I believe that this is perfectly acceptable for entrepreneurs, possibly even necessary. Work-life balance is a great debate between entrepreneurs, small-business owners, and even those attempting to climb the corporate ladder faster than most. Many are of the opinion that living a balanced life is essential for personal 'success,' whatever that may look like. However, I strongly believe that tipping the scales toward building a business is the only way to go.

Question 1 Is work–life balance for everyone?

Question 2 Is work–life balance simply a preference, or is it a necessity when growing a business?

Question 3 As an entrepreneur, would there be areas in your life that you would place at a higher priority than growing a business? Explain.

Experiential Exercises

1. Analyze your own education and experience as qualifications for entrepreneurship. Identify your greatest strengths and weaknesses.

2. Explain your own interest in each type of entrepreneurial reward. Identify which type of incentive is most significant for you personally and explain why.

3. Interview someone who has started a business, being sure to ask for information regarding the entrepreneur's background and age at the time the business was started. In your report of the interview, indicate the entrepreneur's motivations and his or her personality type.

Small Business & Entrepreneurship Resource Center

The Small Business & Entrepreneurship Resource Center offers complete small business management resources through a comprehensive database that covers all major areas of starting, operating, and maintaining a business from financing, management, marketing, accounting, taxes, and more. Go to www.cengagebrain.com and select the Longenecker text for more information on how to access this material.

1. Gaining resources is important for entrepreneurs and small business owners. Bootstrap finance methods provide access to capital, appeal to funding preferences, are widely used, and are often cost-effective. Yet, little is known about the relationship between owner traits and bootstrap financing.

This research identified differences between owners grouped by personal characteristics and the bootstrap approaches they chose. For example, research has shown that higher educational achievement enhanced the ability to obtain a bank loan. After reading this article, discuss whether you think that better insights into an entrepreneur's capital choice tendencies could assist educators in offering better alternatives to satisfy capital needs? Explain your point of view.

2. This study shows the growing importance of gender in small firm research and better understanding of owner characteristics in small firm success. Research has shown that female entrepreneurs rely more heavily than on financing from

family, friends, and personal resources than do males, who prefer commercial loans or the sale of equity. Studies have also shown that female owner-managers use customer-based bootstrapping more regularly than males and act with a greater sense of commitment to supporters. Do you think that this finding reflects women's tendency to manage their businesses through relationships among stakeholders? Explain your answer.

Sources: Neeley, Lynn, and Howard Van Auken. "The relationship between owner characteristics and use of bootstrap financing methods." *Journal of Small Business and Entrepreneurship*, Vol. 22, No. 4 (Fall 2009), p. 399(14). *Small Business Resource Center*. Gale. Higher Education. http://find.galegroup.com/sbrc/start.do?prodId=SBRC, accessed February 25, 2013.

Case 1

DashLocker (P. 645)

In 2010, Robert Hennessy left his job and started his own company, a high-tech laundry service in Manhattan's Upper East Side. What inspired the career change? Hennessy simply saw a need in the market and felt a call to respond. What initially began as a simple coin-operated laundromat grew into a business currently known as DashLocker, a round-the-clock dry cleaning and wash-and-fold service. The case introduces the student to issues faced in deciding whether to start a new business, including such matters as a founder's motivations, the nature of the opportunity, and what is involved in getting started.

Alternative Cases for Chapter 1

Endnotes

1. Clayton Christensen, a Harvard Business School professor, develops this theme in his e-book, *How Will You Measure Your Life?* (New York: HarperCollins, May 2012) (available on Amazon.com). In his book, he says that there is no more noble profession than *being in business*. We believe that what he says is even more true of owning your own business. Reading his book, which is short, will be well worth your time.

2. Jeff Sandefer and Robert Sirico, *A Field Guide for the Hero's Journey* (Grand Rapids, MI: Acton Institute, 2012), p. 5.

3. Paul D. Reynolds and Richard T. Curtin, "Business Creation in the United States: Panel Study of Entrepreneurial Dynamics II, Initial Assessment," *Foundations and Trends in Entrepreneurship*, Vol. 4, No. 3 (2008), p. 158.

4. *Ibid.*, p. 175

5. For an extensive report of the role of small businesses in the U.S. economy, see "The Small Business Economy 2011," United States Government Printing Office, http://www.sba.gov/sites/default/files/SBE_2011_2.pdf, accessed August 15, 2012.

6. Tracy Stapp, "The [10] Most Popular Franchises for Military Veterans," *Entrepreneur*, June 21, www.entrepreneur.com/article/219846, accessed June 30, 2012.

7. Tim Kane, "The Importance of Startups in Job Creation and Job Destruction," Kauffman Foundation Research Series: Firm Formation and Economic Growth, July 2010, pp. 2, 6.

8. The definition of a small business by the SBA varies depending on the industry, but the criterion of 500 employees is the starting point.

9. Contributed by Chia Stewart and Claudia Narvaez, November 16, 2012.

10. Interview with Fan Bi, March 21, 2012; *What Is Blank Label?* www.blanklabel.com/story.aspx, accessed March 10, 2012; K. Dziadul, *New Co-Creation Concept Drives Business Model for Blank Label*, http://bostinnovation.com/2010/09/09/new-co-creation-concept-drives-business-model-for-blank-label/, accessed January 23, 2012; J. Holland, "Two College Entrepreneurs Dress for Success." *Entrepreneur*, March 2011; and Kyle Alspach, "Startup Updates—Blank Label, LevelUp," *Boston Business Journal*, June 2012, www.bizjournals.com/boston/blog/startups/2012/06/blank-label-levelup-cambridge.html, accessed September 8, 2012.

11. Nancy Mann Jackson, "6 Steps to a Successful Business Launch," *Entrepreneur*, June 25, 2012, www.entrepreneur.com/article/223732, accessed September 29, 2012.

12. Stephen Spinelli and Robert Adams, *New Venture Creation: Entrepreneurship for the 21st Century*, 9th ed. (New York, NY: McGraw-Hill/Irwin, 2012), pp. 37–43.

13. As quoted in John Koten, "Everything Will Change," *Inc.*, September 2007, http://ww.inc.com/magazine/20070901/everything-will-change.html, accessed September 16, 2012.

14. This definition is offered in James Austin, Howard Stevenson, and Jane Wei-Skillern, "Social and Commercial Entrepreneurship: Same, Different, or Both?" *Entrepreneurship Theory & Practice*, Vol. 30, No. 1 (2006), pp. 1–22. However, the authors recognize that definitions of the term vary from an emphasis on nonprofit enterprises to corporate philanthropy and many other activities. Indeed, the article identifies key differences between social and commercial entrepreneurship. Using Sahlman's analytical framework [W. A. Sahlman, "Some Thoughts on Business Plans," in W. A. Sahlman, H. Stevenson, M. J. Roberts, and A. V. Bhide (eds.), *The Entrepreneurial Venture* (Boston: Harvard Business School Press, 1996), pp. 138–176], the authors compare the two forms of entrepreneurship across four

factors: the *people,* the *context,* the *deal,* and the *opportunity*. They highlight substantial differences across all four factors. For example, commercial entrepreneurs tend to focus on breakthrough opportunities where new needs are emerging, whereas social entrepreneurs are concerned with opportunities based on long-standing needs that can be served more effectively with innovative approaches. However, they also conclude there are notable similarities. The authors' observations suggest that the concept of social entrepreneurship, though becoming less ambiguous, is still not defined to the satisfaction of many entrepreneurship researchers.

15. "How a Business Can Change the World," *Inc.,* May 2011, pp. 82–94.

16. Kevin Henry, "The Difference Maker," *Baylor Business Review,* Fall 2012, http://bbr.baylor.edu/henry, accessed November 14, 2012.

17. Udo Brixy, Rolf Sternberg, and Heiko Stuber, "The Selectiveness of the Entrepreneurial Process," *Journal of Small Business Management,* Vol. 50, No. 1 (2012), pp. 105–131.

18. Sharon Hadary, "What's Holding Back Women Entrepreneurs?" *The Wall Street Journal,* May 17, 2010, pp. R1, R3.

19. Alicia M. Robb and John Watson, "Gender Differences in Firm Performance: Evidence from New Ventures in the United States, *Journal of Business Venturing,* Vol. 27, No. 5 (September 2012), pp. 544–558.

20. Personal conversation with Ewing Marion Kauffman, October 2005.

21. Jeff Sandefer and Robert Sirico, *A Field Guide for the Hero's Journey* (Grand Rapids, MI: Acton Institute, 2012), p. 11.

22. Quoted in Leigh Buchanan, "What Drives Entrepreneurs?" February 28, 2012, www.inc.com/magazine/201203/motivation-matrix.html, accessed October 1, 2012.

23. Quoted in Lena Basha, "The Entrepreneurial Gene," *MyBusiness,* December/January 2007, p. 15.

24. Ram Charan, "Stop Whining, Start Thinking," *Bloomberg Businessweek,* August 24, 2008, p. 58.

25. Elizabeth Alterma, "Employees Bid Goodbye to Corporate America," *USA Today,* August 20, 2011, www.usatoday.com/money /workplace/story/2011/08/Employees-bid-goodbye-to-corporate -America/50059194/1, accessed May 14, 2012; and http://joyfulplate.com /index.html, accessed August 15, 2012.

26. Very limited academic research has been conducted into the motivations of entrepreneurs. See Alan Carsrud and Malin Brannback, "Entrepreneurial Motivations: What Do We Still Need to Know?" *Journal of Small Business Management,* Vol. 49, No. 1 (2011), pp. 9–26.

27. Personal conversation with Chris DeLeenheer, CEO, Sunzer Consulting Group, November 15, 2012.

28. For a discussion of "making meaning," see Guy Kawasaki, *The Art of the Start* (The Woodlands, TX: Portfolio, 2004), pp. 4–6.

29. Bo Burlingham, "Lessons from a Blue-Collar Millionaire," *Inc.,* February 2010, pp. 56–63.

30. William J. Dennis, Jr. (ed.) "Contributions to Community," *NFIB National Small Business Poll,* Vol. 4, No. 6 (Washington, DC: NFIB Research Foundation, 2004), www.411sbfacts.com/sbpoll.php?POLLID=0025, accessed December 5, 2012.

31. Quoted in Lena Basha, "Like a Good Neighbor," *MyBusiness,* December/ January 2008, p. 28.

32. Personal conversation with Rick Davis, founder of Davaco, Inc., March 16, 2012.

33. Sue LaShellenbargerst, "Plumbing for Joy? Be Your Own Boss," *The Wall Street Journal,* September 2009, pp. D1–D2.

34. *Ibid.*

35. Elizabeth Alterma, "Employees Bid Goodbye to Corporate America," *USA Today,* August 20, 2011. www.usatoday.com/money /workplace/story/2011/08/Employees-bid-goodbye-to-corporate -America/50059194/1, accessed May 14, 2012.

36. Thomas J. Stanley and William D. Danko, *The Millionaire Next Door* (New York, NY: Simon & Schuster, 1996), p. 227.

37. Christensen, *op.cit.*

38. Stephen R. Covey, *The 7 Habits of Highly Effective People* (New York: Free Press, 2004), pp. 95–144.

39. Michael Gerber, *The E-Myth Revisited: Why Most Small Businesses Don't Work and What to Do About It* (New York, NY: HarperCollins, 1995), p. 19.

40. *Ibid.* p. 25.

41. *Ibid.* p. 24

42. *Ibid.* p. 31

43. Thomas L. Friedman, *The World Is Flat* (Waterville, ME: Thorndike Press, 2005).

44. For a number of studies by the Small Business Administration regarding the role of small firms in innovation, see *Innovation in Small Business: Drivers of Change and Value* (2009), www.sba.gov/advo/research/rs342tot .pdf; *An Analysis of Small Business Patents by Industry and Firm Size* (2008), www.sba.gov/advo/research/rstot335.pdf; *Innovation and Small Business Performance: Examining the Relationship Between Technological Innovation and the Within Industry Distributions of Fast Growth Firms* (2006), www .sba.gov/advo/research/rs272tot.pdf; *Small Firms: Why Market-Driven Innovation Can't Get Along Without Them* (2005), www.sba.gov/advo /research/sbe_05_ch08.pdf; *Small Firms and Technology: Acquisitions, Inventor Movement, and Technology Transfer* (2004); www.sba.gov/advo /research/rs233tot.pdf; *Small Serial Innovators: The Small Firm Contribution to Technical Change* (2003), www.sba.gov/advo/research/rs225tot.pdf; and *Influence of R&D Expenditures on New Firm Formation and Economic Growth* (2002), www.sba.gov/advo/research/rs222tot.pdf.

45. Clayton Christensen, *The Innovator's Dilemma* (New York, NY: HarperBusiness, 1997).

46. Amar Bhide, *The Venturesome Economy* (Princeton, NJ: Princeton University Press, 2008).

47. Lindsey Holloway, "The Best Things in Life Are Free," *Entrepreneur,* January 2009, pp. 42–45.

48. Peter Funt, WSJ Opinion, September 20, 2010.Peter Funt, *WSJ Opinion,* September 20, 2010.

49. Alan Murray, "The End of Management," *The Wall Street Journal,* August 21, 2010, p. W3.

50. Comments by Ed Bonneau to an entrepreneurship class, November 20, 2012.

51. *Ibid.*

52. Based on Ty Findley's interview of his dad, Steve Findley, October 15, 2010.

53. Personal conversation with Bernard Rapaport, 2009.

© PortionPac Chemical Corporation

Integrity and Ethics: Foundations for Success in Small Business

© PortionPac Chemical Corporation

In the SPOTLIGHT
PortionPac® Chemical Corporation
www.portionpaccorp.com

After nearly half a century in existence, Chicago-based PortionPac® Chemical Corporation remains a small business, but it is doing just fine with 84 employees and increasing sales. And because of the way PortionPac puts people first, Winning Workplaces (a national nonprofit organization) and *Inc.* magazine named it a "Top Small Company Workplace." The recognition was clearly deserved.

PortionPac specializes in what the company calls Sustainable Solutions®, providing a complete system of safe, effective, and environmentally friendly cleaning products—but that is only a small part of its business formula. When it comes to working with its employees

and customers, the company is clearly exemplary. Who would have guessed that a chemical company would get the "people side" of its business so right?

The company's culture emphasizes three things—trust, satisfaction, and good relationships—and this shows up in the satisfaction and loyalty of its employees. (The company's turnover has been a mere 2 percent, with an average employee tenure of 13 years.) Out of respect for family life, PortionPac never runs a third shift, and it has been known to change work schedules so that employees could spend more time with their kids. The factory floor is more like an atrium than a place to mix chemicals, with natural light pouring in through skylights to bathe a thriving assortment of plants. To help with the long hours the employees spend working together, the machines on the floor were designed to produce less noise, which encourages conversation. Warren Weisberg, co-owner and vice president of the company, spends a lot of time in the factory, learning from the employees and soliciting opinions about their work. When employees request personal time, it is usually granted, and their special needs are always given serious consideration.

But PortionPac's concern for people does not end with its employees—the company also takes care of its customers, with a special focus on custodians, who are the ultimate users of the company's products. To make custodians' work more manageable, the firm has narrowed the range of products it sells from the dozens that typically clutter supply closets to a few color-coded basics that come in portion-controlled packages. Beyond this, PortionPac offers innovative safety and effective cleaning classes for custodians and was the first in the industry to hire a national education director to address their needs. These actions reinforce the message that custodians are part of an honorable occupation, that they are modern-day, chemical-wielding nobility.

Marvin Klein, the company's chairman and co-founder, actually thinks beyond custodial staff when he points out that a clean building can lead to improved student performance and increased office productivity. But the firm's concerns are even more far-ranging—PortionPac is very concerned about the impact of harmful chemicals on the environment. To help with this, the company's products come in premeasured packages to reduce waste. And because they are sold as concentrates that take up only one-tenth the volume of products in their final mix, packaging and shipping require far less energy. Custodians are also encouraged to ease the burden on landfills by reusing the spray bottles and mixing containers for products. Taken together, these features of PortionPac's strategy underscore the firm's uncommon respect for other people and its robust commitment to the well-being of the planet—all without hindering its financial performance.

So, what should be the focus of a well-managed firm? People or profits? PortionPac proves that a company may not have to choose between the two, and that's good news for everyone involved.

Sources: Based on Robert W. Hall, "PortionPac Chemical: Compression Pioneer," www.compression.org/portionpac-chemical-compression-pioneer, accessed July 11, 2012; Leigh Buchanan, "A Look Inside the Un-Factory," *Inc.*, www.inc.com /top-workplaces/2010/a-look-inside-the-un-factory_pagen_2.html, accessed July 11, 2012; and "PortionPac," www.portionpaccorp.com, accessed July 11, 2012.

PortionPac Chemical, this chapter's Spotlight company, is a very unique small business. Its leadership is intensely interested in financial performance but also pays very careful attention to the crucial relationships that make the business tick, especially those involving employees and customers.

Some say that it is precisely because of this emphasis on the people part of the puzzle that PortionPac performs so well. Others claim that the company's emphasis on the environment is also important and plays a key role in generating positive results. The most important point, however, is that PortionPac's leaders have the freedom to emphasize important relationships as they see fit. And consistent with the values of the company's founders, they have chosen to give serious consideration to the needs and interests of those who impact or are impacted by the firm's operations. They see this as a matter of integrity—of being true to the character of the enterprise and those who run it—and the emphasis seems to be paying off in many ways.

But what is integrity, anyway? That's a very important question. In this chapter, we define and discuss this fundamental concept, recognizing that it is the foundation for ethical behavior in small businesses. We also provide frameworks to guide you toward principled management.

2-1 WHAT IS INTEGRITY?

The seeds of business misdeeds are sown when individuals compromise their personal **integrity**—that is, they do not behave in a way that is consistent with the noble values, beliefs, and principles they claim to hold. According to Karl Eller—the highly successful entrepreneur who turned the business of outdoor advertising into

LO
2-1

Define *integrity*, and understand its importance to small businesses.

the revenue powerhouse that it is today—a person has integrity if his or her character remains whole, despite the pressure and circumstances of the worst of situations:

> *[A person of integrity] doesn't fold in a crunch; doesn't lie, cheat, flatter; doesn't fake credentials or keep two sets of books. He doesn't blame others for his mistakes or steal credit for their work. She never goes back on a deal: her handshake matches the tightest contract drawn up by the fanciest law firm in town.*[1]

In other words, **integrity** refers to a general sense of honesty and reliability that is expressed in a strong commitment to doing the right thing, regardless of the circumstances.

Some acts, such as cheating on taxes, clearly violate this standard, while others are less obvious but may be just as inappropriate. For example, one entrepreneur who owned a flooring sales business often sold sheets of linoleum at first-quality prices, even though they were graded as "seconds" by the factory. To hide his deception, he developed an ink roller that changed the factory stamp from "SECONDS" to read "SECONDS TO NONE!" Those who caught the inaccuracy probably figured it was a typo and gave it no more thought, but unsuspecting customers were paying for first-quality flooring, only to receive imperfect goods. By any measure, this shady business practice reveals a lack of integrity on the part of the entrepreneur.

As discussed in Chapter 1, a successful entrepreneur seeks financially rewarding opportunities while creating value, first and foremost, for prospective customers and the firm's owners. This perspective makes clear that relationships are critical and integrity is essential to success. Financial gain is important, but it should not be the only goal. In fact, "doing anything for money" can quickly lead to distortions in business behavior. There are numerous motivations for misconduct in companies, but inappropriate acts such as price fixing, overcharging customers, using pirated software, and a host of others are driven primarily by financial motives. Acting with integrity requires that an individual first consider the welfare of others.

Fortunately, many small business owners strive to live up to the highest standards of honesty, fairness, and respect in their business relationships. Although unethical practices receive extensive attention in the news, most entrepreneurs and other business leaders are people of principle whose integrity regulates their quest for profits.

2-2 INTEGRITY AND THE INTERESTS OF MAJOR STAKEHOLDERS

LO
2-2
Explain how integrity applies to various stakeholder groups.

It is probably evident by now that the notion of integrity is closely tied to ethical issues, which involve questions of right and wrong.[2] Such questions go far beyond what is legal or illegal. Entrepreneurs often must make decisions regarding what is respectful and fair, and these decisions are becoming more important over time.

An honest assessment of the marketplace recognizes that ethical problems sometimes crop up there. A recent Ethics Resource Center survey indicated that employees witness various forms of misconduct in their workplaces. The most frequently observed offenses involve the misuse of company time, abusive behavior, lying to employees, improper use of company resources, and inappropriate Internet use at work (see Exhibit 2.1 for the percentages of workers who observed these and other forms of unethical behavior). These are significant failures. And because a wide range of individuals may be involved and/or affected, it can be challenging for a small business owner to determine how best to address the underlying issues or resolve lingering problems related to such misbehavior.

integrity
A general sense of honesty and reliability that is expressed in a strong commitment to doing the right thing, regardless of the circumstances.

2.1   Frequently Observed Forms of Workplace Misconduct

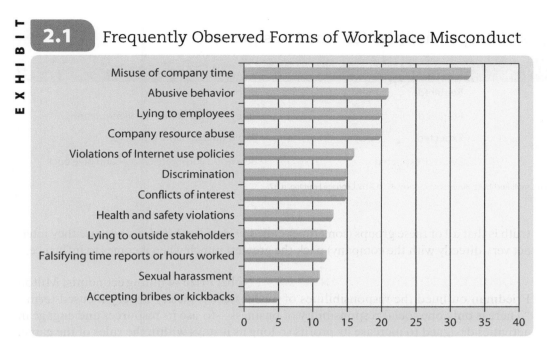

Misuse of company time

Abusive behavior

Lying to employees

Company resource abuse

Violations of Internet use policies

Discrimination

Conflicts of interest

Health and safety violations

Lying to outside stakeholders

Falsifying time reports or hours worked

Sexual harassment

Accepting bribes or kickbacks

0   5   10   15   20   25   30   35   40

Source: Ethics Resource Center, "2011 National Business Ethics Survey: Workplace Ethics in Transition," 2012, pp. 39–40.

When it comes to ethical behavior, small business owners guided by integrity must consider the interests of a number of different groups when making decisions. These groups include owners (or stockholders), customers, employees, the community, and the government, among others. Individuals in these groups are sometimes referred to as stakeholders, indicating that they have a "stake" in the operation of the business. Though definitions vary, **stakeholders** are typically described as those individuals or groups who either can affect the performance of the company or are affected by it.

Because the interests of various stakeholder groups are different, they sometimes conflict; thus, decisions can be very difficult to make. And because there may not be one completely right or wrong position to take, managing the process can be complicated.[3]

As suggested by business ethics and morality scholar Archie Carroll, some of a company's responsibilities cannot be negotiated away (see Exhibit 2.2). For example, a firm must remain profitable to stay in business, and it must also obey the law if it wishes to keep its doors open. Societal expectations regarding a venture's ethical performance may leave a small business owner with a bit more latitude, but it is very limited. Ignoring such expectations, while legal in a strict sense, is likely to tarnish the firm's reputation and can lead to serious repercussions, including negative publicity, consumer protests, or even lawsuits—and these can easily affect financial outcomes. Finally, discretionary responsibilities, such as providing support to the community, are more voluntary and offer greater flexibility. But even here, failing to respond is likely to have negative consequences. The concerns of important stakeholders are fundamental to the management of the business. If neglected, any one group can use its influence to negatively affect the performance of the company. Therefore, stakeholder interests should be carefully considered and wisely balanced.[4]

2-2a   "Big Three" Stakeholders—Owners, Customers, and Employees

Some say companies must follow the Golden Rule—that is, those that hold the gold (owners) make the rules! Others believe that the customer is always right. And how many times have you heard someone say that a company's people are its most important resource? The

stakeholders
Individuals or groups who either can affect or are affected by the performance of the company.

2.2 Four Types of Responsibilities for Small Businesses

Type of Responsibility	Societal Expectation	General Focus
Economic	Required	Be profitable.
Legal	Required	Obey all laws, adhere to all regulations.
Ethical	Expected	Avoid questionable practices.
Discretionary	Desired/Expected	Be a good corporate citizen, and give back.

Source: Adapted with permission from Carroll/Buchholtz, *Business and Society*, 8E. © 2012 Cengage Learning, p. 37.

truth is that all of these groups (sometimes called *primary stakeholders* because they interact very directly with the company) pack the greatest punch when it comes to influence.

PROMOTING THE OWNERS' INTERESTS Nobel Prize–winning economist Milton Friedman outlined the responsibilities of businesses to society in very focused terms: "There is only one social responsibility of business—to use its resources and engage in activities designed to increase its profits so long as it stays within the rules of the game, which is to say, engages in open and free competition without deception or fraud."[5]

Friedman argued that businesses should be expected simply to earn profits honestly; any other use of the firm's resources is justified only if it enhances the firm's value. While we believe that entrepreneurs should adopt a broader view of their social responsibilities, it is undeniable that owners have a clear and legitimate right to benefit from the financial performance of the company.

Many businesses, even small ones, have more than one owner. When this is the case, high standards of integrity require an honest attempt to promote the interests of all the owners, which include a commitment to financial performance and protection of the firm's reputation. Though entrepreneurs should be able to make their own decisions about personal matters, they have an obligation to make choices that protect the financial investment that others have in the company.

In many small businesses, a number of people own a small part of the enterprise but have no direct involvement in its operation. When this is the case, questions concerning proper conduct can show up in a number of areas. For example, entrepreneurs sometimes face ethical issues when reporting financial information. They must decide the extent to which they will be honest and candid. Because a firm has considerable discretion when revealing performance results, financial reports can sometimes be misleading without technically being illegal. But providing misleading financial information could easily persuade owners to make poor decisions regarding their investment in the company. The same could also be said for some who do not have ownership—outsiders such as bankers and suppliers who depend on a firm's financial reports to be accurate. It is always best to make honest disclosures that do not mislead in order to protect critical relationships and the reputation of the firm.

CARING ABOUT CUSTOMERS Customers are obviously one of the most important stakeholder groups that a company must please. The fact that they are central to the purpose of any business has implications for integrity. Owners who take customers seriously and care about them as individuals are apt to have more of them—and those they do have are likely to return often.

It is easy to fall into the habit of seeing every client as merely a dollar sign, but this narrow and self-serving view can lead to a wide range of questionable practices. For example, entrepreneurs are often tempted to take advantage of customers by being less than honest with them. And marketing decisions can be particularly complicated when it comes to ethical issues. Advertising content must sell the product or service but also tell the truth. Salespeople often must walk a fine line between persuasion and deception. In some businesses, a sales representative might obtain contracts more easily by offering improper incentives to buyers or by joining with competitors to rig bids. This is clearly illegal and eventually may result in damage to the company's reputation, which will affect relationships with existing and potential customers.

Companies with integrity recognize the importance of treating their customers with care, but it should be clear by now that this also just makes good sense. At its core, the formula for business success is actually quite simple: When a company delivers an excellent product with excellent service, customer satisfaction and healthy sales are likely to follow.

VALUING EMPLOYEES A firm's level of integrity is also expressed by the value it places on employees. Through management decisions, an owner affects employees' personal and family lives. Issues of fairness, honesty, and impartiality are inherent in decisions and practices regarding hiring, promotions, salary increases, dismissals, layoffs, and work assignments. Employees are also concerned about privacy, safety, and health issues, and these should not be ignored.

In communicating with employees, an owner may be truthful and fair, vague and misleading, or totally dishonest. Some entrepreneurs treat outsiders with great courtesy but display demeaning behavior or attitudes toward subordinates. Showing proper appreciation for subordinates as human beings and as valuable members of the team is an essential ingredient of managerial integrity. It is also wise, since employees are a firm's most important resource.

Many entrepreneurs recognize the great importance of looking after the needs of their employees, creating a positive work environment and rewarding them generously for their contribution. According to recent research, when employees feel that they are valued and socially connected at work, they tend to be highly engaged and much more productive.[6] To complete the picture, employees who are loyal to the business naturally want to pour themselves into their work, which leads to high-quality service, very loyal customers, and ultimately, repeat business and increased profits.[7] So, the owners' interests are well taken care of, and everyone is happy in the end. This really is no mystery—it all works beautifully when you see how the pieces fit together.

But, unfortunately, there are many ways that companies can stray from the integrity track. For example, some small business owners give little thought to the standards of conduct that guide everyday behavior, thinking that a shortcut here and there won't hurt anything. However, lapses in integrity can easily be passed down from superiors to subordinates, replicating like a life-threatening virus that spreads throughout the organization. As this influence expands, employees of small firms are likely to face pressure from various sources to act in ways that conflict with their own sense of what is right and wrong. For example, a salesperson may be pushed to compromise personal ethical standards in order to make a sale. Or an office employee may feel forced by her or his boss to act unethically, perhaps by destroying documents or misrepresenting production data. Such situations are guaranteed to spawn an organizational culture that erodes integrity.

Sometimes, employees may engage in unethical behavior at their employer's expense. They may fail in their ethical obligation to do "an honest day's work." Loafing on the job, working too slowly, and taking unjustified sick leave are all examples of such failure. Some employees even feign injury and draw fraudulent workers' compensation checks, thereby inflating a company's insurance costs.

Living the Dream

The Customer Isn't Always (Doing) Right

While it is important to emphasize the importance of treating customers with care and respect, sometimes it is the customer who is not particularly caring. At least that was the experience of Cecilia Levine, president of MFI International Manufacturing, an El Paso, Texas–based maquiladora operator. She was a single mother raising three children when she decided to launch her business. And as is so often the case, she had very limited resources with which to get her new enterprise off the ground. With the needs of her children constantly on her mind, she realized that there was very little room for error in her business calculations. Things were extremely tight, and that's when an excellent opportunity came into view. "It was an enormous break," recalls Levine, after she won the bid to make an apparel item for a major U.S. clothing firm. "This was going to make all the difference in the world to my struggling, young company."

The president of the apparel firm asked Levine to fly to New York to visit with him about some of the final arrangements regarding the design of the plant and the start of production for the specific item that his company wanted her startup to manufacture. She arranged flights for the trip at her own expense, even though she barely had enough money to pay for the tickets. In her mind, that was clearly the smart thing to do, given the enormous opportunity that seemed to be hers for the taking.

When Levine got to the president's office, there were two copies of a contract waiting for her on the conference table. But as the two went over the agreement together, she noticed that the price she was to receive for each items was 25 cents higher than that to which she had agreed in her proposal. Surprised by the discrepancy, Levine pointed out the apparent error in the price she was to receive for her work—after all, this was a mistake in her favor, and it would be dishonest to accept it.

But it was no mistake, and Levine was shocked at what her counterpart said next. "That isn't really an error, Cecilia," he began. "I'm asking you to add 25 cents to your price and then take that extra money and deposit it in a bank account in Mexico that I want you to open in my name."

A thousand thoughts swirled through Levine's mind as she pondered this request. "I can tell you that I really needed that contract," she now recalls, "but not under those circumstances. With all the wonderful business opportunities in the United States, we don't need to compromise ourselves in ways that would make it hard to sleep at night."

Despite the personal costs, Levine stood up, thanked the stunned executive for the chance to bid on the work, and walked out of his office. It was a moral choice for her—a question of values and integrity—and her conscience was not for sale.

The firm involved in the deal remains a very large, well-known, and highly regarded clothing company—indeed, a household name! Thinking back on the experience, Levine still has a hard time believing what happened. But as a final twist to the story, she knows the competitor who eventually got the contract. While she doesn't know the details of the deal that was struck with the colossal multinational, she knows that her rival was able to build an enormous plant in Mexico after the agreement was struck. But Levine isn't bothered by the way things turned out. "I sleep well at night," she observes with great serenity. It seems you can't put a price on honesty and peace of mind.

Source: Personal communication with Cecilia Levine, September 6, 2012.

According to FBI statistics, employees who steal supplies, merchandise, tools, or equipment from work cost employers as much as $150 billion each year,[8] a figure that does not even include losses from embezzlement (that is, when an employee steals money from the firm). These problems are serious, with some experts estimating that one-third of all new businesses fail because of employee theft of one kind or another.[9]

2-2b Social Responsibility and Small Business

As we discussed in Chapter 1, an ethical business not only treats customers and employees honestly but also acts as a good citizen in its community. These broader obligations of citizenship are called **social responsibilities**.

Some regard social responsibility as the price of freedom to operate independently in a free economy. They believe that the public has certain expectations regarding business behavior, not all of which are required by law. Accordingly, they regard some expenditures on social responsibilities as proper, even when they are costly.

To varying degrees, companies have increasingly accepted responsibility to the communities where they do business. Their contribution starts with creating jobs and adding to local tax revenues, but many entrepreneurs feel a duty to give back even more to the community in return for the local support they enjoy—and they usually benefit from increased goodwill as a result. It is important to recognize that opinions differ as to the extent to which businesses are obligated to engage in socially desirable activities, and the response of small businesses to those obligations also varies.

Contributions to the community can take many different forms. Ryan Allis and Aaron Houghton met when they were still students at the University of North Carolina. Using their experience in Web marketing, Web design, and software development, they started a new company to sell an innovative Web-based e-mail list management tool that Houghton had developed. They called their new venture iContact, and the market loved their product. Because the venture was profitable from its second year in business, Allis and Houghton chose to support charitable enterprises very early on. They established a social responsibility policy called the "4-1s" program: iContact gives away 1 percent of its employee time, 1 percent of its payroll, 1 percent of its product, and 1 percent of its equity to worthy nonprofit organizations. In a single year, iContact gave away 475 days of employee time to 63 organizations, contributed $109,000 in cash donations, and allowed 700 nonprofits to use its product free of charge. The company was recently acquired by a cloud-based marketing software firm called Vocus, so it remains to be seen whether the 4-1s program will be continued, but it has certainly been a very effective program for iContact to date.[10]

Entrepreneurs should think carefully about their community commitments, because building a business on a foundation of "doing good" may add to a small company's financial burden. This is often more than offset by increased loyalty from customers and employees who buy into the mission, which leads to improved productivity and morale. It also sets a company apart from competitors that offer similar products or services but make no charitable contributions. Perhaps most important, this commitment is often rewarded by customers in two ways—repeat sales and a willingness to pay a little more for what they get. These are strong incentives for a company to give serious consideration to its dedication to the community.[11]

But how do small business owners compare with big-business CEOs in their view of social responsibility? The evidence is limited, but research suggests that entrepreneurs who head small growth-oriented companies may be more narrowly focused on profits and therefore less socially sensitive than CEOs of large corporations. With simple survival as the most pressing priority, many small firms see social responsibility as a luxury they simply cannot afford. Small business philanthropy often takes place anyway, but in the form of personal contributions by business owners.

Entrepreneurs must reconcile their social obligations with the need to earn profits. Earning a profit is absolutely essential, and meeting the expectations of society can be expensive. For example, small firms must sometimes make expensive changes to conserve energy or emphasize recycling, and auto repair shops incur additional costs when they dispose of hazardous waste responsibly. It is evident that acting in the public

START UP

Getting Assistance from the SBA
Finding it difficult to get a grasp of your small firm's legal responsibilities? Just go to www.sba.gov, and choose the "Starting and Managing a Business" option to locate helpful government services from federal, state, and local agencies.

social responsibilities
A company's ethical obligations to the community.

Muna Haji, center, joined volunteers from Habitat for Humanity and Women Build as they held up the first wall of what will be her new home, Monday, June 11, 2012. Haji's home is the first to kick off Women Build 2012.

interest often requires spending money, which reduces profits. There are limits to what particular businesses can afford.

Fortunately, many types of socially responsible actions can be consistent with a firm's long-term profit objective.[12] A National Federation of Independent Business study found that 91 percent of small businesses made contributions to their communities through volunteering, in-kind assistance, and/or direct cash donations. The same study reported 74 percent of all small business owners volunteered for community and charitable activities, and the average commitment was just over 12 hours per month (which translates to 18 working days per year).[13] Overall, the evidence on performance impact is far from certain, but it suggests that commitment to the community may very well be good for business.

2-2c Governmental Laws and Regulations

Government at all levels serves a purpose, though there is room to debate whether it has too much power or too little. It intervenes directly in the economy when it establishes laws to ensure healthy competition. But its reach extends into other business matters as well—workplace safety, equal employment opportunities, fair pay, clean air, and safe products, to name a few. Entrepreneurs must comply with governmental laws and regulations if they are to maintain integrity—and avoid spending time behind bars.

One glaring example of unethical behavior by small firm management is fraudulent reporting of income and expenses for income tax purposes. This conduct includes *skimming* (that is, concealing some income), as well as improperly claiming personal expenses to be business-related. We do not mean to imply that all or even most small companies engage in such practices. However, tax evasion does occur, and the practice is common enough to be recognized as a general problem.

Tax avoidance can be flagrant and very intentional, but entrepreneurs often come up short on their tax commitments because of casual accounting systems, single-minded focus on their product or service, or both. One student entrepreneur confesses that he had a close brush with the law because he and his friends were creating clothing in his dorm room and selling it on his campus, but the company did not legally exist, and he was not keeping track of sales and expenses because he didn't take seriously the obligations and advantages of maintaining good records. But after a close encounter with Internal Revenue Service (IRS) agents, this young entrepreneur learned that accurate recordkeeping and legal formalities are necessary to ethical practice and, just as important, to peace of mind.[14]

When the topic of tax avoidance comes up, most people think of income taxes, but employee payroll tax—local, state, and federal obligations such as Social Security, Medicare, and unemployment—and other taxes must also be withheld. These often present the biggest tax burden on small businesses because they are owed regardless of whether the company makes a profit. And because tax authorities like the IRS do not always push hard enough to collect these taxes, small businesses can easily fall behind.[15] In any case, it should be clear that paying

RESOURCES

Avoid Drowning in a Sea of Regulatory Paperwork
Starting a new business may require you to complete, notarize, and file a dozen or more documents. But a new company called License123.com offers a $10 service that will help you locate, fill out, and file all required licenses and permits forms. Given the low price for the service and the serious hassles it can eliminate, that's quite a bargain!

all forms of required taxes is a nonnegotiable feature of integrity, especially for a small business owner who would like to stay in business.

2-3 THE CHALLENGES AND BENEFITS OF ACTING WITH INTEGRITY

LO 2-3

Identify some common challenges and benefits to integrity that arise in small businesses.

Small companies face unique challenges to integrity, especially at such critical stages as getting started and establishing a name, launching online operations, and expanding internationally. Small companies are often vulnerable because of their size and their desire to succeed. But the benefits of integrity are real and can offer small businesses a distinct advantage in the marketplace. Therefore, we will discuss how the payoff from managing with integrity can make a small business, and how lack of it can break one.

2-3a Small Companies and the Legitimacy Lie

Walking the straight and narrow may be more difficult and costly on Main Street than it is on Wall Street. That is, small privately held firms that are not part of the corporate world epitomized by Wall Street may face greater pressures than large businesses do to act unethically. Indeed, because small firms usually do not have the deep pockets and superior resources of their larger competitors, entrepreneurs may find it easier to rationalize, say, inappropriate gift giving or bribery as a way of offsetting what seem to be unfair limitations in order to establish a level playing field. It's easy to cave in to the pressure when your back is against the wall.

Because startups do not have a history and a reputation to lean on when trying to sell customers on their new product or service or to impress other important stakeholders, entrepreneurs often are uniquely tempted to resort to telling what some researchers call *legitimacy lies*.[16] That is, they sometimes misrepresent the facts to mislead others intentionally and earn their confidence. How do you feel about the following situations (which actually took place)?

- An entrepreneur launched his own fundraising business in South Carolina with only a few local projects to work on. Profits were slim, but that didn't stop him from telling everyone that business was great. Consistent with this false storyline, he set up an 800 number and launched a website to create an image of greater scale.[17]

- A small business owner who had just started a trucking company in Michigan sometimes used the phone in "creative ways" to shade customer impressions about the business. For example, "she pretended to transfer customers to different lines and used phony voices to make the company seem bigger."[18]

- Partners in an auto sales startup rented a large lot for their business but could afford only four cars for inventory—a turn-off for would-be buyers. So the partners offered free parking in their lot to any employee of the big firm next door who would allow them to put a false price tag on their car during the day as if it were for sale. Many accepted, and soon the lot was full every morning and mostly empty by late afternoon. Passersby figured the company must be doing a booming business, and predictably, actual sales soon followed.[19]

When small business owners create false impressions to make their companies look good, are they being dishonest or simply resourceful? Pretending to be something they are not can lead small business owners into what is, at best, a gray area. The drive and ingenuity of these entrepreneurs is certainly impressive, but their behavior raises questions about ethical standards. Such moves may save companies, but how would customers feel if they knew they were being manipulated in this way?

Telling legitimacy lies threatens the reputation of the business and the trust that goes along with it. If (when) the truth is revealed, future sales or support could very well be compromised. It would be better—and much more honest—to understand the levers that move customers to confidence in a purchase and provide honest information. Research has shown that customers are less likely to decide to purchase if they have significant questions about the product or service that the new venture is offering, those who represent and/or run the business, and the organization itself.[20] (We call these features *PRO factors*—standing for *P*roducts, *R*epresentatives, and the *O*rganization—to emphasize that they can promote firm performance when customers are satisfied with them.) The concerns of prospective customers include the following:

Because they so often must operate on very limited budgets, many small businesses use social media tools like Facebook to push information about their products or services out to prospective customers.

- Will the *product* (or *service*) serve my needs better than alternatives, and will it be a hassle to change over from the brand I currently buy? (Research indicates that product/service knowledge is the most important of the three factors when customers make purchase decisions.[21])

- Do the company's *representatives* know what they are talking about, and will they (can they) live up to their assurances?

- Will the *organization* still be around to stand behind its product or service if I have a problem with it six months from now?

These are all reasonable concerns, and it is important that the new venture find a way to address them. For example, advertising can help to get product or service information out to prospective customers. But because this can be expensive, many new ventures choose to lean on a well-crafted publicity program, social media tools, or other promotional strategies instead (more on these in Chapter 17).

Often, a small firm's legitimacy is staked on the reputation of its owner, but it is important to highlight and honestly bolster the credibility of anyone who represents the venture. It is best to make the credentials (educational background, expertise, industry experience, etc.) of key employees known, as well as to encourage the participation of those employees in trade, business, and community organizations where they can build important relationships and associations. The business itself can establish legitimacy by setting up a high-quality website, insisting on professional behavior from all customer-contact employees, forming strategic alliances with well-respected partner firms, and taking other, similar measures. The point is that a new venture or small company may be at a legitimacy disadvantage when compared to established competitors, but there are ways to close the gap. And while the focus is primarily on the reactions of customers, many of these principles clearly apply to relationships with investors, suppliers, and other important stakeholders as well.

2-3b Integrity and the Internet

Legitimacy and trust are important to all small businesses, but those using the Internet face a host of ethical issues that are unique to the online marketplace. One issue of great concern to Internet users is personal privacy. In fact, a recent poll found that more than 80 percent of Web users worry about how their personal information is being protected.[22]

Businesses and consumers often disagree about how private the identity of visitors to websites should be. For example, businesses can use cookies (digital "ID tags") to collect data on consumers' buying habits related to a particular Internet address. In this way, a business can create a detailed profile of customers, which it may then sell to media buying companies and other interested groups. While the collection of personal information may allow a business to create a more personalized shopping experience and offer convenience to the buyer, it also opens the door to potential misuse of data. To minimize customer concerns, a company must be honest and transparent with customers about its practices and draft a privacy policy that conforms to the guidelines provided by organizations like the Better Business Bureau (BBB) or through consultation with an attorney.

But it is not just online companies that have to worry about privacy issues. The extent to which an employer may monitor an employee's Internet activity is also hotly debated. Many workers believe it is inappropriate for employers to monitor their e-mail, a practice they consider to be an invasion of privacy. Employers, on the other hand, are concerned that employees may be wasting company time dealing with personal e-mail, shopping online, and surfing the Internet. And it appears there is reason for concern. Business journalist David Freedman reviewed research indicating that accessing the Internet at work for personal reasons is escalating rapidly. In an *Inc.* magazine article, he states,

> *American workers spent the equivalent of 2.3 million years' worth of 40-hour workweeks reading nonwork-related blogs while at work, according to a study by* Advertising Age *magazine. And that's just blogs. Millions more work years were spent shopping online, checking eBay listings, cruising social networks, looking for vacation deals, Googling old flames, and, of course, ogling porn. [This research reports that] employers spend nearly $760 billion a year paying employees to goof off on the Web.*[23]

Many employers are convinced such activity hinders workplace productivity and thus are taking steps to do something about it.[24]

An increasing number of small businesses are installing software to monitor Internet use, and one study found that 38 percent of firms go so far as hiring staff to read or otherwise analyze employees' e-mail.[25] Beyond productivity concerns, companies are very worried these days about leaks of sensitive information and system exposure to risky viruses and malware. But these must be balanced against respect for employee privacy.

In the past, the courts tended to give firms great freedom to monitor personal e-mail accounts accessed from company networks, but that is quickly changing. In a number of cases, the courts have ruled that a firm does not have a legal right to monitor personal e-mail at work unless it has explicitly informed employees that it may do so.[26] Most small companies choose not to monitor workers' Internet use, but those that do should be sure to develop a carefully worded and legally sound policy first, and then ensure that all employees are aware of it.[27] Taking such measures is very practical—it helps head off costly legal challenges—and it also communicates that the firm respects its employees and signals sound commitment to high standards of integrity.

Widespread use of the Internet has also focused attention on the issue of protecting **intellectual property**. Traditionally, protection has been granted to original intellectual creations—inventions, literary works, or artistic products such as music—in the form of patents, copyrights, trademarks, design rights, and trade secrets. The law allows originators of such intellectual property to require compensation for its use. However, the Internet has made it easy for millions of users to copy intellectual property free of charge.

The problem of online intellectual property rights violations were highlighted recently by accusations leveled against eBay, claiming that the auction power-house was in part responsible for rapidly increasing sales of counterfeit goods. When the French company LMVH, a world leader in prestige products, sampled eBay's online listings, it found that 90 percent of the 300,000 Dior and 150,000 Louis Vuitton handbags offered for sale were fake.[28] And when MarkMonitor, a brand protection firm, investigated illicit use of one major luxury brand's products, it found 15,000 websites that were selling "knockoff" version of its offerings.[29] Regardless of the legal liabilities, it is clear that the sale of counterfeit goods is a violation of the law and a breach of integrity. The practice cannot be defended.

Protection of intellectual property is a political as well as an ethical issue. Recent congressional hearings, lawsuits, and proposed legislation suggest that additions or changes to current laws are likely, and international enforcement continues to be a major problem.

2-3c Integrity and Doing Business Abroad

Sooner or later, small business owners operating abroad will confront challenging ethical questions, and they could relate to just about any part of the company's operations. For example, should your firm agree to provide consulting services to a foreign government if it refuses to support basic human rights or represses its citizens politically? Since China's environmental protections are relatively weak, would it be acceptable to use toxic chemicals in production processes there, as long as the local authorities approve it? If giving a gift to a business partner in Bolivia fits with local custom but is considered a bribe by U.S. standards, is there any harm in following such a practice? Such quandaries are bound to come up time and again when doing business abroad.

So what are entrepreneurs to do? Frequently, they simply apply U.S. standards to the situation. But this approach is sometimes criticized for resulting in **ethical imperialism**, an arrogant attempt to impose American values on other societies. Some guidance is provided by restrictions specified in the Foreign Corrupt Practices Act, which makes it illegal for U.S. businesses to use bribery in their dealings anywhere in the world. Regardless of local practices, American firms must comply with these laws, even though "gray areas" exist in which there are no definite answers.

Another viewpoint, sometimes called **ethical relativism**, is troublesome, because it implies that anything goes if the local culture accepts it. To define its ethical landscape and work out its position on difficult issues, a small business must consider the nuances of its particular international environments. Training is also needed to ensure that each employee understands the firm's commitment to integrity, and consulting an attorney in the United States with appropriate expertise is highly recommended.

Also, bear in mind that one-time practices may set a pattern for future behavior. Some business owners have observed that offering a bribe to make a business deal possible often creates expectations for more of the same in the future. Owners who refuse to pay these "fees" say that they may have to deal with frustrating inconveniences in

intellectual property
Original intellectual creations, including inventions, literary creations, and works of art, that are protected by patents or copyrights.

ethical imperialism
The belief that the ethical standards of one's own country can be applied universally.

ethical relativism
The belief that ethical standards are subject to local interpretation.

the short term (for example, shipped products being held up by customs), but it is likely to discourage such demands in the future. This is one of the ways in which integrity in business may offer unanticipated rewards.

2-3d Trust and the Integrity Edge

When it comes to establishing the legitimacy of a startup, taking operations online, expanding internationally, and so many other features of managing a small business, it is not always easy to stay on the high road of proper conduct. Indeed, the price of integrity is high, but the potential payoff is incalculable. The entrepreneur who makes honorable decisions, even when it comes to the smallest of details, can take satisfaction in knowing that she or he did what was right, even if things do not turn out as planned.

But integrity yields other important benefits as well. In his book *Integrity Is All You've Got,* Karl Eller observes that through his long career as a successful entrepreneur, he has seen one constant: the crucial role of integrity to achievement in business. As he puts it, "Those who have [integrity] usually succeed; those who don't have it usually fail."[30] Entrepreneurs with integrity are aware of the importance of the bottom line, but this is not their singular focus. Nonetheless, extraordinary financial performance often follows their efforts.

A growing body of research supports the simple notion that ethical business practices are good for business. Citing specific studies, the advocacy group Business for Social Responsibility (BSR) contends that there are numerous long-term benefits of adopting ethical and responsible business practices. These benefits include the following:[31]

- Improved financial performance
- Enhanced brand image and reputation
- Increased sales and customer loyalty
- Improved productivity and quality
- Better recruitment and reduced employee turnover
- Fewer regulatory inspections and less paperwork
- Improved access to capital

This is consistent with research conducted by the Institute of Business Ethics, which found that firms operating with a "clear commitment to ethical conduct" consistently outperform companies that do not. These findings prompted Philippa Foster Black, director of the institute, to declare, "Not only is ethical behavior in the business world the right and principled thing to do, but it has been proven that ethical behavior pays off in financial returns."[32]

Perhaps the greatest benefit of integrity in business is the *trust* it generates. Trust results only when the stated values of a company and its behavior in the marketplace match. When a small business owner considers the needs of others and follows through on her or his promises, stakeholders notice. Customers buy more of what a firm sells when they realize that the company is doing its best to make sure that its products are of high quality and its customer service is excellent. Employees are much more likely to "go the extra mile" for a small company when it is clear that they are more than simply replaceable parts in an impersonal machine.

And members of the community also respond positively when they are convinced that a firm is living up to its commitments to protect the environment and pay its fair share of taxes. Their support can keep the company going even if it falls on hard times. It all comes down to trust.

LO
2-4

Suggest practical approaches
for building a business with
integrity.

2-4 BUILDING A BUSINESS WITH INTEGRITY

The goal of a small business owner with integrity should be to operate honorably in all areas of practice, which sets the entrepreneur on a path toward crafting the worthy legacy that was discussed in Chapter 1. Those at the top must provide the leadership, culture, and training that support appropriate ethical perspectives and proper behavior.

2-4a The Foundations of Integrity

The business practices that a firm's leaders and employees view as right or wrong reflect their **underlying values**. An individual's beliefs affect what that person does on the job and how she or he acts toward customers and others. Business behavior, then, reflects the level of a person's commitment to honesty, respect, truthfulness, and so forth—in other words, to integrity in all of its dimensions. Such values are often organized into the business enterprise's mission statement.

Values that serve as a foundation for integrity in business are based on personal views of the role of humankind in the universe and, naturally, are part of basic philosophical and/or religious convictions.[33] In the United States, Judeo-Christian ideals have traditionally served as the general body of beliefs underlying business behavior, although there are plenty of examples of honorable behavior based on principles derived from other religions. Since religious and/or philosophical principles are reflected in the business practices of firms of all sizes, a leader's personal commitment to certain basic values is an important determinant of a small firm's commitment to business integrity. A long-time observer of high-tech startups commented on the significance of an entrepreneur's personal standards to investment decisions:

> *I can tell you, even with the smallest high-technology companies, the product had to be good, the market had to be good, the people had to be good. But the one thing that was checked out most extensively by venture capitalists was the integrity of the management team. And if integrity wasn't there, it didn't matter how good the product was, how good the market was—they weren't funded.*[34]

It seems apparent that a deep commitment to basic values affects behavior in the marketplace and gives rise to business practices that are widely appreciated and admired. Without a strong commitment to integrity on the part of small business leadership, ethical standards can easily be compromised.

2-4b Leading with Integrity

In a small organization, the influence of a leader is more pronounced than it is in a large corporation where leadership can become diffused. This fact is recognized by J. C. Huizenga, the founder and CEO of a public school management company called National Heritage Academies, which was ranked as one of the fastest-growing U.S. companies by *Inc.* magazine:

> *The executive of a small company must often face moral challenges more directly, because he or she has more direct contact with customers, suppliers, and employees than an executive in a large corporation who may have a management team to deliberate with. The consequences of his or her choices often affect the business more significantly because of the size of the issue relative to the size of the company.*[35]

underlying values
Beliefs that provide a foundation for ethical behavior in a firm.

© attaphong/Shutterstock.com

In effect, the founder or head of a small business can say, "My personal integrity is on the line, and I want you to do it this way." Such statements are easily understood. And a leader becomes even more effective when she or he backs up such statements with appropriate behavior. In fact, a leader's behavior has much greater influence on employees than her or his stated philosophy does. Everyone watches how the leader behaves, and this conduct establishes the culture of the company, underscoring what is allowed or encouraged and what is prohibited.

In summary, the personal integrity of the founder or owner is the key to a firm's ethical performance. The dominant role of this one person (or the leadership team) provides a powerful voice in shaping the ethical performance of the small company, for good or for ill.

2-4c An Ethical Organizational Culture

Integrity in a business requires a supportive organizational culture. Ideally, every manager and employee should instinctively resolve every ethical issue by simply doing what is right. An ethical culture requires an environment in which employees at every level are confident that the firm is fully committed to honorable conduct. To a considerable degree, strong leadership helps build this understanding. As a small business grows, however, personal interactions between the owner and employees occur less often, creating the need to articulate and reinforce principles of integrity in ways that supplement the personal example of the entrepreneur. A good place to start is to establish an ethics policy for the company.

In their highly influential book *The Power of Ethical Management,* Kenneth Blanchard and Norman Vincent Peale offer insights to guide the development of an ethics policy. They suggest that the policy be based on the following five fundamental principles:[36]

- *Purpose.* The vision for the company and your core values will guide business conduct.
- *Pride.* When employees take pride in their work and their company, they are much more likely to be ethical in their dealings.
- *Patience.* If you push too hard for short-term results, sooner or later acting unethically will seem to be the only way to achieve the outcomes you seek.
- *Persistence.* Stand by your word, which is the foundation of trust. If you are not committed to an ethical framework, your integrity is at risk, as is the reputation of the company.
- *Perspective.* Stop from time to time to reflect on where your business is going, why it is going that way, and how you plan to get there. This will allow you to be more confident that you are on the right track now and will continue to be in the future.

To define ethical behavior in the company more specifically, the owner-manager of a small firm should formulate a **code of ethics** similar to that of most large corporations. A survey of MBA students employed by small and medium-size

code of ethics
Official standards of employee behavior formulated by a business owner.

companies revealed that codes of ethics shape and improve conduct in their organizations in a number of ways:

- By defining behavioral expectations
- By communicating that those expectations apply to employees at all levels in the business
- By helping employees convey the company's standards of conduct to suppliers and customers
- By serving as a tool for handling peer pressure
- By providing a formal channel for communicating with superiors without fear of reprisal.[37]

In other words, a code of ethics identifies conduct that is ethical and appropriate, but it is also a practical tool that can encourage and protect ethical behavior.

A well-written code expresses the principles to be followed by employees of the firm and gives examples of these principles in action. A code of ethics might, for example, prohibit acceptance of gifts or favors from suppliers but point out standard business courtesies, such as a lunch or a couple of movie tickets, that might be accepted without violating the policy.[38] If a code of ethics is to be effective, employees must be aware of its nature and convinced of its importance. At the very least, each employee should read and sign it. As a company grows larger, employees will need training to ensure that the code is well understood and taken seriously.

Entrepreneurs further reinforce ethical culture in the business when they hire and promote ethical people, recognize and correct behavior that is unethical, and lead by example in business dealings, while encouraging all employees to do the same. With training and consistent management, employees can develop the level of understanding needed to act in the spirit of the code in situations not covered by specific rules. However, a code of ethics will be effective only to the degree that the entrepreneur's behavior is consistent with her or his own stated principles. Employees can easily spot hypocrisy, and double standards quickly dull the ethical sensibilities of the organization.

2-4d Better Business Bureaus

Sometimes the business conduct of small companies is shaped by external forces. Because unethical operations reflect adversely on honest members of the business community, privately owned companies in many cities have joined together to form Better Business Bureaus (BBBs). The purpose of such organizations is to promote ethical conduct on the part of all businesses in a region, and they do so in the following ways:

- By providing consumers with free information to help them make informed decisions when dealing with a company
- By creating an incentive for businesses to adhere to proper business practices and earnestly address customer complaints
- By resolving questions or disputes concerning purchases through mediation or arbitration

As a result, unethical business practices often decline in a community served by a Better Business Bureau.

Though BBBs report relevant information to law enforcement agencies, they are not government entities, and they cannot collect money or impose penalties on companies that engage in unethical business practices. However, a BBB can provide information on a company's operating track record, which will affect the firm's reputation and, in turn, its success in the marketplace. This creates an incentive for companies to adopt fair and proper business practices and address customer complaints appropriately in order to avoid losing business.

2-4e The Ethical Decision-Making Process

Ethical decision making often is not a very clear-cut process. In fact, even after much thought and soul searching, the appropriate course of action still may not be apparent in some business situations. The Ethics Resource Center offers a decision-making process that may help with challenging dilemmas. We have adapted this simple six-step process to help small business owners see the issues more clearly and make better, more ethical decisions.[39]

STEP 1: DEFINE THE PROBLEM How you define the problem is important because this will guide where you look for solutions. For example, if you have a customer who is often late paying on the invoices you send him, is this a problem because he does not manage his books well, he is trying to conserve his working capital by forcing you to carry this debt for him for as long as possible, or his own customers are consistently slow paying him for the goods he sells them? If your customer is careless with his books or is just trying to stretch out his accounts payable, a penalty for the delay may correct the problem. However, penalizing that customer is not likely to solve the problem if the delays are actually the result of his cash-strapped customers struggling to find a way to pay him. In fact, penalizing him in this case may only make matters worse. This common example shows that looking for the root of the problem is the best place to start in your search for a solution to a challenging ethical problem.

STEP 2: IDENTIFY ALTERNATIVE SOLUTIONS TO THE PROBLEM It is tempting to go with an "obvious" solution or one that has been used in the past, but often this is not the best answer—even if it is ethical. Be open-minded and consider creative alternatives. Often, an innovative solution is available that is consistent with your personal ethics, protects the interests of other affected parties, and offers superior outcomes. Seeking advice from trusted friends and advisors who have faced similar situations can spur your thinking and lead to options that you might otherwise overlook.

STEP 3: EVALUATE THE IDENTIFIED ALTERNATIVES Rotary Club International, a worldwide organization of business and professional leaders, has set a high standard for business conduct. It calls on its members to ask the following four questions when they prepare to make a decision about the things they think, say, or do:[40]

1. Is it the *truth*?
2. Is it *fair* to all concerned?
3. Will it build *goodwill* and *better friendships*?
4. Will it be *beneficial* to all concerned?

Taking a similar approach, you might ask yourself, "How would I feel if my decision were reported in the daily newspaper?" Or, the question can be even more personal: "How well could I explain this decision to my mother or children?" The answer could help to steer you away from unethical behavior.

Perhaps the most widely recommended principle for ethical behavior is simply to follow the Golden Rule: "Treat others as you would want to be treated." This simple rule is embraced, in one form or another, by most of the world's religions and philosophies,[41] and its influence is very far reaching. For example, the philosopher Immanuel

Kant introduced the so-called categorical imperative, a sophisticated way of asking, "How would it be if everyone decided to do what you intend to do?"[42] Raising such questions can be a very practical way for an entrepreneur to evaluate ethical decisions and guard her or his integrity.

No matter what approach you take, evaluating alternatives requires time and patience. In addition, personal perceptions and biases are likely to cloud the way you see solutions. Therefore, it is important to separate what you *think* is the case from what you *know* to be true. It often helps to write down your thoughts about alternatives so that you can keep track of your concerns as well as important facts and details. You might list the ethical pros and cons of each alternative or identify the impact of each option on every person or company that will be affected. Another possibility is to rank all potential options based on their overall merits and then narrow the list to the two or three best solutions so that you can consider these further. This will allow you to organize your thoughts and make a better selection.

STEP 4: MAKE THE DECISION The next step is to choose the "best" ethical response, based on your evaluation of all possible alternatives. On the surface, this sounds easy enough, but unfortunately no single option will completely solve the problem in most cases. In fact, you may not even be able to identify an obvious winner. No matter how you go about making the decision, keep your vision and core values firmly in mind—this is essential to making solid decisions that do not compromise your ethical standards.

STEP 5: IMPLEMENT THE DECISION This may seem like a "no-brainer," but entrepreneurs sometimes put off responding to ethical challenges because any response will be bad news for someone involved. But avoiding action on the decision may allow a small problem to grow into a major crisis, and it may cause you to spend more time thinking about the problem when other important matters deserve your attention.

STEP 6: EVALUATE THE DECISION The goal of making a decision is to resolve an ethical dilemma. So, has the situation improved, gotten worse, or stayed about the same? Has the solution created ethical issues of its own? Has information come to light indicating that your decision was not the most ethical course of action? Everyone makes mistakes. You may very well need to reopen the matter to make things right. But remember, if your decision was based on the best of intentions and information available at the time, you can wade back into the waters of ethical turmoil with a clear conscience, and there is no substitute for that.

LO
2-5

Define *sustainable small business*, and describe the influence the trend is having on small companies and startup opportunities.

2-5 SMALL BUSINESS AND THE NATURAL ENVIRONMENT

At one time there was little concern for the impact business had on the environment, but that is rapidly changing. For instance, releasing industrial waste into streams, contaminants into the air, and noise into neighborhoods is no longer acceptable. In fact, escalating concern for the environment has spawned a shift toward **sustainable small business**. This trend recognizes that a company must be profitable to stay in business, but it also promotes the use of eco-friendly practices (careful use of resources, energy conservation, recycling, etc.) through all facets of a company's operations. In short, a sustainable enterprise must respond to customer needs while showing reasonable concern for the environment. This is consistent with the concept of integrity outlined in this chapter.

2-5a Sustainability Matters

The interests of small business owners and environmentalists are not necessarily—or uniformly—in conflict. Some business leaders, including many in small companies, have consistently worked and acted for the cause of **environmentalism**, and in many cases this emphasis makes sound financial sense. For example, companies can actually save money by buying or leasing LEED-certified buildings. (This designation stands for "Leadership in Energy and Environmental Design" and is a stamp of approval granted only to those facilities that have been built to strict standards established by the U.S. Green Building Council to promote energy and water conservation, reduce CO_2 emissions, and improve indoor air quality.) Though more expensive to construct, such buildings can decrease energy costs from operations by as much as 20 percent, and healthier workplace environments improve employee productivity, reduce illness and absences, improve recruitment, and raise retention—all of which can create a net savings for the company. One analyst estimates that a 2 percent initial investment in eco-friendly design can generate a tenfold savings in operating costs.[43]

We need to emphasize, however, that the sustainability news for small business is not all good. For example, some firms are adversely affected by new laws passed to protect the environment. Businesses such as fast lube and oil change centers, medical waste disposal operations, self-service car washes, and asbestos removal services have been especially hard hit by expanding environmental regulations. The costs can be punishing. In fact, many companies in these industries and others have closed because of the financial burden of environmental controls. While small companies that enjoy favorable market conditions can often pass higher environmental costs on to their customers, these can easily sink a small, struggling firm with older equipment and limited resources to upgrade.

Regardless of the financial impact, it is critical to follow the environmental regulations that apply to your business. To ignore this responsibility is to violate the law. The authors of "Greening Your Business: A Primer for Smaller Companies" caution businesses to comply with regulations at all levels—federal, state, and local—but their overall message is actually very upbeat: "There are dozens of ways companies of all sizes can reduce their environmental footprints, save money, earn consumer trust and stakeholder confidence, comply with government regulations, be ready to snag new market opportunities, and boost efficiency and productivity."[44]

Win-win solutions are possible. For example, firms whose products leave minimal environmental impact are generally preferred by customers over competitors whose products pollute. And some entrepreneurs are able to build their small business on planet-saving products and services, such as repair shops that service pollution-control equipment on automobiles. Furthermore, compliance with environmental regulations may actually lead to unexpected benefits, such as a reduction in paperwork for companies that can show they are in line with regulations.

sustainable small business
A profitable company that responds to customers' needs while showing reasonable concern for the environment.

environmentalism
The effort to protect and preserve the environment.

Living the Dream

I Love the Taste of Plastic in the Morning

"I'm eyeing the clear packet of hot chocolate—marked CONFIDENTIAL & PROPRIETARY—I just dropped into a mug of steaming water. As I stir, bits of the plasticlike wrapper float to the top. The cocoa creeps out in waves. And then, in an instant, the remnants of the casing simply … disappear."

That's the way a staff editor at *FastCompany* magazine described his first encounter with a MonoSol-encapsuled product—in this case, a dissolvable packet of hot chocolate. Since 1953, Indiana-based MonoSol has been in the business of manufacturing water-soluble films and other products, with considerable success. The company's wrappers can be found all over the world, uniquely encasing a variety of everyday products, from agricultural chemicals to dishwasher detergent to laundry bags.

But now the company is trying to expand the range of its product applications to the food industry. MonoSol's labs have been working hard to create edible films that dissolve when they come into contact with water. They're not there yet, but the company is currently working with major food brands with the hope of seeing its offerings hit store shelves in a year or two.

Driving the company is an enduring interest in serving all of its stakeholders with distinction and great care. MonoSol managers do this by learning about customer needs and expectations, emphasizing high-quality products and exceptional service, and striving to give all employees a sense of meaning and accomplishment in their work. But protecting the environment is also one of the firm's central concerns. In fact, sustainability is a major motivation in perfecting its soluble film products. More than 75 million tons of packaging waste is thrown into landfills every year. MonoSol wants to fundamentally change the way we consume food and drink by getting us to use dissolvable wrappers that will not end up in dumps. In other words, the problem of waste would simply disappear!

One final note: The Japanese manufacturer Kuraray agreed to acquire MonoSol in May of 2012, so the company technically is no longer a small business by SBA standards. However, Kuraray has agreed to allow it to operate as an independent entity, so MonoSol should be able to continue to pursue its goals. For this aggressive company, that is certainly more than mere trash talk.

Sources: Based on Dan Macsai, "Can I Pour You a Pouch?" *FastCompany*, March 2012, pp. 60–62; "MonoSol Vision," www.monosol.com/about.php?p=114, accessed July 23, 2012; and Times Staff, "Kuraray Co. Acquires Merrillville-Based MonoSol," *The Times*, May 22, 2012, www.nwitimes.com/business/local/kuraray-co-acquires-merrillville-based-monosol/article_cbd2fd99-9f48-51aa-8362-7d8ff070bcf6.html, accessed July 23, 2012.

In any case, resources are available to help you avoid the potentially disastrous consequences of noncompliance. The Small Business Administration is prepared to lead you through the sometimes-choppy waters of environmental law, and the U.S. Environmental Protection Agency (EPA) offers the Small Business Gateway, an Internet portal that will connect you to information, technical assistance, and solutions to challenges related to the environment. Also, the EPA provides online access to a guide called "Managing Your Hazardous Waste: A Guide for Small Businesses," which makes compliance much easier to manage.[45]

2-5b Green Opportunities for Small Business

Although they add to the cost of doing business for some small companies, environmental concerns open up great opportunities for others. In fact, many startups have come to life precisely because of "the greening of business" and the potential opportunities that this has created.

The level of interest in ventures that can be labelled "green," "clean," or "sustainable" continues to rise, and this trend has led to the launching of many innovative eco-focused startups. However, according to Joel Makower, executive director of GreenBiz.com and author of *Strategies for the Green Economy*, "Green succeeds only to the extent that it means better—it's cheaper to buy, it operates better, it lasts longer, it's cooler for my image. People want to do the right thing, but they don't want to go out of their way to do it. They love 'change' when it's a noun; they hate it when it's a verb."[46]

Some green businesses are based on sophisticated technologies that run well beyond the reach of the typical small business. However, many opportunities in this category are very accessible to small companies and startups. Here are a few recent green startup stories to inspire you to think about new venture possibilities that could be right for you.

- Bamboo is one of the world's fastest-growing plants, and a number of new ventures have sprouted up to make bicycles out of the sturdy stuff. As owner of Boo Bicycles, Nick Frey builds and sells high-performance bikes with bamboo frames, and business is good. His prices range from $3,000 for a basic frame to $10,000 for a tricked-out racer—he even sold a frame recently as art to a Spanish gallery![47] But beyond aesthetics, the company's website points out that its custom bikes "can be raced successfully at the highest levels but are designed to provide a lively, forgiving ride, which increases stability and traction on descents and reduces fatigue."[48] The product definitely turns heads—and opens wallets, too.

- Joey Santley and Steve Cox launched a company in 2009 called Green Foam Blanks in San Clemente, California, with the goal of overturning half a century of surfboard-making tradition. They developed an innovative process that allowed them to be the first to produce and sell a recycled polyurethane blank (the foam core inside a surfboard) that lacks the cancer-causing materials that all other makers use. Demand has been so strong that the business is struggling to keep up with it.[49]

- When Warren Paul Anderson learned that few tools are available to track water use accurately in a world where 1.1 billion people lack sufficient access to clean drinking water, he started a new business to do something about it. His company, Hydrolosophy, creates software that allows firms to monitor and reduce their water usage by spotting inefficiencies.[50] Firms of all sizes are signing up to cut their utility costs and conserve natural resources at the same time.

Interest in the sustainability trend can take many different forms. For a growing number of small business owners, the ultimate goal is to save the planet; others recognize that sustainable business practices can hold down costs, attract customers, and generate value for shareholders. According to Stuart L. Hart, a professor of strategy at the University of North Carolina, the movement will provide huge opportunities for companies with "moxie" and creativity, as long as they can execute the plan.[51] This sounds like prime territory for small entrepreneurial companies, given their flexibility and innovative thinking. Entrepreneurs may be able to do well financially *and* do good, by guarding the environment and their integrity at the same time.

CLOSED
LOOKING BACK

2-1. Define *integrity*, and understand its importance to small businesses.

- Integrity refers to a general sense of honesty and reliability that is expressed in a strong commitment to doing the right thing, regardless of the circumstances. "Doing anything for money" can quickly lead to distortions in business behavior.
- Many small business owners strive to achieve the highest standards of honesty, fairness, and respect in their business relationships.

2-2. Explain how integrity applies to various stakeholder groups.

- Closely tied to integrity are ethical issues, which go beyond what is legal or illegal to include more general questions of right and wrong.
- The most often reported workplace misbehaviors include the misuse of company time, abusive behavior, lying to employees, abusing company resources, and violating company policy on Internet use.
- When they make business decisions, entrepreneurs must consider the interests of all stakeholder groups, in particular those of owners, customers, employees, the community, and the government.
- A company's owners have a clear and legitimate right to benefit from the financial performance of the business.
- Those companies that take customers seriously and serve them well are likely to have more of them.
- Showing proper appreciation for employees as human beings and as valuable members of the team is an essential ingredient of managerial integrity.
- Most people consider an ethical small business to be one that acts as a good citizen in its community.
- Research suggests that most small business owners exercise great integrity, but some are apt to cut corners when it comes to social responsibilities if profits will be affected.
- Entrepreneurs must obey governmental laws and follow applicable regulations if they want to maintain their integrity and avoid jail time.

2-3. Identify some common challenges and benefits of maintaining integrity in small businesses.

- The limited resources of small firms make them especially vulnerable to allowing or engaging in unethical practices.

- Startups and small companies sometimes resort to telling legitimacy lies, but they can win customers and attract other important stakeholders by paying close attention to the PRO factors (those related to the firm's products, its representatives, and the organization itself).
- Use of the Internet has highlighted such ethical issues as invasion of privacy and threats to intellectual property rights.
- Cultural differences complicate decision making for small firms operating abroad.
- The concept of ethical relativism is troublesome because it implies that ethical standards are subject to local interpretation.
- Research supports the notion that ethical business practices are good for business.

2-4. Suggest practical approaches for building a business with integrity.

- The underlying values and the behavior of business leaders are powerful forces that affect ethical performance.
- An organizational culture that supports integrity is key to achieving appropriate behavior among a firm's employees.
- Small firms should develop codes of ethics to provide guidance for their employees.
- Many small companies join Better Business Bureaus to promote ethical conduct throughout the business community.
- Following an ethical decision-making process can help entrepreneurs protect their integrity and that of their business.

2-5. Define sustainable small business, and describe the influence the trend is having on small companies and startup opportunities.

- A *sustainable small business* is a profitable company that responds to customer needs while showing reasonable concern for the natural environment.
- Some small firms, such as dry cleaners, are adversely affected by costly environmental regulations.
- Win-win outcomes are possible in many cases—the cost of eco-friendly business practices can often be more than offset by operational savings, increased customer interest, and reduced paperwork, for example.
- The SBA, EPA, and other public and private resources stand ready to help small businesses comply with environmental regulations.
- Small companies are sometimes launched precisely to take advantage of opportunities created by environmental concerns. Creating environmentally friendly products and services requires creativity and flexibility, areas in which small businesses tend to excel.

Key Terms

code of ethics p. 47

environmentalism p. 51

ethical imperialism p. 44

ethical relativism p. 44

integrity p. 34

intellectual property p. 44

social responsibilities p. 39

stakeholders p. 35

sustainable small business p. 51

underlying values p. 46

Discussion Questions

1. Define the concept of integrity. What are the major features of integrity?

2. What are the major stakeholder groups that influence and are influenced by small companies? What are the primary interests of each of these groups? How can a small business owner manage potential conflicts between the demands of these groups?

3. Why might small business CEOs focus more attention on profit and less on social goals than large business CEOs do?

4. What is skimming? How do you think owners of small firms might attempt to rationalize such a practice?

5. What is a legitimacy lie? In the case of a startup, how can an entrepreneur use PRO factors to win the confidence of potential customers and investors and avoid telling legitimacy lies?

6. What privacy issues are most important to small businesses? What should a company do to guard against violations of the privacy rights of customers, employees, and others?

7. What are some of the advantages of conducting business with integrity? Some people say they have no responsibility beyond maximizing the value of the firm in financial terms. Can this position be defended? If so, how?

8. Explain the connection between underlying values and integrity in business behavior.

9. What are the six steps in the ethical decision-making process presented in this chapter? What is the practical value of this model to the processing of decisions in a small business?

10. Give some examples of expenditures required on the part of small business firms to protect the environment. In your opinion, do rising concerns for the environment create more costs or more business opportunities for small companies?

You Make the Call

Situation 1

Sally started her consulting business a year ago and has been doing very well. About a month ago, she decided she needed to hire someone to help her since she was getting busier and busier. After interviewing several candidates, she decided to hire the best one of the group, Mary. She called Mary on Monday to tell her she had gotten the job. They both agreed that Mary would start the following Monday and that she could come in and fill out all the hiring paperwork at that time.

On Tuesday of the same week, a friend of Sally's called her to say that she had found the perfect person for Sally. Sally explained that she had already hired someone, but the friend insisted, "Just meet this girl. Who knows, maybe you might want to hire her in the future!"

Rather reluctantly, Sally consented. "Alright, if she can come in tomorrow, I'll meet with her, but that's all."

"Oh, I'm so glad. I just know you're going to like her!" Sally's friend exclaimed.

And Sally did like her. She liked her a lot. Sally had met with Julie on Wednesday morning. She was everything that Sally had been looking for and more. In terms of experience, Julie far surpassed any of the candidates Sally had previously interviewed, including Mary. On top of that, she was willing to bring in clients of her own, which would only increase business. All in all, Sally knew this was a win-win situation. But what about Mary? She had already given her word to Mary that she could start work on Monday.

Question 1 What decision on Sally's part would contribute most to the success of her business?

Question 2 What ethical reasoning would support hiring Mary?

Question 3 What ethical reasoning would support hiring Julie?

Source: www.sba.gov/smallbusinessplanner/manage/lead/SERV_BETHICS.html, accessed September 30, 2010.

Situation 2

Darryl Wilson owns Darryl's Deals on Wheels, a small used-car dealership in Humble, Texas. Wilson started the company three years ago, but he is still struggling to get a solid footing in the industry. The slow economy isn't helping—no one seems to have money to buy cars right now—and there is plenty of competition. The business provides the main source of income for his family, which includes his wife and two teenage daughters. Wilson has to make this business work to keep food on the table and to pay the typical expenses involved in raising a family.

Finding customers is essential to success in the car sales business, but so is holding down costs. This means Wilson has to find "rolling stock" that is in demand and inexpensive, but that is not easy to do because all the other dealers in his area are in the same boat. They, too, are trying to snap up the best deals, and this is driving up the cost of inventory. So, controlling costs means looking at other features of the business, and Wilson thinks he has found something that just may help. The state of Texas requires dealers to report the purchase of all vehicles they acquire for resale, which means the dealer will have to pay a 2.5 percent inventory tax (based on the purchase price) when it sells the car later. But when Wilson buys a car from a private seller, he can usually convince him or her to sign over the title without designating a specific buyer. This allows Wilson to fill in that part of the title and the transfer form with the name of the person who buys the car from him, when that time comes. In the end, the state has no evidence of Wilson's involvement in the transaction, which allows him to avoid paying administrative fees and the inventory tax—a savings of about $250 on a typical sale. The state doesn't catch on, and his customers never seem to notice because they have to pay administrative fees and sales tax anyway when they buy the car and transfer the title into their own names.

So far, Wilson has not run into any problems with this practice. In his mind, this is nothing more than "heads-up business." Furthermore, his profits are so slim right now that playing by the book would probably mean that he would have to go out of business. Even the state would lose money then, because a company that is out of business pays no income taxes and Wilson would have to start collecting unemployment.

Question 1 What are the advantages and possible drawbacks to Wilson's title-transfer scheme?

Question 2 Which stakeholders are affected by this approach, either positively or negatively? How great are their gains/losses?

Question 3 Wilson finds it hard to identify a downside to his approach. What risks might he be overlooking?

Question 4 What would you do if you were in Wilson's shoes? If his competitors are following the same practice (and some of them surely are), would that make any difference to you?

Situation 3

Ben London owns and operates Fantastic Footage, a film-editing company in Los Angeles that does contract work mostly for production companies in Hollywood. Not long ago, a local landscaping business completed nearly $5,500 worth of work around London's offices. While the initial bid now seems a little high for the amount of work that was actually done, there is no question that the work completed was of high quality, and London finally feels comfortable inviting potential clients to meet him at his office to discuss possible deals. However, because of an apparent oversight, the landscaping contractor never submitted a bill. It's been more than 15 months since the completion of the project, and London has come to conclude that the contractor somehow lost track of the project. He is thinking about calling the company to ask for a final invoice so that he can settle up, but business has been really slow over the last year or so, and it hasn't been easy to pay all of the bills as it is. Forking over $5,500 for the landscaping would not be impossible, but it would be pretty challenging to scrape up that kind of money right now. So, he is trying to figure out what he should do.

Question 1 In your opinion, whose responsibility is it to initiate the payment of this debt?

Question 2 What if London is unable to come up with the money to pay the bill when (if) it is finally submitted? What should he do then?

Question 3 What are the options available to London in this case? Assess these using each of the following tests: (1) the Rotary Club's four-questions test, (2) the "newspaper report" test, (3) the "explain it to my mother" test, and (4) the Golden Rule. Do you arrive at the same conclusion when applying each of these? If not, which one should London use to decide what he should do?

Experiential Exercises

1. Examine a recent business periodical online, and report briefly on some lapse in integrity that is in the news. Could this type of problem occur in a small business? Explain.

2. Employees sometimes take sick leave when they are merely tired, and students sometimes miss class for the same reason. Separate into groups of four or five, and prepare a statement on the nature of the ethical issues (if any) in these practices.

3. Based on your experience as an employee, customer, or observer of a particular small business, rate its ethical performance. Outline the evidence or clues you use as a basis for your opinion. How typical are the issues in this case of small businesses in general? Be prepared to offer a summary of your assessment and conclusions.

4. With a current or previous employer in mind, write a simple code of ethics that would show due regard for the interests of all of the company's primary stakeholders (most notably the owners, customers, employees, the community, and the government). How difficult was it to protect and balance the concerns of these groups in the code that you came up with? Report briefly on your findings.

5. Search for "top environmental concerns" on the Internet, and select five concerns that seem to be most relevant to small businesses. Analyze these concerns to determine how they will shape business practice in small firms over the next decade. Then, identify five to ten new venture opportunities that could be created based on the concerns you select. Explain your findings and recommendations.

Small Business & Entrepreneurship Resource Center

The Small Business & Entrepreneurship Resource Center offers complete small business management resources through a comprehensive database that covers all major areas of starting, operating, and maintaining a business from financing, management, marketing, accounting, taxes, and more. Go to www.cengagebrain.com and select the Longenecker text for more information on how to access this material.

1. Collision Experts Incorporated wants to be a preferred provider of professional auto body repair in the Detroit marketplace. The company delivers premium services in the highly competitive automotive services market and prides itself on service integrity. Services are delivered in a manner that dictate doing it right the first time, to keep a customer coming back as opposed to hoping a customer is satisfied and accepts the basic level of quality required to get it out the door. Providing high-quality service ensures repeat customers and fosters a relationship built on trust with each client served. As a family business, Collision Experts realizes that financial integrity is also necessary for success. Policies for financial and resource support of local, school, religious, sporting, and academic activities allow Collision Experts to provide an environment of trust and reciprocity. How do Collision Experts exhibit integrity? What are some ways they make a difference in their community?

2. The mission of Collision Experts Incorporated is to act as an integral part of the business community in providing a valuable service to retail, business, and community clients. The company serves many segments of the community such as retail consumers, churches, nonprofit organizations, and municipal vehicle fleets. Each segment has its own service and quality requirements. The company realizes that its business relationships will make or break the enterprise on a long-term basis. For this reason, Collision Experts must have the ability to work in a coordinated manner with business partners that touch all aspects of the enterprise. For example, its most interdependent business partner is the insurance agency community. After reading this article, explain how entrepreneurs such Collision Experts must consider the interests of all stakeholder groups when making business decisions.

Sources: "Automotive Repair Service: Collision Experts *Inc.*," Lynn M. Pearce (ed.), *Business Plans Handbook*, Vol. 10 (Detroit: Gale, 2004), pp. 1–6; and *Buildings*, Vol. 96, No. 1 (January 2002), p. 6.

Video Case 2

PortionPac® Chemical Corporation (P. 646)

PortionPac manufactures highly concentrated, premeasured cleaning products that reduce resources used and provide sustainable, cost-effective, and environmentally friendly solutions. This case discusses PortionPac's progressive leadership, user-centric educational services, and innovative products and packaging, highlighting its integrity and ethical behavior toward various stakeholder groups, including customers, employees, and the community.

Alternative Cases for Chapter 2

Case 3, The Kollection, p. 648
Case 5, The Avedis Zildjian Company Inc., p. 653
Case 8, Couchsurfing International, p. 657
Case 18, Auntie Anne's Pretzel in China, p. 681

Endnotes

1. Karl Eller, *Integrity Is All You've Got: And Seven Other Lessons of an Entrepreneurial Life* (New York, NY: McGraw-Hill, 2005), p. 89.

2. The terms *integrity* and *ethics* are often used interchangeably, but while closely related conceptually, they are not precisely equivalent. In our view, ethics most often refers to standards of conduct derived from an *externally* created system of rules or guidelines, such as those established by a professional board or industry association. In contrast, integrity is based on an *internal* system of principles that guide behavior, making compliance a matter of choice rather than obligation. However, both can powerfully shape the thoughts and conduct of conscientious individuals.

3. Early on, R. Edward Freeman promoted the stakeholder view in his book, *Strategic Management: A Stakeholder Approach* (Boston, MA: Pitman, 1984), but he recognizes that this framework can make decision making difficult. There usually are no hard-and-fast rules to guide the balancing of stakeholder interests in a given situation. Though others would take issue with Freeman's conclusions, he nonetheless argues that the survival of the firm can be jeopardized if these interests are not kept in balance.

4. See Archie B. Carroll and Ann K. Buchholtz, *Business and Society: Ethics, Sustainability, and Stakeholder Management* (South-Western, 2011) for a more complete discussion.

5. Milton Friedman, *Capitalism and Freedom* (Chicago, IL: University of Chicago Press, 1963), p. 133.

6. April Joyner, "Happiness Begins at the Office," *Inc.*, Vol. 32, No. 4 (2010), p. 8.

7. This is consistent with the findings of a recent and extensive meta-analysis detailing a strong linkage between employee job satisfaction and customer satisfaction [see Steven P. Brown and Sun K. Lam, "A Meta-Analysis of Relationships Linking Employee Satisfaction to Customer Responses," *Journal of Marketing*, Vol. 84, No. 3 (2008), pp. 243–255].

8. "Employee Theft: Legal Aspects—Estimates of Cost," http://law.jrank.org/pages/1084/Employee-Theft-Legal-Aspects-Estimates-cost.html, accessed July 18, 2012.

9. "Employee Theft," www.criminal-law-lawyer-source.com/terms/employee-theft.html, accessed July 18, 2012.

10. "Email and Social Media Marketing You Can Feel Good About," www.icontact.com/about/social-responsibility, accessed July 23, 2012; Ryan Allis, "iContact and Vocus Combine Forces," http://blog.icontact.com/blog/company-announcement, accessed July 23, 2012; and Joel Holland, "Save the World, Make a Million," *Entrepreneur*, April 2010, www.entrepreneur.com/article/205556, accessed July 18, 2012.

11. Raymund Flandez, "Small Companies Put Charity into Their Business Plan," *The Wall Street Journal*, November 20, 2007, p. B3.

12. The popular business press provides numerous examples to support this position, but we recognize that the evidence from academic studies on the subject is mixed. For an excellent review of this research, see Michael L. Barnett, "Stakeholder Influence Capacity and the Variability of Financial Returns to Corporate Social Responsibility," *Academy of Management Review*, Vol. 32, No. 3 (2007), pp. 794–816.

13. William J. Dennis, Jr. (ed.), "Contributions to Community," www.411sbfacts.com/sbpoll.php?POLLID=0025, accessed July 18, 2012.

14. Eric Knopf, "One Step at a Time," in Michael McMyne and Nicole Amare (eds.), *Beyond the Lemonade Stand: 14 Undergraduate Entrepreneurs Tell Their Stories of Ethics in Business* (St. Louis, MO: St. Louis University, 2004), pp. 47–48.

15. Martin Vaughn, "IRS Too Easy on Payroll Taxes, Study Finds," *The Wall Street Journal*, July 29, 2008, p. A8.

16. For an interesting discussion and useful analysis of legitimacy lies, see Matthew W. Rutherford, Paul F. Buller, and J. Michael Stebbins, "Ethical Considerations of the Legitimacy Lie," *Entrepreneurship Theory and Practice*, Vol. 33, No. 4 (2009), pp. 949–964.

17. Paulette Thomas, "Virtual Business Plans Require Human Touch," *The Wall Street Journal*, August 2, 2005, p. B2.

18. Nadine Heintz, "For Rolling Up Her Sleeves," *Inc.*, Vol. 26, No. 4 (2004), pp. 128–129.

19. Miroslav Pivoda, Frank Hoy, Kiril Todorov, and Viktor Vojtko, "Entrepreneurial Tricks and Ethics Surveyed in Different Countries," *International Journal of E-Entrepreneurship and Innovation*, Vol. 2, No. 3 (2011), pp. 46–65.

20. For an in-depth look at the theoretical framework and empirical tests involved in the study mentioned here, see Dean A. Shepherd and Andrew Zacharakis, "A New Venture's Cognitive Legitimacy: An Assessment by Customers," *Journal of Small Business Management*, Vol. 41, No. 2 (2003), pp. 148–167.

21. *Ibid.*

22. Survey results reported in Karen R. Harned, "Why Website Privacy Policies Matter," *MyBusiness*, September/October 2010, p. 39.

23. David H. Freedman, "Worried That Employees Are Wasting Time on the Web? Here's Why You Shouldn't Crack Down," *Inc.*, Vol. 28, No. 8 (2006), pp. 77–78.

24. A study by Salary.com estimated that employees waste about 20 percent of their time at work, and 34.7 percent of the workers surveyed indicated that surfing the Internet was their greatest source of distraction (see Alina Dizik, "Services to Help Us Stop Dawdling Online," *The Wall Street Journal*, January 28, 2010, p. D2).

25. Dionne Searcey, "Some Courts Raise Bar on Reading Employee Email," *The Wall Street Journal*, November 19, 2009, p. A17.

26. *Ibid.*

27. For excellent guidance regarding the legal issues related to Internet use regulation at work, see William P. Smith and Filiz Tabak, "Monitoring Employee E-Mails: Is There Any Room for Privacy?" *Academy of Management Perspectives*, Vol. 23, No. 4 (2009), pp. 33–48.

28. Anonymous, "Handbagged," *The Economist*, Vol. 387, No. 8585 (2008), p. 76, www.economist.com/business/Printer/Friendly.cfm?story_id=11580287.

29. Jayne O'Donnell, "Counterfeits Are a Growing—and Dangerous—Problem," *USA Today*, June 7, 2012, p. 8A.

30. Eller, *op. cit.*, p. 90.

31. This research is cited in Stephen K. Henn, *Business Ethics: A Case Study Approach* (Hoboken, NJ: John Wiley, 2009), pp. 11–12.

32. For more on this, see Robert Moment, "The 7 Principles of Business Integrity," www.successfuloffice.com/the-seven-principles-of-business-integrity.htm, accessed July 24, 2012.

33. A study by Justin G. Longenecker, Joseph A. McKinney, and Carlos W. Moore ["Religious Intensity, Evangelical Christianity, and Business Ethics: An Empirical Study," *Journal of Business Ethics*, Vol. 55, No. 2 (2004), pp. 373–386] provides evidence to support this position. Their results showed that religious values play a part in ethical decision making,

though general religious categorizations (such as Catholic, Protestant, Jewish) do not seem to have similar impact.

34. Nicholas G. Moore, "Ethics: The Way to Do Business," http://cbe.bentley.edu/sites/cbe.bentley.edu/files/images/moore-monograph.pdf, accessed July 24, 2012.

35. Excerpt from an interview with J. C. Huizenga in "Virtuous Business and Educational Practice," *Religion & Liberty*, Vol. 12, No. 5, www.acton.org/pub/religion-liberty/volume-12-number-5/virtuous-business-and-educational-practice, accessed July 24, 2012.

36. Kenneth H. Blanchard and Norman Vincent Peale, *The Power of Ethical Management* (New York, NY: HarperCollins, 1989).

37. J. Michael Alford, "Finding Competitive Advantage in Managing Workplace Ethics," paper presented at the 2005 meeting of the United States Association for Small Business and Entrepreneurship, Indian Wells, CA, January 13–16, 2005.

38. Specific insights and guidance for writing a code of ethics can be found at www.ethics.org/resource/plus-decision-making-model, accessed July 20, 2012.

39. Ethics Resource Center, "The PLUS Decision Making Model," www.ethics.org/resource/plus-decision-making-model, accessed July 24, 2012.

40. "Rotary International: Guiding Principles," www.rotary.org/en/aboutus/rotaryinternational/guidingprinciples/Pages/ridefault.aspx, accessed July 20, 2012.

41. Brian K. Burton and Michael Goldsby ["The Golden Rule and Business Ethics: An Examination," *Journal of Business Ethics*, Vol. 56, No. 3 (2005), pp. 371–383] offer an extended discussion of the history, meaning, and problems of the Golden Rule. They document the appearance of this general principle in the writings of several major world religions and philosophers and provide examples of companies that have used the Golden Rule explicitly as a guide for decision making (e.g., JCPenney and Lincoln Electric Co.). The influence of the Golden Rule is so pervasive that Burton and Goldsby conclude that it "seems to be one of the few candidates for a universally acceptable moral principle."

42. Kant actually offered a critique of the Golden Rule, but only as a footnote to his discussion of the categorical imperative. In his opinion, the categorical imperative is a superior concept for a number of reasons, all of which are related to his expanded view of the imperative [see Immanuel Kant, *Grounding for the Metaphysics of Morals, with a Supposed Right to Lie Because of Philanthropic Concerns*, 3rd ed., trans. J. W. Ellington (Indianapolis, IN: Hackett Publishing, 1993)].

43. Rese Fox, "An Inconvenient Value," www.awarenessintoaction.com/whitepapers/getting-the-true-assessment-of-a-leed-certified-buildings-value.html, accessed July 23, 2012.

44. "Greening Your Business: A Primer for Smaller Companies," www.greenbiz.com/business/research/report/2007/07/18/greening-your-business-primer-smaller-companies, accessed July 23, 2012.

45. "Managing Your Hazardous Waste: A Guide for Small Businesses," www.epa.gov/epawaste/hazard/generation/sqg/handbook/k01005.pdf, accessed July 23, 2012.

46. Jason Daley, "Green Fallout," *Entrepreneur*, Vol. 38, No. 8 (2010), pp. 72–75.

47. Malia Wollan, "Bamboo Bikes Appeal to Earth-Conscious Bikers," *Waco Tribune-Herald*, August 15, 2010, p. A3.

48. "Boo "Bicycles—About," http://boobicycles.com/company, accessed July 23, 2012.

49. Todd Woody, "Surf's Up, Waste's Down," *New York Times*, September 19, 2009, p. A4; and "Green Foam Blanks—About Us," www.greenfoamblanks.com/about.html, accessed July 23, 2012.

50. Alex Lindahl, "The Water Track," *Entrepreneur*, Vol. 38, No. 4 (2010), p. 62.

51. Marc Gunter, "Tree Huggers, Soy Lovers, and Profits," *Fortune*, Vol. 147, No. 12 (2003), pp. 99–104.

CHAPTER 3

© Peshkova/Shutterstock.com

Starting a Small Business

*After studying this chapter,
you should be able to...*

3-1. **Distinguish among the
different types and sources
of startup ideas.**

3-2. **Use innovative thinking
to generate ideas for high-
potential startups.**

3-3. **Describe external and
internal analyses that might
shape the selection of venture
opportunities.**

3-4. **Explain broad-based
strategy options and focus
strategies.**

3-5. **Know how to screen business
ideas to identify those with the
greatest potential.**

3-6. **Assess the feasibility of a
startup idea.**

**OPEN
LOOKING
AHEAD**

Peter Nguyen is founder and CEO of an Internet marketing agency called Brand Ingenuity Group (formerly BizWorks Group) and creator of Advertiser360, a comprehensive course created to help people sell products or services online. His success in business is the result of his quick recognition of new venture opportunities, especially those that stand at the nexus of marketing and the Internet.

Nguyen started his first company, WhizNotes, when he was only 19. As a sophomore at the University of Florida, he realized that there was a great need for a tutoring service that would provide class notes and review sessions before exams in difficult subjects like calculus, biology, and physics. He figured that students would come streaming into the review sessions. But that's not how the story turned out. "We learned one of our first tough lessons in business," Nguyen now recalls. "No matter how great your

**In the SPOTLIGHT
Peter Nguyen**
www.brandingenuitygroup.com

product or service is, if you can't market it, you have no business." In other words, a business opportunity needs more than just interested customers—you also need a way to reach them.

After taking a year off to regroup, Nguyen and his partner decided to sell custom-made t-shirts on their campus.

They called this second company Shox Printing. They knew that one competitor in their city had a near lock on the sale of shirts to student organizations and that they would have to position their company carefully if they were to have a chance to compete. As is sometimes the case with new ventures, price became an entry wedge that allowed their company to get its start. Their competitor was selling shirts for $9 to $12 each, but Nguyen knew a local vendor that would print tees for about $4 to $5 per shirt. That would allow Shox to sell its product for $7 or $8 per shirt, undercut its rival on price, and still make a decent profit. It seemed that a low-cost strategy was clearly the way to go.

But competing on price can set off a price war, a battle that established competitors are more likely to win. So, the two young partners found another lever of competition in the unique access that they had to the student body at their university. Since Nguyen was vice president of the Asian Student Union and personally knew many of the student leaders on campus, they decided to start there. They went to work on building relationships, expanding their clientele list, and generating sales.

The formula worked wonderfully. Soon, Shox Printing evolved into a full-service company that provided printing on almost everything, from key chains to posters to magazines. In a short period of time, the business diversified to add a division called Shox Web, which created websites for local businesses and student organizations. To help the added division grow, they joined forces with a new partner who helped them locate and hire talented programmers from his home in Odessa, Ukraine.

The logical next step was to provide marketing services for local businesses, as the company was becoming a one-stop, full-service operator. It had contracts to work on everything from service engine optimization projects for local businesses to printing thousands of shirts for Rhino Video Games to designing and printing materials to support direct marketing campaigns for Novelis, a large aluminum producer. After only three years of building and expanding, they had added more than 30 people to their team and were recognized for their work, including gold and silver ADDY Awards earned from competing in the world's largest advertising competition. In addition, Nguyen was recognized as one of the top minority business owners of the year by Advertising Specialty Institute and named to *Inc.* magazine's "Top 30 Under 30" list of the most intriguing young business owners in America.

It was a quick, successful start for Nguyen. But the formula for the results he achieves is clear: Recognize high-potential business opportunities and build effective companies around them. The prospects for reward are great.

Sources: Based on Peter Nguyen, *Advertiser360: Learning the Essentials,* (Irvine, CA: AdVentures Group, 2011), pp. 7–9; personal communication with Peter Nguyen, August 19, 2012.

There is no question that entrepreneurs are going to keep coming up with innovative ways of doing things, and the new businesses they create often change the way we live. But to get the ball rolling in the right direction, an entrepreneur must be able to recognize high-potential startup ideas that others have overlooked. This is precisely what Peter Nguyen was able to do when he came up with the concept for his thriving businesses, which are profiled in the opening Spotlight feature. We should emphasize that identifying imaginative new products or services that may lead to promising business ventures is so central to the entrepreneurial process that it has its own name—**opportunity recognition**.

What sets entrepreneurs apart from everyone else is their ability to see the potential that others overlook and then take the bold steps necessary to get businesses up and running. In some cases, the identification of a new business opportunity may be the result of an active search for possibilities or insights derived from personal or work experiences. In other cases, the search for opportunities may be a less deliberate and more automatic process.[1] Economist Israel Kirzner proposed that entrepreneurs have a unique capability, which he called **entrepreneurial alertness**. According to this view, entrepreneurs are not actually the source of innovative ideas. Rather, they are simply "alert to the opportunities that exist *already* and are waiting to be noticed."[2] When these opportunities are aligned with an entrepreneur's knowledge, experience, and aspirations, they are even more likely to be spotted.

A discussion of the finer points of entrepreneurial alertness is beyond the scope of this book, but it is important to understand that being aware of conditions that might lead to new business opportunities can really pay off.[3] Try it for yourself to see if new

opportunity recognition
Identification of potential new products or services that may lead to promising businesses.

entrepreneurial alertness
Readiness to act on existing, but unnoticed, business opportunities.

possibilities for a business become apparent. Over the next week or so, take note of trends, changes, or situations that might support a new business. You will probably be surprised at how many potential opportunities you can identify. If you continue this rather deliberate search, over time you may find that it becomes a habit.[4]

Perhaps you already have a business idea in mind that you would like to pursue. With good planning and the right strategy, you may soon be on your way to success as an entrepreneur. On the other hand, you may have a passionate desire to start your own company but are not sure that you have locked onto the right business idea to get you there. Or maybe you have an *idea* in mind but are not sure if it is a good *business opportunity*. No matter which group you fall into, we will help to get you started on the right foot, with the right idea and the right strategy.

In this chapter, we focus mostly on opportunity recognition and strategy options as these apply to **startups**—that is, businesses that did not exist before entrepreneurs created them. However, the chapters that follow will go beyond a discussion of startups and consider business opportunities that already exist, such as purchasing a franchise or buying an existing business (Chapter 4) or joining a family business (Chapter 5). These can all be high-potential options. As you read this chapter, keep in mind that many of the insights and strategies described here also apply to ongoing small businesses, not just to startups.

3-1 DEVELOPING STARTUP IDEAS

As outlined in Chapter 1, you may choose to become an entrepreneur for any of a number of different reasons. But several motivations may lead you to consider starting an enterprise from scratch rather than pursuing other alternatives. For example, you may have a personal desire to develop the commercial market for a recently invented or newly developed product or service, or you may be hoping to tap into high-potential resources that are uniquely available to you—an ideal location, advanced information technologies, a powerful network of connections, and so on. Some entrepreneurs get "startup fever" because they want the challenge of succeeding (or failing) on their own, or they hope to avoid undesirable features of existing companies, such as unpleasant work cultures or smothering legal commitments. There are almost as many reasons as there are aspiring entrepreneurs!

So how do you get started? It all begins with a promising business idea. But new venture concepts are not all equal, and they can come from many different sources. By recognizing the nature and origin of startup ideas, an entrepreneur can broaden the range of new ideas available for his or her consideration.

3-1a Types of Startup Ideas

Exhibit 3.1 shows the three basic types of ideas from which most startups are launched: ideas to enter new markets, ideas based on new technologies, and ideas that offer new benefits. Each of these has its own unique features.

Numerous startups develop from **new market ideas**—that is, those concerned with providing customers with a product or service that does not exist in a particular market but does exists somewhere else. Randall Rothenberg, an author and the director of intellectual capital at the consulting firm Booz Allen Hamilton, says that this type of startup idea may have the greatest potential: "There's ample evidence that some of the biggest businesses are built by taking existing ideas and applying them in a new context."[5] Because it has so much potential, this angle on new venture ideas should not be overlooked.

Other startups are based on **new technology ideas**, which involve new or relatively new knowledge breakthroughs. This type of business can be high risk because there is

LO 3-1

Distinguish among the different types and sources of startup ideas.

startups
New business ventures created "from scratch."

new market ideas
Startup ideas centered around providing customers with an existing product or service not available in their market.

new technology ideas
Startup ideas involving new or relatively new technology, centered around providing customers with a new product.

3.1 Types of Ideas that Develop into Startups

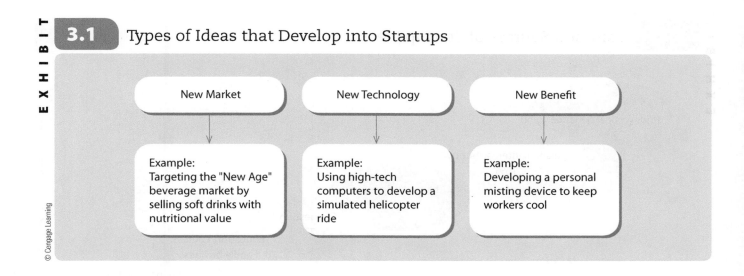

© Cengage Learning

New Market	New Technology	New Benefit
Example: Targeting the "New Age" beverage market by selling soft drinks with nutritional value	Example: Using high-tech computers to develop a simulated helicopter ride	Example: Developing a personal misting device to keep workers cool

usually no definite model of success to follow, but it can also offer tremendous promise. You should pay especially close attention to the fundamental features of a well-conceived new venture of this type. For starters, the technology involved would need to be unique, better than others currently available, feasible to implement, and focused on a market need that is deep enough to generate sufficient sales. Also, the founders would need to have the knowledge, skills, resources, and connections necessary to build a profitable company around the new technology.

Because of the complexities involved with new technology businesses, it often becomes necessary for entrepreneurs to **pivot** at some point after startup. This refers to fundamentally refocusing the startup as it unfolds or completely recreating it if the initial concept turns out to be seriously flawed. According to Kevin Systrom, co-founder of Instagram, the idea behind the pivot is to "try out new ideas, shed them quickly if they don't catch on, and move on to the next new thing."[6] In other words, if the initial idea turns out to be unsound, it is best to fail fast and fail cheap.

New benefit ideas—those based on offering customers benefits from new and improved products or better ways of performing old functions—account for a large number of startups. Consider Nicky Bronner, the 15-year-old founder of Unreal Brands, Inc. To satisfy his sweet tooth without wrecking his health, he set out to "unjunk" snacks by creating and selling his own version of M&Ms, Snickers, Reese's, and other popular candies that are still as tasty but are made of far more wholesome ingredients. Bronner now has contracts to sell his products in Target, Kroger, and other high-profile retailers, so it appears that focusing on new benefits can sometimes lead to really sweet business ideas.[7]

3-1b Common Sources of Startup Ideas

Several studies have identified sources of ideas for small business startups. Exhibit 3.2 shows the results of one such study by the National Federation of Independent Business (NFIB), which found that prior work experience accounted for 45 percent of new ideas. However, there are other important sources. As indicated in the exhibit, the NFIB study found that personal interests and hobbies represented 16 percent of the total, and chance happenings accounted for 11 percent.

Ideas for a startup can come from anywhere, but for now we will focus on three possible sources: personal/work experience, hobbies and personal interests, and accidental discovery.

pivot
To refocus or recreate a startup if the initial concept turns out to be flawed.

new benefit ideas
Startup ideas centered around providing customers with new or improved products or services.

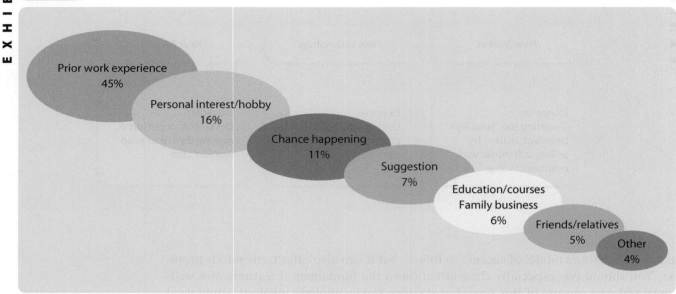

EXHIBIT 3.2 Common Sources of Startup Ideas

Prior work experience 45%

Personal interest/hobby 16%

Chance happening 11%

Suggestion 7%

Education/courses Family business 6%

Friends/relatives 5%

Other 4%

Source: Data developed and provided by the National Federation of Independent Business and sponsored by the American Express Travel Related Services Company, Inc.

PERSONAL/WORK EXPERIENCE One of the primary sources of startup ideas is personal experience. Often, knowledge gleaned from a present or former job allows a person to see possibilities for modifying an existing product, improving a service, becoming a supplier that meets an employer's needs better than current vendors, or duplicating a business concept in a different location. Or personal contacts (your network) may include suppliers that are interested in working with you or customers whose needs are not currently being met. Startup concepts may even result from trying personal circumstances or misfortunes, especially when the entrepreneur can use work experience or technical skills to address the challenge at hand. Regardless of the situation, these insights may lead you to an opportunity with tremendous potential.[8]

That's how it worked for Adrienne Kallweit, whose attempts to find a suitable babysitter for her young child proved to be more challenging than she had expected. From this experience—which reflects a very real need for so many young couples who need safe and reliable child care—Kallweit decided to launch SeekingSitters, which provides "an on-demand babysitter referral service." Apparently, Kallweit's experience was a great predictor of opportunity, because the company has been expanding rapidly since it was launched.[9]

HOBBIES AND PERSONAL INTERESTS Sometimes, hobbies grow beyond being leisure activities to become businesses, and they can add surprising energy to the startup process. For instance, people who love skiing might start a ski equipment rental operation as a way to make income from an activity that they enjoy. Or think about Mark Zuckerberg when he started Facebook. He didn't intend for the venture to grow it into the massive company that it is today; rather, he just "liked having it be this hobby and getting people around [him] excited." But in time, he recognized the business potential of the concept, and you know now that his instincts turned out to be right on the money! While we don't expect all or even most small businesses to grow into life-changing technology giants, Facebook's story proves that fun side projects can sometimes grow into significant new companies with serious profit potential.[10]

ACCIDENTAL DISCOVERY Another source of new startup ideas—accidental discovery—involves something called **serendipity**, a facility for making desirable discoveries by accident. Awareness obviously plays a role here, but anyone may stumble across a useful idea in the course of day-to-day living. That is exactly what happened to a 28-year-old struggling artist in Los Angeles, Simone Gonzales, who came across some interesting fabric and decided to see what she could do with it. "After playing with the thick, mummy-like elastic bands and shaping them into a simple tube skirt—no zipper, hem, or serious tailoring required—Gonzales realized she may be onto something."[11] She decided to make a few skirts from it, which she sold at a friend's boutique. From that small start, Gonzales got enough traction to launch her company, Pleasure Doing Business. Within a few years, things really started to take off, showing that promising business ideas sometimes just happen—even when you're not really looking for them.[12]

serendipity
A facility for making desirable discoveries by accident.

ENTREPRENEURIAL EXPERIENCES

Living the Dream

When Serendipity Creates a Domino Effect

Serendipity can inspire a business startup idea, but it can also spark the transformation of an existing small business by bringing previously overlooked possibilities to light. David Allen experienced this firsthand when his company, Puremco, stumbled upon a company-changing discovery.

With the distinction at the time of being the only wholesale manufacturer of dominoes in the United States, Puremco offered a high-quality product. But to add value, the company customized some of its game sets by silk-screening corporate and college logos on the backs of the 28 tiles. While this was good for marketing, it pushed up costs considerably. The process was tedious and time consuming, as each tile had to be decorated separately and placed in an oven overnight to cure. Puremco's oven could only handle two hundred sets, so production could never exceed that small quantity. On top of that, the decoration/baking sequence had to be repeated for each color in the logo, so a three-color logo would require a full three days of curing time. "We could not produce silk-screened domino sets efficiently enough to take advantage of this value-added operation," recalls Allen.

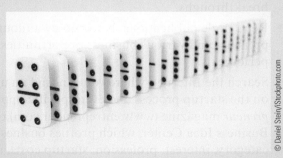
© Daniel Stein/iStockphoto.com

But then serendipity came into play. One day, Allen received a parcel that contained some loose domino tiles that were decorated on the back. The work was very well done, but he could see at a glance that the beautiful artwork had not been added by silk screening. "It immediately struck me that if we used the same process to decorate our own domino sets, it would transform the company," recalls Allen. Fortunately, the sender had enclosed a letter to explain that the work had been done by a company that printed heat transfers for customers (most of them t-shirt vendors). But what did this have to do with Puremco? Some of the heat-transfer company's employees had been playing dominoes on their break one day when one of them wondered if dominoes would accept heat-transfer decorations. He placed some tiles under a transfer, lowered the heat press for a few seconds, and sure enough, the transfer worked perfectly! "What a lucky thing for us that the employees of that company were domino players," Allen declares.

Allen contacted the company and ordered some transfers with a design sized to fit his product and started decorating domino sets with the new process. The designs could be printed on paper with as many colors as desired (even more complicated four-color processes were a snap), so a complete set of dominoes could be decorated in a single, quick operation. As a result of this one small change, Puremco's production capacity increased many-fold. But on top of that, the firm's design capabilities immediately became limitless.

As a result of this one chance discovery, the company was able to develop many stock designs that appeal to a wide variety of customers. The change also allowed Puremco to produce a catalogue of beautifully designed domino sets and sell directly to consumers via mail order. One small adjustment allowed the firm to shift its entire emphasis to selling domino sets as a premium product directly to the end user, and at retail prices that greatly increased profit margins. "It was an accidental discovery, pure and simple," observes Allen. "Serendipity, if you will."

Source: Personal communication with David Allen, August 22, 2012.

OTHER IDEA LEADS If the sources of startup ideas just discussed do not reveal the specific entrepreneurial opportunity that is right for you, examine the following methods, which have been useful to many entrepreneurs:

- Tap personal contacts with potential customers and suppliers, professors, patent attorneys, former or current employees or co-workers, venture capitalists, and chambers of commerce.
- Visit trade shows, production facilities, universities and research institutes, and successful entrepreneurs (in other markets) who are doing what you want to do.
- Observe trends, such as those related to material limitations and energy shortages, emerging technologies, recreational practices, fads, pollution problems, personal security needs, and social movements.
- Pay close attention to all forms of change, including shifts in specific industries and markets, demographic swings, and emerging discoveries or scientific breakthroughs.
- Read trade publications, bankruptcy announcements, and profiles on entrepreneurs and various business opportunities in *Inc., MyBusiness,* and other periodicals.
- Search the Internet, where you can find an unlimited supply of information on the startup process and even specific opportunities. For example, *Entrepreneur* magazine (www.entrepreneur.com) offers such online tools as the Business Idea Center, which profiles business ideas that can be browsed by category, interest, profession, startup costs, and other criteria.

RESOURCES

Spotting Trends
You can spot trends by listening to customers, staying in tune with industry changes, and using such marketing tools as in-person focus groups, social media groups, and chat rooms. Consulting websites like www.trendhunter.com and www.jwtintelligence .com can also help you spot emerging developments and meaningful patterns.

3-2 USING INNOVATIVE THINKING TO GENERATE BUSINESS IDEAS

LO
3-2

Use innovative thinking to generate ideas for high-potential startups.

If you haven't come up with a startup idea from the common sources identified above, you may need to dig deeper. Commit to a lifestyle of creative thinking so that everyday thoughts work in your favor to generate business ideas.[13] Although the following suggestions are designed to help guide your search for that one great idea for a startup, they can also help keep an existing business fresh, alive, and moving forward.

When It Comes to Ideas, Borrow Heavily from Existing Products and Services Or Other Industries. "Good artists borrow; great artists steal," said Pablo Picasso or T.S. Eliot or Salvador Dalí—no one seems to know for sure. This principle launched Apple Computer on the road to greatness when one of its co-founders, Steve Jobs, identified technologies that Xerox had developed but was not using. It can work for you, too, within the limits of the law and ethical conduct. Think deeply about how you might put ideas and practices that you come across to work in launching a startup or accelerating the growth of an existing business. Research shows that this is a powerful starting place for innovation.

Combine Two Businesses to Create a Market Opening. Putting two businesses together can sometimes lead to unique products, services, or experiences that customers can't get elsewhere. Examples include theaters that combine dinner and a movie, and bookstores that add a coffee shop. Andy Levine's company, Sixthman, organizes "floating music festivals" that allow hardcore fans of artists such as KISS, Lynyrd Skynyrd, and Kid Rock to go on cruises with their musical heroes and spend some time hanging out together. These one-of-a-kind vacations have been a tremendous hit, with customers indicating that there is a 60 percent chance that they will be repeating the experience.[14]

At some point, it may make sense to start (or buy) more than one business without merging the operations, a strategy known as *diversification*. Consider Motor City Denim Co., a family firm that is now run by Mark D'Andreta. The Detroit-based enterprise started as a tailor shop but had to shift its focus to making protective covers for robotic machines on auto assembly lines. When the recession hit in 2008 and demand for cars slackened, automakers slashed their orders for the company's product. To make ends meet, D'Andreta started producing handbags, jeans, and other apparel items on some of his machines. The strategy worked, and the firm has staged a bit of a comeback. "To survive," D'Andreta says, "you have to be flexible."[15]

Begin with a Problem in Mind, or Think of a "Pain" That You can Relieve. High-potential business ideas often address problems that people have or a "pain" that a new venture idea could relieve. Think about a significant problem or hassle that people have to deal with, dissect it, chart it out on a sheet of paper, and roll it over and over in your mind while considering possible solutions. Lots of smart business ideas are likely to come to mind. If the pain you are trying to address is your own, the results can be especially good, since you are an expert on the problem and will feel passionate about finding a solution. This notion is validated by Richard Branson, uber-entrepreneur and founder of the Virgin Group empire. "All startups should be thinking, 'What frustrates me and how can I make it better?'" he says. "It might be a small thing or it might be a big thing, but that's the best way for [entrepreneurs] to think. If they think like that, they're likely to build a very successful business."[16]

Recognize a Hot Trend and Ride the Wave. Fads can lead to serious, though sometimes short-lived, money-making opportunities (for example, google Pet Rocks), but *trends* provide a much stronger foundation for businesses because they are connected to a larger change in society. Even more powerful is the product or service that builds on three or four trends as they come together. For example, the outrageous success of Apple's iPad is the result of multiple merging trends: consumer desires for increased mobility, instant gratification, and no hassles all tied together with the product's "coolness" factor.[17]

Also look for countertrends. For example, even in this age of digital addiction, some hotels, resorts, and travel companies have started offering "unplugged" or "digital detox" packages to guests if they surrender their digital devices at check-in. These offers appeal to guests who need an excuse to take a *complete* break from their work.[18] To identify a countertrend, make it a habit to ask those who resist a trend (such as the coffee drinker who refuses to go to Starbucks) what products or services would appeal to them and then see what possibilities come to mind. Set aside your preconceived notions of what "ought to be" and get into the minds of those who resist the flow. If you use the trend as your starting point, you will know better where to look for the countertrend, and that's where you can get ahead of the game.

Study an Existing Product or Service and Explore Ways to Improve Its Function. Almost all suitcases have wheels these days, but that wasn't always the case. The innovation was perfected by Robert Plath, who created what is called the Rollaboard design in 1987. The product was so popular that Plath decided to quit his job as a commercial pilot to start Travelpro International, now a major luggage company.[19] Luggage without wheels is still functional, but adding this feature opened the door to new sales and a new venture.

Think of Possibilities That Would Streamline a Customer's Activities. Many people are busy, so they look to firms that can bear some of the burdens of life for them. That's what keeps businesses like grocery-delivery services going. Take some time to ponder the day-to-day experiences of people in the market segment you would like to serve. What activities would they gladly offload?

Consider Ways to Adapt a Product or Service to Meet Customer Needs in a Different Way. Many new ventures get their start by borrowing a product or service that was already working well somewhere else and adapting it to a different need or situation. For example, eBay's online auction model has been adapted with great success by many startups, such as Etsy.com (to sell handmade goods, vintage products, and art supplies) and HelloLaMode.com (for the resale of luxury products). Or, consider Michelle Marciniak and Susan Walvius's launch of a company called Sheex, which uses the moisture-wicking performance fabrics found in workout clothes to manufacture super-comfortable bedsheets.[20] The possibilities are endless.

Imagine How the Market for a Product or Service Could Be Creatively Expanded. Annie Haven's family ranch in Southern California had few takers for the "fertilizer" that its cattle produced, so she decided to package the growth-stimulating stuff in three- by five-inch pouches (a box of nine bags sells for $27.95) and sell it to gardening enthusiasts. Customers simply steep each bag in one to five gallons of water and use that "tea" to water their plants. Haven has definitely found a way to create a new business by expanding the market for her product, and she is earning a tidy profit, with sales growing at around 30 percent a year![21]

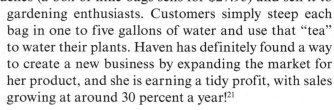

© Courtesy of Authentic Haven Brand

Study a Product or Service to See If You Can Make It "Green." A great surge of effort and investment has been flowing toward ventures that focus on protecting the environment. Examples of recent green startups include a company that strips trouble-making minerals and chemicals from pool water so that it can be reused (Calsaway Pool Services), an upscale paper-saving electronic invitation service for weddings and other formal events (Greenvelope), and "upcyclers" that transform refuse items into high-quality products (LooptWorks).[22] Given the success many of these companies are having, it clearly can pay to think "green."

Keep an Eye on New Technologies. New technologies often open up potential opportunities for startups, but only those who take note of the possibilities can reap the rewards. Read widely, consult industry experts and government offices that promote new technologies, drop by the technology transfer office of a nearby university, or visit with faculty who work at the cutting edge of their fields. Regardless of where you look, be sure to research innovations that have potential commercial value, particularly for new ventures.

These options represent only a few of the many possibilities. We encourage you to seek and size up new venture ideas in whatever circumstances you find yourself. By considering a number of internal and external factors, you should be able to fit together the pieces of the opportunity puzzle.

3-3 USING INTERNAL AND EXTERNAL ANALYSES TO ASSESS NEW BUSINESS IDEAS

LO 3-3

Describe external and internal analyses that might shape the selection of venture opportunities.

Two general approaches can help to identify business ideas—outside-in and inside-out analyses. In other words, entrepreneurs can look for needs in the marketplace and then determine how to use their own capabilities to pursue those opportunities (outside-in), or they can first evaluate their capabilities and then identify new products or services they might be able to offer to the market (inside-out).[23] It is important to understand the finer points of the two methods because they can reveal business ideas that may otherwise be overlooked.

3-3a Outside-In Analysis

Entrepreneurs are more successful when they study a business context in order to identify potential startup opportunities and determine which are most likely to lead to success. This outside-in analysis should consider the general environment, or big picture, and the industry setting in which the venture might do business. It should also factor in the competitive environment that is likely to have an impact. The **general environment** is made up of very broad factors that influence most businesses in a society, while the **industry environment** is defined more narrowly as the context for factors that directly impact a given firm and all of its competitors. The **competitive environment** is even more specific, focusing on the strength, position, and likely moves and countermoves of competitors in an industry.

THE GENERAL ENVIRONMENT The general environment contains a number of important trends, as shown in Exhibit 3.3. *Economic trends* include changes in the rate of inflation, interest rates, and even currency exchange rates, all of which promote or discourage business growth. *Sociocultural trends* refer to societal currents that may affect consumer demand, opening up new markets and forcing others into decline. *Political/legal trends* include changes in tax law and government regulations (perhaps safety rules) that may pose a threat to existing companies or devastate an inventive business concept. *Global trends* reflect international developments that create new opportunities to expand markets, outsource, invest abroad, and so on. As people and

general environment
The broad environment, encompassing factors that influence most businesses in a society.

industry environment
The environment that includes factors that directly impact a given firm and all of its competitors.

competitive environment
The environment that focuses on the strength, position, and likely moves and countermoves of competitors in an industry.

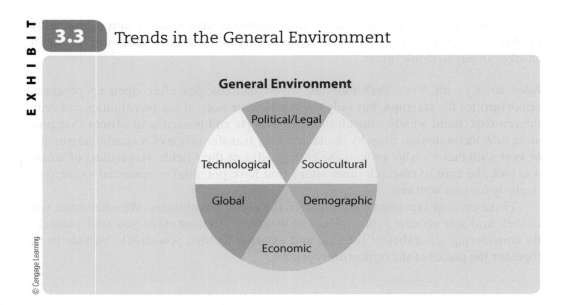

EXHIBIT 3.3 Trends in the General Environment

General Environment

- Political/Legal
- Sociocultural
- Demographic
- Economic
- Global
- Technological

© Cengage Learning

START UP

RESOURCES

Reading Economic Trends

Need a better read on economic trends in order to make better business decisions? VISA Small Business Insights offers a free report on the economic confidence of small business owners based on VISA spending data and responses to a quarterly survey. See current and archived reports at www.visabusinessnetwork.com/spendinsights for data and analysis.

markets around the world become increasingly connected, the impact of the global segment on small business opportunities will increase.

Developments that grow out of *technological trends* spawn—or wipe out—many new ventures. And given the rapid rate of change in this segment of the general environment, it is very important that small business owners stay current on these trends and understand the impact that they may have. Recent technological developments to keep an eye on include the following:

- Web-based or "cloud" computing, mobile technologies, social media, and particularly the merging of these three in inventive ways that pack an especially powerful punch
- Quick response (QR) codes, RFID (radio frequency identification) tags, and other information-compression and delivery systems
- Crowdsourcing methods that provide inexpensive and high-quality solutions to such needs as custom software development, logo and website design, and fundraising
- GPS and other location-based technologies that permit geo-targeting of marketing appeals, information delivery, and other creative applications

Finally, *demographic trends* also play an important role in shaping opportunities for startups. These trends include population size, age structure, ethnic mix, and wage distribution. For example, the focus on aging baby boomers (the 78 million Americans born between 1946 and 1964) may really pay off, given their $2 trillion in annual spending power and willful self-indulgence. And there is no limit to the products and services that can be targeted to this age group. Cell phones with larger keys that can easily be seen in dim lighting and magazines that focus on health issues in the retirement years are business ideas that have emerged with this demographic trend in mind.

Some people believe that evaluation of the general environment is appropriate only for large firms that have corporate staffs to manage the process, but small businesses can also benefit from such analysis. For example, 68 percent of Americans are considered obese or overweight. If current trends persist, the number of overweight/obese Americans will reach a worrisome 86.3 percent by the year 2030.[24] Entrepreneurs have realized that a multitude of business opportunities can be launched based on this rising tide, from weight-loss services to products that help obese people live more comfortably with their condition. Among the many businesses launched by those reading the trend are startups offering airline seatbelt extenders, high-capacity bathroom scales, and oversized furniture.

THE INDUSTRY ENVIRONMENT An entrepreneur will be even more directly affected by the startup's industry than by the general environment. The impact can be substantial, with studies reporting that industry influences can explain anywhere from 8 to 30 percent of firm profitability.[25] To outline these dynamics, Michael Porter lists five factors that determine the nature and degree of competition in an industry:[26]

- *New competitors.* How easy is it for new competitors to enter the industry?
- *Substitute products/services.* Can customers turn to other products or services to replace those that the industry offers?
- *Rivalry.* How intense is the rivalry among existing competitors in the industry?
- *Suppliers.* Are industry suppliers so powerful that they will demand high prices for inputs, thereby increasing the company's costs and reducing its profits?
- *Buyers.* Are industry customers so powerful that they will force companies to charge low prices, thereby reducing profits?

Exhibit 3.4 shows these five factors as weights that offset the potential attractiveness and profitability of a target industry. It illustrates how profits in an industry tend to be inversely related to the strength of these factors—that is, strong factors yield weak profits, whereas weak factors yield strong profits.

EXHIBIT 3.4 Major Factors Offsetting Market Attractiveness

Threat of New Competitors

Threat of Substitute Products or Services

Intensity of Rivalry Among Existing Competitors

Bargaining Power of Suppliers

Bargaining Power of Buyers

Attractiveness and Profitability of a Target Market

© Cengage Learning

Entrepreneurs who understand industry influences can better identify high-potential startup opportunities—situations where, say, rivalry is weak and neither buyers nor suppliers have enough power to drive hard bargains on price. But these insights can also help entrepreneurs to anticipate threats they are likely to encounter and to begin thinking about ways to defend their startups from any downside risk. Entrepreneurs who recognize and understand Porter's five industry factors can position their ventures in a way that makes the most of what the industry offers.

THE COMPETITIVE ENVIRONMENT Within any given industry, it is important to determine the strength, position, and likely responses of rival businesses to newcomers. In fact, experts insist that such analyses are a critical input for the assessment of any business idea. William A. Sahlman of Harvard Business School contends that every aspiring entrepreneur should answer several questions about the competitors he or she is likely to encounter in the marketplace:[27]

- Who would be the new venture's current competitors?
- What unique resources do they control?
- What are their strengths and weaknesses?
- How will they respond to the new venture's decision to enter the industry?
- How can the new venture respond?
- Who else might see and exploit the same opportunity?
- Are there ways to co-opt potential or actual competitors by forming alliances?

This analysis helps an entrepreneur to evaluate the nature and extent of existing competition and to fine-tune future plans. It can also help to identify high-potential business opportunities based on the competitive situation.

Entrepreneurs should take one more step when analyzing the competition: They should identify the thinking that shapes their rivals' moves. As a highly regarded thinker, writer, and consultant on Internet technologies and the new media, Clay Shirky observes that he has sometimes assumed that businesses must operate in a certain way because they always have. For example, he thought he knew that teenagers buy music CDs from stores, that customers have to try on pants before they buy them, and that people read newspapers to catch up on the latest in the world of politics. But then he points out, "In the last 15 years or so, I have had to unlearn every one of [these] things and a million others."[28] To put it another way, innovative entrepreneurs often overtake established rivals by using their commitment to time-honored approaches against them. For example, Blockbuster's old way of doing business left it vulnerable to a startup (Netflix) that challenged conventional wisdom and adopted an inventive set of "rules for the game" (offering videos online or through the mail) to which Blockbuster could not seem to adapt. Blockbuster had to file for bankruptcy in 2010 and continues to struggle for survival.

3-3b Inside-Out Analysis

Identifying opportunities in the external environment is definitely worth the effort, but business concepts make sense only if they fit well with the resources, capabilities, and competencies that an entrepreneur can bring to the world of business. The search for a startup opportunity can actually *begin* with an inside-out analysis, one that catalogues the startup's sources of potential strengths (including those that can reasonably be obtained or created) and the unique competencies that can be formed from them. These can provide a platform from which the fruit of new business opportunities can be reached and harvested.

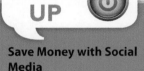

START UP

ACTION

Save Money with Social Media
Want to learn more about what people are saying about your industry, but on a shoestring? Join industry groups on sites like LinkedIn and Facebook, and follow influential industry blogs. Such efforts will help you get a sense of the major players and identify hot button issues.

BUILDING ON INTERNAL RESOURCES AND CAPABILITIES Entrepreneurs who want to start or build a business based on inside-out analysis will first need to have a solid grasp of the resources and capabilities that are available to them and can be used to make this happen. The term **resources** refers to those inputs that an entrepreneur can use to start a business, such as cash for investment, knowledge of critical technologies, access to essential equipment, and capable business partners, to name just a few. A startup or small business can have both tangible and intangible resources. **Tangible resources** are visible and easy to measure. An office building, manufacturing equipment, and cash reserves are all examples of tangible resources. But these are very different from **intangible resources**, which are invisible and difficult to assess. Intangible assets can include intellectual property rights such as patents and copyrights, an established brand, a favorable reputation, and an entrepreneur's personal network of contacts and relationships.

Though the terms are often used interchangeably, *resources* technically are not the same as *capabilities*. Whereas resources are inputs to the work of a business, **capabilities** are best viewed as the company's routines and processes that coordinate the combined use of these productive assets to achieve desired outcomes. Resources can do nothing on their own. Rather, entrepreneurs who figure out how to work with and integrate resources in ways that create value for customers are those most likely to create and build successful ventures.

CORE COMPETENCIES AND COMPETITIVE ADVANTAGE Once entrepreneurs have an accurate view of their resources and capabilities, they will be in a better position to identify core competencies that can be created and used to compete. **Core competencies** are those crucial capabilities that distinguish a company competitively and reflect its general focus and personality. In most cases, these strengths make it possible to achieve a **competitive advantage**, which gives a startup or small business the upper hand by allowing it to provide products or services that customers will choose over available alternatives.

To illustrate how all of this works, consider Starbucks, which offers a nice selection of gourmet coffees. But that is not its only edge in the marketplace. In fact, many of its competitors, large and small, also provide high-quality coffee products. So why has the company been so successful? Most observers believe that it is the premium product, combined with the special "Starbucks experience," that has allowed the coffee icon to grow from a single store in the mid-1980s to more than 17,000 retail locations in over 55 countries today.[29] As one observer put it, "For many of its customers, Starbucks isn't really in the business of selling coffee. Instead, it's offering a place to hang out that happens to sell coffee."[30]

Though the success of Starbucks is undeniable, the company's growth has actually unleashed a torrent of new rivals by whetting the market's appetite for both the product and the experience. But how do small firms compete in a Starbucks-saturated market? By focusing on their own unique core competencies and the advantages they can support. Many small shops thrive in this environment by providing free refills, paying meticulous attention to product quality, emphasizing connections with the local community, or taking other steps to showcase their own unique character and individuality. In other words, they establish core competencies by using resources and capabilities in unique ways that reflect the "personality" of their own enterprises.

3-3c Integrating Internal and External Analyses

A solid foundation for competitive advantage requires a reasonable match between the strengths and weaknesses of a given business and the opportunities and threats present in its relevant environments. This integration is best revealed through

resources
The basic inputs that a firm uses to conduct its business.

tangible resources
Those organizational resources that are visible and easy to measure.

intangible resources
Those organizational resources that are invisible and difficult to assess.

capabilities
A company's routines and processes that can coordinate the combined use of its productive assets in order to achieve desired outcomes.

core competencies
Those capabilities that provide a firm with a competitive edge and reflect its personality.

competitive advantage
A benefit that exists when a firm has a product or service that is seen by its target market as better than those of competitors.

a **SWOT analysis** (standing for *S*trengths, *W*eaknesses, *O*pportunities, *T*hreats), which provides a simple overview of a venture's strategic situation. Exhibit 3.5 lists a number of factors that can be classified by this framework; however, these are merely representative of the countless possibilities that may exist.

In practice, a SWOT analysis provides a snapshot view of current conditions. Outside-in and inside-out approaches come together in the SWOT analysis to help identify potential business opportunities that match the entrepreneur and his or her planned venture. However, because a SWOT analysis focuses on the present, the entrepreneur needs to also consider whether the targeted opportunity will lead to other opportunities in the future (for example, through skillbuilding) and whether pursuit of the opportunity is likely to lead to competitive response by potential rivals. Obviously, the most promising opportunities are those that lead to others (which may offer value and profitability over the long run), promote the development of additional skills that equip the venture to pursue new prospects, and yet do not provoke competitors to strike back.

When potentials in the external environment (revealed through analysis of the general, industry, and competitive environments) fit with the unique resources, capabilities, and core competencies of the entrepreneur (highlighted by internal assessment) and threats outside the startup or weaknesses within it are manageable, the odds of success are greatly improved. As shown in Exhibit 3.6, this is what we call the entrepreneur's "opportunity sweet spot," an area that typically offers the greatest potential for superior business results. With this in mind, we encourage you to be observant and systematic in your search for opportunities and to think carefully about how these opportunities fit your background and skills, as well as your interests and passions. If you do so, you are much more likely to enjoy the adventure.

Clearly, conducting outside-in and inside-out analyses and integrating the results can help you identify potential business opportunities and then build a solid foundation for competitive advantage. With that foundation, an entrepreneur can begin to position the new venture concept or established company with a well-defined strategy that will be more likely to generate superior financial results.

SWOT analysis
An assessment that provides a concise overview of a firm's strategic situation.

3.5 Examples of SWOT Factors

	POSITIVE FACTORS	NEGATIVE FACTORS
Inside the Company	*Strengths*	*Weaknesses*
	• Important core competencies	• Inadequate financial resources
	• Financial strengths	• Poorly planned strategy
	• Innovative capacity	• Lack of management skills or experience
	• Skilled or experienced management	• Inadequate innovation capacity
	• Well-planned strategy	• Negative reputation in the marketplace
	• Effective entry wedge	• Inadequate facilities
	• A strong network of personal contacts	• Distribution problems
	• Positive reputation in the marketplace	• Limited marketing skills
	• Proprietary technology	• Production inefficiencies
Outside the Company	*Opportunities*	*Threats*
	• An untapped market potential	• New competitors
	• New product or geographic market	• Rising demands of buyers or suppliers
	• Favorable shift in industry dynamics	• Sales shifting to substitute products
	• High potential for market growth	• Increased government regulation
	• Emerging technologies	• Adverse shifts in the business cycle
	• Changes allowing overseas expansion	• Slowed market growth
	• Favorable government deregulation	• Changing customer preferences
	• Increasing market fragmentation	• Adverse demographic shifts

3.6 The Entrepreneur's Opportunity "Sweet Spot"

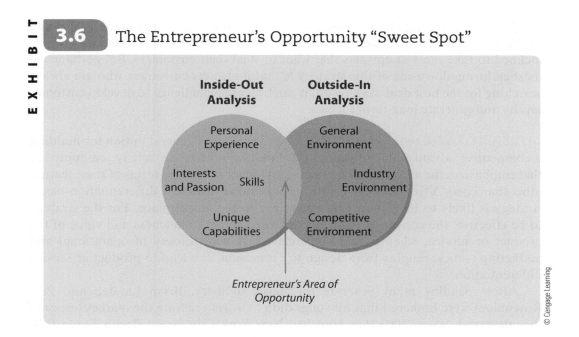

Inside-Out Analysis

- Personal Experience
- Interests and Passion
- Skills
- Unique Capabilities

Outside-In Analysis

- General Environment
- Industry Environment
- Competitive Environment

Entrepreneur's Area of Opportunity

© Cengage Learning

3-4 SELECTING STRATEGIES THAT CAPTURE OPPORTUNITIES

LO 3-4

Explain broad-based strategy options and focus strategies.

A strategy is, in essence, a set of actions that coordinates the resources and commitments of a business to boost its performance. Choosing a strategy that makes sense for a particular entrepreneur and startup is a critical early step toward superior performance. But keeping an eye on strategy options—both broad-based and focus strategies—can also guide established companies toward success.

3-4a Broad-Based Strategy Options

Firms competing in the same industry can adopt very different strategies. Broadly speaking, companies can choose to build their strategies around an emphasis on either low cost or differentiation as they consider how to position themselves relative to their competitors.

© Lair Keiows/Shutterstock.com

COST-BASED STRATEGY To follow a **cost-based strategy**, a firm must hold down its costs so that it can compete by charging lower prices for its products or services and still make a profit. The sources of cost advantages are varied, ranging from low-cost labor to efficiency in operations. Many people assume that cost-based strategies will not work for small companies, and often this is true. However, cost-advantage factors are so numerous and diverse that, in some cases, small businesses may be able to use them with great success. Think about the thousands of small operators who sell used cars on eBay as a primary occupation. Although they lack the scale advantages of the large dealerships against which they compete, they operate with very little overhead by selling exclusively online and handling all features of the transactions involved in order to limit costs. It appears that motivated entrepreneurs can almost always find ways to compete on cost and undercut their much-larger competitors.

strategy
A plan of action that coordinates the resources and commitments of an organization to achieve superior performance.

cost-based strategy
A plan of action that requires a firm to hold down its costs so that it can compete by charging lower prices and still make a profit.

To be sure, taking the low-cost path is not without its risks, especially if doing so sparks a price war with established competitors that have deeper pockets and are inclined to take shots at upstarts that want to steal their customers. But perhaps the most enduring downside of this strategy is that it attracts customers who are always searching for the best deal. As a result, it can be a great challenge to develop customer loyalty and generate long-term success.

DIFFERENTIATION-BASED STRATEGY The second general option for building a competitive advantage is following a **differentiation-based strategy**, an approach that emphasizes the uniqueness of a firm's product or service (in terms of some feature other than cost). A firm that can create and sustain an attractive differentiation-based strategy is likely to be a successful performer in the marketplace. For the strategy to be effective, the consumer must be convinced of the uniqueness and value of the product or service, whether real or perceived. A wide variety of operational and marketing tactics, ranging from design to promotion, can lead to product or service differentiation.

After spending many years in the music industry, Brian Landau and Pete Rosenblum were bothered that hit songs didn't always generate the market response they deserved. So, in 2003 they launched New York City–based Radio Tag, a full-service marketing agency. Right from the start, differentiation was the foundation of their strategy. While most radio stations let the DJs do all the talking, Radio Tag allows artists to introduce their own work via recordings. With this approach, Beyoncé can describe her emotional connection to a song, or members of Coldplay might explain how their latest album came together. "That was really the whole point," says Rosenblum. "Put an artist on the radio and let people become more familiar with who the artist is, what the song is, and how they can buy it." It is clearly a different approach, and a successful one. Radio stations benefit from the free promotional content, artists are able to personally promote their creative works, and the company has profited nicely. Radio Tag is a small business with a well-designed and competently executed differentiation strategy.[31]

3-4b Focus Strategies

If one firm controlled the only known water supply in the world, its sales volume would be huge. Such a business would not be concerned about differences in personal preferences regarding taste, appearance, or temperature. It would consider its customers to be one market. As long as the water product was wet, it would satisfy everyone. However, if someone else discovered a second water supply, the first company's view of the market would change. The first business might discover that sales were drying up and take measures to modify its strategy. In any case, the level of rivalry would likely rise as rivals struggled for position in the same industry space.

If the potential for water sales was enormous, small businesses would eventually become interested in entering the market. However, given their limited resources and lack of experience, these companies would be more likely to succeed if they avoided head-to-head competition with industry giants and sought a protected market segment instead. In other words, they could be competitive if they implemented a **focus strategy** by adapting their efforts to concentrate on the needs of a very limited portion of the market. To get started, these businesses might focus their resources on a narrow slice of the market that was small enough to escape the interest of major players (offering, say, filtered water delivered to individual homes) or even take a completely new approach to permit entry without immediate competitive response (perhaps by filling market gaps resulting from supply shortages).

differentiation-based strategy
A plan of action designed to provide a product or service with unique attributes that are valued by consumers.

focus strategy
A plan of action that isolates an enterprise from competitors and other market forces by targeting a restricted market segment.

Focus strategies represent a strategic approach in which entrepreneurs try to shield themselves from market forces by targeting a specific group of customers who have an identifiable but very narrow range of product or service interests (often called a *market niche*). By focusing on a specialized market, some small businesses develop unique expertise that leads to higher levels of value and service for customers, which is great for business. In fact, this advantage prompted marketing guru Philip Kotler to declare, "There are riches in niches."[32]

The two broad options discussed earlier—cost-based and differentiation-based strategies—can also be used when focusing on a niche market. Although few entrepreneurs adopt a cost-based focus strategy, it does happen. For example, outlets with names like Drinking Water Depot and H2O To Go have opened over the years, with most using an efficient purification system to offer high-quality drinking water to price-sensitive customers at a fraction of the price charged by competitors.

Contrast this approach with the differentiation-based focus strategy that Mark Sikes adopted for his small business, Personalized Bottle Water. Since launching the company in Little Rock, Arkansas, in 1997, he has been selling bottled water featuring custom labels for corporate clients and anyone who wants to celebrate a special occasion, including schools, funeral homes, hotels, and brides and grooms. He has plans to expand the business, but the emphasis will still be on personalization.[33] Without this focus, there is no way that Sikes would be able to compete head to head with a bottling giant like Coca-Cola Company (Dasani), but flexibility and customization—foundations for differentiation—give Personalized Bottle Water a fighting chance.

Entrepreneurs can usually select and implement a focus strategy that will allow them to target a niche market within a sizeable industry, thereby avoiding direct competition with larger competitors. This can be accomplished in a number of ways, as discussed in the next section.

FOCUS STRATEGY SELECTION AND IMPLEMENTATION By selecting a particular focus strategy, an entrepreneur decides on the basic direction of a business, which determines the venture's very nature. A firm's overall strategy is formulated, therefore, as its leader decides how the firm will relate to its environment—particularly to the customers and competitors in that environment. This can involve a delicate balancing act, one that keeps the venture out of the crosshairs of industry heavyweights and yet offers enough market promise to provide the startup with a reasonable shot at getting off the ground.

Selection of a very specialized market is, of course, not the only possible strategy for a small firm. But focus strategies are very popular because they allow a small firm to operate in the gaps that exist between larger competitors. They also leave entrepreneurs with plenty of room to maneuver as they come up with creative new venture ideas. For starters, focus strategies can be set up in the following ways:

- By restricting the target market to a single subset of customers
- By emphasizing a single product or service
- By limiting the market to a single geographical region
- By concentrating on the superiority of the product or service

If a small firm chooses to compete head to head with other companies, particularly large corporations, it must be prepared to distinguish itself in some way in order to make itself a viable competitor. If you want to succeed as a focus player, it's wise to pinpoint a profitable niche and develop great depth of competence in it so that you can *own* it. In the words of Jack Trout, one of the pioneers of the concept of market positioning, the focuser should try to be "like the service guy who repairs only Sub-Zero appliances and becomes the best at that instead of trying to go head to head with Sears in trying to repair everything. Customers will hire [him] because they know he'll have the right parts in stock, have experience with the brand's quirks and be able to complete repairs faster."[34]

Because powerful focus strategies also offer great flexibility, entrepreneurs often find ways to start a number of different specialization strategies within the same industry, with the hope of success for each of them. At the same time, however, they must consider problems stemming from overspecialization and competition, which can threaten to erode the profits of such strategies.

Niche Knockoffs: Sometimes There's Just No Stopping Them

Kickstarter has been famously successful. Since its launch in April of 2009, the fundraising website has collected more than $428 million from 2.5 million people to back 79,314 creative projects. The film-makers, musicians, designers, artists, and others who receive support love it, and those who put up the money are thrilled to be a part of the creative process. Everyone wins, including Kickstarter, which charges fees for certain services related to using its website.

Perhaps that is why so many other crowdfunding sites are starting to pop up. But each newcomer is cleverly focusing on a market niche that will give it a toehold in the industry. Fundly, for example, focuses on raising support for social causes, including political campaigns and various charities, and takes a cut of the total funds raised (less than 5 percent) for its assistance. Appbackr, according to its website, "is the first and only digital wholesale marketplace for the application market." It allows app developers to sell a stake in their planned app projects to buy time to create them. Crowdtilt allows friends to pool money for

group causes, whereas Petridish organizes and promotes fundraising to support a broad range of scientists and their research programs. It seems there is no end to the list of possibilities!

When a business concept proves to be successful, other interested players take notice and come tumbling into the industry with ideas of their own. But those who are smart about it avoid going up against established and stronger competitors whenever possible. Often, that means developing a focus strategy to go after a part of the market that is underserved in some way. And as you can see, this approach can inspire some very interesting startups. So, as you search for a business opportunity, what market niche are you overlooking?

Sources: Based on "Fundly—Features," http://fundly.com/features, accessed August 17, 2012; "AppBackr.com—About Us," http://www.appbackr.com /aboutUs, accessed August 17, 2012; "How Crowdtilt Works," http://www .crowdtilt.com/learn, accessed August 17, 2012; "Kickstarter Stat," http://www .kickstarter .com/help/stats?ref=footer, accessed December 3, 2012; Chris Dannen, "Crowding Around," *FastCompany*, No. 168, (September 2012), p. 38; and personal communication with Dave Boyce, CEO of Fundly on October 4, 2012.

DRAWBACKS OF FOCUS STRATEGIES One small business analyst expresses a word of caution about selecting a niche market:

> *Warning! A firm can be so specialized that it may not have enough customers to be viable. Do not plan to open a pen repair shop, a shoelace boutique, or a restaurant based on the concept of toast (although one based on breakfast cereal has apparently been founded).*[35]

In addition to the dangers of becoming too specialized, firms that adopt a focus strategy tread a narrow path between maintaining a protected market and attracting competition. If their ventures are profitable, entrepreneurs must be prepared to face new competitors. Strategy guru Michael Porter cautions that a segmented market can erode under any of the following four conditions:[36]

- The focus strategy is imitated.
- The target segment becomes structurally unattractive because the structure erodes or because demand simply disappears.
- The target segment loses its uniqueness.
- New firms subsegment the industry.

The experience of Minnetonka, a small firm widely recognized as the first to introduce liquid hand soap, provides an example of how a focus strategy can be imitated. The huge success of its brand, Softsoap, quickly attracted the attention of several giants in the industry, including Procter & Gamble. Minnetonka's competitive advantage was soon washed away. Some analysts believe this happened because the company focused too much on the advantages of liquid soap in general and not enough on the particular benefits of Softsoap. In any case, it should be clear that focus strategies do not guarantee a sustainable advantage. Small firms can boost their success, however, by developing and extending their competitive strengths. Good strategic planning can help point the way through these challenging situations, as well as shape the feasibility of the venture.

3-5 SCREENING NEW BUSINESS IDEAS

With all of the approaches to business idea generation described in this chapter, your problem may not be coming up with an idea for a startup, but coming up with too many. Since you can't pursue multiple startup ideas for now, it is important to narrow your focus to the one that seems most promising. After taking that step, you should complete an in-depth feasibility analysis (discussed on pages 81–82) to determine whether the idea you have selected is viable and merits the investment of time and money that will be necessary to launch it. If your new business idea still seems to be a winner, we will then lead you through the steps required to put together a suitable business plan (discussed in Chapter 6).

At this point, however, you really need to decide on the business idea that you want to consider further. The business idea screening process can help you do this. This process is presented in more detail in Appendix 3.1 (which can be accessed by going to www.cengagebrain.com and selecting the Longenecker text option), where you'll find evaluation forms and instructions that make this initial assessment quick and easy to complete.

It is important to understand that the quality of the final evaluation will only be as good as the information used to generate it. For that reason, running business ideas through the screen will require adequate background research and informed

LO 3-5

Know how to screen business ideas to identify those with the greatest potential.

estimations so that the analysis and conclusions will be based on trustworthy facts and reasonable judgments. The process must be more than a dart-throwing exercise. But it also doesn't need to be time consuming; in most cases, one hour will be enough time to complete the screening for each business idea assessed.[37]

Because the business idea screening tool is designed to provide a quick assessment, it is by no means comprehensive. Rather, it only takes into account the merits of an idea relative to five very important factors:

- *Strength of the business idea:* The best business ideas will meet a definite market need, create value for end users, and offer products or services that customers favor and find easy to use. They also will have no fatal flaws (see page 81).

- *Targeted market and customers:* Businesses are more likely to thrive if they focus on a sizeable market that is easy to identify, growing rapidly, and composed of customers with high levels of purchasing power that they are very willing to use. Further, the best customers will be easily reachable through clear channels of promotion.

- *Industry and competitive advantage:* The most favorable industries for start-ups have few or no competitors, are growing quickly (to allow room for new entrants), and feature high operating margins. They also present few or no barriers to keep new businesses out and would allow your startup to establish and sustain its specific competitive advantage.

- *Capability of founder(s):* In a best-case scenario, the founder(s) will have industry-related experience, skills, and networks, as well as great passion for and fit with the new business.

- *Capital requirements and venture performance:* An entrepreneur will fare best when the venture needs little capital to launch, its anticipated profit potential is great, and similar enterprises perform very well. Low levels of liability and other risks are ideal, as is the ability to start the new business incrementally or test it cheaply before full launch.

The last factor deserves further explanation. If your startup budget is tight (as is so often the case), a business idea's promise is likely to be determined by your ability to launch a limited version of that idea or to test market reactions to gauge its odds for success. This may be more manageable than you realize using free or cheap tools available online or low-tech methods that can get the job done. Many entrepreneurs have tested their ideas on a budget of $100 or less. Examples of their cost-effective methods include using SurveyMonkey.com to contact potential customers and estimate the size of the market, as well as conducting market research at no cost by joining online support groups to probe the depth of interest in a planned service offering (if this is permitted and appropriate). One entrepreneur spent about $45 to test her idea. This included setting up a website for the business using a free template (one approved for commercial use) from Joomla.org, registering a domain name (at $9.95), and spending $10.95 for Web hosting services. After installing Google Analytics (free) to track website traffic and paying for Google AdWords, she then started setting up ads to promote the site. Within a month, she had enough responses to know that her idea was a winner.[38] Testing an idea before launching a business is almost always an advantage.

© mast3r/Shutterstock.com

Finally, you should remember that an idea can be assessed more than once to allow for adjustments that would improve the startup's projected viability. For example, shifting to a narrower market niche might lead to a smaller venture, but it can also reduce the number and strength of competitors, increase the willingness of customers to pay for the product, lower startup costs, boost profitability, and so on.

The screening process presented here cannot provide a *perfect* estimate of the potential of a given business idea. One reason is that all items are weighted equally for the sake of simplicity, even though some may have more impact on an idea's potential than others. Nonetheless, this practical method for assessing multiple ideas will let you efficiently decide which one would be best to pursue. Then, after you have narrowed your focus to the one concept that you want to consider further, you should complete a feasibility analysis to determine its potential in more depth.

3-6 IS YOUR STARTUP IDEA FEASIBLE?

We will show you in Part 3 how to create a business plan that will spell out the details of your planned enterprise and its startup considerations. But it is very important that you take an intermediate step first, one that tells you how *feasible* your business idea may be. A **feasibility analysis** is a preliminary assessment of a business idea that gauges whether or not the venture envisioned is likely to succeed (see Appendix 3.2, which can be accessed by going to www.cengagebrain.com and selecting the Longenecker text option). Of course, it may also indicate that the concept has merit, but only if it is modified in some important way.

Developing a solid feasibility analysis before jumping ahead to the business plan can help ensure that the planned venture will not be doomed by a **fatal flaw**—that is, a circumstance or development that, in and of itself, could render a new business unsuccessful. John Osher, serial innovator and entrepreneur, estimates that nine out of ten entrepreneurs fail because their business concept is deficient. In his words, "They want to be in business so much that they often don't do the work they need to do ahead of time, so everything they do is doomed. They can be very talented, do everything else right, and fail because they have ideas that are flawed."[39] It is important to look deeply and honestly for potential weaknesses in your own startup ideas. No matter how remarkable the business concept may seem to be, moving forward is pointless if it must use a manufacturing process that is patent protected, requires startup capital that cannot be raised, ignores market limitations, or is unsound in some other way.

© Cla78/Shutterstock.com

John W. Mullins is a serial entrepreneur and a professor at the prestigious London Business School. He is also the author of *The New Business Road Test*, a book that underscores the importance of identifying the fatal flaws of a business idea before it is too late:

> *If [entrepreneurs] can find the fatal flaw before they write their business plan or before it engulfs their new business, they can deal with it in many ways. They can modify their ideas—shaping the opportunity to better fit the hotly competitive world in which it seeks to bear fruit. If the flaw they find appears to be a fatal one, they can even abandon the idea before it's too late—before launch, in some cases, or soon enough thereafter to avoid wasting months or years in pursuit of a dream that simply won't fly.*

feasibility analysis
A preliminary assessment of a business idea that gauges whether the venture envisioned is likely to succeed.

fatal flaw
A circumstance or development that alone could render a new business unsuccessful.

Better yet, if, after [questioning] and probing, testing and especially experimenting for answers, the signs remain positive, they embrace their opportunity with renewed passion and conviction, armed with a new-found confidence that the evidence—not just their intuition—confirms their [insight]. Their idea really is an opportunity worth pursuing. Business plan, here we come![40]

Deciding to complete a feasibility analysis before proceeding to the business plan stage can save a lot of time, money, and heartache. Or, as Mullins points out, it may reaffirm the power of a business idea and strengthen the resolve to move forward, providing a reserve of energy and commitment that will come in handy when the going gets tough—and it definitely *will* get tough as the venture unfolds.

Keep in mind that success in entrepreneurship is generally the result of three elements that come together in such a way that the new enterprise gets the thrust it needs to launch and the sustained power to keep it going. These three elements are a market with potential, an attractive industry, and a capable individual or team with the skills and capabilities to pull it all together (see Exhibit 3.7). A feasibility analysis investigates each of these elements.

3-6a Market Potential

It is important to make clear the distinction between a market and an industry, as the two are very different. A market consists of *buyers*, current or potential customers who are interested in purchasing a particular class of products or services to satisfy wants or needs—and they must also have the ability to pay for them. An industry, on the other hand, is composed of *sellers* who compete with one another by offering identical or similar products or services for sale to the same general group of buyers.

EXHIBIT

3.7 A Feasibility Analysis Framework

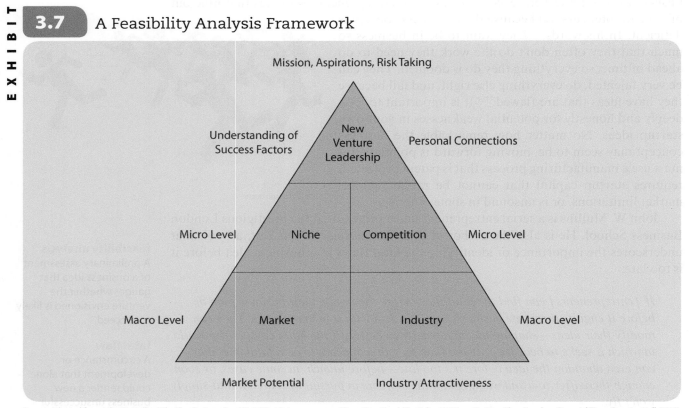

Source: Adapted from John W. Mullins, *The New Business Road Test: What Entrepreneurs and Executives Should Do Before Writing a Business Plan.* (London: Financial Times Prentice Hall, 2006).

When assessing the pool of potential buyers that a business might serve, it is important to think of that market on two levels—the broad macro-market and the fragments or niches (micro-markets) that can be identified within the broader market. Entrepreneurs with limited business aspirations may find attractive niche opportunities acceptable. However, Mullins points out that "it is also important to know which way the tides are flowing."[41] That is, a desirable niche today is likely to lose its luster over time if the broad market from which it is derived is trending toward the negative. In most cases, the health of the macro-market can be a very useful predictor of the future potential of the micro-markets within it.

An entrepreneur with lofty ambitions may be satisfied with an attractive niche only if it can serve as a point of entry into a macro-market with prospects for fast growth and ample long-term potential. The attractiveness of that niche is limited if the fundamental features of the macro-market that support it are not promising. In any case, assessments of the market should be completed on both levels, and each level will be driven by a very different set of questions (see Appendix 3.2, which can be accessed by going to www.cengagebrain.com and selecting the Longenecker text option).

As part of a feasibility analysis, an evaluation of the general environment will help to identify a potential-laden trend that can support promising startup ideas, one of which you will likely select for more thorough consideration. This sets the framework for a macro-market analysis, establishing the boundaries for the research you will need to conduct regarding the number of customers targeted and their overall purchasing power and habits.

The micro-market assessment, however, goes in a very different direction. A startup idea will most likely be tied to a market niche that seems to offer acceptable prospects for growth and, perhaps more important, a path to market entry that is somewhat protected from existing competition. (These dynamics are explained in some detail in our discussion of focus strategies.) Your evaluation of the micro-market should clarify the unique value the startup idea would offer customers, but it should also provide estimates of the size of the niche, its rate of growth, and its long-run prospects.

3-6b Industry Attractiveness

Like markets, industries should be considered from both a "big-picture" and a more focused point of view. A macro-level analysis assesses the overall attractiveness of the industry in which the startup will be established, perhaps summarized best by Michael Porter's model of industry forces (see pages 71–72). This general view of the industry will be further shaped by answers to the associated questions presented in Appendix 3.2 (which can be accessed by going to www.cengagebrain.com and selecting the Longenecker text option). Ultimately, these insights will tell you whether industry conditions would be favorable for the startup you hope to pursue. The more favorable the forces, the more attractive the industry—but keep in mind that a single unfavorable force can be enough to tip the balance toward unattractiveness, so it is important to consider these forces with great care. Foreknowledge of adverse conditions helps an entrepreneur make adjustments to compensate, or it may suggest that it is time to pull the plug on that particular concept. Either way, the feasibility analysis will have served its purpose by highlighting problems in a particular industry setting.

A micro-level industry assessment is focused less on whether industry conditions overall are suitable to launching a new business and more on the probability of a startup's success over the long run. This requires the aspiring entrepreneur to think carefully about the proposed venture to determine whether the advantage it has going for it can be protected from competitive pressures once rivals realize that they have a new challenger. This will be determined mostly by the startup's potential to generate sales and the strength of protective barriers that will shield it from competitors' efforts to replicate its strengths.

3-6c New Venture Leadership

Finally, a new business will only be as strong as its leader, so it is important to assess whether the entrepreneur, or entrepreneurial team, is up to the task. Mullins suggests that three dimensions of capability are important here: (1) the fit of the venture with its leader's mission, aspirations, and level of comfort with the risk involved, (2) the leader's grasp of factors that are critical to the success of the enterprise and her or his ability to execute on these, and (3) the leader's connection to suppliers, customers, investors, and others who will be essential to making the venture work.[42]

Completing a feasibility analysis takes time and effort, but it serves the very important purpose of identifying flaws in a business concept that may be fatal to the proposed startup. While many of these flaws can be corrected by a course adjustment, the analysis might expose major flaws that cannot be addressed or corrected. If it does, you would be wise to abandon the concept and shift your energies to a more attractive alternative. Regardless of the final outcome, completing a feasibility analysis will let you know what needs to be done before you commit time, money, and energy to complete a full-scale business plan. (See Appendix 3.2, which can be accessed by going to www.cengagebrain.com and selecting the Longenecker text option.)

LOOKING BACK

3-1. Distinguish among the different types and sources of startup ideas.

- Entrepreneurs decide to start businesses from scratch for many different reasons.
- New market startup ideas are concerned with products or services that exist but are not present in all markets.
- New technology ideas involve new or relatively new knowledge breakthroughs.
- New benefit ideas are based on new and improved ways of performing old functions.
- Research shows that entrepreneurs claim prior work experience is the leading source of inspiration for startup ideas.
- Personal experience leads many aspiring entrepreneurs to the startup decision.

- Some entrepreneurs start their new ventures based on their hobbies and personal interests, which can add passion and energy to the enterprise.
- Accidental discoveries may also spur startup efforts.

3-2. Use innovative thinking to generate ideas for high-potential startups.

- A commitment to creative thinking can generate many ideas for new businesses.
- Business ideas can also be spurred by borrowing ideas from existing products and services or other industries, combining businesses to create a market opening, focusing on a problem, and responding to a trend.
- Other ideas for new businesses can come from improving an existing product or service, making customers' lives easier, meeting customer needs in a new way, expanding the market for a product or service, making a product or service "green," and tapping into new technologies.

3-3. Describe external and internal analyses that might shape the selection of venture opportunities.

- Outside-in analysis considers the external environment, including the general, industry, and competitive environments.

- Major trends in the general environment are economic, sociocultural, political/legal, global, technological, and demographic in nature.

- The major forces that determine the potential attractiveness and profitability of a target industry include the threat of new competitors, the threat of substitute products or services, the intensity of rivalry among existing competitors, the bargaining power of suppliers, and the bargaining power of buyers.

- Opportunities arise for small businesses that are alert to changes or openings in the general, industry, and competitive environments.

- Inside-out analysis helps the entrepreneur to understand the internal potentials of the business.

- Tangible resources are visible and easy to measure, whereas intangible resources are invisible and difficult to quantify.

- Capabilities refers to a firm's routines and processes that can coordinate the combined use of several resources to achieve desired outcomes.

- Core competencies are those capabilities that can be leveraged to enable a firm to do more than its competitors, thereby leading to a competitive advantage.

- A SWOT analysis provides an overview of a firm's strengths and weaknesses, as well as opportunities for and threats to the organization.

- The entrepreneur's "opportunity sweet spot" is found at the point of overlap of emerging potentials in the external environment and the unique strengths and capabilities of the entrepreneur and the venture.

3-4. Explain broad-based strategy options and focus strategies.

- A competitive advantage can be created using cost-based or differentiation-based strategies, both of which are broad-based strategy options.

- A cost-based strategy requires the firm to become a low-cost provider within the market.

- Product or service differentiation is frequently used as a means of achieving superior performance.

- Focusing on a specific market niche is a strategy that small firms often use successfully.

- A focus strategy may involve restricting focus to a single subset of customers, emphasizing a single product or service, limiting the market to a single geographical region, or concentrating on product or service superiority.

- Entrepreneurs can exploit very different market niches that derive from the same general industry.

- In selecting a particular focus strategy, an entrepreneur determines the basic direction of the business, and this affects the very nature of the venture.

- The benefits of a focus strategy can diminish when the firm becomes too specialized, the strategy is imitated, the target segment becomes unattractive or demand dwindles, the segment loses its uniqueness, or new firms subsegment the industry.

3-5. Know how to screen business ideas to identify those with the greatest potential.

- If too many new business ideas are generated, it will be necessary to use an idea screening process to determine which idea deserves more focused attention.

- The screening of ideas can be performed quickly (usually in an hour or less) and should precede a decision to complete a feasibility analysis on the idea selected.

- The five main factors considered in the screening process include the strength of the idea, the targeted market and customers, industry and competitive advantage issues, founder(s) capabilities and fit with the new business, and capital needs and venture performance.

- There are ways to test many new business ideas in part or "on the cheap," and the practicality of doing this is an important consideration in the screening process.

- An idea can be revised and screened again if doing so will improve its projected viability.

3-6. Assess the feasibility of a startup idea.

- A feasibility analysis should be conducted to identify potentially fatal flaws prior to making the decision to invest the substantial time, energy, and other resources required to put together a full-scale business plan.

- A market consists of all buyers of a product or service; an industry is made up of all sellers who compete for the same market.

- A feasibility analysis should assess the potential of a market on two levels—the broad macro-market and the micro-market—because the long-run potential of a market niche is determined largely by the outlook for the overall market.

- The industry should be assessed for its overall attractiveness (potential for profits) and the specific context of direct competition, which can greatly impact a startup's prospects for success.

- Entrepreneurs are likely to be successful in a startup situation to the degree that the planned venture fits with their mission, aspirations, and risk tolerance.

- Successful entrepreneurs understand and are able to manage the factors that are critical to the operation of the enterprise, and they are able to connect to suppliers, customers, investors, and others whose involvement is crucial to the future performance of the planned venture.

capabilities p. 73

competitive advantage p. 73

competitive environment p. 69

core competencies p. 73

cost-based strategy p. 75

differentiation-based strategy p. 76

entrepreneurial alertness p. 61

fatal flaw p. 81

feasibility analysis p. 81

focus strategy p. 76

general environment p. 69

industry environment p. 69

intangible resources p. 73

new benefit ideas p. 63

new market ideas p. 62

new technology ideas p. 62

opportunity recognition p. 61

pivot p. 63

resources p. 73

serendipity p. 65

startups p. 62

strategy p. 75

SWOT analysis p. 74

tangible resources p. 73

Discussion Questions

1. What are the three basic types of startup ideas? What are the most common sources of inspiration for startup ideas?

2. List and describe the 10 approaches outlined in this chapter that can be used to generate creative new business ideas. What are the most important features of each of these?

3. List the six most important trends of the general environment. What are some ways in which each trend might affect a small business?

4. What are the primary factors that shape competition in an industry, according to Porter's model? In your opinion, which of these factors will have the greatest impact on industry prices and profits?

5. How are tangible and intangible resources related to a venture's capabilities? How are capabilities linked to core competencies? What is the connection between core competencies and competitive advantage?

6. What is a SWOT analysis? How can a SWOT analysis help the entrepreneur match opportunities in the external environment with organizational capabilities?

7. What are the two basic strategy options for creating a competitive advantage?

8. What is meant by the term *focus strategy*? What are the advantages and disadvantages of a focus strategy? What must an entrepreneur know and do to maintain the potential of a focus strategy?

9. Under what circumstances is a new business idea screening process useful? Why? What are the major factors that should be considered when screening new business ideas?

10. Name and describe the major features of feasibility analysis. Why is feasibility analysis important?

You Make the Call

Situation 1

Jonathan Lugar, 17, had just finished helping his mom with a garage sale when it occurred to him that he might create a business to do the same for others and make a little money for college. The idea was to offer a service that would take the headache out of running a garage sale. Lugar would handle all advertising and sale setup, and his experience with other garage sales in the area would allow him to coach sellers on pricing so that items would actually be purchased. He figured he could charge $200 per job for sales that bring in $400 or less, but he and the seller would split sales above $400 on a 50-50 basis. Lugar believes the greatest value added from his services would be from his pricing insights, since most people rarely have a

garage sale and thus have little idea about how much to ask for items. Careful pricing would make his customers happy, since they could maximize their sales and minimize the risk that they would be left with the very items they were trying to get rid of. In fact, Lugar planned to keep track of how much things sold for to fine-tune his pricing advice. He estimates that his startup costs would be minimal and would come mostly from the use of his truck and some fuel.

Question 1 How would you classify Lugar's startup idea? Is it a new market idea, a new technology idea, or a new benefit idea?

Question 2 What was the source of Lugar's startup idea?

Question 3 Would you recommend that he give this startup concept a try? Explain your reasoning.

Situation 2

Nick Anglada is *really* into motorcycles. But his attention is not invested in just any motorized transport that happens to run on two wheels—he likes bikes that are fast, fun, and true works of art. And that is the focus of his startup, Nick Anglada Originals, a company name so good that it immediately gives away the essence of the business. Since the launch of his Oakland, Florida–based company in February 2009, Anglada has ridden his new venture to $2 million in sales by selling bikes (at $25,000 to $100,000 each) that are "tricked out" to the specific tastes of celebrities like Blink-182's Travis Barker. His "rolling art" has graced the covers of dozens of motorcycle magazines.

Uniqueness is key to the company's strategy, but it goes further than that. Anglada elaborates on the firm's emphasis:

> *Customization is a work of art, but ultimately it must be in harmony with the customer's revelation. I like Picasso. Picasso is viewed as a great artist. But not everyone wants a Picasso hanging on [his or her] wall. When you tell people you build bikes, they instantly envision some big, sweaty mean guy covered in tattoos and coveralls. I despise that vision. I am first and foremost an artist; my canvas just happens to be a large, fast machine.*

So Anglada uses stunning paint work, creative pinstriping, and lots and lots of chrome to create breathtaking, one-of-a-kind motorcycles that are guaranteed to turn heads—but designed in each case to the precise tastes of the individual who orders them. "Balancing high performance, functionality, and ground breaking aesthetics, a Nick Anglada Original is the epitome of modern motorcycle design," declares the company's website. There is little question that the product allows purchasers to "transcend the average and become something more," and that is exactly what Anglada has in mind.

Question 1 Based on the frameworks introduced in this chapter, what kind of strategy is Anglada following in his new venture?

Question 2 Identify the strengths upon which this business is built. Do you see any weaknesses that may be of concern to the company?

Question 3 Are there any particular threats that will put Nick Anglada Originals at risk as time goes on? Can you see any opportunities that may allow the company to expand in the future?

Question 4 What resources and capabilities form the foundation for the business? Do you think these will be sufficient to create a *sustainable* competitive advantage for the company? Why or why not?

Sources: Based on "Nick Anglada Originals," http://www.nickangladaoriginals.com, accessed August 14, 2012; "Nick Anglada Originals Appears on Café Racer," http://www.bikerhotline.com/pr/2011/11_nick_anglada_originals_pr, accessed August 14, 2012; and Susan Carpenter, "Switching Gears," *Entrepreneur*, Vol. 38, No. 3 (March 2010), p. 74.

Situation 3

Overcoming jet lag on international trips is crucial to making good decisions when working with overseas counterparts, especially when difficult negotiations are involved. If an executive wants to be refreshed and on top of his or her game, Phillip Sanderson has a solution. Perfect Illuminations, his five-year-old company, has been offering sleep-recovery services through business-class hotels in prime cities around the world. So far, he has worked out deals with eight partner hotels in four cities: New York, Tokyo, London, and Paris. His system provides booths in which guests can bask in 30 minutes of simulated sunshine generated from electronic light boxes. Science has shown that this form of light therapy can help to restore the body's natural sleep rhythms well ahead of the recovery time that it normally takes to reset one's internal clock. The price of the service varies, depending on the city and the specific deal worked out with each partner hotel, but the client response so far has been encouraging. Now Sanderson is trying to identify other cities where he can help weary travelers reset their internal clocks.

Question 1 Will the market for Sanderson's product continue to grow in the years ahead?

Question 2 Given the company's success so far, what sources of competition should he expect?

Question 3 What steps would you recommend that Sanderson take to protect his company from the onslaught of competition that is likely to come?

Experiential Exercises

1. The U.S. Census Bureau provides massive amounts of data that can be used to shape business ideas so that they are compelling and more likely to succeed. Check out its "snapshot" profiles through the QuickFacts feature to get a feel for how useful these data can be (go to http://quickfacts.census.gov/qfd/index.html to learn more).

   On the QuickFacts website, choose a specific city from the drop-down menu, review the data provided, and propose three businesses that would be supported by the demographics of your selected city. Prepare a brief report on your findings, outlining the proposed businesses and rank-ordering them according to your assessment of their potential based on the data. Be prepared to justify each proposed business and your ordering of them.

2. Select a product that is manufactured by a successful small business, and try to determine which features of the general and/or industry environments are the foundation for its creation and success.

3. Visit the website of a business publication, such as *Fortune Small Business, Inc.*, or *The Wall Street Journal*, and describe the type of target market strategy you believe the newspaper or magazine uses.

4. The next time you visit a local small retailer, ask the manager to describe the firm's customer service policies. Do you think these policies are consistent with what you know about the company's primary strategy? Be prepared to present a case defending your conclusions.

5. Working in small groups, write a brief but specific description of the best target market for a new product that is familiar to most of the class. Designate a member of each group to read the group's market profile to the class.

6. Go to the website of a small business, and identify the external factors (such as those in the general, industry, and/or competitive environments) as well as the internal factors around which the business has been created. Does the firm seem to be more sensitive to internal or external dynamics? Given your knowledge of the business, is that good or bad?

7. NYCeWheels sells electrically powered bicycles, like its high-performance line of eZee bikes. Take a look at the information found on the company's website (www.nycewheels.com). Using the terminology introduced in this chapter, identify the specific type of strategy NYCeWheels is using to expand its business.

Small Business & Entrepreneurship Resource Center

The Small Business & Entrepreneurship Resource Center offers complete small business management resources through a comprehensive database that covers all major areas of starting, operating, and maintaining a business from financing, management, marketing, accounting, taxes, and more. Go to www.cengagebrain.com and select the Longenecker text for more information on how to access this material.

1. The Company was founded by Ben Smith after more than 20 years in the beer production and distribution industry. Through his expertise, Smith plans to show a profit within the first year. He intends to develop a highly specialized microbrewery that produces seasonal beers such as stouts, pale ales, porters, and lagers with proprietary formulas. Smith is not only sourcing the required equipment for the business, but also a talented brewmaster who will bring years of experience and specialized recipes to The Company's microbrews. The business expects to distribute approximately 15,000 barrels of beer per year. Smith's dream is to become

a recognized regional (and then national) brewery that provides a variety of beers. Research shows that entrepreneurs claim prior work experience as the leading source of inspiration for startup ideas. Do you agree? Why do you think Smith is well positioned to be successful in this startup?

2. As the microbrewery industry grows, Smith feels that it is important to hire a public relations and marketing firm to position his products regionally and nationally. He will attend festivals and other events that focus on microbrew products. If The Company can produce outstanding beers, it can penetrate the microbrew market with recognition generated from these events. Smith plans to work closely with regional and local microbrew distributors to generate interest in the brand. After reading this article, analyze the competitive nature of this industry using a SWOT analysis. What are the competitive threats and opportunities that Smith's company faces?

Source: BizPlanDB.com. "Microbrewery: Smith Microbrewery, Inc." *Business Plans Handbook.* Ed. Lynn M. Pearce. Vol. 17.

Case 3

The Kollection: From Music Hobby to Startup and Beyond (P. 648)

This case describes the experiences of an entrepreneur who launched a music blog and sharing website to fill a gap in the marketplace and had to work through challenges related to strategic positioning, changes in the competitive landscape, legal/regulatory hang-ups, opportunities for diversification, and generating enough revenue to become profitable.

Alternative Cases For Chapter 3

Case 1, Dashlocker, p. 645
Case 8, Couchsurfing International, p. 657
Case 13, Network Collie, p. 669

Endnotes

1. To read more about an interesting framework that integrates three forms of the search process (deliberate search, industry insight–guided search, and alertness to opportunities), see Robert A. Baron, "Opportunity Recognition as Pattern Recognition: How Entrepreneurs 'Connect the Dots' to Identify New Business Opportunities," *Academy of Management Perspectives,* Vol. 20, No. 1 (February 2006), pp. 104–119.

2. Israel M. Kirzner, *Competition and Entrepreneurship* (Chicago: University of Chicago Press, 1973), p. 74.

3. For an in-depth discussion of the alertness concept and the essence of the mindset of the entrepreneur, see Jeffery S. McMullen and Dean A. Shepherd, "Entrepreneurial Action and the Role of Uncertainty in the Theory of the Entrepreneur," *Academy of Management Review,* Vol. 31, No. 1 (2006), pp. 132–152.

4. The process of opportunity recognition is not entirely driven by thoughts; in fact, feelings and emotions can also play a very important role. For an interesting analysis of the interplay of affect and cognitive processes, see Robert A. Baron, "The Role of Affect in the Entrepreneurial Process," *Academy of Management Review,* Vol. 33, No. 2 (2008), pp. 328–340.

5. Quoted in April Y. Pennington, "Copy That: In Business, Imitation Is More Than a Form of Flattery," *Entrepreneur,* Vol. 34, No. 3 (March 2006), p. 22.

6. Quoted in Lizette Chapman, "'Pivoting' Pays Off for Tech Entrepreneurs," *The Wall Street Journal,* April 26, 2012, http://online.wsj.com/article/SB10001424052702303592404577364171598999252.html, accessed July 30, 2012.

7. Sarah E. Needleman, "A Young Entrepreneur's Sweet Idea," *The Wall Street Journal,* June 14, 2012, http://online.wsj.com/article/SB10001424052702303410404577464700830700754.html, accessed July 30, 2012; and "Unreal Candy," http://getunreal.com/unreal-candy/unreal-54, accessed July 30, 2012.

8. Personal experience can influence the *kind* of startup ideas that entrepreneurs develop, but recent evidence indicates that work experience in general as well as experience with new ventures in particular can improve the *quality* of concepts generated. For more on this, see Maw-Der Foo, "Member Experience, Use of External Assistance and Evaluation of Business Ideas," *Journal of Small Business Management,* Vol. 48, No. 1 (January 2010), pp. 32–43.

9. "SeekingSitters' Business Model," *Inc.,* August 25, 2010, www.inc.com/inc5000/profile/seekingsitters, accessed July 31, 2012; Kevin Manahan, "A Service Born of Necessity," *Entrepreneur,* April 9, 2009, www.entrepreneur.com/article/201166, accessed July 31, 2012; and "SeekingSitters: Easy, Safe Babysitting Solutions," www.seekingsitters.com, accessed July 31, 2012.

10. Colleen Taylor, "Zuckerberg: Facebook Started out as a 'Hobby' and a 'Project,' Not a Company," TechCrunch (October 20, 2012), http://techcrunch.com/2012/10/20/zuckerberg-facebook-started-out-as-a-hobby-and-a-project-not-a-company, accessed March 16, 2013.

11. Erin Weinger, "Selling Short," *Entrepreneur,* Vol. 38, No. 4 (April 2010), p. 19.

12. *Ibid.*

13. To learn more about creativity and the process of business idea generation, see Dimo Dimov, "Idea Generation from a Creativity Perspective," in Andrew Zacharakis and Stephen Spinelli, Jr. (eds.), *Entrepreneurship: The Engine of Growth* (Westport, CT: Praeger Perspectives, 2007), pp. 19–41.

14. "Industry Leader: Travel: Sixthman," *Inc.,* Vol. 33, No. 7 (September 2011), p. 200.

15. Chuck Salter, "This Is How We Do It," *Fast Company,* No. 165 (May 2012), pp. 88–89.

16. Quoted in Jason Ankeny, "The Good Sir Richard," *Entrepreneur,* Vol. 40, No. 6 (June 2012), pp. 30–38.

17. For an interesting analysis of Apple's strategy with products such as the iPad, see Farhad Manjoo, "Apple Nation," *Fast Company,* No. 147 (July/August 2010), pp. 68–112.

18. Anne Tergesen, "When Guests Check In, Their iPhones Check Out," *The Wall Street Journal,* July 5, 2011, p. D1.

19. Joe Sharkey, "Reinventing the Suitcase by Adding the Wheel," *New York Times,* October 4, 2010, www.nytimes.com/2010/10/05/business/05road.html, accessed August 1, 2012.

20. Michelle Juergen, "Sleep Like a Champ," *Entrepreneur,* Vol. 40, No. 3 (March 2012), p. 74.

21. Sarah Kessler, "All Natural—From Her Ranch to Your Backyard," *Inc.,* Vol. 32, No. 4 (May 2010), p. 23; and www.ahavenbrand.com/about_us.html, accessed August 1, 2012.

22. Jodi Helmer, "Paperless Bliss," *Entrepreneur,* Vol. 40, No. 3 (March 2012), p. 76; Jennifer Wang, "One Man's Trash," *Entrepreneur,* Vol. 39, No. 4 (April 2011), pp. 50–53; and Kristin Ohlson, "Save Water, Save Money," *Entrepreneur,* Vol. 36, No. 10 (October 2008), p. 20.

23. As a parallel to the outside-in and inside-out options, Dimo Dimov ["From Opportunity Insight to Opportunity Intention: The Importance of Person-Situation Learning Match," *Entrepreneurship Theory and Practice,* Vol. 31, No. 4 (July 2007), p. 566] mentions two very different opportunity insight–inducing situations. In *demand-driven* situations, the entrepreneur is aware of customer needs but does not know of any products that could meet those needs. *Supply-driven* situations are just the opposite. Here, the entrepreneur is aware of an emerging product, but doesn't know of customer needs that could be satisfied by it.

24. "Fast Facts: Obesity Trends," The George Washington University School of Public Health and Health Services, www.stopobesityalliance.org/wp-content/themes/stopobesityalliance/pdfs/FastFacts_Obesity-Trends5-2010.pdf, accessed August 21, 2012.

25. Bruce R. Barringer, *Preparing Effective Business Plans: An Entrepreneurial Approach* (Upper Saddle River, NJ: Pearson Prentice Hall, 2009), p. 37.

26. Michael Porter, *Competitive Advantage* (New York: Free Press, 1985), pp. 7–29.

27. William A. Sahlman, *How to Write a Great Business Plan* (Boston: Harvard Business School Press, 2008).

28. Clay Shirky, "What Makes Me a Lousy Entrepreneur," http://gawker.com/262145/what-makes-me-a-lousy-entrepreneur, accessed August 2, 2012.

29. "Starbucks Company Profile," http://assets.starbucks.com/assets/5739ef83a25444af98bd14ba1034eb50.pdf, accessed August 6, 2012.

30. Stephan Faris, "Grounds Zero," *Bloomberg Businessweek,* February 9, 2012, www.businessweek.com/magazine/grounds-zero-a-starbucksfree-italy-02092012.html, accessed August 6, 2012.

31. www.getradiotag.com, accessed August 6, 2012; and Sara Wilson, "Maximizing Air Time," *Entrepreneur,* Vol. 36, No. 11 (November 2008), p. 71.

32. Philip Kotler, "Focusing and Niching: Kotler on Marketing," http://dev.hypenotic.com/wordpress/articles/focusing-and-niching-kotler-on-marketing, accessed August 6, 2012.

33. "Personalized Bottle Water: Our Story," www.personalizedbottlewater
.com/our-story.aspx, accessed August 6, 2012.

34. Gwen Moran, "Six Weeks to a Better Bottom Line," *Entrepreneur*, Vol. 38,
No. 1 (January 2010), p. 49.

35. Marc J. Dollinger, *Entrepreneurship: Strategies and Resources* (Lombard,
IL: Marsh Publications, 2008), p. 144.

36. Michael Porter, *op.cit.*, p. 5.

37. Bruce R. Barringer, *op.cit.*, p. 36.

38. Teri Evans, "Have a Business Idea? Test It on the Cheap," October 25, 2010,
http://smallbusiness.foxbusiness.com/entrepreneurs/2010/10/25
/business-idea-test-cheap, accessed August 14, 2012.

39. Quoted in Mark Henricks, "What Not to Do," *Entrepreneur*, Vol. 32, No. 2
(February 2004), pp. 84–90.

40. John W. Mullins, *The New Business Road Test* (London: Financial Times
Prentice Hall, 2010), pp. 3–4.

41. *Ibid.*, p. 10.

42. *Ibid.*, p. 16.

© CBS Photo Archive/Getty Images

Franchises and Buyouts

What comes to mind when you see the word *franchise*? For many, it's a fast-food restaurant. For some, it's the standardization of America—the same product or service wherever you go. For still others, it is a business model with franchisor rules that must be followed. For Dina Dwyer-Owens, however, it's a way of teaching "principles and systems of personal and business success so that all people we touch live happier and more successful lives."

Dwyer-Owens is chairwoman and CEO of The Dwyer Group, a holding company of seven service-based franchise organizations: Aire Serv, Glass Doctor, Mr. Appliance, Mr. Electric, Mr. Rooter, Rainbow International, and The Grounds Guys. Founded in 1981 as Rainbow International, The Dwyer Group's companies were providing services through more than 1,500 franchises in 10 countries by 2012.

Don Dwyer, Dwyer-Owens' father, fit the profile of an entrepreneur. In his youth, he had a newspaper route from which he

earned over $2 million in today's dollars by the time he finished college. Later, he bought a motivational materials franchise. His performance so impressed the franchisor that he made Dwyer part of his management team. Dwyer moved on to head Rainbow International, a carpet dyeing and cleaning company, which became the foundation for the multiple franchise chains that now make up The Dwyer Group.

When Don Dwyer died unexpectedly at age 60 in 1994, the board of directors appointed a nonfamily member to be chief executive officer. A few years later, the board determined that Dwyer-Owens was prepared to assume top leadership, initially

> **In the SPOTLIGHT**
> **The Dwyer Group®: Seven Companies, One Code of Values**
> www.dwyergroup.com

After studying this chapter, you should be able to…

4-1. Define *franchise*, and become familiar with franchise terminology.

4-2. Understand the pros and cons of franchising and the structure of the industry.

4-3. Describe the process for evaluating a franchise opportunity.

4-4. List four reasons for buying an existing business, and describe the process of evaluating an existing business.

appointing her as acting president and CEO. She immediately faced opposition from shareholders and franchisees. One of the key opponents to her appointment told her that she knew nothing about the plumbing service they provided. She confessed to being ignorant, but responded that she knew it as a customer and asked for six months to prove herself. The fact that she continues to be CEO today is testimony to how she performed.

That was not the last time Dwyer-Owens took a risk. In January of 2012, she appeared on the television show *Undercover Boss*. She found it difficult to carry out the tasks of her franchisees and their employees, and her challenges were recorded for all to see. Dwyer-Owens reported afterward that while this experience gave her a deeper appreciation for the work being done, it more importantly gave her reassurance about the model The Dwyer Group presents to franchisees. The model is articulated through the firm's Code of Values (recall the discussion of codes of ethics in Chapter 2), which covers respect, integrity, customer focus, and "having fun in the process!" (See **www.dwyergroup.com/code-of-values.asp** for the entire code.)

When employees of The Dwyer Group or their franchisees hold meetings, their practice is to recite the values before the meeting begins. It is a commitment held by everyone in the organizational network. Dwyer-Owens was surprised by and appreciative of the feedback that her appearance on *Undercover Boss* triggered. Viewers told her that it renewed their hope in humanity, that it showed corporate America was capable of doing good in the world.

Sources: Based on www.dwyergroup.com, accessed September 1, 2012; www.cbs.com/shows/undercover_boss/, accessed September 1, 2012; and personal communication with Dina Dwyer-Owens, April 9, 2012.

"I am convinced that franchise ownership is the best way for the first-time entrepreneur to get started in business."[1] This quote was taken from *Target Success*, written by Don Dwyer. Recall our definition of an entrepreneur from Chapter 1: "A person who is relentlessly focused on an opportunity, in either a new or existing business, to create value while assuming both the risk and the reward for his or her effort." So, buying a business, whether it is independent or part of a chain of franchises, also makes you an entrepreneur. In this chapter, we show you strategies for ownership involving franchises and existing businesses.

4-1 WHAT IS A FRANCHISE?

LO
4-1

Define *franchise*, and become familiar with franchise terminology.

The franchise model has been around for a long time in various forms. Some say the model for modern franchising was the early Roman Catholic Church, when the pope authorized parish priests to collect tithes and remit a portion to the Vatican while retaining the remainder for parish maintenance.[2] Others trace the beginning of franchising to the Middle Ages, when a feudal lord would grant certain rights to laymen in return for a fee and their obedience in carrying out certain community activities, such as operating ferries.[3]

The Singer Sewing Machine company is credited with being the first franchisor in the United States.[4] In 1851, Albert Singer entered agreements with local retailers to give them exclusive rights to sell Singer sewing machines. His contract became the basis for those used by franchisors to this day. Some historians, however, contend that Benjamin Franklin was actually the first U.S. franchisor.[5] They cite the arrangement he made with a printer in South Carolina to reproduce *Poor Richard's Almanac* columns. (An interesting side note is that the widow of the South Carolina printer eventually took over her late husband's business, making her the first female franchisee in North America.)

4-1a Franchising Terminology

If you are considering negotiating to purchase a franchise, you will need to understand the language that is used. Two United States government agencies, the Small

Business Administration (www.sba.gov) and the Federal Trade Commission (www .ftc.gov), along with the International Franchise Association (www.franchise.org) are good sources of definitions of franchising terms.

The SBA defines a **franchise** as a business model that involves one business owner licensing trademarks and methods to an independent entrepreneur.[6] It is a legal and commercial relationship between a **franchisor** (the owner of a trademark, service mark, trade name, or advertising symbol) and a **franchisee** (an individual or group wishing to use that identification in a business). Generally, a franchisee sells goods or services supplied by the franchisor or that meet the franchisor's quality standards. The franchise itself amounts to the right to do business under the franchisor's name and to obtain the use of trademarks, support, and control.

Franchising is based on mutual trust between the franchisor and franchisee. The franchisor provides business expertise (marketing plans, management guidance, financing assistance, site location, training, etc.) that otherwise would not be available to the franchisee. The franchisee brings the entrepreneurial spirit and drive necessary to make the franchise a success.

There are two primary forms of franchising: product and trade name franchising and business format franchising.[7] In **product and trade name franchising**, a franchisor owns the right to a name or trademark and sells that right to a franchisee. Ford automobile dealers, Pepsi-Cola soft drink bottlers, and Chevron convenience stores and service stations are examples of companies engaged in this type of franchising. With **business format franchising**, the franchisor often provides a full range of services, including site selection, training, product supply, marketing plans, and even assistance in obtaining financing. Quick-service restaurants (such as Carl's Jr.), hotels and motels (such as Choice Hotels), and business services (such as Jani-King) typically engage in this type of franchising. Although the common stereotype of business format franchising is represented by the fast-food restaurant, the truth is that companies in over 75 industries make use of this structure.

In order to become a franchisee, you will need to enter into a legal contract with the franchisor spelling out your relationship and obligations to each other. This is known as a **franchise contract**. Before you sign this agreement, the franchisor must provide you with a Franchise Disclosure Document, which will be described later in this chapter. Franchisors do not grow their organizations by waiting for franchisees to come to their door. Rather, they establish organizational structures and designate employees or partners to expand the number of franchised outlets and to monitor their performance. The most frequent means for carrying out these growth strategies are through use of the following:

- A **master licensee**, which is a firm or individual having a continuing contractual relationship with a franchisor to sell its franchises. This independent company or businessperson is a type of middleman or sales agent responsible for finding new franchisees within a specified territory. Master licensees may provide support services such as training and warehousing, which are more traditionally provided by the franchisor. U.S.-based franchisors often use master licensing arrangements to expand into other countries, selecting successful business companies and leaders to open units of their own and sub-franchising to others. The Living the Dream feature discusses an Australian franchisor that found an American master licensee.

- **Multiple-unit ownership**, in which a single franchisee owns more than one unit of the franchised business.

- **Area developers**, who are individuals or firms that obtain the legal right to open several outlets in a given area.

franchise
A business model involving a business owner who licenses trademarks and methods to an independent entrepreneur.

franchisor
The party in a franchise contract that specifies the methods to be followed and the terms to be met by the other party.

franchisee
An entrepreneur whose power is limited by a contractual relationship with a franchising organization.

product and trade name franchising
A franchise agreement granting the right to use a widely recognized product or name.

business format franchising
A franchise arrangement whereby the franchisee obtains an entire marketing and management system geared to entrepreneurs.

franchise contract
The legal agreement between franchisor and franchisee.

master licensee
An independent firm or individual acting as a middleman or sales agent with the responsibility of finding new franchisees within a specified territory.

multiple-unit ownership
Ownership by a single franchisee of more than one franchise from the same company.

area developers
Individuals or firms that obtain the legal right to open several franchised outlets in a given area.

Living the Dream

Greg Carafello—A Franchise Turnaround

Greg Carafello had already been an entrepreneur before joining Cartridge World as a master licensee. For eleven years, Carafello successfully operated a digital printing business in New York. His office was on the 18th floor of the south tower of the World Trade Center (WTC). When a plane hit the building on September 11, 2001, Carafello was able to escape, but his company never rebounded from losing the clients they had in the WTC. It struggled for a few years, but eventually had to close.

Closing down did not mean giving up, however. Carafello became a master licensee for an Australian company called Cartridge World. Cartridge World is in the business of refilling and remanufacturing printing cartridges. Growing globally through franchising, the company has more than 2,000 stores in 60 countries. To expand in North America, Cartridge World sought master licensees, whom they view as partners and management representatives.

Carafello describes himself as being anti-franchise before signing up with Cartridge World. In running his own company, he found it difficult to maintain quality when trying to enter new markets. But that problem was solved when he joined Cartridge World, which required him to adopt its highly refined and well-developed system. He also liked its proven product. Plus, as master licensee for New York and northern New Jersey, he sees himself as a franchisor, helping others become owners of Cartridge World stores. This fits with the expectations of the home office, which wants its master licensees to care about helping others achieve success. And, with the firm's royalty system, Greg recognizes that if his franchisees make less money, so does he.

The executives of Cartridge World know that they must find ways of adding value for their franchisees each year. Once they've learned the operating details of the franchisor, franchisees can become dissatisfied if they feel they are paying for nothing more than the name and trademarks. An initiative of the company in 2012 was to launch a mobile franchise opportunity as a new direct delivery service for business customers. This adds to the portfolio of the master licensee. The mobile service has a lower franchise fee and enables franchisees to enter smaller markets. Additionally, Cartridge World is positioning itself as the environmentally friendly choice in the industry. As Carafello sees it, this keeps customers coming back for more. And it opened his eyes to other franchising opportunities, leading him to become an area developer for Liberty Tax Service. Now he is a true believer in the system.

Sources: Based on Cartridge World, www.cartridgeworld.com/home.aspx, accessed September 2, 2012; "The Fine Print," *Entrepreneur*, March 2012, p. 112; and Laurie Kulikowski, "5 Flourishing Franchisees Provide Insight on Expanding into Multiple Brands," www.nuwireinvestor.com/articles/5-flourishing-franchisees-provide-insight-on-expanding-into-multiple-brands-58788.aspx, accessed December 14, 2012.

- **Piggyback franchising**, which refers to the operation of a retail franchise within the physical facilities of another business. An example of piggyback franchising occurs when Subway operates a restaurant within a truck stop.
- **Multibrand franchising**, which involves operating several franchise organizations within a single corporate structure. The Dwyer Group is a pioneer in this form of franchising (see this chapter's Spotlight feature).
- **Co-branding**, which involves bringing two franchise brands together under one owner. Vas Maniatis, co-founder of Simply Eyebrows (an eyebrow-threading company), struggled with growing the business. His focus was on convenience and value, so he thought he would be a good partner for Walmart. Walmart executives liked the concept but wanted it to be bigger. Maniatis added facials, waxing, nails, and other spa services, and renamed the company Seva. By 2012, Seva franchisees operated their businesses in a dozen Walmart stores, with more locations on the way.[8]

4-1b The Impact of Franchising

Periodically, the International Franchise Association (IFA) sponsors studies of the impact of franchising on the American economy. The mission of the IFA is to protect, enhance, and promote franchising.[9] Founded in 1960, the IFA has more than 1,000 franchisors, 7,000 franchisees, and 350 suppliers as members.[10]

According to the IFA's *The Franchise Business Economic Outlook:2012*, franchised businesses actually provided more jobs than entire industries. Direct employment in 749,499 franchise establishments totaled 8,102,000 jobs. Revenues generated by these businesses amounted to $782 billion, accounting for 3 percent of the gross domestic product of the United States. These figures underestimate the full impact of franchising on the economy, however, because franchising stimulates activity and generates growth in many nonfranchised businesses, such as suppliers and lenders. Use of the franchise model of business formation and growth is expected to increase. Not only are U.S.-based companies expanding internationally, but franchisors headquartered in other countries are also seeking to enter the U.S. market by contracting with franchisees.

piggyback franchising
The operation of a retail franchise within the physical facilities of a host store.

multibrand franchising
The operation of several franchise organizations within a single corporate structure.

co-branding
Bringing two or more franchise brands together under one roof.

4-2 THE PROS AND CONS OF FRANCHISING

"Look before you leap" is an old adage that should be heeded by entrepreneurs who are considering franchising. Weighing the purchase of a franchise against alternative paths to starting a business is an important task, and it deserves careful consideration.

LO 4-2

Understand the pros and cons of franchising and the structure of the industry.

4-2a The Pros

Buying a franchise can be attractive for a variety of reasons. The greatest advantage is the probability of success. Franchisors offer a business model with a proven track record. A reputable franchisor has been through the trials and errors that an entrepreneur might face when starting a business independently. One explanation for the low failure rate of franchises is how selective many franchisors are when granting them;

4.1 Advantages of the Franchise Model

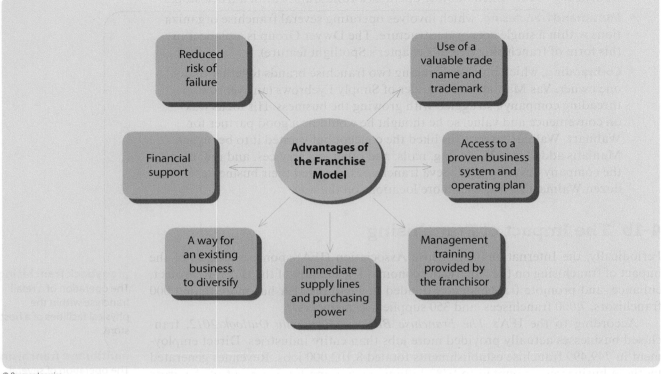

© Cengage Learning

even potential franchisees who qualify financially are sometimes rejected. Exhibit 4.1 lists some of the major advantages you can gain through franchising.

Franchised outlets also have a higher survival rate than independent ventures. Attractive franchises have names that are well known to prospective customers, such as Cinnabon, Curves, Mr. Rooter. When a new franchisee comes on board, franchisors provide detailed operations manuals, so the hard work of blazing a trail has already been done. And they support their franchisees by providing training, reducing purchasing costs, designing promotional campaigns, and assisting in obtaining capital. Naturally, different franchises vary in the depth of support they provide.

TRADE NAMES AND TRADEMARKS When you open your own business, it can take a long time and a lot of money to get your name established and customers in your door or to your website. When you become a franchisee, however, you expect the franchisor to have laid the groundwork. An entrepreneur who enters into a franchising agreement acquires the right to use the franchisor's trademark or brand name. Franchisors that are effective at creating market awareness and acceptance of their company and its brands serve to identify the local franchise with a widely recognized product or service. If customers have been satisfied with the products and services they have received from one unit in a chain, they are likely to do business with another store that carries that company's name.

Success for many businesses results from their intellectual property. Patents usually protect intellectual property, but a trademarked name can be just as valuable if it has become part of common public use. A trademark protects "words, names, symbols, sounds, or colors that distinguish goods and services from those manufactured or sold by others and to indicate the source of the goods. Trademarks, unlike patents, can be renewed forever as long as they are being used in

Consumers' Guide for Buying a Franchise
The Federal Trade Commission (FTC), the nation's consumer protection agency, has prepared *Buying a Franchise: A Consumer Guide* to explain how to shop for a franchise opportunity, the obligations of a franchise owner, and questions to ask before you invest. You can download it at http://business.ftc.gov/documents/inv05-buying-franchise-consumer-guide.

RESOURCES

commerce."[11] Think, for example, of McDonald's Golden Arches, "Oh Thank Heaven for 7-Eleven," and the graphic image of Colonel Sanders of KFC. The Dwyer Group has registered 10 different trademarks.[12] Trademarks and trade names make a business instantly identifiable to prospective customers and clients and can bring them right through the door. You will find more information about trademarks, patents, and copyrights and the value they add in Chapter 15.

A PROVEN BUSINESS SYSTEM AND OPERATING PLAN In addition to a proven line of business and readily identifiable products or services, franchisors offer well-developed and thoroughly tested methods of marketing and management. The manuals and procedures supplied to franchisees enable them to function more efficiently from the start. Reputable firms that grow through franchising begin with company-owned stores, in which they develop their fundamental business model, leading to a tried-and-true method of operating the business. They document the procedures that work, compile them in an operations manual, and provide the manual to franchisees. Guidelines in the manual explain the specific steps required to operate the enterprise profitably.

An operations manual may be the single most valuable tool provided to a franchisee. Following the path laid out in the manual helps the owner avoid mistakes that often occur with a startup business, such as employing unqualified personnel and investing in the wrong equipment or inventory. The franchisee should use the manual to channel his or her energy toward the most productive activities leading to survival and profitability. And the franchisee should expect to be held accountable for following the manual. One of the most critical aspects of franchising is that customers must be able to find the same products, services, and methods of conducting business from one outlet to another. If one franchise is allowed to operate at a substandard level, it could easily destroy customers' confidence in the entire chain.

TRAINING SUPPORT The training received from franchisors is invaluable to many small entrepreneurs because it compensates for weaknesses in their managerial skills. Training by the franchisor often begins with an initial period of a few days or weeks at a central training school and then continues at a franchise site. McDonald's is widely recognized for its off-site franchisee training at Hamburger University. More and more franchisors are providing their training programs online.

Training does not have to be restricted to teaching franchisees about the company and its products. The best franchisors are constantly on the lookout to help their partners stay competitive. In the three-day training they provide to new franchisees, Cathy Deano and Renee Maloney, founders of Painting with a Twist, spend half a day illustrating how to use social media to build the business and interact with customers. Deano and Maloney continue to add more platforms for their franchisees to use.[13]

SUPPLY AND PURCHASING POWER Joining a franchise network makes the entrepreneur part of a larger organization, which provides significant economies of scale. One critical benefit is efficiency in the purchasing function. A franchise network can buy in larger quantities than an individual business can, lowering per-unit costs for franchisees. Additionally, centralized purchasing activities reduce operating expenses for outlets.

Franchisees are often required to contribute to marketing expenses beyond the royalties they pay on sales. These expenses are pooled for the benefit of the entire network. The franchisor is then able to invest in more sophisticated marketing research, higher-quality advertising campaigns, and more extensive media outlets than franchisees could invest in independently. This ability leads to wider and deeper acceptance of brands and trade names and benefits each franchisee.

FINANCIAL SUPPORT Companies such as GNC and Wingstop have formed alliances with banks to create preferred lending programs for franchisees. The International Franchise Association (IFA) encourages franchisors to recruit minorities and veterans as franchisees by offering financial incentives. In order for a franchisor to be listed in the IFA's VetFran Directory, the company must agree to provide initial fee discounts, special financing terms, or other incentives. Over 400 companies are now listed in the directory.[14] Support for franchisees includes programs by AdviCoach, which offers a 15 percent discount off the standard franchise fee, and Mac Tools, which provides $10,000 of free tool inventory.[15]

Many prospective franchisees find that they can work with banks to obtain loans guaranteed by the U.S. Small Business Administration (SBA) in order to finance the franchise fee and startup costs. The SBA maintains a Franchise Registry (www.franchiseregistry.com), which speeds up loan processing for small business franchisees. The Registry attests that the SBA has already reviewed the franchise agreement to confirm that it "does not impose unacceptable control provisions on a franchisee or potential franchisee."[16] This determination not only provides an assurance that the franchisor will not become dictatorial in the business relationship, but also enables lenders to review and process loan applications more quickly for registered franchises.

Although many franchising systems have developed excellent support programs, you should understand that this is by no means universal. The buyer must also be aware of the disadvantages of franchising.

4-2b The Cons

The founders of the International Franchise Association were disturbed by the dishonest and unethical acts of some companies that were growing through franchising and damaging the reputation of the entire industry. These companies also sought to preempt government regulation of franchising. Firms joining the IFA are required to adhere to a code of ethics, the foundational values of which are "trust, truth, and honesty."[17] The code requires IFA members to practice mutual respect and open, frequent communication. The IFA also demands adherence to laws and offers a conflict resolution service for franchisors and franchisees. To this day, however, some franchisors engage in practices that trouble regulators, legislators, and the business community at large. These concerns have led to regulations by the Federal Trade Commission and the passage of laws in a few states, and include financial issues, franchisor competition, and management issues.

FINANCIAL ISSUES Major concerns have arisen regarding the true costs of becoming and remaining a franchisee. New franchisees of some franchise organizations have felt misled about their earnings opportunities. They report being told that they could expect high returns on their investments, only to discover that few, if any, franchisees achieved those results. Current and former franchisees of Quiznos, for example, sued the firm in Illinois, Pennsylvania, and Wisconsin for luring "franchisees into the system by misrepresenting contract terms and financial projections."[18] A settlement for $207 million was reached in 2010. The settlement included credits for purchasing supplies and equipment, and payment was authorized to plaintiffs who chose not to proceed with Quiznos' franchises.[19]

Other criticisms of franchisors that have come to the attention of government agencies include refusing to permit franchisees to sell their businesses in order to invest their money elsewhere and forcing franchisees to purchase products and services from subsidiaries or business associates, resulting in higher-than-market costs. Franchisees of Edible

Arrangements sued the franchisor, accusing the company of unfairly altering business agreements by imposing higher costs and extending hours of operation.[20] There have also been complaints of **churning**, which refers to actions by franchisors to void the contracts of franchisees in order to sell the franchise to someone else and collect an additional fee.

FRANCHISOR COMPETITION Franchisors have actually competed directly against their franchisees on occasion. This can occur when the franchisor opens a corporate-owned store near the franchisee's location or sells products via mail or over the Internet. A variation on this complaint is referred to as **encroachment**. A franchisor is said to encroach on a franchisee's territory when the franchisor sells another franchise location within the market area of an existing franchisee. Such actions can be virtual. For example, H&R Block was sued by a franchisee for selling Internet services within the franchisee's territory without offering any compensation.[21]

Another complaint stems from special clauses inserted into some franchise agreements. A number of franchisors impose noncompete clauses on their franchisees. From the franchisors' perspective, this makes perfect sense—after training and sharing secrets and strategies with a franchisee, they do not want the franchisee to sever the relationship and become a competitor. From the franchisees' perspective, this constitutes restraint of trade, especially if they find the franchisor to be nonresponsive to their needs or if they project that they can make more money on their own. It is only natural to think that the next business you start would evolve from your current experience. Yet the franchisor may keep you from applying those experiential skills by claiming that your new enterprise competes with the franchisor's business.

MANAGEMENT ISSUES The final set of negative issues focuses on the freedom of the franchisee to run his or her own business. As a franchisee, you are not a truly independent business owner. You have a contractual arrangement with the franchisor that stipulates various conditions, and that contract may specify the products you carry, the services you offer, your hours of operation, and other aspects of how you run your company. The contract was drafted by, and most likely favors, the franchisor. Many prospective franchisees fail to recognize that many franchisors are willing to negotiate some portions of the contract. In any case, you should always have an attorney review the contract before you sign it. Some of the most common restrictions imposed on franchisees fall into the following categories:

- Limiting sales territories
- Requiring site approval for the retail outlet
- Imposing requirements regarding outlet appearance
- Limiting goods and services offered for sale
- Limiting advertising and hours of operation

A frequently heard complaint from franchisees is that when their contract expires, they are required to accept new and often costly provisions. Franchisees suspect this is an effort to extract more revenues and/or concessions from them, to force them out in order to sell the franchise to someone else, or to take their business over as a company store. Of course, the franchisor may have another explanation. During the years the contract was in force, the franchisor may have discovered ways to improve the system that were incorporated into more recent franchise contracts. Additionally, franchisors may find that some long-time franchisees have not maintained their facilities or have failed to adapt to new marketing and operating procedures. From the franchisor's point of view, these franchisees need to improve their businesses so that they will not harm the entire network.

churning
Actions by franchisors to void the contracts of franchisees in order to sell the franchise to someone else and collect an additional fee.

encroachment
The franchisor's selling of another franchise location within the market area of an existing franchisee.

4-2c The Costs of Being a Franchisee

If you choose to become a franchisee, you pay for the privilege. You are buying a proven model, and the franchisor will charge you for the benefits being offered. Generally speaking, higher costs characterize the better-known and more successful franchises. Franchise costs have several components, all of which need to be recognized and considered.

1. *Initial franchise fee.* The total cost of a franchise begins with an initial franchise fee, which may range from several hundred to many thousands of dollars. The Dwyer Group's Rainbow International, estimates a total investment ranging from $115, 675 to $189, 100. They offer qualified veterans 25 percent discount off the initial fee.[22]

2. *Investment costs.* Significant costs may be involved in renting or building an outlet and stocking it with inventory and equipment. Certain insurance premiums, legal fees, and other startup expenses must also be paid, and it is often recommended that funds be available to cover personal expenses and emergencies for at least six months.

3. *Royalty payments.* A royalty is a fee charged to the franchisee by the franchisor. It is calculated as a percentage of the gross income that the franchisee receives from customers for selling the franchised products and services. Two Men and a Truck, a moving services company, charges a 6 percent royalty. The royalty fee for America's largest drive-in restaurant business, SONIC Corporation, ranges from 4 to 5 percent.[23]

4. *Advertising costs.* Many franchisors require that franchisees contribute to an advertising fund to promote the franchise. These fees are generally 1 to 2 percent of sales, sometimes even more. Franchisees pay these fees to support the franchisor in establishing the name and reputation of the business in the minds of targeted customers. Successful, well-managed franchise organizations will promote the company and its products and services more cost-efficiently than individual stores could do on their own.

If entrepreneurs could generate the same level of sales by setting up an independent business, they would save the franchise fee and some of the other costs just mentioned. However, if the franchisor provides the benefits previously described, the money that franchisees pay to start and maintain their relationship with the franchisor may well prove to be a very good investment.

4-3 EVALUATING FRANCHISE OPPORTUNITIES

After making a decision to pursue a franchising opportunity, the prospective franchisee must identify a franchising company and investigate it completely. We will use an example in this discussion of the evaluation process—Glass Doctor, a company offering residential, commercial, and auto glass services.

LO
4-3

Describe the process for evaluating a franchise opportunity.

4-3a Selecting a Franchise

With the growth of franchising over the years, the task of selecting an appropriate franchise has become easier. Personal observation frequently sparks interest, or awareness may begin with exposure to an advertisement in a newspaper or magazine or on the Internet. The headlines of these advertisements usually highlight the financial and personal rewards sought by the entrepreneur. *Inc., Entrepreneur,* and *The Wall Street Journal* are only three examples of the many publications that not only print stories about franchising, but also include franchisors' advertisements.

4-3b Investigating the Potential Franchise

The nature of the commitment required in franchising justifies careful investigation of the situation. The investment is substantial, and the business relationship generally continues over many years.

The evaluation process is a two-way effort. The franchisor wishes to investigate the franchisee, and the franchisee obviously wishes to evaluate the franchisor and the type of opportunity being offered. This requires time. You should be skeptical of a franchisor that pressures you to sign a contract without time for proper investigation. Some questions to ask in assessing different franchise opportunities follow:

- Is the franchisor dedicated to a franchise system as its primary means of product and service distribution? That is, does the company primarily distribute its goods and services through corporate-owned stores? If so, will the franchisor give as much attention to franchisees as to its own outlets?

- Does the franchisor produce and market quality goods and services for which there is an established consumer demand?

- Does the franchisor enjoy a favorable reputation and broad acceptance in the industry?

- Will the franchisor offer an established, well-designed marketing plan and provide substantial and complete training to franchisees?

- Does the franchisor have good relationships with its franchisees? Be sure to speak with current and past franchisees. What is/was their working relationship with the franchisor? Would they do it all over again?

- Do franchisees have a strong franchisee organization that has negotiating leverage with the franchisor?

- Does the franchisor have a history of attractive earnings by its franchisees?

There are many sources of information about franchisors to help you in your evaluation. Since many states require registration of franchises, a prospective franchisee should not overlook state offices as a source of assistance. Also, a comprehensive listing of franchisors can be found on the website of the International Franchise Association (www.franchise.org). Exhibit 4.2 displays the listing for Glass Doctor. In assessing published information about franchises, Mark Liston, president of Glass Doctor, cautions:

> As you choose a franchisor remember—this is a marriage … usually for at least 10 years. This is why it is extremely important to understand the culture of the franchisor to determine if this truly will be a partnership with the franchisor and the franchisee interdependent with each other.[24]

The better-known, more successful franchisors are likely to offer a greater chance of long-term survival and prosperity, but they are also in a position to charge premium prices for becoming part of their network. *Entrepreneur* magazine's website contains its ranking of the top-10 franchises in 2012 (see Exhibit 4.3). The rankings are based on a number of factors, with financial strength and stability, growth rate, and system size being the most important.

Glass Doctor

Business Established:	1962
Franchising Since:	1977
Franchised Units:	191
Company Owned Units:	0
Start-up Cost	$20,000 to $125,000
Total Investment:	$107,000 to $260,000

Offering Financial Assistance

In-house financing is available for the initial franchise fee.

Special Incentives

VetFran Participant
International Opportunity Franchise Resale Opportunity
Home Based Franchise

VetFran Incentive

25% of the minimum initial franchise fee for qualified honorably discharged veterans.

Company Details

Description

Established in 1962, Glass Doctor is one of the nation's largest providers of glass services for home, auto and business. Services include repair and replacement of windshields, windows, entry door glass, patio doors, shower enclosures, mirrors, tabletops and storefronts. The company's service vehicles carry complete inventory and supplies. Glass Doctor is part of The Dwyer Group.

Training

Upon becoming a Glass Doctor franchisee, you will attend a proprietary training course where our knowledgeable corporate team assists you in putting financial, marketing, management and customer service strategies to work for you. Two weeks of initial training are required, including seminars at the world headquarters, classroom sessions at the Glass Doctor University training center, hands-on workshops at the Glass Doctor University shop (the only one of its kind in the industry), and job shadowing.

Qualifications

Strong Work Ethic, Financially Qualified, High Achievement Drive, Honesty & Integrity, Strong Image/Self-Esteem, Team Player, Willingness To Learn & Apply Proven Successful Business Systems.

Source: Copied with permission, www.franchise.org/Glass_Doctor_franchise.aspx.

In recent years, franchise consultants have appeared in the marketplace to assist individuals seeking franchise opportunities. Some consulting firms, such as Francorp, conduct seminars on choosing the right franchise. Of course, care should be used in selecting a reputable consultant, and an experienced franchise attorney should evaluate all legal documents.

THE FRANCHISOR AS A SOURCE OF INFORMATION Obviously, the franchisor being evaluated is a primary source of information. However, information provided by a franchisor must be viewed in light of its purpose—to promote the franchise. Mark Liston adds:

[You] must remember that you won't get glowing remarks from everyone. That is good. Although successful franchise organizations have an interdependency, there will be times when they simply disagree. The franchisor has to make decisions that are good for the entire network. Those decisions may not make some individual franchisees happy.[25]

One way to obtain information about franchisors is to review their websites. Most franchisor websites will be directed toward customers, presenting information about products, services, store locations, and so on. The websites should also direct you to information for prospective franchisees. If you enter your contact information, you can expect to receive brochures and marketing materials that contain such information as startup costs and franchisees' testimonials. Your search may also lead you to websites or blogs of disgruntled franchisees, customers, and others.

If you express further interest in a franchise by completing the application form and the franchisor has tentatively qualified you as a potential franchisee, a meeting is usually arranged to discuss the disclosure document. A **Franchise Disclosure Document (FDD)** is a detailed statement of such information as the franchisor's finances, experience, size, and involvement in litigation. The document must inform potential franchisees of any restrictions, costs, and provisions for renewal or cancellation of the franchise. Important considerations related to this document are examined more fully later in this chapter.

EXHIBIT 4.3 Entrepreneur's Top 10 Franchises for 2012

Name/Rank	Startup Costs (2009)
1. Hampton Hotels	$3.7M–13.52M
2. Subway	$85.2K–260.35K
3. 7-Eleven Inc.	$30.8K–1.64M
4. Servpro	$133.05K–181.45K
5. Days Inn	$202.17K–6.76M
6. McDonald's	$1M–2.16M
7. Denny's Inc.	$1.18M–2.4M
8. H&R Block	$35.51K–136.2K
9. Pizza Hut Inc.	$295K–2.15M
10. Dunkin' Donuts	$368.9K–1.74M

Source: "Top Franchises for 2012," www.entrepreneur.com/franchise500/index.html, accessed September 3, 2012.

EXISTING AND PREVIOUS FRANCHISES AS SOURCES OF INFORMATION
There may be no better source of franchise facts than existing and former franchisees. Sometimes, however, the distant location of other franchisees precludes a visit to their place of business. In that case, a telephone call or e-mail can elicit the owner's viewpoint.

4-3c Becoming a Franchisor

After a few years of running your own business, you may conclude that you want to expand and that franchising is a reasonable option for you. It is not unusual for the owners of successful businesses to be approached by individuals who ask to become franchisees. Before entering into an agreement with a potential franchisee, consider the questions discussed in the following subsections.

A REPRODUCIBLE MODEL Is your business replicable? In other words, do you have a model of doing business that someone else could adopt and use successfully in another location? A franchisee purchases an operating system as well as a product or service and a brand name. Is your system efficient, and can it be clearly explained so that others can apply it?

Franchise Disclosure Document (FDD)
A detailed statement that provides the accepted format for satisfying the franchise disclosure requirements of the FTC.

FINANCIAL CONSIDERATIONS How will you finance the growth of the company? Many entrepreneurs think that franchising is a novel mechanism for financing their growing enterprises. They come up with a concept, collect franchise fees, and use those revenues to expand their operations. But franchising is not cost-free for the franchisor. There are legal documents to prepare, an operations manual to write, personnel to hire, and other tasks to be completed. Who will recruit and select franchisees? Who will train them and their managers? Who will monitor their performance to ensure that they conform to contract requirements? Responsible franchisors often find that establishing a franchise costs more than the fee covers and that they only become profitable as a result of the royalties they eventually collect from successful franchisees.

REQUIRED ASSISTANCE What expert assistance will you need to become a franchisor? Successful entrepreneurs learn quickly that they must choose the right experts, individuals who are qualified to provide the necessary help. If you decide to franchise your business, you should have an attorney with knowledge of the franchise method. There are many consultants who specialize in franchising and can assist with drafting operations manuals, preparing disclosure documents, assisting with franchisee selection, and other aspects of the process. A good starting place for any prospective franchisor is becoming a member of the International Franchise Association.

OPERATIONS MANUAL Earlier in this chapter, we looked at the operations manual from the franchisee's point of view. For the franchisor, this is an essential element in the value the business model offers to franchisees. What will go into your operations manual? Many companies that have grown successfully through franchising brought in consultants who specialize in making the business operating model more efficient and easier to replicate prior to writing the manual. You should be able to present an operations manual to your franchisees that spells out what steps to take in daily activities to ensure customer satisfaction while controlling expenses. The operations manual should offer detailed instructions that help franchisees avoid pitfalls and increase sales. It needs to be written from the perspective of the franchisee, who will not know the business as well as the franchisor. It is usually wise to hire a professional technical writer to put the manual together so that it communicates the process effectively. Many new franchisors have found that experts who assist in writing operations manuals also help the businesses improve the efficiencies of their operations, making startup and management easier and lowering the cost for franchisees.

GOVERNMENT REGULATIONS Are you willing to satisfy the government's disclosure requirements? The Federal Trade Commission issued an amended **Franchise Rule** in May 2008. This rule prescribes that the franchisor must disclose certain information to prospective franchisees. Some business owners may decide that they would rather not disclose information that they consider confidential, such as prior bankruptcies, the business experience of the principals, or litigation in which the firm is involved. In such cases, franchising may not be the appropriate method to use for growth.

Franchise Rule
A rule that prescribes that the franchisor must disclose certain information to prospective franchisees.

LONG-TERM VALUE Can you add value for your franchisees year after year? There are many good and successful business models that may provide the right steps for you to follow in order to avoid pitfalls in the startup process. But will your business offer value to prospective franchisees year in and year out?

A franchise agreement is in effect for a long time, typically between 10 and 15 years. What benefits will the franchisees derive from the franchisor each year? Will new products or services be introduced? Will improved marketing strategies be implemented? Will additional, updated training be offered to franchisees and their managers? Why will franchisees want to continue to make royalty payments once they have been up and running and have learned the operating procedures? If the business model does not add value for franchisees each year, franchising is not the right method for growing your company.

4-3d Legal Issues in Franchising

For a business alliance to be successful for both parties, trust is important. But a contract is essential to avoid or resolve problems that may arise.

THE FRANCHISE CONTRACT The basic features of the relationship between the franchisor and the franchisee are embodied in the franchise contract. This contract is typically a complex document of many pages. Because of its importance as the legal basis for the franchised business, the franchise contract should never be signed by the franchisee without legal counsel. In fact, reputable franchisors insist that the franchisee have legal counsel before signing the agreement. An attorney may anticipate trouble spots and note any objectionable features of the contract.

A prospective franchisee should also use as many other sources of help as would be practical. In particular, she or he should discuss the franchise contract in detail with a banker. The prospective franchisee should also obtain the services of a professional accounting firm to examine the franchisor's statements of projected sales, operating expenses, and net income. An accountant can help evaluate the quality of these estimates and identify any projections that may be overstated. These experts are essential to ensure that parties on both sides of the agreement comprehend their obligations. Disagreements between the parties can wind up in courts. For example, Cold Stone Creamery was sued by an association of its franchisees for failure to comply with commitments the franchisor had made in e-mails and meetings with franchisees.[26]

One of the most important features of the franchise contract is the provision relating to termination and transfer of the franchise. Some franchisors have been accused of devising agreements that permit arbitrary cancellation of the franchise relationship. Of course, it is reasonable for the franchisor to have legal protection in the event that a franchisee fails to obtain an appropriate level of operation or does not maintain satisfactory quality standards. However, the prospective franchisee should be wary of contract provisions that contain overly strict or vague cancellation policies. Similarly, the rights of the franchisee to sell the business to a third party should be clearly spelled out. A franchisor who can restrict the sale of the business to a third party could potentially take back ownership of the business at an unfair price. The right of a franchisee to renew the contract after the business has been built up to a successful operating level should also be clearly stated in the contract.

FRANCHISE DISCLOSURE STATEMENTS The offer and sale of a franchise are regulated by both state and federal laws. At the federal level, the minimum disclosure standards are specified by Rule 436 of the Federal Trade Commission (FTC). A guide to the rule can be found on the Federal Trade Commission's website (www.ftc.gov), as can addresses of the state offices that enforce franchise disclosure laws.

The Franchise Disclosure Document (FDD) provides the accepted format for satisfying the requirements of the FTC. In May 2008, the FDD replaced the Uniform Franchise Offering Circular (UFOC) as the legal document satisfying the FTC Franchise Rule. The FDD must include information on a variety of items, including investment requirements and conditions that would affect renewal, termination, and sale of the franchise. Most franchise experts recommend that a franchisee's attorney and accountant review the document.

4-4 BUYING AN EXISTING BUSINESS

LO
4-4
List four reasons for buying an existing business, and describe the process of evaluating an existing business.

Another option for making your dream a reality is buying an existing business. You can be just as entrepreneurial buying an existing enterprise as creating one from scratch. As you look at companies available for purchase, you may discover an opportunity to turn around a company in trouble. Or perhaps you have the skills needed to make an already good business excellent. An existing firm may be the perfect platform on which to build your dream.

Many franchisees actually buy stores that are up and running from the current business owners. When Mark Kauffman was laid off by the hardware company where he had worked as an executive, he bought an existing Maaco Collision Repair & Auto Painting franchise. The profit margins of the shop were not impressive, but Kauffman saw an opportunity. He cut costs, marketed aggressively to new customer groups and boosted sales by 35 percent in his first year.[27]

The decision to purchase an existing business should not be made lightly. It involves serious investment of funds, so you must give careful consideration to the advantages and disadvantages of this option.

4-4a Reasons for Buying an Existing Business

The reasons for buying an existing business can be condensed into the following four general categories:

1. To reduce some of the uncertainties and unknowns that must be faced in starting a business from the ground up
2. To acquire a business with ongoing operations and established relationships with customers and suppliers
3. To obtain an established business at a price below what it would cost to start a new business or to buy a franchise
4. To get into business more quickly than by starting from scratch

Let's examine each of these reasons in more detail.

REDUCTION OF UNCERTAINTIES A successful business has already demonstrated its ability to attract customers, manage costs, and make a profit. Although future operations may be different, the firm's past record shows what it can do under actual market conditions. For example, just the fact that the location must be satisfactory eliminates one major

Capitalizing on an existing business model, Landrie Peterman purchased an Anytime Fitness outlet, and in less than a week, she had changed the franchise rights, renegotiated the lease, and purchased the business. Within six months, she had grown the membership from about 300 to over 1,000 clients.

© Anytime Fitness

uncertainty. Although traffic counts are useful in assessing the value of a potential location, the acid test comes when a business opens its doors at that location. This test has already been met in the case of an existing firm. The results are available in the form of sales and profit data. Noncompete agreements are needed, however, to discourage the seller from starting a new company that will compete directly with the one he or she is selling.

ACQUISITION OF ONGOING OPERATIONS AND RELATIONSHIPS The buyer of an existing business typically acquires its personnel, inventories, physical facilities, established banking connections, and ongoing relationships with trade suppliers and customers. You are also acquiring the goodwill that the prior owner created. Extensive time and effort would be required to build these elements from scratch. Of course, the advantage derived from buying an established firm's assets depends on the nature of the assets. For example, a firm's skilled, experienced employees constitute a valuable asset only if they will continue to work for the new owner. The physical facilities must not be obsolete, and the firm's relationships with banks, suppliers, and customers must be healthy. In any case, new agreements will probably have to be negotiated with current vendors and leaseholders.

A BARGAIN PRICE If the seller is more eager to sell than the buyer is to buy, an existing business may be available at what seems to be a low price. Whether it is actually a good buy, however, must be determined by the prospective new owner. Several factors could make a "bargain price" anything but a bargain. For example, the business may be losing money, the neighborhood location may be deteriorating, or the seller may intend to open a competing business nearby. On the other hand, if research indicates that the business indeed is a bargain, purchasing it is likely to turn out to be a wise investment. And it can be easier to get financing for an ongoing business than for a startup.[28]

A QUICK START Most entrepreneurs are eager to get going in their new business and may not be comfortable waiting the months and years sometimes required to launch a business from scratch. Buying an existing business may be an excellent way to begin operations much more quickly.

4-4b Finding a Business to Buy

Sources of leads about businesses available for purchase include suppliers, distributors, trade associations, and even bankers. Realtors—particularly those who specialize in the sale of business firms and business properties—can also provide leads. In addition, **business brokers** can assist in buying and selling businesses.[29] Entrepreneurs need to be wary of potential conflicts of interest with business brokers, however. For example, if brokers are paid only if a buy–sell transaction occurs, they may be tempted to do whatever it takes to close the deal, even if doing so is detrimental to the buyer. Mark Shelstad's experience with a business broker is described in some detail in the Living the Dream feature.

The Small Business Administration offers the following guidance on finding a business to buy:[30]

1. *Identify your interests.* At a minimum, eliminate businesses that hold no interest for you.
2. *Consider your talents.* You have to give this business your all, so be honest with yourself about your skills and experience.

business brokers
Specialized brokers that bring together buyers and sellers of businesses.

Living the Dream

Buying Someone Else's Idea

"I didn't have a creative idea worthy of starting a business from scratch," admitted Mark Shelstad, who put in years as an equity portfolio manager for different asset management companies. In 2010, he became concerned about the stability of the financial industry and his line of work. He wanted to become his own boss, but coming up with ideas for a new venture wasn't easy.

So, Mark Shelstad decided to use a business broker. Brokers help buyers look for businesses to purchase and help business owners find potential buyers. They advise sellers on how to prepare and price their companies. And they often help buyers arrange for financing. Shelstad's broker even provided assistance in negotiation and handling the detailed paperwork required in closing the sale.

Shelstad knew he couldn't leave everything in the hands of the broker and just sit back and wait for the deal. He found that by frequently contacting the broker, his intention to buy a business was taken more seriously. His broker notified him about a lending-fraud investigation firm within 24 hours of the company being listed for sale. The company had been operating for 23 years, so Shelstad was not looking at a product that was new and untested. He agreed to a purchase price of over $1 million, which he funded from his personal savings and a five-year loan from the seller. (It is not unusual for a seller to become the lender to someone who wants to buy her or his company.)

Shelstad had years of knowledge and experience in finance. He selected a company where he could put that knowledge and experience to work. Armitage Research specializes in financial investigations, providing lenders with factual data about loan prospects. The company also conducts traditional research, including corporate investigations, executive background research, due diligence, and asset validation. These activities match the specialties Shelstad lists for himself on the Armitage Research website: mortgage-backed and asset-backed securities, insurance industry investment regulations and advising, and due diligence portfolio analysis.

Using a business broker should always call for due diligence as well. Keep in mind that the broker's fee is typically paid by the seller, so the buyer must be sure that the deal is fair to all parties.

Sources: Based on BusinessBroker.net, www.businessbroker.net/brokers/brokers.ihtml, accessed September 8, 2012; Armitage Research, http://armitageresearch.com/, accessed September 8, 2012; Armitage Research, http://armitageresearch.com/, accessed September 8, 2012; Mark W. Shelstad, www.linkedin.com/in/shelstad, accessed September 8, 2012; and Sarah E. Needleman, "Buying an Established Business," online.wsj.com/article/SB100014240531119048003045764790019087086.html, accessed September 8, 2012.

3. *List conditions for your business.* Does location matter? How about working hours? How big do you want it to be?

4. *Quantify your investment.* How much can you afford?

4-4c Investigating and Evaluating Available Businesses

Regardless of the source of the lead, a business opportunity requires careful evaluation—what is sometimes called **due diligence**. As a preliminary step, the buyer needs to acquire background information about the business, some of which can be obtained through personal observation or discussion with the seller. Talking with other informed parties, such as suppliers, bankers, and employees of the business, is also important.

due diligence
The exercise of reasonable care in the evaluation of a business opportunity.

The website for the U.S. Small Business Administration provides information for performing due diligence in the purchase of a business. The list of documents that you will need to evaluate (see Exhibit 4.4) may appear long and intimidating, but this assessment is necessary. If a seller cannot supply the documents on this list, you may want to back away. Some items will not exist for every business. For example, not every company will require government certifications. Nevertheless, you should be exhaustive in your efforts to uncover relevant information that could influence the selling price or whether you should even enter into the sale. Otherwise, you may find yourself "on the hook" for unanticipated expenses that show up later.

RELYING ON PROFESSIONALS Although some aspects of due diligence require personal checking, a buyer can also seek the help of outside experts. The two most valuable sources of outside assistance are accountants and lawyers. It is also wise to seek out others who have acquired a business in order to learn from their experience. Their perspective will be different from that of a consultant, and it will bring some balance to the counsel received. The time and money spent on securing professional help in investigating a business can pay big dividends, especially when the buyer is inexperienced. Prospective buyers should seek advice and counsel, but they must make the final decision themselves, as it is too important to entrust to someone else.

FINDING OUT WHY THE BUSINESS IS FOR SALE The seller's *real* reasons for selling may or may not be the *stated* ones. When a business is for sale, always question the owner's reasons for selling. There is a real possibility that the firm is not doing well or that underlying problems exist that will affect its future performance. The buyer must be wary, therefore, of taking the seller's explanations at face value. Here are some of the most common reasons why owners offer their businesses for sale:

- Retirement
- Illness
- Partnership or family disputes
- Unprofitability or failure of the business
- Burnout
- Lack of capital for growth potential

A prospective buyer cannot be certain that the seller-owner will be honest in presenting all the facts about the business, especially concerning financial matters. Background checks on key personnel are essential when conducting due diligence.

EXHIBIT

4.4 Due Diligence for Purchasing a Business

1. Contracts and lease agreements	7. Sales records	13. Payroll, benefits, and employee-pension/profit-sharing information
2. Financial statements	8. Supplier/purchaser lists	
3. Tax returns	9. Contracts	14. Employee roster
4. Real and personal property documents	10. Advertisement materials	15. Certifications by federal, state or local agencies
5. Bank accounts	11. Inventory receipts/lists	16. List of owners
6. Customer lists	12. Organizational charts	

Source: U.S. Small Business Administration, www.sba.gov/content/researching-business-purchase, accessed September 8, 2012.

EXAMINING THE FINANCIAL DATA The first stage in evaluating the financial health of a firm is to review the financial statements and tax returns for the past five years or for as many years as they are available. (*If these statements are not available, think twice before buying the business.*) This review helps to determine whether the buyer and the seller are in the same ballpark on estimates and expectations. If so, the parties can move on to valuing the firm. You will find details on compiling and interpreting financial statements in Chapter 10.

As both a legal and an ethical matter, the prospective buyer may expect to sign a **nondisclosure agreement**. Under the restrictions of such an agreement, the buyer promises the seller that he or she will not reveal confidential information or violate the trust that the seller has offered in providing the information. Buyers are typically allowed to share such information with others, such as a potential lender or legal advisor, on a need-to-know basis.

The buyer should recognize that financial statements can be misleading and may require normalizing to yield a realistic picture of the business. For example, business owners sometimes understate business income in an effort to minimize their taxes. Other financial entries that may need adjustment include personal expenses and wage or salary payments. For example, costs related to the personal use of business vehicles frequently appear as a business expense, and family members may receive excessive compensation or none at all. All entries must be examined to ensure that they relate to the business and are appropriate.

The buyer should also compare the seller's balance sheet to actual assets and liabilities. Property may appreciate in value after it is recorded on the books, but physical facilities, inventory, and receivables may decline in value, so their actual worth may be less than their accounting book value.

4-4d Quantitative Factors in Valuing the Business

Once the initial investigation and evaluation have been completed, the buyer must arrive at a fair value for the firm. **Fair market value** is defined by the United States Internal Revenue Service in Revenue Ruling 59-60 as "the price at which the property would change hands between a willing buyer and willing seller when the former is not under any compulsion to buy and the latter is not under any compulsion to sell, both parties having reasonable knowledge of relevant facts."[31] In valuing firms, the buyer will have to rely on federal tax returns and state sales tax statements. It may also be helpful to scrutinize supplier invoices and customer receipts, as well as the company's bank statements.

Although numerous techniques are used for valuing a company, they are typically derivations of three basic approaches: (1) asset-based valuation, (2) market-comparable valuation, and (3) cash flow–based valuation. These techniques are examined in detail in Appendix B.

4-4e Nonquantitative Factors in Valuing a Business

You should also consider a number of nonquantitative factors in evaluating an existing business. In particular, is it likely that the firm you are considering buying might be subject to change regarding any of the following?

- *Market.* The ability of the market to support all competing business units, including the one to be purchased, should be determined. This requires doing marketing research, studying census data, and personally observing each competitor's place of business.

nondisclosure agreement
An agreement in which the buyer promises the seller that he or she will not reveal confidential information or violate the seller's trust.

fair market value
The price at which the property would change hands between a willing buyer and willing seller, with both parties having reasonable knowledge of relevant facts.

- *Competition.* The prospective buyer should look into the extent, intensity, and location of competing businesses. In particular, the buyer should check to see whether the business in question is gaining or losing in its race with rivals. Additionally, new competitors in the local marketplace (Walmart, for example) may dramatically change an existing small firm's likelihood of success. Past performance is no guarantee of future performance.

- *Future community development.* Future developments in the community that could have an indirect impact on a business include a change in zoning ordinances already enacted but not yet in effect, a change from a two-way traffic flow to a one-way traffic flow, and the widening of a road or construction of an overpass.

- *Legal commitments.* Legal commitments may include contingent liabilities, unsettled lawsuits, delinquent tax payments, missed payrolls, overdue rent or installment payments, and mortgages of record on any of the real property acquired.

- *Union contracts.* The prospective buyer should determine what type of labor agreement, if any, is in force, as well as the quality of the firm's relationship with its employees. Private conversations with key employees and rank-and-file workers can be helpful in determining their job satisfaction and the company's likelihood of success.

- *Buildings.* The quality of the buildings housing the business should be checked, with particular attention paid to any fire hazards. In addition, the buyer should determine whether there are any restrictions on access to the buildings.

- *Product prices.* The prospective owner should compare the prices of the seller's products with those listed in manufacturers' or wholesalers' catalogs and also with the prices of competing products in the locality. This is necessary to ensure full and fair pricing of goods whose sales are reported on the seller's financial statements.

4-4f Negotiating and Closing the Deal

The purchase price of a business is determined by negotiation between buyer and seller. Although the calculated value may not be the price eventually paid for the business, it gives the buyer an estimated value to use when negotiating price. Typically, the buyer tries to purchase the firm for something less than the full estimated value; of course, the seller tries to get more than that value.

In some cases, the buyer may have the option of purchasing the assets only, rather than the business as a whole. When a business is purchased as a total entity, the buyer takes control of the assets but also assumes any outstanding debt, including any hidden or unknown liabilities. Even if the financial records are audited, such debts may not surface. If the buyer instead purchases only the assets, then the seller is responsible for settling any outstanding debts previously incurred. When buying the business as a whole, an indemnification clause in the sales contract may serve a similar function, protecting the buyer from liability for unreported debt.

An important part of the negotiation process is the terms of purchase. In many cases, the buyer is unable to pay the full price in cash and must seek extended terms. At this point, a lender may enter the picture and alter the purchase price. If a bank is providing a loan for buying the business, the bank may require the assets of the company to serve as collateral for the loan. Any lender must perform its own due diligence

© sheff/Shutterstock.com

and estimate a value for the assets, and that value may be at a different level than the buyer and seller have agreed upon.

At the same time, the seller may be concerned about taxes on the profit from the sale. Terms may become more attractive to the buyer and the seller as the amount of the down payment is reduced and/or the length of the repayment period is extended. As with the purchase of real estate, the purchase of a business is closed at a specific time, and a title company or an attorney usually handles the closing. Preferably, the closing will occur under the direction of an independent third party. If the seller's attorney is the closing agent, the buyer should exercise great caution—*a buyer should never go through a closing without the aid of an experienced attorney who represents only the buyer.*

A number of important documents are completed during the closing. These include a bill of sale, tax and other government regulation forms, and agreements pertaining to future payments and related guarantees to the seller. The buyer should apply for new federal and state tax identification numbers to avoid being held responsible for past obligations associated with the old numbers. If you want a happy ending from the purchase and a clear path to your future, do not take short cuts at this stage. Meeting all legal and regulatory requirements secures your investment and your ability to successfully manage the business.

Starting a business, becoming a franchisee, and buying an existing business are all potential paths to your entrepreneurial dream. Although franchising and buying a business are usually considered to be strategies for reducing the risks associated with starting a venture, each path still requires careful research and planning. Whatever your particular circumstances, it is important to keep in mind that business owners must invest themselves, as well as their money, if they want their companies to succeed. As is so often the case in life, it is up to you to devote your time, effort, and resources if you really want to achieve your goals.

LOOKING BACK

4-1. Define *franchise*, and become familiar with franchise terminology.

- According to the U.S. Small Business Administration, a *franchise* is a business model involving a business owner who licenses trademarks and methods to an independent entrepreneur. The franchise governs the method of conducting business between the two parties.
- A franchisee sells goods or services supplied by the franchiser or that meet the franchiser's quality standards.
- The franchisor provides the business expertise (marketing plans, management guidance, financing assistance, site location, training, etc.) that otherwise would not be available to the franchisee.
- The franchisee brings the entrepreneurial spirit and drive necessary to make the franchise a success.
- In product and trade name franchising, the main benefit for the franchisee is the privilege of using a widely recognized product name.
- In business format franchising, entrepreneurs receive an entire marketing and management system.
- A master licensee is an independent firm or individual acting as a middleman or sales agent with the responsibility of finding new franchisees within a specified territory.
- Multiple-unit ownership, in which a single franchisee owns more than one unit of a franchised business, is becoming widely used.
- Some single franchisees are area developers—individuals or firms that obtain the legal right to open several outlets in a given area.
- Piggyback franchising is the operation of a retail franchise within the physical facilities of a host store.
- Multibrand franchising involves operating several franchise organizations within a single corporate structure.
- Co-branding brings two or more franchise brands together within a single enterprise.

4-2. Understand the pros and cons of franchising and the structure of the industry.

- The primary advantage of franchising is its high probability of success.

- Other advantages of franchising include the value of trade names and trademarks, the franchisor's operations manual, training support, immediate access to supply lines and purchasing power, and financial support. It also is a way for existing businesses to diversify.
- Disadvantages of franchising include financial issues, franchisor competition, and management issues.
- Costs associated with franchises include franchise fees, investment costs, royalty payments, and advertising costs.

4-3. Describe the process for evaluating a franchise opportunity.

- Independent third parties such as state and federal government agencies, the International Franchise Association, and business publications can be valuable sources of franchise information.
- The most logical source of the greatest amount of information about a franchise is the franchisor.
- Existing and previous franchisees are also good sources of information for evaluating a franchise.
- Before becoming a franchisor, consider the efficiency of your business model, how you will finance the growth, what expert assistance you will need, what will go into your operations manual, government disclosure requirements, and your ability to add long-term value for franchisees.
- A franchise contract is a complex document and should be evaluated by a franchise attorney, especially the provision relating to termination and transfer of the franchise.
- The Franchise Disclosure Document (FDD) provides the accepted format for satisfying the franchise disclosure requirements of the FTC.

4-4. List four reasons for buying an existing business, and describe the process of evaluating an existing business.

- Buying an existing firm can reduce uncertainties.
- In acquiring an existing firm, the entrepreneur can take advantage of the firm's ongoing operations and established relationships with customers and suppliers.
- An existing business may be available at a bargain price.
- Another reason for buying an existing business is that an entrepreneur may be in a hurry to start an enterprise.
- Investigating a business requires due diligence.
- A buyer should seek the help of outside experts, the two most valuable sources of outside assistance being accountants and lawyers.
- The buyer needs to investigate why the seller is offering the business for sale.
- The financial data related to the business should always be examined.
- Nonquantitative information about the business for sale should also be used in determining its value.

area developers, p. 93

business brokers, p. 107

business format franchising, p. 93

churning, p. 99

co-branding, p. 95

due diligence, p. 108

encroachment, p. 99

fair market value, p. 110

franchise contract, p. 93

Franchise Disclosure Document (FDD), p. 103

franchise, p. 93

franchisee, p. 93

Franchise Rule, p. 104

franchisor, p. 93

master licensee, p. 93

multibrand franchising, p. 95

multiple-unit ownership, p. 93

nondisclosure agreement, p. 110

piggyback franchising, p. 95

product and trade name franchising, p. 93

Discussion Questions

1. What makes franchising different from other forms of business? Be specific.

2. What is the difference between product and trade name franchising and business format franchising?

3. Identify and describe at least four of the key terms in franchising.

4. What are the pros and cons of franchising from the viewpoints of both the potential franchisee and the potential franchisor?

5. Should franchise information provided by a franchisor be discounted? Why or why not?

6. Do you believe that the Franchise Disclosure Document is useful for franchise evaluation? Defend your position.

7. Evaluate loss of control as a disadvantage of franchising from the franchisor's perspective.

8. What are possible reasons for buying an existing company as opposed to starting a new business from scratch?

9. What are some common reasons that cause owners to offer their businesses for sale? Which of these reasons might a buyer consider to be negative?

10. What are some of the nonquantitative factors in valuing a business?

You Make the Call

Situation 1

Although he has owned the Madison, Wisconsin, franchise of 1-800-Got-Junk for seven years, John Patterson claimed he did not know whether he was making profits, breaking even, or even losing money. Still, in February of 2012, Patterson was able to buy an existing 1-800-Got-Junk franchise in the Denver, Colorado, area.

Patterson has reached his dream of recycling 100 percent of what he collects, and he is proud to report that his company has been able to prevent 75 percent of the junk collected from being deposited in landfills. Patterson tries to communicate to customers what he does with the junk they throw away, and they seem interested in knowing that their items are being recycled. And he tries to run his operation in as green a way as possible. He converted a truck using diesel to vegetable oil, and he is moving from using unleaded fuel in some trucks to running them on compressed natural gas instead.

Sources: Based on "Junk in His Trunk," *Entrepreneur*, May 2012, p. 122; www.1800gotjunk.com/us_en/locations/junk-removal-denver, accessed September 8, 2012; and www.1800gotjunk.com/us_en/locations/junk-removal-madison/; accessed September 8, 2012.

Question 1 Do you think that Patterson really does not know or care whether or not he is making money? Can he succeed in two locations if that is his attitude?

Question 2 What type of background do you think you would need to run a 1-800-Got-Junk franchise?

Question 3 If you were Patterson, what support would you expect to get from the franchisor?

Situation 2

Siler Chapman worked in a Pizza Works franchise while he was a student at the University of North Carolina. When he saw people losing jobs in an economic downturn, he decided he'd rather be his own boss than find himself fired by someone else. So he opened (what else?) a pizza place. While building his business, he also found that he had a talent for tossing pizzas and became part of a U.S. team that won the Pizza Olympics in Italy four years in a row.

Tossing pizzas was fun, and Chapman found it to be a good marketing tool, but he also found the day-to-day management demands of growing a business to be hard. When Chapman was approached by Donato's Pizzeria, he decided to convert his three stores to Donato's franchises. Within two years, his three stores had expanded to fifteen. And Chapman is planning 200 more!

Sources: Based on Jason Daley, "Acrobat of Pizza," *Entrepreneur*, Vol. 38, No. 11 (November 2010), p. 140; and www.donatos.com/about_donatos/index.asp, accessed October 30, 2010.

Question 1 If Siler Chapman had so much trouble running three restaurants as an independent owner, why do you think he was able to manage so many more as a franchisee?

Question 2 From a franchisor's perspective, why might you choose to convert an existing chain of stores to your model instead of having franchisees who start from scratch?

Situation 3

After earning his engineering degree at a top university, Phil had numerous job offers at high salaries. He accepted a position with a well-established manufacturing company and quickly moved up the ranks. Then, he was recruited to be part of the top management team of a construction company. Life has been good, but Phil has been thinking that he'd really like to run his own business. He's established a strong reputation for both his technical and his leadership skills. He has been speaking with business brokers and with some owners that he feels might be willing to negotiate a sale, but nothing has felt right so far.

Question 1 Why do you think Phil is thinking about business ownership after the success he has achieved working in other companies? Why do you think he wants to buy instead of start a business?

Question 2 What questions do you think Phil should ask of a seller if he finds a business that he likes?

Experiential Exercises

1. Interview a local owner-manager of a franchise. What was the process by which the owner obtained the franchise? Would she or he do it all over again?

2. Select a franchise in an industry that interests you and visit that company's website. Read what it says about becoming a franchisee with the organization, and report back to the class on what it's like to be a franchisee there.

3. Does a franchise operate on your campus? Who is the franchisee? Interview the official who is responsible for that contract. Why did the school decide to have the outlet on campus?

4. Consult the Yellow Pages of your local telephone directory or search local business listings online to determine if there is a business broker in your community. Interview the broker, and report to the class on how he or she values businesses.

The Small Business & Entrepreneurship Resource Center

The Small Business & Entrepreneurship Resource Center offers complete small business management resources through a comprehensive database that covers all major areas of starting, operating, and maintaining a business from financing, management, marketing, accounting, taxes, and more. Go to www.cengagebrain.com and select the Longenecker text for more information on how to access this material.

1. The Chophouse, Inc., founded by James Ellery, is a New York–based company that plans to develop restaurant franchises in the greater New York metropolitan area. The menu consists of steak plus seafood, chicken, ribs, burgers, sandwiches, and a salad bar. The Chophouse will generate revenues from franchise licenses, royalty fees, and company-owned restaurants. The franchise industry has changed, shifting toward franchisors becoming providers of services and financing for franchisees in return for 8 percent of all gross receipts. In addition, a franchisor exercises much authority over franchisees. What do you see as the pluses and minuses of becoming a franchisee of The Chophouse?

2. Two high-profile strikes in New York and Chicago gained national attention by assailing quick-service restaurants for creating only dead-end, minimum-wage-paying jobs, perpetuating the image of the industry as one populated chiefly by underpaid burger flippers. The stubborn myth that restaurants provide only jobs with little or no career potential has been around for decades, but the economic downturn has forced operators to defend themselves against increased criticism. Chipotle, for example, showcases its Restaurateurs on local news broadcasts or YouTube. Sahul Flores rose from crew member to general manager in nine months, became a Restaurateur, and is now responsible for over 50 restaurants. What do you think would change perceptions of the industry? How could social media be used to change minds?

Sources: "Restaurant Franchise System: The Chophouse," Michelle Lee (ed.), *Business Plans Handbook* (Detroit: Gale, 2012); and Brandau, Mark. "Industry Aims to Make Over Employer Image," Nation's Restaurant News 47. 9 (May 13, 2013): 3(2).

Two Men and a Truck (P. 651)

Two Men and a Truck started in the early 1980s as a way for two brothers to make extra money while they were in high school. Now, over 20 years later, the company has grown to more than 200 locations worldwide and is the nation's largest franchised local moving company.

Alternative Case for Chapter 4

Case 18, Auntie Anne's Pretzels in China, p. 681

Endnotes

1. Don Dwyer, "How We Began," www.dwyergroup.com/how-we-began.asp, accessed September 2, 2012.

2. Arthur G. Sharp, www.referenceforbusiness.com/encyclopedia/For-Gol/Franchising.html, accessed September 2, 2012.

3. Roy Seaman, www.theukfranchisedirectory.net/page/history-of-franchising.php, accessed September 2, 2012.

4. Don Daszkowski, "The History of Franchising," http://franchises.about.com/od/franchisebasics/a/history.htm, accessed September 2, 2012.

5. Hilary Strahota, "Benjamin Franklin: Father of Franchising?" *Franchising World*, September 2007.

6. U.S. Small Business Administration, www.sba.gov/content/franchising-businesses#, accessed September 2, 2012.

7. *Ibid.*

8. Jason Daley, "Playing Well Together," *Entrepreneur*, April 2012, pp. 87–92; and Seva, www.sevabeauty.com, accessed September 8, 2012.

9. http://franchise.org/aboutifa.aspx, accessed September 2, 2012.

10. http://franchise.org/faq.aspx, accessed September 2, 2012.

11. www.uspto.gov/main/glossary/index.html#trademark, accessed September 3, 2012.

12. www.dwyergroup.com/privacy.asp, accessed September 3, 2012.

13. Jason Daley, "On the Same Page," *Entrepreneur*, June 2012, pp. 96–98; and "Painting with a Twist," www.paintingwithatwist.com, accessed September 8, 2012.

14. www.franchise.org/Veteran-Franchise.aspx, accessed September 3, 2012.

15. Tracy Stapp, "Military Intelligence," *Entrepreneur*, July 2012, pp. 98–107.

16. http://franchiseregistry.com/sba_eligibility/, accessed September 3, 2012.

17. http://franchise.org/industrysecondary.aspx?id=3554, accessed September 3, 2012.

18. "Legal Briefs," *Franchise Times*, Vol. 14, No. 7 (August 2008), p. 51.

19. http://qnationalsettlement.com/, accessed September 3, 2012.

20. Elizabeth Sile, "Edible Arrangements in Legal Hot Water," www.inc.com/news/articles/201107/edible-arrangements-lawsuit.html, accessed September 3, 2012.

21. Jonathon Bick, "Internet-Based Franchise Encroachment Runs Rampant," *New Jersey Law Journal*, Vol. 202, No. 12, http://bicklaw.com/e-Franchiseproblems.htm, accessed September 3, 2012.

22. http://franchise.org/Rainbow_International_franchise.aspx, accessed September 3, 2012.

23. www.sonicdrivein.com/business/franchise/own.jsp, accessed September 3, 2012.

24. Personal communication with Mark Liston, October 27, 2010.

25. *Ibid.*

26. "Franchisees' Complaint," http://online.wsj.com/article/SB10001424052970204136404577211522730549042.html?mod=WSJ_Franchising_MIDDLETopNews, accessed September 8, 2012.

27. Sarah E. Needleman, "Buying an Established Business," http://online.wsj.com/article/SB10001424053111904800304576479001908 7086.html, accessed September 9, 2012.

28. Rieva Lesonsky, "Is It Time to Sell Your Business or Buy a New One?" http://smallbiztrends.com/2012/05/sell-business-buy-a-new-one.html, accessed September 8, 2012.

29. "Business Broker," www.entrepreneur.com/encyclopedia/term/82270.html, accessed September 8, 2012.

30. U.S. Small Business Administration, www.sba.gov/content/choosing-business, accessed September 8, 2012.

31. U.S. Small Business Administration, www.sba.gov/content/determing-value-business, accessed September 8, 2012.

MC 58-C
USDOT 694
Fla. Reg. IM # 1221
PBC#M772

4439 Westroads Dr.
West Palm Beach, FL 33407

TWO MEN
AND A
TRUCK
"Movers Who Care."
www.twomenandatruck.com

Packing & Moving
Supplies
• Tape
• Markers
• Paper Products

© ZUMA Press/Alamy

The Family Business

Brig and Jon Sorber were just 17 and 15 years old, respectively, when they began hauling junk for customers in a pickup truck in 1981. After their first ad in a local paper, they started getting calls from people who wanted their households moved. This work gave them some spending money, but they left the company in their mother's hands when they started college.

Mary Ellen Sheets had invested $350 in Two Men and a Truck when she bought her sons an old bread delivery truck. When the boys went off to college, she hired a couple of workers to keep the business going. As Sheets struggled to build the company, she found that she could rely on her mother, whom everyone called Grandma Eb, to help in the office and keep the business organized. Mary Ellen was inspired by what her mother always told her: "Treat everyone with dignity, respect, and patience." That became the "Grandma Rule" and guides the company to this day.

 In the SPOTLIGHT
Two Men and a Truck
www.twomen.com

When Sheets decided to grow the company by franchising, she recruited her daughter, Melanie Bergeron, to take over running the corporate headquarters so that Sheets could turn her attention to other interests (although she did remain a franchisee). In 1994, Bergeron took the title of company president at no salary. At that time, the firm was doing about $6 million in revenue. In addition to being

© Two Men and a Truck

OPEN
LOOKING
AHEAD

After studying this chapter, you should be able to...

5-1. Explain the forces that can keep a family business moving forward.

5-2. Describe the complex roles and relationships involved in a family business.

5-3. Identify management practices that enable a family business to function effectively.

5-4. Describe the process of managerial succession in a family business.

5-5. Describe the process of managerial succession in a family business.

president, Bergeron had her own Two Men franchise. She proved to be a good student, learning from mentors in the franchising industry and from an advisor in a major accounting and consulting firm. Two Men and a Truck overcame obstacles, grew, and prospered.

One day, Bergeron decided she wanted to spend more time with her husband and two sons and less at the office. Her brothers had rejoined the company as franchisees, so she called her brother Brig, asked if he was ready to be president, and then handed him the baton. Today, Brig Sorber serves as CEO. Jon Sorber is executive vice president, Bergeron chairs the board of directors, and Sheets carries the title of founder.

By 2012, when Two Men and a Truck was operating from 200 locations in 34 states, Brig made a decision similar to the one his sister made in 2009. He decided it was time to share leadership in the company. With the approval of the board of directors, a nonfamily member was chosen to serve as

president. Randy Shacka had been with Two Men for 10 years, proving himself in franchise development and operations. The owners had been impressed with how Randy applied his engineering education to organizational and budget management. He also proved to have interpersonal skills that matched the culture of the company.

Sheets looks back on the organization that she and her children grew and feels incredibly blessed, especially proud of creating good jobs for so many people. Bergeron reports that the company expresses her mother's values in its new motto, "Move People Forward." She explains that means more than physically moving customers' belongings. It is also a statement that the company wants to help their franchisees and all employees achieve the goals they want from life.

Sources: Based on http://www.twomen.com, accessed November 18, 2012; personal communication with Melanie Bergeron, October 18 and 20, 2010, and September 18, 2012; and personal communication with Mary Ellen Sheets, September 20, 2012.

H ave you heard someone call a small firm a "mom and pop business"? Has anyone ever told you not to go into business with family members, or to take a job with a professionally managed company, not a family business? So how is it that most businesses in the United States and the rest of the world are family owned and operated?

It is well documented that a majority of businesses in most free-market economies fit some definition of family ownership. The largest family businesses include such publicly traded companies as Walmart, Ford Motor Co., Comcast, News Corp., and HCA Hospital Corporation of America.[1] Although the stereotypical entrepreneur may not intentionally start a family enterprise, he or she often relies on family members to obtain the resources necessary for the startup and to pitch in when a problem arises. Family members are usually the first people to lend you money or make an investment in your company, or to step in if you get sick or if an essential employee suddenly quits. Many times, it is a family member who knows and accepts your strengths and weaknesses and is willing to work long hours, often at no pay.

But family members are not always cordial, cooperative, and compatible. They know how to make you mad, to make you feel guilty, to embarrass you. Such actions have caused the downfall of many a family enterprise, large and small. In this chapter, we investigate how family and business interact, what makes them strong, and what can destroy them. From extensive research into family firms, we introduce strategies that have helped family businesses succeed.

5-1 WHAT IS A FAMILY BUSINESS?

W hat exactly is a family? This may seem like a silly question to ask, but definitions of *family* vary in different parts of the world. They include the classic "nuclear" family, restricted to parents and children, and an "extended" family, comprising an entire community of extended relatives. No doubt you have seen many versions of families on television, in movies, and possibly in your own life. Given the

LO
5-1

Define the terms *family* and *family business*.

Part 2 Starting from Scratch or Joining an Existing Business interest and involvement that family members have in each other's lives, it shouldn't be surprising that they have opinions about a business owned by one or more members, whether they are officially connected with the company or not.

In this book, the word **family** refers to a group of people bound by a shared history and a commitment to share a future together, while supporting the development and well-being of individual members.[2] This definition acknowledges that there can be considerable differences in the compositions of families. They can vary according to blood relationships, generational representation, and legal status. A **family business** can be defined as an organization "in which either the individuals who established or acquired the firm or their descendants significantly influence the strategic decisions and life course of the firm. Family influence might be exerted through management and/or ownership of the firm."[3]

Experts on family businesses try to sort through family relationships and apply labels to firms as they evolve from one generation to another. An **owner-managed business** is a venture that is operated by a founding entrepreneur. If the children of the founder become the owners and managers of the business, that second generation is referred to as a **sibling partnership**. A **cousin consortium** describes a business in the third and subsequent generations when children of the siblings take ownership and management positions. But whichever generation is leading a company, the influence of other generations is felt. Beyond their personal relationships with their mother, the siblings involved in Two Men and a Truck continue to feel the presence of their grandmother, who allowed their mother to use her farm as a place to park trucks, who helped with business paperwork, and who held onto the cash the drivers collected. And they share that legacy with employees and franchisees who partner with the company.

5-1a Family and Business Overlap

Families and businesses exist for fundamentally different reasons. The family's primary function is the care and nurturing of family members, while the business is concerned with the production and distribution of goods and/or services. And while the family's focus is on creating value for family members and emphasizing cooperation, unity, and stability, the business's goal is to create value for customers and emphasize competition, diversity, and flexibility.

Individuals involved in a family business have interests and perspectives that differ according to their particular situations. The model in Exhibit 5.1 (a Venn diagram) shows the ways in which individuals may be involved—as owners, members of the family, employees of the business, and various combinations of these. In addition, the configuration of roles can affect the way these individuals think about the enterprise. For example, whereas a family member who works in the firm and has an ownership interest (segment 7) might favor reinvesting in order to grow the business, a family member with an ownership share but who works elsewhere (segment 5) might want dividend payouts, and an employee with neither family nor ownership interest (segment 2) might seek higher wages.

Competing interests can complicate the management process, creating tension and sometimes leading to conflict. Relationships among family members in a business are more sensitive than relationships among unrelated employees. For example, disciplining an employee who consistently arrives late is much more problematic if he or she is also a family member. Or, consider a performance review session between a parent-boss and a child-subordinate. During his college years, Edward Wimmer paid no attention when his father told him to wear some type of identification when practicing for a marathon. Not long after that, he was almost hit by a truck. He breathed

family
A group of people bound by a shared history and a commitment to share a future together, while supporting the development and well-being of individual members.

family business
An organization in which *either* the individuals who established or acquired the firm *or* their descendants significantly influence the strategic decisions and life course of the firm.

owner-managed business
A venture operated by a founding entrepreneur.

sibling partnership
A business in which children of the founder become owners and managers.

cousin consortium
A business in third and subsequent generations, when children of the siblings take ownership and management positions.

5.1   The Three-Circle Model of Family Firms

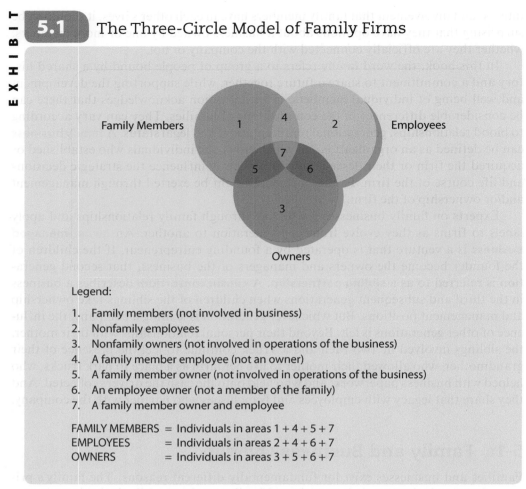

Family Members

Employees

Owners

Legend:

1. Family members (not involved in business)
2. Nonfamily employees
3. Nonfamily owners (not involved in operations of the business)
4. A family member employee (not an owner)
5. A family member owner (not involved in operations of the business)
6. An employee owner (not a member of the family)
7. A family member owner and employee

FAMILY MEMBERS = Individuals in areas 1 + 4 + 5 + 7
EMPLOYEES   = Individuals in areas 2 + 4 + 6 + 7
OWNERS   = Individuals in areas 3 + 5 + 6 + 7

Sources: Based on Frank Hoy and Pramodita Sharma, *Entrepreneurial Family Firms* (Boston: Prentice Hall, 2010); and James J. Chrisman, Franz W. Kellermanns, Kam C. Chan, and Kartono Liano, "Intellectual Foundations of Current Research in Family Business: An Identification and Review of 25 Influential Articles," *Family Business Review*, Vol. 23 (2010), pp. 9–26.

a sigh of relief, then realized that his dad was right. That stayed with him when he and his father started a business together. They knew from the beginning that respect and communication would be critical for them to make their company, Road ID, a success.[4] The existence of a family relationship adds an emotional factor that strongly supports (or vastly complicates) the working relationship.

5-1b Advantages and Disadvantages of a Family Business

If family relationships are so likely to cause trouble, why are most enterprises family owned and/or controlled? For some entrepreneurs, it is purely accidental. Gary Hirshberg co-founded Stonyfield Farm as a farming school, growing it to a producer of yogurt and other products that are sold nationwide, and eventually selling the company to Danone. The early years were a struggle. Hirshberg's wife, Meg, worked in the business, and her mother wrote checks at critical points when Stonyfield was losing $25,000 a week. Hirshberg saw himself as having responsibility for making the business a success, but it is hard to see how the firm could have survived without the family pitching in.[5]

Problems with family firms can easily blind people to the unique advantages that come with participating in a family business. The benefits associated with family involvement should be recognized and discussed when recruiting both relatives and nonfamily members to work in the family firm. One primary benefit derives from the strength of family relationships. Family members have a unique motivation: Business success is also family success.

Businesses that are family owned often highlight this feature in their promotional materials to set themselves apart from competitors. On the Carlson website, for example, the firm presents itself as "a vibrant, global, family-owned hospitality and travel company" operating in more than 150 countries.[6] Management obviously believes that emphasizing family ownership sends an important message to customers.

And such messages are not only for customers. Family businesses can convey a sense of tradition and achievement to relatives who are considering joining the firm and to nonfamily employees who have become part of the story. After all, any company that has achieved generational succession has undoubtedly overcome countless challenges and threats. Everyone who accepts a position with the business should learn the heritage and accomplishments of those who created and grew the company. They should be proud to be accepted into the extended family.

But we must not ignore the disadvantages. Even before a venture is created, conflict may arise among family members. The spouse, parents, in-laws, or others may accuse a budding entrepreneur of putting the family at risk in launching the business. When this happens between married couples, the eventual result is often the failure of either the business or the marriage. From the perspective of the opposing family members, the entrepreneur may be gambling with retirement savings, the children's college funds, or the home mortgage.

Many companies have policies against hiring family members. The assumption is that employees and executives may show favoritism toward their relatives, regardless of competence or performance. This is sometimes referred to as **nepotism**, which is the practice of employing relatives. In fact, many family businesses do provide employment to relatives regardless of their qualifications, and may keep them on the payroll even after their poor performance has become obvious to everyone. Not only is the effectiveness of the company diminished, but these practices also demoralize competent employees.

Positives and negatives associated with family businesses are summarized in Exhibit 5.2. The fact that so many family firms are able to survive generational transitions, however, demonstrates that the disadvantages can be overcome.

nepotism
The practice of employing relatives.

EXHIBIT 5.2 Positives and Negatives of Family Businesses

Positives (+)	Negatives (−)
Trust among family members	Mistrust by nonfamily employees of incompetent family employees
Loyalty to the family	Lack of loyalty to the firm
Commitment	Entitlement
Knowledge	Lack of knowledge
Long-range thinking	Demand for instant gratification
Close communication	Failure to communicate

Sources: Based on Priscilla M. Cale and David C. Tate, *Sink or Swim: How Lessons from the* Titanic *Can Save Your Family Firm* (Santa Barbara, CA: Praeger, 2011); Frank Hoy and Pramodita Sharma, *Entrepreneurial Family Firms* (Boston: Prentice Hall, 2010); Peter Leach, *Family Business: The Essentials* (London: Profile Books, 2007).

5-2 DYNAMIC FAMILY BUSINESSES

On average, family businesses survive longer than nonfamily firms. Recent research findings suggest that companies that are successful in transferring ownership and management from one generation to the next are characterized by entrepreneurial behavior. That means the new leaders need to act on their own, take risks, and introduce or support innovations. For family businesses, a key issue in the transfer of ownership and management is the retention or modification of the **organizational culture**, a pattern of behaviors and beliefs that characterize a particular firm.

The culture of the family firm deserves special attention because it can serve as either an advantage or a disadvantage. On the positive side, it can be a strategic resource that promotes an entrepreneurial orientation. This prevents successive leaders from thinking of themselves simply as administrators who are expected to continue the practices of the founder.

5-2a The Imprint of Founders on the Family Business Culture

Founders leave a deep impression on the family businesses they launch.[7] And the distinctive values that motivate and guide an entrepreneur in the founding of a company may help create a competitive advantage for the new business. Business founders are often innovators who may meet customers' needs in a special way and emphasize customer service as a guiding principle for the company. Founders often imprint their own personalities on their companies. They hire the first employees and, even as the company grows, may know everyone in the organization and their family members.

Of course, there is always a darker possibility—an overly controlling founder who won't listen to others or share information or allow others to make decisions. These attitudes can harm the business by creating a general feeling of superiority and a sense of complacency that spreads throughout the organization. At a minimum, such founders fail to prepare others for leadership. While contributions of founders deserve proper acknowledgment, any negative legacy must be avoided.

organizational culture Patterns of behaviors and beliefs that characterize a particular firm.

5-2b The Commitment of Family Members

In family firms, when the founder turns over the reins of leadership (most often, to a new generation), the continuity of the business depends, in large part, on those next-generation family members and their level of commitment to the business. Recent research suggests that family members coming into a business do so for a variety of reasons, and these reasons shape the strength and nature of their commitment to the company.[8]

The model pictured earlier in Exhibit 5.1 on p. 120 is often used to summarize the complexities of dealing with the family firm's interactive components: the business, the family, and the owner. This model can help founders recognize that they have to balance their obvious interest in the business, their personal aspirations, and the needs of their family. Next-generation family members who choose to pursue a career in the business must also deal with these challenges, and their commitment to the company will likely determine the value of their contributions, the financial benefits they create for the family, and their personal satisfaction in work-related roles.

START UP

TRANSFORM

The Spirit of the Founder
Read the biography of a founder who put his or her name on a company: L.L. Bean, Ford, Hilton. These are names of people and enterprises that have survived and grown from on generation to another. You will be fascinated by their stories.

SOCIOEMOTIONAL WEALTH One of the newest theories regarding family businesses is the finding that the commitment of family members to the firm relates to what is called **socioemotional wealth**. The idea is that gains and losses in nonfinancial characteristics of the relationship between the family and the business affect strategic and policy decisions regarding the company. The socioemotional involvement of family members can include the exercise of personal authority, the enjoyment of family influence, and close identification with a firm that may be carrying the family name.

Jennifer Silence Rankin worked in her parents' lawn care business when she was a teenager. She hated the sweeping and laundry cleaning, and vowed not to join the company. But after studying marketing and communication in college, she started to look at the company in a different way. As Rankin put it, "It hit me how much sweat, blood and tears my parents have put into this place.... I would not be OK with it being handed over to someone else."[9] Rankin chose this business for more than the salary she receives or the wealth it might create.

The socioemotional commitment of family members to the firm occurs along five dimensions, shown in Exhibit 5.3. The acronym for the dimensions is FIBER: *family* control, *identification* with the firm, *binding* social ties, *emotional* attachment, and *renewal* of family bonds through dynastic succession.

THE FEAR OF COMMITMENT Greg McCann, founding director of the Family Business Center at Stetson University, has learned from students and the family firms that he has coached that members of the succeeding generation in family firms may have emotional resistance to joining the firm. Typical fears include the following:[10]

1. **Fear of failure.** *If I really take ownership of my life, I might fail.* Realize that if emotional resistance prevents your progress, you are destined to fail.

2. **Fear of success.** *If I succeed, then others will expect more of me in the future.* It's true that successful people have to deal with the pressure of high expectations. But isn't this pressure preferable to others having no expectations of you? Or worse yet, having no expectations of yourself?

3. **Fear of commitment.** *If I never really try, then I will never really fail.* Avoiding a decision may feel safe, but many people don't understand that not deciding *is* a decision, and it is a poor one.

4. **Fear of disappointing your parents.** *It would break my dad's heart if I worked for another company instead of the family business.* Your parents want you to be happy, and if you are working to achieve that, almost all parents will be happy with your decision. Beyond that, you have to decide whether being authentic is important to you. If it is, you will have to confront this fear.

5. **Fear of disappointing others.** *If I don't go with all my friends to an internship in Chicago, I might lose their friendship.* This fear is similar to the last one, but it

> **socioemotional wealth**
> Nonfinancial factors in a family firm that affect the commitment of family members to the business.

EXHIBIT 5.3 Dimensions in Socioemotional Commitment

Family control and influence. Specifically, family members exert control over strategic decisions.
Identification of family members with the firm. The firm may be seen as an extension of the family itself.
Binding social ties. Family members feel closeness and solidarity.
Emotional attachment of family members. The history and knowledge of past events influence and shape current activities.
Renewal of family bonds to the firm through dynastic succession. There is an intention to hand the business down to future generations.

Source: Based on Pascaul Berrone, Cristina Cruz, and Luis Gomez-Mejia, "Socioemotional Wealth in Family Firms: Theoretical Dimensions, Assessment Approaches, and Agenda for Future Research," *Family Business Review,* Vol. 25, No. 3 (2012), pp. 258–279.

plays out with friends, mentors, colleagues, and bosses. It is a real and understandable fear, but you need to look at it more deeply to determine what pleasing others costs you and to question the assumption that you know what they want. Remember, you are responsible for your own happiness.

McCann's final advice is that each individual should make her or his own decisions and not let emotional resistance influence those decisions. How each person handles fears is often influenced by the sense of unity within her or his family.

COMMITMENT THROUGH UNITY MassMutual Financial Group, in conjunction with Kennesaw State University and the Family Firm Institute, conducted a survey of family business owners to assess the relationship of family unity to a company's success. The findings follow:[11]

- Family unity and cohesion were found to be critical to family business success, especially when family members identified unity as an important goal. In particular, 87 percent of respondents said family members share the same values. Agreement on values, attitudes, and beliefs indicates family unity and cohesion.

- Considering business matters such as strategy, ownership, and management, 82.9 percent of the owners said that they were completely or very unified as an ownership group.

- Unity of the ownership group is significantly associated with family commitment to the business in each generation, predictions of sales growth, and demonstrations of past growth. It is important to note that family unity was positively correlated with previous growth and projected growth.

- Family unity affects other stakeholders as well. Unified families reported they were more likely to share their values with customers and employees, with 85 percent sharing to a large extent with both groups.

In summary, the researchers concluded that the overlap between individual and organizational values may result in increased levels of employee loyalty, commitment, and organizational citizenship behavior.

5-3 FAMILY ROLES AND RELATIONSHIPS

**LO
5-3**

Describe the complex roles and relationships involved in a family business.

According to columnist Meg Cadoux Hirshberg, "People start companies to do their own things, while marriage is about doing things together…. [T]here is no tension a business can't make worse."[12] Hirshberg provides this as a warning to couples who are thinking about going into business together. This dim view of the family enterprise is not shared by everyone. However, significant conflicts can result when family roles and business interests collide, and anticipating these challenges and planning for them can really pay off. This section examines a few of the many possible family roles and relationships that can contribute to managerial complexity in a family business.

5-3a Co-Preneurs

Some family businesses are owned and managed by couples teams. Such couples are popularly known as **co-preneurs**. Their roles vary depending on their backgrounds and expertise. Whatever the arrangement, both individuals are integral parts of the business.

co-preneurs
Couples teams who own and manage businesses.

One potential advantage of a couples team is the opportunity to work with someone you really trust and to share more of your lives together. For some couples, however, the benefits can be overshadowed by problems related to the business. Differences of opinion about business matters can carry over into family life. And the energy of both parties may be so spent by working long hours in a struggling company that little zest remains for a strong family life. There is a recent trend of couples starting Web-based businesses, often from home. In some of these cases, the co-preneurs have found that there can be too much togetherness, in which case they must establish rules for time apart.[13]

1) Many couples have had to set boundaries and develop routines to cope with the demands of everyday life (like raising children) and still have sufficient time for the business. Dr. Ken Blanchard is internationally known for writing *The One Minute Manager* and over thirty other books. He and his wife, Dr. Marjorie Blanchard, are co-owners of The Ken Blanchard Companies. They founded their business in 1979. By 2012, it had over 300 employees and was labeled on the company website as a family-owned firm. The Blanchards acknowledge that the original goals for their company apply to their relationship as well: (1) working with people they love, (2) wanting to make a difference, (3) striving to walk the talk, and (4) having fun.[14]

Family members may think simple rules or guidelines or goals are unnecessary, but for many people working with relatives, such goals can keep a focus on what they want both the business and the family to become.

5-3b Mom or Dad, the Founder

Many entrepreneurs expect to pass the enterprise on to a son or a daughter. The idea is that the business and the family will grow and prosper together. Entrepreneurs with children think naturally in terms of handing the business on to the next generation. Some of the approaches taken to prepare prospective successors for ownership and leadership include the following:

- Demonstrating the founders' commitment to both the business and the family through both actions and words.
- Permitting and supporting entrepreneurial behavior by the children; letting them take calculated risks and encouraging them to learn from failure.
- Supporting educational efforts that contribute to skills for leading the business while helping the children to develop their own special talents.
- Helping the children recognize that rules and responsibilities have their place in both business and life.

Of all the relationships in a family business, the parent–child relationship has been recognized for generations as the most troublesome. Parents sometimes have difficulty accepting that their children may choose a different path than joining the business. In recent years, the problems inherent in the relationship have been addressed by counselors, seminars, and books too numerous to count. In spite of all this attention, however, the parent–child relationship continues to disrupt many families involved in family businesses.

5-3c Sons and Daughters

Should sons and daughters be recruited for the family business, or should they pursue careers of their own choosing? Experts recommend introducing children to the family

© altrendo images/Getty Images

firm at an early age. Parents may take small children to the firm on occasion, then hire them as interns on weekends or during summer breaks. This exposes the children to the lives their parents are living and to what the company is contributing to the family. Parents can make a conscious effort to teach their children that a successful enterprise demands hard work and is not just an inheritance.

Another issue is personal freedom. Today's society values the right of the individual to choose his or her own career and way of life. If this value is embraced by a son or daughter, that child must be granted the freedom to select a career of his or her own choosing. In the entrepreneurial family, the natural tendency is to think in terms of a family business career and to push a child, either openly or subtly, in that direction. Little thought may be given to the child's talent, aptitude, and temperament. He or she may prefer music or medicine to the world of business and may fit the business mold very poorly. It is also possible that the abilities of the son or daughter may simply be insufficient for a leadership role.

A son or daughter may feel a need to go outside the family business, for a time at least, to prove that he or she can make it without help from the family. Family business consultants typically give this advice to parents. Grown children who find they can succeed on their own are likely to have more self-confidence in their abilities if they choose to join the family firm at a later date. And nonfamily employees may respect the new entrant if the son or daughter was hired after demonstrating competence in a different organization.

America's oldest family firm,[15] the Avedis Zildjian Company of Norwell, Massachusetts, manufacturer of cymbals and associated products, proudly traces the firm's origin to the year 1623 and provides biographies on its website of those who led the company through the centuries.[16] For generations, the oldest males in succeeding generations were groomed to take the reins and lead the company forward. In 1999, leadership passed to a daughter, who was named chief executive officer. The Living the Dream feature, on page 121, profiles a representative of the 15th generation of the Zildjian family.

5-3d Sibling Cooperation, Sibling Rivalry

It is not unusual for more than one child to take positions within the company as they enter the workforce or make a career change. Even if they do not work in the business, brothers and sisters of those who do may be more than casual observers on the sidelines. They may have a stake as heirs or partial owners.

At best, siblings work as a smoothly functioning team, each contributing services according to his or her respective abilities. Just as families can experience excellent cooperation and unity in their relationships with one another, some family businesses benefit from effective collaboration among brothers and sisters.

However, business issues tend to generate competition, and this affects family, as well as nonfamily, members. Siblings, for example, may disagree about business policy or about their respective roles in the business. And, in some cases, the conflicts can spiral seriously out of control.[17]

Nonfamily members can play a key role in resolving or avoiding conflict among siblings. Sometimes, nonfamily executives become mentors when a family member joins the firm. This can occur formally or informally. Mentoring is often job-related, focusing on developing work and leadership skills. But the mentor can also guide the son or daughter on the culture and values that underlie the company and its success. A member of the firm's board of directors or board of advisors may play a similar

Living the Dream

Nature or Nurture?

Was it Cady Zildjian MacPherson's choice to join the family firm, or was her fate chosen for her?

The Avedis Zildjian Company of Norwell, Massachusetts, proudly describes itself on the company website "as the oldest family-owned business in America." The first Avedis founded the company in 1623 in what was then Constantinople (now Istanbul, Turkey), using a "secret alloy to create cymbals of spectacular clarity and power." Avedis III brought the firm to the United States in 1929. Today, the company is led by CEO Craigie Zildjian and her sister Debbie, who is vice president of human resources. They are members of the family's 14th generation.

Debbie's daughter, Cady, interned with Zildjian while in high school. Her first assignment was as a receptionist. After completing her studies at Colgate University, she worked part-time for Zildjian, then joined SmartPak Equine, LLC, as a senior marketing assistant. For three years, Cady was part of a team that included registered pharmacy technicians, in a firm funded by venture capitalists. She found this experience to be valuable in understanding how professionals operate and evolve in their working relationships.

© Lee Martin/Alamy

According to Cady, no pressure was placed on her to join the family firm. Although she says that she always knew it would be hard to work with family, she found the attraction to be part of the Zildjian tradition was irresistible. Cady joined the company in April 2007 and in 2012 held the position of associate product manager. She says her only regret is that she would have liked more outside experience.

Cady describes steps that the company leadership has taken as important in enabling family members to work together successfully. The Zildjians relied on outside advisors to help them set up guidelines for the family and firm. They created a family council and developed written policies for entry to the business. Cady considers effective communication to be essential. The company holds quarterly meetings for shareholders, and family members make a point of spending time together that is not for business purposes.

Cady now watches with interest as her sister and her cousin complete their college degrees. Will they be part of the Avedis Zildjian story, or will they follow a different path?

Sources: Based on http://zildjian.com, accessed July 27, 2012; personal interview with Cady Zildjian MacPherson, May 21, 2012.

role. While these mentors should not be seen as referees, they have the potential of coaching siblings in reaching agreement on issues by setting lifetime memories and resentments aside.

Another sibling dilemma has been labeled the *predator/parasite conflict*. Family members working in the firm are sometimes seen by relatives who work outside the company as predators—extracting money from the business that the outsiders believe is rightfully theirs. From the inside, family members external to the firm are seen, in turn, to be parasites. That is, they have ownership rights, receive dividends, or make other claims on the business without contributing to its success.

There are many stories about siblings who destroyed their families' businesses. Adolf and Rudolf Dassler appeared to have complementary skills that should have been perfect for collaboration—one was reserved and a sports fanatic; the other was an outgoing salesperson. But they battled over everything, eventually going separate ways. Adolf founded Adidas and Rudolf launched Puma, and their companies continued the fights.[18] The Disney brothers, Walt and Roy, were similarly known to argue, but they recognized each other's talent and proved to be the right team to build the Disney empire.[19]

Later in the chapter, you will learn that many enterprises have sought to preempt conflicts by formalizing structures. Some have implemented written guidelines by way of constitutions, while others have formed structures such as family business councils.

5-3e In-Laws In and Out of The Business

You are born or adopted into a *family of origin*, the relatives who form your world in your childhood. When you partner with another individual, you discover yourself with a new *family of attachment*, which refers to the new, separate relationship you just formed plus the family connections you acquire from your partner. Suddenly, the members of your family of origin find themselves linked to your new family, with its own values and traditions. For many family firms, the families of attachment may influence the business in one way or another. In-laws may become directly or indirectly involved in the firms. They may have been employed in the company and married a family member. They may have accepted a position in the company following their marriage. At a minimum, they will have opinions about the family business and their spouses' relatives, which they are likely to express.

When an in-law joins a company, effective collaboration may be achieved by assigning family members to different branches or roles within the company. But competition for leadership positions may eventually force decisions that distinguish among the children and in-laws employed in the business. Being fair and maintaining family loyalty become more difficult as the number of family employees increases.

In-laws who are on the sidelines also have considerable influence on the business and the family. They are keenly interested in family business issues that impact their spouses. When family frustrations come up at work, spouses tend to hear all about it at home, often just before the couple goes to bed. The family member vents, then feels better, and goes to sleep. The spouse, on the other hand, is just hearing about the situation and spends the rest of the night worried, angry, or both. Then, when everything is sorted out at the office the next morning, no one even thinks about phoning the spouse to let him or her know that everything is fine. Spouses tend to hear only one side of the story—the bad side—and it shades their view of the business. So, the criticism they receive for having a bad attitude about the family and its enterprise is often undeserved.[20]

5-3f The Entrepreneur's Spouse

Not every couple becomes co-preneurs. But even if a spouse does not work in the business, he or she may still play a critical role behind the scenes. Traditionally, this role has been fulfilled by the male entrepreneur's wife and the mother of his children. However, many husbands have now assumed the role of entrepreneur's spouse.

In order for the spouse to play a supporting role in the entrepreneur's career, there must be effective communication between them. The spouse needs to hear what's going on in the business. Otherwise, she or he may begin to feel detached and respond by competing with the business for attention. As Meg Cadoux Hirshberg describes it, "Slide into bed with an entrepreneur and you wind up cuddling with his business." In her book,

For Better or for Work, Hirshberg tells the entrepreneur not to act like the boss at home, the spouse to give the entrepreneur some space, and couples to give priority to communication. It is worth noting that Hirshberg's husband, Gary, started Stonyfield Farm from scratch. Today, that company is the largest yogurt company in the world, with sales of $350 million.[21]

© Michael Neelon/Alamy

As a parent, the spouse helps prepare the children for possible careers in the family business. Researchers have found that one of the most frequent and stressful roles performed by the spouse is to serve as a mediator in business relationships between the entrepreneur and the children. A strategy taken by some parents is to involve their children directly in the business at young ages:

> *Packing boxes after school or counting inventory on weekends is often a terrific first job. Laboring alongside a parent, children feel proud of the family business—this is ours! We are making this! And they watch their parents acting as leaders, taking responsibility for both their own lives and the lives of others.*[22]

Ideally, the entrepreneur and her or his spouse form a team committed to the success of both the family and the family business. Such teamwork does not occur automatically—it requires a collaborative effort by both parties in the marriage.

5-4 GOOD GOVERNANCE IN THE FAMILY FIRM

LO
5-4

Identify management practices that enable a family business to function effectively.

Family businesses sometimes face the stereotype of not being professionally managed. Yet several research studies have shown that publicly traded family firms perform as well as or better than nonfamily corporations.[23] As with all companies facing global competition and rapidly changing markets, family businesses have to look carefully at family members who want leadership positions in the enterprise and determine whether they are up to the task. The complex relationships in family firms require the oversight of competent and professional management, whether from inside or from outside the family. Allowing unprepared or incompetent family members to be managers weakens the firm. Compromising in this way runs counter to the interests of both the firm and the family.

The family firm is a competitive business. Practicing good management will help the business thrive and permit the family to function as a family. Failing to do so poses a threat to the business and strains family relationships.

5-4a Nonfamily Employees in a Family Firm

Nonfamily members often discover that they have limited opportunities in a family firm. In some cases, promotions are missed because of the presence of family members who may have the inside track. Few parents will promote an outsider over a competent daughter or son who is being groomed for future leadership, and this is understandable. But this limits the potential for advancement of nonfamily employees, which may lead them to become frustrated, to feel cheated, or to leave the firm.

Those outside the family are sometimes caught in the crossfire between family members who are competing with each other. It is difficult for outsiders to maintain strict neutrality in family feuds. If a nonfamily executive is perceived as siding with one of those involved in the feud, she or he may lose the support of other family members. Hardworking employees often feel that they deserve hazard pay for working in a firm plagued by family conflict.

The extent of limitations on nonfamily employees depends on the number of family members active in the business and the number of managerial or professional positions in the business to which nonfamily employees might aspire. It also depends on the extent to which the owner demands competence in management and maintains an atmosphere of fairness in supervision. To avoid future problems, the owner should make clear, when hiring nonfamily employees, the extent of opportunities available to them and identify the positions, if any, that are reserved for family members.

The leader of a family-owned enterprise might decide to bring in a nonfamily member as an executive with the firm for the following reasons:

- To bridge the gap between generations
- To set a new direction for the firm
- To deal with change
- To provide new skills and expertise

Brig Sorber chose Randy Shacka as his replacement as president of Two Men and a Truck (see this chapter's SPOTLIGHT feature), because he recognized that Shacka had a set of organizational skills that he felt were right for moving the company ahead. The rest of the family agreed that Shacka had demonstrated a commitment to values that paralleled their own. Owners often look for certain traits in nonfamily leaders: maturity, facilitation skills, mentoring skills, emotional sensitivity, trustworthiness, and the ability to understand and share the values of the family.

5-4b Family Retreats

It would be great if founders thought about how the business and the family would affect each other from the time they start on their adventure. The truth is, however, that most owners don't start thinking about how the two will interact until some problem comes up, often when the business matures and has created wealth. One of the first steps experts recommend for building a healthy family-to-business relationship is to hold a retreat. A **family retreat** is a meeting of family members (often including in-laws), usually held away from company premises, to discuss family business matters. In most cases, the atmosphere is informal to encourage family members to communicate freely and discuss their concerns about the business in an environment that does not pit family members against each other. The retreat is not so much an *event* as it is the *beginning of a process* of connecting family members. It presents an opportunity to celebrate the founders and their sacrifices, as well as highlight the legacy they wanted to pass down to future generations of the family.

The prospect of sitting down together to discuss family business matters may seem threatening to some family members. As a result, some families avoid open communication, fearing it will stir up trouble. They assume that making decisions quietly or secretly will preserve harmony. Unfortunately, this approach often covers up serious differences that become increasingly troublesome. Family retreats are designed to improve lines of communication and to bring about understanding and agreement on family business issues.

Honest and candid discussion can be difficult, so it is standard for family leaders to invite an outside expert or facilitator to coordinate early sessions. The facilitator can help develop an agenda and set ground rules for discussion. While chairing early sessions, the moderator can establish a positive, nonthreatening tone that emphasizes family achievements and encourages rational consideration of sensitive issues. Family members who are able to develop an atmosphere of neutrality, however, may be able to chair the sessions without using an outsider.

family retreat
A gathering of family members, usually at a remote location, to discuss family business matters.

To ensure the success of a family business retreat, David Lansky, CEO of a family business consulting firm, suggests that these guidelines be followed:[24]

1. *Be clear about the purpose of the retreat.* The "Miracle Question" is "If the meeting accomplished everything you could possibly hope for, what would that look like?"

2. *Set small, attainable goals.* Don't look at the retreat as having to accomplish all possible goals.

3. *Use an agenda and stick to it.* Schedule the meeting for a fixed period of time, and appoint someone to take notes.

4. *Give everyone a chance to participate.* This is a critical step in establishing trust among the participants. People need to feel that they have been heard.

5. *Know the difference between consensus and agreement.* Participants don't have to see things the same way (agreement) in order to concur on a course of action (consensus).

When families hold retreats, they need time for play and rest as well as discussing the business.

© Ariel Skelley/Blend Images/Glow Images

But the talk at family retreats is not always about business. After a retreat, families often speak of the joy of sharing family values and stories of past family experiences. Thus, retreats can turn into vacations with participants enjoying each other's company socially. When members of an extended family grow to like each other, it strengthens the family as well as the company.

5-4c Family Councils

A logical follow-up to the retreat is the creation of a **family council**, in which family members meet to discuss values, policies, and a direction for the future. A family council is the organizational and strategic planning arm of a family. It provides a forum for listening to the ideas of all members and discovering what they believe in and want from the business. A family council formalizes the participation of the family in the business to a greater extent than a family retreat does. It can also be a focal point for planning the future of individual family members, the family as a whole, and the business, as well as how each relates to the others.

A council isn't a casual get-together. It should be a formal organization that provides governance for family members in their relationship with the business. Council members are normally elected by the extended adult family members. The representatives hold regular meetings, keep minutes, and make suggestions to the firm's board of directors. During the first several meetings, an acceptable mission statement is usually generated, as well as a family constitution.

Family businesses that have such councils find them useful for developing family harmony. The meetings are often fun and informative and may include speakers who discuss items of interest. Time may be set aside for sharing achievements, milestones, and family history. The younger generation is encouraged to participate because much of the process is designed to increase their understanding of family traditions and business interests and to prepare them for working effectively in the business.

5-4d Family Business Constitutions

As we just explained, family councils may be charged with the responsibility of writing a **family business constitution**, which is a statement of principles intended to guide a family firm through times of crisis and change, including the succession process. This

family council
An organized group of family members who gather periodically to discuss family-related business issues.

family business constitution
A statement of principles intended to guide a family firm through times of crisis and change.

is not usually a legally binding document, but it helps preserve the intentions of the founder and ensures that the business survives periods of change largely intact. When a transfer between generations occurs and there is no guiding document, issues such as ownership, performance, and compensation can become flash points for conflict.[25]

When Randall Clifford's father died in 1994, the ownership and control of Ventura Transfer Company, the oldest trucking company in California, were suddenly called into question. Clifford's stepmother sued him and his three brothers for an interest in the business. Then, to make matters worse, the four Clifford brothers began to struggle among themselves for control of the company. After a drawn-out legal battle, the sons decided to enlist the help of a consultant to draft a family business constitution. The resulting document helped the family sort out many of the issues that had plagued the transition process.[26]

A family business constitution, sometimes called a *family creed*, provides the framework for a family's system of governance of the firm and may include the following topics:[27]

- The core values that all family members should follow
- A process for decision making
- The benefits that family members may receive from the business
- A mechanism for introducing younger members to the family business and its governance structures
- A dispute resolution procedure
- The philanthropic ambitions of the family

© PaulPaladin/Shutterstock

At the end of her first year as owner of Two Men and a Truck, Mary Ellen Sheets found that she had accumulated a $1,000 profit. She immediately wrote 10 checks to various charities. Not realizing what her business was destined to become, Sheets did not draft a constitution at that point, but she did set the precedent. Today, giving back to the community is a core value of the company.[28]

A family business constitution cannot foresee every eventuality, but like any such document it can be amended as needed. The important point is that this document can smooth any transitions, including a change in leadership, which is the subject of the next section.

5-5 THE PROCESS OF LEADERSHIP SUCCESSION

LO 5-5
Describe the process of managerial succession in a family business.

The task of preparing family members for careers, leadership, and ownership within the business is difficult and sometimes frustrating. Professional and managerial requirements are intertwined with family feelings and interests. Making the process work can take years.

In a 2012, PriceWaterhouseCoopers (PwC) surveyed 1,952 family business owners in over thirty countries. They investigated many characteristics of family businesses and the plans of their owners. Succession was identified as the critical issue. Just over 40 percent of the responding firms intended to pass ownership and management to the next generation, but only about half of those felt the prospective successors had the skills and enthusiasm to take over.[29]

Because everyone is so uncomfortable with the subject, plans for succession often are not well developed or at least are poorly communicated. It is hard for the entrepreneurial owner to think of not being around and in charge. And the succeeding generation finds it difficult to confront mom and dad with the prospect of death. The successor may feel that she or he is appearing to be mercenary.

But ignoring the prospect of death does not make it go away. Failing to act can result in disaster. According to Barbara Spector, editor of *Family Business* magazine:

> *In a family business, poor succession planning can have implications for the future of the family as well as the company. Optimally, succession is a process, not a one-time event. Next-generation members are taught to develop a sense of stewardship so they understand that the needs of the business, not their personal desires, take top priority.*[30]

The process begins with the determination of whether appropriate talent exists within the family.

5-5a Available Family Talent

Companies that survive long enough to face a generational transition generally have talented, visionary leadership. But the leadership that made the business successful at one time may not be right as conditions change. A business is dependent, therefore, on developing or attracting effective leaders for the future. If the available talent is not sufficient, the owner must bring in outside leadership or supplement family talent to avoid a decline in the business under the leadership of second- or third-generation family members.

The question of competency is both critical and sensitive. With experience, individuals can improve their abilities. Therefore, younger family members should not be judged too harshly early on. In fact, learning from mistakes may be essential for later success. Parents may be overly cautious about delegating authority to their children, but how will those children be ready if they haven't tested their wings? When Richard A. Lumpkin asked his father to authorize him to create a holding company that would allow their firm to break into other businesses, his dad answered, "Son, I wouldn't be for that even if I thought it was a good idea." Lumpkin found the board of directors to be more receptive, and they convinced his father to allow the change. Twenty-five years later, Lumpkin's company, Consolidated Communications, Inc., was the 14th largest telephone company in the United States.[31]

In some cases, a younger family member's skills may actually help to rescue the company, especially when the business becomes mired in the past and fails to keep up with changing technology and emerging markets. Charles Johnson Jr. and his sister Jessica took control of Johnson Security Bureau following the unexpected death of their father in 2008. The company had been founded by their grandparents in 1962. There had been conflict between the second and third generations before Charles Sr. died. Charles Sr. was informal in bidding on projects and avoided technology, opposing a company website. After taking charge, Jessica and Charles Jr. moved forward with the website and formalized procedures, taking the company to a new level.[32]

A family firm should not accept the existing level of family talent as unchangeable. The business should find development programs to teach younger family members and improve their skills. It is not unusual for firms to specify training programs and other requirements in formal documents, such as a family business constitution. Some firms include mentoring as a part of such programs. **Mentoring** is the process by which a more experienced person guides and supports the work, progress, and professional relationships of a new or less-experienced employee. In the family business, a mentor and protégé have the opportunity to navigate and explore family as well as business-related roles and responsibilities.[33]

Perhaps the fairest and most practical approach to leadership development is to recognize the right of family members to prove themselves. A period of development and testing may occur either in the family business or, preferably, in another organization. If children show themselves to be capable, they earn the right to increased leadership responsibility. If potential successors are found to have inadequate leadership abilities, preservation of the family business and the welfare of family members demand that they be passed over for promotion. The appointment of competent outsiders to these jobs, if necessary, increases the value of the firm for all family members who have an ownership interest in it.

5-5b Preparing for Succession

Age creeps up faster than we expect, so parents and children should not wait too long to talk about succession

© Purestock/Getty Images

Sons or daughters do not typically assume leadership of a family firm at a particular moment in time. Instead, a long, drawn-out process is involved. This process can be intentionally designed and implemented, or it can simply occur as all parties age. In the latter case, no one should be surprised if the next generation is not prepared at the time a transition is necessary. Successful management and ownership transitions require thoughtful action by both the current and the future leadership teams. Family business educator Greg McCann proposed actions for both generations, as discussed in the following subsections.[34]

RESPONSIBILITIES OF THE SENIOR GENERATION Listed below are some topics that the senior generation should consider and some steps it should take:

1. *Communication.* Parents need to listen and ask questions. Communication can be used to build trust and to convey values. Providing support and feedback are important, but not just in a one-way direction.

2. *Planning.* Not only should the company's vision be articulated, but also the family's values and even the plan for settling the estate of the senior generation. Planning should encompass family members, employees, and owners.

3. *Accountability.* The senior generation engages in roles as both parent and business owner. In each case, there should be investments in and support for the development of the succeeding generation. That means holding the next generation accountable for their actions, especially those that relate to credibility and integrity.

4. *Owner development.* To prepare the next generation to participate in the governance of the firm, the senior generation should be specific about the job structure of an active owner-manager or board member.

5. *Long-term planning.* When asking the next generation to develop long-term plans that will prepare them for leadership, the current generation of leaders must simultaneously prepare their own plans. Such plans should take into account future business development, boards of directors and advisors, family councils, and other structures.

mentoring
The process by which a more-experienced person guides and supports the professional progress of a new or less-experienced employee.

Part 2 Starting from Scratch or Joining an Existing Business

Because members of the junior generation sometimes have trouble seeing the senior generation as managers rather than parents, many seniors decide to bring in outside experts to help work through these steps.

RESPONSIBILITIES OF THE JUNIOR GENERATION If prospective future leaders of the family enterprise expect to advance to executive positions, they must proactively share in their preparation by doing the following:

1. *Be open to communication.* The succeeding generation should understand the values that led to the creation and growth of the family enterprise and to its current mission. If they believe change is necessary, their actions should result from conscious decisions. They should seek to be fully informed about the history and direction of the company.

2. *Develop a personal action plan.* At this stage, prospective successors should seriously assess whether they have addressed such questions as Who am I? What are my core values? What are the most important areas of my personal and professional life that I should work on?

3. *Implement the personal action plan.* This involves pursuing relevant education, training, and experience. Actions should lead to the establishment of personal credibility and marketability. The junior generation should not be joining the family business simply because they lack alternatives.

4. *Prepare for ownership.* Future leaders need to develop basic management skills, such as the ability to comprehend financial statements and to effectively supervise employees. They must grasp the role of a board of directors in terms of its relationship to the management team of the firm. And they need to understand the relationship between the business and the family.

5. *Design life plans.* Life plans are for both the individual and the business. What should the résumé of the family company CEO look like in five or ten years?

A key responsibility of the junior generation members is to keep in mind that they are not entitled to a leadership position. Such positions need to be earned.

5-5c Transfer of Ownership

The succession process for a surviving family firm eventually requires the **transfer of ownership**. Questions of inheritance affect not only the leadership successor but also other family members who have no involvement in the business. In distributing their estate, parent-owners typically wish to treat all their children fairly, both those involved in the business and those on the outside. And for many family-controlled enterprises, nonfamily members may have shares of ownership in the firm.

Family business specialist Richard Salomon advises, "Don't worry about 'fairness' and treading on toes: Put a definitive governance mechanism in place."[35] Salomon contends that family members may believe that consensus can be achieved, but he has observed too many cases where deadlocks have paralyzed the ability of businesses to function.

One step taken by some parents to avoid such deadlocks involves changing the ownership structure of the firm. Those children active in the firm's management, for example, might be given common (voting) stock and others given preferred (nonvoting) stock.

Typically, a variety of legal issues need to be resolved. Tax considerations are relevant, and they tend to favor gradual transfer of ownership to all heirs. As noted, however, transfer of equal ownership shares to all heirs may be inconsistent with the

transfer of ownership
Passing ownership of a family business to the next generation.

future successful operation of the business. Tax advantages should not be allowed to blind one to possible adverse effects on management.

There are also government regulations to protect minority shareholders. Outside investors, business partners, and even employees who may hold stock are not necessarily interested in watching the value of their stock lie dormant or deteriorate. Careless decisions by family members may lead to actions in civil courts.

Ideally, the founder has been able to arrange his or her personal holdings to create wealth outside the business as well as within it. This is an area where outside experts who grasp financial and estate planning, as well as tax law and accounting, can be invaluable. Planning and discussing the transfer of ownership is not easy, but it is strongly recommended. Over a period of time, the owner must reflect seriously on family talents and interests as they relate to the future of the firm. The plan for transfer of ownership can then be firmed up and modified as necessary when it is discussed with the children or other potential heirs. In discussing exit strategies in Chapter 13, we explain a variety of possible financial arrangements for the transfer of ownership.

In this chapter, we have tried to make one message very clear to prospective family business owners—families and family businesses are interrelated. Trying to separate them would be like trying to unscramble eggs. The better you understand that going in, the more successful you can be in both areas of your life. Despite what many people believe, family members can work together successfully and happily. Advance planning can help avoid a lot of problems, as well as boost the success of the business.

LOOKING BACK

5-1. Define the terms *family* and *family business*.

- The word *family* refers to a group of people bound by a shared history and a commitment to share a future together while supporting the development and well-being of individual members.
- Most businesses in the United States and other countries with free-market economies are family-owned and controlled.
- A *family business* is an organizational entity in which either the individuals who established or acquired the firm or their descendants significantly influence the strategic decisions and life course of the firm.
- A family business comprises the individual owner, the family, and the organization, yet each maintains an independent identity.

5-2. Explain the forces that can keep a family business moving forward.

- The organizational culture of a family business is composed of the patterns of behaviors and beliefs that emerge from the interaction of family and business.
- The founder often leaves a deep imprint on the culture of a family firm.
- The long-term survival of the business is dependent on the commitment of family members. They may be committed to the family business for different reasons, and these reasons will likely determine the nature and strength of that commitment.
- Because commitments among individuals can vary, family unity becomes an important factor in moving the business forward.

5-3. Describe the complex roles and relationships involved in a family business.

- Couples known as co-preneurs join in business together, which can strengthen or weaken their relationship.
- A primary and sensitive relationship exists between a founder and her or his son or daughter.
- Siblings and other relatives may similarly strengthen or weaken their working and personal relationships through a family business.

- In-laws play a crucial role in the family business, either as direct participants or as sideline observers.

- The role of the founder's spouse is especially important, as he or she often serves as a mediator in family disputes and helps prepare the children for possible careers in the family business.

5-4. Identify management practices that enable a family business to function effectively.

- Good management practices are as important as good family relationships in the successful functioning of a family business.

- Motivation of nonfamily employees can be enhanced by open communication and fairness.

- Family retreats bring all family members together to discuss business and family matters.

- Family councils provide a formal framework for the family's ongoing discussion of family and business issues.

- Family business constitutions can guide a company through times of crisis or change.

5-5. Describe the process of managerial succession in a family business.

- Discussing and planning the transfer of leadership is sometimes difficult.

- The quality of leadership talent available in the family determines the extent to which outside managers are needed.

- Succession is a long-term process starting early in the successor's life.

- The succession process requires actions and effective communication on the part of both the senior generation and the succeeding generation.

- Transfer of ownership involves issues of fairness, taxes, and managerial control.

Key Terms

co-preneurs p. 124

cousin consortium p. 119

family p. 119

family business p. 119

family business constitution p. 131

family council p. 131

family retreat p. 130

mentoring p. 134

nepotism p. 121

organizational culture p. 122

owner-managed business p. 119

sibling partnership p. 119

socioemotional wealth p. 123

transfer of ownership p. 135

Discussion Questions

1. How are family businesses different from nonfamily businesses? In what ways are they the same?

2. Suppose that you, as the founder of a business, have a sales representative position open. Your sister has a stepdaughter who is looking for a job and asks you to hire the young woman. What action would you take? Why?

3. What advantages result from family involvement in a business? What are some disadvantages?

4. You have been offered a job with a family-owned company. You are not related to anyone in that business. What factors should you consider in deciding whether or not to take accept the offer?

5. If you start a venture and expect some of your family members to join you, what rules do you think you should write down in advance?

6. With a college-level business degree, you are headed for a job in your family's business. You have learned some of the latest management practices, but know that these new ideas

have not been adopted in the company. Still, the business is showing a good return on investment. How should you proceed in updating what you see as obsolete approaches? Should you attempt to update these approaches at all?

7. Describe a family business with which you are familiar. What strengths or weaknesses do you see in the business relationships among the members active in the company?

8. Should a son or daughter feel an obligation to carry on a family business? What might happen if that prospective successor chooses not to join the firm?

9. Assume that you are an ambitious, nonfamily manager in a family firm and that one of your peers is the son or daughter of the founder. What, if anything, would keep you interested in pursuing a career with this company?

10. In making decisions about transferring ownership of a family business from one generation to another, how much emphasis should be placed on estate tax laws and other concerns that go beyond the family? Why?

You Make the Call

Situation 1

Twin brothers Stefan and Dillon inherited the fruit canning factory founded by their father just before they turned 30. It turned out they made a great team—one outstanding at production and operations, the other a natural at marketing and sales. Over the next three decades, they tripled the size of the enterprise. And they enjoyed each other's company, often vacationing together and making sure that their kids grew up more like siblings than cousins.

The brothers were in excellent health as they approached 60. They weren't thinking about retirement, but they had spent time and effort in developing the next generation for leadership. Then, out of the blue, they received an offer from a multinational corporation to buy their business at a huge premium.

The brothers turned to their children for their opinions. For Stefan's son and daughter, this was a no-brainer—take the money and move on. Dillon's son was of a different mind, though. He had always wanted to lead the family firm in its third generation. Stefan liked the idea of financial security and was happy with his children's reaction. Dillon was ready to step aside for a more comfortable life style, but wanted what was best for his son. A series of conversations and meetings began to turn ugly.

Question 1 What would you do if you were Stefan? What would you do if you were Dillon?

Question 2 What advice would you offer to Stefan and Dillon to maintain strong family relationships?

Situation 2

It took five tries, but Morris and Ellen finally succeeded as co-preneurs. They had tried businesses in different industries, but none was able to do more than put bread on the table—and they had five children to feed! But the fifth venture took off. They started a printing company specializing in designing and producing promotional brochures and grew it into the largest producer in their region.

The time they spent in the businesses took its toll, however. At one time or another, each of their children joined the firm, and at one time or another, each was fired. The couple was distant from three of their children. Two children returned to the family business after working for other firms and learning that their parents were not that different from other business owners. Their oldest son was a good technician, but invariably failed with any projects he took on independently. The younger son was recognized by employees and customers as skilled both in management and in interpersonal communication. Unfortunately, he had a felony conviction for drug trafficking and was prohibited from driving motor vehicles.

Morris recently suffered a heart attack and has realized that he cannot continue forever. He and Ellen have to make a decision about the continuity of the business. Compounding their dilemma is the fact that they are in a declining industry, one in which electronic production is rapidly replacing paper.

Question 1 What advice do you have for Morris and Elena?

Question 2 What recommendations do you have for preparing children to lead changes in a company?

Situation 3

Brothers Sebastian and Alfonso grew up competing for their parents' attention, so everyone was surprised when they decided to go into business together. Alfonso was the reserved one. An engineer, he had developed the product that was the basis of their venture. Sebastian was outgoing, a born salesman. He was CEO of the company, while Alfonso worked in the laboratory, overseeing research and development. The business took off, but building it into a national competitor required that all profits be invested in product development and market expansion. After a few years, Sebastian wanted to know where his share of the profits were. He knew sales were growing exponentially. What was his brother doing with his money? One day, the brothers' dad called and offered to come in and run the business. He would make sure that everyone got their fair share.

Question 1 What would you recommend to Sebastian at this point?

Question 2 What would you recommend to Alfonso?

Experiential Exercises

1. Interview someone in your community who has grown up in a family business about the ways she or he has been trained or educated, both formally and informally, for entry into the business. Prepare a brief report, identifying whether he or she carried out the five responsibilities of the junior generation that were discussed in this chapter.

2. Interview a college student who has grown up in a family business about parental attitudes toward

his or her possible entry into the business. Submit a one-page report describing the extent of pressure on the student to enter the family business and the direct or indirect ways in which family expectations have been communicated.

3. Identify a family business and prepare a brief report on its history, including its founding, family involvement, and any leadership changes that have occurred.

4. Read and report on a biography or autobiography about a family in business.

Small Business & Entrepreneurship Resource Center

The Small Business & Entrepreneurship Resource Center offers complete small business management resources through a comprehensive database that covers all major areas of starting, operating, and maintaining a business from financing, management, marketing, accounting, taxes, and more. Go to www.cengagebrain.com and select the Longenecker text for more information on how to access this material.

1. After traveling with their young children and trying keep them happy with a small selection of toys that could be packed into suitcases or under the seat of a car, Alex and Jenny Johnston decided to open a toy rental store in the community where Alex's parents, Jim and Kay Johnston, had retired. In retirement communities, grandparents host grandchildren, but the kids get bored due to a lack of interesting toys. Granny's Attic is a private, family-owned business, with four members of the Johnston family investing equally and being equally responsible for the business. Jim Johnston spent 40 years as a CPA, and Kay was an elementary school teacher and principal for 35 years. Their son, Alex, is an attorney, and their daughter-in-law, Jenny, is a stay-at-home

mom. If you were advising the Johnston family about making Granny's Attic a success, what would you say?

2. Castellini Manufacturing is a small furniture company owned and operated by Tony and Tanya Castellini, husband and wife. Tony develops and designs products, while Tanya manages the company as president. Tanya had a successful career in retail before becoming half-owner of Castellini Manufacturing. She was an area manager of Trinkets and Things, a buyer for Youth Styles, and a merchandising assistant for the Sports Store. She has a degree in business from Penn State. Tony oversees design and development, assembly, and manufacturing. Tony designed furniture for Oaken Accents before becoming half owner of Castellini Manufacturing. He also has a business degree from Penn State. As co-preneurs, how can Tony and Tanya reap the benefits of working together while avoiding the dilemma of having differences of opinion carry over into their family life?

Sources: Heidi Denler, "Toy Rental Business: Granny's Attic," Michelle Lee (ed.), *Business Plans Handbook* (Detroit: Gale, 2012); and Gerald Rekve, "Home Furnishing Manufacturer: CASTELLINI MANUFACTURING," Lynn M. Pearce (ed.), *Business Plans Handbook*, Vol. 14 (Detroit: Gale, 2009).

Case 5

The Avedis Zildjian Company Inc. (P. 653)

The Avedis Zildjian Company case describes how the oldest family business in the United States has survived through the generations. In 1999, a female family member became CEO for the first time. The case addresses succession issues, innovation, and future challenges facing a family-owned business.

Alternative Cases for Chapter 5

Video Case 4, Two Men and a Truck, p. 651

Case 22, Pearson Air Conditioning & Service, p. 689

Endnotes

1. Stan Luxenberg, "America's Largest Family Companies," *Family Business Magazine*, Agenda 2011.

2. Frank Hoy and Pramodita Sharma, *The Entrepreneurial Family Business* (Upper Saddle River, NJ: Pearson Prentice Hall, 2010).

3. *Ibid.*

4. Margaret Littman, "Father Knows Best," *Entrepreneur*, March 2012, p. 19.

5. Leigh Buchanan, "Gary Speaks," *Inc.*, March 2012, pp. 34–37.

6. Carlson Company, www.carlson.com, accessed October 7, 2012.

7. Michael A. Klein, *Trapped in the Family Business* (Northampton, MA: MK Insights, 2012).

8. Tim Barnett, Kimberly Eddleston, and Franz Willi Kellermanns, "The Effects of Family Versus Career Role Salience on the Performance of Family and Nonfamily Firms," *Family Business Review,* Vol. 22, No. 1 (March 2009), pp. 39–52; and Frank Hoy and Pramodita Sharma, *Entrepreneurial Family Firms* (Boston: Prentice Hall, 2010).

9. Sarah E. Needleman, "Where Every Day Is Father's Day," *The Wall Street Journal*, http://online.wsj.com/article/SB100014240527023038231045 76391841138964286.html, accessed November 18, 2012; and Al's Lawn Care Products & Service Inc., www.alslawncare.com, accessed November 18, 2012.

10. Greg McCann, *When Your Parents Sign the Paychecks* (Indianapolis: JIST Works, 2007), p. 63.

11. Bill Glavin, Joe Astrachan, and Judy Green, *2007 American Family Business Survey* (Springfield, MA: Massachusetts Mutual Life Insurance Company, 2007).

12. Meg Cadoux Hirshberg, "Breaking Up's Not Hard to Do," *Inc.,* November 2010, p. 47.

13. Pia Chatterjee, "Making Beautiful Startups Together," *Business 2.0*, September 2007, pp. 42–44.

14. The Ken Blanchard Companies, www.kenblanchard.com, accessed November 18, 2012.

15. Barbara Spector, "America's Oldest Family Companies," www .familybusinessmagazine.com/index.php?/articles/single/americas _oldest_family_businesses_introduction, accessed October 29, 2012.

16. Avedis Zildjian Company, http://zildjian.com/, accessed October 31, 2010.

17. Stephanie Clifford, "Splitting Heirs," *Inc.,* August 2007, pp. 103–110.

18. Barbara Smit, *Sneaker Wars* (New York: HarperCollins, 2008).

19. Jan Sutcliffe, *Walt Disney* (Minneapolis: Lerner Publishing Group, 2009).

20. John L. Ward, "Family Humor," proceedings of the Fifth Annual Kellogg Family Business Invitational Conference, Evanston, IL, May 16–17, 2006, p. 45.

21. Meg Cadoux Hirshberg, *For Better or for Work* (Austin, TX: Greenleaf Book Group, 2012); Meghan Casserly, "Surviving the Startup: 20 Simple Rules for Relationship Success," *Forbes*, www.forbes.com/sites /meghancasserly/2012/03/05/surviving-startups-meg-cadoux-hirshberg -20-simple-rules-relationships/, accessed November 18, 2012; and Stonyfield Farm, www.stonyfield.com/, accessed November 18, 2012.

22. Meg Cadoux Hirshberg, "Minding the Kids," *Inc.,* Vol. 32, No. 2 (March 2010), pp. 39–41.

23. Per-Olaf Bjuggren and Johanna Palmberg, "The Impact of Vote Differentiation on Investment Performance in Listed Family Firms," *Family Business Review*, Vol. 23, No. 4 (December 2010), pp. 327–340.

24. David Lansky, "Family Meetings: Some Guidelines," www.efamilybusiness .com/index.cfm?md=Content&sd=ViewArticle&MatterID=18&WebArticle ID=590, accessed November 29, 2010.

25. Drew S. Mendoza, Stephen L. McClure, and John L. Ward, *Family Business Succession: The Final Test of Greatness*, 2nd ed. (Hampshire, England: Palgrave Macmillan, 2010).

26. Matthew Fogel, "A More Perfect Business," www.inc.com/magazine /20030801/familybusiness.html, accessed December 16, 2012.

27. Ken McCracken, Charlie Tee, and Matthew Woods, "Governance and Management," in Ian MacDonald and Jonathon Sutton (eds.), *Business Families and Family Businesses* (London: Globe Business Publishing, 2009), pp. 179–192.

28. Two Men and a Truck, www.twomen.com/mary-ellen-sheets, accessed November 29, 2010.

29. PriceWaterhouseCoopers, "Family Business Survey 2012," www.pwc.com /us/en/private-company-services/publications/2012-family-business -survey.jhtml, accessed November 19, 2012.

30. Barbara Spector, "Succession and Stewardship: Challenges for the Next Generation," *The Family Business Shareholder's Handbook* (Philadelphia: Family Business Publishing, 2008), p. 119.

31. Hoy and Sharma, *Entrepreneurial Family Firms, op. cit.*

32. Johnson Security Bureau, www.johnsonsecruitybureau.com, accessed November 19, 2012; and Adriana Gardella, "This Is Not Your Father's Company," http://boss.blogs.nytimes.com/2011/12/16/this-is-not -your-fathers-company/?scp=1&sq=This%20Is%20Not%20Your%20 Father%E2%80%99s%20Company&st=cse, accessed November 19, 2012.

33. For an extended discussion of various aspects of mentoring in the family firm, see Barbara Spector (ed.), *The Family Business Mentoring Handbook* (Philadelphia: Family Business Publishing Co., 2004). Only one of many resources on mentoring, this book contains articles outlining a number of proven mentoring strategies, as well as case examples of family companies that have used these approaches to achieve effective succession transitions. It addresses processes and strategies as they apply specifically to family businesses.

34. Greg McCann, "Cultivating Ownership in the Next Generation," in Spector, *The Family Business Shareholder's Handbook, op. cit.*, pp. 120–121.

35. Richard Salomon, "Setting a Standard for Future Generations," in Spector, *The Family Business Shareholder's Handbook, op. cit.*, p. 123.

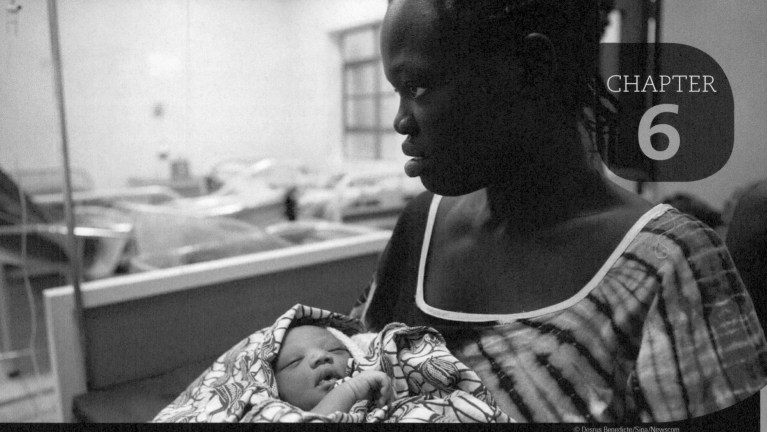

© Desrus Benedicte/Sipa/Newscom

The Business Plan: Visualizing the Dream

According to the World Health Organization (WHO), approximately 1,000 women die every day from preventable causes linked to pregnancy and childbirth. A full 99 percent of these deaths occur in developing countries, with women in poor rural communities most at risk. Most of these problems can be avoided through skilled care during childbirth.

Meg Wirth spent five years with Commons Capital, where she identified challenges in global health. Based on her research, Wirth founded Maternova in 2009 as a mission-driven, for-profit organization. The company adopted a two-pronged approach to driving revenue: (1) the aggregation and sales of select low-tech medical devices in a pioneering e-commerce marketplace, and (2) the addition of an innovative

In the SPOTLIGHT
Maternova
http://maternova.net

open-source platform, where health-care workers can connect globally.

Looking for capital to fund this new enterprise, Wirth and her small team entered business plan competitions and two startup incubators in hopes of gaining visibility and needed cash. In fact, entering business plan competitions has served as part of the team's overall bootstrapping strategy. In the process, they have discovered that the chance to present a business plan to the right audience makes entering these competitions a no-brainer.

OPEN
LOOKING
AHEAD

After studying this chapter, you should be able to...

6-1. Explain the purpose and objectives of business plans.

6-2. Give the rationale for writing (or not writing) a business plan when starting a new venture.

6-3. Describe the preferred content and format for a business plan.

6-4. Offer practical advice on writing a business plan.

6-5. Explain the concept and process for developing a firm's business model.

6-6. Identify available sources of assistance in preparing a business plan.

6-7. Maintain the proper perspective when writing a business plan.

Through their participation in business plan competitions, the Maternova team has garnered a number of benefits, including the following:

- Growth in business relationships and an expanded international network of partners
- Valuable press coverage nationally and internationally
- Annual compounded revenue growth of over 200 percent
- Positioning of the company on government contracts
- Expanded product lines and improved online capabilities to drive client revenue

The Maternova team credits using an online business-planning software called *LivePlan* for helping them turn their business model into a winning business plan. (*LivePlan* was developed by Palo Alto Software to walk an entrepreneur through the process of writing a plan, along with providing advice when needed.)

The Maternova team offers these tips for anyone considering entering a business plan competition:

- *Do your research:* It pays off to apply to competitions that are the best fit for your company.
- *Use good business plan software:* The format for your business plan should be very professional and help you easily convey business goals, current and future capabilities, and mission.
- *Know your audience:* Select an audience that will be aligned with your mission.

To find out about business plan competitions, you don't have to look far. Many universities and colleges with business and entrepreneurship programs sponsor them annually. Also, a large number of online resources provide directories and calendars of national and international competitions.

Sources: Written by Sherisa Aguirre, Senior Content Strategist, Palo Alto Software. Sources used include http://maternova.net/, accessed January 25, 2013; www.liveplan.com, accessed January 25, 2013; and www.bizplancompetitions.com, accessed January 25, 2013.

When you mention an idea for a new business to a friend who's also a business owner, she says, "You'll need to prepare a business plan." While the business idea sounds great, spending hours writing some formal document is not exactly your idea of fun, and you wonder if it is really necessary. After all, you know an entrepreneur who started and successfully grew a company based on an idea developed on the back of a napkin over dinner at a local restaurant. And isn't it true that the founders of such notable companies as Microsoft, Dell Computers, *Rolling Stone* magazine, and Calvin Klein all started their businesses without business plans?

6-1 AN OVERVIEW OF THE BUSINESS PLAN

LO 6-1

Explain the purpose and objectives of business plans.

To answer the question of whether or not you should write a business plan, you'll first need to understand its purpose and objectives, and that there is no one correct formula for preparing a business plan. Opportunities are so diverse in size as well as growth potential that no single plan will work in all situations. But, in general, a **business plan** is a document that outlines the basic concept underlying a business—specifically, what problem will be solved—and describes how you will execute your plan to solve the problem. A business plan can also be thought of as an entrepreneur's game plan. It gives shape to the dreams and hopes that have motivated the entrepreneur to take the startup plunge. The plan should lay out your basic idea for the venture and include descriptions of where you are now, where you want to go, and how you intend to get there. John Mullins, the author of *The New Business Road Test*, says that the following three key elements should be in every business plan:[1]

business plan
A document that outlines the basic concept underlying a business and describes how.

- A logical statement of a problem and its solution
- A significant amount of cold, hard evidence
- Candor about the risks, gaps, and assumptions that might be proved wrong.

Writing a business plan is an opportunity to assess if a good idea is also a good investment opportunity. It needs to provide evidence that your business can sell enough products or services to make a satisfactory profit. Also, as emphasized in Chapter 1, your personal aspirations and motivations deserve careful thought. *If the business does not align with your personal goals, you are not likely to succeed, and you certainly will not enjoy the journey.*

A business plan, if done well, is a tool to be used by company *insiders* for direction and to aid in the development of relationships with *outsiders* who could help the company achieve its goals. Exhibit 6.1 provides an overview of those who might have an interest in a business plan for a proposed venture.

The first group consists of the internal users of the plan: the entrepreneur and the new firm's management and employees. The business plan provides a framework that helps the entrepreneur and the management team focus on important issues and activities for the new venture. And it helps the entrepreneur communicate his or her vision to current and prospective employees of the firm.

The business plan can also be helpful with outsiders. To make the company successful, the entrepreneur must convince outsiders—prospective customers, suppliers, lenders, and investors—to become linked with the firm. Why should they do business with your startup, rather than with an established firm? They need evidence that you will be around in the future. Professor Amar Bhide at Tufts University, who conducts extensive research in strategy and entrepreneurship, explains, "Some entrepreneurs may have an innate capability to outperform their rivals, acquire managerial skills, and thus build a flourishing business. But it is difficult for customers (and others) to identify founders with these innate capabilities."[2]

6-2 WILL WRITING A PLAN MAKE A DIFFERENCE?

Will writing a business plan make a difference? That all depends. The justification often used for not writing a business plan goes something like this: "Companies that start up based on business plans are no more successful than those

LO
6-2

Give the rationale for writing (or not writing) a business plan when starting a new venture.

EXHIBIT

| 6.1 | Users of Business Plans |

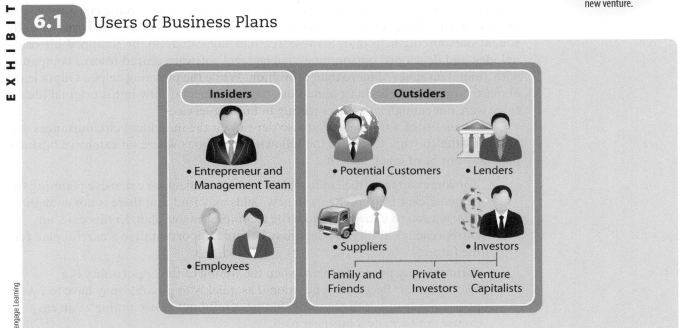

© Cengage Learning

that do not." It is true that studies attempting to measure the success of entrepreneurs with business plans against the success of those without them have produced mixed results. Some findings suggest a relationship; others find none.

6-2a The Balance Between Planning and Executing

Given what we know about companies that were started without business plans, having a plan is clearly not an absolute prerequisite for success. *But this simply tells us that the business plan is not the business.* Some entrepreneurs spend hours writing a 60-page business plan with another 50 pages of appendices but are not effective at executing the plan. In such cases, we can say confidently that writing the plan was a waste of time. Only if you effectively *execute* the business plan does it have a chance of making a difference. Thomas Stemberg, the founder of Staples, who later became a venture capitalist, says it well:

> *In my experience, entrepreneurs often confuse envisioning what a business will be with laying the foundation for what it could be. So they dream big dreams and construct detailed business plans, which is fine. But it's nowhere near as important as putting in place as early as humanly possible the people and systems that will carry them through their journey, no matter what unexpected directions changing markets or technology force them to take. To me, business plans are interesting chiefly as indications of how an entrepreneur thinks…. If you have the right management team and an exciting market, the rest will take care of itself.*[3]

Thus, an entrepreneur must find the right balance between planning and becoming operational. No matter how well your plan has been thought out, unexpected events will happen. One of the key attributes of a successful entrepreneur is adaptability, regardless of what the business plan says to do. Boxer, Mike Tyson, once commented, "Everybody has a plan until they get punched in the face." Starting a business can be a bit like a prizefight.[4] You plan, but then you have to adapt to the obstacles that will surely arise.

Vinay Gupta spent six months attending conferences, meeting with consultants, and writing a 60-page business plan before launching an outsourcing consulting firm for mid-sized businesses. It soon became clear that far fewer mid-sized firms actually sought outsourcing help than his research had suggested. So, he scrapped his original idea and developed outsourcing-management software geared toward companies with annual revenues of more than $1 million. While the planning helped Gupta learn about the industry, it hadn't pointed out the fundamental flaw in his original idea—there were not enough customers willing to buy his services.[5]

The benefits of a business plan also depend on the individual circumstances surrounding the startup. Consider the following situations where an extensive business plan may not be of much benefit:

- For some startups, the environment is too turbulent for extensive planning to be beneficial. Entrepreneurs in new fields may find that there is not enough information to allow them to write a comprehensive plan. In this case, an entrepreneur's ability to adapt may be more important than a careful plan for the future.

- Planning may pose a problem when the timing of the opportunity is a critical factor. Becoming operational as quickly as possible may have to take priority over in-depth planning, but be careful not to use timing as an easy excuse not to write a business plan.

- A business may be so constrained by a shortage of capital that planning is not an option. In a study of firms identified by *Inc.* magazine as the fastest-growing firms in the United States, Amar Bhide concluded that planning may not make sense for some companies: "Capital-constrained entrepreneurs cannot afford to do much prior analysis and research. The limited profit potential and high uncertainty of the opportunity they usually pursue also make the benefits low compared to the costs."[6]

Although there are times when writing a carefully documented business plan is not needed, more often than not entrepreneurs resist writing a business plan because they lack the discipline to do so. Frank Moyes, a successful entrepreneur who for many years taught courses on business planning at the University of Colorado, offers the following observation:

> *Perhaps the most important reason to write a business plan is that it requires you to engage in a rigorous, thoughtful and often painful process that is essential before you start a venture. It requires you to answer hard questions about your venture. Why is there a need for your product/service? Who is your target market? How is your product/service different than your competitor's? What is your competitive advantage? How profitable is the business and what are the cash flows? How should you fund the business?*[7]

So, a business plan may not be needed in some situations, especially if you are the only person working in the business. But if you want to capture the future potential of an opportunity and make a difference in lives, planning is the rule, not the exception. Remember Ewing Marion Kauffman's words from Chapter 1, "You should not choose to be a common company. It is your right to build an uncommon company if you can."[8] Building an uncommon company requires thoughtful planning and then execution. Deciding what you want the business to be and to accomplish is vital and deserves considerable thought. Above all, be intentional, which comes from having to justify your beliefs and assumptions about your startup—that is what a business plan is all about.

START UP

TOOLS

Should You Write a Business Plan?
Before you decide not to write a plan, give some thought to the following question. A lender or other investor demands to see a business plan before investing. Wouldn't you require the same before investing your personal savings or, even more important, your family's savings?

6-2b What Form Will the Business Plan Take?

For most entrepreneurs, the issue is not *whether* to plan but *how* to engage in effective planning, given the situation. As already observed, different situations lead to different needs—and to different levels of planning.

The real issue is more about deciding how to plan and the form that the planning will take. In starting a business, an entrepreneur has to make some trade-offs, as preparing a plan requires time and money, two resources that are always in short supply. At the extremes, an entrepreneur has two basic choices when it comes to writing a business plan: the *short plan* or the *comprehensive plan*.

THE SHORT PLAN As noted earlier, extensive planning may be of limited value when there is a great amount of uncertainty in the environment or when timing is a critical factor in capturing an opportunity. A **short plan** is an abbreviated form of the traditional business plan that addresses only the most important issues in a firm's success, such as:

- The problem needing to be solved for customers
- The strategy

short plan
An abbreviated business plan that presents only the most important issues and projections for the business.

- Measures used to gauge success
- Milestones to be met
- Tasks and responsibilities of the team
- The business model (to be described shortly)

A short plan will frequently satisfy an investor who is trying to determine if he or she has any interest in investing in the business and eventually seeing a full-length plan. When presenting a business plan to investors, the short plan is typically in the form of a PowerPoint presentation, limited to no more than 15 to 30 minutes. If investors continue to have an interest, they most likely will request an in-depth business plan, including all the supporting material. (See Appendix 6A, which can be found at www.cengage-brain.com, for a short PowerPoint presentation to prospective investors by the founders of Boomerang's Hand-Held Aussie Pies.)

THE COMPREHENSIVE PLAN When entrepreneurs and investors speak of a business plan, they are usually referring to a **comprehensive plan**, a complete business plan that provides an in-depth analysis of the critical factors that will determine a firm's success or failure, along with all the underlying assumptions. Such a plan is beneficial when you are describing a new opportunity (startup), facing significant change in the business or the external environment (changing demographics, new legislation, developing industry trends), or explaining a complex business situation. In the remainder of this book, we will be discussing the comprehensive business plan.

6-3 PREPARING A BUSINESS PLAN: THE CONTENT AND FORMAT

LO 6-3

Describe the preferred content and format for a business plan.

comprehensive plan
A complete business plan that provides an in-depth analysis of the critical factors that will determine a firm's success or failure, along with all the underlying assumptions.

Like writing a term paper or report, getting started writing a business plan is usually the hardest part. Recall that in Chapter 3, we emphasized the importance of first conducting a feasibility analysis and then writing a business plan only if your idea seems viable. Three elements must be evident from the feasibility analysis before you move on to the business plan: (1) strong market potential, (2) an attractive industry, and (3) the right individual or team to execute the plan.[9]

Once the feasibility analysis is completed, it's time to begin the process of writing a business plan. For this, two issues are of primary concern: (1) the content and format of the plan, and (2) the effectiveness of the written presentation.

When considering the content of a business plan, continue to think first and foremost about the opportunity, as identified by your feasibility analysis. Strategies and financial plans will follow naturally if the opportunity is a good one. The business plan should give thorough consideration to the following basic factors (presented graphically in Exhibit 6.2):

1. The *opportunity* should reflect the potential and the attractiveness of the market and industry.

2. *Critical resources* include not just money, but also human assets (suppliers, accountants, lawyers, investors, etc.) and hard assets (accounts receivable, inventories, etc.). An entrepreneur should think of ways to minimize the resources necessary for startup.

3. The *entrepreneurial team* must possess integrity, and breadth and depth of experience.

4. The *financing structure*—how a firm is financed (debt versus equity) and how the ownership percentage is shared by the founders and investors—will have a significant impact on an entrepreneur's incentive to work hard. The goal is to find a win-win deal.

5. The *context* (or external factors) of an opportunity includes the regulatory environment, interest rates, demographic trends, inflation, and other factors that inevitably change but cannot be controlled by the entrepreneur.

Thus, the business plan will need to demonstrate that the entrepreneur has pulled together the right opportunity, the right resources, the right people, and the right financing structure, all within the right context. Admittedly, there will always be uncertainties and ambiguities; the unanticipated is bound to happen. But by making decisions about these key factors, you can be sure that you are dealing with the important issues, and this will help you in determining the appropriate content to include in the plan.

There is no single format to be followed in writing a business plan. However, investors want to see a format that is familiar to them. So, you do not want to write a business plan that is fundamentally different from what they are accustomed to seeing. Deviating significantly from this format would be a mistake.

EXHIBIT 6.2 A Business Plan Identifies the Key Factors for Success

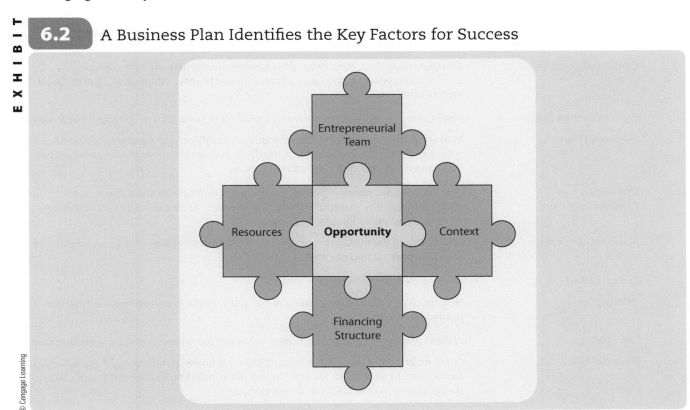

© Cengage Learning

Exhibit 6.3 summarizes the major sections common to most business plans. A brief overview of each of these sections follows.[10] (Chapters 7 through 13 take an in-depth look at each section of the business plan.)

6-3a Cover Page

The cover page should contain the following information:

- Company name, address, phone number, fax number, and website
- Tagline and company logo
- Name of contact person (preferably the president) with mailing address, phone number, fax number, and e-mail address
- Date on which the business plan was prepared
- If the plan is being given to investors, a disclaimer that the plan is being provided on a confidential basis to qualified investors only and is not to be reproduced without permission
- Number of the copy (to help keep track of how many copies have been given out)

EXHIBIT

6.3 Abbreviated Business Plan Outline

Section Heading	Information Provided
Cover Page	Company name, logo, tagline, contact information, copy number, date prepared, and disclaimer (if needed)
Table of Contents	Listing of the key sections of the business plan
Executive Summary	One- to three-page overview of the significant points, intended to motivate the reader to continue reading
Industry, Target Customer, and Competitor Analysis	Key characteristics of the industry, including the different segments, and the niche where you plan to compete
Company Description	Company objectives, the nature of the business, its primary product or service, its current status (startup, buyout, or expansion) and history (if applicable), and the legal form of organization
Product/Service Plan	Justification for why people will buy the product or service, based on its unique features
Marketing Plan	Marketing strategy, including the methods of identifying and attracting customers, selling approach, type of sales force, distribution channels, types of sales promotions and advertising, and credit and pricing policies
Operations and Development Plan	Operating or manufacturing methods, operating facilities (location, space, and equipment), quality-control methods, procedures to control inventory and operations, sources of supply, and purchasing procedures
Management Team	Description of the management team, outside investors and/or directors, and plans for recruiting and training employees
Critical Risks	Any known inherent risks in the venture
Offering	How much capital the entrepreneur needs and how the money will be used (section used to attract investors)
Exit Strategy	Ways an investor—and the entrepreneur—may be able to harvest their business investment
Financial Plan	Contemplated sources of financing; any historical financial statements, if available; pro forma financial statements for three to five years, including income statements, balance sheets, cash flow statements, and cash budgets
Appendix of Supporting Documents	Various supplementary materials and attachments to expand the reader's understanding of the plan

6-3b Table of Contents

The table of contents provides a sequential listing of the sections of the plan, with page numbers. This allows the reader to spot-read the plan (a common practice) rather than reading it from front to back. Exhibit 6.4 presents the table of contents of the business plan for BlueAvocado, a company that produces environmentally friendly, reusable shopping bags. (The firm was featured as the Spotlight company in Chapter 1. The complete business plan is available in Appendix A online at www.CengageBrain.com.) While the table of contents for BlueAvocado's business plan does not follow exactly the general format presented in Exhibit 6.3, it has much of the same content.

6-3c Executive Summary (Overview)

The **executive summary**, or **overview**, is often thought to be the most important section of the business plan. If you don't catch the readers' attention in the executive summary, most likely they will not continue reading. At the very outset, it must convey a clear and concise picture of the proposed venture and, at the same time, create a sense of excitement regarding its prospects. This means that it must be written—and, if necessary, rewritten—to achieve clarity and create interest. Even though the executive summary comes at the beginning of the business plan, it provides an overview of the entire plan and should be written last. In no more than three (preferably two) pages, the executive summary should include the following subsections:

- A description of the opportunity
- An explanation of the business concept
- An industry overview
- The target market
- The competitive advantage you hope to achieve in the market

EXHIBIT 6.4 Table of Contents for BlueAvocado Business Plan

Table of Contents	
1.0	Introduction
2.0	The Company
3.0	Market Opportunity
4.0	Product Overview
5.0	Lauren Conrad Partnership
6.0	Technology Initiatives
7.0	Supply Chain
8.0	Marketing/Sales Plan
9.0	Financial Overview
10.0	People
11.0	Sustainability Issues
12.0	Conclusion/Contact Appendices

Source: BlueAvocado, Co. Reprinted with permission.

executive summary (overview)
A section of the business plan that conveys a clear and concise overall picture of the proposed venture and creates interest in the venture.

- The economics of the opportunity
- The management team
- The amount and purpose of the money being requested (the "offering"), if you are seeking financing

Depending on the situation and the preference of the entrepreneur, the executive summary may be in the form of a synopsis or a narrative. A *synopsis* briefly covers all aspects of the business plan, giving each topic relatively equal treatment. It relates, in abbreviated fashion, the conclusions of each section of the completed business plan. Although it is easy to prepare, the synopsis can be rather dry reading for the prospective investor.

Because the *narrative* tells a story, it can convey greater excitement than the synopsis. However, composing an effective narrative requires a gifted writer who can communicate the necessary information and generate enthusiasm without crossing the line into hype. A narrative is more appropriate for businesses that are breaking new ground with a new product, a new market, or new operational techniques. It is also a better format for ventures that have one dominant advantage, such as holding an important patent or being run by a well-known entrepreneur. Finally, the narrative works well for companies with interesting or impressive backgrounds or histories.

Exhibit 6.5 shows the overview that appears in BlueAvocado's business plan. It was written in the narrative form.

6-3d Company Description

The company description informs the reader of the type of business being proposed, the firm's objectives, where the firm is located, and whether it will serve a local or international market. If the business is already in existence, its history should be included. In many cases, legal issues—especially those concerning the firm's form of organization—are addressed in this section of the plan. (Legal issues regarding the form of organization are discussed at length in Chapter 8.) In writing this section, the entrepreneur should answer the following questions:

1. When and where is the business to be started?
2. What is the history of the company?
3. What are the firm's objectives?
4. What changes have been made in structure and/or ownership?
5. In what stage of development is the firm—for example, seed stage or full product line?
6. What has been achieved to date?
7. What is the firm's competitive advantage, or what we might call distinctive competence?
8. What are the basic nature and activity of the business?
9. What is its primary product or service?
10. What customers will be served?
11. What is the firm's form of organization—sole proprietorship, partnership, limited liability company, corporation, or some other form?
12. What are the current and projected economic states of the industry?
13. Does the firm intend to sell to another company or an investment group? Does it plan to be a publicly traded company, or do the owners want to transfer ownership to the next generation of the family?

6.5 BlueAvocado Overview

BlueAvocado™ is a woman-owned, sustainable business with a vision to invite millions to reduce their environmental impact and carbon footprint with eco-chic lifestyle products. In 2008, the company introduced a patent-pending reusable shopping bag system, the gro-pak® to the US market to eliminate the use of 1,000 plastic bags and avoid 35 pounds of carbon dioxide emissions annually. The gro-pak includes 5 stylish, machine-washable bags that include ventilated bags for produce, insulated bag for hot/cold items, and durable hauling bags that collapse into one kit. Since then, the company has expanded its portfolio, offering reusable lunch kits and continues to invest in next-generation products that reduce our environmental waste and inspire joy.

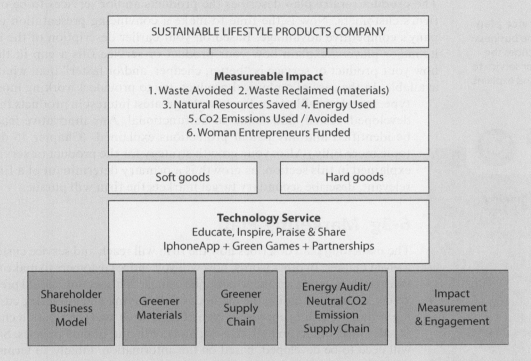

With its unique stylish kit and commitment to sustainability, BlueAvocado has successfully captured mind share and market share throughout the US. The company and its products have been featured in *Real Simple, Better Homes & Gardens, InStyle, PARADE, CNN, MSNBC, Shape, Parenting*, and *USA Today*. The company has received numerous accolades, including a Top Pick at the International Home & Housewares show in the Chicago Tribune (2009) and a top "Green Product Finalist" at the Natural Products Expo (2009). In June 2010, BlueAvocado was featured in *Fast Company* as a green company to watch, after being selected as a finalist at the Sustainable Brands Conference Innovation Open. In August 2010 it was a sustainable brand finalist at the New York International Gift Fair. BlueAvocado products are available in more than 700 retail outlets throughout the US states, Canada, and Italy at key retailers, including The Container Store, Sur La Table, Whole Foods, Amazon, and the Home Shopping Network.

Source: BlueAvocado, Co. Reprinted with permission.

6-3e Industry, Target Customer, and Competitor Analysis

The primary purpose of this section is to present the opportunity and demonstrate why there is a significant market to be served. You should describe the broader industry in which you will be competing, including industry size, growth rate, fundamental trends, and major players. Next, identify the different segments of the industry, and then describe in detail the niche in which you plan to participate. It is tempting to begin describing your own company at this point. Instead, you should provide the context of the opportunity and demonstrate that a market segment is being underserved. There will be an opportunity later to introduce your product and/or service.

The next step is to describe your target customers in terms of demographics and psychological variables, such as their values, their attitudes, and even their fears. The more clearly you can identify your customer, the more likely it is that you will provide a product or service that is actually in demand. Finally, knowing who your customer is will serve as the basis for understanding who your competitors are. You should analyze competitors in terms of product or service attributes that they offer or are failing to provide.

6-3f Product/Service Plan

The **product/service plan** describes the products and/or services to be offered to the firm's customers. Now is the time to make a convincing presentation of your company's competitive advantage. Based on your earlier description of the industry and its major players, explain how your product or service fills a gap in the market or how your product or service is "better, cheaper, and/or faster" than what is currently available. In the case of a physical product, try to provide a working model or prototype. Investors will naturally show the greatest interest in products that have been developed, tested, and found to be functional. Any innovative features should be identified and any patent protections explained. (Chapter 15 discusses this topic more fully.) Also, your growth strategy for the product or service should be explained in this section, as growth is a primary determinant of a firm's value. If relevant, describe secondary target markets the firm will pursue.

6-3g Marketing Plan

The **marketing plan** describes how the firm will reach and service customers within a given market. In other words, how will you entice customers to make the change to your product or service and to continue using it? This section should present the marketing strategy, including the methods of identifying and attracting customers; pricing strategies, selling approach, type of sales force, and distribution channels; types of sales promotions and advertising; and credit and pricing policies. Sales forecasts will need to be developed, based on this information. Finally, in terms of servicing the customer, this section should describe any warranties, as well as planned product updates. (Chapter 7 provides in-depth coverage of the marketing plan.)

6-3h Operations and Development Plan

The **operations and development plan** offers information on how the product will be produced or the service provided. Here, you will explain how the operations will contribute to the firm's competitive advantage—that is, how its operations will create value for the customer. This section discusses such items as location and facilities, including how much space the business will need and what type of equipment it will require. It is important to describe the choice between in-house production and outsourcing in order to minimize costs. Remember, however, that you should never plan to outsource a part of operations that contributes to your competitive advantage. The operations and development plan should also explain the firm's proposed approach to assuring quality, controlling inventory, and using subcontractors for obtaining raw materials. (Read Chapters 9 and 21 for further discussion the issues to be addressed in this section.)

6-3i Management Team

Prospective investors look for well-managed companies. Of all the factors they consider, the quality of the management team is paramount. Some investors say that they would rather have an "A" management team and a "B" product or service than a "B" team and an "A" product. But it can also be said that the right management in the wrong market is likely headed for failure. For success, you must have a good team working in a growth market.

The **management team** section should detail the proposed venture's organizational structure and the backgrounds of those who will fill its key positions. Ideally, a well-balanced management team—one that includes financial and marketing expertise as well as production experience and innovative talent—will already be in place. Managerial experience in related enterprises and in other startup situations is particularly valuable. (The factors involved in preparing the management team section are discussed in greater detail in Chapter 8.)

Having a team that brings different skills and experiences to the task of starting a new business can make the difference between failure or success.

6-3j Critical Risks

The business plan is intended to tell a story of success, but there are always risks associated with starting a new venture. Thus, the plan would be incomplete if it did not identify the risks inherent in the venture. The **critical risks** section identifies the potential pitfalls that may be encountered by an investor. Common risks include a lack of market acceptance (customers don't buy the product as anticipated), competitor retaliation, longer time and higher expenses than expected to start and grow the business, inadequate financing, and government regulations.

6-3k Offering

If the entrepreneur is seeking capital from investors, an **offering** should be included in the plan to indicate clearly how much money is needed and when. It is helpful to convey this information in a *sources and uses table* that indicates the type of financing being requested (debt or equity) and how the funds will be used. For example, for a firm needing $500,000, including any money borrowed and the founder's investment, the sources and uses table for the first year might appear as follows:

Sources:	
Bank debt	$100,000
Equity:	
New investors	300,000
Founders	100,000
Total sources	$500,000
Uses:	
Product development	$125,000
Personnel costs	75,000
Working capital:	
Cash	20,000
Accounts receivable	100,000
Inventory	80,000
Machinery	100,000
Total uses	$500,000

management team
A section of the business plan that describes a new firm's organizational structure and the backgrounds of its key players.

critical risks
A section of the business plan that identifies the potential risks that may be encountered by an investor.

offering
A section of the business plan that indicates to an investor how much money is needed, and when and how the money will be used.

If equity is being requested, the entrepreneur will need to decide how much ownership of the business she or he is willing to give up—not an easy task in most cases. Typically, the amount of money being raised should carry the firm for 12 to 18 months—enough time to reach some milestones. Then, if all goes well, it will be easier and less costly to raise more money later. (These issues will be explained in greater detail in Chapters 11 and 12.)

6-3l Exit Strategy

If a firm is using the business plan to raise equity financing, investors will want to know the possible options for cashing out of their investment, or what is called the **exit strategy**. Most equity investors absolutely will not invest in a startup or early-stage business if they are not reasonably confident that at some time in the future there will be an opportunity to recover their principal investment, plus a nice return on the investment. (In Chapter 13, we will explain the issue of crafting an exit strategy, or what we call the *harvest*.)

6-3m Financial Plan

The **financial plan** presents financial forecasts as pro forma statements. This section of the business plan should show that the proposed business can be self-supporting and, ultimately, profitable. To do this, the entrepreneur needs to be honest with himself or herself, and fully consider the company's financial outlook.

Pro forma statements, which are projections of the company's financial statements, should be presented for at least three years and possibly up to five years. The forecasts ideally include balance sheets, income statements, and statements of cash flows on an annual basis for three to five years, as well as cash budgets on a monthly basis for the first year and on a quarterly basis for the second and third years. It is vital that the financial projections be supported by well-substantiated assumptions and explanations of how the figures have been determined. And as Rudy Garza, a venture capitalist in Austin, Texas, explains, "While I may not have much confidence in the entrepreneur's financial forecasts, the financial plan helps me understand the entrepreneur's thought processes about the opportunity. That is very important in my estimation."[11]

While all the financial statements are important, the statement of cash flows deserves special attention, because a business can be profitable but fail if it does not produce positive cash flows. A well-prepared statement of cash flows identifies the sources of cash—that is, how much will be generated from operations and how much will be raised from investors. It also shows how much money will be devoted to investments in such areas as inventories and equipment. The statement of cash flows should clearly indicate how much cash is needed from lenders and prospective investors and for what purpose. (The preparation of pro forma statements and the process of raising needed capital are discussed in Chapters 11 and 12.)

6-3n Appendix of Supporting Documents

The appendix should contain various supplementary materials and attachments to expand the reader's understanding of the plan. These supporting documents include

exit strategy
A section of the business plan that focuses on options for cashing out of the investment.

financial plan
A section of the business plan that projects the company's financial position based on well-substantiated assumptions and explains how the figures have been determined.

Pro forma statements
Projections of a company's financial statements for up to five years, including balance sheets, income statements, and statements of cash flows, as well as cash budgets.

any items referenced in the text of the business plan, such as (1) the résumés of the key investors and owners/managers, (2) photographs of products, facilities, and buildings (3) professional references, (4) marketing research studies, (5) pertinent published research, (6) and signed contracts of sale.

The fact that it appears at the end of the plan does not mean that the appendix is of secondary importance. The reader needs to understand the assumptions underlying the premises set forth in the plan. And nothing is more important to a prospective investor than the qualifications of the management team.

Each chapter in this section (Part 3) of the book, with the exception of Chapter 10, ends with a special set of exercises to walk you through the process of writing a business plan. These exercise sets consist of questions to be thoughtfully considered and answered. They are entitled "The Business Plan: Laying the Foundation," because they deal with issues that are important to starting a new venture and provide guidelines for preparing the different sections of a business plan.

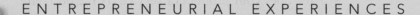

ENTREPRENEURIAL EXPERIENCES

Living the Dream

Accelerated Ventures

A large number of colleges and universities, including Baylor University, offer business plan competitions. Baylor also has the *Accelerated Ventures* program, where selected teams of students are provided seed capital to start actual companies. The program enables them to start real companies and receive actual ownership in the businesses they found.

As of December 2012, all twelve of the companies that were started earlier in the year were still in operation, and more than half of the students had chosen to run their businesses as their primary career pursuit after graduation. A number of the teams have also attracted various sponsors from the local and regional community. These sponsors have provided valuable resources to the young entrepreneurs through advertising and marketing assistance, office space, and much more.

Below are profiles of two of the twelve groups of students who have participated in the program.

Whol-E: The founders of Whol-E seek to educate the planet on alkaline hydration. Their water boasts a pH of

10.4, making it one of the most alkaline ionized waters on the market. But it doesn't stop there. It also has chelated minerals essential for body function and well-being. With a scientifically proven blend of calcium, magnesium, sodium, potassium, and phosphorus, Whol-E water provides the most complete hydration possible. Their slogan, "Be Happy. Be Healthy. Be Whol-E," invites consumers to join with them in the movement to educate the planet on alkaline hydration.

My Wedding Connector: This online resource recommends elite vendors in the wedding industry by region, and puts those vendors in direct contact with brides-to-be. Visitors to the website request free quotes from the best local wedding photographers, cake designers, videographers, venues, and more. While many wedding directories simply list all local vendors, My Wedding Connector's vendors are notified of the leads to their business and are given contact information of interested buyers. The founders seek to connect engaged couples with quality local wedding professionals for a stress-free way to plan a wedding.

6-4 ADVICE FOR WRITING A BUSINESS PLAN

An effective written presentation ultimately depends on the quality of the under-lying business opportunity. Remember, *the plan is not the business*. A poorly conceived new venture idea cannot be rescued by a good presentation. However, a good concept may be destroyed by a presentation that fails to communicate effectively. Below are recommendations that will help you avoid some of the common mistakes.

6-4a Analyze the Market Thoroughly

In analyzing the market for your product or service, you must answer some basic questions. Investors and lenders require answers to these questions, and so should you.

- What is your target market?
- How large is the target market?
- What problems concern the target market?
- Are any of these problems greater than the one you're addressing?
- How does your product or service fix the problem?
- Who will buy your product or service?
- How much are they willing to pay for it?
- Why do they need it?
- Why would they buy from you?
- Who are your competitors?
- What are their strengths and weaknesses?

As we have already said, your presentation should be the result of evidence-based statements. Nowhere in the business plan is it more important to provide hard evidence to support your claims than when presenting your analysis of the market. Gathering secondary data about the market is important, but if you are not out talking to prospective customers, then your analysis has no credibility.

Be prepared to revise your plan based on what you learn from customers. Eric Ries, an entrepreneur and author of *The Lean Startup*, recommends an iterative process summarized as the *build-measure-learn loop*. You begin small, try it out in the market, then make changes based on what you learn from customers. Ries contends that if you don't learn quickly about a plan's core assumptions through inexpensive data-driven experiments, the traditional business plan is a waste of time.[12]

Finally, understand that everyone has competitors. Saying "We have no competition" is almost certain to make readers skeptical. You must show in your plan where your business will fit in the market and what your competitors' strengths and weaknesses are. If possible, include estimates of their market shares and profit levels.

6-4b Provide Solid Evidence for Any Claims

Factual support must be supplied for any claims or assurances made. In short, the plan must be believable. *Think of your assumptions and original beliefs not as facts, but as hypotheses to be tested.*

Page after page of detailed computer-generated financial projections suggest—intentionally or unintentionally—that the entrepreneur can predict with great accuracy what will happen. Experienced investors know this isn't the case. They want to know what is behind the numbers, as this allows them to see how the entrepreneur thinks and if he or she understands the key factors that will drive success or failure. To determine this information, investors often ask a common question: "What is your business model?" This key question will be discussed later in the chapter.

6-4c Think Like an Investor

Many small firms do not seek outside capital, except in the form of small loans. But whether or not you are preparing a business plan in order to seek outside financing, you would benefit from understanding the world as an investor sees it—that is, you should think as an investor thinks. As Jeffrey Bussgang, who has been both an entrepreneur and a venture capitalist, advises, "You should think like [an investor] and act like an entrepreneur."[13] In this way, you bring to the analysis both the energy of the entrepreneur and the discipline of an investor.

At the most basic level, prospective investors have a single goal: to maximize potential return on an investment through cash flows that will be received, while minimizing the risk they are taking. Even investors in startups who are thought to be risk takers want to minimize their exposure to risk. For one thing, they look for ways to shift risk to others, usually to the entrepreneur. Given the fundamentally different perspectives of the investor and the entrepreneur, the important question becomes "How do I write a business plan that will satisfy what a prospective investor wants to know?" There is no easy answer, but two facts are relevant: Investors have a short attention span, and certain features attract investors while others repel them.

Because most investors receive so many business plans, they cannot possibly read them all in any detailed fashion. To illustrate, one of the authors delivered an entrepreneur's business plan to a prospective investor with whom he had a personal relationship. The plan was well written, clearly identifying a need. While the investor was courteous and listened carefully, he made a decision not to consider the opportunity in a matter of five minutes. A quick read of the executive summary did not spark his interest, and the discussion quickly changed to other matters.

Furthermore, investors are more *market-oriented* than *product-oriented*, realizing that most patented inventions never earn a dime for the inventors. The essence of the entrepreneurial process is to identify new products or services that meet an identifiable customer need. Thus, it is essential for the entrepreneur to appreciate investors' concerns about target customers' responses to a new product or service and to reach out to prospective customers.

6-4d Don't Hide Weaknesses—Identify Potential Fatal Flaws

One difficult aspect of writing a business plan is effectively dealing with problems or weaknesses—and every business has them. An entrepreneur, wanting to make a good impression, may become so infatuated with an opportunity that he or she cannot see potential fatal flaws.

For instance, an entrepreneur might fail to ask, "What is the possible impact of new technology, e-commerce, or changes in consumer demand on the proposed venture?" If there are weaknesses in the plan, the investors will find them. At that point, an investor's question will be "What else haven't you told me?" The best way to properly handle weaknesses is to consider thoroughly all potential issues, to be open and

© mast3r/Shutterstock.com

straightforward about those issues, and to have an action plan that effectively addresses any problems. To put it another way, *integrity matters*.

6-4e Maintain Confidentiality

When presenting your business plan to outsiders (especially prospective investors), prominently indicate that all information in the plan is proprietary and confidential. Number every copy of the plan, and account for each outstanding copy by requiring all recipients of the plan to acknowledge receipt in writing.

When a startup is based on proprietary technology, be cautious about divulging certain information—for example, the details of a technological design or the highly sensitive specifics of a marketing strategy—even to a prospective investor.

While you should be cautious about releasing proprietary information, *do not become fixated on the notion that someone may take your idea and beat you to the market with it*. Remember, the plan is not the key to your success; your execution is what matters! If someone can "out-execute" you, then you may not be the right person to start the business.

6-4f Pay Attention to Details

Paying attention to the details may seem minor to you but likely is not to others who read the plan to decide whether to be associated with the firm. The following suggestions will help you attend to the "little things":

1. *Use good grammar.* Nothing turns off a reader faster than a poorly written business plan. Find a good editor, and then review and revise, revise, revise.

2. *Limit the presentation to a reasonable length.* The goal is not to write a long business plan, but to write a good business plan. People who read business plans appreciate brevity and view it as an indication of your ability to identify and describe in an organized way the important factors that will determine the success of your business. In all sections of your plan, especially the executive summary, get to the point quickly.

3. *Go for an attractive, professional appearance.* To add interest and aid readers' comprehension, make liberal but effective use of visual aids, such as graphs, exhibits, and tabular summaries. The plan should be in a three-ring loose-leaf binder to facilitate future revisions, as opposed to being bound like a book and printed on shiny paper with flashy images and graphs.

4. *Describe your product or service in lay terms.* Entrepreneurs with a technical background tend to use jargon that is not easily understood by individuals who are unfamiliar with the technology or the industry. That is a big mistake! Present your product and/or service in simple, understandable terms, and avoid the temptation to use too much industry jargon.

If you choose to ignore these recommendations, the business plan will detract from the opportunity itself, and you may lose the chance to capture it. We suggest that you have trusted and experienced entrepreneurs critique the business concept and the effectiveness of the business plan presentation; they know the minefields to avoid.

6-5 UNDERSTANDING THE BUSINESS MODEL[14]

LO
6-5

Explain the concept and process for developing a firm's business model.

The term *business model* has become a popular phrase in business, especially among entrepreneurs and their investors. Ramon Casadesus-Masanell and Joan Ricart at Harvard University emphasize the significance of developing an effective business model:

> There has never been so much interest in business models as there is today; seven out of 10 companies are trying to create innovative business models, and 98 percent are modifying existing ones, according to a recent survey.... Strategy has been the primary building block of competitiveness over the past three decades, but in the future, the quest for sustainable advantage may well begin with the business model.[15]

While it is widely discussed in business circles, business models are little understood by most businesspeople in small and large firms alike. Author Joan Magretta defined a business model as "the story that tells how an enterprise will work."[16] Basically, a **business model** explains in a systematic and clear way how a business will generate profits and cash flows, given a firm's (1) revenue sources, (2) cost and expense structures, (3) the required size of investment in the business, and (4) the sources of risk. It is the "nuts and bolts" of how a business will make money. As such, it measures the anticipated results of the core business decisions and all the trade-offs that determine a company's profits and cash flows. It is important to understand that the eventual success or demise of a business model depends in large part on how the business model interacts with those of competitors in the industry.

Some business models are easy to understand. A firm produces a product and/or service and sells it to customers; if sales exceed expenses, the company makes a profit. Other models are less straightforward. For instance, television broadcasting is part of a complex network of distributors, content creators, advertisers, and viewers. How the eventual profits and cash flows are created and shared depends on a number of competing factors, which are not always clear at the outset. Furthermore, e-commerce is giving rise to new business models. Consider auctions, one of the oldest ways for setting prices for such things as agricultural commodities and antiques. Today, the Internet has popularized the auction model and broadened its use to a wide array of goods and services.

In a startup, where there is so much uncertainty, a business model forces the entrepreneur to be more disciplined and avoid wishful thinking about financial projections. When it comes time to create a business plan, the entrepreneur needs to know the drivers that will determine the firm's future profits and cash flows. Thus, a business model can provide the best evidence on whether a business concept can be translated into a viable, profitable business and how large of an investment will be required to make it happen. Exhibit 6.6 provides a basic overview of the process for building a business model for a company with three sources of revenues.

As shown at the top of Exhibit 6.6, an entrepreneur should begin by developing the venture's mission statement, its strategic goals, and the principles that are to guide its operations. Four key elements then make up the business model: (1) the revenue model, (2) cost structures, (3) maximum investment, and (4) business model risk. Let's briefly consider each element.

6-5a Revenue Model

The **revenue model** defines the nature and types of a company's sources of revenue. Before discussing the more common types of revenue models, it is essential to first understand whether the business model is based on a single or a hybrid *revenue stream*

START UP

RESOURCES

Business Models
For a comprehensive and easy-to-read source about business models, see Alexander Osterwalder and Yves Pigneur, *Business Model Generation* (Hoboken, NJ: John Wiley & Sons, 2010).

business model
An analysis of how a firm plans to create profits and cash flows given its revenue sources, its cost structures, the required size of investment, and sources of risk.

revenue model
A component of the business model that identifies the different types of revenue streams a firm expects to receive.

EXHIBIT **6.6** Basic Business Model Framework

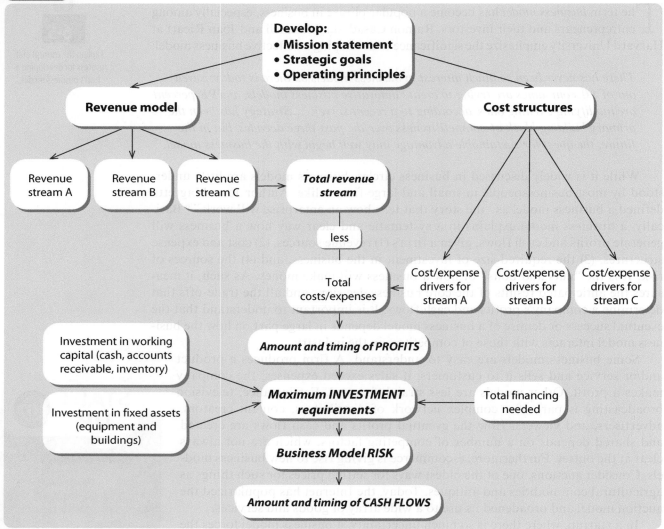

© Cengage Learning

Types of revenue streams typically include (1) a *single stream*, where a firm's revenues come from a single product or service, (2) *multiple streams*, where a business realizes revenues from a combination of multiple products and services, (3) *interdependent streams*, where a company's revenues come from selling one or more products and/ or services as a way to generate revenues from other products and/or services, such as printers and printer cartridges, and (4) *loss leader*, where one or several revenue streams are sold at a loss in order to create sales in a profitable revenue stream.

The more common types of revenue models include the following:

- *Volume or unit-based revenue model.* Customers pay a fixed price per unit in exchange for a product or service.

- *Subscription/membership revenue model.* Customers pay a fixed amount at regular intervals, prior to receiving a product or service.

- *Advertising-based revenue model.* Customers pay only a fraction of the true value of the product or service.

- *Licensing revenue model.* Customers pay a one-time licensing fee to be able to use or resell the product or service.

When forecasting revenues, an entrepreneur will find that the answers to a number of key questions can provide the rationale for future sales estimates:

1. Who are your most likely customers?
2. How are they different from the general population?
3. What events will trigger the need or desire for your type of product or service?
4. When will this trigger occur? Can it be predicted?
5. How will customers make decisions on whether or not to buy your product or service?
6. What will be the key decision factors?
7. How will your product or service compare to that of the competition on these key factors?
8. Will these differences be meaningful to the customer?
9. Are these differences known to the customer?
10. How can your product or service be exposed to your most likely potential customers?

Additional questions should be developed based on the product or service, the industry, and the customers being served. Your understanding of the answers to such questions will help in making financial projections that are believable and achievable. But even if the questions don't provide the answers you were hoping for, you had better understand why your financial projections may not be realized and what needs to be done to improve the forecasts.

6-5b Cost Structures

Cost structures consist of the drivers that affect a firm's costs and expenses. These expenses can vary with either time or volume of sales. Common types of cost drivers include unit cost of goods sold, payroll, marketing activities, administrative costs, and marketing expenses. Expenses and costs that are useful in making projections are frequently classified as follows:

- *Fixed costs.* Costs that do not vary at all with volume, such as rent expenses.
- *Variable costs.* Expenses that vary directly and proportionately with changes in volume, for example, sales commissions.
- *Semi-variable costs.* Expenses that include both variable costs and fixed costs. These costs vary in the direction of, but not proportionately with, changes in the volume of sales, such as certain types of payrolls that change as a firm becomes larger but do not change proportionally with sales changes.

The core business decisions and trade-offs of a company's business model can be better understood if the entrepreneur knows the key cost drivers, in both type and importance, as well as whether any of the cost drivers provide a strategic cost advantage.

6-5c Maximum Investment

Another key component of a business model is the **maximum investment** required for a company to achieve positive cash flows and profits. It not only includes the amount of investment in hard assets, such as equipment and buildings but, equally important, the amount of working capital in the form of operating cash, accounts receivable, and inventory.

Once a business model has been developed and used to provide pro forma financial statements, it is worthwhile for an entrepreneur to change the different assumptions being made to identify the factors that are critical to the company's success. Only

cost structures
A component of the business model that provides a framework for estimating the nature and types of costs and expenses a firm may incur.

maximum investment
A component of the business model that provides estimates of the types and amounts of investment required to achieve positive profits and cash flows.

by doing so will the business model yield its greatest value in determining if the venture has a reasonable chance of success. (This explanation of a business model will be illustrated further in Chapter 11, when we look at projecting a firm's financial requirements.)

6-5d Managing Business Model Risk

When designing a business model, an entrepreneur must anticipate **business model risk**; that is, she or he must consider changes that can affect the level of risk in a given business model and how the model can adjust to them. It is not enough to have a business model that provides a competitive advantage given the present circumstances. Consideration must be given as to how the model will be affected by changing circumstances, such as changes in demand for and supply of your products or services, or how the competition responds to your entry into the market. In other words, an

business model risk
A component of the business model that identifies risks in the model and how the model can adjust to them.

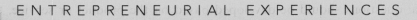

ENTREPRENEURIAL EXPERIENCES

Living the Dream

Changing the Business Model

When Jen Falso and Lisa Assenza met in 1998, the two quickly became great friends and came up with the idea of painting furniture and glassware to make some extra cash. Falso and Assenza began selling their HuePhoria hand-painted goods at local fundraisers and through word of mouth to get their hobby-turned-business into motion. At the outset, they painted wine glasses that were more creative than what they were seeing in stores—and more durable.

After selling more than 5,000 glasses in two years, they hit a point where they could not keep up with demand. Also, they could not offer the glasses to retail stores at a wholesale price that would keep them in business. So, in 2005 they partnered with another friend, Kathy Berger, to help HuePhoria glassware make the leap into mass production.

The partners thought they had a winning business model, selling their product to upscale gift boutiques. But when U.S. consumer spending shriveled in 2008, upscale gift stores that sold products like HuePhoria's drastically cut back their inventory.

The founders had been attending about four gift shows a year in New York and Atlanta in order to reach prospective buyers. Each show cost the four-employee

company about $10,000. In previous years, the shows had paid off through dozens of new store orders. But by late 2008, Berger estimated that nearly 40 percent of their independent retail customers were struggling financially, with some even filing for bankruptcy. So, they decided to focus on selling through HuePhoria's website. They added a greater variety of partyware products and developed relationships with customers that were willing to manage the inventory and ship product on-demand. It was a way to expand product offerings without the expense of housing the inventory.

And they looked for ways to capitalize on HuePhoria's loyal customer base of moms. They launched the "Ball Mom" program, which offered women startup kits so that they could host parties and sell HuePhoria products for 25 percent of sales.

The new strategies paid off. Sales in the first quarter of 2011 increased 72 percent from the previous year. The partners credit their improved financials to their willingness to try a new business model when the old one wasn't working.

Sources: Based on www.huephoria.com; and Kelly K. Spors, "Banking on a New Business Model," *Entrepreneur*, April 25, 2011, www.entrepreneur.com /article/219530, accessed January 5, 2013.

entreprenuer must continually be anticipating what can go wrong with the firm's business model and what can be done if it does.

6-6 RESOURCES FOR BUSINESS PLAN PREPARATION

LO
6-6
Identify available sources of assistance in preparing a business plan.

When writing a business plan, it is important to know what works and what does not work. A variety of books, websites, and computer software packages offer extensive guidance on preparing a business plan, even step-by-step instruction. (A listing of some of these materials appears in Appendix 6B, which you can find at www.cengagebrain.com.) Such resources can be invaluable. However, resist the temptation to adapt an existing business plan for your own use.

6-6a Computer-Aided Business Planning

A number of business plan software packages have been designed to help an entrepreneur think through the important issues in starting a new company and organize her or his thoughts to create an effective presentation. Maternova, our Spotlight company, used LivePlan, a leading software package. But while they can facilitate the process, software packages in and of themselves are not capable of producing a unique plan. In fact, they can actually limit an entrepreneur's creativity and flexibility if not used properly.

One of the authors recently received a business plan that was almost 80 pages long. When questioned about the excessive length, the entrepreneur responded, "By the time I answered all the questions in the software package, that's how it turned out." Only you as the entrepreneur can say what should and should not be in the plan. If you don't know, then you are not ready to write one. Remember, there is no simple procedure for writing a business plan, no "magic formula for success." If you recognize their limitations, however, you can use business plan software packages to facilitate the process.

6-6b Professional Assistance in Business Planning

Company founders are most notably doers—and evidence suggests that they had better be, if the venture is to be successful. But some small business owners lack the breadth of experience and know-how, as well as the inclination, needed for planning.

A small business owner who is not able to answer tough questions about the business may need a business planning advisor—someone accustomed to working with small companies, startups, and owners who lack financial management experience. Such advisors include accountants, marketing specialists, attorneys (preferably with an entrepreneurial mindset), incubator organizations, small business development centers (SBDCs), and regional and local economic development offices.

An investment banker or financial intermediary can draw up a business plan as part of a firm's overall fundraising efforts. Also, a well-chosen advisor will have contacts you lack and may even

© Fuse/Jupiter Images

help you reformulate your business plan entirely. However, using a business planning advisor will cost you. They frequently charge an hourly fee as well as a contingency percentage based on the amount raised.

The Small Business Administration (SBA) and the Service Corps of Retired Executives (SCORE) can also be helpful. Both organizations have programs to introduce business owners to volunteer experts who will advise them. SCORE, in particular, is a source for all types of business advice, such as how to write a business plan, investigate market potential, and manage cash flows. SCORE counselors work out of local chapters throughout the United States and can be found by contacting the national office.

Another source of assistance is the FastTrac Entrepreneurial Training Program sponsored by the Kauffman Center for Entrepreneurial Leadership in Kansas City, Missouri. Located in universities, chambers of commerce, and SBDCs across the country, the FastTrac program teaches the basics of product development, concept recognition, financing strategies, and marketing research, while helping entrepreneurs write a business plan in small, well-organized increments.

You definitely have options when it comes to getting business plan assistance. However, if you choose to hire a consultant, the following suggestions may help you avoid some costly mistakes:[17]

- *Get referrals.* Ask colleagues, acquaintances, and professionals such as bankers, accountants, and lawyers for the names of business plan consultants they recommend. A good referral goes a long way to easing any concerns you may have. In any case, few consultants advertise, so referrals may be your only option.

- *Look for a fit.* Find a consultant who is an expert in helping businesses like yours. Ideally, the consultant should have lots of experience with companies of similar size and age in related industries. Avoid general business experts or those who lack experience in your particular field.

- *Check references.* Get the names of at least three clients the consultant has helped to write business plans. Call the former clients and ask about the consultant's performance. Was the consultant's final fee in line with the original estimate? Was the plan completed on time? Did it serve the intended purpose?

- *Get it in writing.* Have a legal contract outlining the consultant's services. It should state in detail the fee, when it will be paid, and under what circumstances. And make sure you get a detailed written description of what the consultant must do to earn the fee. Whether it's an hourly rate or a flat fee isn't as important as each party's knowing exactly what's expected of them.

Keep in mind that securing help in business plan preparation does not relieve the entrepreneur of the responsibility of being the primary planner. Her or his ideas remain essential to producing a plan that is realistic and believable.

6-7 KEEPING THE RIGHT PERSPECTIVE

Writing a business plan should be thought of as an ongoing process and not as the means to an end. In fact, when it comes to writing a plan, the process is just as important as the final outcome. Some entrepreneurs have difficulty accepting this, given their orientation to "bottom-line" results. But this point deserves to be repeated: *Writing a business plan is primarily an ongoing process and only secondarily the means to an outcome. The process is just as important as—if not more so than—the finished product.*

Part 3 Developing the New Venture Business Plan

While your plan will represent your vision and goals for the firm, it will rarely reflect what actually happens. With a startup, too many unexpected events can affect the final outcome. Thus, a business plan is in large part an opportunity for an entrepreneur and management team to think about the potential key drivers of a venture's success or failure. Anticipating different scenarios and the ensuing consequences can significantly enhance an entrepreneur's adaptability—an essential quality, when so much is uncertain.

Now that you are aware of the role of the business plan in a new venture, you are ready to move on to Chapters 7 through 13, which will closely examine each of the plan's components.

6-1. Explain the purpose and objectives of business plans.

- A business plan is a document that sets out the basic idea underlying a business and describes related startup considerations. It should describe where the entrepreneur is presently, indicate where he or she wants to go, and outline how he or she proposes to get there.

- A business plan has three key elements: (1) a logical statement of a problem and its solution, (2) a significant amount of hard evidence, and (3) candor about the risks, gaps, and assumptions that might be proved wrong.

- The objectives of a business plan include assessing whether a good idea is also a good investment opportunity, determining whether the business aligns with your personal goals, providing direction for insiders, and convincing outsiders to enter into a relationship with the company.

6-2. Give the rationale for writing (or not writing) a business plan when starting a new venture.

- Studies attempting to test whether entrepreneurs who have business plans do better than those who don't have produced mixed results. Some findings suggest a relationship; others do not.

- What ultimately matters is not writing a plan, but implementing it. The goal is to execute the plan.

- An entrepreneur must find the right balance between planning and becoming operational.

- The benefits of a business plan depend on the individual circumstances surrounding a startup.

- Most entrepreneurs need the discipline that comes with writing a business plan. A written plan helps to ensure systematic, complete coverage of the important factors to be considered in starting a new business.

- A business plan helps an entrepreneur communicate his or her vision to current and prospective employees of the firm.

- By enhancing the firm's credibility, a business plan serves as an effective selling tool with prospective customers and suppliers, as well as investors.

- A short plan is an abbreviated form of a traditional business plan that presents only the most important issues and projections for the business.

- A comprehensive plan is a complete business plan that provides an in-depth analysis of the critical factors that will determine a firm's success or failure, along with the underlying assumptions.

6-3. Describe the preferred content and format for a business plan.

- The opportunity, the critical resources, the entrepreneurial team, the financing structure, and the context of an opportunity are all interdependent factors that should be given consideration when thinking about the content of a business plan.

- Key sections of a business plan are the (1) cover page, (2) table of contents, (3) executive summary (overview), (4) company description, (5) industry, target customer, and competitor analysis, (6) product/service plan, (7) marketing plan, (8) operations and development plan, (9) management team, (10) critical risks, (11) offering, (12) exit strategy, (13) financial plan, and (14) appendix of supporting documents.

6-4. Offer practical advice on writing a business plan.

- Analyze the market thoroughly.
- Provide solid evidence for any claims.

- Understand how investors think.
- Don't hide weaknesses; try to identify potential fatal flaws.
- Maintain confidentiality, when appropriate.
- Pay attention to the details.

6-5. Explain the concept and process for developing a firm's business model.

- The term *business model* has become a popular phrase in business, especially among entrepreneurs and their investors.
- The business model measures the anticipated results of the core business decisions and all the trade-offs that determine a company's profits and cash flows.
- Understanding the business model is especially important in a startup, where there is so much uncertainty.
- A business model explains in a systematic and clear way how a business will generate profits and cash flows, given its revenue sources, its cost structures, the required size of investment, and its sources of risk.

6-6. Identify available sources of assistance in preparing a business plan.

- A variety of books, websites, and computer software packages are available to assist in the preparation of a business plan.
- Professionals with planning expertise, such as attorneys, accountants, and marketing specialists, can provide useful suggestions and assistance in the preparation of a business plan.
- The Small Business Administration (SBA), the Service Corps of Retired Executives (SCORE), and the FastTrac Entrepreneurial Training Program can also be helpful.

6-7. Maintain the proper perspective when writing a business plan.

- Writing a business plan should be thought of as an ongoing process and not the means to an end.
- The plan rarely reflects what actually happens with the business.
- A business plan can be viewed as an opportunity for the entrepreneur and the management team to think about the potential key drivers of a venture's success or failure.

Key Terms

business model p. 159

business model risk p. 162

business plan p. 142

comprehensive plan p. 146

cost structures p. 161

critical risks p. 153

executive summary p. 149

exit strategy p. 154

financial plan p. 154

management team p. 153

marketing plan p. 152

maximum investment p. 161

offering p. 153

operations and development plan p. 152

product/service plan p. 152

pro forma statements p. 154

revenue model p. 159

short plan p. 145

Discussion Questions

1. What do entrepreneurs usually mean when they talk about a business plan?

2. When should you write a business plan? When might it not be necessary or even advisable to write a plan?

3. What are the two types of business plans? In what situation(s) would you use each type of plan?

4. Why is the executive summary so important?

5. How might an entrepreneur's perspective differ from that of an investor in terms of the business plan?

6. Describe the major sections to be included in a business plan.

7. If the income statement of a financial plan shows that the business will be profitable, why is there a need for a statement of cash flows?

8. What are some common mistakes that entrepreneurs make in writing a business plan?

9. Investors are said to be more market-oriented than product-oriented. What does this mean? What is the logic behind this orientation?

10. What is a business model, and why is it important?

You Make the Call

Situation 1

You want to start an online clothing store and need information about the size of the market for the marketing section of your business plan. From a Google search, you found that Americans spent $18.3 billion online for apparel, accessories, and footwear last year and that the forecast for their spending on these items in the coming year is $22.1 billion. You have also researched publicly traded apparel companies, like Gap, to discover trends in online sales for these firms.

Question 1 Why is your research thus far inadequate for what you need to know?

Question 2 Do you think it will be difficult to find all the information you need?

Question 3 What else might you do to find the necessary information?

Situation 2

You recently visited with a friend who knew you had taken a small business course when you attended college. During your visit, she made the comment, "I plan to open a business this summer. I won't be applying for a bank loan to fund this company, so I don't have a business plan. Do I need one?"

Question 1 What would you need to know in order to answer her question?

Question 2 If she decides to write a business plan, what advice would you give her?

Situation 3

John Martin and John Rose decided to start a new business to manufacture noncarbonated soft drinks. They believed that their location, close to high-quality water, would give them a competitive edge. Although Martin and Rose had never worked together,

Martin had 17 years of experience in the soft drink industry. Rose had recently sold his firm and had funds to help finance the venture; however, the partners needed to raise additional money from outside investors. They spent almost 18 months developing their business plan. The first paragraph of their executive summary reflected their excitement:

> The "New Age" beverage market is the result of a spectacular boom in demand for drinks with nutritional value from environmentally safe ingredients and waters that come from deep, clear springs free of chemicals and pollutants. Argon Beverage Corporation will produce and market a full line of sparkling fruit drinks, flavored waters, and sports drinks that are of the highest quality and purity. These drinks have the same delicious taste appeal as soft drinks while using the most healthful fruit juices, natural sugars, and the purest spring water, the hallmark of the "New Age" drink market.

With the help of a well-developed plan, the two men were successful in raising the necessary capital to begin their business. They leased facilities and started production. However, after almost two years, the plan's goals were not being met. There were cost overruns, and profits were not up to expectations.

Question 1 What problems might have contributed to the firm's poor performance?

Question 2 Although several problems were encountered in implementing the business plan, the primary reason for the low profits turned out to be embezzlement. Martin was diverting company resources for personal use, even using some of the construction materials purchased by the company to build a house. What could Rose have done to avoid this situation? What are his options after the fact?

Experiential Exercises

1. Appendix A, which can be found at www.cengagebrain.com, provides most of the business plan for BlueAvocado. Based on what you learned in this chapter, write a one-page report on what you like about BlueAvocado's plan and what you do not like.

2. A former chef wants to start a business to supply temporary kitchen help (such as chefs, sauce cooks, bakers, and meat cutters) to restaurants in need of staff during busy periods. Prepare a one-page report explaining which section or

   sections of the business plan would be most crucial to this new business and why.

3. Suppose that you wish to start a tutoring service for college students in elementary accounting courses. List the benefits you would realize from preparing a written business plan.

4. Interview a person who has started a business within the past five years. Prepare a report describing the extent to which the entrepreneur engaged in preliminary planning and his or her views about the value of business plans.

Small Business & Entrepreneurship Resource Center

The Small Business & Entrepreneurship Resource Center offers complete small business management resources through a comprehensive database that covers all major areas of starting, operating, and maintaining a business from financing, management, marketing, accounting, taxes, and more. Go to www.cengagebrain.com and select the Longenecker text for more information on how to access this material.

1. An area of great interest is the ownership of student-generated intellectual property. Students involved in business plan courses and competitions have immense potential to conceive and prototype product, process, system, and service concepts within the university environment. Faculty members facilitate the innovation process in the context of their employment as university professionals. This research focuses on who actually owns the intellectual property generated. Surveys show that students feel that they own their ideas and are reluctant to share ownership with their faculty mentors. Do you agree that students own student-generated intellectual property? Explain.

2. Combating the decline in fresh potato sales and the "yield plateau" are the two key priorities outlined by the Potato Council in its latest three-year plan. The draft "Business Plan 2013–2016" said one problem was identifying land of sufficient quality to produce good yields. In fresh potatoes, shoppers were trading down to economy lines as shopping budgets came under pressure. "We have what we believe to be a well-balanced and highly focused plan that takes the industry on a journey towards profitability and sustainability," said chairman Allan Stevenson. The plan is open for consultation. Explain how writing this business plan is an ongoing process and how it offers the Potato Council an opportunity to anticipate different scenarios and consequences.

Sources: Silvernagel, Craig, Richard R. Schultz, Steven B. Moser and Marie Aune. "Student-Generated Intellectual Property: Perceptions of Ownership by Faculty and Students." *Journal of Entrepreneurship Education* 12. (Annual 2009): 13(21); and Richard Ford, "Potato Council Sets Out Recovery Plan," *Grocer*, November 24, 2012, p. 34.

Case 6

Hyper Wear®, Inc. (P. 655)

Hyper Wear was founded in 2008 to participate in the functional fitness market, along with such recognized brands as CrossFit and Zumba. The market had been growing at an 11 percent annual rate from 2007 to 2012. In 2011, the firm raised money from outside investors and hired Denver Fredenburg as its CEO. By 2012, sales were approximately $1 million, and the firm needed more money to fund its growth. Fredenburg wrote a business plan to be used in raising the needed money.

Alternative Cases for Chapter 6

Case 3, The Kollection, p. 648
Video Case 6: KindSnacks [website only]

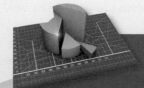

Business Plan

LAYING THE FOUNDATION

Part 3 (Chapters 6 through 13) deals with issues that are important in starting a new venture. This chapter presented an overview of the business plan and its preparation. Chapters 7 through 13 focus on major segments of the business plan, such as the marketing plan, the organizational plan, the location plan, the financial plan, and the exit plan, or what we call the harvest.

After you have carefully studied these chapters, you will have the knowledge you need to prepare a business plan.

Since applying what you study facilitates learning, we have included at the end of each chapter in Part 3 (except Chapter 10), a list of important questions that need to be addressed in preparing a particular section of a business plan. Appendix 6B, which can be found at www.cengagebrain.com, includes lists of books, websites, and software packages useful in preparing business plans.

Company Description Questions

Now that you have learned the main concepts of business plan preparation, you can begin the process of creating a business plan by writing a general company description. In thinking about the key issues in starting a new business, respond to the following questions:

1. When and where is the business to start?
2. What is the history of the company?
3. What are the company's objectives?
4. What changes have been made in structure and/or ownership?
5. In what stage of development is the company?
6. What has been achieved to date?
7. What is the company's distinctive competence?
8. What are the basic nature and activity of the business?
9. What is its primary product or service?
10. What customers will be served?
11. What is the company's form of organization?
12. What are the current and projected economic states of the industry?
13. Does the company intend to become a publicly traded company or an acquisition candidate, or do the owners want to transfer ownership to the next generation of the family?

Endnotes

1. John Mullins, *The New Business Road Test* (London: Financial Times Prentice Hall, 2010).
2. Amar Bhide, *The Origin and Evolution of New Businesses* (New York: Oxford University Press, 2000), p. 53.
3. Thomas Stemberg, "What You Need to Succeed," *Inc.*, Vol. 29, No. 1 (January 2007), pp. 75–77.
4. Taken from San Hogg, "Pull No Punches," *Entrepreneur*, July 2012, p. 74.
5. Kelly Spors, "Do Start-Ups Really Need Formal Business Plans?" *The Wall Street Journal*, January 9, 2007, p. B9.
6. Bhide, *op. cit.*, p. 70.
7. Stephen Lawrence and Frank Moyes, "Writing a Successful Business Plan," http://leeds-faculty.colorado.edu/moyes/html/resources.htm, accessed October 10, 2012.
8. Personal communication with Ewing Marion Kauffman, March 2004.
9. An alternative framework for a feasibility analysis is provided by Frank Moyes, a former professor at the University of Colorado, at http://leeds-faculty.colorado.edu, accessed January 5, 2012.
10. Portions of the content in this section draw on Andrew Zacharakis, Stephen Spinelli, and Jeffry A. Timmons, *Business Plans That Work* (New York: McGraw-Hill, 2011).
11. Personal conversation with Rudy Garza, November 29, 2012.
12. Eric Ries, *The Lean Startup: How Today's Entrepreneurs Use Continuous Innovation to Create Radically Successful Businesses* (New York: Crown Business, 2011).
13. Jeffrey Bussgang "Think Like a VC, Act Like an Entrepreneur," *Bloomberg Businessweek*, www.businessweek.com/stories/2008-08-26/think-like-a-vc-act-like-an-entrepreneur, accessed December 2, 2012.
14. The explanation of business models in this section draws heavily from a variety of sources, primarily Richard G. Hamermesh, Paul W. Marshall, and Taz Pirmohamed, "Note on Business Model Analysis for the Entrepreneur," Harvard Business School (9-802-048), January 22, 2002; Karan Girotra and Serguel Netesskine, How to Build Risk into Your Business Model," *Harvard Business Review*, May 2011, pp. 100–105; Peter Weill, Thomas W. Malone, and Thomas G. Apel, "The Business Models Investors Prefer," MIT Sloan Management, Vol. 52, No. 4 (2011), pp. 17–19; Vivek Wadhwa, "Before You Write a Business Plan," *Bloomberg Businessweek*, www.businessweek.com/stories/2008-01-07/before-you-write-a-business-planbusinessweek-business-news-stock-market-and-financial-advice, accessed September 30, 2012; Michael Rappa, "Business Models on the Web," www.digitalenterprise.org/models/models.html, accessed February 10, 2012; Vivek Wadhwa, "Countdown to Product Launch (Part II)" *Bloomberg Businessweek*, May 12, 2006, www.businessweek.com/print/smallbiz/content/may2006/sb20060512_948264.htm, accessed January 31, 2011; Karen E. Klein, "Do You Really Need a Business Plan?" *Bloomberg Businessweek*, www.businessweek.com/stories/2008-03-12/do-you-really-need-a-business-plan-businessweek-business-news-stock-market-and-financial-advice, accessed December 6, 2012; and Rob Adams, "Taking the Trouble to Research Your Market," *Bloomberg Businessweek*, www.businessweek.com/smallbiz/content/oct2004/sb20041020_9945.htm, accessed October 14, 2012.
15. Ramon Casadesus-Masanell and Joan E. Ricart, "How to Design a Winning Business Model," *Harvard Business Review*, January–February 2011, p. 100.
16. *Ibid.*, p. 101.
17. "Get Help with Your Plan," *Entrepreneur*, March 2, 2001, www.entrepreneur.com/startingabusiness/businessplans/article38314.html, accessed August 14, 2010.

© Monkey Business Images/Shutterstock.com

CHAPTER 7

The Marketing Plan

OPEN
LOOKING
AHEAD

When you are serious about starting your own business, you can find many sources of help. One of those sources is Startup Professionals, who purpose is "to help startup founders find necessary resources, mentoring, and expertise to get their company incorporated, build a business plan, file patents, and find funding."

Recognizing the number of startups in the country each year and the number of failures, Martin Zwilling and co-founder, Ernst Gemassmer, launched Startup Professionals, Inc., in 2008. Both partners had extensive experience at executive levels and in venture creation. Having been a CEO, president, and general manager of various electronics and computer companies, Gemassmer, board chairman of Startup Professionals, had also founded manufacturing and consulting enterprises. Zwilling, its CEO, had a degree in accounting, but began his career in sales and marketing with IBM, where he advanced steadily. He moved on to

In the SPOTLIGHT
Startup Professionals
www.startupprofessionals.com

leadership positions in other firms, gaining experience in software development and applications, eventually serving as managing partner of Southwest Software Ventures and Consulting.

© Martin Zwilling Photo Courtesy of Startup Professionals, Inc.

But why take on a new venture when both men were already successful in their careers? The founders of Startup Professionals understood that there was "pain" in the marketplace, and they could see it in the numbers. Each year, about 750, 000 new companies are started in the United States. Most never seek financing from investors to grow their businesses. But of those that do, only 1 out of 100 new businesses is successful in obtaining funds from angel groups and venture capitalists. While it is healthy for an economy to have many startups each year, it is the startups with significant growth potential (sometimes called *gazelles*) that have the biggest impact on job generation and wealth formation. The partners formed Startup Professionals in the belief that many of the 99 percent of companies that weren't getting capital were capable of high growth but needed help in developing their growth strategies and in presenting themselves to investors.

Startup Professionals offers a range of products and services to clients, including the Early Stage Startup Starter Kit, which contains a sample business plan, executive presentation, and financial model. The company also helps clients with incorporating a business, preparing a full business plan, and more. Zwilling recognized that startups need to avoid the mistakes that entrepreneurs typically make when they initiate and grow their companies. While the products provided by Startup Professionals help business owners solve many of their problems, the core of the enterprise is the advisors that mentor clients. This service, called Executive Mentoring, is designed through a custom agreement. Zwilling has described the advisors as "luminaries in the fields of banking, accounting, recruiting, venture financing, and legal representation." A key lesson that small business owners must learn is how to build a network of contacts that can help them test ideas, find customers, locate financing, and so on. Zwilling's plan drew from the networks that he and Gemassmer had formed over the years to organize a group of associates who provide services to the entrepreneurs who contact them for assistance.

The plan for attracting entrepreneurs stemmed from Zwilling's expertise in software applications and his grasp of Internet marketing. While many businesses use Facebook, Linkedin, Twitter, and another social media to promote their products and service, Zwilling instead proved that he could become a regular contributor to *Forbes* and The Huffington Post, as well as being published in *Inc.*, *Entrepreneur*, *Fortune*, and many other business magazines. These tactics attract many prospects to the Startup Professionals website, resulting in customers for the company's products and services. By practicing what they were coaching, Zwilling and Gemassmer made their own business a success, while helping others grow theirs.

Sources: Based on www.startupprofessionals.com, accessed December 8, 2012; www .sba.gov, accessed December 8, 2012; and www.facebook.com/startuppro, accessed December 8, 2012.

Entrepreneurs are often passionate about their product or service. They can talk about its features all day, but they sometimes ignore the fact that customers buy a product or service because they get a benefit from it. Owners need to put themselves in the shoes of their customers and figure out why customers buy what they do. In other words, they need a marketing plan.

The features that we discuss in this chapter are important components of any well-written plan. First, it is appropriate to answer a few basic questions about marketing:

- How can marketing be defined for a small business?
- What are the components of an effective marketing philosophy?
- What does having a consumer orientation imply about a business?

7-1 WHAT IS SMALL BUSINESS MARKETING?

The practice of marketing has a much broader scope than simply selling a product or service. And it is not just advertising. It consists of many activities, some of which occur even before a product is produced and made ready for distribution and sale. Entrepreneurs need to be sure that a market exists for what they plan to sell before they ever launch their companies.

Small business marketing consists of those business activities that direct the creation, development, and delivery of a bundle of satisfaction from the creator to the targeted user. This definition emphasizes the benefits customers will gain from a

LO
7-1

Describe small business marketing.

small business marketing
Business activities that direct the creation, development, and delivery of a bundle of satisfaction from the creator to the targeted user.

ACTION

product or service. It may be helpful to view a product or service as having three levels: core product/service, actual product/service, and augmented product/ service. The **core product/service** is the fundamental benefit or solution sought by customers. The **actual product/service** is the basic physical product and/or service that delivers those benefits. The **augmented product/service** is the basic product and/or service plus any extra or unsolicited benefits to the consumer that may prompt a purchase. In the case of shoes, for example, the core product is basic protection for the feet; the actual product is the shoe itself. The augmented product might be increased running speed, greater comfort, or less wear and tear on feet and legs. Augmentation could also be reflected in how the customer feels. Do the shoes offer style, prestige, social identity?

Because smaller firms generally cannot afford the talented marketing experts that large corporations employ, they conduct many trials and endure numerous problems. A marketing plan will not enable you to avoid all missteps, but it can drastically reduce the number of errors by forcing you to think through available options, given the resources you have.

To be successful today, a business must solve someone's "pain." In other words, a business provides a bundle of satisfaction to its customers, not merely the tangible product or intangible service that is the focus of the exchange. By offering a bundle of satisfaction, you don't just make a sale, you retain your customers, resulting in multiple purchases over time. Jessica Kim's first business was BabbaCo, selling baby products on the Internet. When Kim discovered that her customers continued to visit her Facebook page even though their children were out of diapers, she added another business. BabbaBox is a subscription service that delivers activities and storybooks to customers each month. Now, parents post photos of their kids and exchange parenting tips on the BabbaBox Facebook page.[1]

7-1a Marketing Philosophies Make a Difference

A firm's marketing philosophy determines how its marketing activities are developed in the marketing plan and used to achieve business goals. Three different marketing perspectives guide most small businesses: the production-oriented, sales-oriented, and consumer-oriented philosophies. The first two philosophies are used most often, as they are associated with the experience and aptitudes of entrepreneurs who may have a manufacturing or technology-based background, or who may have had a career in sales.

A *production-oriented philosophy* emphasizes the product as the single most important part of the business. The firm concentrates resources on developing the product in the most efficient manner, even if promotion, distribution, and other marketing activities are slighted. This is the classic "build a better mousetrap" approach. But do customers understand what makes your mousetrap special, or do they even know about your product? On the other hand, a *sales-oriented philosophy* deemphasizes production efficiencies and customer preferences in favor of a focus on "pushing product." Achieving sales goals becomes the firm's highest priority. In contrast, a firm adopting a *consumer-oriented philosophy* believes that everything, including production and sales, centers on the consumer and his or her needs. The result: All marketing efforts begin and end with the consumer.

7-1b A Consumer Orientation—The Right Choice

Consumer orientation is put into practice by applying a two-stage process that underlies all marketing efforts: identifying customer needs and satisfying those needs. This simple formula is easy to understand but difficult to implement, given the competitive

core product/service
The fundamental benefit or solution sought by customers.

actual product/service
The basic physical product and/or service that delivers those benefits.

augmented product/ service
The basic product and/or service plus any extra or unsolicited benefits to the consumer that may prompt a purchase.

nature of most markets. But this is what it takes for a company to be successful in the long term. We strongly recommend that all new businesses begin with a consumer orientation. Customer satisfaction is not a means to achieving a goal—it *is* the goal!

Why don't all firms adopt a consumer orientation when the benefits seem so obvious? The answer lies in three key factors. First, if there is little or no competition and if demand exceeds supply, a firm is tempted to emphasize production. This is usually a short-term situation, however, and concentrating on production to the exclusion of marketing can lead to disaster in due time.

Second, an entrepreneur may have a strong background in production or in selling but be weak other areas. It is natural for an owner to play to his or her strength. Third, some small business owners are simply too focused on the present. What is "hot" today may not be hot five years from now. The better course of action is to identify ways to please consumers in the long term.

We can find many examples of both production- and sales-oriented philosophies that generate short-term success. However, a consumer orientation not only recognizes production efficiency goals and professional selling but also adds concern for customer satisfaction. In effect, a firm that adopts a consumer orientation incorporates the best of each marketing philosophy.

Once a small firm makes a commitment to a customer orientation, it is ready to develop a marketing strategy to support this goal. Marketing activities include taking the steps necessary to locate and describe potential customers—a process called **market analysis**. Marketing activities also encompass product and/or service, pricing, promotion, and distribution, which combine to form the **marketing mix**.

Exhibit 7.1 depicts the major components of the marketing plan (market analysis, the competition, and marketing strategy) and the marketing activities required to generate the information needed for the plan (marketing research, market segmentation, and sales forecasting). In the remainder of the chapter, we will take a more in-depth look at these plan components and marketing activities.

market analysis
The process of locating and describing potential customers.

marketing mix
The combination of product/service, pricing, promotion, and distribution activities.

EXHIBIT 7.1   The Marketing Plan and Supporting Marketing Activities

© Cengage Learning

LO 7-2

Identify the components of a formal marketing plan.

7-2 THE FORMAL MARKETING PLAN

After an entrepreneur completes a feasibility study (described in Chapter 3) and determines that the venture idea is a viable opportunity, he or she is ready to prepare the formal marketing plan. Each business venture is different, so each marketing plan must be unique. A cloned version of a plan created by someone else should be avoided. But certain subjects—market analysis, the competition, and marketing strategy—must be covered.

The following discussion is not intended to be complete or comprehensive. In fact, more detailed treatment of marketing activities and strategies for both new and established small businesses is provided in Part 4, in Chapters 14 through 18. The material in those chapters can also help you in writing your marketing plan.

7-2a Market Analysis

A critical section of the marketing plan describes the market the entrepreneur is targeting. A **customer profile** identifies the key demographic and psychological characteristics of the customers you consider most likely to be qualified purchasers of your products and services. Marketing research information, compiled from both secondary and primary data, can be used to construct this profile.

If a business owner envisions several target markets, each segment must have a corresponding customer profile. Likewise, different target markets may call for a corresponding number of related marketing strategies. Typically, however, a new venture will initially concentrate on a select few target markets—or even just one. Attempting to reach all potential customers would be way too costly for a small business.

customer profile
A description of potential customers in a target market.

A detailed discussion of the major benefits to customers provided by the new product or service should also be included in this section of the plan. Obviously, these benefits must be reasonable and consistent with statements in the product/service section of the plan.

Spira Footwear produces running and walking shoes that contain a patented WaveSpring technology. Spira's management team can talk at length about the product's lateral stability, height and size, weight and appearance.[2] But they also understand that customers buy their shoes more for the benefits they receive than for the features that the designers love. Excerpts from the company's marketing plan concentrate on those benefits:[3]

Comfort
Management believes that shoes incorporating the WaveSpring® technology are extremely comfortable, perhaps the most comfortable ever produced. Consumers report that WaveSpring® feels like walking on a cushion of air or a moving sidewalk in an airport. Superior cushioning combined with a significant energy return generated by the WaveSpring® technology creates this remarkable sensation.

Heel and Forefoot Applications
The WaveSpring® technology can be placed both in heel and forefoot of the shoe.
The WaveSpring® allows for tremendous cushioning while still providing the necessary energy return for use as a propulsive force in both heel and forefoot.

© Spira Footwear

174

Part 3 Developing the New Venture Business Plan

Performance Enhancement

Management believes that one is able to participate in physical activities for longer periods of time at higher exertion levels as a result of the WaveSpring® technology. World class athletes and everyday users report tremendous benefits from the shoe and technology.

Another major component of market analysis is the actual sales forecast. It is usually desirable to include three sales forecasts covering the "most likely," "best-case," and "worst-case" scenarios. These alternatives provide investors and the entrepreneur with different numbers on which to base their decisions.

It is always difficult to forecast. Anyone who has followed global business cycles knows that it is not possible to predict all the variables that will affect how a company sells its product or service. Forecasting sales for a new venture is even more difficult. While it is necessary to make assumptions during forecasting, these should be minimized. The forecasting method should be fully described and backed up by data whenever feasible.

7-2b The Competition

Existing competitors should be studied carefully. The more you know about their key management personnel, the better you can anticipate the actions they will take. A brief discussion of competitors' overall strengths and weaknesses should be a part of the competition section of the plan. Also, related products currently being marketed or tested by competitors should be noted. The entrepreneur should also assess the likelihood that any of these firms will enter the targeted market. Performing a SWOT analysis at this point is always a good idea (see Chapter 3). It is important that your company have a clear understanding of what it does well (*strengths*), what it doesn't do so well (*weaknesses*), available market *opportunities*, and *threats* from competitors as well as from changes in the company's operating environment (social, technological, economic, political, and other environmental variables).

Every company must address its distinct set of competitors. Spira's founders knew they were up against major competitors who would not politely give up market share in the shoe markets. But they could easily track Nike, Reebok, Asics, New Balance, and others. They could learn how these companies react when existing competitors introduce new products or attempt to enter new markets. Startup Professionals, on the other hand, had to analyze the practices of relatively small, highly segmented firms. Given the relatively low cost to enter the industry, even the government (through the SBA and agencies in every state) was a competitor for Startup Professionals.

7-2c Marketing Strategy

The information on marketing strategy forms the most detailed section of the marketing plan and, in many respects, is subject to the closest scrutiny from potential investors. Marketing strategy plots the course of the marketing actions that will make or break the owner's vision. It's one thing to know that a large target market exists for a product or service. It's another to be able to explain why customers will buy that product or service from you.

The marketing mix of the "4 Ps" highlights the areas that a company's marketing strategy should address: (1) *product* decisions that will transform the basic product or service idea into a bundle of satisfaction, (2) *place* (distribution) activities that will determine the delivery of the product to customers, (3) *pricing* decisions that will set an acceptable exchange value on the total product or service, and (4) *promotional* activities that will communicate the necessary information to target markets.

The limited resources of small businesses have a direct bearing on the emphasis given to each of these areas. Additionally, a service business will not have the same distribution problems as a product business, and the promotional challenges facing a retail store will be quite different from those faced by a manufacturer. Despite these differences, we can offer a generalized format for presenting strategies in a marketing plan for those who will carry out those strategies.

THE PRODUCT/SERVICE SECTION The product/service section of the marketing plan includes the name of the product and/or service and the name of the business and why they were selected. Any legal protection that has been obtained for the names should be described. It is also important to explain the logic behind the name selection. An entrepreneur's family name, if used for certain products or services, can sometimes make a positive contribution to sales. The Dwyer Group carries the family name, making a statement that the family is ready to put its reputation on the line with regard to the actions of its enterprises. But each of the franchise chains owned by The Dwyer Group is labeled according to the services provided: Aire Serv Heating & Air Conditioning, Glass Doctor, The Ground Guys Landscape Management, etc. (see Chapter 4).[4]

A good name is simple, memorable, and descriptive of the benefit provided by the product or service. (We will look at this in more depth in Chapters 14 and 15.) Whatever the logic behind the choice of names, the selection should be defended and the names registered with the appropriate agencies so that they are protected.

Sometimes, names selected for a business or a product or service may be challenged, even many years later, particularly if they haven't been registered. In fact, this happened to Apple Computer, a company that can afford all the legal advice anyone could ask for. The iPad trademark in Europe is owned by STMicroelectronics, a Swiss semiconductor corporation that uses it as an acronym for "integrated passive and active devices."[5] A small business that changes its name or the name of a key product or service may find that advertising, packaging, and other materials become prohibitively expensive.

In the marketing plan, other components of the total product, such as the packaging, should be presented via drawings. It may be desirable to use professional packaging consultants to develop these drawings in some cases. Customer service plans such as warranties and repair policies also need to be discussed in this section. All of these elements of the marketing strategy should be tied directly to customer satisfaction. (Chapter 14 further examines the importance of creating and maintaining good customer relationships.)

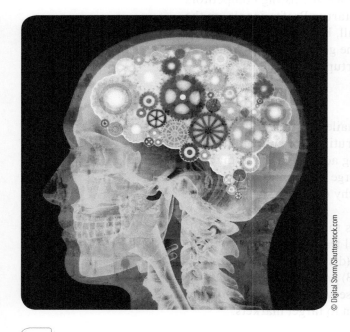

Another legal issue that many small business owners face relates to unique features of their products or services. These features affect the reasons customers buy your product and why someone might invest in your company. To protect these special features, companies obtain patents, trademarks and copyrights, which are used to differentiate products and images from those of competitors and to prevent rivals from stealing a competitive advantage.

Rather than patenting their products or technologies, some enterprises prefer to maintain trade secrets. We all have heard the stories of the secret Coca-Cola formula and of KFC's mysterious 11 herbs and spices. These trade secrets fall under the term *intellectual property.* Many companies build their marketing strategies around their intellectual property, promoting the idea that only they can offer a particular benefit to customers.

PLACE—THE DISTRIBUTION SECTION Quite often, new ventures use established intermediaries to handle the distribution of their product. This strategy reduces the investment necessary for launch and helps the new company get its products to customers faster. How those intermediaries will be persuaded to carry the new product should be explained in the distribution section of the marketing plan. Any intention the new business may have of licensing its product or service should also be covered in this section.

Some retail ventures require fixed locations; others need mobile stores. For many, the Internet is their location, but they may rely on others in a distribution chain to transport and/or warehouse merchandise. Layouts and configurations of retail outlets should be described in this section of the marketing plan. Questions such as the following should be addressed:

Will the customer get the product by regular mail or by express delivery? Will the service be provided from the entrepreneur's home or office, or from the location of a licensed representative? How long will it take between order placement and actual delivery?

USING TECHNOLOGY

Living the Dream

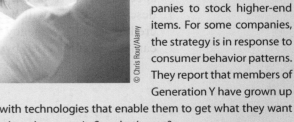

What's Next?

The whole notion of "place" has taken on new meaning, thanks to advancing technologies. Can a bricks-and-mortar location compete successfully without a Web presence? Will the predicted demise of desktops and laptops lead to an all-mobile society? What will the location options be for your company 10 years or 20 years from now?

In December of 2012, *Entrepreneur* magazine published a series of articles under the heading "Trends 2013." One asked whether you will be running your company from your own office or from Starbucks. The key is to have Internet access. Why not videoconference with your team?

Technology is also changing how consumers obtain products from manufacturers and distributors. We have seen multiple delivery specialty companies arise to compete

© Chris Rout/Alamy

with the U.S. Postal Service in order to put products in stores or the hands of consumers. But what about vending machines as advanced delivery systems? New designs have resulted in vending sales of ballet slippers, fresh-cut flowers, works of art, pieces of 24-karat gold, and many other novel examples. Electronic payment technologies have encouraged companies to stock higher-end items. For some companies, the strategy is in response to consumer behavior patterns. They report that members of Generation Y have grown up with technologies that enable them to get what they want when they want it. So, what's next?

Sources: Based on Matt Villano, "Reimagining the Workspace," *Entrepreneur*, December 2012, p. 71; Jennifer Wang, "The Digital Doctor Is In," *Entrepreneur*, December 2012, p. 78; Kara Ohngren, "Automation Nation," *Entrepreneur*, December 8, 2012, p. 77.

When a new firm's method of product delivery is exporting, the distribution section must discuss the relevant laws and regulations governing that activity. Knowledge of exchange rates between currencies and distribution options must be reflected in the material discussed in this section. (Distribution concepts are explained in greater detail in Chapter 15, and exporting is discussed in Chapter 18.)

THE PRICING SECTION At a minimum, the price of a product or service must cover the cost of bringing it to customers. Therefore, the pricing section must calculate both production and marketing costs. Naturally, forecasting methods used for analysis in this section should be consistent with those used in preparing the market analysis section.

Break-even computations, which indicate the points at which revenues and costs are equal, should be included for alternative pricing. However, setting a price based exclusively on break-even analysis is not advisable, as it ignores other important aspects. If the entrepreneur has found a truly unique niche, he or she may be able to charge a premium price—at least in the short run. There's no perfect way of doing it, but your objective is to determine what purchasers are willing to pay for your product or service, then work backward to make sure you can produce and distribute it in a way that allows you to make a profit.

Competitors should be studied to learn what they are charging. To break into a market, an entrepreneur will usually have to price a new product or service within a reasonable range of that of the competition. Many new business owners think their best strategy is to underprice the competition in order to gain market acceptance and boost sales. It is important to keep in mind, however, that existing competitors probably have more resources than you do. If they consider your business to be a threat and engage you in a price war, they can probably outlast you. In addition, do you really want your customers to come to you only because you sell a cheaper product or service? That's no way to build loyalty; you will lose those customers to the next company that prices lower than you do. (Chapter 16 examines break-even analysis and pricing strategy in more depth.)

THE PROMOTION SECTION The promotion section of the marketing plan should describe the entrepreneur's approach to creating customer awareness of the product or service and explain why customers will be motivated to buy. Among the many promotional options available to the entrepreneur are personal selling (that is, direct person-to-person selling) and advertising. You will read more about personal selling and advertising in Chapter 17.

If personal selling is appropriate, the section should outline how many salespeople will be employed and how they will be compensated. The proposed system for training the sales force should also be mentioned. If advertising is to be used, a list of the specific media to be employed should be included and advertising themes should be described. If you will be using the services of an advertising agency, the name and credentials of the agency should be provided, as well as a brief mention of successful campaigns supervised by the agency.

7-3 MARKETING RESEARCH FOR THE SMALL BUSINESS

LO 7-3

Discuss the nature of the marketing research process.

Many small business owners base their marketing plans on intuition or on their personal, limited experiences and observations. If you are serious about meeting the needs of your customers, collect and evaluate marketing research data before writing the marketing plan. A plan based on research will be stronger than a plan with intuition and personal observations as its foundation.

7-3a The Nature of Marketing Research

Marketing research may be defined as the gathering, processing, interpreting, and reporting of market information. It is all about finding out what you want to know. A small business typically conducts less marketing research than a big business does, partly because of the expense involved but also because the entrepreneur often does not understand the basic research process. Therefore, our discussion of marketing research focuses on the more widely used and practical techniques that entrepreneurs can employ as they analyze potential target markets and make preparations to develop their marketing plans. A word of caution: Don't use research techniques that you've heard about but haven't really studied. You can mislead yourself and make bad decisions.

Although a small business can conduct marketing research without the assistance of an expert, the cost of hiring such help is often money well spent, as the expert's advice may help increase revenues or cut costs. Marketing researchers are trained, experienced professionals, and prices for their research services typically reflect this. On the other hand, companies such as SurveyMonkey (www.surveymonkey.com) are now reducing overall research costs by taking advantage of the Internet to offer Web-based surveys and online focus groups.

marketing research
The gathering, processing, interpreting, and reporting of market information.

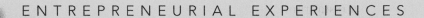

ENTREPRENEURIAL EXPERIENCES

Living the Dream

Research Keeps Going and Going and Going

Sam Arbesman is not a serial entrepreneur. He chose an academic career, accepting an appointment as a Fellow at Harvard University. He is also a senior scholar in research and policy at the Ewing Marion Kauffman Foundation. He does not create or run businesses, but he has a lot to say that small business owners need to know.

In his book, *The Half-Life of Facts*, Arbesman argues that you should never take facts for granted or assume that knowledge is permanent. What we think we know becomes obsolete and is replaced with new facts. Consider, for example, smoking, red wine, mammograms, uranium atoms, parenting—the list goes on.

What are the implications of Arbesman's findings for you in running your own business? Do you think that the research you conducted to identify a market for your startup will be accurate the day

© Samuel Arbesman/NTI/Landow

you open your doors? Will the buying habits of your customers always remain the same? Will competitors stick with the same strategies year in and year out?

In a blog for the *Harvard Business Review*, Arbesman pointed out that new facts and ideas are not spread easily because people are intellectually stubborn. We are not ready to weigh all the evidence, to accept change when it contradicts the values and behaviors we've lived by.

Imagine the advantage you would gain by gathering and analyzing data about your market and the competitive environment, and then constantly testing your beliefs and updating your plan. The marketing research process does not have an expiration date.

Sources: Based on Samuel Arbesman, *The Half-Life of Facts* (New York: Penguin Group, 2012); Samuel Arbesman, "Why Do Great Ideas Take So Long to Spread?" HBR Blog Network, blogs.hbr.org/cs/2012/11/why_do_great_ideas_take_so_lon.html, accessed December 9, 2012.

Before committing to research, however, an entrepreneur should always estimate the projected costs of marketing research and compare them with the benefits expected. Such analysis is never exact, but it will help the entrepreneur to decide how much and what kind of research should be conducted.

7-3b Steps in the Marketing Research Process

The typical steps in the marketing research process are (1) identifying the informational need, (2) searching for secondary data, (3) collecting primary data, and (4) interpreting the data gathered.

STEP ONE: IDENTIFYING THE INFORMATIONAL NEED The first step in marketing research is to identify and define what you need to know. The fact is that small business owners sometimes conduct or commission surveys without pinpointing the specific information they need. Broad statements such as "Our need is to know if the venture will be successful" or "We want to know why our customers make their buying decisions" will do little to guide the research process, but even a more specific goal can easily miss the mark. For example, an entrepreneur thinking about a location for a restaurant may decide to conduct a survey to ascertain customers' menu preferences and reasons for eating out when, in fact, what he or she needs to know most is how often residents of the target area eat out and how far they are willing to drive to eat in a restaurant.

Keep in mind that your marketing plan has to fit with your entire business strategy. What resources do you have to draw from? How efficient are your operations? What is your current competitive advantage and how long will it last? You must understand how your business operates in order to determine who your customer segments are and should be, and what relationships you want to build with those customers.

secondary data
Market information that has been previously compiled.

STEP TWO: SEARCHING FOR SECONDARY DATA Information that has already been compiled is known as **secondary data**. Generally, collecting secondary data is much less expensive than gathering new, or primary, data. Therefore, after defining their informational needs, entrepreneurs should exhaust available sources of secondary data before going further into the research process. It may be possible to base much of the marketing plan for the new venture solely on secondary data. A massive amount of information is available in libraries throughout the United States and on the Internet. The libraries of higher education institutions can be especially valuable. Not only do they have access to numerous databases containing business-related information, but they also have librarians with the skills necessary to guide you through those databases.

Software programs and hundreds of websites (many offering free information) can help an entrepreneur research customers for her or his product or service. Like all repositories of information, the Internet is most helpful when used in tandem with other sources. Be very careful to verify the accuracy of all secondary data gathered from the Internet and other sources. Blogs have become a very popular means of conveying information, but not all of that information is factually correct.

A particularly helpful source of secondary data for the small firm is the Small Business Administration, which publishes information on many topics that could prove valuable to you, including marketing research. For example, search for "market research" on the SBA website, and you will be directed to a detailed explanation of how to conduct marketing research.

Unfortunately, the use of secondary data has several drawbacks. One is that the data may be outdated. Another is that the units of measure in the secondary data may not fit the current problem. For example, a firm's market might consist of individuals with incomes between $50,000 and $75,000, while secondary data may report only the number of individuals with incomes between $50,000 and $100,000, skewing the information toward people who may be looking for products and services at a different quality level or in different locations than what you propose to offer.

Finally, the question of credibility is always present. Some sources of secondary data are less trustworthy than others. Mere publication of data does not in itself make the data valid and reliable. It is advisable to compare several different sources to see whether they are reporting similar data. Professional research specialists can also help assess the credibility of secondary sources.

STEP THREE: COLLECTING PRIMARY DATA If the secondary data are insufficient, a search for new information, or **primary data**, is the next step. Observational methods and questioning methods are two techniques used in accumulating primary data. Observational methods avoid interpersonal contact between respondents and the researcher, while questioning methods involve some type of interaction with respondents. We encourage drawing on the expertise of research specialists when gathering primary data.

Observational Methods. Observation is probably the oldest form of research in existence. A simple but effective form of observational research is mystery shopping. Mystery shoppers gather observational data by going into a store (yours or a competitor's) and looking at how items are displayed, checking out in-store advertising, and assessing other features of the store. Mystery shopping can also be used to test employee product knowledge, sales techniques, and more. The results of such activities are used to make important changes in store design and merchandising, as well as to reward good employees.[6]

Jaynie L. Smith is CEO of Smart Advantage, a marketing consulting firm, and author of the book *Relevant Selling*. Smith says that when she asks company executives what they think their customers want and compares their answers to what the customers say, 90 percent of the time the executives are wrong. To make things worse, what existing customers want is often different from what prospective customers want, resulting in mismatched marketing strategies.[7] Be careful about seeing only what you want to see and drawing incorrect conclusions about why customers are buying your products.

Questioning Methods. Surveys and experimentation are questioning methods that involve contact with respondents. Surveys can be conducted by mail, telephone, the Web, or personal interview. Mail surveys are often used when target respondents are widely dispersed. However, they usually yield low response rates—only a small percentage of the surveys sent out are typically returned. Telephone surveys and personal interview surveys achieve higher response rates. But personal interviews are very expensive, and individuals are often reluctant to grant such interviews if they think a sales pitch is coming. Some marketing researchers, such as iThink, are now specialists in online surveys. For many target market segments, Internet surveys will be the preferred approach.

A questionnaire is the basic instrument guiding the researcher who is administering the survey and the respondent who is taking it. It should be developed carefully and pretested before it is used in the market. Poorly designed questionnaires may lead

primary data
New market information that is gathered by the firm conducting the research.

to results that cause you to make bad decisions. Here are several considerations to keep in mind when designing and testing a questionnaire:

- Ask questions that relate directly to the issue under consideration. A good test of relevance is to assume an answer to each question and then ask yourself how you would use that information.
- Select the form of question, such as open-ended or multiple-choice, that is most appropriate for the subject and the conditions of the survey.
- Carefully consider the order of the questions. Asking questions in the wrong sequence can produce biased answers to later questions.
- Ask the more sensitive questions near the end of the questionnaire. Age and income, for example, are usually sensitive topics.
- Carefully select the words in each question. They should be as simple, clear, and objective as possible.
- Pretest the questionnaire by administering it to a small sample of respondents who are representative of the group to be surveyed.

It is important to remember that formal marketing research is not always necessary. The business owner's first decision should be whether to conduct primary research at all. It may be best not to conduct formal research in the following situations:[8]

- Your company doesn't have the resources to conduct the research properly or to implement any findings generated from the proposed research.
- The opportunity for a new business or product introduction has passed. If you've been beaten to the punch, it may be wise to wait and see how the early entrant to the market fares.
- A decision to move forward has already been made. There's no need to spend good money on a decision that has already been made.
- You can't decide what information is needed. If you don't know where you are going, any road will take you there.
- The needed information already exists (that is, secondary information is available).
- The cost of conducting the research outweighs the potential benefits.

Bloomberg Businessweek journalist John Tozzi suggests several ways entrepreneurs can do their own research with very little money.[9]

1. Conduct your research in the same way that you sell your product or service. Salespeople who make personal calls can gather information while they are out. If sales are over the phone, survey over the phone. If you market primarily online, conduct Web surveys.
2. Mine public sources. Use government sites, such as that of the U.S. Census Bureau. After all, you've paid for this information through your taxes.
3. Enlist students from local colleges to help stretch your limited research budget. In addition, their professors may prove to be good sources of research interpretation expertise.

STEP FOUR: INTERPRETING THE DATA GATHERED After the necessary data have been gathered, they must be transformed into usable information. Without interpretation, large quantities of data are only isolated facts. Methods of summarizing and simplifying information for users include tables, charts, and other graphics. Descriptive statistics (for example, the average response) are most helpful during this step in the research procedure. Inexpensive personal computer software, such as Excel, is now available to perform statistical calculations and generate report-quality graphics.

As important as marketing research is, it should be viewed as a supplement to, not a replacement for, good judgment and cautious experimentation in launching new products and services. Ultimately, the marketing plan should reflect the entrepreneur's educated belief about the best marketing strategy for her or his firm.

7-4 UNDERSTANDING POTENTIAL TARGET MARKETS

To prepare the market analysis section of the marketing plan, an entrepreneur needs a proper understanding of the term *market*, which means different things to different people. It may refer to a physical location where buying and selling take place ("They went to the market"), or it may be used to describe selling efforts ("We must market this product aggressively"). Still another meaning is the one we emphasize in this chapter: A market is a group of customers or potential customers who have purchasing power and unsatisfied needs. Note carefully the three ingredients in this definition of a market:

1. A market must have buying units, or *customers*. These units may be individuals or business entities.

2. Customers in a market must have *purchasing power*. Those who lack money and/or credit do not constitute a viable market because no transactions can occur.

3. A market must contain buying units with *unsatisfied needs*. Customers, for instance, will not buy unless they are motivated to do so—and motivation can occur only when a customer recognizes his or her unsatisfied needs.

In light of our definition of a market, determining market potential is the process of locating and investigating buying units that have both purchasing power and needs that can be satisfied with the product or service that is being offered.

7-4a Market Segmentation and Its Variables

In Chapter 3, cost- and differentiation-based strategies were described as they apply to marketplaces that are relatively homogeneous, or uniform, in nature. As discussed, these strategies can also be used to focus on a market niche within an industry. In his book *Competitive Advantage*, Michael Porter refers to this type of competitive strategy—in which cost- and differentiation-based advantages are achieved within narrow market segments—as a *focus strategy*.[10]

A focus strategy depends on market segmentation and becomes a consideration in competitive markets. Formally defined, market segmentation is the process of dividing the total market for a product or service into smaller groups with similar needs, such that each group is likely to respond favorably to a specific marketing strategy. A generation ago, telephones were purely a landline technology. Today, there are cell

LO 7-4

Define *market segmentation*, and discuss its related strategies.

market
A group of customers or potential customers who have purchasing power and unsatisfied needs.

market segmentation
The division of a market into several smaller groups with similar needs.

phone and smartphone configurations targeted at young versus older segments, tech-oriented versus non-tech-oriented customers, business versus home features. And voice communication can be achieved through technologies that bear no resemblance to phones.

In order to divide the total market into appropriate segments, an entrepreneur must consider **segmentation variables**, which are parameters that distinguish one form of market behavior from another. Two broad sets of segmentation variables that represent the major dimensions of a market are benefit variables and demographic variables.

BENEFIT VARIABLES The definition of a market highlights the unsatisfied needs of customers. **Benefit variables** are related to customer needs since they are used to identify segments of a market based on the benefits sought by customers. For example, a single health club may offer services that are used for different reasons and in different ways by different market segments. Senior citizens might want cardiovascular exercise, young men might be interested in bodybuilding, and young girls may attend gymnastics classes there.

DEMOGRAPHIC VARIABLES It is impossible to implement forecasting and marketing strategy with benefit variables alone. Therefore, small businesses commonly use **demographic variables** as part of market segmentation. These variables refer to certain characteristics that describe customers, their purchasing power, their consumption patterns, and other factors. They include age, marital status, gender, occupation, and income.

7-4b Marketing Strategies Based on Segmentation Considerations

There are several types of strategies based on market segmentation efforts. The three types discussed here are the unsegmented approach, the multi-segment approach, and the single-segment approach. Few companies engage in all three approaches simultaneously. Small businesses often lack the resources that these strategies tend to require. But for some, a marketing strategy based on segmentation considerations is the best route to take.

THE UNSEGMENTED STRATEGY When a business defines the total market as its target, it is following an **unsegmented strategy** (also known as **mass marketing**). This strategy can sometimes be successful, but it assumes that all customers desire the same basic benefit from the product or service. This may hold true for water but certainly does not hold true for shoes, which satisfy numerous needs through a wide range of styles, prices, colors, and sizes. With an unsegmented strategy, a firm develops a single marketing mix—one combination of product, price, promotion, and distribution. Its competitive advantage must be derived from either a cost- or a differentiation-based advantage. For example, Two Men and a Truck "offers you any home moving services you need," and provides local and long-distance services. This company targets both commercial and residential customers, offering similar services to each.[11] Exhibit 7.2 represents its strategy.

THE MULTISEGMENT STRATEGY With a view of the market that recognizes individual segments with different preferences, a firm is in a better position to tailor marketing mixes to various segments. If a firm determines that two or more market

segmentation variables
The parameters used to distinguish one form of market behavior from another.

benefit variables
Specific characteristics that distinguish market segments according to the benefits sought by customers.

demographic variables
Specific characteristics that describe customers, their purchasing power, their consumption patterns, and other factors.

unsegmented strategy (mass marketing)
A strategy that defines the total market as the target market.

EXHIBIT

7.2   An Unsegmented Market Strategy

Two Men and a Truck

Product and Marketing Strategy

Product: Local and Long-Distance Moving
Promotion: Online and Through Social Media,
              Public Relations, and Direct Mail
Media: Mass Media by Event Organizer

Market
Businesses and Homes

© Cengage Learning 2014

multi-segment strategy
A strategy that recognizes different preferences of individual market segments and develops a unique marketing mix for each.

single-segment strategy
A strategy that recognizes the existence of several distinct market segments but focuses on only the most profitable segment.

segments have the potential to be profitable and then develops a unique marketing mix for each segment, it is following a **multisegment strategy**.

In the Spotlight feature in Chapter 16, you will be introduced to Dyn, a global Internet infrastructure service provider. Its clients include both businesses and home users, and it identifies four primary customer segments, as shown in Exhibit 7.3.

THE SINGLE-SEGMENT STRATEGY When a firm recognizes that several distinct market segments exist but chooses to concentrate on reaching only the most potentially profitable segment, it is following a **single-segment strategy**. Once again, a competitive advantage is achieved through a cost- or differentiation-based strategy. Startup Professionals provides products and services that have value for students, retirees, hobbyists, and more, but the founders chose to focus their energies on high-growth-potential ventures. Its market strategy is illustrated in Exhibit 7.4.

The single-segment approach is probably the wisest strategy for small businesses to use during initial marketing efforts. It allows a small firm to specialize and make better use of its limited resources. Then, once its reputation has been established, the firm will find it easier to enter new markets.

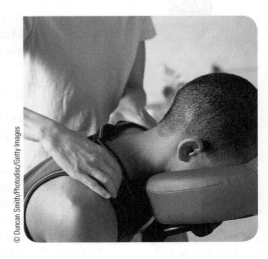

© Duncan Smith/Photodisc/Getty Images

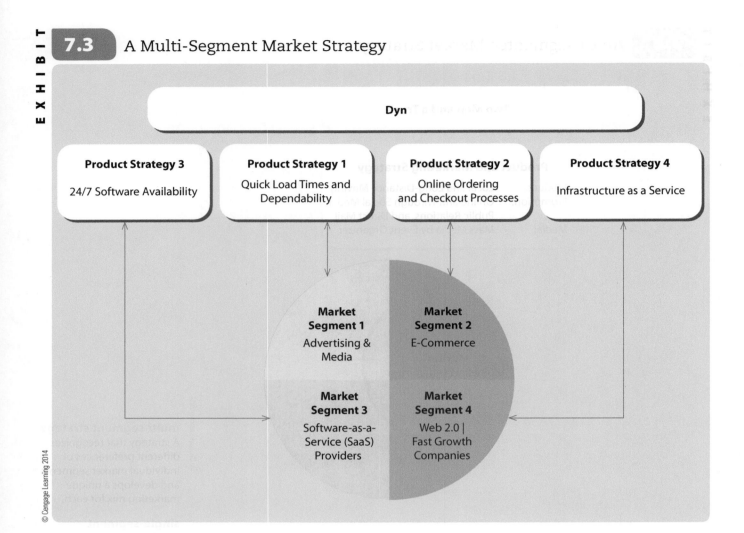

LO 7-5

Explain the different methods of forecasting sales.

7-5 ESTIMATING MARKET POTENTIAL

A small business can be successful only if sufficient market demand exists for its product or service. A sales forecast is the typical indicator of market adequacy, so it is particularly important to complete this assessment prior to writing the marketing plan. Many types of information are required to gauge market potential. This section discusses these information needs as it examines the forecasting process.

7-5a The Sales Forecast

A **sales forecast** is an estimate of how much of a product or service can be sold within a given market in a defined time period. The forecast can be stated in terms of dollars and/or units.

Because a sales forecast revolves around a specific target market, that market should be defined as precisely as possible. Don't make the mistake of forecasting sales that exceed the size of the market you are serving. If the market for desks is described as "all offices," the sales forecast will be extremely large. But you are probably only selling to a smaller segment, such as "government agencies seeking solid wood desks priced between $800 and $1200." That will result in a much smaller but more useful forecast.

sales forecast
A prediction of how much of a product or service will be purchased within a given market during a specified time period.

EXHIBIT **7.4** A Single-Segment Market Strategy

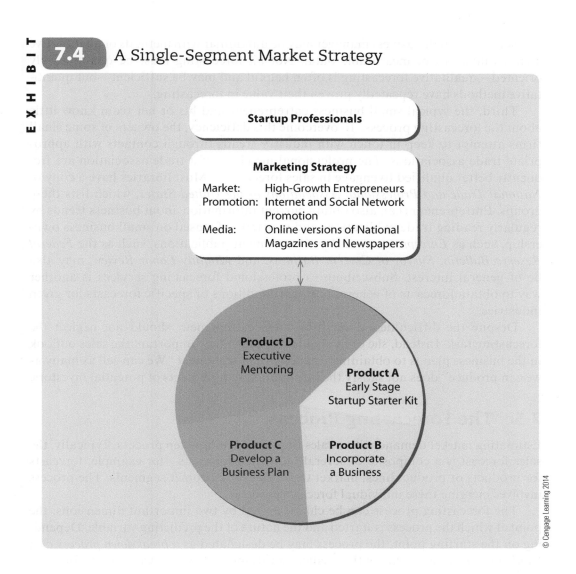

One sales forecast may cover a period of time that is a year or less, while another may extend over several years. Both short-term and long-term forecasts are needed for a well-constructed marketing plan.

A sales forecast is an essential component of the marketing plan because it is critical to assessing the feasibility of a new venture. If the market is insufficient, the business is destined for failure. A sales forecast is also useful in other areas of business planning. Production schedules, inventory policies, and personnel decisions all start with a sales forecast. Obviously, a forecast can never be perfect, and entrepreneurs should remember that a forecast can be wrong in either direction, by either underestimating or overestimating potential sales.

7-5b Limitations of Forecasting

For a number of practical reasons, forecasting is used less frequently by small firms than by large firms. First, for any new business, forecasting circumstances are unique. Entrepreneurial inexperience, coupled with a new idea, represents the most difficult forecasting situation. An ongoing business that requires only an updated forecast for its existing product is in the most favorable forecasting position.

Second, a small business manager may be unfamiliar with methods of quantitative analysis (analysis of measurable data). Not all forecasting must be quantitatively oriented—qualitative forecasting is often helpful and may be sufficient—but quantitative methods have repeatedly proven their value in forecasting.

Third, the typical small business entrepreneur and his or her team know little about the forecasting process. To overcome this deficiency, the owners of some small firms attempt to keep in touch with industry trends through contacts with appropriate trade associations. The professional members of a trade association are frequently better qualified to engage in sales forecasting. Most libraries have a copy of *National Trade and Professional Associations of the United States*, which lists these groups. Entrepreneurs can also obtain current information about business trends by regularly reading trade publications and magazines focused on small business ownership, such as *Entrepreneur* and *Inc*. Government publications, such as the *Federal Reserve Bulletin*, *Survey of Current Business*, and *Monthly Labor Review*, may also be of general interest. Subscribing to professional forecasting services is another way to obtain forecasts of general business conditions or specific forecasts for given industries.

Despite the difficulties, a small business entrepreneur should not neglect the forecasting task. Instead, she or he should remember how important the sales outlook in the business plan is to obtaining financing. The statement "We can sell as many as we can produce" does not satisfy the information requirements of potential investors.

7-5c The Forecasting Process

Estimating market demand with a sales forecast is a multi-step process. Typically, the sales forecast is a composite of several individual forecasts—for example, forecasts for products or product lines, market territories, or customer segments. The process involves merging these individual forecasts properly.

The forecasting process can be characterized by two important dimensions: the point at which the process is started and the nature of the predicting variable. Depending on the starting point, the process may be designated as a *breakdown process* or a *buildup process*. The nature of the predicting variable determines whether the forecasting is *direct* or *indirect*.

THE STARTING POINT The **breakdown process**, sometimes called the **chain-ratio method**, begins with a variable that has a very large scope and systematically works down to the sales forecast. This method is frequently used for consumer products forecasting. The initial variable might be a population figure for the target market. Through the use of percentages, an appropriate link is built to generate the sales forecast.

David Goldsmith cautions his New York University students against making a general forecast of the future, recommending activity-based forecasting instead.[12] This approach breaks the whole into its parts or activities, forecasts each of those, and then brings them together to get a better picture of what's to come.

One source of data available to every small business owner is the U.S. Census Bureau, which compiles statistics on various population segments by, for example, gender, age, geographic location, and household income. Additional data on customer segments may be obtained through state and local government agencies, chambers of commerce, trade associations, and private enterprise sources.

In contrast to the breakdown process, the **buildup process** calls for identifying all potential buyers in a target market's submarkets and then adding up the estimated demand. For example, a local dry-cleaning firm that is forecasting demand for cleaning high school letter jackets might estimate its market share within each

breakdown process (chain-ratio method)
A forecasting method that begins with a large-scope variable and works down to the sales forecast.

buildup process
A forecasting method in which all potential buyers in a target market's submarkets are identified and the estimated demand is added up.

area school as 20 percent. Then, by determining the number of high school students obtaining a letter jacket at each school—perhaps from school yearbooks—an analyst could estimate the total demand.

The buildup process is especially helpful for industrial goods forecasting. To estimate potential, forecasters often use data from the Census of Manufactures by the U.S. Department of Commerce. The information can be broken down according to the North American Industry Classification System (NAICS), which classifies businesses by type of industry. Once the code for a group of potential industrial customers has been identified, the forecaster can obtain information on the number of establishments and their geographic location, number of employees, and annual sales. A sales forecast can be constructed by summing this information for several relevant codes.

THE PREDICTING VARIABLE In **direct forecasting**, which is the simplest form of forecasting, sales is the forecasted variable. Many times, however, sales cannot be predicted directly and other variables must be used. **Indirect forecasting** takes place when surrogate variables are used to project sales. For example, if a firm lacks information about industry sales of baby cribs but has data on births, the strong correlation between the two variables allows planners to use the figures for births to help forecast industry sales for cribs.

For a new business, there are few things as important as identifying your market—nothing happens until someone buys something from your company. And if you plan to grow your business, understanding your market is essential. In this chapter, we introduced you to the steps necessary for putting together a marketing plan. The plan will be a living document for you as you manage your business. Every day, you will learn more about your market and how you can meet customer needs. And the marketing plan has an impact on many other areas of your business. In later chapters, you will see that your marketing strategy affects how many people you employ and what skills they need, the volume and selection of your inventory, the production processes you use, and many other business functions.

direct forecasting
A forecasting method in which sales is the estimated variable.

indirect forecasting
A forecasting method in which variables related to sales are used to project future sales.

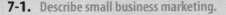

7-1. Describe small business marketing.

- Small business marketing consists of business activities that direct the creation, development, and delivery of a bundle of satisfaction from the creator to the targeted user.
- The product or service as a bundle of satisfaction has three levels: (1) core product/service, (2) actual product/service, and (3) augmented product/service.

- Three distinct marketing philosophies are the production-, sales-, and consumer-oriented philosophies.
- A small business should adopt a consumer orientation to marketing, as that philosophy is most consistent with long-term success.
- Small business marketing activities include market analysis and determining the marketing mix.

7-2. Identify the components of a formal marketing plan.

- The formal marketing plan should include sections on market analysis, the competition, and marketing strategy.
- The market analysis should include a customer profile.
- A SWOT analysis is helpful in assessing the competition.
- The "4 Ps" of marketing strategy that should be discussed in the marketing plan are (1) product decisions affecting the total product and/or service, (2) place (distribution) activities, (3) pricing decisions, and (4) promotional activities.

7-3. **Discuss the nature of the marketing research process.**

- Marketing research involves the gathering, processing, interpreting, and reporting of marketing information.
- The cost of marketing research should be evaluated against its benefits.
- The steps in the marketing research process are identifying the informational need, searching for secondary data, collecting primary data, and interpreting the data gathered.

7-4. **Define** *market segmentation*, **and discuss its related strategies.**

- A focus strategy relies on market segmentation, which is the process of dividing the total market for a product or service into smaller groups with similar needs, such that each group is likely to respond favorably to a specific marketing strategy.
- Broad segmentation variables that represent major dimensions of a market are benefit variables and demographic variables.
- Three types of market segmentation strategies are (1) the unsegmented approach, (2) the multi-segment approach, and (3) the single-segment approach.
- The unsegmented strategy—when a business defines the total market as its target—is also known as mass marketing.

- A firm that determines that two or more market segments have the potential to be profitable and then develops a unique marketing mix for each segment is following a multi-segment strategy.
- A firm that follows a single-segment strategy recognizes that several distinct market segments exist but chooses to concentrate on reaching only the segment that promises the greatest profitability.

7-5. **Explain the different methods of forecasting sales.**

- A sales forecast is an estimate of how much of a product or service will be purchased within a given market during a defined time period.
- The forecasting process may be either a breakdown or a buildup process and may be either direct or indirect, depending on the predicting variable.
- The breakdown process, or chain-ratio method, begins with a variable that has a very large scope and systematically works down to the sales forecast.
- The buildup process calls for identifying all potential buyers in a target market's submarkets and then adding up the estimated demand.
- In direct forecasting, sales is the forecasted variable. In indirect forecasting, surrogate variables are used to project sales.

Key Terms

actual product/service p. 172

augmented product/service p. 172

benefit variables p. 184

breakdown process (chain-ratio method) p. 188

buildup process p. 188

core product/service p. 172

customer profile p. 174

demographic variables p. 184

direct forecasting p. 189

indirect forecasting p. 189

market p. 183

market analysis p. 173

marketing mix p. 173

marketing research p. 179

market segmentation p. 183

multi-segment strategy p. 185

primary data p. 181

sales forecast p. 186

secondary data p. 180

segmentation variables p. 184

single-segment strategy p. 185

small business marketing p. 171

unsegmented strategy (mass marketing) p. 184

Discussion Questions

1. What is the scope of small business marketing? What do you think the differences in marketing might be if you were a manager in a large corporation?

2. How do the three marketing philosophies differ? Select a product and discuss marketing tactics that could be used to implement each philosophy.

3. What are the obstacles to adopting a consumer orientation in a small firm?

4. Briefly describe each of the components of a formal marketing plan.

5. What are the steps in the marketing research process? Which step do you feel would be the hardest for you to take? Why?

6. What are the major considerations in designing a questionnaire?

7. Briefly explain the three components of the definition of a market, as presented in this chapter.

8. What types of variables are used for market segmentation? Would a small firm use the same variables as a large business? Why or why not?

9. Explain the difference between a multi-segment strategy and a single-segment strategy. Which one is more likely to be appealing to a small firm? Why?

10. Explain why forecasting is used more widely by large firms than by small ones.

You Make the Call

Situation 1

What is your strategy for e-commerce? That's a question Michael Maher, Barrett Purdum, and Mike Armenta asked each other when they launched Taylor Stitch, a custom shirt manufacturer and retailer in San Francisco. They decided that their strengths were in designing, manufacturing, and marketing their products, not in designing a Web platform for their business. After researching options available, they chose Shopify, which helps companies set up online stores. It sells or configures domain names, sets up and hosts websites, provides shopping cart features enabling customers to browse and buy, and offers other e-commerce products and consulting services. The owners of Taylor Stitch credit the Shopify platform with spurring sales through a well-integrated system.

Question 1 What factors should business owners consider when deciding to manage their own website and online sales instead of contracting for the service?

Question 2 Taylor Stitch has both a bricks-and-mortar store and an online store. What are the advantages and disadvantages of this strategy?

Sources: Based on www.taylorstitch.com, accessed December 13, 2012; and www.shopify.com, accessed December 13, 2012.

Situation 2

Every company wants to use "word of mouth" to promote their business. The Internet has taken that to a whole new level. People read endorsements from others through networks they have found reliable. Gregory E. Alden manages the chain of Woodside Hotels in Northern California. Positioned in the luxury hotel category, Woodside properties rely on being ranked high by their customers on such websites as Yelp, TripAdvisor, Expedia, and others. But monitoring all those services can be seriously time consuming. Alden found a better way to monitor how satisfied customers were and what they were communicating about the hotels by contracting with Revinate. Revinate provides a software platform for hotels and other companies in the hospitality industry. The platform allows Alden to track online reviews and to use social media to learn what travelers want. He can spot trends and act on criticisms immediately, bringing customers back and attracting new ones.

Question 1 How do you think Gregory Alden found out about Revinate? Given all the online companies that might help your business connect you with customers, how would you choose one?

Question 2 Do you report your experiences with businesses on any social networks? Why or why not?

Sources: Based on Gwen Moran, "Chatter Master," *Entrepreneur*, December 2012, p. 62; www.woodsidehotels.com, accessed December 13, 2012; and www.revinate.com, accessed December 13, 2012.

Situation 3

Ricardo De La Blanca Brigati is CEO of the DLB Group, a full-service marketing company with about 10 million in revenues operating throughout the Americas and in Spain. He encourages his clients to focus on African American, Hispanic, Asian American, and Native American consumers. He sees the buying power of these segments, but few small businesses are making adjustments to serve them. DLB's website offers examples of how the company helps clients, both in the United States and abroad, develop comprehensive marketing strategies that set them apart by adapting to (and respecting) other cultures.

Question 1 Identify a minority group to which you do not belong. What steps could you take to learn about that market segment in order to sell those consumers a product or service?

Question 2 Suppose your small business was contacted by a company in another country that wanted to sell your products in its market. What would you want to know about that market before going into it? Choose any country besides the United States and determine what changes you would have to make to your marketing plan to adjust to the different culture.

Sources: Based on www.dlbgroup.com/, accessed January 23, 2011; and Karen E. Klein, "What Companies Get Wrong When Marketing to Minorities," www.businessweek.com/smallbiz/content/dec2010/sb20101213_643259.htm, accessed January 23, 2011.

Experiential Exercises

1. View the website of a local small business. Interview the owner of that business about how the website fits into his or her overall marketing plan.

2. Assume you are planning to market a new breath mint. What social media do you think would be the best to get the word out about your product? Describe the strategy you would use.

3. Interview someone from a small business assistance organization (e.g., Small Business Development Center, Service Corps of Retired Executives, chamber of commerce, etc.). Does she or he help clients or members with marketing research or with sales forecasting? What does she or he consider to be the best sources of market information?

Small Business & Entrepreneurship Resource Center

The Small Business & Entrepreneurship Resource Center offers complete small business management resources through a comprehensive database that covers all major areas of starting, operating, and maintaining a business from financing, management, marketing, accounting, taxes, and more. Go to www.cengagebrain.com and select the Longenecker text for more information on how to access this material.

1. New and smaller firms create the most jobs in the U.S. economy. The facts speak for themselves. The vast majority of these job-creating companies are fast-growing businesses. David Birch of Cognetics, Inc., has named these firms "gazelles." A *gazelle*, by Birch's definition, is a business establishment with at least 20 percent sales growth every year (for five years), starting with a base of at least $100,000. Gazelles have shown extraordinary performance. After reading this article, discuss the following misconceptions about gazelles: Gazelles are all high-tech; gazelles get venture

capital; gazelles are small; and gazelles are both national and international.

2. 3M Company identifies segments of consumers based on their preferences for product features. Similarly, 3M identifies eight segments of employees based on motivation for working at 3M. "We found a cluster of midcareer employees looking more for experiences, not money per se," says a 3M manager. Segmentation helps managers revamp or create benefits, or develop talent programs. Behind segmentation is the idea that employees are not all the same. By using data, data mining and statistical analysis, 3M aims to understand the hopes, aspirations, and needs of employees. How would you feel about working for 3M or another company that used market segmentation methods for employees? Explain your answer.

Sources: Donald F. Kuratko and Richard M. Hodgetts, "The Age of the Gazelles," *Entrepreneurship: Theory, Process, Practice*, 6th ed. (Mason, OH: Thomson South-Western, 2004); and BillRoberts, "Celebrate Differences: Meet Diverse Needs Through Employee Segmentation," *HR Magazine*, Vol. 57, No. 12 (December 2012), pp. 24–28.

Video Case 7

Readymade Magazine (P. 656)

ReadyMade markets itself as a magazine catering to GenNest, the group of consumers ages 25 to 35 who are just settling down after college. But *ReadyMade* appeals to a wide variety of readers, with subscribers in all age groups. This diversity offers a unique challenge to *ReadyMade* as it tries to promote itself to advertisers who need to know what sort of people will be reached through advertisements in the publication.

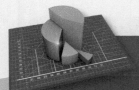

Business Plan

LAYING THE FOUNDATION

As part of laying the foundation for your own business plan, respond to the following questions regarding the marketing plan, marketing research, market segmentation, and sales forecasting.

Marketing Plan Questions

1. How will you identify prospective customers?
2. What is the customer profile for your product and/or service?
3. Who is your competition?
4. Have you conducted a SWOT analysis?
5. What geographic area will you serve?
6. What are the distinguishing characteristics of your product and/or service?
7. What steps have already been taken to develop your product and/or service?
8. What do you plan to name your product and/or service?
9. Will there be a warranty?
10. How will you set the price for your product and/or service?
11. What type of distribution plan will you use?
12. Will you export to other countries?
13. What type of selling effort will you use?
14. What special selling skills will be required?
15. What types of advertising and sales promotion will you use?
16. Can you use the Internet to promote your company and product/service?

Marketing Research Questions

1. What research questions do you need answers to?
2. What types of research should be conducted to collect the information you need?
3. How much will this research cost?
4. What sources of secondary data will address your informational needs?
5. What sources of relevant data are available in your local library?
6. What sources of outside professional assistance would you consider using to help with marketing research?
7. Is there information available on the Internet that might be helpful?
8. What research questions do you need answers to?

Market Segmentation Questions

1. Will you focus on a limited market within the industry?
2. What segmentation variables will you use to define your target market?
3. If you determine that several distinct market segments exist, will you concentrate on just one segment?

Forecasting Questions

1. How do you plan to forecast sales for your product and/or service?
2. What sources of forecasting assistance have you consulted?
3. What sales forecasting techniques are most appropriate to your needs?
4. What is the sales forecast for your product and/or service?
5. How reliable is your sales forecast?

Endnotes

1. Rachel Kaufman, "Loyal Customers, One Box at a Time," *Inc.*, April 2012, p. 112.

2. Based on www.spira.com/wavespring-technology-w6.aspx, accessed December 8, 2012.

3. *Ibid.*

4. www.dwyergroup.com/dwyer-group-companies.asp, accessed December 8, 2012.

5. Brad Stone, "What's in a Name? For Apple, iPad Said More Than Intended," *The New York Times*, January 29, 2010, pp. A1, A3.

6. Carl McDaniel and Roger Gates, *Marketing Research*, 8th ed. (Hoboken, NJ: John Wiley & Sons, 2009).

7. Christopher Hann, "Your Wish Is My Command," *Entrepreneur*, December 2012, p. 28.

8. McDaniel and Gates, *op. cit.,* pp. 94–95.

9. John Tozzi, "Market Research on the Cheap," *Bloomberg Businessweek*, www.businessweek.com/smallbiz/content/jan2008 /sb2008019_352779.htm, accessed January 12, 2011.

10. Michael Porter, *Competitive Advantage* (New York: Free Press, 1985), p. 5.

11. www.twomenandatruck.com, accessed December 9, 2012.

12. David Goldsmith, "For a Finer Forecast, Pull Apart the Future," *Fast Company*, www.fastcompany.com/3001941/finer-forecast-pull -apart-future, accessed December 9, 2012; and David Goldsmith, *Paid to Think: A Leader's Toolkit for Redefining Your Future* (Dallas, TX: BenBella Books, 2012).

© sdecoret/Shutterstock.com

The Organizational Plan: Teams, Legal Structures, Alliances, and Directors

Startups that succeed famously tend to be founded by teams, and more new ventures are moving in that direction as a result. In new team relationships, however, emotions and unchecked optimism may take over in the beginning, while crucial considerations are set aside. That can be a serious mistake. New venture stories that start with wise team selections and carefully considered incorporation or partnership agreements are more likely to have a happy ending.

Justin Moore is founder and CEO of Axcient, which provides client firms with an easy-to-use platform for data backup, business continuity, and disaster recovery services. Based on his experience as a serial entrepreneur, Moore has observed, "Where there's ambiguity, there's conflict." Having precisely defined relationships from the outset can dissolve troubling uncertainties. What if a co-founder quits, relocates, or dies?

In the SPOTLIGHT
Axcient, Sapience Knowledge Systems, and Velocent Systems
www.axcient.com
www.velocent.com

What if the company is to be sold or must shut down? These and many other possible scenarios need to be considered and spelled out in legal agreements. Moore's advice: Choose your team wisely, spend more time on the front end defining your relationships with them, and hire an attorney to get the agreement right. Cutting corners on this is likely to cost you much more over the long run.

Moore's counsel is echoed by Biju Nair, who sold his startup, Sapience Knowledge Systems, to Synchronoss Technologies in 2011. Nair set up

OPEN
LOOKING
AHEAD

After studying this chapter, you should be able to...

8-1. Describe the characteristics and value of a strong management team.

8-2. Explain the common legal forms of organization used by small businesses.

8-3. Identify factors to consider in choosing among the primary legal forms of organization.

8-4. Discuss the unique features and restrictions of five specialized organizational forms.

8-5. Understand the nature of strategic alliances and their uses in small businesses.

8-6. Describe the effective use of boards of directors and advisory boards.

Sapience to develop software that helps companies collect, process, manage, and interpret customer relationship management information. But he knows the importance of having sound agreements in place to protect the interests of the founders and to improve daily operations. Those who have a clear sense of their ownership interest in a company are likely to put more effort into their work, which will boost venture performance. Such definition will also head off misunderstandings that can ruin friendships, destroy reputations, and cost the firm money.

Bruce Peterson is founder and CEO of Velocent Systems, which develops customer-monitoring solutions for mobile broadband operators. He takes Nair's advice one step further in his company, requiring all business partners and employees to list each of the inventions they created before signing on with Velocent so that there are no questions about who has a legitimate right to what. Once again, spelling out relationships upfront allows the firm to define work demands and shape expectations for rewards from the start.

Each of these entrepreneurs recognizes the importance of choosing business associates wisely, defining relationships with them in advance and with care, and drafting agreements that will protect everyone's interests, while also providing documentation that may be needed to resolve misunderstandings that surface later. Their ventures are all relatively sophisticated. Your startup may be much simpler, but it still makes sense to consider carefully the advice that these entrepreneurs are giving. A front-end investment will pay enormous dividends in the form of an entrepreneurial team that is content, motivated, and naturally committed to outstanding performance.

Sources: Based on "Axcient—Company Profile," www.axcient.com/about-us.html, accessed August 29, 2012; "Company Overview of Velocent Systems," http://investing.businessweek.com/research/stocks/private/snapshot.asp?privcapId=30613229, accessed August 30, 2012; Ann C. Logue, "Beyond the Handshake," *Entrepreneur*, Vol. 40, No. 6 (June 2012), pp. 91–95; and "Sapience Knowledge Systems—At a Glance," http://sapienceknowledge.com/uploads/4/2/5/5/4255077/sapience_at_a_glance_v4.pdf, accessed August 29, 2012.

One of the most enduring myths in American business is that of the lone entrepreneur who defies the odds by taking a creative business idea and turning it into reality by sheer force of will and personality. It makes a great story, but does it reflect reality?

To be sure, plenty of solo entrepreneurs are starting new businesses, but evidence is mounting to show that team-founded ventures tend to outperform their solo-founded counterparts. Entrepreneurship experts Stephen Spinelli and Robert Adams emphasize this point: "Owning and running the whole show effectively puts a ceiling on growth. . . . It is extremely difficult to grow a higher-potential venture by working single-handedly. Higher-potential entrepreneurs build a team, an organization, and a company."[1]

Unfortunately, team leadership in a small enterprise all too often presents its share of heartaches, especially when partners are hastily chosen, work and reward relationships are unclear, and formal agreements are poorly conceived or confusing (as highlighted in the Spotlight feature to this chapter). The high hopes of partnership and camaraderie in business can easily be dashed on the rocks of real life. People are imperfect, after all, so working closely with others is bound to lead to a certain amount of disappointment. But in all but the simplest of businesses, the entrepreneur's personal talents often need to be supplemented with the experience and abilities of other individuals. A venture's prospects typically are most promising when its leadership is composed of competent, resourceful, and tenacious individuals who are committed to doing their best.[2] With that in mind, it is important for an entrepreneur to identify and attract a strong management team. An organizational plan that provides for effective leadership is appealing to both potential investors and prospective managerial personnel.

This chapter also discusses the selection of an appropriate ownership structure, often called a legal form of organization. The direction of the business will be powerfully shaped by an entrepreneur's decision to organize as a sole proprietorship, a partnership, a corporation, or one of the other available forms. The organizational form should match the needs of the business, but getting it right can be a challenge. Also included in the organizational plan are strategic alliances, which are becoming increasingly popular among small businesses and can be vitally important to their performance. Finally, we describe the role of boards of directors or advisors for small businesses and provide insights on how to make the most of them.

All of these elements of a small business should be carefully considered in the organizational plan. The quality of an entrepreneur's decisions on these issues can greatly enhance the performance of the company—or doom it to failure. We will show you how to navigate the potentially dangerous waters of planning for these facets of the business and guide you toward improved odds for success.

8-1 BUILDING A MANAGEMENT TEAM

LO 8-1

Describe the characteristics and value of a strong management team.

If a firm is extremely small, the founder will probably be the key manager and perhaps the only manager. In most firms, however, others share leadership roles with the owner, which creates opportunities to leverage their combined networks and resources for the good of the company. In general, the **management team** consists of individuals with supervisory responsibilities, as well as nonsupervisory personnel who play key roles in the business.[3] For example, members of a management team might include a financial manager who supervises a small office staff and another person who directs the marketing effort.

If you should find that you don't have your "dream team" in place when you are just getting started, understand that the team arrangement does not have to be permanent. Though it can be difficult to do, sometimes you have to respectfully and appropriately let individuals go when they cannot or will not effectively support the business. New members can be added to the team as the need arises.[4]

Strong management can make the best of a good business idea by securing the resources needed to make it work. Of course, even a highly competent management team cannot rescue a firm that is based on a weak business concept or that lacks adequate resources. But the importance of strong management to startups is evident in the attitudes of prospective investors, who consider the quality of a new venture's management to be one of the most important factors in decisions to invest or to take a pass. In other words, investors know that enterprises typically perform poorly if they are guided by weak or incapable managers.

As indicated earlier, a management team often can bring greater strength to a venture than an individual entrepreneur can. One reason for this is that a team can provide a diversity of talent to meet various managerial needs, which can be especially helpful to startups built on new technologies that must manage a broad range of factors. In addition, a team can provide greater assurance of continuity, since the departure of one member of a team is less devastating to a business than the departure of a solo owner.

The competence required in a management team depends on the type of venture and the nature of its operations.[5] For example, a software development firm and a restaurant require very different types of business experience. Whatever the business, a small firm needs managers with an appropriate combination of education, experience, and skills. The qualifications of an applicant for a key position should complement those of members already on the team.

In many cases, a startup owner stacks the management team with family and friends, rather than seeking balanced expertise. This has a definite upside. The owner knows these people well and trusts them, they often work for less compensation (despite the elevated risk of joining a new venture), and they are more likely to make personal sacrifices to keep the business alive. The downside is that the team can quickly become very homogeneous, lack complementary strengths, entertain feelings of entitlement, and carry the baggage of family dysfunction into the enterprise. All of these factors—the negative and the positive—should be taken into consideration when hiring family and friends.

management team
Managers and other key persons who give a company its general direction.

8-1a Achieving Balance

Not all members of a management team need competence in all areas—the key is balance. As one small business observer put it, "You want someone who knows as much as you do, just not about the same things."[6] If one member has expertise in finance, another should have an adequate marketing background. And the venture will need someone who can supervise employees effectively.[7] This diversity in perspectives and work styles is what enables the completion of complex tasks, but it can also lead to serious conflict, which can squeeze all the energy and enthusiasm out of a venture.[8]

Even when entrepreneurs recognize the need for team members with varying expertise, they frequently look for qualities that reflect their own personalities and management styles. Interpersonal compatibility and cooperation among team members are necessary for effective collaboration, and cohesive teams tend to perform better.[9] However, experience suggests that a functionally diverse and balanced team will be more likely to cover all the business bases, giving the company a competitive edge.

To ensure balance, a management team should comprise both competent insiders and outside specialists. For example, a small firm will benefit greatly by developing working relationships with a commercial bank, a law firm, and an accounting firm. (A number of outside sources of managerial assistance are identified and discussed in Chapter 19.) In addition to providing counsel and guidance to the management team, an active board of directors or advisors (discussed later in this chapter) can also help connect the venture with external sources of expertise and assistance. It is simply a matter of tapping into board members' existing networks of business relationships. The value of a good board, in this regard, cannot be overstated.

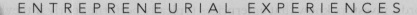

Living the Dream

It Can Be Lonely at the Top

Despite the advantages of forming a team to start a business, the truth is that many entrepreneurs would rather go it alone. And emerging technologies makes this option increasingly manageable today. Business support services that used to cost thousands of dollars are now available online for free or for a small monthly charge, and hiring help from around the world can require nothing more than a few mouse clicks. These tools can replace the assistance that might otherwise be available only by taking on a skilled business partner.

Harvey Manger-Weil found a way to go into business without the hassles that come from having a physical location, partners, or other fixed features. As a former enrollment director at Dartmouth College, he had seen many smart students be rejected by the colleges of their choice due to mediocre SAT scores. So, he developed a tutoring method that would allow applicants to improve their exam results dramatically. And after perfecting his system, Manger-Weil used it to launch The College Wizard, an

© Siamionau Pavel/Shutterstock.com

online training company that gets extremely high marks from those who have used it.

The College Wizard is growing at a healthy clip, but Manger-Weil is able to keep up with it as a solo business owner by following principles that he learned from Entrepreneur-in-Residence at Yale University and go-it-alone guru, Bruce Judson. The secret, says Judson, is relatively simple: "Systematize everything you can. Look at your business and see what pieces you can automate and outsource. Ultimately, every business is a repetitive system, and you need to automate that so you can spend your time doing the things that really add value."

Bibby Gignilliat is another Judson disciple who has chosen to follow the path of self-reliance. Her San Francisco–based venture, Parties That Cook, runs cooking classes as team-building exercises for Fortune 500 companies. She has grown the venture to 12 employees in four cities and more than $2 million in revenue by focusing on what she does best and delegating or outsourcing other necessary functions, such as hiring. This makes her solo work manageable.

In the final analysis, entrepreneurial teams can achieve great things and may, at times, be necessary. But they're not for everyone. Taking on a partner means giving up the freedom to make your own decisions, being dependent on others to get things done, and pursuing a dream that you may not fully share. In other words, the price can be steep, and many entrepreneurs are unwilling to pay it.

Sources: Based on Josh Kaufman, "Go It Alone—Bruce Judson," http://personalmba.com/review/go-it-alone, accessed August 31, 2012; Jason Daley, "Well Enough Alone," *Entrepreneur*, Vol. 40, No. 4 (April 2012), pp. 81–85; http://thecollegewizard.net, accessed August 31, 2012; www.partiesthatcook.com, accessed August 31, 2012; "Employee Turned Entrepreneur—Bibby Gignilliat," www.breakingthe9to5jail.com/employee-turned-entrepreneur-bibby-gignilliat, accessed August 31, 2012; personal communication with Harvey Manger-Weil on October 5, 2012; and personal communication with Bibby Gignilliat on October 5, 2012.

8-1b Expanding Social Networks

Sometimes it's not *what* you know but *whom* you know that matters. Management team members help the venture obtain investment and technology resources. But they can also connect the enterprise with a social network that provides access to a wide range of resources beyond the reach of individual team members. A **social network** is the web of relationships that a person has with other people, including roommates or other acquaintances from college, former employees and business associates, and contacts through community organizations like the Rotary Club and religious groups. But it doesn't end there. A friend from college may not have what you need, but he or she may know someone who does. It is often said that business is all about relationships, a principle that is not lost on successful entrepreneurs. And the power of social networks is expanded tremendously as well-connected people are added to the management team.

What does an entrepreneur need from his or her network? That all depends on the situation. Howard Aldrich and Nancy Carter, two highly regarded experts on building management teams and social networks, have found that nearly half of those who are starting businesses use their networks to access information or get advice. About one-fourth use their networks to gain introductions to other people. Finally, a much smaller percentage use connections to obtain money, business services, physical facilities and equipment, help with personal needs, and other forms of assistance.[10] Clearly, a healthy system of personal relationships can help a small business access the resources it needs to get established and grow.

Beyond providing access to resources, social networks can be especially helpful in communicating legitimacy and jump-starting sales. Reputable firms may hesitate to do business with a company that doesn't have a demonstrated track record for reliable delivery or quality products or services. But influential advocates can use their pull to help a small business acquire one or more high-profile customers, which may persuade others to give a relatively unknown company a shot at their business, too. For an entrepreneur, having a healthy social network and a management team with helpful connections can be critical in establishing a solid reputation.

social network
An interconnected system of relationships with other people.

Some small business owners are tapping into the expanding universe of social media tools to attract customers, connect with peers, and share advice about common problems. In fact, a recent study found that the rate of adoption of social media tools by small companies has been doubling each year, which greatly expands the reach of their network-building efforts.[11] The more popular social media choices include the following:

- *LinkedIn:* Allows users to record contact details of people they know and trust in business; excellent for recruiting professionals or for connecting with groups of individuals who share common interests.
- *Twitter:* Enables people to send brief updates, or microblogs, to those signed up to receive them via computer or cell phone; a powerful tool for sending out information and doing mobile marketing.
- *Yelp:* Permits users to rate and comment on local businesses; good for getting feedback from customers; cheaper than surveys.
- *Facebook:* Lets users join networks organized by city, workplace, school, or region; superb for connecting with business contacts users seldom see and for observing how people interact in social networks.

Keeping up with the rapid growth of social media is a challenge. However, these alternatives can help you make connections easier, faster, and more conveniently—but only if you use them.

Regardless of how you pull it together, an active and robust social network is necessary for building **social capital**, which we refer to as the advantage created by an individual's connections within a network of social relationships. But this advantage doesn't develop overnight or by accident. It takes years to build social capital, and the building blocks that support it are well known—being reliable as a friend, being fair in your dealings, being true to your word.

The principle of reciprocation can be extremely helpful in adding to whatever social capital you already have. In his popular book on influence, Robert Cialdini defines **reciprocation** as a subtle but powerful sense of obligation, deeply embedded in every society, to repay in kind what another person has done for us or provided to us.[12] In general, people naturally feel that they should return favors. You can easily prime the pump of social capital by being the first to lend a hand and then watch those you assist come to your rescue when you run up against a challenge and ask for help. You don't have to fake it; just slow down a bit, and take a genuine interest in the needs of your friends and acquaintances. And helping others doesn't have to be costly. In today's information economy, passing along an important bit of news or insight is easy and free—but it can be as good as gold! So, think ahead, and reach out to help where you can. Your social capital is sure to increase, binding friends and contacts to you and providing a solid foundation for building a business.

social capital
The advantage created by an individual's connections in a social network.

reciprocation
A powerful sense of obligation to repay in kind what another has done for or provided to us.

RESOURCES

Network Development
Reid Hoffman, "the guru of networking," offers some great insights on how to build your personal network. He has been involved in the startup or early stages of sky-high performers like LinkedIn, Facebook, and Zynga, so he knows a great deal about building connections. To learn more about his networking insights and advice, read *The Start-Up of You*, by Reid Hoffman (New York: Crown Business, 2012).

8-2 COMMON FORMS OF LEGAL ORGANIZATION

LO
8-2

Explain the common legal forms of organization used by small businesses.

When launching a new business, an entrepreneur must choose a legal form of organization, which will determine who the actual owners of the business are. The most basic options are the sole proprietorship, partnership, and C corporation. More specialized forms of organization exist, but many small businesses find one of these common forms suitable for their needs. After outlining the primary options, we look first at some criteria for choosing among them and then introduce a number of specialized forms (see Exhibit 8.1) that offer their own unique features and advantages.

EXHIBIT **8.1** Forms of Legal Organization for Small Businesses

© Cengage Learning

8-2a The Sole Proprietorship Option

A **sole proprietorship**, the most basic business form, is a company owned by one person. An individual proprietor has title to all business assets and is subject to the claims of creditors. He or she receives all of the firm's profits but must also assume all losses, bear all risks, and pay all debts. Although this form certainly is not right for everyone, forming a sole proprietorship is nonetheless the simplest and cheapest way to start operation. Most states do not even require such companies to have a business license. Because of the ease of startup, the majority of small businesses (62.6 percent)[13] adopt this legal structure (see Exhibit 8.2).

In a sole proprietorship, an owner is free from interference by partners, shareholders, and directors. However, a sole proprietorship lacks some of the advantages of other legal forms. For example, there are no limits on the owner's personal liability—that is, the owner of the business has **unlimited liability**, and thus his or her personal assets can be taken by business creditors if the enterprise fails. For this reason, the sole proprietorship form is usually the practical choice only for very small businesses. In addition, sole proprietors are not employees of the business and cannot benefit from

sole proprietorship
A business owned by one person, who bears unlimited liability for the enterprise.

unlimited liability
Liability on the part of an owner that extends beyond the owner's investment in the business.

8.2 Percentage of Small Businesses by Legal Form of Organization

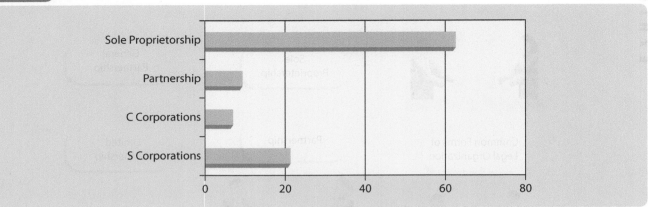

Sources: Internal Revenue Service, "Table 1A. Calendar Year Projections of Individual Returns by Major Processing Categories for the United States," www.irs.gov/pub/irs-soi/p6187t1a.xls (data for sole proprietorships), accessed September 6, 2012; and Internal Revenue Service, "Table 1. Fiscal Year Projections of the Number of Returns to Be Filed with the IRS," www.irs.gov /pub/irs-pdf/p6292.pdf (data for partnerships, C corporations, and S corporations), accessed September 6, 2012.

the advantage of many tax-free fringe benefits, such as insurance and hospitalization plans, which are often provided by corporations for their employees.

The death of the owner terminates the legal existence of a sole proprietorship. Thus, the possibility of the owner's death may cloud relationships between a business and its creditors and employees. It is important that the owner have a will, because the assets of the business minus its liabilities will belong to her or his heirs. In a will, a sole proprietor can give an executor the power to run the business for the heirs until they can take it over or it can be sold.

Also of concern is the possible incapacity of the sole proprietor. For example, if she or he were badly hurt in an accident and hospitalized for an extended period, the business could be ruined. A sole proprietor can guard against this contingency by giving a competent person legal power of attorney to carry on in such situations.

In some cases, circumstances argue against selecting the sole proprietorship option. If the nature of a business involves exposure to legal liability—for example, the manufacture of a potentially hazardous product or the operation of a child-care facility—a legal form that provides greater protection against personal liability is likely to be a better choice. For most companies, however, various forms of insurance are available to deal with the risks of a sole proprietorship, as well as those related to partnerships. (Liability insurance and other forms of protection are discussed further in Chapter 23.)

8-2b The Partnership Option

A **partnership** is a legal entity formed by two or more co-owners to operate a business for profit. Because of a partnership's voluntary nature, owners can set it up quickly, avoiding many of the legal requirements involved in creating a corporation. A partnership pools the managerial talents and capital of those joining together as business partners. As in a sole proprietorship, however, the owners share unlimited liability.

Operating a business as a partnership has benefits, but it is also fraught with potential problems, enough that most experts discourage the use of this form of organization as a way to run a business. The benefits of partnerships include the ability to share the workload as well as the emotional and financial burdens of the enterprise and to gain management talent that might otherwise break the budget. And it should not be overlooked that partners can add companionship to life in a small business.

However, many believe that the personal conflicts common in partnerships more than offset the benefits, and partners often fall short of one another's expectations.

partnership
A legal entity formed by two or more co-owners to operate a business for profit.

Of course, decision making is more complicated in partnerships because leadership is shared, and owners must also share their equity position in the business, which naturally dilutes the control of each partner. While some of the difficulties of partnerships are financial in nature, most are relational—for example, coping with a partner's dishonesty or dealing with differing priorities. Partnerships clearly have both disturbing and redeeming qualities. Therefore, *a partnership should be formed only if it appears to be the best option after considering all features of the enterprise.*

QUALIFICATIONS OF PARTNERS Any person capable of contracting may legally become a business partner. Individuals may become partners without contributing capital or having a claim to assets at the time of dissolution. Such persons are partners only in regard to management and profits. The formation of a partnership involves consideration not only of legal issues but also of personal and managerial factors. A strong partnership requires partners who are honest, healthy, capable, and compatible. The following suggestions may help entrepreneurs make the most of this form of organization:

- *Choose your partner carefully.* Partnerships are like marriages—they work best when you pick the right partner. Many sources are available to help you find that "perfect someone"—trade magazines, client contacts, professional associations, even online matching services like BusinessPartners.com and PartnerUp.com. But identifying a promising partner is just a start. You also need to be sure that your goals, values, and work habits are compatible and that your skills are complementary before committing to the deal. Above all, team up with a person you can trust, since the actions of your partner can legally bind you, even if a decision is made without your knowledge or consent.[14]

- *Be open, but cautious, about partnerships with friends.* Valued relationships can take a quick turn for the worse when a business deal gets rocky. A Dr. Jekyll friend can sometimes transform into a Mr. Hyde business associate when money enters the picture.

- *Test-drive the relationship, if possible.* Try more limited forms of business collaboration before jumping in with both feet. For example, you can cooperate on a small project or share a booth at a trade show and observe the behavior, style, and work habits of your prospective partner. This allows you to assess his or her strengths and weaknesses before committing to a long-term relationship.

- *Create a combined vision for the business.* Partners must be on the same page when it comes to forming the business concept they hope to develop together. This takes time, patience, and a lot of conversation. Other specific matters you should discuss before joining forces include the expectations of all partners (contributions of time, money, expertise, etc.), planned division of work, anticipated vacation time, and the sharing of profits and losses.

- *Prepare for the worst.* Keep in mind that more than half of all partnerships fail. That is why most experts recommend having an exit strategy for the partnership from the beginning. What looks like a good business arrangement at the outset can quickly fall apart when market conditions shift, a partner becomes involved in another business venture, or personal circumstances change. For example, the birth of a child, a sudden divorce, or the unexpected death of a spouse can alter everything. If it becomes necessary, exiting a partnership is far more difficult when plans for such an unfortunate outcome were not considered early on.

Failure to take suggestions like these seriously can derail efforts to build an effective working relationship or doom an otherwise workable partnership to an unnecessary or painful demise.

RIGHTS AND DUTIES OF PARTNERS An oral partnership agreement is legal and binding, but memory is always less than perfect. In his book *Legal Guide for Starting and Running a Small Business*, author and practicing business attorney Fred S. Steingold strongly recommends that partners sign a written **partnership agreement** to avoid problems later on.[15] This document, which explicitly spells out the partners' rights and duties, should be drawn up before the venture is launched. Though the partners may choose to have an attorney draft the agreement in order to ensure that all important features are included, many other sources of assistance also are available to guide you through this process. For example, another book by Steingold, *Legal Forms for Starting and Running a Small Business*,[16] provides a lengthy outline and description of a proper agreement.

Unless the articles of the partnership agreement specify otherwise, a partner is generally recognized as having certain implicit rights. For example, partners share profits or losses equally, unless they have agreed to a different ratio. But these rights are also balanced against serious liabilities. In a general partnership, each party bears **joint and several liability**, which means that a business decision by one partner binds all other partners, even if they were not consulted in advance, didn't approve the agreement or contract in question, or didn't even know about it![17] And as with a sole proprietorship, the unlimited personal liability of the partners can be terrifying. The assets of the business are at risk, of course, but so are the personal assets of the partners, including their homes, cars, and bank accounts. Good faith, together with reasonable care in the exercise of managerial duties, is required of all partners in the business.

Unfortunately, complications can arise even if partners have been careful to match their expectations at the start of the partnership and the arrangement has been formalized through a partnership agreement. When problems emerge, partners should move quickly to try to resolve the underlying issues. If they cannot do so, they should consider hiring a business mediator. Working with a mediator can be expensive, but the dissolution of the partnership is likely to be far more costly.

partnership agreement
A document that states explicitly the rights and duties of partners.

joint and several liability
The liability of each partner resulting from any one partner's ability to legally bind the other partners.

TERMINATION OF A PARTNERSHIP Death, incapacity, or withdrawal of a partner ends a partnership and requires liquidation or reorganization of the business. Liquidation often results in substantial losses to all partners, but it may be legally necessary. A partnership represents a close personal relationship of the parties that cannot be maintained against the desire of any one of them.

When one partner dies, loss due to liquidation may be avoided if the partnership agreement stipulates that surviving partners can continue the business after buying the decedent's interest. This option can be facilitated by having each partner carry life insurance that names the other partners as beneficiaries.

Partnerships sometimes have immediate concerns to address when a partner decides to leave the business, especially if the departure was unexpected. Aaron Keller, Brian Adducci, and a third partner started a marketing and design firm in Minneapolis called Capsule. Eighteen months later, when their partner decided to leave the business and start a competing company (taking several employees and clients with him), Keller and Adducci knew they would have to move quickly to avoid serious losses. As part of a sound

Entering a partnership can offer certain advantages, but they sometimes have to be terminated for a variety of reasons.

© Teun van den Dries/iStockphoto.com

response plan, they were advised to take several measures: First, cut off the departing partner's access to bank accounts, physical facilities, and company assets to avoid loss or damage to equipment critical to the business. Then, quickly assess that partner's role in the enterprise and take steps to fill his shoes to get the business back to normal as soon as possible. Once these very pressing matters are under control, sort out any legal issues that remain, such as abiding by any exit agreements that may have been signed. With time and a lot of hard work, Keller and Adducci were able to regain their footing, but the experience helped them to understand just how fragile a partnership can be—and how important it is to have a rapid-response plan when things go wrong.[18]

8-2c The C Corporation Option

In 1819, Chief Justice John Marshall of the United States Supreme Court defined a **corporation** as "an artificial being, invisible, intangible, and existing only in contemplation of the law." With these words, the Supreme Court recognized the corporation as a **legal entity**, meaning that it can file suit and be sued, hold and sell property, and engage in business operations that are stipulated in the corporate charter. In other words, a corporation is a separate entity from the individuals who own it, which means that the corporation, *not* its owners, is liable for the debts of the business. The implications of this arrangement for risk taking and business formation are profound and far-reaching, prompting one highly influential business executive to declare the creation of the modern corporation to have been the single greatest innovation in the last several hundred years, at least where wealth creation is concerned.[19] The ordinary corporation—often called a **C corporation** to distinguish it from more specialized forms—is discussed in this section.

THE CORPORATE CHARTER To form a corporation, one or more persons must apply to the secretary of state (at the state level) for permission to incorporate. After completing preliminary steps, including payment of an incorporation fee, the written application (which should be prepared by an attorney) is approved by the secretary of state and becomes the **corporate charter**. This document—sometimes called *articles of incorporation* or *certificate of incorporation*—shows that the corporation exists.

A corporation's charter should be brief, in accord with state law, and broad in its statement of the firm's powers. Details should be left to the *corporate bylaws*, which outline the basic rules for ongoing formalities and decisions of corporate life, including the size of the board of directors, the duties and responsibilities of directors and officers, the scheduling of regular meetings of the directors and shareholders, the means of calling for a special meeting of these groups, procedures for exercising voting rights, and restrictions on the transfer of corporate stock.

RIGHTS AND STATUS OF STOCKHOLDERS Ownership in a corporation is evidenced by **stock certificates**, each of which stipulates the number of shares owned by a stockholder. An ownership interest does not confer a legal right to act for the firm or to share in its management. It does, however, provide the stockholder with the right to receive dividends in proportion to stockholdings, but only when the dividends are properly declared by the firm. Ownership of stock typically carries a **preemptive right**, or the right to buy new shares in proportion to the number of shares already owned before new stock is offered for public sale.

The legal status of stockholders is fundamental, of course, but it may be overemphasized. In many small corporations, the owners typically serve both as directors and as managing officers. The person who owns most or all of the stock can control a business as effectively as if it was a sole proprietorship. Thus, this form of organization can work well for individual- and family-owned businesses, where maintaining control of the firm is important.

corporation
A business organization that exists as a legal entity and provides limited liability to its owners.

legal entity
A business organization that is recognized by the law as having a separate legal existence.

C corporation
An ordinary corporation, taxed by the federal government as a separate legal entity.

corporate charter
A document that establishes a corporation's existence.

stock certificate
A document specifying the number of shares owned by a stockholder.

preemptive right
The right of stockholders to buy new shares of stock before they are offered to the public.

LIMITED LIABILITY OF STOCKHOLDERS For most stockholders, their limited liability is a major advantage of the corporate form of organization. Their financial liability is restricted to the amount of money they invest in the business. Creditors cannot require them to sell personal assets to pay the corporation's debts. However, a bank that makes a loan to a small firm may insist that the owners assume personal liability for the firm's debts. If the corporation is unable to repay the loan, the banker can then look to the owners' personal assets to recover the amount of the loan. In this case, the corporate advantage of limited liability is lost.

Why would owners agree to personally guarantee a firm's debt? Simply put, they may have no choice if they want the money. Most bankers are unwilling to loan money to an entrepreneur who is not prepared to put his or her own personal assets at risk.

DEATH OR WITHDRAWAL OF STOCKHOLDERS Unlike a partnership interest, ownership in a corporation is readily transferable. Exchange of shares of stock is sufficient to transfer an ownership interest to a different individual.

Stock of large corporations is exchanged continually without noticeable effect on the operation of the business. For a small firm, however, a change of owners, though legally similar, can involve numerous complications. For example, finding a buyer for the stock of a small company may prove difficult. Also, a minority stockholder in a small firm is vulnerable. If two of three equal shareholders in a small business sold their stock to an outsider, the remaining shareholder would then be at the mercy of that outsider.

The death of a majority stockholder can have unfortunate repercussions in a small firm. An heir, the executor, or a purchaser of the stock might well insist on direct control, with possible adverse effects for other stockholders. To prevent problems of this nature, legal arrangements should be made at the outset to provide for management continuity by surviving stockholders and fair treatment of a stockholder's heirs. As in the case of a partnership, taking out life insurance ahead of time can ensure the ability to buy out a deceased stockholder's interest.

MAINTAINING CORPORATE STATUS Certain steps must be taken if a corporation is to retain its standing as a separate entity. For example, the corporation must hold annual

EXHIBIT

8.3 Comparison of Basic Legal Forms of Organization

Form of Organization	Initial Organizational Requirements and Costs	Liability of Owners	Continuity of Business
Sole proprietorship	Minimum requirements; generally no registration or filing fee	Unlimited liability	Dissolved upon proprietor's death
General partnership	Minimum requirements; generally no registration or filing fee; written partnership agreement not legally required but strongly suggested	Unlimited liability	Unless partnership agreement specifies differently, dissolved upon withdrawal or death of partner
C corporation	Most expensive and greatest requirements; filing fees; compliance with state regulations for corporations	Liability limited to investment in company	Continuity of business unaffected by shareholder withdrawal or death
Form of organization preferred	Proprietorship or partnership	C corporation	C corporation

© Cengage Learning

(*Continued*)

meetings of both the shareholders and the board of directors, keep minutes to document the major decisions of shareholders and directors, maintain bank accounts that are separate from owners' bank accounts, and file a separate income tax return for the business.

8-3 CONSIDERATIONS IN CHOOSING AN ORGANIZATIONAL FORM

Choosing a legal form for a new business deserves careful attention because of the various, sometimes conflicting features of each organizational option. Depending on the particular circumstances of a specific business, the tax advantages of one form, for example, may offset the limited liability advantages of another form. Some trade-offs may be necessary. Ideally, an experienced attorney or knowledgeable accountant should be consulted for guidance in selecting the most appropriate form of organization.

LO 8-3

Identify factors to consider in choosing among the primary legal forms of organization.

Some entrepreneurship experts insist that the two most basic forms of business—sole proprietorship and partnership—should *never* be adopted. While these forms clearly have drawbacks, they are workable. And fortunately there are other basic forms to consider, such as the C corporation. Exhibit 8.3 summarizes the main considerations in selecting one of these three primary forms of ownership.

INITIAL ORGANIZATIONAL REQUIREMENTS AND COSTS Organizational requirements and costs rise as the formality of the organization increases. That is, a sole proprietorship is typically less complex and less expensive to form than a partnership, and a partnership is less complex and less expensive to form than a corporation. In view of the relatively modest costs, however, this consideration is of minimal importance in the long run.

LIABILITY OF OWNERS Liability risks are among the most important factors to consider when selecting an organizational form. As discussed earlier, a sole proprietorship and a partnership have the built-in disadvantage of unlimited liability for the owners. With these forms of organization, there is no distinction between the firm's

EXHIBIT 8.3 Comparison of Basic Legal Forms of Organization (*Continued*)

Transferability of Ownership	Management Control	Attractiveness for Raising Capital	Income Taxes
May transfer ownership of company name and assets	Absolute management freedom	Limited to proprietor's personal capital	Income from the business is taxed as personal income to the proprietor
Requires the consent of all partners	Majority vote of partners required for control	Limited to partners' ability and desire to contribute capital	Income from the business is taxed as personal income to the partners
Is easily transferred by transferring shares of stock	Shareholders have final control, but usually board of directors controls company policies	Usually the most attractive form for raising capital	The C corporation is taxed on its income and the stockholder is taxed if and when dividends are received
Depends on the circumstances	Depends on the circumstances	C corporation	Depends on the circumstances

© Cengage Learning

assets and the owners' personal assets. In contrast, setting up a corporation limits the owners' liability to their investment in the business.

Two cautions are in order regarding liability and organizational forms. First, incorporation will not protect a firm's owners from liability if it is used to perpetuate a fraud, skirt a law, or commit some wrongful act. In such cases, the courts may decide that there is no legal separation between the owners and the corporate entity, a concept known as **piercing the corporate veil**. Protection from financial liability may be jeopardized if, for example, (1) the company is bankrupt, but its owners knowingly take on debt, (2) the board of directors does not meet as required by law or observe other corporate formalities, or (3) business and personal accounts are not kept separate and company funds are used to pay an owner's personal expenses. Legal action is taken most often against smaller, privately held business entities and "sham corporations" that are set up with the specific goal of deceiving others.[20] Of course, some forms of organization offer no shield against liability in the first place.

Second, no form of organization can protect entrepreneurs from *all* forms of liability. For example, if an owner causes a traffic accident and is declared personally liable for damages or injuries in court, he or she will have to pay the judgment, even if it means selling personal assets to satisfy the ruling. If, on the other hand, an employee caused the accident while on company business, the assets of the business will be at risk, but the personal assets of the owner will be shielded from liability—*but only if the business is organized as a corporation or limited liability company* (which will be discussed later in the chapter). This protection does not extend to the owner(s) of a sole proprietorship or a partnership, whose personal assets would also be at risk.

As indicated previously, most banks and many suppliers require small business owners to sign a personal guarantee before loaning money or extending credit to them, regardless of the form of organization. Entrepreneurs have to pay off these obligations if their businesses are unable to, even if doing so requires the use of personal assets. This is the lender's way of trying to ensure that debts are repaid, but it illustrates a practical limitation of organizational forms when it comes to liability protection.[21]

CONTINUITY OF BUSINESS A sole proprietorship is immediately dissolved on the owner's death. Likewise, a partnership is terminated on the death or withdrawal of a partner, unless the partnership agreement states otherwise. A corporation, on the other hand, offers continuity. The status of an individual investor does not affect the corporation's existence.

TRANSFERABILITY OF OWNERSHIP Ownership is transferred most easily in a corporation. The ability to transfer ownership, however, is not necessarily good or bad—it all depends on the owners' preferences. In some businesses, owners may want the option of evaluating any prospective new investors. Under other circumstances, unrestricted transferability may be preferred.

MANAGEMENT CONTROL A sole proprietor has absolute control of the firm. Control within a partnership is normally based on the majority vote, so it follows that an increase in the number of partners reduces each partner's voice in management. Within a corporation, control has two dimensions: (1) the formal control vested in the stockholders who own the majority of the voting common shares and (2) the functional control exercised by the corporate officers in conducting daily operations. In a small corporation, these two forms of control usually rest with the same individuals.

ATTRACTIVENESS FOR RAISING CAPITAL A corporation has a distinct advantage when raising new equity capital, due to the ease of transferring ownership through the sale of common shares and the flexibility in distributing the shares. In contrast, the

piercing the corporate veil
A situation in which the courts conclude that incorporation has been used to perpetuate a fraud, skirt a law, or commit some wrongful act and thus remove liability protection from the corporate entity.

unlimited liability of a sole proprietorship and a partnership discourages new investors.

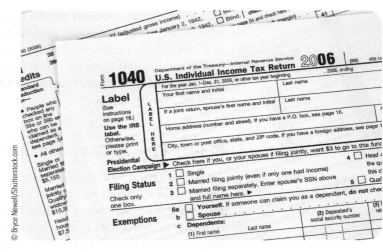
© Bryce Newell/Shutterstock.com

INCOME TAXES Income taxes frequently have a major effect on an owner's selection of a form of organization. To understand the federal income tax system, you must consider this twofold question: Who is responsible for paying taxes, and how is tax liability determined? The three major forms of organization are taxed in different ways:

- *Sole proprietorship.* Self-employed individuals who operate a business as a sole proprietorship report income from the business on their individual federal income tax returns. They are then taxed on that income at the rates set by law for individuals.

- *Partnership.* A partnership reports the income it earns to the Internal Revenue Service, but the partnership itself does not pay any taxes. The income is allocated to the partners according to their agreement. The partners each report their own shares of the partnership's income on their personal tax returns and pay any taxes owed.

- *C corporation.* The C corporation, as a separate legal entity, reports its income and pays any taxes related to these profits. The owners (stockholders) of the corporation must report on their personal tax returns any amounts paid to them by the corporation in the form of dividends. (They must also report capital gains or losses, but only at the time they sell their stock in the company.) Keep in mind that dividends are, in essence, taxed twice—first as part of a corporation's earnings and then as part of the owners' personal income.

The IRS's small business website at www.irs.gov/businesses/small/index.html provides links to tax information on the different organizational forms, insights related to important small business topics, and answers to industry-specific questions, as well as forms and publications that will help with tax planning and preparation.

limited partnership
A partnership with at least one general partner and one or more limited partners.

general partner
A partner in a limited partnership who has unlimited personal liability.

8-4 SPECIALIZED FORMS OF ORGANIZATION

The majority of small businesses use one of the three major ownership structures just described—the sole proprietorship, partnership, or C corporation. However, other specialized forms of organization are also used by small firms. Five of these alternatives merit further consideration: the limited partnership, the S corporation, the limited liability company, the professional corporation, and the nonprofit corporation.

LO
8-4
Discuss the unique features and restrictions of five specialized organizational forms.

8-4a The Limited Partnership

The **limited partnership** is a special form of partnership involving at least one general partner and one or more limited partners. The **general partner** remains personally liable for the debts of the business, but **limited partners** have limited personal liability as long as they do not take an active role in the management of the partnership. In other words, limited partners risk only the capital they invest in the business. An individual

limited partner
A partner in a limited partnership who is not active in its management and has limited personal liability.

with substantial personal wealth can, therefore, invest money in a limited partnership without exposing his or her personal assets to liability claims that might arise through activities of the business. If a limited partner becomes active in management, however, his or her limited liability is lost. To form a limited partnership, partners must file a certificate of limited partnership with the proper state office, as state law governs this form of organization.

8-4b The S Corporation

The designation **S corporation**, or **Subchapter S corporation**, is derived from Subchapter S of the Internal Revenue Code. This organizational form permits a business to retain the limited liability feature of a C corporation while offering more favorable tax treatment on income. To obtain S corporation status, a corporation must meet certain requirements, including the following:

- No more than 100 stockholders are allowed.[22]
- All stockholders must be individuals or certain qualifying estates and trusts.[23]
- Only one class of stock can be outstanding.
- Fiscally, the corporation must operate on a calendar-year basis.
- Partnerships, corporations, and nonresident aliens cannot be shareholders.[24]

An S corporation does not pay income taxes but instead passes taxable income or losses on to the stockholders. This allows stockholders to receive dividends from the corporation without double taxation on the firm's profit (once through a corporate tax and again through a personal tax on received dividends). A competent tax attorney should be consulted before selecting S corporation status, as tax law changes have considerable effect on this form.

8-4c The Limited Liability Company

The **limited liability company** is a relatively new form of organization. It has grown in popularity because it offers the simplicity of a sole proprietorship and the protection of a corporation to shield the personal assets of owners. A limited liability company can have an unlimited number of owners (even having a single owner is permitted in most states), and these may include non-U.S. citizens.[25] This form differs from the C corporation in that it avoids double taxation. Like S corporations, limited liability companies are not taxed but simply pass their income on to their owners, who pay taxes on it as part of their personal income.[26]

According to many attorneys, the limited liability company is usually the best choice for new businesses. Compared to most other forms, it is easier to set up, is more flexible, and offers some significant tax advantages. But a limited liability company isn't always the best way to go. For example, under the following conditions, it would be better to use a C corporation:

- *You want to provide extensive fringe benefits to owners or employees.* The C corporation can deduct these benefits, and they are not treated as taxable income to the employees.
- *You want to offer stock options to employees.* Since limited liability companies do not have stock, they cannot offer such incentives.

S corporation (Subchapter S corporation)
A type of corporation that offers limited liability to its owners and passes taxable income or losses on to stockholders.

limited liability company
A form of organization in which owners have limited liability but pay personal income taxes on business profits.

- *You hope to go public or sell the business at some time in the future.* A C corporation can go public or be sold to another corporation in a tax-free, stock-for-stock exchange.

- *You plan to convert to a C corporation eventually.* You cannot change from a pass-through entity like a limited liability company without paying additional taxes.

8-4d The Professional Corporation

Have you noticed the initials PC or PA as part of the corporate name on the letterhead or signage of your doctor, dentist, or attorney? These letters indicate that the practice is set up as a **professional corporation** in order to offer professional services. Though its meaning varies from state to state, the term *professional* usually applies to those individuals whose professions require that they obtain a license before they can practice, so this would include doctors, chiropractors, lawyers, accountants, engineers, architects, and other highly trained individuals. But unlike other liability-shielding organizational forms, the professional corporation does not protect a practitioner from her or his own negligence or malpractice. Rather, it shields owners in the practice from one another's liability. In some states, a different business structure called a *limited liability partnership* can serve the same purpose and may have additional advantages. Obviously, the professional corporation applies to a fairly narrow range of enterprises, but it is usually the best option for businesses that fall into that category. In fact, many state laws require this form of organization before a practice can operate.

8-4e The Nonprofit Corporation

For some ventures, the most practical form of organization is the **nonprofit corporation**. Most elect to become 501(c)(3) organizations, which are created to serve civic, educational, charitable, or religious purposes. To qualify for 501(c)(3) status, the money-raising concern, fund, or foundation must be a corporation—the IRS will not grant this option to an individual or partnership. In the application process, the officers need to submit articles of organization that spell out and limit the range of activities of the enterprise. For a tax exemption to be granted, the organization must pass the **organizational test** ("IRS-speak" for verification that the organization is staying true to the articles filed). A nonprofit corporation must establish a board of directors or trustees to oversee its operations, and if it should dissolve, it is required to transfer its assets to another nonprofit corporation.

Though social entrepreneurs certainly do not have to charter their enterprises as nonprofit corporations, they often choose this option. Matthew Gutschick and Ben Whiting started a social enterprise called MagicMouth Theatre, to teach theater and magic to young people and offer opportunities for them to perform. As Gutschick recalls, when they selected a business structure, the two entrepreneurs "decided to go nonprofit because it gave us a larger measure of credibility and authenticity."[27] In other words, choosing to structure an organization as a nonprofit corporation can be a way to reinforce the message and work of the organization.

professional corporation
A form of corporation that shields owners from liability and is set up for individuals in certain professional practices.

nonprofit corporation
A form of corporation for enterprises established to serve civic, educational, charitable, or religious purposes; not for generation of profits.

organizational test
Verification of whether a nonprofit organization is staying true to its stated purpose.

TOOLS

The B Corporation
Are you hoping to use the power of business to solve a social or environmental problem? If so, the B Corporation may be exactly the form you need to adopt. The performance and accountability standards are demanding, sustainability must be a primary thrust, and transparency is forced through B Impact Reports that have to be filed. But according to the certifying organization, the outcomes more than justify the costs: "Individuals will have great economic opportunity, society will move closer to achieving a positive environmental footprint, more people will be employed in great places to work, and we will have built stronger communities at home and around the world." To learn more, visit http://www.bcorporation.net.

Living the Dream

Doing Good and Doing Well, with Organizational Forms to Match

Many entrepreneurs are committed to making two things at the same time: (1) money and (2) a difference in the world—and not necessarily in that order. If you assume that a company must select one organizational form or another, it may seem like multifaceted dreams will be difficult to reach. A few examples show how hybrid forms can be set up with very successful results.

Mozilla Foundation was created in 2003 as a nonprofit organization to manage efforts to fuel extraordinary innovative development of Web browsers and "promote openness, innovation, and opportunity on the Internet." It has definitely succeeded. Its best known product, Firefox, now holds more than 20 percent of the world's market for Web browsers. And that popularity provided some of the justification for the foundation's formation of Mozilla Corporation in 2005, which is a for-profit subsidiary that brings in more than $100 million a year from revenue-sharing agreements it has with search partners like Google and Yahoo. But the nonprofit side of the combined entity is still very active and receives around $222,000 annually in charitable contributions, which are given to support open-source software development.

Hybrid forms work for smaller entrepreneurial ventures as well. Story Pirates is a nonprofit launched in 2003 by graduates of Northwestern University "to celebrate the words and ideas of young people" and "make learning more engaging and effective." Its after-school story-writing and drama programs have grown in popularity and now are offered at more than 200 schools from coast to coast. Because of its rising popularity, the founders had to figure out how to handle the rapid growth in ticket sales. Forming a for-profit with the same name was a huge step in the right direction. The two organizations now are able to share the name and content through licensing agreements that allow them to make the most of various high-potential opportunities that come their way.

Nicole Betancourt and Sarah Schenk faced similar challenges and decided to launch "sister entities" with the singular mission of "answer[ing] parents' questions about food and creat[ing] a world that nurtures healthy, thriving children." They set up a for-profit arm called Parent Earth, Inc., to generate income that would then be used to bankroll its nonprofit alter ego, Parent Earth Foundation, until it raised enough support to stand on its own. The nonprofit is tax exempt and can accept foundation grants, which is a huge plus. But for-profit entities have much more flexibility when it comes to raising investment, generating income, and paying the salaries necessary to attract top-flight talent. And, of course, they can also make tax-deductible contributions to their nonprofit partners.

Hybrid forms come with some hassles that must be managed—such as maintaining separate boards and management teams and being prepared to prove that transactions between entities reflect true market value. But as one writer put it, "You get to have your cake and save the whales, too." What more could a small business owner ask for?

Sources: Based on www.mozilla.org/about/history.html, accessed September 13, 2012; Issie Lapowsky, "The Social Entrepreneurship Spectrum: Hybrids," *Inc.*, Vol. 33, No. 4 (May 2011), pp. 86–88; www.parentearth.com/about, accessed September 13, 2012; and www.storypirates.org/about, accessed September 13, 2012.

8-5 FORMING STRATEGIC ALLIANCES

LO 8-5
Understand the uses of strategic alliances in small businesses.

A strategic alliance is an organizational relationship that links two or more independent business entities in some common endeavor. Without affecting the independent legal status of the participating business partners, it provides a way for companies to improve their individual effectiveness by sharing certain resources. And these alliances can take many forms, from informal information exchanges to formal equity- or contract-based relationships and everything in between. Exhibit 8.4 shows some types of alliances that are most popular with small businesses.

Strategic alliances are increasing in importance to small businesses today, and more entrepreneurs are finding creative ways to use these cooperative strategies to their advantage. In fact, statistics show that nearly two-thirds of small businesses use alliances, and three-fourths of these companies report having positive experiences with them.[28] Given the escalating pace of competition and the rising costs of developing essential capabilities, alliances provide a way for small companies to access another firm's first-rate resources so that they can be more competitive. Since a competitive advantage often goes to the entrepreneur who is quick to exploit it, many small business owners see strategic alliances as an essential part of their plan for growth. These cooperative strategies represent one way to keep up with the accelerating pace of change in today's business environment. (See Chapter 18 for a discussion of strategic alliances as these apply to global enterprises.)

8-5a Strategic Alliances with Large Companies

Small business owners often assume that their ventures have nothing to offer larger companies, but the truth is that they can play an essential role in helping corporations address some of their most pressing challenges. Typically, these alliances are formed to join the complementary skills and expertise of the partnered firms, in order to promote the competitive edge of both (or all) parties. For example, large manufacturers sometimes team up with innovative small manufacturers in product development efforts, and giant retailers form alliances with smaller suppliers to

strategic alliance
An organizational relationship that links two or more independent business entities in a common endeavor.

EXHIBIT 8.4 Most Popular Small Business Alliances by Type

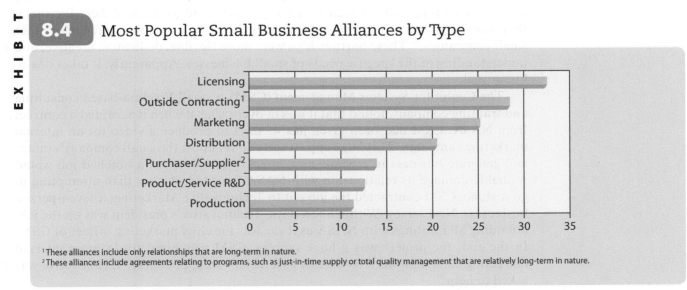

¹ These alliances include only relationships that are long-term in nature.
² These alliances include agreements relating to programs, such as just-in-time supply or total quality management that are relatively long-term in nature.

Source: Based on William J. Dennis, Jr. (ed.), "Strategic Alliances," *National Small Business Poll*, Vol. 4, No. 4 (Washington, DC: NFIB Research Foundation, 2004), pp. 1–8.

achieve specific quality requirements and meet demanding delivery schedules. Combining the speed, flexibility, and creative energy of a small business with the industry experience, production capabilities, and market reach of a large corporation can be a winning strategy.

While alliances with large firms can give a tremendous boost to performance, some small businesses discover that bigger isn't always better. The advantages created by joining forces with large firms must be weighed against the risk of being squeezed financially or of running into smothering bureaucratic complications. One small company, for example, jumped at the chance to form an alliance with a major multinational firm in the same industry. Everything seemed to be running smoothly until the small firm learned that a simple invoice discrepancy was holding up a $1.2 million payment that it desperately needed to meet future expansion commitments. The money was small change to the multinational, but it was critical to its small partner. The two companies reached a stalemate, the alliance failed, and the small business was never able to recover $300,000 of the money that it was owed.

Forming alliances with prestigious partners may offer a substantial boost to status and market access, but the parties' strategic priorities may not mesh, and a major corporation can wield enormous power over a small, struggling enterprise. Also, some large firms have a track record of misbehavior as partners, and you need to know this *before* entering an alliance with them. The guidelines provided in Chapter 4 for the evaluation of a franchisor (see pages 100–103) can be helpful when deciding whether to take on a particular strategic partner. For example, it would be wise to investigate whether the corporation has been a good, ethical partner for other small companies. Knowing this in advance will help you to make an informed and profitable decision.

RESOURCES

Building Business Alliances

It is crucial that you select a strategic partner who won't damage your reputation and will help boost your venture's performance. For an excellent primer on partner selection, see Donna Peek's advice in "Evaluating and Selecting a Strategic Partner," at www.entrepreneurship .org/en/resource-center /evaluating-and-selecting -a-strategic-partner.aspx.

8-5b Strategic Alliances with Small Companies

Small businesses can also form strategic alliances with partners that are similar in size, in ways that enhance mutual competitive strength. Studies have indicated that about half of all small businesses maintain one or more strategic alliances with companies that are smaller or equal in size.[29] When *Inc.* researchers asked dozens of entrepreneurs which alliance partners had performed best for them, they were surprised to learn that the most enthusiastic anecdotes were about other small companies.[30] These partnerships were more flexible, dedicated, creative, and understanding of the specific needs of small businesses. Apparently, it takes one to know one!

The Center for Systems Management (CSM), a small Virginia-based consulting and training company, found that it was in over its head when it accepted a contract from NASA. CSM had been given just 45 days to produce a video for an internal marketing campaign. This huge opportunity could boost the small company's image and generate business in a whole new category of work, but a botched job would probably damage its relationship with NASA for good. Rather than attempting to go it alone, CSM contracted the job out to Technovative Marketing, a seven-person business in New Jersey. Within a few days, Technovative's president was on the job, attending all meetings with NASA as if she was the chief marketing officer of CSM. In the end, the project was a huge success. CSM was hired to do more internal marketing campaign work for NASA as a result—and, of course, Technovative was asked to help.[31]

8-5c Setting Up and Maintaining Successful Strategic Alliances

An alliance strategy can be powerful for growing companies—it spreads the risk of entering new markets and helps small players with unattractive balance sheets appear stable to the end buyer. It can also provide a fast track to reaching the critical mass required for pre-sale and post-sale support. Entrepreneurs should select partners with a "division of labor" mentality that allows all parties to focus their efforts on what they do best. For example, identifying intersections between product lines and expertise opens up the potential for cross-selling that creates growth opportunities for everyone involved.

Working closely with other companies can also introduce significant hazards. Because alliance partners are in a unique position to learn about your strategy and customer base, they can become competitors overnight. Therefore, it is crucial to select partners with care and to structure contracts to ensure growth, including an "easy out" clause if the alliance does not work out.

While strategic alliances often are not easy to set up, they can be even more difficult to maintain. Research has shown that many small businesses are pleased with the results of their strategic alliances,[32] but a number of alliances run into trouble and, in time, fail. Fortunately, when setting up alliances, entrepreneurs can take the following steps to improve their chances for success:

- *Establish a healthy network of contacts.* These people can lead you to still other contacts, and eventually to the one you need. Tap into leads through industry analysts, executive recruiters, public relations agencies, business reporters, and even the government.

- *Identify and contact individuals within a firm who are likely to return your call.* "Dialing high" (calling contacts at the vice-presidential level or higher) works in small or medium-size firms, but in large firms you may need to call managers or other mid-level employees to get a response.

- *Do your homework and win points just for being prepared.* You should be able to clearly outline the partner's potential financial benefits from the alliance. If possible, show that your firm can deliver value to the alliance across several fronts.

- *Learn to speak and understand the "language" of your partner.* You will not pick up on subtle messages in conversations with partners unless you know how they communicate. This can eventually make or break the alliance.

- *Make sure any alliance offer is clearly a win–win opportunity.* Only those agreements that benefit all participating parties will endure.

- *Monitor the progress of the alliance to ensure that goals and expectations are being met, and make changes as they become necessary.*

The goal is to form strategic alliances that are beneficial to all partners and to manage these alliances effectively. In their book *Everyone Is a Customer*, Jeffrey Shuman, Janice Twombly, and David Rottenberg point out that a key to successful strategic alliances is understanding the true nature of the relationship: "Relationships are advertised as being between companies, whereas in reality relationships are built between people. And that's a very important distinction."[33] Cultivating relationships is essential to business success in general, and these can be promoted through an effective board of directors or advisors, the topic to which we turn next.

LO
8-6

Describe the effective use of boards of directors and advisory boards.

8-6 MAKING THE MOST OF A BOARD OF DIRECTORS

In entrepreneurial firms, the **board of directors** tends to be small (usually five or fewer members[34]) and serves as the governing body for corporate activity. In concept, the stockholders elect the board, which in turn chooses the firm's officers, who manage the enterprise. The directors also set or approve management policies, consider reports on operating results from the officers, and declare any dividends.

All too often, the majority stockholder in a small corporation (usually the entrepreneur) appoints a board of directors only to fulfill a legal requirement (since corporations are required by law to have a board of directors) or as mere window dressing for investors. Such an entrepreneur often will select personal friends, relatives, or businesspersons who are too busy to analyze the firm's circumstances and are not inclined to disagree with the owner. Entrepreneurs who take a more constructive approach find an active board to be both practical and beneficial, especially when the members are informed, skeptical, and independent.

8-6a Selection of Directors

An entrepreneur who is attempting to assemble a cooperative and experienced group of directors needs to consider the value of an outside board, one with members whose income does not depend on the firm. The firm's attorney and banker, local management consultants, and other business executives might all be considered as potential directors but usually lack the independence needed to critically review an entrepreneur's plans. Also, in many cases the owner is already paying for their expertise.

Objectivity is a particularly valuable contribution of outside directors. They can look at issues more dispassionately than can insiders who are involved in daily decision making. Outside directors, for example, are freer to evaluate and to question a firm's ethical standards. Some operating executives, without the scrutiny of outside directors, may rationalize unethical or illegal behavior as being in the best interest of the company. In a family business, an outside board can help mediate and resolve issues related to leadership succession, in addition to providing more general direction. As outsiders, they bring to the business a measure of detachment from potentially explosive emotional differences.

Working with outside board members is not always easy, but an entrepreneur who is advised by the board to make tough decisions may find that those decisions are required to move the business forward. For example, the board may keep bringing the conversation back to issues that are easy to avoid, such as the need to build long-term relationships with important individuals in the banking community or the value of converting intentions for the company's future into a formal business plan that can be studied, debated, perfected, and used as a tool to attract crucial resources to the enterprise. Entrepreneurs often spend as much as 20 percent of their time on board-related activities, but the time commitment is worth the cost if the directors are doing their jobs well.

The nature and needs of a business help determine the qualifications required in its directors. For example, a firm that faces a marketing problem may benefit greatly from the counsel of a board member with a marketing background. Business prominence in the community is not an essential quality for board members, although it may help to give the company credibility and enable it to attract other well-qualified directors. Directors with a broad network of influential business friends and associates can contribute greatly, as long as they are willing to reach out to their contacts on behalf of the company.

After deciding on the qualifications to look for, a business owner must seek suitable candidates as board members. Effective directors are honest and accountable, offer

board of directors
The governing body of a corporation, elected by the stockholders.

valuable insights based on business experience, and enhance the company's credibility with its stakeholders (especially customers and suppliers). Suggestions for such candidates may be obtained from the firm's accountant, attorney, banker, and other associates in the business community. Owners or managers of other, noncompeting small companies, as well as second- and third-level executives in large companies, are often willing to accept such positions. Before offering candidates positions on the board, however, a business owner would be wise to do some discreet background checking.

8-6b Contributions of Directors

The growing complexity of small businesses, arising in part from globalization and technological developments, makes the expertise of well-chosen directors especially valuable. In a family business, outsiders can play a unique role in helping evaluate family talent and mediating differences among family members. And a strong board of directors can help the entrepreneur look beyond the next few months to make important, long-term strategic decisions. In other words, good directors will be able to help entrepreneurs keep their eyes on the big picture.

By virtue of their backgrounds, directors can fill gaps in the expertise of a management team and monitor its actions. The board should meet regularly to provide maximum assistance to the chief executive. In board meetings, ideas should be debated, strategies determined, and the pros and cons of policies explored. In this way, the chief executive is informed by the unique perspectives of all the board members. Their combined knowledge makes possible more intelligent decisions on issues crucial to the firm.

By utilizing the experience of a board of directors, the chief executive of a small corporation is in no way giving up active control of its operations. Instead, he or she is simply drawing on a larger pool of business knowledge. A group will typically make better decisions than will a single individual working alone.

An active board of directors serves management by reviewing major policy decisions, advising on external business conditions and on proper reaction to the business cycle, providing informal advice from time to time on specific problems that arise, and offering access to important personal contacts. With a strong board, a small firm may gain greater credibility with the public, as well as with business and financial communities.

8-6c Compensation of Directors

The compensation paid to board members varies greatly, and some small firms pay no fees at all. If compensation is provided, it is usually offered in the form of an annual retainer, board meeting fees, and pay for committee work. (Directors may serve on committees that evaluate executive compensation, nominate new board members, and oversee the work of the company's auditors.) Annual retainers for board work at established small firms typically range from $5,000 to $10,000, and board meeting fees can run from $500 to $2,000 per meeting. These costs to the firm are usually in addition to reimbursements for travel expenses related to board meetings and the financial burden of providing Directors and Officers Liability Insurance, which protects board members if they should be sued in the course of carrying out their duties as directors.[35] Sometimes, board members are also given a small percentage of the company's profits as a bonus for their participation, and some cash-strapped businesses may grant them stock (often 1 percent, but as high as 2 percent or more to lure top talent) in lieu of compensation.[36]

The relatively modest compensation offered for the services of well-qualified directors suggests that financial reward is not their primary motivation for serving on a board. But keep in mind that it is not uncommon for some directors to serve for free because of their interest in seeing a new or small business prosper. Reasonable compensation is appropriate, however, if directors are making important contributions to the firm's operations. In any case, it is good to keep in mind that you usually get what you pay for.

8-6d An Alternative: An Advisory Board

Some individuals are reluctant to join a board of directors because outside directors may be held responsible for illegal company actions, even though they are not directly involved in wrongdoing. Thus, many small companies use an **advisory board** as an alternative to a board of directors. Qualified outsiders are asked to serve on a board as advisors to the company. This group then functions in much the same way as a board of directors does, except that its actions are only advisory in nature. In other words, it has no legal authority over the owner or the company.

The legal liability of members of an advisory board is not completely clear. However, limiting their compensation and power is thought to lighten, if not eliminate, the personal liability of members. Since its role is advisory in nature, the board also may pose less of a threat to the owner and possibly work more cooperatively than a board of directors.

Without a doubt, a well-selected board of directors or advisors can do a great deal for a small company, but bear in mind that this is only one part of an effective organizational plan. The success of any business depends on the quality of its people, who must also be well organized and skillfully led. That's why having a balanced management team, selecting an organizational form that makes sense for the enterprise and its circumstances, and joining advantageous strategic alliances are all so important. This chapter has touched on each of these topics to help you think through key factors involved in developing a solid organizational plan that will give your business a good running start and help to ensure its long-term success.

advisory board
A group that serves as an alternative to a board of directors, acting only in an advisory capacity.

LOOKING BACK

8-1. Describe the characteristics and value of a strong management team.

- A strong management team nurtures a good business idea and helps provide the necessary resources to make it succeed.
- The skills of management team members should complement each other, forming an optimal combination of education and experience.
- A small firm can enhance its management by drawing on the expertise of competent insiders and outside specialists.

- Social media tools can be very helpful in attracting customers, connecting with peers, and sharing advice about common problems.
- Building social capital through networking and goodwill is extremely helpful in developing a small business.

8-2. Explain the common legal forms of organization used by small businesses.

- The most basic legal forms of organization used by small businesses are the sole proprietorship, partnership, and C corporation.
- In a sole proprietorship, the owner receives all profits and bears all losses. The principal disadvantage of this form is the owner's unlimited liability.
- In a partnership, which should be established on the basis of a written partnership agreement, success depends on the partners' ability to build and maintain an effective working relationship. The partners share unlimited liability.
- C corporations are particularly attractive because of their limited liability feature. The fact that ownership is easily transferable makes them well suited for combining the capital of numerous owners.

8-3. Identify factors to consider in choosing among the primary legal forms of organization.

- Currently, 62.6 percent of all new businesses are organized as sole proprietorships, 9.3 percent are set up as partnerships, and 7 percent are established as C corporations.

- The key factors in choosing an organization form are initial organizational requirements and costs, liability of the owners, continuity of the business, transferability of ownership, management control, attractiveness for raising capital, and income tax considerations.

- Self-employed individuals who operate businesses as sole proprietorships report income from the businesses on their individual tax returns.

- A partnership reports the income it earns to the Internal Revenue Service, but the partnership itself does not pay income taxes. The income is allocated to the owners according to their partnership agreement.

- A C corporation reports its income and pays any taxes due on this corporate income. Individual stockholders must also pay personal income taxes on dividends paid to them by a corporation.

8-4. Discuss the unique features and restrictions of five specialized organizational forms.

- In a limited partnership, general partners have unlimited liability, while limited partners have only limited liability as long as they are not active in the firm's management.

- S corporations, also called Subchapter S corporations, enjoy a special tax status that permits them to avoid the corporate tax but requires individual stockholders to pay personal taxes on their proportionate shares of the business profits.

- In limited liability companies, individual owners have the advantage of limited liability but pay only personal income taxes on the firm's earnings.

- Professional corporations are set up for those who offer professional services (usually those that require a license), to protect them from the liability of other owners in the practice.

- Some enterprises (especially those with a social focus) benefit from greater credibility and authenticity when they organize as nonprofit corporations, such as 501(c)(3) organizations.

8-5. Understand the nature of strategic alliances and their uses in small businesses.

- Strategic alliances allow business firms to combine their resources without compromising their independent legal status.

- Strategic alliances may be formed by two or more independent businesses to achieve some common purpose. For example, a large corporation and a small business or two or more small businesses may collaborate on a joint project.

- Entrepreneurs can improve their chances of creating and maintaining a successful alliance by establishing productive connections, identifying the best person to contact, being prepared to confirm the long-term benefits of the alliance, learning to speak the partner's "language," ensuring a win–win arrangement, and monitoring the progress of the alliance and making necessary changes.

8-6. Describe the effective use of boards of directors and advisors.

- To be most effective, a board of directors should include properly qualified, independent outsiders.

- Boards of directors can assist small corporations by offering counsel and assistance to their chief executives.

- One alternative to an active board of directors is an advisory board, whose members are not personally liable for the company's actions.

Key Terms

advisory board p. 218

board of directors p. 216

C corporation p. 205

corporate charter p. 205

corporation p. 205

general partner p. 209

joint and several liability p. 204

legal entity p. 205

limited liability company p. 210

limited partner p. 209

limited partnership p. 209

management team p. 197

nonprofit corporation p. 211

organizational test p. 211

partnership agreement p. 204

partnership p. 202

piercing the corporate veil p. 208

preemptive right p. 205

professional corporation p. 211

reciprocation p. 200

S corporation (Subchapter S corporation) p. 210

social capital p. 200

social network p. 199

sole proprietorship p. 201

stock certificate p. 205

strategic alliance p. 213

unlimited liability p. 201

Discussion Questions

1. Why would investors tend to favor a new business led by a management team over one headed by a lone entrepreneur? Is this preference justified?

2. What are the merits of each of the three most basic legal forms of organization?

3. Does the concept of limited liability apply to a sole proprietorship? Why or why not?

4. Suppose a partnership is set up and operated without a formal partnership agreement. What problems might arise from this? Explain.

5. How do the three most basic forms of organization differ in terms of management control by the owner and the sharing of the firm's profits?

6. What is an S corporation, and what are its principal advantages?

7. Why are strategic alliances helpful to many small businesses? What steps can an entrepreneur take to create effective strategic alliances and to prevent their failure?

8. How might a board of directors be of value to management in a small corporation? What personal qualities and business qualifications are most important for a director?

9. What may account for the failure of most small companies to use boards of directors as more than "rubber stamps"? What impact is this likely to have on the business?

10. How do advisory boards differ from boards of directors? Which of the two would you recommend to a small business owner? Why?

You Make the Call

Situation 1

Just recently, Donny Eckols came up with the idea of starting an online service that would help investors who are looking for rental properties on the cheap to get connected with homeowners who really need to sell their houses fast. This opportunity holds special appeal for Eckols, whose parents have been involved in the real estate industry for decades. Eckols doesn't want to start this new business by himself, however, so he keeps prodding his friend John Starner to partner with him.

While Starner thinks this potential startup could very well turn out to be a smash hit, he just can't quite see himself in the real estate business. To him, it sounds a lot like sales, and that's more Eckols's thing, with his upbeat style and his natural ability to read people and anticipate their reactions. Starner's personality is very different, focusing on technology more than people and on ideas more than interactions. So far, he and Eckols have had a great friendship, but Starner is beginning to wonder if the good times will continue to roll once money is on the line and the pressure begins to mount. He knows that Eckols leans heavily on Starner's computer skills, even as Starner looks to Eckols to make life interesting and keep him connected.

Starner also fears that Eckols might begin to take over the business once it gets going. After all, he would bring a lot of industry insight to the new venture, given his family background, and it was his idea in the first place. How could he not take on a sense of ownership? Starner knows that his programming skills and ease with technology will fill in important gaps in what Eckols brings to the table, but will that be enough to keep him in the game? He has to decide soon. Eckols wants to launch the new company before the end of the month.

Question 1 How relevant are the individual personalities to the success of this entrepreneurial team? Do you think Starner and Eckols have a chance to survive a potential partnership? Why or why not?

Question 2 Do you consider it an advantage or a disadvantage that the members of this team are about the same age?

Question 3 On balance, is it good or bad that the company will be started by two men who are also very close friends? What are the potential benefits and drawbacks of mixing business and friendship in this case?

Situation 2

Matthew Freeman started a business in 2007 to provide corporate training in project management. He initially organized his business as a sole proprietorship. Until recently, he did most of his work on a contract basis for Corporation Education Services (CES). Under the terms of his contract, Freeman was responsible for teaching 3- to 5-day courses to corporate clients—primarily Fortune 1000 companies. He was compensated according to a negotiated daily rate, and expenses incurred during a course (hotels, meals, transportation, etc.) were reimbursed by CES. Although some expenses were not reimbursed by CES (such as those for computers and office supplies), Freeman's costs usually amounted to less than 1 percent of his revenues.

In 2013, Freeman increasingly found himself working directly with corporate clients rather than contracting with CES. Over the years, he had considered incorporating but had assumed the costs and inconveniences of this option would outweigh the benefits. However, some of his new clients said that they would prefer to contract with a corporation rather than with an individual.

And Freeman sometimes wondered about potential liability problems. On the one hand, he didn't have the same liability issues as some other businesses—he worked out of his home, clients never visited his home office, all courses were conducted in hotels or corporate facilities, and his business involved only services. But he wasn't sure what would happen if a client ended up being dissatisfied with the content and outcomes of his instruction. Finally, he wondered whether there would be tax advantages to incorporating.

Question 1 What are the advantages and disadvantages of running the business as a sole proprietorship? As a corporation?

Question 2 If Freeman decides to incorporate his business, which types of corporations could he form? Which type would you recommend? Why?

Situation 3

Julie Patton is co-founder and president of PM Meals, a food-services business that prepares and sells boxed meals and convenience snacks to hotels, convention operators, corporate clients, and community event planners. Patton makes most of the business decisions related to the company and is in charge of generating new accounts. The firm's other co-founder, Angela Marks, has culinary training and oversees the meal-preparation side of the operation. The food they offer represents relatively simple fare, but it is flavorful and attractively presented, exceeding by far what most clients would expect from a boxed-meal provider.

The company has entered a growth phase, which has attracted the attention of a high-potential investor. PM Meals could certainly use the money to support its growing business, but the investment would come with major strings attached. For example, even though the company has been performing nicely without a board of directors, the investor insists that it form one and that he be given a seat on the new board. In his words, "If I am going to put up money for the business, I want to be able to influence how my money is being used."

Patton and Marks are concerned that forming a board and including at least one outside investor (the one who insists on having a seat) will undermine their control and paralyze the business. As they weigh alternatives, they are leaning toward forming a three-person board and accepting the new investment—but they are far from certain as to what they should do.

Question 1 Would you accept the investment and the conditions that go along with it, or refuse it and go a different direction?

Question 2 Can one outside member on a board of three make any real difference in the way the board operates?

Question 3 If you were the owners, whom would you include on the board?

Question 4 If Patton and Marks decide to form a board of directors, what will determine its usefulness or effectiveness? Do you predict that it will be helpful? Why or why not?

Experiential Exercises

1. Prepare a one-page résumé of your personal qualifications to launch a software instruction business at your college or university. Then write a critique that might be prepared by an investor, evaluating your strengths and weaknesses, as shown on the résumé. Identify in the critique any gaps or weaknesses you have that could be covered by forming a management team to start the business.

2. Interview an attorney whose clients include small businesses. Inquire about the legal considerations involved in choosing the form of organization for a new business. Report your findings to the class.

3. Interview a small business owner who is involved in a strategic alliance with another firm. Ask which factors or issues he or she thought about most when deciding whether to enter into the alliance. In what ways did he or she structure the deal to protect against any of the concerns that were considered? Report your findings to the class.

4. Discuss the contributions of directors to small firms with a corporate director, attorney, banker, or business owner. Prepare a brief report on your findings. If you discover a particularly well-informed individual, suggest that person to your instructor as a possible guest speaker.

Small Business & Entrepreneurship Resource Center

The Small Business & Entrepreneurship Resource Center offers complete small business management resources through a comprehensive database that covers all major areas of starting, operating, and maintaining a business from financing, management, marketing, accounting, taxes, and more. Go to www.cengagebrain.com and select the Longenecker text for more information on how to access this material.

1. Martin Productions is a home-based sole proprietorship. As an art director for an automotive company, Douglas Martin has 25 years of experience creating presentations for the company, its advertising agencies, and investors. Following an early retirement due to the slump in the economy, Martin formed the company to create presentations. His work will be outsourced by automakers, businesses of all sizes, and

nonprofits that cannot afford to maintain a department or art director position. Within three years, Martin expects to add a partner and have an extensive Internet presence. He plans to have enough business to hire an assistant, who could then become a partner. Then, the sole proprietorship would become a partnership, a corporation, or an LLC. After reading this article, what advice would you give Martin about his sole proprietorship and expansion to a partnership, corporation, or LLC? What pitfalls should he avoid?

2. TeleCommunication Systems (TCS) and Johannesburg, South Africa–based Cellfind Ltd. have partnered to offer services solutions in Africa. Cellfind's offerings will include the location-based services solution provided by TCS. Mobile

operators can enable location services and generate revenue almost immediately by using TCS's platform and Cellfind's applications. This is the first agreement between the two companies and the first for TeleCommunication Systems in Africa. Wireless operators will benefit from a comprehensive, cost-effective solution, while consumers will benefit from emergency location tracking, tracking of goods in transit, and more. Do you think that this new partnership is a strategic fit for both companies? Explain your answer in pointing out the advantages and disadvantages of this agreement.

Sources: Heidi Denler, "Digital Presentations: Martin Productions," *Business Plans Handbook*, Lynn M. Pearce (ed.) (Detroit: Gale, 2011); and "TeleCommunication Systems Partners with Cellfind to Offer Location-Based Services Solution in Africa," *Internet Business News*, February 22, 2013.

Case 8

Couchsurfing International: A Story of Startup, Growth, and Transformation (P. 657)

This case highlights important features of high-performing ventures, including the make-up and coordinated roles of the founding team, the selection of an organizational form, and the formation of a board of directors or advisors.

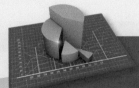

Business Plan

LAYING THE FOUNDATION

As part of laying the foundation to prepare your own business plan, respond to the following questions regarding your management team, legal form of organization, strategic alliances, and board of directors.

1. Who are the members of your management team? What skills, education, and experience do they bring to the team?

2. What other key managers do you plan to recruit?

3. Do you plan to use consultants? If so, describe their qualifications.

4. What are your plans for future employee recruitment?

5. What will be the compensation and benefit plans for managers and other employees?

6. What style of management will be used? What will be the decision-making process in the company? What mechanisms are in place for effective communication between managers

and employees? If possible, present a simple organizational chart.

7. How will personnel be motivated? How will creativity be encouraged? How will commitment and loyalty be developed?

8. What employee retention and training programs will be adopted? Who will be responsible for job descriptions and employee evaluations?

9. Who will have an ownership interest in the business?

10. Will the business function as a sole proprietorship, partnership, or corporation? If a corporation, will it be a C corporation, an S corporation, a limited liability company, a professional corporation, or a nonprofit corporation?

11. What are the liability implications of this form of organization?

12. What are the tax advantages and disadvantages of this form of organization?

13. If a corporation, where will the corporation be chartered and when will it be incorporated?

14. What attorney or legal firm has been selected to represent the firm? What type of relationship exists with the company's attorney or law firm?

15. What legal issues are presently or potentially significant?

16. What licenses and/or permits may be required?

17. What strategic alliances are already in place, and what others do you plan to establish in the future? Describe the nature of these alliances. What are the responsibilities of and benefits to the parties involved? What are the exit strategies if an alliance should fail?

18. Who are the directors of the company? What are their qualifications? How will they be compensated?

Endnotes

1. Stephen Spinelli and Robert Adams, *New Venture Creation: Entrepreneurship for the 21st Century* (New York: Irwin McGraw-Hill, 2012), p. 46.

2. Our position is consistent with recent research showing that the quality of business ideas generated in a business idea competition were related to the characteristics of the entrepreneurial teams that came up with those ideas. The quality was higher for larger teams, those with more years of work experience, and those that received outside assistance from experienced venture founders. For more on this research, see Maw-Der Foo, "Member Experience, Use of External Assistance and Evaluation of Business Ideas," *Journal of Small Business Management*, Vol. 48, No. 1 (January 2010), pp. 32–43.

3. Current views see management team members as those with financial ownership and significant decision-making responsibilities in the venture [see Gaylen N. Chandler, "New Venture Teams," in Andrew Zacharakis and Stephen Spinelli, Jr. (eds.), *Entrepreneurship: The Engine of Growth* (Westport, CT: Praeger Perspectives, 2007), pp. 75–76]. Other definitions are more restrictive and emphasize such factors as being a founder of the venture [see Iris Vanaelst, Bart Clarysse, Mike Wright, Andy Lockett, Nathalie Moray, and Rosette S'Jegers, "Entrepreneurial Team Development in Academic Spinouts: An Examination of Team Heterogeneity," *Entrepreneurship Theory and Practice*, Vol. 30, No. 2 (March 2006), p. 251]. At the other end of the spectrum, some entrepreneurs consider all employees and advisors to be a part of the team. Because our discussion is focused on those who hold important leadership positions in the small business but may not share ownership in the firm, we use the broader term *management team* rather than *entrepreneurial team* to reflect this more general view.

4. For an interesting study of the addition of members to the management team, see Daniel P. Forbes, Patricia S. Borchert, Mary E. Zellmer-Bruhn, and Harry J. Sapienza, "Entrepreneurial Team Formation: An Exploration of New Member Addition," *Entrepreneurship Theory and Practice*, Vol. 30, No. 2 (March 2006), pp. 225–248.

5. This may explain why research using Panel Study of Entrepreneurial Dynamics data found that around three-fourths of *solo* entrepreneurs were starting service firms (49 percent) or retail businesses (26 percent). These types of startups tend to be less complicated than technology-based firms or manufacturing businesses, so a single founder is more likely to have the knowledge and experience necessary to get the business going. A more complex startup may well require the combined expertise and insight of a *team* of entrepreneurs. For a closer look at the data, see *Expected Costs of Startup Ventures*, a consulting report prepared for the SBA's Office of Advocacy by Blade Consulting Corporation, Vienna, Virginia, November 2003.

6. Ross McCammon, "We're Better Together," *Entrepreneur*, Vol. 40, No. 6 (June 2012), pp. 20–21.

7. Research has not always supported the view that functional balance leads to improved venture performance. Some studies have found that functional heterogeneity is correlated with small firm growth, while others offer no evidence to indicate a relationship with team performance (see Chandler, *op. cit.*).

8. Andy Lockett, Deniz Ucbasaran, and John Butler, "Opening Up the Investor-Investee Dyad: Syndicates, Teams, and Networks," *Entrepreneurship Theory and Practice*, Vol. 30, No. 2 (March 2006), p. 119.

9. Chandler, *op. cit.*, p. 71.

10. Howard E. Aldrich and Nancy M. Carter, "Social Networks," in William B. Gartner, Kelly G. Shaver, Nancy M. Carter, and Paul D. Reynolds (eds.), *Handbook of Entrepreneurial Dynamics: The Process of Business Creation* (Thousand Oaks, CA: Sage, 2004), p. 331.

11. Jennifer Van Grove, "How Small Business Is Using Social Media," http://mashable.com/2010/03/02/small-business-stats, accessed January 16, 2013.

12. Robert B. Cialdini, *Influence: Science and Practice* (Needham Heights: MA: Allyn & Bacon, 2009).

13. This percentage from the IRS includes enterprises organized as limited liability companies (LLCs; an organizational form that is introduced later in the chapter). This inclusion is probably inconsequential, as other sources indicate the number of startups formed as LLCs is still quite small.

14. Fred S. Steingold, *Legal Guide for Starting and Running a Small Business* (Berkeley, CA: Nolo Press, 2011).

15. *Ibid*.

16. Fred S. Steingold, *Legal Forms for Starting and Running a Small Business* (Berkeley, CA: Nolo Press, 2012).

17. Ira Nottonson, *Forming a Partnership: And Making It Work* (Irvine, CA: Entrepreneur Press, 2007), pp. 6–7.

18. Nichole L. Torres, "Left in the Lurch?" *Entrepreneur*, Vol. 34, No. 5 (May 2006), p. 108.

19. John Seely Brown, as quoted in Stephen J. Dubner, "How Can We Measure Innovation? A Freakonomics Quorum," April 25, 2008, www.freakonomics .com/2008/04/25/how-can-we-measure-innovation-a-freakonomics -quorum, accessed September 7, 2012.

20. "Piercing the Corporate Veil," www.residual-rewards.com /piercingthecorporateveil.html, accessed September 7, 2012.

21. David Newton, "Personal Loan Guarantees," www.entrepreneur.com /article/55544, accessed September 7, 2012.

22. For tax years beginning after 2004, the law increased the maximum number of shareholders permitted in an S corporation from 75 to 100. (Note that husband and wife count as one stockholder.)

23. The rules have been modified in recent years to allow more types of trusts to hold Subchapter S stock.

24. Internal Revenue Service, "S Corporations," www.irs.gov/Businesses/Small -Businesses-&-Self-Employed/S-Corporations, accessed September 7, 2012.

25. Internal Revenue Service, "Limited Liability Company (LLC)," www.irs .gov/Businesses/Small-Businesses-&-Self-Employed/Limited-Liability -Company-(LLC), accessed September 11, 2012.

26. For a description of the tax advantages of the limited liability company, see Steingold, *Legal Guide, op. cit.*

27. Nichole L. Torres, "Lofty Ideals," *Entrepreneur*, Vol. 34, No. 6 (June 2006), pp. 150–151.

28. William J. Dennis, Jr. (ed.), "Strategic Alliances," *NFIB National Small Business Poll*, Vol. 4, No. 4 (Washington, DC: NFIB Research Foundation, 2004), p. 4.

29. *Ibid.,* pp. 9–14.

30. Michael Fitzgerald, "Turning Vendors into Partners," *Inc.*, www.inc.com /magazine/20050801/vendors.html, accessed September 12, 2012.

31. *Ibid.*

32. Dennis, *op. cit.*, p. 7.

33. Jeffrey Shuman, Janice Twombly, and David Rottenberg, *Everyone Is a Customer: A Proven Method for Measuring the Value of Every Relationship in the Era of Collaborative Business* (Chicago: Dearborn Trade Publishing, 2002).

34. In many states, the number of board members required depends on the number of shareholders in the business. A corporation with one shareholder may need only one director to satisfy this demand, with two directors being required when there are two shareholders and three directors when there are three. However, no state requires a corporation to have more than three directors on its board (see Steingold, *Legal Guide, op. cit.*).

35. The compensation figures provided here are consistent across many sources, but the ranges are wide enough to indicate that the variation among small businesses is considerable.

36. Kent Romanoff, "Board of Directors Compensation," http:// theperfectpayplan.typepad.com/the_salary_sage/board-compensation, accessed September 12, 2012.

© KB Studio/Shutterstock.com

The Location Plan

We tend to think of most small business location selections as permanent decisions, but this notion is becoming increasingly outdated. While many small companies still operate out of a fixed place of business, the list of location alternatives grows longer each year. For example, more and more small business owners are choosing their homes as the center of their entrepreneurial world. But even at home, the true location varies—from a bedroom office one day, to the back patio the next, and to the kitchen table the day after that. In other cases, the location of the venture will be *permanently temporary*. For entrepreneurs who start businesses on the Internet, everyday work life may be a mix of tapping into the wireless at a local Starbucks and renting office or conference room space on an as-needed basis. The point is that small businesses have a lot of options from which to choose.

In the SPOTLIGHT
VaVaVroom and Clayton Fear Farm
www.vavavroomonline.com
www.claytonfearfarm.com

You may notice a lot more "pop-up stores" opening up these days. They may look like regular stores, but they are open for only a few months—and that is by design. Small business owners use this strategy for a number of reasons, such as to spread the word on a brand, to test a new line of products, or to try out a new sales channel. Denise Maple used this approach to increase exposure for her company and its products. Maple is owner of VaVaVroom, a fashion company that sells to "female motorcycling enthusiasts who crave the best-designed, best-made, and most fashionable cycling clothing on the planet." To rev up sales,

After studying this chapter, you should be able to...

9-1. Describe the five key factors in locating a brick-and-mortar startup.

9-2. Discuss the challenges of designing and equipping a physical facility.

9-3. Recognize both the attraction and the challenges of creating a home-based startup.

9-4. Understand the potential benefits of locating a startup on the Internet.

she joined a few other fashion designers and launched a pop-up store on Chicago's Michigan Avenue, a trendy shopping area. The 16-day pop-up was all about exposure—that is, getting new customers to see her designs so that they might become long-term buyers in the years ahead.

Some small businesses have permanent facilities, but they use them only for part of every year. Clayton Fear Farm provides a useful example of this type of seasonal operation. When Glenn Boyette was afraid that he was going to lose his family farm, he went into the business of scaring others! He has built three haunted houses and other Halloween attractions on his 150-acre farm in Clayton, North Carolina. Now, 35,000 visitors from September to January drop by to check out his haunted houses, corn maze, Christmas light show, and other seasonal attractions. For these experiences, Boyette charges between $12 and $25 a person, depending on the attraction, which means that revenues have doubled from what he made by farming alone. It's just a different cash crop.

Sources: Based on "Clayton Fear Farm," www.claytonfearfarm.com, accessed September 19, 2012; National Federation of Independent Businesses, "Should You Open a Pop-Up Store?" www.nfib.com/business-resources/business-resources -item?cmsid=5902, accessed September 24, 2012; personal communication with Glenn Boyette of Clayton Fear Farm, January 25, 2013.

A new venture idea begins to take shape materially as an entrepreneur works through all of the basic parts of the business plan. And that idea becomes even more real as resources are committed to the implementation of the plan, including the selection of a business location and any facilities and equipment. But, as you can see from this chapter's Spotlight feature, the location-related possibilities for small businesses are growing in number and variety. At the leaner end of the spectrum, these can be nothing more than a cell phone, some desk space at home, and a website. Locating on the Internet has changed everything for many startups. It offers global market reach at minimal cost, which provides a tremendous boost to budding ventures that desperately need customers but are short on funding. The rise of the Internet-based venture has been a game-changing phenomenon.

Entrepreneurs at the other end of the location continuum, however, might need a new building and/or a fully stocked warehouse facility and perhaps even forklifts and other equipment to get their planned operations off the ground. It all depends on the nature of the business. But, regardless of the specific resources involved, every location decision should be based on certain fundamental principles that can guide the process and minimize mistakes.

Those who purchase an existing business or a franchise usually receive considerable location guidance from members of the acquired firm or the franchisor. But entrepreneurs who choose to start a venture from scratch will quickly find that the location decision can be very time consuming. To help make the task more manageable, this chapter addresses some of the major factors that should be considered when choosing a location and setting up physical facilities. And because starting a home-based business and launching on the Internet have become such popular options, these alternatives are also covered in some detail. (Although we recognize that the Internet can be an integral part of operations for both a traditional and a home-based business, we treat e-commerce ventures in a separate category because of the Internet's significance as a sole sales outlet for these small businesses.)

Regardless of how the selection is made, a discussion of key location factors and how they support the location decision should be included in the business plan. This chapter will guide you through that process. But keep in mind that the depth of this discussion will vary from plan to plan, depending on the nature and form of the new venture.

9-1 LOCATING THE BRICK-AND-MORTAR STARTUP

LO
9-1

Describe the five key factors in locating a brick-and-mortar startup.

The choice of a location for a physical facility is often a one-time decision, but a small business owner may later relocate a venture to reduce operating costs, be closer to customers, or tap other advantages. A recent survey found that 42 percent of entrepreneurs in the United States believe their current location is best for their business, but nearly half of those polled said they would consider a move if it would help their companies.[1] That ability to be flexible led Marty and Avery Walker to relocate their Volvo Rents business from Austin to College Station, Texas. Since their venture rents and sells heavy equipment to construction companies and other businesses, it made sense to move 100 miles from the saturated rental market in Austin to be closer to the steady building activity in College Station. And the Walkers cashed in on their change of address, with company revenues increasing from $1.1 to $4 million in less than two years.[2] Location decisions can be complicated, but if carefully planned and wisely made, the payoff can be fantastic.

9-1a The Importance of the Location Decision

The importance of the initial decision as to where to locate a traditional physical building—a **brick-and-mortar facility**—is underscored by both the high cost of such a place and the hassle of pulling up stakes and moving an established business. Also, if the site is particularly poor, the business may never become successful, even with adequate financing and superior managerial ability. The importance of location is so clearly recognized by national chains that they spend hundreds of thousands of dollars investigating sites before establishing new facilities.

The choice of a good location is much more vital to some businesses than to others. For example, the site chosen for a clothing store can make or break the business because it must be convenient for customers. The physical location of a painting contractor's office, on the other hand, is of less importance, since customers do not need frequent access to the facility. But even painting contractors may suffer if their business site is poorly chosen. For example, some communities are more willing or able than others to invest resources to keep their properties in good condition, thereby providing greater opportunities for painting jobs.

9-1b Key Factors in Selecting a Good Location

Five key factors, shown in Exhibit 9.1, guide the location selection process: customer accessibility, business environment conditions, availability of resources, the entrepreneur's personal preference, and site availability and costs. Other factors relevant to the location decision include the following:[3]

- *Neighbor mix:* Who's next door?
- *Security and safety:* How safe is the neighborhood?
- *Services:* Does the city provide trash pickup, for example?
- *Past tenants' fate:* What happened to previous businesses in that location?
- *Location's lifecycle stage:* Is the area developing, stagnant, or in decline?

For a particular business and its unique situation, one factor may carry more weight than others. However, each of the five key factors should always have some influence on the final location decision.

brick-and-mortar facility
The traditional physical facility from which businesses have historically operated.

EXHIBIT

9.1 Five Key Factors in Determining a Good Business Location

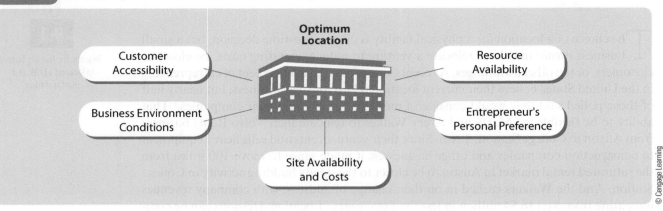

CUSTOMER ACCESSIBILITY For many businesses, customer accessibility is an extremely important consideration in selecting a location. It is vital in industries in which the cost of shipping the finished product is high relative to the product's value. Products such as packaged ice and soft drinks, for example, must be produced near consuming markets because of the excessive transportation costs involved. Retail outlets and service firms (such as tire repair companies and hair stylists) must be located where they can provide handy access for targeted purchasers to avoid losing business to more conveniently placed competitors.

Rarely will customers be willing to travel long distances on a repeat basis just to shop. That's why Glenn Campbell and Scott Molander decided to sell hats in high-traffic areas through their startup, Hat World, Inc. (selling mostly under the Lids brand). Each store, located in a shopping mall or airport, offers a vast assortment of officially licensed baseball-style hats. And this positioning works. From its start in 1995, and after some consolidation moves, the total operation has grown to more than 1,000 stores nationwide and in Canada and Puerto Rico.[4]

Choosing the best location for a retail store used to be a hit-or-miss proposition. The recent emergence and growing popularity of site-selection software has removed much of the guesswork. Some products worth a look include an entry-level version of The Right Site by Easy Analytics Software, MapInfo AnySite Online, or geoVue's iSITE package. If you are searching for an ideal location for an office, REgis software by SitesUSA can be especially helpful. But in any case, before you invest your hard-earned dollars, try to arrange a test run, if possible, to see if the software is right for your business. And always ask about Web-based versions, which often are less expensive.

Site-selection programs can give users access to demographic information such as age, income, and race for specific neighborhoods, as well as details about other businesses located nearby, climate conditions, traffic flow, and much more. Just keep in mind that these software packages also have their limitations. For example, many emphasize traffic counts and geographic distance, which can easily overlook factors like slowdowns from rush-hour traffic conditions, the potential of railroads or interstates to divide buying clusters, and similar issues.

If you want to go it alone but still capture the power of detailed data to make your decision, it may be helpful to visit the United States Census Bureau at www.census.gov. Don't let all of the options presented on this site discourage you. If you are patient and work your way through some of the links, you will be amazed by the depth of helpful information you can uncover. We also suggest that you visit the website of *Site Selection* magazine (www.siteselection.com), which offers online tools for researching locations and demographics.

Convenient access for customers is one reason that many small businesses have successfully established a strong presence on the Internet. With a suitable computer connection, customers can access a small company's home page from anywhere in the world. (Locating a startup on the Internet is discussed later in this chapter.)

Living the Dream

Some Entrepreneurs Want to Keep on Truckin'

To suit their active lifestyles, people are demanding mobile services of all kinds—communications, advertising, information access, and so many others—and entrepreneurial companies are lining up to provide them. They smell opportunity.

But the mobile trend also has implications for the small business location decision and its related costs. In most cases, starting a business on wheels is far cheaper than occupying a traditional brick-and-mortar facility. It is inexpensive and fast to buy and outfit a truck, and it is easy to harness the power of social media to let customers know where it will be so that they can show up and buy. The fact that a mobile business can provide products or

© Arun Nevader/FilmMagic/Getty Images

services wherever customers need them definitely adds the fuel of convenience to the fire of demand, but the low initial investment seems to be the primary driving factor for most entrepreneurs. Food-service expert Kevin Higar observes, "Somebody in the food-truck business who wants five or six or seven units rolling along can get them up and running at a price point that's much lower than a brick-and-mortar store." But the same can be said for mobile operators in almost any industry.

The super-low startup costs bode well for new venture profitability. Vanessa Lurie set up a clothing boutique on wheels to troll the streets of Portland, Oregon, selling apparel items that range in price from $5 to $80. Her startup turned a profit its first year in business. For Joey Wolffer, owner of The Styleliner, a truck from which she sells international designer apparel and accessory items in New York City and the Hamptons, venture performance is a primary consideration.

She reveals that The Styleliner turned a profit after its first summer in operation, and reports indicate that sales from the truck and its related website doubled over the following year. Operating by mobile clearly can be a powerful business model.

But going mobile also presents some challenges that should not be overlooked. For example, in response to the outcry from established restaurants with physical facilities, some cities have put the brakes on food trucks by enacting laws that restrict where they can set up to do business and how long they can remain there. In New Orleans, mobile food vendors cannot park in any one location for longer than 45 minutes. And according to Texas law, such sellers have to use a "commissary" (a licensed kitchen apart from the owner's home that can service the food truck or trailer), and it must be inspected twice a year. These are serious limitations, and the patchwork of regulations differs dramatically from city to city, which only adds to the confusion and frustration.

Still, the trend is spreading quickly to other industries, including auto repair, dog grooming, hair stylists, ice cream, florists—even drug testing. According to Aaron Novishen, co-founder of Mobi Munch, a mobile operator with several food trucks in California, "Ten percent of the top 200 restaurant chains will have a mobile presence [soon]." That is sure to create a stir—and perhaps a lot of traffic jams.

Sources: Based on Jason Daley, "Franchise A-Go-Go," *Entrepreneur*, Vol. 39, No. 8 (August 2011), pp. 99–103; Wendy Gragg, "Food Truck Hits Speed Bumps," *Waco Tribune-Herald*, August 19, 2012, p. 5B; Louie Lee, "Chained to the Road," *The Wall Street Journal*, November 14, 2011, p. R7; Hadley Malcolm, "Entrepreneurs Keep on Truckin'," *USA Today*, June 28, 2012, p. 8A; and Sarah E. Needleman, "Street Fight: Food Trucks Versus Restaurants," *The Wall Street Journal*, August 9, 2012, p. B8.

BUSINESS ENVIRONMENT CONDITIONS A startup business is affected in a number of ways by the environment in which it operates. Weather is one important environmental feature that influences the location decision, as well as the demand for products such as air conditioners and outdoor swimming pools. Such factors are particularly important to entrepreneurs like Trey Cobb, owner of a high-performance car parts maker called COBB Tuning. In 2002, Cobb took the bold step of moving his entire small company from Texas to a custom-built facility in Utah. This particular move was all about climate—in this case, improving product-testing conditions. Cobb recognized the advantages of locating the company in an area that provided access to the varied geographic and weather conditions that would be necessary to fully test the car parts that his company manufactures.[5]

Competition, legal requirements, and tax structure are a few of the other critical environmental factors. Entrepreneurs need profits to sustain their businesses. Therefore, all factors affecting the financial picture are of great concern. State and local governments can help or hinder a new business by forgiving or levying taxes. State corporate income tax rates vary considerably across the United States, with only a few states having no such tax. To rank the states in terms of the costs of their tax systems on small business (based on a composite score pulled together from 18 different tax measures), the Small Business & Entrepreneurship Council publishes a "Business Tax Index" each year. In its 2012 report, the council found that the five states with the most favorable tax systems, in order, were (1) South Dakota, (2) Texas, (3) Nevada, (4) Wyoming, and (5) Washington.[6]

Tax relief for the business is important, but don't forget to factor in the impact of a state's personal income tax rates, which will affect the pay your employees ultimately receive for their labor. These taxes will determine how far wage dollars will go and, in turn, the benefit and satisfaction your workers receive from the business.[7] And there are other important elements in the equation, such as the overall cost of living. A lower *cost of living* can mean a higher *standard of living* for employees. To do cost-of-living research yourself, consult websites like http://money.cnn.com and http://salary.com, or contact local economic development agencies and request data on this and other factors, which they will provide free of charge.[8]

Governments don't always do everything they could to help new businesses get started and flourish. And the barriers can run far beyond issues of taxation. Consider these "wrinkles in the law" that have thwarted entrepreneurial aspirations:[9]

- Esmeralda Rodriguez had to pay rent while waiting for permits to open a play center in Chicago. After a year of delays, and with her savings running out, she had to give up.

- James Tia, a former lawyer, sold meatless burritos in Washington, D.C.— that is, until the city shut the operation down "because his rice was not on the list of approved foods." It took a year and a half of lobbying, guided by Tia's expert legal skills, and favorable test results from a food-safety expert to finally get the business back on track.

- In Miami, jitney van services flourished briefly because of an accidental legal loophole. But the county responded swiftly, closing the gap in the law by requiring jitney startups first to prove that they would not be cutting into the business of existing competitors.

- Philadelphia required Ramesh Naropanth to spend $8,000 to install unnecessary gates on his convenience store before approving a permit for him to sell sandwiches.

Stories like these are not all that uncommon. And such setbacks can easily doom a small business, especially if it is new, lacks momentum, and is short on resources.

Still, most state and city governments go to great lengths to support startups; after all, their economic futures depend on new venture creation. Nonetheless, nearly all cities have regulations that restrict new business operations under certain circumstances. For example, some cities have **zoning ordinances** that may limit the operations of home-based businesses. These ordinances often apply to factors related to traffic and parking, signage, nonrelated employees working in a home, the use of a home more as a business than as a residence, the sale of retail goods to the public, and the storage of hazardous materials and work-related equipment.[10]

AVAILABILITY OF RESOURCES Access to raw materials, suitable labor, crucial suppliers, and transportation are some of the factors that have a bearing on location selection. Proximity to important sources of raw materials and an appropriate labor supply are particularly critical considerations in the location of most manufacturing businesses, whereas access to key suppliers is more likely to influence site selections for retail outlets and restaurant operations.

If raw materials required by a company's operations are not readily available in all areas, then regions in which these materials abound will offer significant location advantages. This is especially true for businesses that are dependent on bulky or heavy raw materials that lose much of their size or weight in the manufacturing process. A sawmill is an example of a business that must stay close to its raw materials in order to operate economically.

The suitability of the labor supply for a manufacturer depends on the nature of its production process. Labor-intensive operations need to be located near workers with appropriate skills and reasonable wage requirements. A history of acceptable levels of labor productivity and peaceful relations with employers are also important factors. Companies that depend on semiskilled or unskilled workers usually locate in an area with surplus labor, while other firms may need to be close to a pool of highly skilled labor. If the required talent is unavailable, relocation may be necessary, even it if means moving to another state. According to Tim Nitti, a location expert with a major site-selection firm, "Probably the single biggest emerging reason why anyone is moving companies . . . is access to talent."[11]

A road junction at Hangzhou

Access to good transportation is important to many companies. For example, good highways and bus systems provide customers with convenient access to retail stores, which encourages sales. For small manufacturers, quality transportation is especially vital. They must carefully evaluate all trucking routes, considering the costs of both transporting supplies to the manufacturing location and shipping the finished product to customers. It is critical that they know whether these costs will allow their product to be competitively priced.

PERSONAL PREFERENCE OF THE ENTREPRENEUR As a practical matter, many entrepreneurs tend to focus primarily on their personal preference and convenience when locating a business. Statistics hint at this, showing that nearly half of all entrepreneurs (47 percent) live no more than a five-minute drive from their venture's location.[12] And, despite a world of alternatives, small business owners often choose to stay in their home community. Just because an individual has always lived in a particular town, however, does not automatically make the town a satisfactory business location.

On the other hand, locating a business in one's home community may offer certain unique advantages that cannot be found elsewhere. From a personal point of view, an

zoning ordinances
Local laws regulating land use.

entrepreneur will generally appreciate and feel comfortable with the atmosphere of his or her home community. As a practical business matter, he or she may find it easier to establish credit with hometown bankers who know that entrepreneur's personal background and reputation. Having personal connections in the local business community can also lead to invaluable business advice. If local residents are potential customers, the prospective entrepreneur probably has a better idea of their tastes and preferences than would an outsider. And it doesn't hurt that friends and relatives in the community may be quick to buy the product or service and gladly spread positive reports about it to others. Though such decisions are usually based on emotion, there are clearly some potential benefits of locating a startup close to home.

The personal preferences that drive the location decision are as varied as the entrepreneurs who make it. Sometimes entrepreneurs choose a location offering unique lifestyle advantages, such as being close to a favorite golf course or a trustworthy babysitter. But while personal preference is important and should not be ignored, it would be unwise to allow this to take priority over obvious location weaknesses that are almost certain to limit or even doom the success of the enterprise. The location decision must take all relevant factors into consideration.

SITE AVAILABILITY AND COSTS Once an entrepreneur has settled on a certain area for her or his business, a specific site must still be chosen. Many small business owners recognize the value of seeking professional assistance (for example, local realtors) in determining site availability and appropriateness.

If an entrepreneur's top location choices are unavailable, other options must be considered. One alternative is to share facilities with other enterprises. In recent years, business incubators have sprung up in all areas of the country. A **business incubator** is a facility that rents space to new businesses or to people wishing to start businesses. Incubators are often located in repurposed buildings, such as abandoned warehouses or schools. They serve fledgling businesses by making space available, offering management advice, and providing other forms of assistance (including clerical support), all of which help reduce operating costs. An incubator tenant can be fully operational the day after moving in, without buying phones, renting a copier, or hiring office employees.

Most incubators can accommodate different kinds of early-stage ventures, but some are beginning to focus on a specific business niche, such as fashion, food, or design. Many provide access to industry-specific resources. Hot Bread Kitchen Incubates, for example, provides food startups with access to "seven kitchens complete with industrial trial-size convection ovens, deep fryers, blenders, kettles, grills and a host of other devices."[13] Client businesses also receive recipe scale-up assistance, training in kitchen-use efficiency, supervised production time, general business training, and solid partnership opportunities with other startups in the incubator.[14] To avoid renting space to new ventures that are apt to compete directly with one another, most specialty incubators accept no more than two startups that target the same market. Nonetheless, this arrangement can still lead to its share of complications—for example, similar businesses sometimes try to tie up crucial pieces of equipment for their own use and advantage. But despite the drawbacks, locating in a niche incubator must be worth the trouble, because spaces are reportedly in short supply.[15]

The purpose of business incubators is to see new businesses hatch, grow, and leave the incubator, so the situation is temporary *by design*. But it appears that many businesses are looking for permanent shared-office arrangements. Regus, a leading provider of shared office space, finds that its business is booming. The firm currently operates more than 1,200 business centers in 550 cities spread over nearly 100 countries.[16]

business incubator
A facility that provides shared space, services, and management assistance to new businesses.

Part 3 Developing the New Venture Business Plan

Perhaps you are more of a free spirit. One variation on the shared-office-space theme is the "co-working" movement, which involves shared working spaces (sometimes an office) that allow mostly freelancers, consultants, artists, and other independent workers "to work and connect under the same roof." Office Nomads is one such place. Cofounded by Jacob Sayles and Susan Evans, this Seattle-based facility "combines the best of a home office, an Internet café and a traditional office" to give its tenants prospects for greater interaction, a sense of camaraderie, and networking opportunities. It also has reciprocal agreements with co-working establishments in 17 states and 13 countries for members who need access while on the road. With typical rates running from $25 a day to around $500 a month, co-working facilities can be a real bargain.[17] They're not for everyone, but they are a good working alternative for some entrepreneurs.

When it comes to site selection—whether permanent or more flexible—the process should factor in all relevant costs. Unfortunately, an entrepreneur is frequently unable to afford the *best* site. The costs involved in building on a new site may be prohibitive, or the purchase price of an existing structure may exceed the entrepreneur's budget.

Assuming that suitable building space is available, the entrepreneur must decide whether to lease or buy. More small business owners choose to purchase rather than lease their buildings (57 percent, according to one study[18]), but the benefits of leasing can sometimes outweigh the gains of owning:

- A large cash outlay is avoided, which can be especially important for a new small firm that lacks adequate financial resources.

- Risk is reduced by minimizing investment and by postponing commitments for space until the success of the business is assured and facility requirements are better known.

- It is usually more affordable to lease in a high-image area compared to buying in a prime location.

- Leasing allows the entrepreneur to focus on running the business rather than managing properties.

But there are clearly disadvantages to leasing as well. For example, those who buy will benefit financially when a well-selected property appreciates in value, and their facilities costs will be stable and predictable over time. Just as important, they won't need to ask permission to make future changes or additions to the property.

If entering a lease agreement seems to be the way to go, the entrepreneur first should check the landlord's insurance policies to be sure there is proper coverage for various types of risks. If not, the lessee should seek coverage under his or her own policy. It is also wise to have the terms of the lease agreement reviewed by an attorney. She or he may be able to add special provisions to a lease, such as an escape clause that allows the lessee to exit the agreement under certain conditions. An attorney can also ensure that an entrepreneur will not be unduly exposed to liability for damages caused by the gross negligence of others. Consider the experience of one firm that wished to rent 300 square feet of storage space in a large complex of offices and shops. On the sixth page of the landlord's standard lease, the firm's lawyer found language that could have made the firm responsible for the entire 30,000-square-foot complex if it burned down, regardless of blame! Competent legal counsel may not be cheap, but the services that it provides can certainly save an entrepreneur a lot of money and heartache.

START UP

RESOURCES

Beginning on a Budget
When searching for a location to lease for your business, be sure to use a broker who understands your business, knows what you can afford, and is on your side. Pair the broker with an attorney who can make sure that you understand the lease implications, and your team is ready to go! For more information and important specifics on leasing, see Julie Bennett, "How to Negotiate a Lease," *Entrepreneur*, Vol. 38, No. 5 (May 2010), pp. 75–83.

Living the Dream

Doing Business Without the Big Corner Office—or Any Office at All!

Buying or leasing office space for a small business can be very expensive, which is why so many companies now are looking for alternatives. It has prompted many entrepreneurs to search for ways to make more efficient use of office space or to figure out how to operate with no such space at all.

According to a survey conducted by CoreNet Global, a corporate real estate association, the average amount of facility space allotted per employee has fallen from 225 square feet in 2010 to 176 in 2012, and that figure will probably be closer to 100 square feet by the year 2017. According to one CoreNet representative, the idea is to squeeze more results out of the same or less space by creating "smarter but smaller" offices to hold costs down while promoting "collaborative and team-oriented" behavior through the resourceful and flexible design and use of space.

The model for small companies seems to be coming from fast-moving entrepreneurial firms like online shoe and apparel giant Zappos, where "office-like work" can take place nearly anywhere in the facility, including on couches and at shared tables—or even at the coffee shop around the corner. The company's staff is "more concerned about being around other people who do cool things than how big their desks are," says Zappos executive Zach Ware. "Our workspace has become our laptops." Younger employees seem to welcome the new open floor plans, as do forward-thinking small business owners, since they can house more workers in less space and still boost worker satisfaction and productivity, thereby reducing overall facility costs.

But if your company is just getting started, you might not be able to afford *any* permanent office space. Co-working space provider Launchpad leases 11,000 square feet of collaborative workspace to small businesses (mostly tech startups and creative endeavors) that want to join a community of like-minded and similarly-driven individuals. Although the company offers private offices, many clients prefer to spend far less (around $275 per month) to come in on any day of the week to use whichever desk is available. This arrangement is made special by the mix of people Launchpad brings into the space. As co-founder Barre Tanguis puts it, "If you need your LLC started, there's a lawyer upstairs; if you want to get your books down, there's an accountant right there; if you want a commercial start on the Web, there's a filmmaker in house." This makes it easy to get the support that an entrepreneur might need at any given time, which saves time and promotes success.

If co-working space would still be too much of a drag on your startup budget, you could try to go office-less. Automattic, Inc., a web services company, has grown its way to hiring 123 people working in 26 countries, all without buying or leasing offices or entering co-working contracts (except for one office in San Francisco that is used

© Jupiterimages/Comstock Images/Getty Images

occasionally). Its employees work at home. This approach has its drawbacks (some people can't handle the lack of personal contact, or they may struggle to keep work and home life separate), but it allows the company to tap a wider pool of talent (since location is not a factor) and save a lot of money on real estate.

Nobody knows exactly how many "office-less companies" there are, but the number of workers who declare home as their primary place of work is rapidly rising, increasing 66 percent in the five-year period ending in 2010. This seems to signal that more small businesses may be headed in this same direction. So the question is not whether an increasing number of people will work from home in the years ahead—this number will definitely rise. The real question is whether your venture should be added to the count.

Sources: Based on Emily Glazer, "Can't Afford an Office? Rent a Desk for $275," *The Wall Street Journal*, October 4, 2011, p. B4; Matt Krantz, "What Office? Laptops Are Workspace," *USA Today*, June 7, 2012, pp. 6A, 7A; "Launchpad—Our Story," www.launchpadnola.com/story, accessed October 14, 2012; and Rachel Emma Silverman, "Step into the Office-Less Company," *The Wall Street Journal*, September 5, 2012, p. B6.

9-2 DESIGNING AND EQUIPPING THE PHYSICAL FACILITIES

LO 9-2

Discuss the challenges of designing and equipping a physical facility.

A well-written location plan should describe the physical space in which the business will be housed and include an explanation of any equipment needs. The plan may call for a new building or an existing structure, but ordinarily a new business that needs physical space will occupy an existing building, perhaps after some minor or major remodeling.

9-2a Challenges in Designing the Physical Facilities

When specifying building requirements, an entrepreneur must avoid committing to a space that is too large or too luxurious for the company's needs. At the same time, the space should not be so small or limiting that operations are hindered or become inefficient. Buildings do not produce profits directly; they merely house the operations and personnel that do so. Therefore, the ideal building will be practical, not extravagant.

The general suitability of a building for a given type of business operation depends on the functional requirements of the enterprise. For example, a restaurant should ideally be on one level to make service manageable; a manufacturer's interlinked production processes should be in the same building and located near one another in order to be efficient. Other important factors to consider include the age and condition of the building, potential fire hazards, the quality of heating and air conditioning systems, the adequacy of lighting and restroom facilities, and appropriate entrances and exits. Obviously, these factors are weighted differently for a factory than for a wholesale or retail operation. But in every case, the comfort, convenience, and safety of the business's employees and customers should be taken into consideration.

9-2b Challenges in Equipping the Physical Facilities

The final step in arranging for physical facilities is the purchase or lease of equipment and tools. The National Federation of Independent Business has reported that, overwhelmingly, owners of small businesses would rather own their equipment than lease it (see Exhibit 9.2). The majority believe that, in the long run, it is cheaper to buy than

9.2 Small Business Owners Choose Buying over Leasing

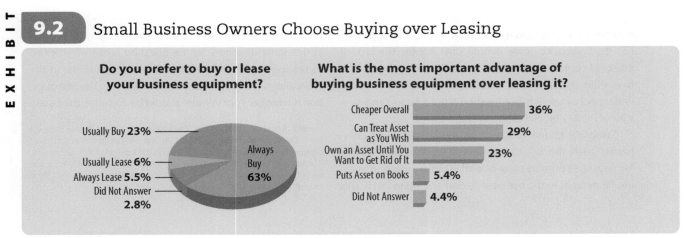

Do you prefer to buy or lease your business equipment?

Usually Buy **23%**

Usually Lease **6%**

Always Lease **5.5%**

Did Not Answer **2.8%**

Always Buy **63%**

What is the most important advantage of buying business equipment over leasing it?

Cheaper Overall **36%**

Can Treat Asset as You Wish **29%**

Own an Asset Until You Want to Get Rid of It **23%**

Puts Asset on Books **5.4%**

Did Not Answer **4.4%**

Source: Based on data from National Federation of Independent Business, "Reinvesting in the Business," http://www.411sbfacts.com/files/reinvesting.pdf, accessed October 2, 2012.

to lease. Having the flexibility to use the equipment as they wish and to keep it until it is no longer needed are also important reasons why small business owners prefer to own rather than lease. Still, the leasing option has advocates as well. So what should a small business owner do? To make an informed decision on this, use an equipment lease-versus-buy calculator, which can be found online with a simple Internet search. It's also a good idea to check with an accountant to be sure that any tax consequences of your decision to lease or buy are considered.

MANUFACTURING EQUIPMENT Machines used in factories can include either general-purpose or special-purpose equipment. **General-purpose equipment** requires minimal investment and is easily adapted to various operations. Small machine shops and cabinet shops, for example, use this type of equipment, which can be set up to handle two or more shop operations using the same piece of machinery. This offers flexibility, which is most important to industries in which products are so new that the technology is not yet well developed or there are frequent design changes. **Special-purpose equipment**, such as bottling machines and manufacturing robots used in factories, offers a more narrow range of possible applications and is more expensive to buy or lease. But a small firm can use special-purpose equipment economically only if it makes a standardized product on a fairly large scale. Upgrades via special tooling can lead to greater output per machine-hour of operation and reduce the labor cost per unit of product even further. On the downside, though, it is important to remember that this equipment has little or no resale value, due to its narrow range of possible applications.

RETAILING EQUIPMENT Small retailers need merchandise-display racks or counters, storage racks, shelving, mirrors, seats for customers, shopping carts, cash registers, and other items to facilitate selling. Such equipment may be costly, but it is usually less expensive than that necessary for a factory operation. And enterprising entrepreneurs often find ways to reduce startup or expansion costs by purchasing used equipment, making their own, or finding other ways to improvise.

If a store is intended to serve a high-income market, its fixtures should signal this by displaying the elegance and style expected by such customers. For example, polished mahogany showcases with bronze fittings can help to create an upscale setting. Indirect lighting, thick rugs, and oversized easy chairs also communicate luxury to clients. In contrast, a store that caters to lower-income

general-purpose equipment
Machines that serve many functions in the production process.

special-purpose equipment
Machines designed to serve specialized functions in the production process.

customers should concentrate on simplicity. Luxurious fixtures and plush seating would suggest an atmosphere that is inconsistent with low prices and only add to the cost of the operation, making it more difficult to keep prices down.

OFFICE EQUIPMENT Every business office—even a home office— needs furniture, filing and storage cabinets, and other such items. Major manufacturers of office furniture can certainly provide the necessary desks, chairs, and cabinetry, but so can scores of smaller vendors. Check out local sources of used office furniture, which may have items for sale that are still very presentable but a lot less expensive. And always make your decisions with the future in mind. If you select furnishings that are simple, free-standing, and detachable, then, when your business takes off, you can easily move them all to a larger facility.

© Jeffrey Liao/Shutterstock.com

Selecting office equipment that can help a business operate efficiently can be challenging. Be sure to choose computers, multifunction printers, and telephone systems that reflect the latest technological advances applicable to a particular business.

A company's major equipment needs should be identified in the location plan. This can ensure that the financial section of the plan will include funds for their purchase.

9-2c Business Image

All new ventures should be concerned with projecting the most appropriate image to customers and the public at large. The look and "feel" of the workplace should create an impression that says something about the quality of a firm's product or service and about the way the business is operated in general. For a small firm, and especially a startup, it is important to use the physical facilities to convey the image of a stable, professional company.

Factors as basic as color and interior design should be considered. Even before the first customer shows up, companies sometimes find that their financial backers are unwilling to hand over investment dollars until an office or retail store is perceived as attractive and inviting. If the image aspect of the facilities equation is beyond your expertise and insight, you may need to consult a design professional with a trained eye who can help you to make decisions that work.

Image is the engine of sales, so carefully consider how to mold your space to create a distinct and appropriate impression, yet still provide plenty of space, allow easy traffic flow, pass building inspections, and more—all in keeping with your budget and business goals. The way your facilities, customers, and employees come together will be critical to the success of your new business.

RESOURCES

Equipping a New Business on a Shoestring
You don't need the flashiest equipment and the best of furnishings to get started, just stuff that works. With deals on sites like Craigslist and Freecycle, you could save a bundle. If you need computers and would prefer to buy new rather than used, you can often save money by going to sites like www.techbargains.com or www.bradsdeals.com. And you can often find a wide selection and good deals on new furniture at www.overstock.com.

9-3 LOCATING THE STARTUP IN THE ENTREPRENEUR'S HOME

Rather than lease or buy a commercial site, many entrepreneurs choose instead to use their basement, garage, or spare room for their operations, creating a **home-based business**. In the past, a home location for a business was almost always

LO 9-3

Recognize both the attraction and the challenges of creating a home-based startup.

considered second-rate. But times have changed. Despite the limitations and potential for image problems, home-based entrepreneurs no longer feel embarrassed about their location. In fact, recent research has shown that home-based businesses may actually enjoy an advantage over other companies when it comes to certain dimensions of financial performance (for example, achieving a first sale).[19] The home office, once viewed as a passing phase on the path to growth for many businesses, has become a viable permanent option for some.

9-3a The Attraction of Home-Based Businesses

According to government surveys, more than half of all U.S. business owners chose to run their businesses primarily out of a home.[20] Why do many entrepreneurs find operating a business at home so appealing? Motivations vary, but the main attractions of a home-based business relate to financial and family lifestyle considerations such as the following:[21]

- Get a business up and running quickly and cheaply.
- Have something interesting to do, and get paid for doing it.
- Be your own boss, and reap the rewards from your efforts.
- Spend more time with family and friends.
- Save time and money wasted on daily commutes.

FINANCIAL CONSIDERATIONS Like most ventures, a home-based business has an important goal—earning money—and locating at home helps increase profits by reducing costs. For example, a freelance writer of magazine articles may need only a computer, a few office supplies, and an Internet connection to launch a business from home. Since most writers own a computer, the true startup costs for such a business may be only a few hundred dollars.

This option can certainly limit the cost and therefore the risk of testing market demand for a new product or service. With the ups and downs of the advertising industry, Donnovan Andrews and Stephen Smyk thought it would be best to start their fledgling agency, called Performance Bridge Advertising, in their home. "[We] built the business slowly and were conservative until we got to the point where we had excess capital," says Andrews. This cautious approach worked well. Andrews and Smyk moved into office space in a professional building only four months after they started the business.[22]

FAMILY LIFESTYLE CONSIDERATIONS Many young entrepreneurs remain in a family business because of close ties to relatives. Similarly, entrepreneurs who locate business operations in the home are frequently motivated by the desire to spend more time with family members, sometimes even including them in the work.

Marissa Shipman, founder and CEO of Shipman Associates, Inc., launched her cosmetics business from her home in 2001. "I love working from home," she says. But she also reveals that her home has had to change several times to accommodate her growing business. And Shipman Associates is a true family affair, as Shipman's sister, Jordana, is executive vice president with marketing responsibilities. At one point, Shipman even had her father on the payroll. It has worked out well enough for Shipman to conclude that a home is a great place to start a business. "If you have something you think could work," she says, "do it on a small scale and see."[23]

home-based business
A business that maintains its primary facility in the residence of its owner.

9-3b The Challenges of Home-Based Businesses

Just as most businesses located at commercial sites have their problems, home-based businesses face special challenges because of their location. We briefly examine two of these issues—business image and legal considerations. A third challenge—family and business conflicts—was discussed in Chapter 5.

PROFESSIONAL IMAGE Maintaining a professional image when working at home is a major challenge for many home-based entrepreneurs. Allowing young children to answer the telephone, for example, may undermine a company's image. Likewise, a baby crying or a dog barking in the background during a phone call can be distracting to a client and discourage sales.

If clients or salespeople visit the home-based business, it is critical that a professional office area be maintained. Space limitations sometimes make this difficult. For example, when you own a home-based business, house guests can create a real problem. Unless you want Aunt Zerelda wandering into a client meeting in her bathrobe or your nephew Jimmie playing his electric guitar during a work call, ground rules need to be set for house guests. Otherwise, major disruptions to the business are bound to occur. But establishing appropriate boundaries between home and business is easier said than done. Consider one successful work-at-home small business owner's take on this:

> *The moment you create a business, you step into a twilight zone where the barrier between what is work and what is not starts to break down. The deterioration accelerates for entrepreneurs who work out of their homes. You may start off with a home-based business but soon find yourself with a business where you and your family also happen to live.*[24]

So, it's not just a matter of preventing family members from spoiling business opportunities. Family life is paramount and should be shielded, in reasonable ways, from the creeping reach of the company's operations. The groan of extra car traffic, the presence of strangers (customers and employees) wandering through the house, inconvenient stacks of inventory and packing materials cluttering common areas, brusquely rejected invitations to break the focus on work to join one's spouse for lunch— these and many other hassles and inconveniences are everyday fare for the family of a home-based entrepreneur. And they call for patience and an extra dose of understanding from everyone involved.

LEGAL CONSIDERATIONS Local laws can sometimes pose serious problems for home-based businesses. Zoning ordinances, discussed earlier, regulate the types of enterprises permitted to operate within certain areas, and some cities outlaw any type of home-based business within city limits.

Many zoning laws, dating as far back as the 1930s, have never been updated. The intent of such laws is to protect a neighborhood's residential quality by forbidding commercial signs, limiting noise, and preventing parking problems. The neighborhood you live in may have a homeowners' association that can limit your ability to run a home-based business. Some entrepreneurs first become aware of these zoning laws when neighbors initiate zoning enforcement actions.

There are also tax issues related to a home-based business. For example, a separate space must be clearly devoted to the activities of the business if an entrepreneur is to claim a tax deduction. A knowledgeable accountant can help explain these tax regulations.

And don't forget the insurance considerations that may affect a home-based business. A homeowner's policy is not likely to cover an entrepreneur's business activities, liabilities, and equipment. Therefore, he or she should always consult a trustworthy insurance agent about policy limitations to avoid unpleasant surprises down the road.

The bad news for home-based businesses is that they often face significant hassles and limitations, such as those outlined above. The good news is that these ventures now have access to powerful business-application technologies that can help them compete against rivals, even those with a commercial site. With this in mind, in the next section we examine the potential of the Internet as a place to host a new business.

LO
9-4

Understand the potential benefits of locating a startup on the Internet.

9-4 E-COMMERCE: LOCATING A STARTUP ON THE INTERNET

What does the term *e-commerce* really describe? **E-commerce** refers to electronic commerce, or the buying or selling of products or services over the Internet. It is an alternative means of conducting business transactions that traditionally have been carried out by telephone, by mail, or face to face in a brick-and-mortar facility. Following the crash of Web-based enterprises more than a decade ago, Internet businesses are now growing in new ways and faster than ever—and with good reason. Locating on the Web can fundamentally reshape the way small firms conduct business. Far more than a simple alternative to the brick-and-mortar facility, the Internet can significantly boost a small company's financial performance.[25]

9-4a Benefits of E-Commerce to Startups

Electronic commerce can benefit a startup in many ways. It certainly allows a new venture to compete with bigger businesses on a more level playing field. Because of their limited resources, small firms often cannot reach beyond local markets. So those small firms confined to the brick-and-mortar world typically can serve only a restricted region. But the Internet blurs geographic boundaries and expands a small company's reach. In fact, e-commerce allows any business access to customers almost anywhere.

The experience of Beauty Encounter, a company that sells perfumes and beauty products, shows how the Internet is proving to be a great equalizer, giving small firms a presence comparable to that of marketplace giants. The business is an extension of three physical stores that were started by a Vietnamese couple who immigrated to the United States in 1980. Their daughter, Jacquelyn Tran, recognized the limitations of such operations and decided to carve out her own space in the global marketplace by establishing an online presence in 1999. Since then, the company has done nothing but grow. It now offers 1,100 unique brands, with new products being added daily, proving that small companies now can play in the big leagues.[26] Going online can unlock the door of opportunity for these companies, regardless of the industry.

It should also be pointed out that an e-commerce operation can help the startup with early cash flow problems by compressing the sales cycle—that is, reducing the time between receiving an order and converting the sale to cash. E-commerce systems can be designed to generate an order, authorize a credit card purchase, and contact a supplier and shipper in a matter of a few minutes, all without human assistance. The shorter cycle translates into quicker payments from customers and improved cash flows to the business.

E-commerce
Electronic commerce, or the buying and selling of products or services over the Internet.

Beyond the advantages outlined above, e-commerce enables small firms to build on one of their greatest strengths—customer relationships. The Internet has brought new life and technology to bear on the old-fashioned notion of customer service. **Electronic Customer Relationship Marketing (eCRM)** is an electronically based system that helps a company handle its customer relationships more effectively. At the heart of eCRM is a customer-centric data warehouse. A typical eCRM system allows an e-commerce firm to integrate data from websites, call centers, sales force reports, and other customer contact points, with the goal of building customer satisfaction and loyalty. (You will learn more about customer relationship management in Chapter 14, which focuses on this very important topic.)

9-4b E-Commerce Business Models

One of the fundamental features of an online operation is the business model upon which it is built. As discussed in Chapter 6, a business model is an analysis of how a firm plans to create profits and cash flows given its revenue sources, its cost structures, the required size of investment, and sources of risk. Online companies differ in their decisions concerning which customers to serve, how best to become profitable, and what to include on their websites. Exhibit 9.3 shows some possible alternatives for e-commerce business models. None of these models can currently be considered dominant, and some of the more complex Internet operations cannot be described by any single form. In reality, the world of e-commerce contains endless combinations of business models. To help you grasp the possibilities, we first outline e-commerce business models according to the type of customer served and then describe models based on the nature of a company's online presence. As you consider a direction for your small business and its online aspirations, keep in mind that a poorly devised business model is often the primary cause of an online company's failure.

TYPE OF CUSTOMERS SERVED Marketing frameworks classify traditional brick-and-mortar facilities as manufacturers, wholesalers, or retailers, depending on the

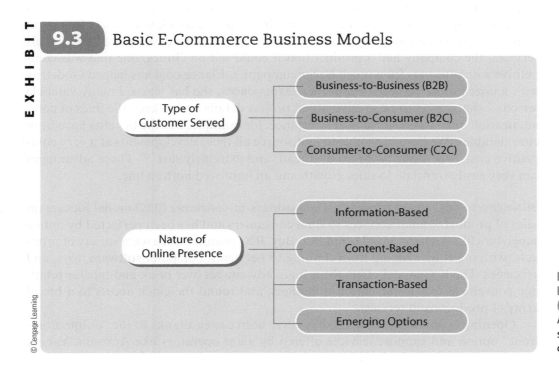

EXHIBIT 9.3 Basic E-Commerce Business Models

- Type of Customer Served
  - Business-to-Business (B2B)
  - Business-to-Consumer (B2C)
  - Consumer-to-Consumer (C2C)

- Nature of Online Presence
  - Information-Based
  - Content-Based
  - Transaction-Based
  - Emerging Options

© Cengage Learning

Electronic Customer Relationship Marketing (eCRM)
An electronically based system that emphasizes customer relationships.

customers they serve. In a similar way, e-commerce businesses also are commonly distinguished according to customer focus. There are three major categories of e-commerce business models: business-to-business (B2B), business-to-consumer (B2C), and consumer-to-consumer (C2C). In this section, we examine some strategies used by e-commerce firms within these three categories.

Business-to-business models. The dollar amounts generated by firms using a **business-to-business (B2B) model** (selling to business customers) are significantly greater than those for firms with a business-to-consumer (B2C) model (selling to final consumers). Because B2B success stories generally receive less publicity than B2C ventures do, the potential of B2B opportunities is often overlooked. But aspiring entrepreneurs should be sure to consider B2B options.

B2B operations "come in all shapes and sizes," but the most popular form of this strategy emphasizes sales transactions. By using online capabilities, a B2B firm can achieve greater efficiency in its buying and selling activities. For example, by dealing directly with its business clients online, International Business Machines (IBM) is able to build its computer systems and related products to meet the specific needs of its customers. The company relies heavily on the Internet to deliver its business solutions, but it also has an extensive sales force and consulting services to deliver value to its many customers worldwide.

A unique form of B2B trade involves work outsourcing, which helps connect freelancers and other specialists with companies that need their services. One market research firm estimates that close to 100 online marketplaces for work outsourcing already exist, and the market continues to grow rapidly, with sales increasing around 20 percent each year.[27] Some of the better known sites include Elance.com, Freelancer. com, oDesk.com, Guru.com, and Sologig.com, which allow you to "hire, manage, and pay remote contractors as if they were in your office."[28] Now, the market for global talent is as close as your computer. While work-outsourcing marketplaces help freelancers reach the clients they need to build their businesses, they can also help entrepreneurs locate the support services necessary to improve their own operations.

Danielle Godefroy, co-founder of Lingolook Publishing, first used Elance.com to connect with a software developer in Colorado, who contracted to make the language-pronunciation flashcards that the company then was able to sell to travelers for use on their iPhones. Once Godefroy paid the iPhone applications developer $5,000 for his services, the company had a product that it could sell on iTunes, one that was competitive with offerings from much larger companies. Elance.com has helped Godefroy with a dozen other projects. From these experiences, she has learned many valuable lessons—that it pays to be specific about project details and to keep the lines of communication open when working at a distance, for example. But the benefits have been considerable. "We have been able to [out]source all these developments at a very competitive cost," she says, "with no overhead, and extremely fast."[29] These advantages can very easily translate to sales growth and an improved bottom line.

Business-to-consumer models. The **business-to-consumer (B2C) model** focuses on sales of products and/or services to final consumers and has been perfected by online superstars like Amazon, Apple, and Best Buy. B2C ventures sell a wide variety of products, with offerings ranging from clothing to pet items, computer software, toys, and groceries. The B2C model offers three main advantages over brick-and-mortar retailing: convenient use, immediate transactions, and round-the-clock access to a broad array of products and services.

Opening up an online business has never been easier, thanks to the "online storefront" option and support services offered by giant operators like Amazon, Yahoo,

business-to-business (B2B) model
A business model based on selling to business customers electronically.

business-to-consumer (B2C) model
A business model based on selling to final consumers electronically.

and eBay. Some companies do business only through such a storefront, though many others also establish their own independent website and sell through both. When he launched his online store, Oliver's Pet Care, Shaheed Khan signed up for Amazon Webstore (http://webstore.amazon.com), which provides all of the tools needed to build an online business. It allows sellers to list their items alongside those offered by Amazon and to use the Fulfillment by Amazon program to handle product packing and shipping. The fulfillment program makes it possible for Kahn's customers to combine orders of his products with Amazon's and to receive Super Saver Shipping, customer service, and returns support directly from Amazon. Kahn says these services make his life manageable and have boosted Oliver's Pet Care sales to thousands of dollars a day.[30]

B2C e-commerce businesses certainly face unique challenges (payment security risks, customers who refuse to purchase a product without first seeing it or trying it on, etc.), but they also enjoy the advantages of flexibility. For example, they are able to change merchandise mixes and prices quickly, and they can easily modify the appearance of their online store. Traditional merchants located in brick-and-mortar stores would find such changes to be very costly and time-consuming, making it nearly impossible for them to keep up with fast-moving markets.

Gilt Groupe, started in 2007, exploits the flexibility edge that online businesses can have. As one of a handful of popular "flash sale" websites, this fashion retailer makes e-commerce fun and exciting by offering "invitation-only access to highly coveted products and experiences at insider prices."[31] Gilt's website provides its members with a unique selection of apparel, accessories, and lifestyle items that change every day—and that is the secret to the company's success. Susan Lyne, now chairman of the company, explains what sets Gilt Groupe apart from the competition:

> *Most online shopping mirrors brick-and-mortar stores. They're not taking advantage of what's uniquely possible online, the heightened sense of entertainment and competition. A big part of the Gilt brand promise is discovery: you come every day and it's new every day.*[32]

All indications are that the formula is working like a charm: Gilt's sales grew six-fold in a single year![33] By changing its product offerings daily, customers are drawn to the website often to see what's new, and the pages can be changed to keep up with shifts in consumer demand and product availability. This capacity for flexibility provides a substantial edge over brick-and-mortar operations—at least for those online businesses that position themselves to take advantage of it.

In some cases, market conditions or opportunities persuade wholesalers to bypass the retailer and take their product or service directly to the final consumer through online operations, a strategy sometimes referred to as **disintermediation**. Eli Mechlovitz and his family had been selling glass and tile as a wholesaler in New York for more than two decades, but slowing sales forced Mechlovitz to reconsider the company's strategy. In 2007, he decided to launch GlassTileStore.com to sell custom tiles and mosaics directly to consumers who were looking for deals on the Internet. Through this channel, the company can sell products at much lower prices (sometimes as much as 50 percent below their cost in retail stores), and website sales now exceed those typical during the best of months before online operations began.[34] That's the power of the online option—it offers market reach and flexibility that would not otherwise be available.

As B2C e-commerce models continue to develop and evolve, new alternatives will emerge, which is bound to catch established rivals off guard. Even some very large competitors find it difficult to keep up with the online game. For example, Google's

disintermediation
A B2B wholesaler's bypassing of a "middleman" to sell its product or service directly to the final consumer.

creative service offerings have forced Microsoft to reconsider how it prices its software, and full-service travel agencies are still trying to figure out how to adjust their approaches to deal with more recent competitors like Kayak.com and CheapOAir.com. An alert entrepreneur will monitor movement in the marketplace to be able to respond quickly to potential risks and identify emerging opportunities.

Consumer-to-consumer models. A growing number of entrepreneurs who sell their wares over the Internet do so without creating either a website or a storefront. Instead, they use auction sites, which fall under what is sometimes called the **consumer-to-consumer (C2C) model**. This model is usually set up around Internet **auction sites** that allow individuals and companies to list products available for sale to potential bidders.

Online auctions have become one of the most celebrated success stories on the Internet. And eBay, founded in 1995 by computer programmer Pierre Omidyar, is the 900-pound gorilla of auction sites. To provide a few statistics to show you what an amazing phenomenon eBay has become, the company has more than 104 million active users around the world and sells over $2,000 in goods *every second*. It may also surprise you to know that $18 billion was sold on eBay in a recent three-month period, and the most expensive item sold to date was a private business jet (for $4.9 million).[35]

You can buy or sell nearly anything on eBay, and it's incredibly easy. For a fee, auction-site consultants will coach you on how to be a successful seller. You can also attend eBay University, in person or via online tutorials, to learn the ins and outs of operating an eBay business. To show you how easy it is to get started, Exhibit 9.4 provides a simple five-step procedure for selling items on eBay. As easy as it is to sell a few items on eBay, it is a very different matter to actually make money as an ongoing business on the site. As in the more conventional forms of retailing, a well-thought-out business plan is helpful in turning your business idea (or hobby) into a money-making proposition.

Auction sites like eBay generate most of their revenue through listing fees and commissions. To continue its rapid growth, eBay is expanding its services and entering additional markets across the globe through new sites, acquisitions, and shared ventures. Overall, eBay does business in 39 countries (including the United States),[36] and PayPal, eBay's global payments platform, has 110 million total accounts.[37] But it is no longer the only show in town. Today, eBay faces competition from the likes of UBid.com, Bidz.com, and OnlineAuction.com.

The company is also taking steps to expand the eBay Stores side of its business, which gives sellers access to millions of shoppers worldwide. This option helps eBay Store sellers achieve success by providing powerful tools to help them build, manage, promote, and track their eBay presence. And they can create a listing, with full search exposure, for as little as $0.03.[38] To hold on to its position at the top of the heap, the company has harnessed the power of the smartphone revolution by perfecting a new generation of powerful mobile-shopping technologies that have sharply increased sales.[39]

consumer-to-consumer (C2C) model
A business model usually set up around Internet auction sites that allow individuals and companies to list items available for sale to potential bidders.

auction sites
Web-based businesses offering participants the ability to list products for consumer bidding.

EXHIBIT **9.4** Selling Your Item on eBay

Step 1: Set up an eBay seller's account, which is free of charge.
Step 2: Create a listing for the item to be offered for sale.
Step 3: Manage your listing to see if anyone has bid on or purchased your item.
Step 4: Wrap up with the sale with your buyer by receiving payment, shipping the item, and leaving feedback.

Source: Based on "Getting Started Selling on eBay," http://pages.ebay.com/help/sell/sell-getstarted.html, accessed October 10, 2012.

NATURE OF ONLINE PRESENCE A second broad way of categorizing e-commerce models relates to a firm's intended level of online presence. The role of a website can range from merely offering information and basic content to enabling complex business transactions.

Information-based model. A website built on the **information-based model** offers information about a business, its products, and other related matters but doesn't charge for its use. It is typically just a complement to an existing brick-and-mortar facility. Many small businesses use this model for their online operations. Your dentist or plumber may have a website that simply describes the services offered but probably will require a phone call to set up an appointment. These sites often feature a "Contact Us" link that will take the user to a separate Web page displaying the company's address and phone number and, in many cases, offer "click-through" access that allows the user to get in touch with the business via e-mail.

Research has shown that the Internet has become the first stop for consumers who need information on a local business.[40] So it makes sense for small companies to create websites that can then be picked up by consumer searches. They should also list their businesses on local platforms offered by major search engines, which can be done by going to www.google.com/places or http://local.yahoo.com, to mention only two of the available options.

Content-based model. The **content-based model** of e-commerce is a variation of the information-based alternative in that it also features a website that provides access to information but not the ability to make purchases. Rather than selling products or services, a content-based website provides information (content) for those who visit it, usually with the hope of attracting a healthy stream of visitors. In most cases, this online traffic can be "monetized" (turned into a source of revenue), assuming that is what the creator has in mind. For example, it is easy enough to have Google place ads or banners on your website; you would then earn money each time a visitor clicks on them (see www.google.com/adsense for details). Ad revenue is usually disappointingly low, but another option is to become an online affiliate. Affiliate programs (sometimes called *associate programs*) arrange for online merchants to pay a commission to websites for any traffic that they can send to them. For example, Amazon's Associates Program pays referral fees of up to 10 percent on qualified sales of its products that are initiated through links on an affiliate's website. As a bonus, the program is easy to use, and the company will show you more than a dozen options for building links and ads for Amazon products on your site.[41] But this is just one example of hundreds of affiliate programs that you could choose to join.

Transaction-based model. In a **transaction-based model** of e-commerce, a website is set up to provide a mechanism for buying or selling products or services. The transaction-based model could be considered the center of the e-commerce universe, with online stores where visitors go to shop, click, and buy.

Many Internet ventures sell a single product or service. For example, Huber and Jane Wilkinson market their reading comprehension program, IdeaChain, through their MindPrime, Inc., website (www.mindprime.com). Other ventures are direct extensions of a brick-and-mortar store, creating what is sometimes called a bricks-and-clicks or a clicks-and-mortar strategy. For example, if you wanted to purchase a new printer, you might research options on Office Depot's website and then either buy your selection online or pick up the printer at your neighborhood Office Depot store. Although Office Depot is a large corporation with millions of customers, small businesses can follow the same general model with excellent results.

information-based model
A business model in which a website provides information about a business, its products, and other related matters but doesn't charge for its use.

content-based model
A business model in which a website provides information (content) that attracts visitors, usually with the hope of generating revenue through advertising or by directing that traffic to other websites.

transaction-based model
A business model in which a website provides a mechanism for buying or selling products or services.

Many e-commerce companies generate a lot of sales by merging the content- and transaction-based models into one website. Launched in 1999, BodyBuilding.com is probably the most visited bodybuilding and fitness website in the world. Its 25,000 pages of content, most of which plugs products that are sold on the site through its transaction features, attracts more than 250,000 unique visitors each day, enough traffic to generate more than 6 million orders to date.[42]

But this raises a thorny ethical question: How can an online company feature content that is so closely tied to its own products? To maintain integrity in this situation, the company should be transparent and make sure that all claims are legitimate. After all, the long-term performance of the company will depend on it. According to Peter Nguyen, the Internet entrepreneur profiled in Chapter 3's Spotlight feature, websites that get extraordinary results usually do at least one of the following three things:[43]

- Create *meaningful value* in the form of valuable information, incentives, or services.
- Provide *remarkable experiences* that create entertainment that can be shared.
- Offer *impactful solutions* that help people improve themselves, their businesses, or their communities.

It follows that online entrepreneurs who create the most benefit for their customers are far more likely to succeed. Websites that make false or overstated claims are usually short-lived, as the news of their misdeeds spreads quickly on the Internet. As with brick-and-mortar operations, enduring and impactful online businesses must have integrity and deliver genuine value to their customers.

Emerging options. The Internet world is known for how fast it moves, and entrepreneurial minds are constantly finding new ways to cash in on its potential. In most cases, these are variations on the content-based model discussed earlier.

Bloggers produce online journals to trade comments with friends and other readers, but these can also be managed as a money-making venture. Small firms have found blogs easy to use and thus an attractive platform from which to promote the sale of an overstocked item or to give an employee special recognition. But Web traffic on a blog can also generate substantial income from advertising and paid links. The amount earned is dependent on such factors as how much traffic the site generates, the trustworthiness of the content offered, and how relevant the ads are to those who visit. Rhett Butler quit his job as a production manager in 2003 when he realized just how much money could be generated through his environmental conservation blog, Mongabay. "The rainforest has always been my passion," says Butler, "but I never expected to make a living off of it." At one point, he was making between $15,000 and $18,000 a month in ad revenue from the 1.3 million unique visitors drawn to his website each month.[44]

Another option is to create podcasts, audio or video files that are distributed over the Internet and can draw a listenership of around 38 million. Comedian, former radio personality, and multimedia ranter Adam Carolla launched his podcast venture in 2009 and now records crude, radio-like episodes that he archives online. More than 2.8 million listeners tune in each month to see what he has to say, and that translates to substantial profit. Carolla and other podcasters can make money by peddling ads and sponsorships, asking for donations, selling subscriptions, and charging for access to live events.[45]

Still other entrepreneurs are cashing in on the Web by exploiting the reach of YouTube or Pinterest to create a following that can be turned into profit. YouTube has organized a Partner Program that allows high-traffic content creators to display Google ads on their videos and earn a percentage of the revenues generated whenever a visitor clicks on one of those ads. Hundreds of partners earn six figures a year from

TOOLS

Ensuring Website Usability

It makes no sense to spend money on a website if online visitors find it difficult to use and choose to shop elsewhere. For $200 (or less), services like UserTesting.com, OpenHallway.com, and BetaBreakers.com can help you identify problems and suggest ways to improve your online presence. It's a great bargain!

the program, according to Kevin Yen, YouTube's director of strategic partnerships.[46] Pinterest first launched its social image bookmarking website in 2010 and is still trying to figure out how to make money from it. But that hasn't stopped some of its more popular "pinners" from finding a way to cash in. For example, 31-year-old designer Satsuki Shibuya has more than a million followers, exposure that has prompted some companies to pay her anywhere from $150 to $1,200 just for pinning an image of one of their products. "It's a smart move [for the paying brands]," she says. "They're already putting ads in magazines, and there are 10 times as many people looking at Pinterest."[47] As these examples demonstrate, new online business concepts are being created all the time, and alert entrepreneurs are finding ways to cash in on them.

9-4c Internet-Based Businesses and the Part-Time Startup Advantage

When an entrepreneur launches a new company, many times she or he has to decide whether to give up an existing job and jump full-time into the startup or hold on to the job while getting a part-time business going on the side. There are advantages and drawbacks to each approach, of course, but research shows that most entrepreneurs prefer to launch a part-time enterprise to keep the income flowing until they can afford to make a complete transition to the new business. Though many kinds of businesses can be started on a part-time basis, a growing number of small business owners are finding that the flexibility and low cost of launching an online business make this a very attractive option.

Brian Eddy and Chad Ronnebaum chose the part-time startup path back in 1999. These long-time friends decided to keep their successful careers *and* launch Q3 Innovations, a product design, development, and distribution company that creates personal safety and monitoring devices.[48] As with most startups, launching Q3 Innovations was a very satisfying, but grueling, experience. Eddy and Ronnebaum were booking 90- to 100-hour work weeks during the company's six-year startup phase (only about half of those hours were spent at their regular jobs), so the "part-time" business was tying up their weekends and most of their evenings, too. The startup grew so much that Eddy decided to leave his legal practice to become the company's full-time CEO, and Ronnebaum set aside his career as a pharmacist to become the full-time president of the venture a few years later.[49]

The part-time strategy followed by Q3's founders took much of the risk out of making the transition to life as entrepreneurs. And the decision to use the Internet as a business platform played a significant part in making their Q3 Innovations dream a reality.[50] (The company was acquired by Quest Products, Inc. in 2010, but the enterprise remains intact, and the venture's line of products is still being sold on the Q3 Innovations website.[51])

Clearly, the location decision is complicated, but it is extremely important to get it right. If your business needs a physical facility, can you find a location that is convenient to customers, offers a supportive business climate, and provides access to necessary resources? As the owner of the business, would you be happy to show up to work at that location, day after day and year after year? When you think of the costs involved, does the location make sense? If you have decided to locate your business at home, can you keep the business and your home life manageably separate? Also, can you abide by zoning restrictions and maintain a favorable company image? If the Internet is the right place for your startup, can you identify the type of customer you will serve and the business model you will adopt? There are many questions to be answered, but there are also many sources of information to help you decide what location will work best for your planned venture. Don't get impatient—just take your time, do your research, and make a wise choice. A world of endless business opportunities awaits you.

9-1. Describe the five key factors in locating a brick-and-mortar startup.

- Customer accessibility is a key location factor in industries with high transportation costs, as well as those that must provide handy access for targeted customers to avoid losing those customers to more conveniently located competitors.
- Climate, competition, legal requirements, and the tax structure are types of environmental factors affecting the location decision.
- Availability of resources such as raw materials, a suitable labor supply, and transportation can be important to location decisions.
- Though it can interfere with sound decision making, the entrepreneur's personal preference is a practical consideration in selecting a location.
- An appropriate site must be available and priced within the entrepreneur's budget.

9-2. Discuss the challenges of designing and equipping a physical facility.

- The general suitability of a building depends on the functional requirements of the business; it should be neither too large and extravagant nor too small and restrictive.
- The comfort, convenience, and safety of the business's employees and customers must not be overlooked.
- Deciding whether to purchase or lease equipment is an important choice many entrepreneurs face.
- Most small manufacturing firms must use general-purpose equipment, but some can use special-purpose equipment for specialized operations.
- Small retailers must have merchandise display racks and counters, storage racks, shelving, mirrors, shopping carts, cash registers, and other equipment that facilitates selling.
- Fixtures and other retailing equipment should create an atmosphere appropriate for customers in the retailer's target market.

- Entrepreneurs should select office equipment that reflects the latest advances in technology applicable to a particular business.
- All new ventures, regardless of their function, should project an image that is appropriate to and supportive of the business and its intentions.

9-3. Recognize both the attraction and the challenges of creating a home-based startup.

- Home-based businesses are started both for financial reasons and to accommodate family lifestyle considerations.
- Operating a business at home can pose challenges beyond family and business conflict, particularly in the areas of business image and legal considerations.
- Technology, especially the Web, has made it possible to operate many types of businesses from almost any location.

9-4. Understand the potential benefits of locating a startup on the Internet.

- E-commerce offers small firms the opportunity to compete with bigger companies on a more level playing field.
- Internet operations can help small firms with early cash flow problems by compressing the sales cycle.
- E-commerce enables small firms to build stronger customer relationships.
- Business-to-business (B2B) companies generate far more sales than ventures following alternative models.
- The three main advantages of online business-to-consumer (B2C) firms are convenient use, immediate transactions, and continuous access to products and services.
- Internet auction sites, like eBay, are based on the consumer-to-consumer (C2C) model and can help even the smallest of businesses access a worldwide market with great convenience.
- The role of a website can range from merely offering information and content to permitting the buying and selling of products and services online.
- Emerging platforms for online ventures include blogging, podcasting, and creating a following on YouTube or Pinterest to generate revenue from ads and sponsorships, donations, subscription charges, or fees for access to live events.
- Internet-based businesses can be started on a part-time basis, which reduces the personal risk of the entrepreneur if the venture should fail.

Key Terms

auction sites p. 244

brick-and-mortar facility p. 227

business incubator p. 232

business-to-business (B2B) model p. 242

business-to-consumer (B2C) model p. 242

consumer-to-consumer (C2C) model p. 244

content-based mode p. 245

disintermediation p. 243

E-commerce p. 240

Electronic Customer Relationship Marketing (eCRM) p. 241

general-purpose equipment p. 236

home-based business p. 238

information-based model p. 245

special-purpose equipment p. 236

transaction-based model p. 245

zoning ordinances p. 231

Discussion Questions

1. What are the key attributes of a good business location? Which of these would probably be most important for a retail location? Why?

2. Which resource factors might be most vital to a new manufacturing venture that produces residential home furniture? Why?

3. Is the hometown of the business owner likely to be a good location? Is it logical for an owner to allow personal preferences to influence a decision about business location? Explain your answers.

4. Under what conditions would it be most appropriate for a small business to buy rather than lease a building for its operations?

5. What is the difference between general-purpose equipment and special-purpose equipment? What are the advantages and disadvantages of each?

6. What factors should an entrepreneur evaluate when considering a home-based business? Be specific.

7. How might zoning and tax laws impact the decision to start a home-based business?

8. Define and describe B2B, B2C, and C2C businesses. What is the major thrust of each of these three models?

9. What are the primary features of the information-based, content-based, and transaction-based models of e-commerce? Which of these offers the greatest business potential? Explain your answers.

10. What are some of the emerging options for making money in an Internet-based business? Which of these has the greatest potential for profits and long-term growth?

You Make the Call

Situation 1

Entrepreneurs Joe Stengard and his wife, Jackie Piel, had a decision to make. Located just outside of St. Louis, Missouri, their five-year-old company, S&P Crafts, was growing rapidly, and they were in desperate need of more space to make their custom-ordered craft kits.

A move always involves a certain measure of risk, so the couple was hesitant to transfer the company's operations. However, an economic development organization in Warren County, Missouri, offered attractive incentives in the form of tax breaks and financial assistance if they would move to a new facility in the rural town of Hopewell. Initial research indicated that a local workforce was readily available and had skills appropriate to the operation, so Stengard and Piel decided to move.

Since the change of address, company sales have tripled. And the new facility has grown from 10,000 square feet to 40,000 square feet in just two short years.

Question 1 How important was the location decision for these two entrepreneurs? Why?

Question 2 What types of permits and zoning ordinances did Stengard and Piel need to consider before deciding to relocate?

Question 3 How could Stengard and Piel use the Internet to expand their business?

Situation 2

Eliza Roundtree, a single parent, wants to start an interior design business to help support her two young children. She works in the banking industry but has always had a desire to start a business. She enjoys decorating her own home and is often asked, "Have you ever considered doing this professionally? You have such a good sense of colors and how they blend together with fabrics, furnishings, and design."

Roundtree is unsure whether she should locate in a commercial site or in her home, which is in rural central Texas. She is leaning toward locating at home because she wants more time with her children. However, she is concerned that the home-based location is too far from the closest city, which is where most of her potential customers live.

Initially, her services would include planning for mid-market residential interior design projects, which would involve estimating project options and costs and consulting with clients on colors, fabrics, and furnishings. Eventually, she would like to specialize in creating luxury interiors for owners of upscale homes. But she has a lot to learn before she will be ready for that.

Question 1 What are some potential problems that Roundtree will face if she locates her new business at home?

Question 2 What do you see as the major benefits for Roundtree of a home-based business?

Question 3 How could Roundtree use technology to help operate a home-based business?

Situation 3

The SUBWAY restaurant chain now has nearly 38,000 locations in 99 countries, so it knows a thing or two about deciding where to set up shop. But in 2009, the company elected to take its location expertise to new heights. *SUBWAY Restaurant News* reported it this way:

> *Richard Schragger is a multi-unit SUBWAY franchisee in the New York City area. For the next two years, his newest store* will be located on top of the world! Richard's newest SUBWAY restaurant will be on a crane, rising alongside the construction of One World Trade Center—also known as the Freedom Tower—providing meals for construction workers as the structure rises 108 stories. At 1,776 feet, it will be the tallest building in the United States and one of the tallest buildings in the world.

The location of this restaurant allowed the hundreds of iron workers and tradesmen working on the structure to enjoy meals aloft and avoid the 45-minute elevator ride required to reach the ground. DCM Erectors, the construction company overseeing work on the tower, welded together 36 shipping containers to create the new restaurant. That metal shell, along with the food to be served and the equipment needed to serve it, was hoisted by crane, level by level, so that it was always positioned near the workers as they riveted, welded, and fabricated the new structure. When mealtime rolled around (breakfast, lunch, and dinner for this unique shop), employees did not have far to go to grab a bite. No matter how you slice it, this was an unusual location for a restaurant chain.

Question 1 What are the major advantages that Schragger enjoyed as the result of having this most unique site?

Question 2 What major disadvantages and special challenges did the company likely run into as a result of this towering location?

Question 3 Do you think it was a good idea for Schragger to locate a SUBWAY franchise in this way? What other uncommon locations can you think of that small businesses have used or are using to their advantage?

Sources: Based on Jason Daley, "A Tall Order," *Entrepreneur*, Vol. 38, No. 4 (April 2010), p. 124; and "SUBWAY—Explore Our World," www.subway.com/subwayroot/exploreourworld.aspx, accessed October 16, 2012.

Experiential Exercises

1. Search for articles online that provide rankings of states or cities as business locations. What definite trends do you notice? Report on your findings.

2. Identify and evaluate a local site that is now vacant because of a business closure. Point out the strengths and weaknesses of that location for the former business and comment on the part that location may have played in the closure.

3. Interview a small business owner concerning the strengths and weaknesses of his or her business's location. Prepare a brief report summarizing your findings.

4. Consider a local small business that might benefit from adding e-commerce as a supporting feature of its business strategy. Prepare a report on the reasons that this particular business is not involved in e-commerce and recommend an e-commerce strategy that would help to boost its performance.

5. Do some research online to determine what e-commerce assistance is available to small firms. Report on your findings.

Small Business & Entrepreneurship Resource Center

The Small Business & Entrepreneurship Resource Center offers complete small business management resources through a comprehensive database that covers all major areas of starting, operating, and maintaining a business from financing, management, marketing, accounting, taxes, and more. Go to www.cengagebrain.com and select the Longenecker text for more information on how to access this material.

1. Shopping online is a revealing act. Websites know what catches visitors' fancy, how long they linger, and where to find them when they leave. Traditional shopkeepers are blind by comparison. Who enters their stores and how they behave are mysteries, which are only partly solved when someone buys something. Brick-and-mortar retailers would like to level the playing field. Clothing chains want the same analytics in-store as they can get online. The equipment is already there: security cameras look for thieves and Wi-Fi networks pick up mobile-phone signals. Testing is going on to see if technology can help retailers understand customers and boost profits. For example, mannequins look at customers with camera eyes, noting sex, age, and ethnicity. One noticed Asian shoppers arriving at the same time every day, prompting the manager to post Asian salespeople to receive them. After reading this article, do you think that brick-and-mortar retailers should use every advantage to compete with price-chopping websites? Or do cameras invade a shopper's privacy? Explain your answer.

2. Operating a one-man mobile transport refrigeration business specializing in 24-hour service is challenging. Resources are limited; it requires a huge investment in parts, tools, and equipment and one person can accomplish only so much in a day. Productivity is reduced when a service call is far away, because driving eats up work time. Yet, no company wants to turn away business. Three small 24-hour mobile transport refrigeration repair services in Georgia found a solution to be more effective and productive. Rather than turn away business, they refer service calls to one another. They try to distinguish themselves from the competition by providing superior service with more personal attention in a timely manner. What are the advantages and disadvantages of a mobile business? Evaluate the collaboration among these three businesses.

Sources: "We Snoop to Conquer: Retail Technology," *The Economist*, February 9, 2013, p. 64; and "Mobile Repair Businesses Co-op to Expand Services, Coverage," *Refrigerated Transporter*, Vol. 44, No. 9 (February 1, 2009).

Video Case 9

Cookies-n-Cream (P. 660)

This case highlights the importance of the location decision to the success of a small business, illustrating specifically how nontraditional location options, like the use of mobile vending trucks, can open up opportunities for a startup.

Alternative Case for Chapter 9

Case 3, The Kollection, p. 648

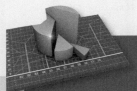

Business Plan

LAYING THE FOUNDATION

As part of laying the foundation for preparing your own business plan, respond to the following questions regarding location.

Brick-and-Mortar Startup Location Questions

1. How important are your personal reasons for choosing a location?

2. What business environment factors will influence your location decision?

3. What resources are most critical to your location decision?

4. How important is customer accessibility to your location decision?

5. How will the formal site evaluation be conducted?

6. What laws and tax policies of state and local governments need to be considered?

7. What is the cost of the proposed site?

Physical Facility Questions

1. What are the major considerations in choosing between a new and an existing building?

2. What is the possibility of leasing a building or equipment?

3. How feasible is it to locate in a business incubator?

4. What is the major objective of your building design?

5. What types of equipment do you need for your business?

Home-Based Startup Location Questions

1. Will a home-based business be a possibility for you?

2. For the venture you are planning, what would be the advantages and disadvantages of locating the business in your home?

3. Have you given consideration to family lifestyle issues?

4. Will your home project the appropriate image for the business?

5. What zoning ordinances, if any, regulate the type of home-based business you want to start?

Internet Startup Questions

1. What type of customers will be served by the Internet startup?

2. What technical limitations (such as the cost of designing and developing a website or constantly changing software needs) might hinder the company you plan to launch?

3. How will you deal with nontechnical issues (privacy concerns, website security, dealing with global languages and cultures, etc.) that may limit the success of your online business?

4. Do you plan to open a storefront hosted by Amazon, eBay, or one of the other online giants, or would an independent website be better suited to the needs of your business?

5. What will be the nature of the online presence you hope to establish—information-based, content-based, transaction-based, or some other form?

6. Will you start the business on a part-time basis, or do you plan to be involved full-time?

Endnotes

1. Jessica Bruder, "The Best Places to Launch," *Fortune Small Business*, Vol. 19, No. 9 (November 2009), pp. 56, 58.

2. Jason Daley, "Move, or Lose," *Entrepreneur*, Vol. 39, No. 6 (June 2011), p. 122.

3. Adapted from J. D. Ryan and Gail P. Hiduke, *Small Business: An Entrepreneur's Business Plan*, 8th ed. (Mason, OH: South-Western Cengage Learning, 2009), pp. 148–150.

4. "About Lids—Company Info," www.lids.com, accessed October 1, 2012.

5. COBB Tuning—History, www.cobbtuning.com/company-info-history-s/50300.htm, accessed October 1, 2012.

6. Small Business & Entrepreneurship Council, "Business Tax Index 2012," www.sbecouncil.org/uploads/BTI2012FINAL.pdf, accessed October 1, 2012.

7. Jacquelyn Lynn, "Tax Relief," *Entrepreneur*, Vol. 36, No. 7 (July 2008), p. 24.

8. Jacquelyn Lynn, "What's It Worth?" *Entrepreneur*, Vol. 36, No. 3 (March 2008), p. 32.

9. As reported in Chip Mellor and Dana Berliner, "Small Businesses Losing Out to Red Tape," *USA Today*, October 25, 2010, http://usatoday30.usatoday.com/news/opinion/forum/2010-10-21-mellor26_st_N.htm, accessed October 2, 2012.

10. Rieva Lesonsky, *Start Your Own Business: The Only Start-Up Book You'll Ever Need* (Irvine, CA: Entrepreneur Press, 2007), p. 251.

11. As quoted in Jacquelyn Lynn, "Location Is Key," *Entrepreneur*, Vol. 36, No. 11 (November 2008), p. 26. See also Craig S. Galbraith, Carlos L. Rodriguez, and Alex F. DeNoble, "SME Competitive Strategy and Location Behavior: An Exploratory Study of High-Technology Manufacturing," *Journal of Small Business Management*, Vol. 46, No. 2 (April 2008), pp. 183–202.

12. National Federation of Independent Businesses, "411 Small Business Facts," www.411sbfacts.com/sbpoll.php?POLLID=0048&KT_back=1, accessed November 24, 2010.

13. Sarah E. Needleman, "Start-Up Programs Find Niche," *The Wall Street Journal*, November 18, 2010, p. B7.

14. "HBK Incubates," http://hotbreadkitchen.org/hbk-incubator, accessed October 2, 2012.

15. Needleman, *op. cit.*

16. "Regus—Where We Operate," www.regus.com/search/where-we-operate.aspx, accessed October 2, 2012; and Gwendolyn Bounds, "My Office Is Your Office: Small Firms Share Space," *The Wall Street Journal*, March 18, 2008, p. B4.

17. David Port, "Solo, but Not Alone," *Entrepreneur*, Vol. 37, No. 10 (October 2009), pp. 99–103.

18. National Federation of Independent Businesses, "411 Small Business Facts—Energy Consumption," www.411sbfacts.com/sbpoll .php?POLLID=0047&KT_back=1, accessed October 2, 2012.

19. See Candida G. Brush, Linda F. Edleman, and Tatiana S. Manolova, "The Effects of Initial Location, Aspirations, and Resources on Likelihood of First Sale in Nascent Firms," *Journal of Small Business Management*, Vol. 46, No. 2 (April 2008), pp. 159–182.

20. Chuck Green, "My Home Is Not Your Home," *The Wall Street Journal*, November 14, 2011, http://online.wsj.com/article/SB10001424052702303 36580457643205148459760.html, accessed October 3, 2012.

21. Ken Harthun, "Top 5 Reasons for Starting a Home-Based Business," April 14, 2010, www.examiner.com/article/top-5-reasons-for-starting-a-home-based-business, accessed October 2, 2012.

22. Nichole L. Torres and April Y. Pennington, "Home Court Advantage," www .entrepreneur.com/article/77660-2, accessed October 3, 2012.

23. Nicole L. Torres, "Shipman Associates," www.entrepreneur.com/ article/78440, accessed October 3, 2012.

24. Meg Cadoux Hirshberg, "Bed and Boardroom," *Inc.*, Vol. 32, No. 1 (February 2010), pp. 31–33.

25. For the details of supporting research, see David A. Johnson, Michael Wade, and Ron McClean, "Does eBusiness Matter to SMEs? A Comparison of the Financial Impacts of Internet Business Solutions on European and North American SMEs," *Journal of Small Business Management*, Vol. 45, No. 3 (July 2007), pp. 354–361.

26. "Beauty Encounter—About Us," www.beautyencounter.com/about-us, accessed October 3, 2012.

27. Raymund Flandez, "Help Wanted—and Found," *The Wall Street Journal*, October 13, 2008, http://online.wsj.com/article/SB122347721312915407 .html, accessed October 9, 2012.

28. The National Association of Local Advertisers, "Virtual Assistants and Contractors," http://thenala.com/marketing/marketplace, accessed October 9, 2012.

29. Flandez, *op. cit.*

30. "New Video About Oliver's Pet Care," http://blog.oliverspetcare .com/amazon-interview, accessed October 10, 2012. "Fulfillment by Amazon," http://www.amazon.com/gp/help/customer/display .html?nodeId=200229160, accessed October 10, 2012.

31. "About Gilt," www.gilt.com/company/about, accessed December 7, 2010.

32. Kate Rockwood, "Gilt Groupe," *Fast Company*, No. 143 (March 2010), p. 77.

33. *Ibid.*

34. Shelly Banjo, "Wholesalers Set Up Shop Online to Tap Customers," *The Wall Street Journal*, http://online.wsj.com/article/SB122168658509949417 .html, accessed October 10, 2012.

35. "eBay Marketplace Fast Facts," http://pages.ebay.in/community/ aboutebay/news/infastfacts.html, accessed October 10, 2012.

36. *Ibid.*

37. "PayPal—Corporate Fast Facts," www.paypal-media.com/assets/pdf/ fact_sheet/PPFastFactsQ12012.pdf, accessed October 10, 2012.

38. "eBay Stores," http://pages.ebay.com/storefronts/faq.html, accessed October 10, 2012.

39. Dan Mascai, "eBay Dials M for Makeover," *FastCompany*, No. 151 (January 2011), pp. 42–44.

40. Ashley DeVecht, "Click Here for Profits," *MyBusiness*, September/October 2010, pp. 27–31.

41. "Amazon Associates," https://affiliate-program.amazon.com, accessed October 11, 2012.

42. "BodyBuilding.com—About Our Company," www.bodybuilding.com/fun/ comp.htm, accessed October 11, 2012.

43. Peter Nguyen, *Advertiser360: Learning the Essentials*, (Irvine, CA: Ad Ventures Group, 2011), p. 19.

44. Kelly K. Spors, "New Services Help Bloggers Bring in Ad Revenue," *TheWall Street Journal*, January 15, 2008, p. B6.

45. Ellen McGirt, "Pod Star," *Fast Company*, No, 144 (April 2010), pp. 79–83.

46. Mark Borden, "The New Influentials," *Fast Company*, No. 150 (November 2010), pp. 125–131.

47. Max Chafkin, "Starring Ben Silbermann As the Pinup Kid," *Fast Company*, No. 169 (October 2012), pp. 90–96, 146–147.

48. "Q3 Innovations—Our Products," http://www.q3i.com/products.php, accessed October 15, 2012.

49. Nichole L. Torres, "Weekenders," *Entrepreneur*, Vol. 33, No. 8 (August 2005), p. 80; and personal conversation with Chad Ronnebaum, February 7, 2007.

50. Q3 Innovations—About Us, www.q3i.com/aboutus.php, accessed January 6, 2009.

51. "Q3 Innovations—Personal Safety and Monitoring Devices," www.q3i .com, accessed October 15, 2012; and "Quest Products, Inc., Acquires Assets of Q3 Innovations, LLC," http://media.q3i.com/page/2, accessed October 15, 2012.

© Zurijeta/Shutterstock.com

CHAPTER 10

Understanding a Firm's Financial Statements

After studying this chapter, you should be able to …

10-1. Describe the purpose and content of an income statement.

10-2. Explain the purpose and content of a balance sheet.

10-3. Explain how viewing the income statement and balance sheets together gives a more complete picture of a firm's financial position.

10-4. Use the income statement and balance sheets to compute a company's cash flows.

10-5. Analyze the financial statements using ratios to see more clearly how decisions affect a firm's financial performance.

 OPEN LOOKING AHEAD

Johnny Stites is CEO of J&S Construction Company, Inc., in Cookeville, Tennessee. After graduating from college, Johnny served in the U.S. Navy for three years and then returned home to work in the family business. Several years later, his younger brother, Jack, joined him in the business and now serves as the company's president.

Johnny and Jack have grown the business into one of the most successful construction firms in the Southeast, if not the United States. A visitor to their business is immediately struck by the passion and sattention to detail they give to who they want to be and how they choose to operate their company. When asked how they use financial information to run the business, Johnny made the following observations:

When you start and run your own business, it no longer matters

> In the SPOTLIGHT
> **J&S Construction Company**
> www.jsconstruction.com

whether you were a marketing, management, finance, or any other specific major. As an entrepreneur, you have to know how a business operates, which requires more than having knowledge in a specific academic field. So whatever your major, you had best know the basics of accounting and finance. You do not need to be an accountant, but you had better be able to read and understand financial statements. Sure, you can hire an accountant, but if you do not understand what the numbers are telling you, you are in big trouble.

© Valentyn Volkov/Shutterstock.com

Entrepreneurs do not start companies so that they can learn accounting—that's for certain. In fact, for many students and aspiring entrepreneurs, accounting is not their favorite subject. But if you have or plan to start a business, you had better learn some accounting, sooner rather than later. Norm Brodsky, a serial entrepreneur and noted columnist for *Inc.*, puts it plainly:

> When I started out, I thought that CEOs ran businesses with the help of their top executives. What I didn't realize is that a business is a living entity with needs of its own, and unless the leaders pay attention to those needs, the business will fail. So how do you know what those needs are? There's only one way: by looking at the numbers and understanding the relationships between them. They will tell you how good your sales are, whether you can afford to hire a new salesperson or office manager, how much cash you will need to deal with new business coming in, how your market is changing, and on and on. You can't afford to wait until your accountant tells you these things. Nor do you have to become an accountant. You do have to know enough accounting, however, to figure out which numbers are most important in your particular business, and then you should develop the habit of watching them like a hawk.[1]

Understanding accounting has to do more with experience than ability. In this chapter, you will learn how to construct an *income statement*, a *balance sheet*, and a *cash flow statement*. Equally important, you will learn some basics of interpreting what these **financial statements**, or **accounting statements**, tell you about your business. This chapter is presented as simply as possible, without sacrificing the content that a small business owner needs. In addition, you will find the following by going to www.cengage.com and selecting the Longenecker text:

1. A spreadsheet that provides all the numerical tables within the chapter, along with computations.

2. Lecture modules that complement, but do not replace, you reading of the chapter.

3. Additional problems that can be used to further your understanding of financial statements.

4. Answers to the "Let's Check for Understanding" features found at the end of each section.

Before we begin a systematic study of financial statements, we will lay a foundation by telling a story about two young sisters who started their own small business, a lemonade stand.

financial statements (accounting statements)
A firm's income statement, balance sheets, and cash flow statement.

THE LEMONADE KIDS

Cameron and Ashley Bates, ages 13 and 15, wanted to buy an iPad to share, which they estimated would cost $360. Their parents said they would pay most of the cost, but that the two girls would need to contribute $100 to the purchase price.

To earn money, the girls decided to operate a lemonade stand for two Saturdays in a nearby park frequented by walkers and runners. To start the business, they each invested $5 from their savings. Their mom, Krista, liked the girls' idea and said she would loan them any additional money they would need with two conditions: (1) The girls would have to repay her in two weeks, and (2) she would keep the books for their business and expect them to learn what the numbers meant. Krista thought this would provide the girls a valuable opportunity to learn about business.

Setting Up the Business

A balance sheet, Krista explained to the girls, is a table that shows on a specific date (1) the dollar amount of the assets owned by the business, and (2) the sources of the money used to pay for the assets. She continued to say that there are two sources of money to pay for assets. The girls could either borrow money or, as the owners of the business, they could put their own money into the business. The first means of paying for assets is called *debt* and the second is the *owner's equity*. It's a bit like buying a house for $100,000, borrowing $70,000 from a bank, and then using $30,000 from your savings to pay the remaining part of the purchase price. The $30,000 is your equity in the home. Similarly, companies usually borrow money (debt) to supplement the owners' investment of their own money in the business (equity). Thus, a company's total assets will always equal the total debt plus the owners' equity they have invested in the business; that is,

Total assets = Money borrowed from others + Money invested by the owners

or

Total assets = Debt + Owners' equity

For instance, the girls' beginning $10 in cash represented their only asset and, since it was their own money, it was also their equity in the business. Krista then wrote out a simple balance sheet:

Assets		**Loans (debt) and owners' equity**	
		Loans	$ 0
Cash	$10	Cameron & Ashley's equity	10
Total assets	$10	Total loans & equity	$10

After thinking about what they would need in supplies to operate the lemonade stand, the girls requested a $40 loan from their mother. After the loan was made, the new balance sheet appeared as follows:

Assets		**Loans (debt) and owners' equity**	
		Loan from Mom	$40
Cash	$50	Cameron & Ashley's equity	10
Total assets	$50	Total loans & equity	$50

$40 increase in cash $40 increase in debt

In preparing for their opening day, the girls bought $40 of "premium pink lem-onade mix" and paper cups. Krista explained that the lemonade mix and cups con-stituted their *inventory* of supplies. After the girls paid for the inventory, the resulting balance sheet was as follows, where cash decreased and inventory increased by $40:

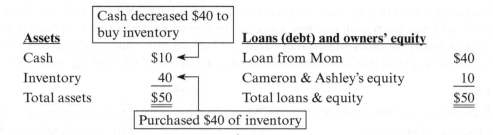

Assets		Loans (debt) and owners' equity	
Cash	$10	Loan from Mom	$40
Inventory	40	Cameron & Ashley's equity	10
Total assets	$50	Total loans & equity	$50

Opening Day

Being astute young entrepreneurs, Cameron and Ashley were aware that not all pass-ersby carried cash. So they created a sign-up sheet where customers could record their contact information for payment later in the week. They then chose a prime location for their lemonade stand and prepared to serve some very fine ice-cold pink lemonade.

By the end of the day, they had sold 60 cups at $1 each—30 cups that were bought on "credit" and 30 with cash. Since the lemonade only cost the girls 25 cents a cup, they made 75 cents per cup in profits, for a total of $45 in profit [$45 = ($1 sales price per cup − $0.25 cost per cup) × 60 cups]. Krista told the girls that an income statement reports the results of a firm's operations over a period of time—in this case, for a day. So the income statement for their first Saturday of selling looked like this:

Sales (60 cups × $1 per cup sales price)	$65
Cost of lemonade sold (60 cups × $0.25 cost per cup)	(15)
Profits	$45

Their balance sheet at the end of the day was as follows:

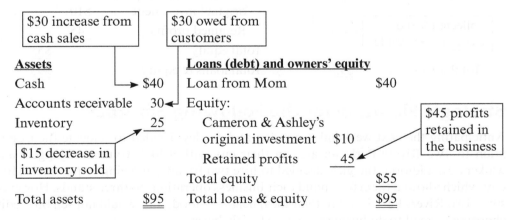

Assets		Loans (debt) and owners' equity	
Cash	$40	Loan from Mom	$40
Accounts receivable	30	Equity:	
Inventory	25	Cameron & Ashley's original investment	$10
		Retained profits	45
		Total equity	$55
Total assets	$95	Total loans & equity	$95

This time, cash increased from $10 to $40, as a result of the cash sales of $30—even though they had sold $60 of lemonade. The remaining $30 was still owed by their credit customers; the girls hoped to collect this money during the coming week. These assets, they learned, were called "accounts receivable." Also, there was a $15 decline in inventory, the result of the lemonade sold. Finally, the girls' equity increased by $45, the amount of the day's profits.

When Ashley looked at the income statement and balance sheet, she questioned why cash had only increased $30, even though profits were $45 for the day. Why were they not the same? Krista told her that she was about to learn an important lesson: *Computing a company's cash flows will require you to look both at the income statement and at the changes in the balance sheet.* For one thing, they did not collect $30 of their sales, which resulted in $30 of accounts receivable, instead of cash. Second, the $15 cost of goods sold was not a cash outflow, since the inventory that was sold had been purchased previously. In other words, they "sold" $15 of inventory and received the cash. Thus, reconciling their profits with the change in cash requires the following calculation:

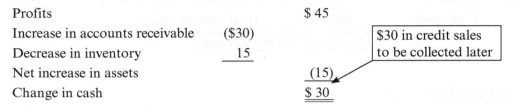

Profits		$ 45
Increase in accounts receivable	($30)	
Decrease in inventory	15	
Net increase in assets		(15)
Change in cash		$ 30

$30 in credit sales to be collected later

Collecting Accounts Receivable

Not wanting to let their accounts receivable go uncollected too long, the girls hired their little sister, Erin, for $5 to make calls during the week on their credit customers. To their delight, by Friday night Erin (accompanied by a few of her friends) had collected all the money they were owed. With the money collected, cash increased $30 with a corresponding $30 decrease in accounts receivable. As a result, the balance sheet appeared as follows:

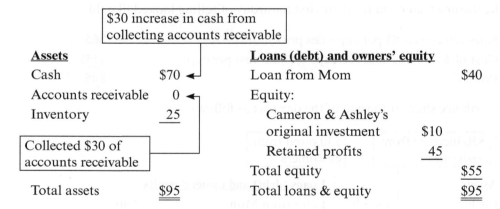

$30 increase in cash from collecting accounts receivable

Assets		**Loans (debt) and owners' equity**		
Cash	$70	Loan from Mom		$40
Accounts receivable	0	Equity:		
Inventory	25	Cameron & Ashley's original investment	$10	
		Retained profits	45	
		Total equity		$55
Total assets	$95	Total loans & equity		$95

Collected $30 of accounts receivable

Strategic Planning for the Following Saturday

Anticipating the next weekend, Cameron and Ashley decided to relocate their operation to Two Rivers Park, an area in their city with a high volume of joggers and walkers. In addition, the girls decided to hire two friends, agreeing to pay each $10 a day, which allowed them to expand their business operations to three stands. However, since Two Rivers Park is not in their local neighborhood, they would not sell on credit, choosing instead to do business on a cash-only basis.

The Second Saturday of Business

Cameron and Ashley arrived at Two Rivers Park with their two friends early Saturday morning and soon found themselves surrounded by customers. By mid-afternoon, they had sold 100 cups of lemonade, depleting their entire inventory! After paying their two friends $10 dollars each and Erin $5 for her collection work, the girls were delighted to see that they had made $50 in profits—their income statement for the second day looked like this:

Sales ($1 sales price per cup × 100 cups)	$100
Cost of lemonade ($0.25 cost per cup × 100 cups)	(25)
Salaries (2 friends × $10 + $5 paid to Erin)	(25)
Profits	$50

The balance sheet at the end of the day appeared as follows:

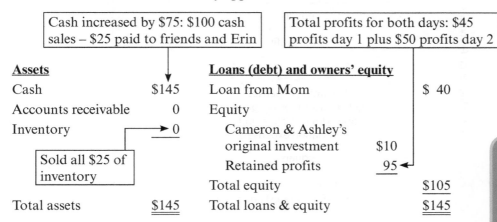

Cash increased by $75: $100 cash sales – $25 paid to friends and Erin

Total profits for both days: $45 profits day 1 plus $50 profits day 2

Assets

		Loans (debt) and owners' equity	
Cash	$145	Loan from Mom	$ 40
Accounts receivable	0	Equity	
Inventory	0	Cameron & Ashley's original investment	$10
		Retained profits	95
		Total equity	$105
Total assets	$145	Total loans & equity	$145

Sold all $25 of inventory

Cash assets had now increased to $145, a $75 increase as a result of the $100 in cash sales less the $25 paid to Erin and the girls' two friends. Inventory was now zero, and the girls' equity once again increased by the day's profits, in this case, $50.

The girls had accomplished their goal! They had enough to pay for their portion of the iPad ($100), repay the $40 loan to their mom; and still had $5 to split. When they went to bed that night, they discussed the possibility of starting a summer business. The entrepreneurial flame had been lit, and they had big dreams for their next venture.

The hypothetical story of Cameron and Ashley and their lemonade stand provides an uncomplicated way of thinking about accounting statements. If you understand—really understand—the Lemonade Kids' financial results, you are ready to move on to the next step. This will not make you an accountant, but it will give you the skill needed to manage a small business by the numbers. Our starting point is the income statement.

10-1 THE INCOME STATEMENT

An **income statement**, or **profit and loss statement**, indicates the amount of profits or losses generated by a firm *over a given time period*, usually monthly, quarterly, or yearly. In its most basic form, the income statement may be represented by the following equation:

$$\text{Sales (revenue)} - \text{Expenses} = \text{Profits (income)}$$

(In this text, we generally use the term *profits*, instead of *earnings* or *income*, but all three terms can be used interchangeably. For example, *profits before taxes* are the same thing as *earnings before taxes*.)

A more complete overview of an income statement is presented in Exhibit 10.1. As shown in the exhibit, you begin with sales (for example, the number of lemonade

START UP

SKILLS

Avoiding Failure
Research convincingly shows that insufficient capital is one of the main reasons for small business failure, along with lack of experience, poor location, poor inventory management, and overinvestment in fixed assets. With three of the five primary reasons for failure being financial, you should understand your financial capacities if you want to improve the odds in your favor.

LO
10-1

Describe the purpose and content of an income statement.

income statement (profit and loss statement)
A financial report showing the amount of profits or losses from a firm's operations over a given period of time.

EXHIBIT 10.1

The Income Statement: An Overview

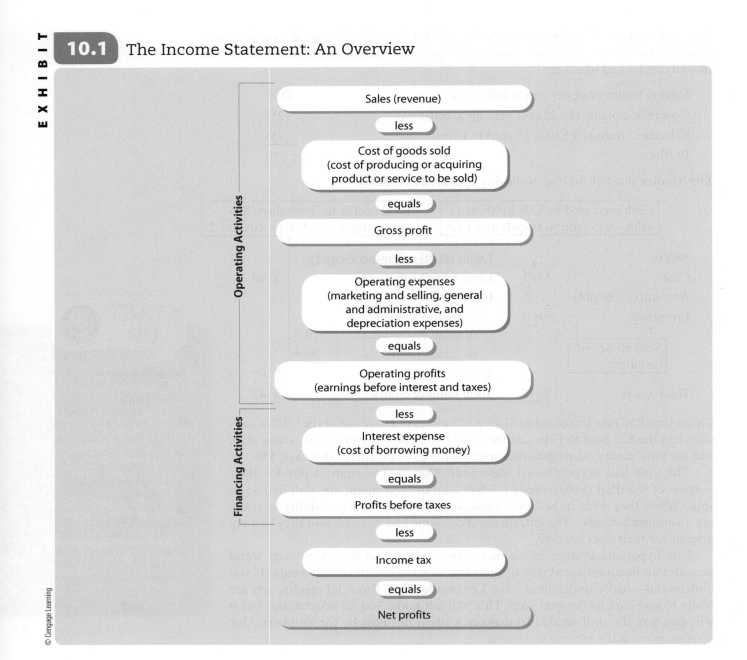

Sales (revenue)

less

Cost of goods sold
(cost of producing or acquiring
product or service to be sold)

equals

Gross profit

less

Operating expenses
(marketing and selling, general
and administrative, and
depreciation expenses)

equals

Operating profits
(earnings before interest and taxes)

less

Interest expense
(cost of borrowing money)

equals

Profits before taxes

less

Income tax

equals

Net profits

Operating Activities

Financing Activities

© Cengage Learning

cost of goods sold
The cost of producing or acquiring goods or services to be sold by a firm.

gross profits
Sales less the cost of goods sold.

operating expenses
Costs related to marketing and selling a firm's product or service, general and administrative expenses, and depreciation.

drinks sold times the sales price per cup). You then subtract the **cost of goods sold** (e.g., the cost per cup of lemonade times the number of cups sold) from sales to compute the firm's **gross profits**. Next, **operating expenses**, consisting of marketing and selling expenses, general and administrative expenses, and depreciation expense are deducted from gross profits to determine **operating profits**. (The amount that Cameron and Ashley paid their friends and Erin to work for them was an operating expense.) As shown in the exhibit, operating profits reflect only the decisions the owner has made relating to sales, cost of goods sold, and operating expenses. How the firm is financed, debt versus equity has no effect on operating profits.

From the firm's operating profits, we deduct any **interest expense** incurred from borrowing money (debt) to find **profits before taxes**, or **taxable profits**—a company's taxable income. A firm's income taxes are calculated by multiplying profits before taxes by the applicable tax rate. For instance, if a firm has profits before taxes of $100,000 and its tax rate is 28 percent, then it will owe $28,000 in taxes (0.28 × $100,000 = $28,000).

The number that results when taxes are subtracted from profits before taxes represents **net profits**, or profits that may be reinvested in the firm or distributed to the owners—provided, of course, the cash is available to do so. As you will come to understand, *positive net profits in an income statement does not necessarily mean that a firm has generated positive cash flows.*

Exhibit 10.2 shows the 2013 income statement for Houser & Associates, Inc., an equipment leasing company owned by sisters Lauren and Caitlin Houser. The company had sales of $850,000 for the 12-month period ending December 31, 2013. The cost of goods sold was $550,000, resulting in a gross profit of $300,000. The company had $200,000 in operating expenses, which included marketing expenses, general and administrative expenses, and depreciation expense. **Depreciation expense** is the cost of a firm's equipment and building, allocated over the asset's useful life. For example, if a business paid $10,000 for a piece of equipment with a four-year life expectancy, the depreciation expense each year would be $2,500 ($10,000 ÷ 4 years = $2,500). So, after total operating expenses were subtracted, the company's operating profits would amount to $100,000. To this point, we have calculated profits based *only* on expenses related to the firm's operations—and not those affected by how the firm finances its assets.

Houser & Associates' interest expense of $20,000 (the expense it incurred from borrowing money) is deducted from operating profits to arrive at the company's profits before taxes, or taxable income, of $80,000. Given a 25 percent tax rate, the company paid $20,000 in income taxes ($80,000 profits before tax × 0.25 tax rate = $20,000), leaving net profits of $60,000.

The net profits of $60,000 are the profits that the business earned for its owners after paying all expenses—cost of goods sold, operating expenses, interest expense, and

operating profits
Earnings after operating expenses but before interest and taxes are paid.

interest expense
The cost of borrowed money.

profits before taxes (taxable profits)
Earnings after operating expenses and interest expenses but before taxes.

net profits
Earnings that may be distributed to the owners or reinvested in the company.

depreciation expense
The cost of a firm's building and equipment, allocated over the asset's useful life.

10.2 Income Statement for Houser & Associates, Inc., for the Year Ending December 31, 2013

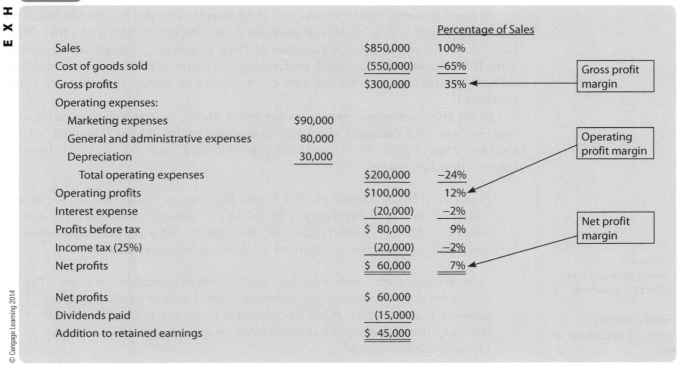

		Percentage of Sales	
Sales	$850,000	100%	
Cost of goods sold	(550,000)	−65%	Gross profit margin
Gross profits	$300,000	35%	
Operating expenses:			
Marketing expenses	$90,000		
General and administrative expenses	80,000		Operating profit margin
Depreciation	30,000		
Total operating expenses	$200,000	−24%	
Operating profits	$100,000	12%	
Interest expense	(20,000)	−2%	Net profit margin
Profits before tax	$ 80,000	9%	
Income tax (25%)	(20,000)	−2%	
Net profits	$ 60,000	7%	
Net profits	$ 60,000		
Dividends paid	(15,000)		
Addition to retained earnings	$ 45,000		

income taxes. Now the owners have to decide what to do with these profits. They can let the company pay them a **dividend** out of the profits, which represents a withdrawal of capital from the business (assuming cash is available to do so). Or, they can retain the profits in the business to help finance the firm's growth. Of course, they can combine the two choices by taking a smaller dividend and retaining the rest of the profits in the business.

In the last column in Exhibit 10.2, we have expressed each amount in the income statement as a percentage of sales. Also, we show what is called **profit margins**—gross profit margins, operating profit margins, and net profit margins—which simply express a firm's profits as a percentage of sales. Specifically, Houser & Associates has a gross profit margin of 35 percent, an operating profit margin of 12 percent and a net profit margin of 7 percent. For every $100 of sales, the company earns $35 in gross profits, $12 in operating profits, and $7 in net profits. Company owners need to track these numbers very carefully.

So what did the Houser sisters, as the firm's owners, do with their profits? As shown at the bottom of Exhibit 10.2, $15,000 in dividends was distributed to them; the remaining $45,000 ($60,000 net profits less $15,000 in dividends) was retained by the firm—an amount you will see later in the balance sheet. *Dividends paid to a firm's owners, unlike interest expense, are not considered an expense in the income statement.* Instead, they are viewed as a return of principal to the owners.

In summary, the income statement answers the question "How profitable is the business?" In providing the answer, the income statement reports financial information related to five broad areas of business activity:

1. Sales (revenue)
2. Cost of producing or acquiring the goods or services sold by the company
3. Operating expenses, such as marketing expenses, rent, managers' salaries, and depreciation expense
4. Interest expense
5. Tax payments

A small business owner should pay close attention to the income statement to determine trends and to make comparisons with competitors and with other firms that are considered to provide examples of "best practices"—companies we all can learn from. As already suggested, profit margins (profits ÷ sales) should be watched carefully. Large expenses should also be monitored to ensure that they are being controlled.

Being able to measure profits, as explained above, isn't enough; you must also consider how your decisions affect your company's profits. Philip Campbell, a CPA and the author of *Never Run Out of Cash: The 10 Cash Flow Rules You Can't Afford to Ignore,* offers this advice:

> *If you ask a business owner whether he runs his company to make money, the answer will always be "Yes." The reality is, he doesn't . . . . More often than not, you hear words like "brand," "market share," or "shelf space." When you hear those words, you can be sure that you've just found an opportunity to make some money.*
>
> *Why? Because those words always are used to justify unprofitable decisions. They are big red flags that you are not making decisions based on a common-sense approach to profitability. When you hear those words, ask yourself this simple question, "Are we making this decision based on profitability or for some other (possibly hidden) reason?"*[2]

dividend
A distribution of a firm's profits to the owners.

profit margins
Profits as a percentage of sales.

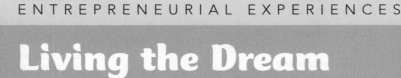

ENTREPRENEURIAL EXPERIENCES

Living the Dream

The Little Things Are the Big Things When It Comes to Managing Finances

As an entrepreneur, you have to be an effective manager of your time AND your firm's finances. No one will watch your company's money like you will or should. After all, it's your money.

According to Russell Allred, a business growth consultant, "If you don't know where you're wasting money this month, it's too late to figure it out at the end of the year."

By checking his monthly expenses closely, Eli Mechlovitz, co-founder of GlassTileStore.com, found a number of unnecessary subscriptions, warranty programs, fee-based website analytics programs, utility bill errors, and other incorrect or unwanted charges. According to Mechlovitz, eliminating these wasteful expenses has saved his company approximately $4,000 per month.

So, it's important that entrepreneurs not only understand what the financial statements tell them, but also act on what they learn.

Source: Adapted from Gwen Moran, "How to Clean Up Your Business," *Entrepreneur*, May 2011, pp. 76–78.

© Africa Studio/Shutterstock.com

LO
10-2

Explain the purpose and
content of a balance sheet.

10-2 THE BALANCE SHEET

While an income statement reports the results of business operations over a period of time, a **balance sheet** provides a snapshot of a business's financial position at a *specific point in time.* Thus, a balance sheet captures the cumulative effects of all earlier financial decisions up to a specific date. It shows the assets a firm owns, the liabilities (or debt) outstanding or owed, and the amount the owners have invested in the business (owners' equity) on that date. In its simplest form, a balance sheet follows this formula:

$$\text{Total assets} = \text{Debt} + \text{Owners' equity}$$

That is, for every dollar of assets, there must be a dollar of financing in the form of debt or owner's equity.

Exhibit 10.3 illustrates the elements in the balance sheet of a typical firm. Each of the three main components of the balance sheet—assets, debt, and owners' equity—is discussed in the following sections.

balance sheet
A financial report showing a firm's assets, liabilities, and owners' equity at a specific point in time.

EXHIBIT 10.3 The Balance Sheet: An Overview

Assets	Debt (Liabilities) and Owners' Equity (Net Worth)
Current Assets Cash Accounts receivable Inventory	**Debt** *Current (Short-Term) Debt* Accounts payable Accrued expenses Short-term notes *Long-Term Debt* Long-term notes Mortgages
plus	*plus*
Fixed Assets Machinery and equipment Buildings Land	**Owners' Equity** Sole proprietors' net worth or Partnership equity or Common stock-holders' equity
plus	
Other Assets Long-term investments Patents	
equals	*equals*
Total Assets	**Total Debt and Equity**

(center: equals)

© Cengage Learning 2014

10-2a Assets

Assets, shown on the left side of Exhibit 10.3, are what the company owns that has a monetary value. They are always grouped into three categories: (1) current assets, (2) fixed assets, and (3) other assets.

CURRENT ASSETS **Current assets (working capital)**, which are always listed first in a balance sheet, include those assets that are relatively liquid—that is, assets that can be converted into cash relatively quickly. Current assets primarily include cash, accounts receivable, and inventory.

1. **Cash** is money in the bank and may include some type of marketable security, such as a short-term government security, that can be sold very quickly. Every firm must have cash for current business operations.

2. **Accounts receivable** are like a loan to customers. When a firm sells its products or services, customers may pay in cash or be given credit terms (a loan), such as being allowed 30 days to pay for purchases. Accounts receivable need to be monitored carefully, since they have a lot to do with the cash that will (or will not) come into the business. Creditors are likely to be watching it as well.

3. **Inventory** comprises the raw materials and the products being held by a firm for sale in the ordinary course of business. Service companies typically have little or no inventory, but nearly every other company—manufacturers, wholesalers, retailers—does. As with accounts receivable, the business owner had better manage inventory carefully; otherwise, performance of the business will suffer.

As mentioned earlier, current assets are also called working capital, because these assets are vital in providing the needed capital for day-to-day operations. *A firm cannot survive without adequate working capital.* Exhibit 10.4 illustrates the **working capital cycle**, a process where inventory is purchased or produced, and then sold for cash or on credit (accounts receivable). The accounts receivable are later converted into cash when collected. The cycle is then repeated, over and over.

FIXED ASSETS (PROPERTY, PLANT, AND EQUIPMENT) The second type of assets in the balance sheet is the set of more permanent assets in a business. **Fixed assets**, also called **property, plant, and equipment (PPE)**, include land, buildings, machinery, trucks, computers, and every other physical asset a company owns. The balance sheet lists a firm's facilities and equipment at the original cost, when they were purchased. Some businesses are more capital-intensive than others—for example, a manufacturer is more capital-intensive than a gift store—and, therefore, it will have a greater amount invested in fixed assets.

Most fixed assets are also **depreciable assets**; that is, they wear out or become obsolete over time. The original cost of these assets is shown on the balance sheet when they are purchased. Each year, the assets are depreciated over their expected useful life.

Assume, for example, that a business purchased a truck for $20,000 with an expected useful life of four years. When the firm buys the truck, the original cost of $20,000 is shown on the balance sheet as a **gross fixed asset**. We would then depreciate the cost of the truck over its useful life of four years. A depreciation expense of $5,000 would be shown annually in the income statement ($20,000 ÷ 4 years = $5,000). Each year, the cumulative depreciation expense, or what is called **accumulated depreciation**,

current assets (working capital)
Assets that can be converted into cash relatively quickly.

cash
Money in the bank and may include a security that can be sold very quickly, such as a government security.

accounts receivable
The amount of credit extended to customers that is currently outstanding.

inventory
A firm's raw materials and products held in anticipation of eventual sale.

working capital cycle
The process of converting inventory to cash.

fixed assets (property, plant and equipment [PPE])
Physical assets that will be used in the business for more than one year, such as equipment, buildings, and land.

depreciable assets
Assets whose value declines, or depreciates, over time.

gross fixed assets
Depreciable assets at their original cost, before any depreciation expense has been taken.

accumulated depreciation
Total (cumulative) depreciation expense taken over an asset's life.

10.4 The Working Capital Cycle

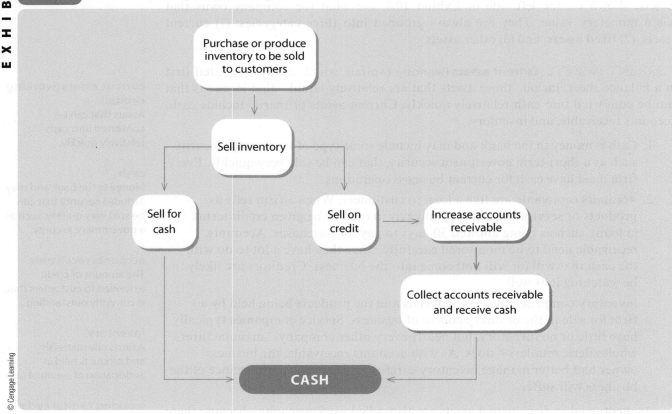

© Cengage Learning

is subtracted from the original cost of the fixed asset to yield the **net fixed asset**. In this instance, the balance sheet at the end of each year would appear as follows:

	Year 1	Year 2	Year 3	Year 4
Gross fixed asset	$20,000	$20,000	$20,000	$20,000
Accumulated depreciation	(5,000)	(10,000)	(15,000)	(20,000)
Net fixed asset	$15,000	$10,000	$ 5,000	$ 0

OTHER ASSETS The third category of assets, **other assets**, includes patents, copyrights, and goodwill. For a startup company, organizational costs—costs incurred in organizing and promoting the business—may also be included in this category.

10-2b Debt and Equity

The right side of the balance sheet in Exhibit 10.3 (on page 264), showing debt and equity, indicates how a firm is financing its assets. Financing comes from two main sources: debt (liabilities) and owners' equity (net worth). Debt is money that has been borrowed and must be repaid at some predetermined date. Owners' equity, on the other hand, represents the owners' investment in the company—money they have personally put into the firm without any specific date for repayment. Owners recover their investment by withdrawing money from the firm in the form of dividends or by selling their ownership in the firm.

DEBT **Debt** is financing provided by a creditor. As shown in Exhibit 10.3, it is divided into (1) current, or short-term, debt and (2) long-term debt.

net fixed assets
Gross fixed assets less accumulated depreciation.

other assets
Intangible assets, such as patents, copyrights, and goodwill.

debt
Financing provided by creditors.

Current Debt. Current debt (short-term liabilities) is borrowed money that must be repaid within 12 months. Sources of current debt may be classified as follows:

- **Accounts payable (trade credit)** represent credit extended by suppliers to a firm when it purchases inventory. For example, when a firm buys $10,000 in inventory, the supplier (seller) may allow the purchasing company 30 or 60 days to pay for it. Thus, along with the $10,000 in increase in inventory in the balance sheet, accounts payable would increase by a like amount.

- **Accrued expenses** are operating expenses that have been incurred and are owed but not yet paid. The amount of the expense is included in the income statement and also shown as a liability (accrued expense) in the balance sheet. For example, consider an employee who is owed $4,000 for work performed in April, but who will not be paid until May 1. The $4,000 would be recorded as an expense in the income statement for April, but since no payment is made in April, it would be shown as a liability (accrued wages) in the balance sheet on April 30. When the employee is paid on May 1, the accrued expenses are decreased by $4,000, along with a $4,000 decrease in cash.

- **Short-term notes** represent cash amounts borrowed from a bank or other lending source for 12 months or less. Short-term notes are a primary source of financing for most small businesses. Assume, for example, that you borrow $50,000 from a bank for 90 days (one quarter of a year) to purchase inventory during a peak season. If the interest rate on the loan is 8 percent, you will incur $1,000 in interest ($1,000 = $50,000 principal owed × 0.08 interest rate × ¼ year). The interest paid on the loan would be shown as interest expense in the income statement and the principal amount borrowed as a liability in the balance sheet.

Long-Term Debt. Loans granted for longer than 12 months from banks or other financial institutions comprise **long-term debt**. When a firm borrows money for five years to buy equipment, it signs an agreement—a **long-term note**—promising to repay the loan plus interest over five years. As with short-term notes, the interest is an expense shown in the income statement and the amount of the principal is a liability reported on the balance sheet.

When a firm borrows money, say, for 30 years to purchase a warehouse or office building, the real estate usually serves as collateral for the long-term loan, which is called a **mortgage**. If the borrower is unable to repay the loan, the lender can take the real estate in settlement.

10-2c Owners' Equity

Owners' equity is money that the owners invest in a business, whether it is a sole proprietorship, partnership, or corporation. For corporations, shares of **common stock** are issued to the investors, which represent their ownership in the corporation. In addition to investing directly in a business by writing a check to the company, owners can invest indirectly simply by leaving all or part of the firm's profits in the business to be reinvested. The cumulative amount of *net profits* that have been retained and reinvested in a business over the entire life

current debt (short-term liabilities)
Borrowed money that must be repaid within 12 months.

accounts payable (trade credit)
Outstanding credit payable to suppliers.

accrued expenses
Operating expenses that have been incurred but not paid.

short-term notes
Agreements to repay cash amounts borrowed from banks or other lending sources within 12 months or less.

long-term debt
Loans from banks or other sources with repayment terms of more than 12 months.

long-term notes
Agreements to repay cash amounts borrowed from banks or other lending sources, plus interest, for periods longer than 12 months.

mortgage
A long-term loan to purchase a building or land.

owners' equity
Owners' investments in a company plus cumulative net profits retained in the firm.

© BKMCphotography/Shutterstock.com

of the company—profits not paid out to the owners in dividends—is called **retained earnings**. Thus, the basic formula for owners' equity is as follows:

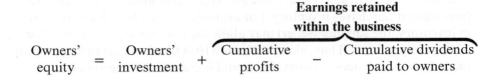

$$\text{Owners' equity} = \text{Owners' investment} + \overbrace{\text{Cumulative profits} - \text{Cumulative dividends paid to owners}}^{\text{Earnings retained within the business}}$$

common stock
Stock shares that represent ownership in a corporation

retained earnings
Profits not paid out as dividends over the life of a business.

Exhibit 10.5 presents balance sheets for Houser & Associates for December 31, 2012, and December 31, 2013, along with dollar changes in the balance sheets for the same time periods. By referring to the columns representing the two balance sheets, you can see the financial position of the firm at the beginning *and* at the end of 2013.

The 2012 and 2013 year-end balance sheets for Houser & Associates show that the firm began 2013 (ended 2012) with $800,000 in total assets and ended 2013 with total assets of $920,000. We see how much has been invested in current assets (cash, accounts receivable, and inventory) and in fixed assets. We also observe how much debt and equity were used to finance the assets. Note that about half of the equity came

EXHIBIT 10.5 Balance Sheets for Houser & Associates, Inc., for December 31, 2012 and 2013

	2012	2013	Changes
Assets			
Current assets:			
Cash	$ 45,000	$ 50,000	$ 5,000
Accounts receivable	75,000	80,000	5,000
Inventory	180,000	220,000	40,000
Total current assets	$300,000	$350,000	$ 50,000
Fixed assets:			
Gross fixed assets	$860.000	$960,000	$100,000
Accumulated depreciation	(360,000)	(390,000)	(30,000)
Net fixed assets	$500,000	$570,000	$ 70,000
TOTAL ASSETS	$800,000	$920,000	$120,000
Debt (Liabilities) and Equity			
Current liabilities:			
Account payable	$ 15,000	$ 20,000	$ 5,000
Short-term notes	60,000	80,000	20,000
Total current liabilities (debt)	$ 75,000	$100,000	$ 25,000
Long-term debt	150,000	200,000	50,000
Total debt	$225,000	$300,000	$ 75,000
Owners' equity			
Common stock	$300,000	$300,000	$ 0
Retained earnings	275,000	320,000	45,000
Total owners' equity	$575,000	$620,000	$ 45,000
TOTAL DEBT AND EQUITY	$800,000	$920,000	$120,000

from investments made by the owners (common stock), and the other half came from reinvesting profits in the business (retained earnings). Referring back to the income statement in Exhibit 10.2, note that the $45,000 increase in retained profits, shown in the Changes column in Exhibit 10.5, is the firm's net profits for the year ($60,000) less the dividends paid to the owners ($15,000).

Finally, a balance sheet helps the small business owner know the financial strength and capabilities of the business—something that cannot be known in any other way. It helps answer such key questions as

- Is the business in a position to expand?
- Can the firm easily handle the ebb and flow of sales and expenses?
- Is the firm collecting its accounts receivable as planned and efficiently managing inventory?
- Can accounts payable be paid more slowly to forestall an inevitable cash shortage, without hurting the entrepreneur's credit reputation?

The entrepreneur is not the only one who needs to be well versed about the balance sheet. Lenders such as bankers, investors, and suppliers, who are considering how much credit to grant rely heavily on a firm's balance sheet in their decision making.

Let's Check for Understanding

Understanding the Balance Sheet

Answer the questions below:

1. Give an example of accounts receivable.
2. What relationship would you expect between inventory and accounts payable?
3. What is the difference between common stock and retained earnings?
4. Construct a balance sheet, using the following information. What are the firm's current assets, net fixed assets, total assets, current liabilities, long-term debt, total owners' equity, and total debt and equity?

Gross fixed assets	$75,000
Cash	$10,000
Other assets	$15,000
Accounts payable	$40,000
Retained earnings	$15,000
Accumulated depreciation	$20,000
Accounts receivable	$50,000
Long-term note	$5,000
Mortgage	$20,000
Common stock	$100,000
Inventory	$70,000
Short-term notes	$20,000

(Go to www.cengagebrain.com and select the Longenecker text to access the answers to these questions.)

LO
10-3

How do financial statements show a firm's financial position?

10-3 VIEWING THE INCOME STATEMENT AND BALANCE SHEET TOGETHER

Thus far, we have discussed the income statement and the balance sheet as separate reports. But they actually complement each other to give an overall picture of the firm's financial situation. Because the balance sheet is a snapshot of a firm's financial condition at a specific point in time, such as on the exact day of December 31, and the income statement reports results over a given period, such as the period from January 1 through December 31, both are required to determine a firm's financial position.

Exhibit 10.6 shows how the income statement and the balance sheet fit together. To understand how a firm performed during 2013, you must know the firm's financial position at the beginning of 2013 (balance sheet on December 31, 2012), its financial performance during the year (income statement for 2013), and its financial position at the end of the year (balance sheet on December 31, 2013).

To illustrate the relationship between the balance sheets and income statement, consider the two balance sheets and income statement shown below for Maness Corporation. The first balance sheet was prepared on December 31, 2012, which can also be thought of as the beginning of 2013. (Whatever a firm ends with in 2012, it starts with in 2013.) From the combined financial statements, we can see the company's financial position as it started 2013 (the balance sheet as of December 31, 2012), how the firm did in its operations throughout 2013 (presented in the income statement), and the firm's financial position at the end of 2013 (the balance sheet as of December 31, 2013).

EXHIBIT 10.6 The Fit of the Income Statement and Balance Sheet

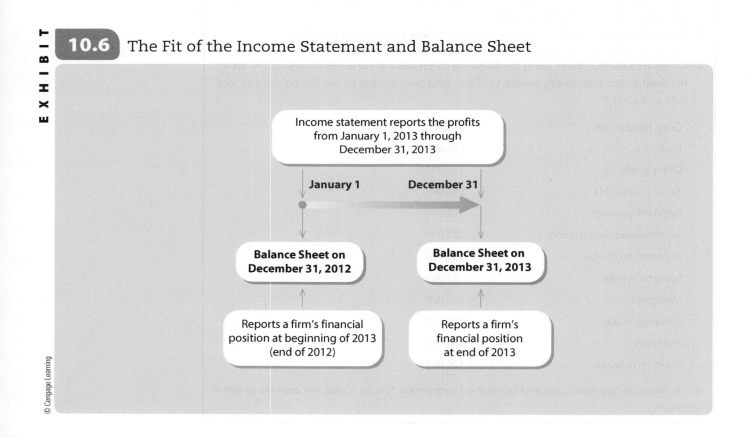

Balance Sheets as of December 31, 2012, and December 31, 2013

	2012	2013	Changes
Assets			
Cash	$ 150,000	$ 125,000	$ (25,000)
Accounts receivable	350,000	375,000	25,000
Inventory	475,000	550,000	75,000
Total current assets	$ 975,000	$1,050,000	$ 75,000
Gross fixed assets	$2,425,000	$2,750,000	$325,000
Accumulated depreciation	(1,000,000)	(1,200,000)	(200,000)
Net fixed assets	$1,425,000	$1,550,000	$125,000
TOTAL ASSETS	$2,400,000	$2,600,000	$200,000
Debt (Liabilities) and Equity			
Accounts payable	$ 200,000	$ 150,000	$ (50,000)
Short-term notes	0	150,000	150,000
Total current liabilities	$ 200,000	$ 300,000	$100,000
Long-term debt	600,000	600,000	0
Total debt	$ 800,000	$ 900,000	$100,000
Owners' equity			
Common stock	$ 900,000	$ 900,000	$ 0
Retained earnings	700,000	800,000	100,000
Total owners' equity	$1,600,000	$1,700,000	$100,000
TOTAL DEBT AND EQUITY	$2,400,000	$2,600,000	$200,000

Income Statement for the Year Ending December 31, 2013

Sales	$1,450,000
Cost of goods sold	(850,000)
Gross profits	$ 600,000
Operating expenses	(240,000)
Operating profits	$ 360,000
Interest expense	(64,000)
Profits before taxes	$ 296,000
Taxes	(118,000)
Net profits	$ 178,000
Net profits	$ 178,000
Dividends paid	(78,000)
Addition to retained earnings	$ 100,000

(Note: The addition to retained earnings represents the change in retained earnings in the balance sheets.)

10-4 THE CASH FLOW STATEMENT

An entrepreneur once told us how intimidated she felt when her accountant presented the firm's monthly financial reports and she had difficulty understanding cash flows. Our advice was to get a new accountant—one who would explain the statements carefully—and also to spend the time necessary to gain a solid understanding of the financial statements and the firm's cash flows.

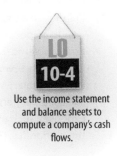

LO 10-4

Use the income statement and balance sheets to compute a company's cash flows.

Effectively managing cash flows is critical for small business owners. In the words of Philip Campbell, a CPA and former CFO of several companies, "Despite the fact that cash is the lifeblood of a business—the fuel that keeps the engine running—most business owners don't truly have a handle on their cash flow. Poor cash-flow management is causing more business failures today than ever before."[3]

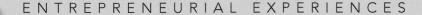

Living the Dream

Surviving Tough Times Means Effectively Managing Your Finances

In 2006, after managing a commercial interior design business, Rose Corrick founded Art of Cloth, a producer of hand-dyed fashion textiles. By summer 2008, sales had never been higher, as an increasing number of boutiques were buying Corrick's clothing. In preparation for anticipated growth, she moved from her basement into a 4,500 square-foot facility, signing a three-year lease. She then bought the necessary equipment to manufacture her clothes in greater quantities.

But when the recession hit in late 2008, customers began canceling orders, even though Art of Cloth had already made some custom products. The result was $30,000 in lost revenues. Corrick felt she had little legal recourse, as she did not want to cut off customers who might return in better economic times. The business began having major cash flow issues. As Corrick explained, "All of a sudden, we couldn't pay our bills. Being such a small company, it was very painful."

In response to the changing conditions and the cash flow problems, Corrick negotiated more favorable payment terms with several of her suppliers. She stopped paying herself a salary and was forced to lay off people. Finally, she used her personal credit card to pay for some company expenses, such as travel to trade shows. Corrick established three priorities: (1) Cut expenses that would affect revenues

the least, (2) make the firm's products more marketable, given the economic realities, and (3) carefully monitor the company's cash flows.

Accordingly, she cut prices on several higher-priced items by 15 to 30 percent, based on feedback from her customers. To offset the lost revenues, she found a way to cut manufacturing costs and improve efficiency by speeding up the dyeing process. But she continued to attend design shows in major U.S. cities to gain exposure to prospective buyers, spending $1,000 to $4,000 to attend each one.

By late 2009, her efforts were paying off. Although the number of boutiques carrying her apparel had decreased slightly, sales remained at about the same level as in 2008—$362,000. Then, by 2010 sales nearly doubled to about $715,000 and were expected to be $1.2 million in 2011.

If there is a moral to Corrick's story, it would have to be the importance of her understanding the relationship between revenues and different types of expenses. When times are good, inefficiencies can develop and not even be noticed. But when times are bad, only those who understand the finances of their business can survive.

Sources: Based on Kelly K. Spoors, "A Fashion Startup Survives Cash-Flow Problems and Redesigns Itself for a Comeback," *Entrepreneur*, May 9, 2011, www.entrepreneur.com/article/219579 May 9, 2011, accessed January 12, 2013; and John Sung Kim, "How Rose Corrick Made Her Small Business Comeback," May 17, 2011, www.halloo.com/Blog/index.php/how-rose-corrick-made-her-small-business-comeback, accessed January 19, 2013.

For this reason, a small firm owner must understand the sources and uses of the firm's cash. A **cash flow statement** is a financial report that shows the sources of a firm's cash and its uses of the cash. In other words, it answers the questions "Where did the cash come from?" and "Where did the cash go?"

10-4a Profits versus Cash Flows

Entrepreneurs need to be aware that *the profits shown on a company's income statement are not the same as its cash flows!* In the words of author Jan Norman, "Even profitable companies can go broke. That's a difficult truth for some business owners to swallow. But the sooner you learn that when you're out of cash, you're out of business, the better your chances for survival will be."[4] Many a business that showed a profit on its income statement has had to file for bankruptcy because the amount of cash coming in did not compare with the amount of cash going out. Without adequate cash flows, little problems become major problems!

An income statement is not a measure of cash flows because it is calculated on an *accrual* basis rather than a *cash* basis. This is an important point to understand. In **accrual-basis accounting**, profits are recorded when earned—whether or not the profits have been received in cash—and expenses are recorded when they are incurred—even if money has not actually been paid out. In **cash-basis accounting**, profits are reported when cash is received and expenses are recorded when they are paid. For a number of reasons, profits based on an accrual accounting system will differ from the firm's cash flows:

1. Sales reported in an income statement include both *cash* sales and *credit* sales. Thus, total sales do not correspond to the actual cash collected. A company may have had sales of $1 million for the year, but may not have collected on all of them. If accounts receivable increased $80,000 from the beginning of the year to the end of the year, then we would know that only $920,000 of the sales had been collected ($920,000 = $1,000,000 sales − $80,000 increase in accounts receivable).

2. Cash spent for inventory doesn't represent all inventory purchases since some inventory is financed by credit. Consider a business that purchased $500,000 in inventory during the year, but the supplier extended $100,000 in credit for the purchases. The actual cash paid for inventory would be only $400,000 ($400,000 = $500,000 total inventory purchases − $100,000 credit granted by the supplier).

3. The depreciation expense shown in the income statement is a noncash expense. It reflects the costs associated with using an asset that benefits the firm's operations over a period of several years, such as a piece of equipment used over five years. Thus, if a business had profits of $250,000 that included depreciation expenses of $40,000, then the cash flows would be $290,000 ($290,000 = $250,000 profits + $40,000 depreciation expense).

So the question—and its answer—that every small business owner should ask and understand is "How do I compute my firm's cash flows?"

10-4b Measuring a Firm's Cash Flows

It's time to return to our young entrepreneurs, Cameron and Ashley, and their lemonade stand. To develop a report that explained the cash flows from their

cash flow statement
A financial report showing a firm's sources of cash as well as its uses of cash.

accrual-basis accounting
An accounting method of recording profits when earned and expenses when incurred, whether or not the profits have been received in cash or the expenses paid.

cash-basis accounting
An accounting method of recording profits when cash is received and recording expenses when they are paid.

lemonade business, you could simply list all the cash inflows and outflows and see what happened to their cash balance. Here is what it would look like:

Cameron and Ashley's initial investment	$ 10
Loan from their mom	$ 40
Purchased inventory	(40)
Cash collected from the first Saturday's sales	$ 30
Collection of accounts receivable	$ 30
Cash collected from the second Saturday's sales	$100
Salaries expense	(25)
Ending cash	$145

They began with a $10 investment in the business and ended with $145 in cash, before repaying their mom the $40 loan and contributing $100 toward the iPad purchase. This works quite well in the world of lemonade stands. But the report would become overwhelming in a business of any significant size, where thousands of transactions are recorded in the financial statements each year. Also, there's a better approach to learning what activities contribute to a firm's cash flows. We can explain the cash inflows and outflows of a business by looking at three **cash flow activities**:

1. *Generating cash flows from day-to-day business operations.* It is informative to know how much cash is being generated in the normal course of operating a business on a daily basis, beginning with purchasing inventory on credit, selling on credit, paying for the inventory, and finally collecting on the sales made on credit.

2. *Buying or selling fixed assets.* When a company buys (or sells) fixed assets, such as equipment and buildings, cash outflows (or inflows) result. These cash flows are not part of the regular day-to-day operations and, consequently, are not included in the income statement. They appear only as changes from one balance sheet to the next.

3. *Financing the business.* Cash inflows and outflows occur when the company borrows or repays debt; when it distributes money to the owners, such as when dividends are paid; or when the owners put money into the business in the form of additional equity.

cash flow activities
Operating, investing, and financing activities that result in cash inflows or outflows.

If we know the cash flows from the activities listed above, we can explain a firm's total cash flows. To illustrate how this is done, we use Houser & Associates' income statement (Exhibit 10.2) and balance sheets (Exhibit 10.5).

ACTIVITY 1: CASH FLOWS FROM DAY-TO-DAY BUSINESS OPERATIONS To convert the company's income statement from an *accrual* basis to a *cash* basis, we take two steps: (1) Add back depreciation to net profits, since depreciation is not a cash expense, and (2) subtract any uncollected sales (increase in accounts receivable) and payments for inventory (increases in inventory less increases in accounts payable).

The reason we add back depreciation should be clear. The changes in accounts receivable, inventory, and accounts payable may be less intuitive. Two comments might be helpful for your understanding:

1. A firm's sales are either cash sales or credit sales. If accounts receivable increase, that means customers did not pay for everything they

© Anna Kucherova/Shutterstock.com

purchased. Thus, any increase in accounts receivable needs to be subtracted from total sales to determine the cash that has been collected from customers. Remember the Lemonade Kids: On their first day, they sold $60 in lemonade, but they only collected $30. The remainder was accounted for by an increase in accounts receivable.

2. The other activity occurring in the daily course of business is purchasing inventory. An increase in inventory shows that inventory was purchased, but if accounts payable (credit extended by a supplier) increase, then we may conclude that the firm did not pay for the entire inventory purchased. The net payment for inventory is equal to the increase in inventory less what has not yet been paid for (increase in accounts payable).

Referring back to Houser & Associates' income statement (Exhibit 10.2) and balance sheets (Exhibit 10.5), we can perform the conversion from accrual basis to cash basis as follows:

Net profits	$60,000	
Add back depreciation	30,000	
Profits before depreciation		$90,000
Less increase in accounts receivable (uncollected sales)		(5,000)
Less payments for inventory consisting of:		
Increase in inventory	($40,000)	
Less increase in accounts payable (inventory purchased on credit)	$ 5,000	
Cash payments for inventory		(35,000)
Cash flows from operations		$50,000

ACTIVITY 2: INVESTING IN FIXED ASSETS The second cash flow activity occurs when a company purchases or sells fixed assets, such as equipment or buildings. These activities are shown as a change in *gross* fixed assets (not *net* fixed assets) in the balance sheet. An increase means the company spent cash buying fixed assets, while a decrease means it received cash from selling fixed assets. For instance, Houser & Associates spent $100,000 on new plant and equipment in 2013, based on the change in gross fixed assets from $860,000 to $960,000, as shown in its balance sheets (Exhibit 10.5).

ACTIVITY 3: FINANCING THE BUSINESS The cash flows associated with financing a business are as follows:

1. A cash inflow when a company borrows more money (increases short-term and/or long-term debt).
2. A cash outflow when a firm repays debt (decreases short-term and/or long-term debt).
3. A cash inflow when the owners invest in the business to increase their equity.
4. A cash outflow when the owners withdraw money from the business. In sole proprietorships and partnerships, the owner(s) would simply write a check on the firm's bank account to take the money out. In a corporation, the company would either pay a dividend to the owners or repurchase the owners' stock.

Note that when we talk about borrowing or repaying debt when financing the business, accounts payable and accrued expenses are not included. These sources of financing were included in activity 1, when we computed cash flows from operations. Here, in activity 3, only debt from such sources as banks in the form of short-term notes and long-term debt is included.

The income statement of Houser & Associates (Exhibit 10.2) showed that $15,000 in dividends was paid to the owners. From its balance sheets (Exhibit 10.5), we see that short-term debt increased $20,000 and long-term debt increased $50,000, both sources of cash flow. Thus, in net, Houser & Associates raised $55,000 in financing cash flows:

Increase in short-term notes	$20,000
Increase in long-term debt	50,000
Less dividends paid to owners	(15,000)
Financing cash flows	$55,000

TIPS FOR COMPUTING CASH FLOWS When measuring cash flows:

1. Work on the three parts of the cash flow statement individually, and then put it all together. That helps you focus on what needs to be done without being overwhelmed.

2. Use only depreciation expense and net profits from the income statement.

3. It is necessary that you understand how the changes in a firm's balance sheets have implications for its cash flows. *Sources of cash* are represented in a balance sheet by a decrease in an asset—for example, selling inventory or collecting receivables—and by an increase in liability or equity—for example, borrowing funds or selling stock. *Uses of cash* are represented by an increase in an asset—for example, investing in fixed assets or buying inventory—and by a decrease in a liability or equity—for example, paying off a loan or buying back stock.

4. Use every change in the company's balance sheet, with two exceptions: (a) Ignore accumulated depreciation and net fixed assets since they involve the noncash item of depreciation, and use only the change in *gross* fixed assets. (b) Ignore the change in retained earnings since it equals net profits and dividends paid, two items that are captured elsewhere.

To summarize, Houser & Associates generated $50,000 in cash flows from operations, invested $100,000 in gross fixed assets (gross property, plant, and equipment), and received a net $55,000 from financing activities, for a net increase in cash of $5,000. This change in cash can be verified from the balance sheets (see Exhibit 10.5), which show that the firm's cash increased by $5,000 during 2013 (from $45,000 to $50,000). Stated somewhat differently, Houser & Associates had positive cash flows from (1) their day-to-day business operations (cash flow from operations) and (2) borrowing money from a bank. These cash inflows were used to pay for fixed assets and to increase the firm's cash. The complete statement of cash flows for Houser & Associates is presented in Exhibit 10.7.

10.7 Cash Flow Statement for Houser & Associates, Inc., for the Year Ending December 31, 2013

Operating activities:		
Net profits	$60,000	
Add back depreciation	30,000	
Profits before depreciation		$ 90,000
Less increase in accounts receivable (uncollected sales)		($ 5,000)
Less payments for inventory consisting of:		
Increase in inventory	(40,000)	
Less increase in accounts payable (inventory purchased on credit)	5,000	
Payments for inventory		($ 35,000)
Cash flows from operations		$ 50,000
Investment activities:		
Less increase in gross fixed assets		($100, 000)
Financing activities:		
Increase in short-term notes	20,000	
Increase in long-term debt	50,000	
Less dividends paid to owners	(15,000)	
Financing cash flows		$ 55,000
Increase in cash		$ 5,000
Beginning cash (December 31, 2012)	$45,000	
Ending cash (December 31, 2013)	$50,000	

Let's Check for Understanding

Understanding Cash Flows

Earlier in the chapter, we used Maness Corporation's financial data to illustrate the connections between a company's income statement and its balance sheets. The company's financial statements are shown again below, along with the changes in the balance sheets between 2012 and 2013 (numbers you will need). Use this data again to prepare a cash flow statement, and then answer the following questions:

1. How much of Maness Corporation's cash flows are from operating activities, from investment activities, and from financing activities?
2. What was the change in cash between December 31, 2012, and December 31, 2013?
3. Look at your answers for questions 1 and 2, and describe what you learned about the company's cash flows.

Balance Sheets as of December 31, 2012, and December 31, 2013

	2012	2013	Changes
Assets			
Cash	$ 150,000	$ 125,000	$ (25,000)
Accounts receivable	350,000	375,000	25,000
Inventory	475,000	550,000	75,000
Total current assets	$ 975,000	$1,050,000	$ 75,000
Gross fixed assets	$ 2,425,000	$2,750,000	$ 325,000
Accumulated depreciation	(1,000,000)	(1,200,000)	(200,000)
Net fixed assets	$ 1,425,000	$1,550,000	$ 125,000
TOTAL ASSETS	$2,400,000	$2,600,000	$ 200,000
Debt (Liabilities) and Equity			
Accounts payable	$ 200,000	$ 150,000	$ (50,000)
Short-term notes	0	150,000	150,000
Total current liabilities	$ 200,000	$ 300,000	$ 100,000
Long-term debt	600,000	600,000	100,000
Total debt	$ 800,000	$ 900,000	$ 100,000
Owners' equity			
Common stock	$ 900,000	$ 900,000	$ 0
Retained earnings	700,000	800,000	100,000
Total owners' equity	$1,600,000	$1,700,000	$ 100,000
TOTAL LIABILITIES AND OWNERS' EQUITY	$2,400,000	$2,600,000	$ 200,000

Income Statement for the Year Ending January 1 – December 2013

Sales	$1,450,000
Cost of goods sold	(850,000)
Gross profits	$ 600,000
Operating expenses	(240,000)
Operating profits	$ 360,000
Interest expense	(64,000)
Profits before taxes	$ 296,000
Taxes	(118,000)
Net profits	$ 178,000
Net profits	$ 178,000
Dividends paid	(78,000)
Increase in retained earnings	$ 100,000

(Go to www.cengagebrain.com and select the Longenecker text to access the answers to these questions.)

LO 10-5

Analyze the financial statements using ratios to see more clearly how decisions affect a firm's financial performance.

10-5 EVALUATING A FIRM'S FINANCIAL PERFORMANCE

Once a firm's owner understands the content of the accounting statements, she or he wants to know how management decisions impact the financial situation of a business. An entrepreneur's decisions play out primarily in four ways when it comes to finances:

1. *The firm's ability to pay its debt as it comes due.* In other words, does the company have the capacity to meet its short-term (one year or less) debt commitments?

2. *The company's profitability from assets.* Is the business providing a good rate of return on its assets? There is no more important question when it comes to determining if a business is strong economically.

3. *The amount of debt the business is using.* Using debt increases a firm's risk, but may also increase the expected rate of return on the owners' equity investment.

4. *The rate of return earned by the owners on their equity investment.* All decisions ultimately affect the rate of return earned by the owners on their equity investment in the business.

Exhibit 10.8 provides a list of financial ratios as they relate to the four issues just listed. The name of each ratio is given, along with how it is computed. We illustrate the ratios by using the 2013 financial data for Houser & Associates, as presented in Exhibit 10.2 (income statement) and Exhibit 10.5 (balance sheets). Finally, the last column shows an industry average for each ratio, which comes from financial publications, such as Robert Morris & Associates. Let's look at the ratios as they apply to Houser & Associates.

10-5a Liquidity (Ability to Pay Its Debt)

A business—or a person, for that matter—that has enough money to pay off any debt owed is described as being *liquid*. The **liquidity** of a business depends on the availability of cash to meet maturing debt obligations. The **current ratio** is traditionally used to measure a company's liquidity. This ratio compares a firm's *current assets* to its *current liabilities*, as follows:

$$\text{Current ratio} = \frac{\text{current assets}}{\text{curent liabilities}}$$

As you can see in Exhibit 10.8, for Houser & Associates the current ratio is 3.50, compared to an industry norm of 2.70. In other words, the firm has $3.50 in current

liquidity
The degree to which a firm has working capital available to meet maturing debt obligations.

current ratio
A measure of a company's relative liquidity, determined by dividing current assets by current liabilities.

EXHIBIT 10.8 Financial Ratio Analysis for Houser & Associates, Inc.

Financial ratios	Houser & Associates	Industry Norm
1. Ability to pay debt as it comes due:		
Current ratio $= \dfrac{\text{Current assets}}{\text{Current liabilities}}$	$\dfrac{\$350,000}{\$100,000} = 3.50$	2.7
2. Company's profitability on its assets:		
Return on assets $= \dfrac{\text{Operating profits}}{\text{Total assets}}$	$\dfrac{\$100,000}{\$920,000} = 10.87\%$	13.2%
Operating profit margin $= \dfrac{\text{Operating profits}}{\text{Sales}}$	$\dfrac{\$100,000}{\$850,000} = 11.76\%$	11.0%
Total asset turnover $= \dfrac{\text{Sales}}{\text{Total assets}}$	$\dfrac{\$850,000}{\$920,000} = 0.92$	1.2
3. The amount of debt the company uses:		
Debt ratio $= \dfrac{\text{Total debt}}{\text{Total assets}}$	$\dfrac{\$300,000}{\$920,000} = 32.61\%$	40.0%
4. Rate of return earned by the owners on their equity investment:		
Return on equity $= \dfrac{\text{Net profits}}{\text{Owners' equity}}$	$\dfrac{\$\ 60,000}{\$620,000} = 9.68\%$	12.5%

assets for every $1 of short-term debt, compared to an industry average of $2.70 of current assets for every $1 in short-term debt. Thus, based on the current ratio, Houser & Associates is more liquid than the average firm in the industry.

10-5b Profitability on Assets

A vitally important question to a firm's owners is whether a company's operating profits are sufficient relative to the total amount of assets invested in the company. A firm's assets are invested for the express purpose of producing operating profits. A comparison of operating profits to total assets reveals the rate of return that is being earned on the firm's total assets, which represent the total amount of investment in the business. We compute the **return on assets** as follows:

$$\text{Return on assets} = \frac{\text{Operating profits}}{\text{Total assets}}$$

As shown in Exhibit 10.8, Houser & Associates' return on assets of 10.87 percent is less than the industry norm of 13.2 percent, indicating that Houser & Associates is generating less operating profits on each dollar of assets than its competitors. That is not good!

To gain more understanding about why Houser & Associates is not doing very well in generating profits on the firm's assets, you can separate the return on assets into two components: (1) the operating profit margin and (2) the total asset turnover. The equation for the return on assets can be restated as follows:

$$\text{Return on assets} = \frac{\text{Operating profits}}{\text{Total assets}} = \overset{\substack{\text{Operating} \\ \text{Profit Margin}}}{\frac{\text{Operating profits}}{\text{Sales}}} \times \overset{\substack{\text{Total Asset} \\ \text{Turnover}}}{\frac{\text{Sales}}{\text{Total assets}}}$$

The first component of the expanded equation, the **operating profit margin** (operating profits ÷ sales), shows how well a firm is controlling its cost of goods sold and operating expenses relative to a dollar of sales. The second component of a firm's return on assets, the **total asset turnover** (sales ÷ total assets), indicates how efficiently management is using the firm's assets to generate sales.

The operating profit margin and total asset turnover for Houser & Associates, along with industry averages, are presented in Exhibit 10-8 and shown again below. You can also see how they relate to Houser & Associates' return on assets, as well as to the industry:

		Operating Profit Margin	×	Total Asset Turnover	=	Return on Assets
Return on assets$_{\text{Houser}}$	=	11.76%	×	0.92	=	10.87%
Return on assets$_{\text{Industry}}$	=	11.00%	×	1.20	=	13.20%

Based on the operating profit margin, Houser & Associates is competitive when it comes to managing its income statement—that is, keeping costs and expenses low relative to sales. However, Houser & Associates' total asset turnover shows why the firm is not earning a good return on its assets. The firm is not using its assets efficiently. The company's problem is that it generates $0.92 in sales per dollar of assets, while the

return on assets
A measure of a firm's profitability relative to the amount of its assets, determined by dividing operating profits by total assets.

operating profit margin
A measure of how well a firm is controlling its cost of goods sold and operating expenses relative to sales, determined by dividing operating profits by sales.

total asset turnover
A measure of how efficiently a firm is using its assets to generate sales, calculated by dividing sales by total assets.

competition produces $1.20 in sales from every dollar in assets. Management needs to assess what is causing the problem, looking carefully at how they are managing the different types of assets, namely, the accounts receivable, inventory, and fixed assets. The low total asset turnover, showing that Houser & Associates is using more assets per sales dollar than its competitors, possibly indicates one or more of the following problems:

1. The firm is not collecting its accounts receivable as quickly as the competition. By collecting its receivables on a more timely basis, it would release money that is currently tied up.

2. Given the amount of sales, the owners have too much money tied up in inventory, which suggests that some inventory is slow moving or even obsolete.

3. It is possible that the company has overinvested in fixed assets (such as facilities) compared to the competition.

Clearly, the Houser sisters need to investigate why their firm is not competitive when it comes to managing assets. After all, entrepreneurship is about doing more with less when it comes to managing resources.

10-5c Use of Debt Financing

How much debt, relative to the total assets, is used to finance a business is extremely important. For one thing, the more debt a business uses, the more risk it is taking because the debt has to be repaid no matter how much profit the firm earns; it is a fixed cost. However, if a company earns a higher return on its investments than the interest rate being paid on its debt, the owners benefit from using debt.

The **debt ratio** tells us what percentage of the firm's assets is financed by debt and is computed as follows:

$$\text{Debt ratio} = \frac{\text{Total debt}}{\text{Total assets}}$$

Refer again to Exhibit 10.8, which shows Houser & Associates' debt ratio as 32.61 percent, compared to an industry norm of 40.0 percent. Since Houser & Associates uses less debt than the average firm in the industry, it has less risk. After all, borrowed money must be repaid regardless of how much money the business makes. All is well if the company prospers and repays the loan. But if not, *watch out*!

10-5d Return on Owners' Equity

The last financial ratio considered here is the rate of return that the owners are receiving on their equity investment, or the **return on equity**. It is computed as follows:

$$\text{Return on equity} = \frac{\text{Net profits}}{\text{Total owner' equity}}$$

As you can see in Exhibit 10.8, the return on equity for the Houser sisters is 9.68 percent, while the industry average for return on equity is 12.5 percent. Thus, it appears that the Houser sisters are not receiving a return on their investment equivalent

debt ratio
A measure of what percentage of a firm's assets is financed by debt, determined by dividing total debt by total assets.

return on equity
A measure of the rate of return that owners receive on their equity investment, calculated by dividing net profits by owners' equity.

to that of owners of comparable businesses. Why not? To answer this question, consider the following:

1. A firm with a high (low) return on *assets* will have a high (low) return on *equity*. It simply is not possible to have a good return on equity if you are not earning a good return on your assets.

2. As the amount of a firm's debt increases, its return on equity will increase, *provided that the return on assets is higher than the interest rate paid on any debt.*

In the case of Houser & Associates, the firm has a lower return on *equity* in part because it has a lower return on *assets*. It also uses less debt than the average firm in the industry, causing its return on equity to be lower than that of other firms. However, using less debt does reduce the firm's risk.

Here's another example: If a business earns a 15 percent return on *assets* but only has to pay 6 percent on its bank debt, the owners will receive 15 percent on the amount of their equity investment plus the 9 percent difference between the return on assets and what they pay the bank (15% − 6% = 9%). The more debt and the less equity they use, the more the owners' return on equity will be; it's called **financial leverage**.

It's very important to understand that the return on equity will be lower if the return on assets falls below the interest rate on the loan (e.g., if the return on assets is 8 percent, but the interest rate on debt is 10 percent). That is called negative financial leverage. These relationships will be explained further in Chapter 12, when we discuss sources of financing.

Our analysis of financial statements is now complete. Hopefully, you are now better prepared to know what financial statements can tell you about a business—knowledge that can be found in no other way than by interpreting the numbers.

In this chapter, we focused on understanding financial statements related to a firm's historical financial performance. We were essentially looking back to see how a business performed in a previous time period. In the next chapter, we will continue to work with financial statements, but this time we will be looking forward. In writing a business plan, you need to show convincingly how your plans will play out in terms of the firm's financial future.

financial leverage
The impact (positive or negative) of financing with debt rather than with equity.

Let's Check for Understanding

Understanding How to Evaluate a Firm's Financial Performance

Let's return once again to Maness Corporation's financial data to illustrate how to use financial ratios to evaluate a firm's performance. Using the data for 2013, which are shown below, and the industry norms, compute the financial ratios that were discussed in this chapter. Once you have computed the ratios, answer the following questions:

1. Is Maness Corporation more or less liquid than the average company in the industry?
2. Is the company doing a good job of earning a return on its assets? Explain.
3. How does the owner finance the business in terms of debt and equity?
4. Is Maness receiving a good return on equity? Explain.

Balance Sheet as of December 31, 2013

Assets	2013
Cash	$ 125,000
Accounts receivable	$ 375,000
Inventory	550,000
Total current assets	$ 1,050,000
Gross fixed assets	2,750,000
Accumulated depreciation	(1,200,000)
Net fixed assets	$ 1,550,000
TOTAL ASSETS	$ 2,600,000

Debt (Liabilities) and Equity	
Accounts payable	$ 150,000
Short-term notes	150,000
Total current liabilities	$ 300,000
Long-term debt	600,000
Total debt	$ 900,000
Common stock	$ 900,000
Retained earnings	800,000
Total owners' equity	$ 1,700,000
TOTAL LIABILITIES AND OWNERS' EQUITY	$ 2,600,000

Income Statement for the Year ending December 31, 2013

Sales	$ 1,450,000
Cost of goods sold	(850,000)
Gross profits	$ 600,000
Operating expenses	(240,000)
Operating profits	$ 360,000
Interest expense	(64,000)
Profits before taxes	$ 296,000
Taxes	(118,000)
Net profits	$ 178,000

Industry norms

Current ratio	3.25
Return on assets	15.0%
Operating profit margin	20.0%
Total asset turnover	0.75
Debt ratio	0.20
Return on equity	9.0%

(Go to www.cengagebrain.com and select the Longenecker text to access the answers to these questions.)

CLOSED LOOKING BACK

10-1. Describe the purpose and content of an income statement.

- An income statement is, in its most basic form, represented by the equation: Profits (income) = Sales (revenue) − Expenses

- An income statement answers the question "How profitable is the business?" by looking at five broad areas of business activity: (1) sales, (2) cost of producing or acquiring goods or services, (3) operating expenses, (4) interest expense, and (5) tax payments.

10-2. Explain the purpose and content of a balance sheet.

- A balance sheet provides a snapshot of a firm's financial position at a specific point in time.

- It shows the assets a firm owns, its liabilities, and the amount of owners' equity.

- In its most simple form, the balance sheet is represented by the formula:

    Total assets = Debt + Owners' equity

- Total assets include current, fixed, and other assets.

- Debt is financing provided by creditors.

- Owners' equity is the owners' investment in the business, both in terms of actual cash invested and earnings that have been retained in the business.

10-3. Explain how viewing the income statement and balance sheets together gives a more complete picture of a firm's financial position.

- Because the balance sheet offers a snapshot of a firm's financial condition at a specific point in time and the income statement reports a firm's performance over a period of time, both are needed to fully evaluate a firm's financial position.

- Three financial reports are needed to evaluate a firm's performance over a given time period: a balance sheet showing a firm's performance at the beginning of a year, a balance sheet for the end of the year, and an income statement spanning the time period between the two balance sheets.

10-4. Use the income statement and balance sheets to compute a company's cash flows.

- A cash flow statement shows the sources of a firm's cash as well as its uses of cash.

- A cash flow statement is comprised of three sections: (1) cash flows from daily operations (operating activities), (2) cash flows related to the investment in fixed assets (investing activities), and (3) cash flows related to financing the firm (financing activities)

- Cash flows from operations are calculated by adding back the depreciation expense to the net profits and then subtracting any uncollected sales and payments for inventory.

- Investments in fixed assets are recorded in the statement of cash flows as a change in gross fixed assets.

- Financing a business involves borrowing money, repaying debts, investing by owners, and paying dividends or selling/repurchasing stock.

10-5. Analyze the financial statements using ratios to see more clearly how decisions affect a firm's financial performance.

- Financial ratios help examine a firm's (1) ability to pay debt as it comes due, (2) profitability from assets, (3) use of debt, and (4) rate of return to owners.

- A firm's ability to pay debt as it comes due is most often evaluated by looking at a firm's current ratio (current assets divided by current liabilities).

- A company's profitability on assets is measured by calculating a company's return on assets (operating profits divided by total assets).

- The debt ratio is used to evaluate the total amount of debt used by the company to finance its assets (total debt divided by total assets).

- The return on equity, which is the rate of return earned by owners on their equity investment, is driven by a firm's return on assets and its debt ratio (net profits divided by total owners' equity).

Key Terms

accounts payable (trade credit) p. 267

accounts receivable p. 265

accrual-basis accounting p. 273

accrued expenses p. 267

accumulated depreciation p. 265

balance sheet p. 264

cash p. 265

cash-basis accounting p. 273

cash flow activities p. 274

Discussion Questions

1. Explain the purposes of the income statement and balance sheets.

2. What determines a company's profitability?

3. Distinguish among (a) gross profits, (b) operating profits, and (c) net profits.

4. The balance sheet reports information on a firm's (1) assets, (2) debt, and (3) equity. What is included in each of these reported categories?

5. How are owners' equity and debt different?

6. Distinguish between common stock and retained earnings.

7. What is the relationship between an income statement and a balance sheet?

8. Why aren't a firm's cash flows equal to its profits?

9. Describe the three major components of a cash flow statement.

10. What questions do financial ratios help answer about a firm's financial performance?

You Make the Call

Situation 1

The Donahoo Western Furnishings Company was formed on December 31, 2012, with $1,000,000 in equity plus $500,000 in long-term debt. On January 1, 2013, all of the firm's capital was held in cash. The following transactions occurred during January 2013:

- January 2: Donahoo purchased $1,000,000 worth of furniture for resale. It paid $500,000 in cash and financed the balance using trade credit that required payment in 60 days.

- January 3: Donahoo sold $250,000 worth of furniture that it had paid $200,000 to acquire. The entire sale was on credit terms of net 90 days.

- January 15: Donahoo purchased more furniture for $200,000. This time, it used trade credit for the entire amount of the purchase, with credit terms of net 60 days.

- January 31: Donahoo sold $500,000 worth of furniture, for which it had paid $400,000. The furniture was sold for 10 percent cash down, with the remainder payable in 90 days. In addition, the firm paid a cash dividend of $100,000 to its stockholders and paid off $250,000 of its long-term debt.

Question 1 What did Donahoo's balance sheet look like at the outset of the firm's life?

Question 2 What did the firm's balance sheet look like after each transaction?

Question 3 Ignoring taxes, determine how much income Donahoo earned during January. Prepare an income statement for the month. Recognize an interest expense of 1 percent for the month (12 percent annually) on the $500,000 long-term debt, which has not been paid but is owed.

Question 4 What was Donahoo's cash flow for the month of January?

Situation 2

At the beginning of 2013, Mary Abrahams purchased a small business, the Maitz Company, whose income statement and balance sheets are shown below.

Income Statement for the Maitz Company for 2013

Sales		$175,000
Cost of goods sold		(105,000)
Gross profits		$ 70,000
Operating expenses:		
Depreciation	$ 5,000	
Administrative expenses	$20,000	
Selling expenses	$26,000	
Total operating expenses		$ (51,000)
Operating profits		$ 19,000
Interest expense		(3,000)
Profits before taxes		$ 16,000
Taxes		(8,000)
Net profits		$ 8,000

Balance Sheets for the Maitz Company for 2012 and 2013

Assets	2012	2013
Current assets:		
Cash	$ 8,000	$ 10,000
Accounts receivable	$15,000	$ 20,000
Inventory	$22,000	$ 25,000
Total current assets	$45,000	$ 55,000
Fixed assets:		
Gross fixed assets	$ 50,000	$ 55,000
Accumulated depreciation	(15,000)	(20,000)
Net fixed assets	$ 35,000	$ 35,000
Other assets	$ 12,000	$ 10,000
TOTAL ASSETS	$ 92,000	$100,000

Debt (Liabilities) and Equity

Current debt:		
Accounts payable	$ 10,000	$ 12,000
Accruals	$ 7,000	$ 8,000
Short-term notes	$ 5,000	$ 5,000
Total current debt	$ 22,000	$ 25,000
Long-term debt	$ 15,000	$ 15,000
Total debt	$ 37,000	$ 40,000
Equity	$ 55,000	$ 60,000
TOTAL DEBT AND EQUITY	$ 92,000	$100,000

The firm has been profitable, but Abrahams has been disappointed by the lack of cash flows. She had hoped to have about $10,000 a year available for personal living expenses. However, there never seems to be much cash available for purposes other than business needs. Abrahams has asked you to examine the financial statements and explain why, although they show profits, she does not have any discretionary cash for personal needs. She observed, "I thought that I could take the profits and add back depreciation to find out how much cash I was generating. However, that doesn't seem to be the case. What's happening?"

Question 1 Given the information provided by the financial statements, what would you tell Abrahams? (As part of your answer, calculate the firm's cash flows.)

Question 2 How would you describe the cash flow pattern for the Maitz Company?

Situation 3

Philip Spencer, the owner of Wholesome Foods, has hired you to evaluate his firm's financial performance. The firm's financial data is provided below, along with an average for the financial ratios that Spencer collected on several competing peer firms.

Question 1 Compute the financial ratios discussed in the chapter for Wholesome Foods for 2012 and 2013.

Question 2 Prepare a cash flow statement for the firm for 2012 and 2013.

Question 3 Interpret your findings, both for the firm's financial ratios compared to those of the peer group and for the cash flow statement.

Assets	2011	2012	2013
Cash	$ 21,000	$ 20,200	25,000
Accounts receivable	42,000	33,000	46,000
Inventory	51,000	84,000	96,000
Prepaid rent	1,200	1,100	2,000
Total current assets	$ 115,200	$ 138,300	$ 169,000
Gross property, plant, and equipment	650,000	664,000	740,000
Accumulated depreciation	(364,000)	(394,000)	(434,000)
Net property, plant, and equipment	$ 286,000	$ 270,000	$ 306,000
TOTAL ASSETS	$ 401,200	$ 401,300	$ 475,000

Debt (Liabilities) and Equity	2011	2012	2013
Accounts payable	$ 48,000	$ 57,000	$ 52,400
Accrued expenses	9,500	9,000	12,000
Short-term notes	11,500	9,000	20,000
Total current liabilities	$ 69,000	$ 75,000	$ 84,400
Long-term debt	160,000	150,000	185,000
Common stock	$ 22,200	$ 22,200	$ 34,500
Retained earnings	150,000	161,100	171,100
Total owners' equity	$ 172,200	$ 183,300	$ 205,600
TOTAL DEBT AND EQUITY	$ 401,200	$ 401,300	$ 475,000

Income Statement	2012	2013
Sales	$ 600,000	$ 650,000
Cost of goods sold	(460,000)	(487,500)
Gross profits	$ 140,000	$ 162,500
Operating expenses:		
General and administrative expenses	$ 30,000	$ 37,500
Depreciation expense	30,000	40,000
Total operating expenses	$ 60,000	$ 77,500
Operating profits	$ 80,000	$ 85,000
Interest expense	(10,000)	(12,000)
Profits before taxes	$ 70,000	$ 73,000
Taxes	(27,100)	(30,000)
Net profits	$ 42,900	$ 43,000
Net profits	$ 42,900	$ 43,000
Dividends paid	(31,800)	(33,000)
Addition to retained earnings	$ 11,100	$ 10,000

Financial Ratios (Averages)	Peer Companies
Current ratio	1.80
Return on assets	16.8%
Operating profit margin	14.0%
Total asset turnover	1.20
Debt ratio	0.50
Return on equity	18.0%

Experiential Exercises

1. Interview an owner of a small firm about the financial statements she or he uses. Ask the owner how important financial data are to her or his decision making.

2. Acquire a small firm's financial statements. Review the statements and describe the firm's financial position. Find out if the owner agrees with your conclusions.

3. Dun & Bradstreet and Robert Morris Associates compile financial information about many companies. They provide, among other information, income statements and balance sheets for an average firm in an industry. Go to a library and look up, or search online for, financial information on two industries of your choice, and compute the following data for each industry:

   a. The percentages of assets in (1) current assets and (2) fixed assets (property, plant, and equipment)

   b. The percentages of financing from debt financing and owners' equity

   c. The gross profits and the operating profits as percentages of sales

Small Business & Entrepreneurship Resource Center

The Small Business & Entrepreneurship Resource Center offers complete small business management resources through a comprehensive database that covers all major areas of starting, operating, and maintaining a business from financing, management, marketing, accounting, taxes, and more. Go to www.cengagebrain.com and select the Longenecker text for more information on how to access this material.

1. The statement of cash flows is one of the three statements used to report and understand the performance of a business. By no means is it third in importance, as it provides vital information that's not provided in the balance sheet or income statement. The statement of cash flows reports the cash flow generated over time and the sources and uses of cash. When cash is needed, businesses borrow money or sell equity. When cash is invested and results in a positive cash flow, owners pay down debt and return equity to the owners. The financing section of the statement of cash flows calculates and presents the cash impact of these activities. After reading this article, explain why it is important for business owners to understand how changes in balance sheet items affect cash flow.

2. You record your income and expenses, tally a "bottom line," and provide the report to your banker. Is that it for the income statement? A report of bottom-line profit or loss for a period? If that's what you think, you are missing the boat. Your income statement should be an indispensable tool for you. It is a source of insight into how you can improve the profitability of your business. In fact, if you are not skilled at organizing and mining your income statement for information of value in managing your business, it's likely your business isn't very profitable. Discuss the three important purposes of financial statements as outlined in this article. What kinds of information do financial statements provide?

Sources: "The Statement of Cash Flows," *The Business Owner*, Vol. 36, No. 6 (November–December 2012, pp. 3–4; and "The Income Statement," *The Business Owner*, Vol. 36, No. 5 (September–October 2012), pp. 3–5.

Case 10

Harper & Reiman, LLC (P. 661)

Haprer & Reiman, LLC caters to non-profit organizations. The company has experienced significant growth, with sales approaching $29 million in 2014—far beyond anything Harper & Reiman could have imagined. For one thing, the firm distinguished itself in the industry by designing a payment system that serve non-profits by allowing them to make payments in seasons when donations are the highest. This case allows students to evaluate the firm's financial performance. This case was prepared by Lauren Houser, April 2013.

Alternative Case for Chapter 10

Video Case 10, B2B CFO [website only]

Endnotes

1. Norm Brodsky, "Secrets of a $110 Million Man," *Inc.*, October 2008, p. 77.

2. Philip Campbell, "Are You Really Focused on Profits?" *Inc.*, June 2008, www.inc.com/resources/finance/articles/20080601/campbell.html, accessed December 15, 2012.

3. Quoted in "How to Manage Cash Flows," www.inc.com/encyclopedia /cashflow.html, accessed February 3, 2011.

4. Jan Norman, "You're Making Sales, but Are You Making Money?" *Entrepreneur*, March 2004, www.entrepreneur.com/article/0,4621,228680,00.html, accessed January 11, 2013.

© Metta image/Alamy

CHAPTER 11

Forecasting Financial Requirements

OPEN LOOKING AHEAD

Managing rapid growth can become an entrepreneur's worst nightmare. Unhappy customers and employees, a lack of cash, and the inability to fill orders can overwhelm a small business owner, who hasn't prepared for the challenges that growth brings. "They're too busy working in the business to work on the business," observes Jeff DeGraff, professor at the Ross School of Business at the University of Michigan. But taking the time to plan for growth, especially when it's unexpected, can keep a small business on track.

When Ahmed Khattak arrived at Yale University as an international student with no credit and no ability to access the traditional cell phone market, he was unable to call his family in Pakistan. In response to the problem, Khattak revolutionized the cell phone industry through his company, GSM Nation, allowing not only himself but

> In the SPOTLIGHT
> **The Need to Manage Growth**
> www.gsmnation.com

others like him an easy way to purchase cellular phones without the hassle of binding contracts.

Khattak's first hurdle was to obtain seed funding for his startup. An initial loan of $30,000 came from his family and friends, followed by an investment from GSM Nation's co-founder, Junaid Shams. The new venture proved to be successful from the very beginning. Khattak says,

It's hard to put a finger on a particular occasion when I thought we were going to be

© Michael Ransburg/Shutterstock.com

successful because we have surpassed our wildest imaginations. I mean, think of it, in excess of $50 million in sales in just over two years. We have taken such huge leaps that every six months we have a new aim and we literally treat that as our starting point.

The fast-paced growth, however, brought with it significant financial forecasting challenges, particularly involving the projection and management of cash flow. According to co-founder Junaid Shams,

[T]he biggest mistake we made in the early going was not having as much funding as we originally thought we needed. We were growing so fast the first six to 12 months, faster than what even we had expected, that we didn't have the funding at the time necessary to allow us to grow at the same pace.

Today, the co-founders' concerns are about managing growth, making certain that the products keep moving and cash flows stay positive.

Despite challenges in the industry and days that are sometimes 20 hours long, Khattak finds running his own company to be a very rewarding experience. Founding GSM Nation also proved to be a great career move during the economic downturn. Khattak notes,

Everyone wants to work in a startup. It's the only thing that's sort of recession proof. A lot of startups have done really well in the recession.

GSM Nation now serves a wide variety of consumers, including the State Department and the United Nations, and was named one of the top 25 most-promising companies in 2011 by *Businessweek*, reaching annual sales of $25 million in 2011.

Sources: Excerpts from Marty Jerome, "Young Entrepreneur Changes the U.S. Cell Phone Market," *Entrepreneur*, December 2012, www.entrepreneur.com/article/224539, accessed January 27, 2013; http://empact100.com/company/1067-gsm-nation-llc, accessed April 11, 2013; and Elaine Pofeldt, "They're Young, They're Smart—And You Probably Couldn't Pay Them Enough to Work at Your Company," www.forbes.com/sites/elainepofeldt/2012/03/20/theyre-young-and-smart-and-you-probably-couldnt-pay-them-enough-to-work-at-your-company, accessed April 11, 2013.

A *good idea may or may not be a good investment opportunity.* As we discussed in Chapter 3, a good investment opportunity requires a product or service that meets a definite customer need and creates a sustainable competitive advantage. To be attractive, an opportunity must generate strong profits relative to the required amount of investment. Therefore, projections of a venture's profits, its asset and financing requirements, and its cash flows are essential in determining whether a venture is economically viable.

11-1 THE PURPOSE OF FINANCIAL FORECASTING

LO
11-1

Describe the purpose of financial forecasting.

I n Chapter 10, we followed the Lemonade Kids to see the accounting implications of what was happening in their venture. In that very simple world, there was really no need to plan for the future. Everything just worked out okay. But that is not the case when starting and operating a business with any complexity. In the real world, you need to forecast, as best you can, the financial outcomes that could result from your decisions.

Granted, the numbers never work out the way you planned. But the process allows you to understand what drives your numbers, and that's very important to lenders and investors. Whether you are applying for your first (or tenth) bank loan or pitching investors, sooner or later you will have to prepare a set of financial projections. Lenders will look at what the numbers say about the likelihood of repayment. Investors will attempt to value your company based on the numbers.

The purpose of **pro forma financial statements** is to answer three questions:

1. How profitable can you expect the firm to be, given the projected sales levels and the expected sales–expense relationships?

2. How much and what type of financing (debt or equity) will be needed to finance a firm's assets?

3. Will the firm have adequate cash flows? If so, how will they be used? If not, where will the additional cash come from?

Preparing historical financial statements, such as income statements, balance sheets, and cash flow statements, is not a difficult task. However, *projecting* what may happen to a business in the future in terms of profits and cash flows are another matter.

For an established firm, you at least have the benefit of past data, both in terms of past revenues and what your costs and expenses have been. You basically need to anticipate how your market could change and what you will be doing differently in the future and how the changes will affect the financial numbers. The main difficulty here is predicting sales, which can be greatly affected by influences outside of the business itself.

When starting a new business, however, there is limited, if any, past experience on which to base your numbers. You make assumptions, which may feel like no more than educated guesses. But it can be done, as business plan consultant Rhonda Abrams explains:

> *The best place to start is by speaking with others in your industry, attending trade shows, and contacting your industry association. Another excellent source is the Risk Management Association Annual Statement Studies, which look at actual financial statements of companies in certain industries.*[1]

Once financial projections have been prepared, the process should not stop there. Because of the uncertainty of what can happen, the small business owner should always be asking, "What could go wrong, and if it does happen, what will I do?" For instance, you want to plan how to respond if sales are significantly lower or higher than projected. A firm can get into trouble not only when sales are inadequate, but also when the firm is experiencing high growth.

When seeking financing, an entrepreneur must be able to give informed answers about the firm's needs, including the amount of money needed, the purposes for which it will be used, and when and how the lender or creditor will be paid back. Only careful financial planning can provide answers to these questions.

Let's take a look at the process for projecting a firm's profitability, asset and financing requirements, and cash flows. This process should be based on a carefully developed *business model* (see Chapter 6, pages 159–163).

11-2 FORECASTING PROFITABILITY

LO 11-2

Develop a pro forma income statement to forecast a new venture's profitability.

pro forma financial statements
Statements that project a firm's financial performance and condition, including a firm's projected profits, assets and financing requirements, and cash flows.

Profits reward an owner for investing in a company and constitute a primary source of financing for future growth. Therefore, it is critical for an entrepreneur to understand the factors that drive profits (see also Exhibit 10.1, on page 260):

1. *Amount of sales.* The dollar amount of sales equals the price of the product or service times the number of units sold or the amount of service rendered.

2. *Cost of goods sold.* Cost of goods sold is the cost of producing or purchasing the firm's products or services. These costs can be either *fixed* (those that do not vary with a change in sales volume) or *variable* (those that change proportionally with sales).

3. *Operating expenses.* These expenses relate to marketing and distributing the product, general and administrative expenses, and depreciation expenses. Like cost of goods sold, operating expenses can be fixed or variable in nature.

4. *Interest expense.* An entrepreneur who borrows money agrees to pay interest on the loan principal. For example, a loan of $25,000 for a full year at a 12 percent interest rate results in an interest expense of $3,000 for the year ($3,000 = 0.12 × $25,000).

5. *Taxes.* A firm's income taxes are figured as a percentage of profits before taxes, or what is also called taxable profits.

A hypothetical example demonstrates how to estimate a new venture's profits.[2] David Allen is planning to start a new business called **D&R Products, Inc.**, which will do wood trim work for luxury homes. In thinking about how to build a company that is economically viable in terms of profits and cash flows, Allen envisions a *revenue model* based on two complementary revenue streams: product design and product sales/installations.

1. *Product design.* For customers who want to be engaged in the creation of their own wood trim for new homes or renovations, D&R will provide user-friendly design software. In addition, the firm has developed alliances with professional interior designers who would work with the customer to create a design that is not only aesthetically pleasing but also architecturally sound. Finally, an open platform will allow customers to interface with other customers designing their own wood trim. D&R will receive 10 percent of the interior designers' revenue stream resulting from working with D&R contacts. While Allen does not see this revenue stream as a major source of sales, he does expect it to lead to increased product sales and installations.

2. *Product sales/installations.* The primary source of revenues for D&R will be the actual sale and installation of product in new and renovated homes, with plans to eventually expand to larger commercial projects.

In terms of the company's *cost structure,* Allen has carefully identified expected fixed and variable costs of goods sold and operating expenses. The firm will have a cost advantage in the form of a newly developed lathe that will allow it to adapt to varying design specifications in a very economical manner. Finally, Allen has determined the asset investments that would be required in order to gain positive cash flows.

After extensive interviews with prospective customers, building contractors, and suppliers, along with industry research, Allen has made the following estimates for the first two years of operations:

1. *Amount of sales.*

   a. *Year 1*: Allen already has contracts for 10 jobs and expects to acquire another 10, or 20 jobs in total, by the end of the first year at an average price of $12,500 per job. Thus, revenue from product sales and installations is projected to be $250,000 in the first year, computed as follows:

   20 jobs × $12,500 average price per job = $250,000

   Allen further estimates that revenue from product design will only amount to $10,000 in this first year. So total revenues for year 1 are projected to be $260,000:

Product sales and installation	$250,000
Product design	10,000
Total revenues	$260,000

b. *Year 2*: Allen forecasts 30 jobs in the second year, again believing that the average revenue per job will be $12,500. He also expects $25,000 in product design sales, for total revenues of $400,000:

Product sales and installation	$375,000
(30 jobs × $12,500 average price per job)	
Product design	25,000
Total revenues	$400,000

2. *Cost of goods sold*. For product and installation sales, the fixed cost of goods sold (including production costs and employee salaries) is expected to amount to $100,000 per year, while the variable costs of production will be around 20 percent of product sales and installation. In addition, there will be fixed costs of $10,000 related to product design.

3. *Operating expenses*. The firm's fixed operating expenses (marketing expenses, general and administrative expenses) are estimated to be $46,000 per year. In addition, depreciation will be $4,000 annually. The variable operating expenses will be approximately 30 percent of product sales and installation. There will be no operating costs for product designs.

4. *Interest expense*. Based on the anticipated amount of money to be borrowed and the corresponding interest rate, Allen expects interest expense to be $8,000 in the first year, increasing to $12,000 in the second year.

5. *Taxes*. Income taxes will be 25 percent of profits before taxes (taxable profits).

Given the above estimates, we can forecast D&R Products' profits, as shown in the pro forma income statement in Exhibit 11.1. We first enter our assumptions in a spreadsheet (rows 3–18). Then, in rows 20–44, we see the two years of pro forma income statements (columns B and C) and the equations used to compute the numbers (columns D and E), where

- Rows 22 and 23 show the projected revenues for product sales and installations (row 22) and for product design activities (row 23).
- Row 24 shows total sales.
- Rows 28–30 provide the cost of goods sold for product sales and installations.
- Row 31 gives us the expected costs of $10,000 for product design.
- Row 32 then sums the costs of goods sold for both product sales and installations and product design to arrive at the total cost of goods sold.
- Row 33 gives us gross profits, which equals total sales less total cost of goods sold.
- Rows 36–39 present the anticipated operating expenses associated with product sales and installations; there are no operating expenses related to product design.
- Row 40, operating profits, equals gross profits less total operating expenses.
- Row 41 shows the interest expense for borrowing money.
- Row 42 is profits before taxes (operating profits less interest expense).
- Row 43 equals the tax expense. Since D&R Products is expected to have a loss in the first year, the taxes will be zero. The taxes in the second year are calculated as the tax rate (25 percent) multiplied by the profits before taxes. (In reality, the firm would not expect to pay taxes in the second year either,

START
UP

ACTION

"What If" Scenarios
When it comes to financial forecasting and budgeting, you should always prepare at least three scenarios: one with an aggressive forecast for sales increases, another using more conservative assumptions, and a third with worst-case scenarios. This is particularly important in an environment where future demand is unclear, as in the last economic downturn. Remember that a spreadsheet is a great tool to evaluate "what if" scenarios when forecasting profits and cash flows.

11.1 Pro Forma Income Statements for D&R Products, Inc.

	A	B	C	D	E
3	INCOME STATEMENT ASSUMPTIONS:				
4		**Year 1**	**Year 2**		
5	Product sales and installations:				
6	Number of projected jobs	20	30		
7	Average selling price per job	$ 12,500	$ 12,500		
8	Fixed cost of goods sold	$100,000	$100,000		
9	Fixed operating expenses	$ 46,000	$ 46,000		
10	Depreciation expense	$ 4,000	$ 4,000		
11	Interest expense	$ 8,000	$ 12,000		
12	Variable cost of goods sold	20%	20%		
13	Variable operating expenses	30%	30%	**Equations based on**	
14	Product design:			**assumptions**	
15	Projected design revenues	$ 10,000	$ 25,000		
16	Fixed design costs	$ 10,000	$ 10,000		
17					
18	Income tax rate	25%	25%	↓	↓
19				*Equations for:*	
20				*Year 1*	*Year 2*
21	Sales:				
22	Product sales and installations	$250,000	$375,000	=B6*B7	=C6*C7
23	Product design	10,000	25,000	=B15	=C15
24	Total sales	$260,000	$400,000	=SUM(B22:B23)	=SUM(C22:C23)
25					
26	Cost of goods sold:				
27	Cost of goods sold: product sales and installations				
28	Fixed cost of goods sold	$100,000	$100,000	=B8	=C8
29	Variable cost of goods sold (20% of product sales)	50,000	75,000	=B22*B12	=C22*C12
30	Total cost of goods sold: product sales and installations	$150,000	$175,000	=SUM(B28:B29)	=SUM(C28:C29)
31	Total cost of goods sold: product design	10,000	10,000	=B16	=C16
32	Total cost of goods sold	$160,000	$185,000	=SUM(B30:B31)	=SUM(C30:C31)
33	Gross profits	$100,000	$215,000	=B24-B32	=C24-C32
34					
35	Operating expenses: product sales and installations				
36	Fixed operating expenses	$ 46,000	$ 46,000	=B9	=C9
37	Variable operating expenses (30% of product sales)	75,000	112,500	=B13*B22	=C13*C22
38	Depreciation expense	4,000	4,000	=B10	=C10
39	Total operating expenses: product sales and installations	$125,000	$162,500	=SUM(B36:B38)	=SUM(C36:C38)
40	Operating profits	$ (25,000)	$ 52,500	=B33-B39	=C33-C39
41	Interest expense (interest rate 12%)	8,000	12,000	=B11	=C11
42	Profits before taxes	$ (33,000)	$ 40,500	=B40-B41	=C40-C41
43	Taxes (25% of profits before tax)	0	10,125	0	=C42*C18
44	Net profits	$ (33,000)	$ 30,375	=B42-B43	=C42-C43

since tax laws allow a firm to carry losses in one year forward into future years. However, we are ignoring this reality in order to provide a simple example.)

- Row 44 shows the firm's projected net profits—profits before taxes minus income taxes

These computations indicate that D&R Products is expected to have a $33,000 net loss in its first year, followed by a positive net profit of $30,375 in its second year. A startup typically experiences losses for a period of time, frequently as long as two or three years.[3] In a real-world situation, an entrepreneur should project the profits of a new company at least three years into the future (or five years into the future, if it can be done with some degree of confidence).

Let's now shift our attention from forecasting profits to estimating asset and financing requirements.

The exhibits in this chapter can also be found online by going to www.cengage-brain.com and selecting the Longenecker text for more information on how to access this material.

LO
11-3
Determine a company's asset and financing requirements using a pro forma balance sheet.

11-3 FORECASTING ASSET AND FINANCING REQUIREMENTS

The amount and types of assets required for a new venture will vary, depending on the nature of the business. High-technology businesses—such as computer manufacturers, designers of semiconductor chips, and pharmaceutical companies—often require millions of dollars in investment. Most service businesses, on the other hand, require minimal initial capital. For example, IRM Corporation, an information technology firm serving the food and beverage industry, has little in the way of assets. The firm leases its office space and has no inventory. Its only asset of any significance is accounts receivable.

Most firms of any size need both working capital (cash, accounts receivable, inventory, etc.) and fixed assets (property, plant, and equipment). For instance, a food store requires operating cash, inventory, and possibly limited accounts receivable. In addition, the owner will have to acquire cash registers, shopping carts, shelving, office equipment, and a building. The need to invest in assets results in a corresponding need for financing.

Working capital is another term used in the business world for current assets—namely, cash, accounts receivable, and inventory that are required in the day-to-day operations of the business. *It has nothing to do with property, plant, and equipment.* Also, the term is sometimes used loosely to mean current assets less current liabilities, which is really **net working capital**. Net working capital is a measure of a company's liquidity—that is, the greater a firm's net working capital, the greater its ability to pay on any debt commitment as it comes due.[4]

© Africa Studio/Shutterstock.com

Too frequently, small business owners tend to underestimate the amount of capital the business requires. Consequently, the financing they get may be inadequate. Without the money to invest in assets, they try to do without anything that is not absolutely essential and to spend less money on essential items. When Dan Cassidy started Baha's Fajita Bar, a restaurant aimed at serving college students, his goal was

net working capital
Current assets less current liabilities.

to raise $100,000 in capital. However, he opened the restaurant when he had raised only $70,000. In six months, he ran out of cash and had to close the restaurant. The problem became critical when students went home for spring break and were slow to eat at restaurants in the week following their return to school. Cassidy's unfortunate experience shows just how risky it can be for a small business to ignore the potential for unexpected challenges and underestimate its capital needs.[5]

While being undercapitalized is rarely, if ever, a good decision, the goal of the entrepreneur should be to minimize and control, rather than maximize and own, resources. To the greatest extent possible, the entrepreneur should use other people's resources—for instance, leasing equipment rather than buying, negotiating with suppliers to provide inventory "just in time" to minimize tied-up inventory, and arranging to collect money owed the firm before having to pay its bills. As discussed in Chapter 1, this is called *bootstrapping*, and it's one of the most common ways entrepreneurs accomplish more with less. When Cecilia Levine, the owner of MFI International, a manufacturing firm, had the opportunity to get a contract to make clothing for a Fortune 500 company, she became a master of bootstrapping.

> *I never expected the fast growth and demand that my services would have. To finance the growth, debt financing would have been helpful, but it was not an option. The definition of credit in the dictionary reads, "The ability of a customer to obtain goods or services before payment, based on the trust that payment is going to be made in the future." What it does not say is that for a banker, trust means having collateral, and without collateral you don't get credit. But I still had children to feed and the desire to succeed so I looked for another form of financing—bootstrapping.*
>
> *I had a major customer who believed in me, and who had the equipment I needed. He sold me the equipment and then would reduce his weekly payment of my invoices by an amount to cover the cost of the equipment. Also, the customer paid me each Friday for what we produced and shipped that week. Everyone who worked for me understood that if we didn't perform and finish the needed production for the week, we didn't get paid by our customer. When I received the payment from the customer, I was then able to pay my employees. We were a team, and we understood the meaning of cash flow. Therefore, we performed.[6]*

Working with a limited amount of capital makes forecasting all the more important because you have less room for error. Moreover, the uncertainties surrounding an entirely new venture make estimating asset and financing requirements difficult. Even for an established business, forecasts are never perfect. There are always surprises—you can count on it.

In gathering needed information for financial forecasting, an entrepreneur should search for relevant information from a variety of sources. Robert Morris Associates, Dun & Bradstreet, banks, trade associations, and similar organizations compile financial information for a variety of industries.

Along with public data, common sense and educated guesswork should also be used. Continually ask yourself, "Does this make economic sense?" and "What could go wrong?" However, no source of information can compare with talking to prospective customers. Sitting in a room with your computer, without ever getting out and talking to potential customers, is a certain way to miss the obvious.

The determination of how much financing will be needed should also take into consideration the owner's personal financial situation, especially if no other income is available to make ends meet. Whether or not the owner's personal living expenses during the initial period of operation are part of the business's capitalization, they must be considered in the financial plan. Inadequate provision for personal expenses will inevitably lead to a diversion of business assets and a departure from the plan. Therefore, failing to incorporate these expenses into the financial plan as a cash outflow raises a red flag to any prospective investor.

In fact, a real danger exists that a small business owner will neglect personal finances later as well. As a firm grows, an increasing percentage of the owner's net worth is tied up in the firm. For many entrepreneurs, well over half of their net wealth is invested in their businesses. Even more do not plan adequately for their long-term personal financial health. For 25 years, Ed Bonneau, a successful entrepreneur by any standard, essentially had two major assets in his personal portfolio: his home and his business. Over all those years, his company had grown steadily and predictably. Then the president of his largest customer embezzled $500 million from that company. This customer owed Bonneau a lot of money, which was a total loss. At that point, Bonneau realized that he was putting his family's financial welfare at risk by not owning other investments outside of his company. He needed to diversify his personal investments.[7]

The key to effectively forecasting financing requirements is first to understand the relationship between a firm's projected sales and its assets. A firm's sales are the primary force driving future asset needs. Exhibit 11.2 depicts this relationship, which can be expressed simply as follows: *The greater a firm's sales, the greater the asset requirements will be and, in turn, the greater the need for financing.*

11-3a Determining Asset Requirements

Since asset needs increase as sales increase, a firm's asset requirements are often estimated as a percentage of sales. Therefore, if future sales have been projected, a ratio of assets to sales can be used to estimate asset requirements. Suppose, for example, that a firm's sales are expected to be $1 million. If assets in the firm's particular industry tend to run about 50 percent of sales, the firm's asset requirements would be estimated to be 0.50 × $1,000,000, or $500,000.

Although the assets-to-sales relationship varies over time and with individual businesses, it tends to be relatively constant within an industry. For example, assets as a percentage of sales average 20 percent for grocery stores, compared with 65 percent for oil and gas companies. This method of estimating asset requirements is called the **percentage-of-sales technique**. It can also be used to project figures for individual assets, such as accounts receivable and inventory.

To illustrate the percentage-of-sales technique, let's return to D&R Products, Inc., where we will estimate the firm's asset requirements for the first two years, given the company's sales projections. In Exhibit 11.1, the firm's pro forma income statements, product

percentage-of-sales technique
A method of forecasting asset requirements.

11.2 Assets-to-Sales Financing Relationships

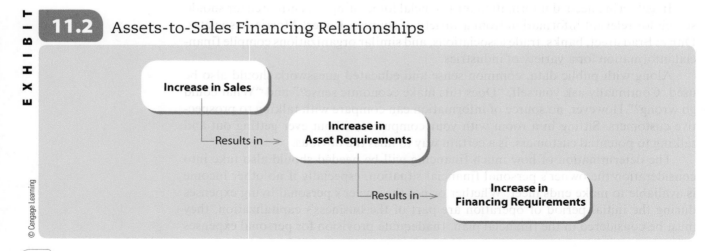

© Cengage Learning

and installation sales (not including the $10,000 of design revenues) were forecasted to be $250,000 and $375,000 in years 1 and 2, respectively. After considerable investigation of the opportunity, Allen estimated the firm's current asset requirements (cash, accounts receivable, and inventory) as a percentage of product and installation sales:

Assets	Percentage of Sales
Cash	4%
Accounts receivable	10%
Inventory	25%

Allen will need equipment, that will cost $10,000. Also, he has found a building suitable for a manufacturing facility for $40,000. Combined, these two items total $50,000 and will be reflected in a balance sheet as *gross fixed assets*.

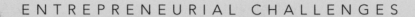

ENTREPRENEURIAL CHALLENGES

Living the Dream

Forecasting in an Uncertain Economy

Forecasting a company's sales is a difficult process in the best of circumstances, much less at the beginning of a recession. Near the end of 2008, when consumers were spending less and customers were pulling out of big contracts at the last minute, smaller companies encountered even more difficulty in forecasting sales. To illustrate, Seth Early of Early & Associates was 15 minutes from closing a $100,000 sale, just waiting for the customer to send a purchase order. Instead, he received a call from the customer saying, "The boss said don't sign anything."

During unpredictable economic downturns, many entrepreneurs have learned to make more frequent adjustments to their forecasts and take a more conservative approach. After forecasting for the year, the management team for an advertising agency T3, based in Austin, Texas, adjusts forecasted sales every month based on their account directors' advice. COO Lee Gaddis says, "We go to each of them every month and ask them to give us a 12-month projection. We ask everyone to be conservative." At the end of each month, the firm's CFO, Charles Kiley, meets with the account directors to

© cosmonaut/Daniel Deitschel/iStockphoto.com

compare the forecast to the actual invoices and reports back to senior management. Then, the team decides whether to "buy, hold, or sell" on hiring and expenses.

Uncontrollable variables in a business can also create real problems when it comes to sales forecasts. For example, Terry McBride is CEO of Burns & McBride Home Comfort, a $25-million heating oil distributing company. McBride explains that weather and the price of oil can cause havoc to forecasting the firm's sales. He says they were always off 7 to 8 percent in their forecasts from being too optimistic. Then, "we'd always blame it on the weather." McBride worked with grad students from Marquette University to create software that measures consumption and plots it with the weather. This made more accurate predictions on oil usage, which in turn lowered delivery costs and increased customer satisfaction. The software decreased the errors in forecasting sales down to 1 to 2 percent.

Source: Based on Donna Fenn, "How to Forecast Sales in an Uncertain Economy," *Inc.*, November 1, 2010, www.inc.com/guides/2010/10/how-to -forecast-sales-in-2011.html, accessed December 3, 2012.

Net fixed assets is equal to gross fixed assets minus accumulated depreciation. Since the depreciation expense reported in the income statement (Exhibit 11.1) is $4,000 per year, then the accumulated depreciation will be $4,000 in year 1, increasing (accumulating) to $8,000 the next year. Given the anticipated sales and the assets-to-sales relationships, Allen is able to forecast the asset requirements for his venture. If product and installation sales are $250,000 in year 1 and $375,000 in year 2, Allen estimates the following:

Assets	Assumptions	Year 1	Year 2
Cash	4% of sales	$ 10,000	$ 15,000
Accounts receivable	10% of sales	25,000	37,500
Inventory	25% of sales	62,500	93,750
Total current assets		$ 97,500	$146,250
Gross fixed assets	Equipment and building costs	$ 50,000	$50,000
Accumulated depreciation	$4,000 annually	(4,000)	(8,000)
Net fixed assets		$ 46,000	$42,000
TOTAL ASSETS		$143,500	$188,250

So Allen expects to need $143,500 in assets by the end of the first year and $188,250 by the conclusion of the second year. However, at this point, he should test how sensitive the results of the model are to changes in the assumptions being made. He needs to determine which assumptions have the greatest impact on the outcomes. Then he can focus his research on what matters most.

At this point, Allen has a sense of the asset investments required to achieve the forecasted profits. Now, he needs to consider how these assets will be financed.

11-3b Determining Financing Requirements

There must be a corresponding dollar of financing for every dollar of assets. Stated another way, debt plus equity must equal total assets. To forecast a company's financing needs effectively, an entrepreneur must understand certain basic principles that govern the financing of firms, which can be stated as follows:

1. The more assets a business needs, the greater its financing requirements. Thus, a firm that is experiencing rapid sales growth requires more assets and, consequently, faces greater pressure to find financing—and that pressure can be unbearable if not managed carefully.

2. A company should finance its growth in such a way as to maintain adequate liquidity. (*Liquidity* measures the degree to which a firm has current assets available to meet maturing short-term debt.) The need for adequate liquidity in small firms deserves special emphasis. As already mentioned, a common weakness in small business financing is the tendency to maintain a disproportionately small investment in liquid assets, or what was defined earlier as *net working capital* (current assets − current liabilities). Even more specifically, in Chapter 10 we used the *current ratio* (current assets ÷ current liabilities) as a measure of liquidity that compares a firm's current assets to its current liabilities on a relative basis. To ensure payment of short-term debts as they come due, small business owners should, as a general rule, maintain a current ratio of at least 2—that is, have current assets of at least two times the amount of current liabilities—or have a good reason for not doing so.

3. The amount of money that a firm can borrow is dependent in part on the amount of money the owners put into the business in the form of owners' equity. A bank

would never provide *all* of the necessary financing for a firm. For example, a bank might specify that at least half of the firm's financing must come from owners' equity, while the rest can come from debt. In other words, the owners would have to limit the firm's *debt ratio* (total debt ÷ total assets) to 50 percent.

4. Some types of short-term debt—specifically, *accounts payable* and *accrued expenses*—maintain a relatively constant relationship with sales. For example, as sales increase, more inventory will be required. If the inventory is purchased on credit, accounts payable will increase as well. As a result, accounts payable will track increases in sales. If sales increase by $1, accounts payable might increase by $0.15, or 15 percent of sales. So, if you expect a $1,000 increase in sales, you can also expect accounts payable to increase by $150, which is 15 percent of the increase in sales. The same holds true for accrued expenses. More business means more expenses, some of which will be accrued as liabilities, rather than being paid immediately. Given the "spontaneous" relationship of these types of liabilities with sales, they are sometimes called **spontaneous debt financing**. While not the more formal type of debt, such as bank loans, these accrued liabilities can be a significantly large source of financing for many small companies. The rest of debt financing must come from loans by banks and other lending sources.

5. Owners' equity in a business comes from two sources: (1) investments the owners make in the business, and (2) profits that are retained within the company rather than distributed to the owners, or *retained earnings*. For the typical small firm, retained earnings are the primary source of equity capital for financing growth. (Be careful not to think of retained earnings as a cash resource. As already noted, a firm may have significant profits but no cash to reinvest.)

So the essence of the foregoing principles can be captured in the following equation:

$$\begin{array}{c} \text{Total asset} \\ \text{requirements} \end{array} = \begin{array}{c} \text{Total sources} \\ \text{of financing} \end{array} = \begin{array}{c} \text{Spontaneous} \\ \text{debt financing} \end{array} + \begin{array}{c} \text{Loans from} \\ \text{banks} \end{array} + \begin{array}{c} \text{Owners'} \\ \text{investment} \end{array} + \begin{array}{c} \text{Retained} \\ \text{earnings} \end{array}$$

Small business owners who thoroughly understand these five principles and their relationships with each other will be effective in forecasting their firm's financial requirements—and they will be effective in acquiring needed financing.

Recall that Allen projected asset requirements of $143,500 and $188,250 for years 1 and 2, respectively. He then made estimates of the financing requirements, based on the following facts and assumptions:

1. Allen negotiated with a supplier to receive 30 days' credit on inventory purchases, which results in accounts payable running about 8 percent of sales.

2. Allen also estimates that accrued expenses that will be shown as short-term liabilities in the balance sheet will amount to about 4 percent of sales. This approximation comes from his evaluation of accrued expenses in similar businesses.

3. Allen plans to invest $110,000 of his personal savings to provide the needed startup equity for the business. He will receive common stock in return for his investment.

4. A bank has agreed to provide a short-term line of credit of $25,000 to D&R Products. A **line of credit** is simply a short-term loan to help with temporary needs, such as seasonal increases in inventory. It works like a credit card—the company has the option to borrow up to the limit (in this case, $25,000) as needed and then pay it down when it is no longer needed.

spontaneous debt financing
Short-term debts, such as accounts payable, that automatically increase in proportion to a firm's sales.

line of credit
A short-term loan.

5. The bank has also agreed to help finance the purchase of a building for manufacturing and warehousing the firm's products. Of the $40,000 needed to purchase the building, the bank will lend the firm $30,000, with the building serving as collateral for the loan. The loan will be repaid over 10 years in equal principal payments of $3,000 plus interest on the remaining note balance each year.

6. As part of the loan agreement, the bank has imposed two restrictions: (1) The firm's current ratio must remain at 2.0 or above, and (2) no more than 50 percent of the firm's financing may come from debt, both short-term and long-term (that is, total debt should be no more than 50 percent of total assets). Failure to comply with either of these conditions will cause the bank loan to come due immediately.

With this information, Allen can now estimate the sources of financing for D&R Products. If sales resulting from product and installations are $250,000 in year 1 and $375,000 in year 2, Allen estimates the following:

Sources of Financing	Assumptions	Year 1	Year 2
Accounts payable	8% of sales	$20,000	$ 30,000
Accrued expenses	4% of sales	$10,000	$15,000
Mortgage	$30,000 – $3,000 annual payments	$27,000	$24,000
Common stock	Owner's investment	$110,000	$110,000

Any remaining financing, up to $25,000, can come from the bank line of credit. If the line of credit is inadequate to meet the firm's needs, Allen will have to put more equity into the business.

Based on this information, Allen can now develop pro forma balance sheets for D&R Products. Exhibit 11.3 shows the assumptions made, the equations underlying the numbers, and the actual balance sheets, as developed in a spreadsheet. To help you visualize the results more easily, the balance sheets are also shown graphically in Exhibit 11.4. In looking at this exhibit, you need to remember two things:

1. Total assets and total sources of financing (debt and equity) must always balance. Note that D&R Products' total asset requirements of $143,500 for the first year and $188,250 for the second year are the same as the firm's total debt and equity.

2. To bring sources of financing into balance with total assets, D&R Products will need to borrow on the company's $25,000 line of credit. By the end of the first year, $9,500 of the line of credit is needed to bring the total debt and equity to $143,500. In the second year, line-of-credit borrowing will increase to $11,875 to gain the $188,250 in total financing needed.

Finally, based on Allen's projections, the firm should be able to satisfy the bank's loan restrictions, maintaining both a current ratio of 2.0 or more and a debt ratio of less than 50 percent. The computations are as follows:

Ratio	Computation	Year 1	Year 2
Current ratio =	$\dfrac{\text{current assets}}{\text{current liabilities}}$	$\dfrac{\$97,500}{\$39,500} = 2.47$	$\dfrac{\$146,250}{\$56,875} = 2.57$
Debt ratio =	$\dfrac{\text{total debt}}{\text{total assets}}$	$\dfrac{\$66,500}{\$143,500} = 0.46 = 46\%$	$\dfrac{\$80,375}{\$188,250} = 0.43 = 43\%$

We have now completed the process for forecasting a company's profitability and its asset and financing needs, as reflected in the income statement and balance sheets, respectively. We will now consider the third and final key financing issue: projecting cash flows.

11.3 Pro Forma Balance Sheets for D&R Products, Inc.

	A	B	C	D	E
3	*BALANCE SHEET ASSUMPTIONS*	**Year 1**	**Year 2**		
4	Projected revenues: product sales and installations	$250,000	$375,000		
5	Cash/sales	4%	4%		
6	Accounts receivable/sales	10%	10%		
7	Inventory/sales	25%	25%		
8	Gross fixed assets	$ 50,000	$ 50,000	**Equations based**	
9	Accounts payable/sales	8%	8%	**on assumptions**	
10	Accrued expenses/sales	4%	4%		
11	Cost of equipment	$ 10,000	$ 10,000		
12	Building cost	$ 40,000	$ 40,000		
13				↓ *Equations for:* ↓	
14	**Assets**			*Year 1*	*Year 2*
15	Cash	$ 10,000	$ 15,000	=B4*B5	=C4*C5
16	Accounts receivable	25,000	37,500	=B4*B6	=C4*C6
17	Inventory	62,500	93,750	=B4*B7	=C4*C7
18	Total current assets	$ 97,500	$146,250	=SUM(B15:B17)	=SUM(C15:C17)
19	Gross fixed assets	$ 50,000	$ 50,000	=B8	=C8
20	Accumulated depreciation	(4,000)	(8,000)	Depreciation expense for year 1	Accumulated depreciation expense for years 1 and 2
21	Net fixed assets	$ 46,000	$ 42,000	=B19+B20	=C19+C20
22	TOTAL ASSETS	$143,500	$188,250	=B18+B21	=C18+C21
23					
24	**Debt (Liabilities) and Equity**				
25	Accounts payable	$ 20,000	$ 30,000	=B4*B9	=C4*C9
26	Accrued expenses	10,000	15,000	=B4*B10	=C4*C10
27	Short-term line of credit	9,500	11,875	Required financing	Required financing
28	Total current liabilities	$ 39,500	$ 56,875	=SUM(B25:B27)	=SUM(C25:C27)
29	Mortgage	27,000	24,000	Original loan of $30,000 – annual payment of $3,000	Year 1 balance of $27,000 – annual payment of $3,000
30	Total debt	$ 66,500	$ 80,875	=SUM(B28:B29)	=SUM(C28:C29)
31	Ownership equity				
32	Common stock	$110,000	$110,000	Given	Given
33	Retained earnings	(33,000)	(2,625)	Year 1 loss	Year 1 loss + year 2 profit
34	Total ownership equity	$ 77,000	$107,375	=SUM(B32:B33)	=SUM(C32:C33)
35	TOTAL DEBT AND EQUITY	$143,500	$188,250	=SUM(B30:B33)	=SUM(C30:C33)
36					
37	Current ratio	$ 2.47	$ 2.57	=B18/B28	=C18/C28
38	Debt ratio	46%	43%	=B30/B35	=C30/C35

© Cengage Learning

11.4 Pro Forma Balance Sheets for D&R Products, Inc.

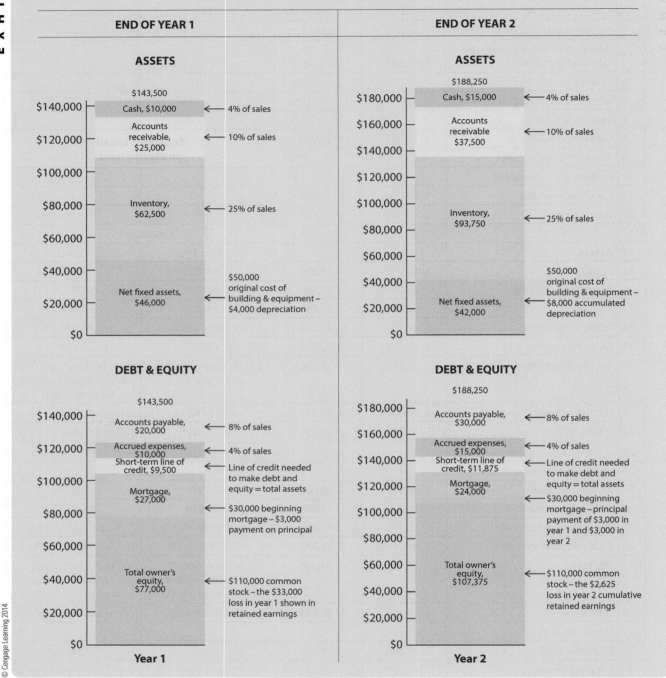

END OF YEAR 1

ASSETS

$143,500

- $140,000 — Cash, $10,000 ← 4% of sales
- $120,000 — Accounts receivable, $25,000 ← 10% of sales
- $100,000
- $80,000 — Inventory, $62,500 ← 25% of sales
- $60,000
- $40,000
- $20,000 — Net fixed assets, $46,000 ← $50,000 original cost of building & equipment – $4,000 depreciation
- $0

DEBT & EQUITY

$143,500

- $140,000 — Accounts payable, $20,000 ← 8% of sales
- $120,000 — Accrued expenses, $10,000 ← 4% of sales
- Short-term line of credit, $9,500 ← Line of credit needed to make debt and equity = total assets
- $100,000 — Mortgage, $27,000
- $80,000 — ← $30,000 beginning mortgage – $3,000 payment on principal
- $60,000
- $40,000 — Total owner's equity, $77,000 ← $110,000 common stock – the $33,000 loss in year 1 shown in retained earnings
- $20,000
- $0

Year 1

END OF YEAR 2

ASSETS

$188,250

- $180,000 — Cash, $15,000 ← 4% of sales
- $160,000 — Accounts receivable $37,500 ← 10% of sales
- $140,000
- $120,000
- $100,000
- $80,000 — Inventory, $93,750 ← 25% of sales
- $60,000
- $40,000 — $50,000 original cost of building & equipment – $8,000 accumulated depreciation
- $20,000 — Net fixed assets, $42,000
- $0

DEBT & EQUITY

$188,250

- $180,000 — Accounts payable, $30,000 ← 8% of sales
- $160,000
- $140,000 — Accrued expenses, $15,000 ← 4% of sales
- Short-term line of credit, $11,875 ← Line of credit needed to make debt and equity = total assets
- $120,000 — Mortgage, $24,000 ← $30,000 beginning mortgage – principal payment of $3,000 in year 1 and $3,000 in year 2
- $100,000
- $80,000
- $60,000 — Total owner's equity, $107,375 ← $110,000 common stock – the $2,625 loss in year 2 cumulative retained earnings
- $40,000
- $20,000
- $0

Year 2

11-4 FORECASTING CASH FLOWS

LO 11-4

Forecast a firm's cash flows.

As we have mentioned numerous times, profits and cash flows are not the same thing. A business can have positive profits and be running out of cash—or it can incur losses, as shown in the income statement, and have positive cash flows. The income statement simply does not give the small business owner the information he or she needs to know about the firm's cash flows. Forecasting cash flows is *critical* for the small business owner: If the business runs out of money, the consequences can be devastating.

Projecting a company's cash flows can be accomplished in one of two ways. First, we can use the information from the pro forma income statement and balance sheets to develop a pro forma statement of cash flows, similar to what we did in Chapter 10 to compute Houser & Associates' cash flows. Second, we can prepare a cash budget, which is simply a listing of expected cash inflows and outflows.

In forecasting cash flows, an owner must consider the time period used for projections. In a statement of cash flows that covers an entire year, everything may look great on paper, but the firm could very well run out of cash during certain months in that year. This scenario is particularly true for a business whose sales are seasonal. For instance, a wholesale sunglass company orders inventory in the spring, but most of its sales occur in the summer. Furthermore, the company will extend credit to its customers and not be paid until the end of the summer. If we look at the company's cash flows on an annual basis, all may be well. But during the spring and early summer, there will be large investments in accounts receivable and inventory, putting extreme pressure on the firm's cash flows. In this instance, the owner would want to forecast cash flows on a monthly basis—maybe even on a weekly basis.

© Victoria Brassey/Shutterstock.com

In the next two sections, we use D&R Products, Inc., to illustrate how to forecast cash flows. First, we prepare pro forma statements of annual cash flows. Then, we illustrate how to prepare a monthly cash budget.

11-4a Pro Forma Statement of Cash Flows

The pro forma income statement and balance sheets for D&R Products, Inc., that we prepared earlier are now used to prepare a pro forma statement of cash flows (see Exhibit 11.5). Pay particular attention to cash flows from operating activities, cash flows from investing activities, and cash flows from financing activities, which are shown in boxes in the exhibit. Looking at these numbers, we can see the following:

1. In the first year, the business is expected to have negative cash flows from operations of $86,500 and will be investing $50,000 in the building and equipment. To cover these negative cash flows, Allen expects to raise $146,500 in financing from his personal investment of $110,000, $9,500 on the line of credit from the bank, and $27,000 from the mortgage on the building after making the annual $3,000 payment on the principal. The firm would then end the year with $10,000 in cash. (Note that the change in the pro forma balance sheet for year 1 is the same as the year-end balance shown in the balance sheet, since the business did not exist in the prior year. The balance at the beginning of year 1 would have been zero.)

2. In the second year, the firm's cash flow operations are expected to be $5,625. (Notice that while the business is expected to have $5,625 in cash flows from operations, Allen anticipates having profits of $30,375. Remember, *cash flows and profits are not the same thing.*) Moreover, there are no plans to invest in fixed assets in the second year. Given his underlying assumptions, Allen would need to increase the line of credit (short-term debt) from the bank from $9,500 in year 1 to $11,875 in year 2, for an increase of $2,375, and pay $3,000 on the mortgage. The balance result of all the cash flows would be a $5,000 increase in cash, for an ending cash balance of $15,000.

11.5 Pro Forma Cash Flow Statements for D&R Products, Inc.

	Year 1		Year 2	Sources of Information
Operating activities:				
Net profits		($ 33,000)	$ 30,375	Pro forma
Depreciation		4,000	4,000	income
Increase in accounts receivable (cash outflow)		($ 25,000)	($ 12,500)	statement
Increase in inventory (cash outflow)	($62,500)		($31,250)	
Increase in accounts payable (cash inflow)	20,000		10,000	
Cash payments for inventory (cash outflow)		($ 42,500)	($ 21,250)	
Increase in accrued expenses (cash inflow)		10,000	5,000	
Cash flows from operations		**($ 86,500)**	**$ 5,625**	Changes in
Investing activities:				projected bal-
				ance sheets
Increase in gross fixed assets (cash outflow)		($ 50,000)	$ 0	from founding
Cash flows from investing		**($ 50,000)**	**$ 0**	of business to
				year 1 and from
				year 1 to year 2
Financing activities:				
Increase in short-term line of credit		$ 9,500	$ 2,375	
Increase (decrease) in mortgage		27,000	(3,000)	
Increase in stock		110,000	0	
Cash flows from financing		**$146,500**	**($ 625)**	
Increase (decrease) in cash		$ 10,000	$ 5,000	
Beginning cash		$ 0	$ 10,000	
Ending cash (as shown in the balance sheets)		**$ 10,000**	**$15,000**	

© Cengage Learning

Allen now has a good estimate of the cash flows for each year as a whole and an idea of what contributes to the cash inflows and outflows. But there is also a need to track the firm's cash flows for a shorter time period, usually on a monthly basis.

11-4b The Cash Budget

The **cash budget** is one of the primary tools that a small business owner can use to manage cash flows. The budget is concerned specifically with dollars both received and paid out. *No single planning document is more important in the life of a small company, either for avoiding cash flow problems when cash runs short or for anticipating short-term investment opportunities if excess cash becomes available.*

To help you understand the process of preparing a cash budget, let's continue with the example of D&R Products. In the previous section, we prepared a pro forma statement of cash flows for the year. But Allen realizes that he also needs to have a sense of the timing of the cash flows throughout the year, so he has decided to prepare a monthly cash budget for the first year of operations. We will look at only the first three months of the cash budget to understand how it was prepared. While Allen predicts that the firm will have $250,000 in annual sales in the first year, his sales projections for the first three months are as follows:

January	$4,000
February	6,000
March	9,000

In addition, the following assumptions will be made:

cash budget
A listing of cash receipts and cash disbursements, usually for a relatively short time period, such as a week or a month.

1. Of the firm's sales dollars, 40 percent are collected the month of the sale, 30 percent one month after the sale, and the remaining 30 percent two months after the sale.

2. Inventory will be purchased one month in advance of the expected sale and will be paid for in the month in which it is sold.

3. Inventory purchases will equal 60 percent of projected sales for the next month's sales.

4. The firm will spend $3,000 each month for advertising.

5. Salaries and utilities for the first three months are estimated as follows:

	Salaries	Utilities
January	$5,000	$150
February	6,000	$200
March	6,000	$200

6. Allen will be investing $110,000 in the business from his personal savings.

7. The firm will be investing $10,000 for needed equipment and $40,000 for the purchase of a building, for a total investment of $50,000. However, the bank has agreed to finance $30,000 of the building purchase price in the form of a mortgage.

Based on this information, Allen has prepared a monthly cash budget for the three-month period ending March 31. Exhibit 11.6 shows the results of his computations, which involve the steps shown on the next page:

EXHIBIT 11.6 Three-Month Cash Budget for D&R Product, Inc., for January–March

Assumptions:
Anticipated sales collections:
In the month of sale	40%	
1 month later	30%	
2 months later	30%	

	December	January	February	March
Monthly sales	$ 0	$4,000	$6,000	$9,000
Inventory purchases on credit	$2,400	$3,600	$5,400	

		December	January	February	March
Monthly sales		$0	*$ 4,000	$ 6,000	$ 9,000
Cash receipts					
Step 1:	Collection of sales				
	In month of sale		$ 1,600	$ 2,400	$ 3,600
	1 month later			1,200	1,800
	2 months later				1,200
	Total cash receipts		$ 1,600	$ 3,600	$ 6,600
Step 2:	**Operating cash disbursements**				
Step 2a:	Payments on inventory purchases		$ 2,400	$ 3,600	$ 5,400
	Advertising		3,000	3,000	3,000
Step 2b:	Wages and salaries		5,000	6,000	6,000
	Utilities		150	200	200
	Total operating cash disbursements		$10,550	$12,800	$14,600
Step 3:	**Cash flows from operations**		($8,950)	($9,200)	($8,000)
Step 4:	Allen's personal investment		110,000		
Step 5:	Purchase of equipment and building		(50,000)		
Step 6:	Mortgage (loan from the bank to buy the building)		30,000		
Step 7:	Beginning cash balance		0	81,050	71,850
Step 8:	**Ending cash balance**		$81,050	$71,850	$63,850

*For example, January sales of $4,000 are collected as follows: (40%) $1,600 in January, (30%) $1,200 in February, (30%) $1,200 in March.

Step 1. Determine the amount of collections each month, based on the projected sales patterns just provided.

Step 2. Estimate the amount and timing of the following cash disbursements:

a. Inventory purchases and payments. The amount of the purchases is shown in the boxed area at the top of the table. However, the actual payment for inventory will not be made until one month later.

b. Advertising, wages and salaries, and utilities are paid in the month incurred.

Step 3. Calculate the *cash flows from operating activities*, which equals the cash receipts (collections from sales) less cash disbursements.

Step 4. Recognize the $110,000 investment in the business by Allen.

Step 5. Note the $50,000 investment in the building and equipment.

Step 6. Show the $30,000 loan from the bank to help pay for the building.

Step 7. Determine the beginning-of-month cash balance (ending cash balance from the prior month).

Step 8. Compute the end-of-month cash balance.

Based on the cash budget, Allen now has a sense of what to expect for the first three months of operations, which could not be seen from the annual pro forma statement of cash flows presented in Exhibit 11.5. He knows now that he will be "burning" somewhere between $8,000 and $9,200 of cash per month for the first three months of operations. Given that he will have almost $64,000 in cash remaining at the end of March, he will run out of cash in about seven or eight months if the cash flows from operations continue to be negative $8,000 or $9,000 each month. At that time, he will have to start borrowing on the bank line of credit.

© Minerva Studio/Shutterstock.com

One final thought about the cash budget. Once it has been prepared, an entrepreneur has to decide how to use it. Entrepreneurship is about seeking opportunities, and there is a real danger that a cash budget may lead to inflexibility. A strict cost-containment strategy in order to "make the budget" can discourage managers from being creative and shifting their approach when it makes sense to do so. An inflexible budget can lead to a "use it or lose it" mentality, where managers spend remaining budgeted money at year's end so that allocations will not be cut the following year. Such a mindset negatively impacts the entrepreneurial process.

11-5 USE GOOD JUDGMENT WHEN FORECASTING

LO 11-5

Provide some suggestions for effective financial forecasting.

The forecasting process requires an entrepreneur to exercise good judgment in planning, particularly when the planning is providing the basis for raising capital. The overall approach to forecasting is straightforward—entrepreneurs make assumptions and, based on these assumptions, determine financing requirements. But entrepreneurs may be tempted to overstate their expectations in order to acquire much needed financing. So how do you get it right? Here are some practical suggestions about making financial forecasts:[8]

1. *Develop realistic sales projections.* Entrepreneurs often think they can accomplish more than they actually are able to, especially when it comes to forecasting future sales. When graphed, their sales projections for a new venture often resemble a hockey stick—the sales numbers are flat or rise slightly at first (like the blade of a hockey stick) and then soar upward (like a hockey stick's handle). Such projections are always suspect—only the most astonishing changes in a business or market can justify such a sudden, rocket-like performance.

2. *Build projections from clear assumptions about marketing and pricing plans.* Don't be vague, and don't guess. Spell out the kinds of marketing you plan to do—for example, state specifically how many customers you expect to attract.

3. *Do not use unrealistic profit margins.* Projections are immediately suspect if profit margins (profits ÷ sales) or expenses are significantly higher or lower than the average figures reported by firms in the industry with similar revenues and numbers of employees. In general, a new business should not expect to exceed the industry average in profit margins. Entrepreneurs frequently assume that as their company grows it will achieve economies of scale, and gross and operating profit margins will improve. In fact, as the business grows and increases its fixed costs, its operating profit margins are likely to suffer in the short run. If you insist in your projections that the economies can be achieved quickly, you will need to explain your position.

4. *Don't limit your projections to an income statement.* Entrepreneurs frequently resist providing a projected balance sheet and cash flow statement. They feel comfortable projecting sales and profits but do not like having to commit to assumptions about the sources and uses of capital needed to grow the business. Investors, however, want to see those assumptions in print, and they are particularly interested in the firm's cash flows—and you should be as well.

5. *Provide monthly data for the upcoming year and annual data for succeeding years.* Many entrepreneurs prepare projections using only monthly data or annual data for an entire three- or five-year period. Given the difficulty in forecasting accurately beyond a year, monthly data for the later years are not particularly believable. From year 2 on, annual projections are adequate.

6. *Avoid providing too much financial information.* Computer spreadsheets are extremely valuable in making projections and showing how different assumptions affect the firm's financials. But do not be tempted to overuse this tool. Instead, limit your projections to two scenarios: the most-likely scenario (base case) and the break-even scenario. The base case should show what you realistically expect the business to do; the break-even case should show what level of sales is required to break even.

7. *Be certain that the numbers reconcile—and not by simply plugging in a figure.* All too often, entrepreneurs plug a figure into equity to make things work out. While everyone makes mistakes, that's one you want to avoid because it can result in a loss of credibility.

8. *Follow the plan.* After you have prepared the pro forma financial statements, check them against actual results at least once a month, and modify your projections as needed.

These suggestions, if followed, will help you avoid overpromising and underdelivering. Given the nature of starting a business, entrepreneurs at times simply have to have faith that they will be able to deliver on what they promise, even though it may not be clear exactly how this will be accomplished. Risk is part of the equation, and often things will not go as planned. But integrity requires you to honor your commitments, and that cannot be done if you have made unrealistic projections about what you can accomplish.

The information on financial planning provided in this chapter and in Chapter 10 will serve as a foundation for the examination of an entrepreneur's search for specific sources of financing in Chapter 12.

CLOSED LOOKING BACK

11-1. Describe the purpose of financial forecasting.

- The purpose of pro forma financial statements is to determine (1) future profitability based on projected sales levels and expected sales–expense relationships, (2) how much and what type of financing will be needed, and (3) whether the firm will have adequate cash flows.
- Accurate financial forecasting is important not only for ensuring that a firm has the resources it needs to grow, but also for managing growth.

11-2. Develop a pro forma income statement to forecast a new venture's profitability.

- It is important for an entrepreneur to understand the drivers of a firm's profits, especially the specific ways in which each factor applies to a unique firm.
- A firm's net profit is dependent on (1) amount of sales, (2) cost of goods sold, (3) operating expenses, (4) interest expense, and (5) taxes.
- In a real-world situation, an entrepreneur should project the profits of a company for at least three years into the future.

11-3. Determine a company's asset and financing requirements using a pro forma balance sheet.

- The amount and type of assets required for a venture will vary according to the nature of the business. However, all firms need to understand how much working capital and fixed assets will be required.
- An entrepreneur should try to bootstrap as many resources as possible in order to minimize a firm's investment while simultaneously ensuring adequate resources.

- Funding for a new venture should cover asset requirements and also the personal living expenses of the owner.
- A direct relationship exists between sales growth and asset needs: As sales increase, more assets are required. For every dollar of assets needed, there must be a corresponding dollar of financing.
- A firm's financing is determined by considering its (1) asset requirements, (2) need to maintain adequate liquidity, (3) debt ratio, (4) sources of spontaneous debt financing, and (5) owners' equity.

11-4. Forecast a firm's cash flows.

- Forecasting cash flows can be accomplished in two ways: (1) by preparing a pro forma statement of cash flows, and/or (2) by developing a cash budget. Ideally, an entrepreneur would do both.
- A firm's cash flows involve three activities: operating, investing, and financing activities.
- A cash budget is concerned specifically with dollars both received and paid out.
- A cash budget should provide boundaries but should not limit creativity and flexibility. The entrepreneurial process is all about seizing opportunity.

11-5. Provide some suggestions for effective financial forecasting.

- Develop realistic sales projections, and build projections from clear assumptions about marketing and pricing plans.
- Do not use unrealistic profit margins. In general, new businesses do not exceed industry average profit margins in their first years.
- Do not limit your projections to an income statement. Investors want to see pro forma balance sheets and a cash flow statement as well.
- Provide monthly data for the upcoming year and annual data for succeeding years.
- Avoid providing too much financial information. Limit projections to two scenarios: the most-likely scenario (base case) and the break-even scenario.
- Be certain that the numbers reconcile.
- Follow the plan, and measure how actual performance compares with forecasted performance so that modifications to future forecasts will be more accurate.

Key Terms

cash budget p. 306

line of credit p. 301

net working capital p. 296

pro forma financial statements p. 292

percentage-of-sales technique p. 298

spontaneous debt financing p. 301

Discussion Questions

1. What determines a company's profitability?

2. Discuss how asset and financing requirements might differ among a retail business, a service company, and an information system–based venture.

3. Why is it important to consider an entrepreneur's personal finances when conducting the short- and long-term financial forecasts of a firm?

4. Describe the process for estimating the amount of assets required for a new venture.

5. What are some of the basic principles that govern the financing of a firm? Why are they important?

6. How are a startup's financing requirements estimated?

7. Describe two ways for projecting a venture's cash flows, and discuss when each is appropriate to use.

8. When forecasting cash flows, why is it important to consider the time period covered by the forecast? What issues should the entrepreneur consider when doing financial forecasts?

9. Why is it important for an entrepreneur not only to create a cash budget, but also to decide how it will be used within the firm?

10. Choose three of the practical suggestions for making financial forecasts. Discuss their importance, as well as the potential consequences of ignoring these suggestions.

You Make the Call

Situation 1

D&R Products, Inc., used as an example in this chapter, is an actual firm (although some of the facts were changed to maintain confidentiality). David Allen bought the firm from its founding owners and moved its operations to his hometown. Although he has estimated the firm's asset needs and financing requirements, he cannot be certain that these projections will be realized. The figures merely represent the most-likely case. Allen also made some projections that he considers to be the worst-case and best-case sales and profit figures. If things do not go well, the firm might have sales of only $200,000 in its first year. However, if the potential of the business is realized, Allen believes that sales could be as high as $325,000. If he needs any additional financing beyond the existing line of credit, he could conceivably borrow another $5,000 in short-term debt from the bank by pledging some personal investments. Any additional financing would need to come from Allen himself, thereby increasing his equity stake in the business.

Question If all of D&R Products' other relationships hold, how will Allen's worst-case and best-case projections affect the income statement and balance sheet in the first year? [(To help you in your analysis, D&R Product's pro forma statements

as presented in Exhibits 11.1, 11.3, and 11.4 are available at www.cengagebrain.com (select the Longenecker text)].

Situation 2

Philip Spencer of the Spencer Corporation wants you to forecast the firm's financing needs over the fourth quarter (October through December). He has made the following observations relative to planned cash receipts and disbursements:

- Interest on a $75,000 bank note (principal due next March) at an 8 percent annual rate is payable in December for the three-month period just ended.

- The firm follows a policy of paying no cash dividends.

- Actual historical and future predicted sales are as follows:

Historical Sales		Predicted Sales	
August	$150,000	October	$200,000
September	175,000	November	220,000
		December	180,000
		January	200,000

- The firm has a monthly rental expense of $5,000.
- Wages and salaries for the coming months are estimated at $25,000 per month.
- Of the firm's sales, 25 percent is collected in the month of the sale, 35 percent one month after the sale, and the remaining 40 percent two months after the sale.
- Merchandise is purchased one month before the sales month and is paid for in the month it is sold. Purchases equal 75 percent of sales.
- Tax prepayments are made quarterly, with a prepayment of $10,000 in October based on earnings for the quarter ended September 30.
- Utility costs for the firm average 3 percent of sales and are paid in the month they are incurred.
- Depreciation expense is $20,000 annually.

Question 1 Prepare a monthly cash budget for the three-month period ending in December.

Question 2 If the firm's beginning cash balance for the budget period is $7,000, and this is its desired minimum balance, determine when and how much the firm will need to borrow during the budget period. The firm has a $50,000 line of credit with its bank, with interest (10 percent annual rate) paid monthly. For example, interest on a loan taken out at the end of September would be paid at the end of October and every month thereafter as long as the loan was outstanding.

Situation 3

Julia Chase is in the process of starting a new business and wants to forecast the first year's income statement and balance sheet. She has made a number of assumptions, which are shown below:

a. Chase has projected the firm's sales will be $1 million in the first year.

b. She believes that the operating and gross profit margins will be 20 percent and 50 percent, respectively.

c. For working capital, Chase has estimated the following:
   Accounts receivable as a percentage of sales: 12%
   Inventory as a percentage of sales: 15%
   Accounts payable as a percentage of sales: 7%
   Accruals as a percentage of sales: 5%

d. A bank has agreed to loan her $300,000, consisting of $100,000 in short-term debt and $200,000 in long-term debt. Both loans will have an 8 percent interest rate.

e. The firm's tax rate will be 30 percent.

f. Chase will need to purchase $350,000 in plant and equipment.

Chase will provide any other financing needed.

Question 1 Based on Chase's assumptions, prepare a pro forma income statement and balance sheet.

Question 2 If her estimates are correct, what will be the firm's current ratio and debt ratio? Explain the meaning of these ratios.

Small Business & Entrepreneurship Resource Center

The Small Business & Entrepreneurship Resource Center offers complete small business management resources through a comprehensive database that covers all major areas of starting, operating, and maintaining a business from financing, management, marketing, accounting, taxes, and more. Go to www.cengagebrain.com and select the Longenecker text for more information on how to access this material.

1. Many firms face financial difficulties or even bankruptcy while earning a continuously larger income. One reason for this is the failure to adequately budget future operating expenses and to forecast future cash needs. The cyclical nature of many businesses causes cash inflows and outflows to be inconveniently timed. For example, before sales increase, production must increase, but increased production requires increased cash expenditures. Because of this problem, expanding businesses are often cash starved. According to this article, how can forecasting financial needs lead to effective management?

2. Budgeting for cash is a critical part of safeguarding a firm's financial future. Fortunately, many liquidity problems can be avoided through effective planning. The cash budget is one of the primary tools that a small business owner can use to manage cash flows. After reading this article, explain how cash budgets enable management to foresee when cash problems are likely to arise and to arrange for funds to meet the cash requirements of these periods.

Source: Brian Carpenter and Laura Ellis, "Budgeting for the Future: Why Firms Need to Forecast and Budget Their Cash Flows," *The National Public Accountant,* Vol. 45, No. 6 (August 2000), p. 14.

Ashley Palmer Clothing Inc. (P. 664)

Ashley Palmer Clothing, Inc. designs apparel for the modern woman's shape rather than using a standardized size as traditionally done. The firm was launched in June 2009 by Ashley Jantz and Amanda Palmer, both graduates of a liberal arts college in Boston, followed by graduate studies in business. The firm has experienced significant growth over the past four years. But Jantz and Palmer are expecting the growth rate to double in 2014. The case is aimed at forecasting the firm's financial requirements for 2014.

Alternative Cases for Chapter 11

Case 22, Pearson Air Conditioning & Service, p. 689

Video Case 10, B2B CFO [website only]

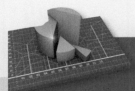

Business Plan

LAYING THE FOUNDATION

As part of laying the foundation to prepare your own business plan, you will need to develop the following:

1. Historical financial statements (if applicable) and three to five years of pro forma financial statements, including balance sheets, income statements, and statements of cash flows.

2. Monthly cash budgets for the first year and quarterly cash budgets for the second year.

3. Profit and cash flow break-even analysis. (See Chapter 16 for an explanation of break-even analysis.)

4. Financial resources required now and in the future, with details on the intended use of funds being requested.

5. Underlying assumptions for all pro forma statements.

6. Current and planned investments by the owners and other investors.

Endnotes

1. Rhonda Abrams, "How Can I Make Financial Projections in My Business Plan When I Have No Solid Numbers?" *Inc.*, September 2000, www.inc.com/articles/2000/09/20226.html, accessed December 15, 2012.

2. This example is based on an actual situation; however, the name of the founder has been changed, as have some of the numbers.

3. Investors also look to financial projections to determine the sales level necessary for the firm to break even. A firm's break-even point, while important from a financial perspective, is also important for pricing its products or services. The issue of pricing and the break-even point are discussed in Chapter 16.

4. In Chapter 10, we used the *current ratio* to measure a company's ability to meet maturing obligations, which was measured as current assets *divided* by current liabilities. Thus, the current ratio is a relative measure (current assets *relative* to current liabilities), which allows us to compare firms of different sizes. *Net working capital* (current assets *less* current liabilities) is an *absolute* dollar measure of liquidity used by many bankers.

5. Personal conversation with Dan Cassidy September 6, 2009.

6. Personal communication with Cecilia Levine, October 15, 2011.

7. As told by Ed Bonneau, October 4, 2012.

8. Information in this section was taken from Linda Elkins, "Real Numbers Don't Deceive," *Nation's Business*, Vol. 85, No. 3 (March 1997), pp. 51–52; and Paul Broni, "Persuasive Projections," *Inc.*, Vol. 22, No. 4 (April 2000), pp. 183–184.

CHAPTER 12

© Dasha Petrenko/Shutterstock.com

A Firm's Sources of Financing

After studying this chapter, you should be able to …

12-1. Describe how a firm's characteristics affect its available financing sources.

12-2. Evaluate the choice between debt financing and equity financing.

12-3. Identify the typical sources of financing used at the outset of a new venture.

12-4. Discuss the basic process for acquiring and structuring a bank loan.

12-5. Explain how business relationships can be used to finance a small firm.

12-6. Describe the two types of private equity investors who offer financing to small firms.

12-7. Distinguish among the different government loan programs available to small companies.

12-8. Explain when large companies and public stock offerings can be sources of financing.

12-9. Describe how crowdfunding can be used by some small businesses to raise capital.

OPEN
LOOKING
AHEAD

The easiest way to secure equity financing is to have a great idea. It sounds simple but is difficult to execute. For one thing, investors look for business ideas that can create barriers of entry to prevent competitors from easily entering the market. A venture capitalist explains:

"We like really strong barriers to entry, like unique intellectual property or complexity with the operation, so that it's not very likely that 10 other competitors are going to jump into the market and eat their lunch."

4moms, a producer of innovative juvenile products, is a business that has done just that. The company is recognized for its sleek easy-to-use baby stroller, washing tub, play crib, and infant seat. In 2003, founders Rob Daley and Henry Thorne came up with an idea for a digital shower controller that received a negative reaction from concerned moms. This failure

In the Spotlight
4moms
www.4moms.com

led them to pursue their now tremendously successful venture, 4moms, which has grown 200–400 percent each year.

Despite the company's strong revenue growth, Daley and Thorne knew they needed to look for external sources of financing in order to position the company for long-term growth. This included

© AP Photos/Roberto Pfeil/dapd

investments in more research and development and a larger supply chain. Daley recalls, "We [had] 13 wish-list projects, but we could only [actively] develop five of them,"

In August 2012, 4moms hit it big, raising $20 million in funding from Bain Capital. The funding was to provide the company with resources for product development. The Bain investment team was also helping 4moms find someone to lead the marketing department. Scott Friend, managing director of Bain Capital Ventures, noted:

> We've been long-time observers of the juvenile product category....The team at 4moms ... built the first products in decades that truly disrupt[ed] this industry, combining a rare blend of Apple-like design brilliance with world-leading robotics and engineering expertise from Carnegie Mellon. The results are products like nothing the world has ever seen.

Despite the strength of the product, 4moms spent considerable time and effort developing the business and laying the groundwork to seal the deal with the right investors. Thorn explains:

> We targeted them.... [We had been] looking at VC firms of their size for years but hadn't achieved enough revenue to merit considering that magnitude of VC.... We were planning on raising money, and we alerted the VC groups about it. We'd be launching our new product, and we knew our revenue would be much larger and would merit the interest of investors the size of Bain. But Bain did a huge amount of research on us and diligence in our company, and we were so impressed with them and they were so impressed with us that we decided to go and do a deal.

Sources: Based on Gwen Moran, "How a New Take on the Stroller Snagged $20 Million in Funding," Inc.com, January 14, 2013, http://www.entrepreneur.com /article/225016, accessed February 15, 2013; "4moms® Announces $20M in Funding with Bain Capital Ventures," PR Newswire, August 9, 2012, www .prnewswire.com/news-releases/4moms-announces-20m-in-funding-with-bain -capital-ventures-165563796.html, accessed February 15, 2013; and "Cash Infusion Primes the Product Pump at 4moms," *The Business Journals*, August 24, 2012, www .bizjournals.com/pittsburgh/print-edition/2012/08/24/cash-infusion-primes -product-pump-4moms.html?page=all, accessed February 15, 2013.

In Chapter 11, we addressed *how much* financing is needed and *what types* of financing are available for small businesses. In this chapter, we discuss two sources of financing: spontaneous debt financing and external financing.

Spontaneous debt financing, such as accounts payable and accruals, increase in response to increases in sales. For example, as a firm's sales grow, it purchases more inventory and suppliers extend more credit, which increases accounts payable—a primary source of debt for many small businesses that requires no interest payments if paid on time. *External financing* comes from outside lenders and investors. Lenders (such as bankers) provide debt capital, and investors (such as common stockholders, partners, or sole proprietors) provide equity financing.

First, let's consider how a firm's characteristics affect the way it will be financed. An understanding of this core issue is critical to identifying appropriate sources of financing.

12-1 FIRM CHARACTERISTICS AND SOURCES OF FINANCING

At times, financing a business can weigh heavily on small business owners. In recent years, acquiring needed financing became increasingly difficult for small firms as financial institutions struggled and the economy faltered. But even when the economy improved, aspiring entrepreneurs needed persistence and discipline to get a business off and running.

Four basic firm characteristics significantly affect how a business is financed: (1) the firm's economic potential, (2) the size and maturity of the company, (3) the nature of its assets, and (4) the personal preferences of the owners with respect to the trade-offs between debt and equity. Without understanding how these characteristics come into play in financing your business, you stand little chance of getting the necessary financing (see Exhibit 12.1).

LO
12-1

Describe how a firm's characteristics affect its available financing sources.

12.1 Firm Characteristics and Available Sources of Financing

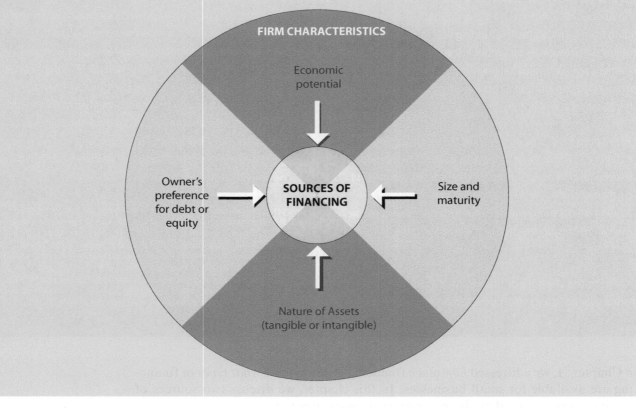

FIRM CHARACTERISTICS

Economic potential

Owner's preference for debt or equity

SOURCES OF FINANCING

Size and maturity

Nature of Assets
(tangible or intangible)

12-1a Firm's Economic Potential

A firm with potential for high growth and large profits has more possible sources of financing than does a firm that provides a good lifestyle for the owner but little in the way of returns to investors. Only firms with a high rate of return on investment create value for the investor. In fact, most investors in startup companies focus on firms that offer potentially high returns within a 5- to 10-year period. Clearly, a company that provides a comfortable lifestyle for its owner but insufficient profits to attract outside investors will find its options for alternative sources of financing limited.

START UP

ACTION

Before approaching an investor, (1) clean up your personal credit, (2) identify your management team, (3) write an effective business plan, (4) decide what type of outside financing you need, and (5) do careful research on potential investors.

12-1b Company Size and Maturity

Larger and older firms have access to bank credit that may not be available to younger and smaller companies. Also, smaller firms tend to rely more on personal loans and credit cards for financing. In the early years of a business, most entrepreneurs bootstrap their financing—that is, they depend on their own initiative to come up with the necessary capital. Only after the business has an established track record will most bankers and other financial institutions be willing to provide financing.

You have probably read about venture capitalists who helped finance such firms as Yahoo, eBay, and Apple. But even venture capitalists limit how much they will invest in startup companies. Many such investors believe the additional risk associated with startups is too great relative to the returns they expect to receive. On average, about three-fourths of a venture capitalist's investments are in later-stage businesses—only a few focus heavily on startups. Similarly, bankers demand evidence that the business will be able to repay a loan—and that evidence usually must be based on what the firm has done in the past and not what the owner says it will achieve in the future. So, a firm's life-cycle position is a critical factor in raising capital.

12-1c Nature of Firm's Assets

A banker specifically considers two types of assets when evaluating a firm for a loan: tangible assets and intangible assets. Tangible assets, which can be seen and touched, include inventory, equipment, and buildings. The cost of these assets appears on the firm's balance sheet, which the banker receives as part of the firm's financial statements. Tangible assets are great collateral when a firm is requesting a bank loan. While intangible assets, such as goodwill or past investments in research and development, is important to an investor, they have little value as collateral when it comes to getting a loans a result, companies with substantial tangible assets have a much easier time borrowing money than do companies with intangible assets.

12-1d Owner Preferences for Debt or Equity

The owner of a company faces the question "Should I finance with debt or equity, or some mix of the two?" The answer depends, in part, on his or her personal preference. The ultimate choice between debt and equity involves certain trade-offs, which will be explained in the next section.

12-2 DEBT OR EQUITY FINANCING?

Most providers of financial capital specialize in *either* debt *or* equity financing. Furthermore, the choice between debt and equity financing must be made early in a firm's life cycle and may have long-term financial consequences. To make an informed decision, a small business owner needs to recognize and understand the trade-offs between debt and equity with regard to potential profitability, financial risk, and voting control (see Exhibit 12.2). Let's consider each of these trade-offs in turn.

LO
12-2

Evaluate the choice between debt financing and equity financing.

12-2a Potential Profitability

Anyone who owns a business wants it to be profitable. Of course, profits can be measured as a dollar amount, such as $500,000, or as a percentage return on the investment. But the really important question is how much profit the business makes relative to the size of the investment. In other words, the owner is primarily interested in the rate of return on the investment. Making $500,000 in profits may sound great, but not if the owner must invest $50 million to earn it. It would be better to purchase a certificate of deposit that earned, say, 2 percent. Any rate over 1 percent would provide income greater than $500,000.

To see how the choice between debt and equity affects potential profitability, consider the Daley Company, a new firm that's still in the process of raising needed capital.

- The owners have already invested $100,000 of their own money in the new business. To complete the financing, they need another $100,000.
- They are considering one of two options for raising the additional $100,000: (1) investors who would provide $100,000 for a 30 percent share of the

12.2 Trade-Offs Between Debt and Equity

High Equity and Low Debt Financing

EQUITY

DEBT

Results:
Voting Control: Owners must share control with other equity investors who buy the stock or make a large investment.
Financial Risk: Lower
Potential Profitability: Lower potential return on investment for the owners

High Debt and Low Equity Financing

DEBT

EQUITY

Results:
Voting Control: Owners maintain control without having to make a large investment.
Financial Risk: Higher
Potential Profitability: Higher potential return on investment for the owners

firm's outstanding stock, or (2) a bank that would lend the money at an interest rate of 8 percent, so the interest expense each year would be $8,000 = (0.08 × $100,000).

- The firm's operating profits (earnings before interest and taxes) are expected to be $28,000 based on the following forecast:

Sales	$150,000
Cost of goods sold	80,000
Gross profit	$ 70,000
Operating expenses	42,000
Operating profits	$ 28,000

- With the additional $100,000 in financing, the firm's total assets would be $200,000 ($100,000 original equity plus $100,000 in additional financing).

- Based on the projected operating profits of $28,000 and total assets of $200,000, the firm expects to earn a 14 percent *return on assets*, computed as follows.

$$\text{Return on assets} = \frac{\text{operating profits}}{\text{total assets}} = \frac{\$28,000}{\$200,000} = 0.14 = 14\%$$

If the firm raises the additional $100,000 in equity, its balance sheet will appear as follows:

| Total assets | $200,000 |

Debt	$ 0
Equity (founders' and new investors')	200,000
Total debt and equity	$200,000

But if the firm instead borrows $100,000, the balance sheet will look like this:

| Total assets | $200,000 |

Debt (8% interest rate)	$100,000
Equity (founders')	100,000
Total debt and equity	$200,000

If we assume no taxes (just to keep matters simple), we can use the above information to project the firm's net profits when the additional $100,000 is financed by either equity or debt:

	Equity	**Debt**
Operating profits	$28,000	$28,000
Interest expense	0	(8,000) = (0.08 × $100,000)
Net profits	$28,000	$20,000

From these computations, we see that net profits are greater if the firm finances with equity ($28,000 in net profits) than with debt ($20,000 in net profits). But the owners would have to invest *twice* as much money ($200,000 rather than $100,000) to avoid the $8,000 interest expense and get the higher net profits.

Should owners always finance with equity to get higher net profits? Not necessarily. The return on the owners' investment, or *return on equity*, is a better measure of performance than the absolute dollar amount of net profits.

$$\text{Return on equity} = \frac{\text{Net profits}}{\text{Total owners' equity}}$$

So when the firm uses *all* equity financing, the return on equity is 14 percent, computed as follows:

$$\text{Return on equity} = \frac{\text{Net profits}}{\text{Total owners' equity}} = \frac{\$28,000}{\$200,000} = 0.14 = 14\%$$

But if the additional financing comes from debt, leading to interest expense of $8,000 and equity investment of only $100,000, the rate of return on equity is 20 percent, calculated as follows:

$$\text{Return on equity} = \frac{\text{Net profits}}{\text{Total owners' equity}} = \frac{\$20,000}{\$100,000} = 0.20 = 20\%$$

Thus, Daley's return on equity is higher if half of the firm's financing comes from equity and half from debt. By using only equity, Daley's owners will earn $0.14 for every $1 of equity invested. By using debt, they will earn $0.20 for every $1 of equity invested. So, in terms of a rate of return on their investment, Daley's owners get a better return by borrowing money at 8 percent interest than by using equity financing. That makes sense, because the firm is earning 14 percent on its assets but only paying

12.3 Debt Versus Equity at the Daley Company

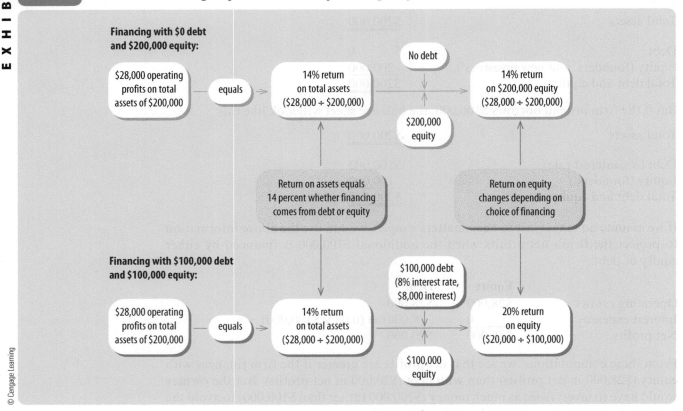

Financing with $0 debt and $200,000 equity:

$28,000 operating profits on total assets of $200,000 → equals → 14% return on total assets ($28,000 ÷ $200,000)

No debt

$200,000 equity

14% return on $200,000 equity ($28,000 ÷ $200,000)

Return on assets equals 14 percent whether financing comes from debt or equity

Return on equity changes depending on choice of financing

Financing with $100,000 debt and $100,000 equity:

$28,000 operating profits on total assets of $200,000 → equals → 14% return on total assets ($28,000 ÷ $200,000)

$100,000 debt (8% interest rate, $8,000 interest)

$100,000 equity

20% return on equity ($20,000 ÷ $100,000)

© Cengage Learning

creditors at an 8 percent rate. Daley's owners benefit from the difference. These relationships are shown in Exhibit 12.3.

As a general rule, *as long as a firm's rate of return on its assets (operating profits ÷ total assets) is greater than the cost of the debt (interest rate), the owners' rate of return on equity will increase as the firm uses more debt.*

12-2b Financial Risk

If debt is so beneficial in terms of producing a higher rate of return for the owners, why shouldn't Daley's owners use as much debt as possible—even 100 percent debt—if they can? Then the rate of return on the owners' equity investment would be even higher—unlimited, in fact, if the owners did not have to invest any money.

That's the good news. The bad news: *Debt is risky.* If the firm fails to earn profits, creditors still insist on being repaid, regardless of the firm's actual performance. In extreme cases, creditors can force firms into bankruptcy if they fail to honor their financial obligations. Equity, on the other hand, is less demanding. If a firm is not profitable, an equity investor must accept the disappointing results and hope for better results next year. Equity investors cannot demand more than what is earned.

Another way to view the negative side of debt is to contemplate what happens to the return on equity if a business has a bad year. Suppose that instead of earning 14 percent on its assets, or $28,000 in operating profits, the Daley Company earns a mere $2,000—only 1 percent on its assets of $200,000. The return on equity would again depend on whether the firm used debt or equity to finance the second $100,000 investment in the company. The results would be as follows:

	Equity	**Debt**
Operating profits	$2,000	$2,000
Interest expense	0	(8,000) = (0.08 × $100,000)
Net profits	$2,000	($6,000)

If the added financing came in the form of equity, the return on equity would be a disappointing 1 percent:

$$\text{Return on equity} = \frac{\text{Net profits}}{\text{Total owners' equity}} = \frac{\$2,000}{\$200,000} = 0.01 = 1\%$$

But if debt were used, the return on equity would be a painful negative 6 percent:

$$\text{Return on equity} = \frac{\text{Net profits}}{\text{Total owners' equity}} = \frac{-\$6,000}{\$100,000} = 0.06 = -6\%$$

If only 1 percent is earned on the assets, the owners would be better off if they financed solely with equity. Thus, debt is a double-edged sword. If debt financing is used and things go well, they will go *very* well for the owners. But if things go badly, they will go *very* badly for the owners. In short, debt financing makes business more risky.

12-2c Voting Control

The third issue in choosing between debt and equity is the degree of control retained by owners. Raising new capital through equity financing would mean giving up a part of the firm's ownership, and most owners of small firms resist giving up control to outsiders. They do not want to be accountable in any way to minority owners, much less take the chance of possibly losing control of the business. Out of an aversion to losing control, many small business owners choose to finance with debt rather than with equity. They realize that debt increases risk, but it also permits them to retain full ownership of the firm.

With an understanding of the basic trade-offs to be considered when choosing between debt and equity, let's now look at specific sources of financing. Where do small business owners go to find the money to finance their companies?

12-3 SOURCES OF EARLY FINANCING

When initially financing a small business, an owner will typically rely on personal savings and then seek financing from family and friends. If these sources are inadequate, the owner may in certain circumstances turn to more formal channels of financing, such as banks and outside investors.

Exhibit 12.4 gives an overview of the sources of financing of smaller companies. As indicated, some sources of financing—such as banks, business suppliers, asset-based lenders, and the government—are essentially limited to providing debt financing. Equity financing for most small business owners comes from personal savings and, in rare instances, from selling stock to the public. Other sources—including friends and family, other individual investors, venture capitalists (rarely), and large corporations—may provide either debt or equity financing, depending on the situation. Keep in mind that the use of these and other sources of funds are not limited to a startup's initial financing. Such sources will also be used to finance a firm's day-to-day operations and business expansions.

LO
12-3

Identify the typical sources of financing used at the outset of a new venture.

12.4 Sources of Funds

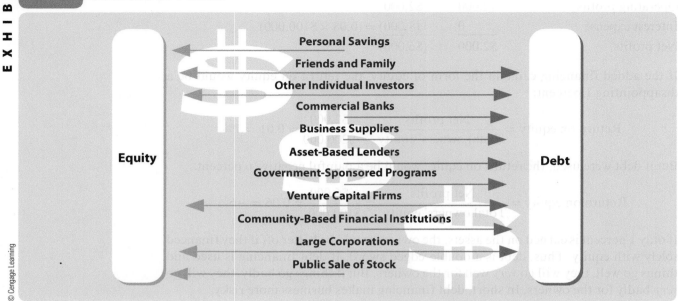

Equity		Debt
	Personal Savings	
	Friends and Family	
	Other Individual Investors	
	Commercial Banks	
	Business Suppliers	
	Asset-Based Lenders	
	Government-Sponsored Programs	
	Venture Capital Firms	
	Community-Based Financial Institutions	
	Large Corporations	
	Public Sale of Stock	

© Cengage Learning

© Anna Ts/Shutterstock.com

To gain insight into how startups are financed, consider the responses given by owners of Inc. 500 firms—the 500 fastest-growing, privately held firms in the United States—when they were asked about the financing sources they used to start their firms. Even for these high-growth firms, 70 percent of the startup financing came from the founders' personal savings, with another 10 percent coming from friends and family and 8 percent from bank loans. The remaining sources of financing were relatively insignificant in starting the firms. However, within five years the Inc. 500 entrepreneurs had, on average, raised 17 percent of their financing from private investors and 12 percent from venture capitalists.[1]

Let's now consider specific sources of financing for smaller companies, beginning with sources "close to home"—personal savings, friends and family, and credit cards.

12-3a Personal Savings

It is imperative for an entrepreneur to have some personal investment in the business, which typically comes from personal savings. Indeed, personal savings is by far the most common source of equity financing used to start a new business, which needs equity to allow for a margin of error. In its first few years, a firm can ill afford large fixed outlays for debt repayment. Also, a banker—or anyone else—is unlikely to loan money if the owner does not have his or her own money at risk.

A problem for many people who want to start a business is that they lack sufficient personal savings for this purpose. It can be very discouraging when the banker asks, "How much will you be investing in the business?" or "What do you have for collateral to secure the loan you want?" There is no easy solution to this problem, which is faced by an untold number of entrepreneurs. Nonetheless, many individuals who lack personal savings for a startup find ways to own their own companies without spending large amounts of money. And they figure out how to grow the business—perhaps by using the cash flows being generated from the firm's operations, by using other people's resources, or by finding a partner or friends and relatives who will provide the necessary financing.

12-3b Friends and Family

While personal savings serve as the *primary* source of financing for most small business startups, friends and family are a distant second. They provide almost 80 percent of startup capital beyond the entrepreneur's personal savings.[2] Entrepreneurs who acquire financing from friends and family are putting more than just their financial futures on the line—they're putting important personal relationships at risk, too. "It's the highest-risk money you'll ever get," says David Deeds, professor of entrepreneurship at The University of St. Thomas in Minneapolis. "The venture may succeed or fail, but either way, you still have to go to Thanksgiving dinner."[3]

At times, loans from friends or relatives may be the only available source of new financing. Such loans can often be obtained quickly, because they are based more on personal relationships than on financial analyses. *But you should accept money from a friend or relative only if that person will not be hurt financially to any significant extent if the entire amount is lost.* In other words, do not borrow money from your brother if he cannot afford the loss, much less from your grandmother's retirement savings.

Friends and relatives who provide business loans sometimes feel that they have the right to offer suggestions concerning the management of the business. And hard business times may strain the relationship. But if relatives and friends are the only available source of financing, the entrepreneur may have no other alternative. To minimize the chance of damaging important personal relationships, the entrepreneur should plan to repay such loans as soon as possible. In addition, any agreements should be put in writing. It is best to clarify expectations up front, rather than be disappointed or angry later.

Some good advice comes from James Hutcheson, president of Regeneration Partners, a consulting group that specializes in family-owned businesses. He says that entrepreneurs should approach their relatives only after they have secured investments or loans from unbiased outside sources.

> *Go and get matching funds. If you need $25,000, then first get $12,500 from others before asking your family for the rest. If you can't do it that way—and if you don't have your own skin in the game—then you need to think twice about why you're asking someone you love to give you money. I believe you should get others to back the idea as well, so a parent or relative doesn't feel as though the money is a gift but rather a worthwhile investment. It puts a higher level of accountability into the entire process.*[4]

So, borrow from friends and family very cautiously. Do it, if necessary, but do it carefully and meticulously clarify expectations.

12-3c Credit Cards

Prior to the 2008–2009 financial crisis, unsolicited offers of "free" credit cards arrived in the mail almost daily for many individuals. Using credit cards to help finance a small business became increasingly common among entrepreneurs. It has been estimated that approximately half of all entrepreneurs have used credit cards at one time or another to finance a startup or business expansion. Even though credit card companies began experiencing huge losses in 2009, credit cards remain a significant source of financing for many small business owners.

For someone who cannot acquire traditional financing like a bank loan, credit card financing may be an option—not a great option, but a necessary one. The interest costs can become overwhelming over time, especially because of the tendency to borrow beyond the ability to repay. So it is essential that an entrepreneur using credit card financing be extremely self-disciplined to avoid becoming overextended. Steven Fischer provides an example. Unable to get a line of credit from a bank, Fischer used

his personal credit cards to keep his business operating after he was unable to collect receivables from some of his clients. He anticipated using his cards to keep his company afloat until they were paid. However, paying wages and bills proved to be more expensive than he had anticipated. Also, mixing his personal credit cards with business loans and expenses created problems. In the end, Fischer's company didn't survive.[5] After laying off employees and paying all of the business's bills, Fischer found himself personally liable for $80,000 in credit card debt.

So why use credit cards? At times the only option open to a small business entrepreneur, credit cards also have the advantage of speed. A lender at a bank has to be convinced of the merits of the business opportunity, and that involves extensive

© NAN728/Shutterstock.com

preparation on the part of the entrepreneur. Credit card financing, on the other hand, requires no justification of the use of the money.

In practice, credit cards are a significant source of financing for a number of entrepreneurs, particularly early in the game. But the eventual goal is to use credit cards as a method of payment and not as a source of credit. In other words, the sooner you can pay your credit card balance in full each month, the sooner you can grow a profitable business.

12-4 BANK FINANCING

LO 12-4

Discuss the basic process for acquiring and structuring a bank loan.

In 2010, lending by banks and other financial institutions to small businesses had decreased by $40 billion from two years earlier.[6] Many small business owners caught in the middle of a severe recession were not just frustrated about being unable to grow their business, some were also fearful of not being able to survive. Their inability to get loans from banks was their greatest concern. By mid-year 2011, the problem had eased somewhat. But even in early 2013, many small firms were still facing an uncertain future, both in their businesses and in acquiring bank financing. This uncertainty was reflected in the *2012 Year-End Economic Report* by the National Small Business Association (NSBA). Based on a survey of small business owners, the NSBA found that company owners were feeling less optimistic about the outlook of their own firms and the overall U.S. economy than they were [in 2012].[7] The most recent recession clearly affected the world of small business owners.

Commercial banks are a primary provider of debt capital to *established* firms. Quite simply, they want firms with proven track records and plenty of collateral in the form of hard assets. Bankers are reluctant to loan money to finance losses, R&D expenses, marketing campaigns, and other "soft" assets. Such expenditures should be financed by equity sources. Nevertheless, it is wise to cultivate a relationship with a banker sooner rather than later, and well in advance of making a loan request.

12-4a Types of Loans

Bankers primarily make business loans in one of three forms: lines of credit, term loans, and mortgages.

LINES OF CREDIT A **line of credit** is an informal agreement or understanding between a borrower and a bank as to the maximum amount of funds the bank will provide the borrower at any one time. Under this type of agreement, the bank has no legal obligation to provide the capital. (A similar arrangement that *does* legally commit the bank is a *revolving credit agreement*.) The entrepreneur should arrange for a line of credit in advance of an actual need, as banks are reluctant to extend credit on the spur of the moment.

TERM LOANS Under certain circumstances, banks will loan money on a 5- to 10-year term. Such **term loans** are generally used to finance equipment with a useful life corresponding to the loan's term. Since the economic benefits of investing in such equipment extend beyond a single year, banks can be persuaded to lend on terms that more closely match the cash flows to be received from the investment. For example, if equipment has a useful life of seven years, it might be possible to repay the money needed to purchase the equipment over, say, five years. It would be a mistake for a firm to borrow money for a short term, such as six months, when the equipment being purchased is expected to last for seven years. *Failure to match the loan's payment terms with the expected cash inflows from the investment is a frequent cause of financial problems for small firms.* The importance of synchronizing cash inflows with cash outflows when structuring the terms of a loan cannot be overemphasized.

Some loans call for term payments that include principal and interest, others for interest only with lump sum principal reductions. If in doubt, ask your banker for advice: "I want to expand. Here's the loan I think I need. What do you think?"

MORTGAGES Mortgages, which represent a long-term source of debt capital, can be one of two types: chattel mortgages and real estate mortgages. A **chattel mortgage** is a loan for which certain items of inventory or other movable property serve as collateral. The borrower retains title to the inventory but cannot sell it without the banker's consent. A **real estate mortgage** is a loan for which real property, such as land or a building, provides the collateral. Typically, these mortgages extend up to 25 or 30 years.

line of credit
An informal agreement between a borrower and a bank as to the maximum amount of funds the bank will provide at any one time.

term loan
Money loaned for a 5- to 10-year term, corresponding to the length of time the investment will bring in profits.

chattel mortgage
A loan for which items of inventory or other movable property serve as collateral.

real estate mortgage
A long-term loan with real property held as collateral.

© alexsl/iStockphoto.com

12-4b Understanding a Banker's Perspective

To be effective in acquiring a loan, an entrepreneur needs to understand that a banker has three priorities when making a loan. They are listed below in their order of importance to the banker:

1. *Recouping the principal of the loan.* A banker is not rewarded adequately to assume large amounts of risk and will, therefore, design loan agreements so as to reduce the risk to the bank. First and foremost, the banker has to protect depositors' capital.

2. *Determining the amount of income the loan will provide the bank*, both in interest income and in other forms of income, such as fees.

3. *Helping the borrower be successful and then become a larger customer.* Only if the relationship is a win-win for both parties will the bank do well.

In making a loan decision, a banker gives serious consideration to what they call the "five C's of credit": (1) the borrower's *character*, (2) the borrower's *capacity* to repay the loan, (3) the *capital* being invested in the venture by the borrower, (4) the *collateral* available to secure the loan and (5) the *conditions* of the industry and economy. Of course, no banker would ever make a loan to a borrower whose character is in question. Here, the borrower's relationships and credit scores are used as indicators. But while good character is vital, it is not sufficient to receive a loan. In fact, a loan committee will spend little time talking about a prospective borrower's character unless unless they become aware of somereason to question it. The conversation about the person will more likely center on the her or his ability and achievements, and the nature of the borrower's relationship with the bank. Exhibit 12.5 illustrates the coming together of the five C's for a decision. While we place character at the center, all the criteria (C's) are important, as reflected in the exhibit.

12.5 Five C's: The Foundation for Getting a Loan

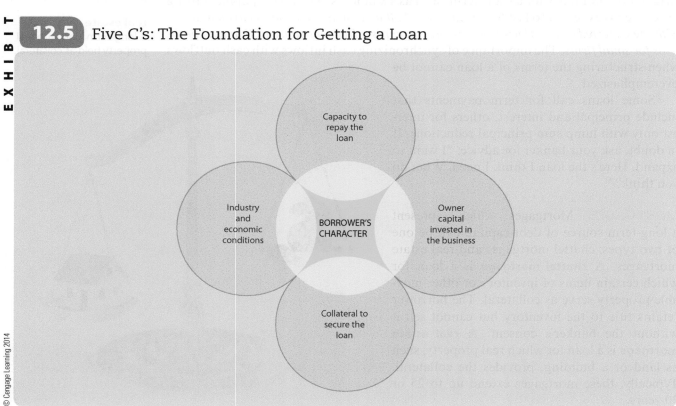

These issues are apparent in the six questions Jack Griggs, a banker and long-time lender to small businesses, wants six questions answered before he will make a loan:[8]

- Does the borrower have strong character and reasonable ability?
- Do the purpose and amount of the loan make sense, both for the bank and for the borrower? For example, the loan may be too small to be profitable for the bank or may be in an industry in which the bank has no lending experience.
- Does the loan have a certain primary source of repayment? This usually means proven cash flows.
- Does the loan have a certain secondary source of repayment? This would be the collateral that the borrower can offer in case the loan cannot be repaid.
- Can the loan be priced profitably for the customer and for the bank?
- Are this loan and the relationship good for both the customer and the bank?

A banker's review of a loan request includes analysis of financial considerations. When seeking a loan, a small business owner will be required to provide certain information in support of the request. Failure to provide this information will almost certainly result in rejection by the banker. Presenting inaccurate information or not being able to justify assumptions made in forecasting financial results is sure to make the banker question the entrepreneur's business acumen.

A well-prepared loan request is absolutely necessary. Capturing the firm's history and future in writing suggests that the entrepreneur has given thought to where the firm has been and where it is going. As part of the presentation, the banker will want to know early on the answers to the following questions:

- How much money is needed?
- What is the venture going to do with the money?
- When is the money needed?
- When and how will the money be paid back?

An example of a written loan request is provided in Exhibit 12.6. A banker also will want, if at all possible, to see the following detailed financial information:

- Three years of the firm's historical financial statements, if available, including balance sheets, income statements, and cash flow statements
- The firm's pro forma financial statements (balance sheets, income statements, and cash flow statements), in which the timing and amounts of the debt repayment are included as part of the forecasts
- Personal financial statements showing the borrower's net worth (net worth = assets − debt) and estimated annual income. A banker simply will not make a loan without knowing the personal financial strength of the borrower.

ACTION

Bankers Don't Like Surprises
Never surprise your banker with bad news. Tell your banker immediately if you are having a problem, and let him or her work with you. Avoiding your banker when things go wrong may cause you to be perceived as not being forthright, and you may lose your banker's trust.

12-4c Selecting a Banker

For a typical small firm, the provision of checking-account facilities and the extension of short-term (and possibly long-term) loans are the two most important services of a bank. Normally, loans are negotiated with the same bank in which the firm maintains its checking account. In addition, the firm may use the bank's safe-deposit vault or its services in collecting notes or securing credit information. An experienced banker can also provide management advice, particularly in financial matters, to a new entrepreneur.

EXHIBIT 12.6

Sample Written Loan Request

Date of Request:	December 15, 2012
Borrower:	Prestige & DeLay, Inc.
Amount:	$1,000,000
Use of Proceeds:	Accounts receivable $ 400,000
	Inventory 200,000
	Marketing 100,000
	Officer loans due 175,000
	Salaries 75,000
	Contingencies 50,000
	$1,000,000
Type of Loan	Revolving Line of Credit
Closing Date	January 3, 2013
Term	12 months
Rate	8.5%
Takedown	$400,000 at closing
	$300,000 at March 1, 2013
	$200,000 at June 1, 2013
	$100,000 on September 1, 2013
Collateral	70 percent of accounts receivable under 90 days
	50 percent of current inventory
Guarantees	Guarantees to be provided by Prestige & DeLay
Repayment Schedule	Principal and all accrued interest due on anniversary of note
Source of Funds for Repayment	a. Excess cash from operations (see cash flow)
	b. Renewable and increase of line if growth is profitable
	c. Conversion to three-year note
Contingency Source	Sale and leaseback of equipment

© Cengage Learning

For convenience in making deposits and conferring about loans and other matters, a bank should be located in the same general vicinity as the firm. All banks are interested in their home communities and, therefore, tend to be sympathetic to the needs of local business firms. Except in very small communities, two or more local banks are usually available, thus permitting some freedom of choice.

Banks' lending policies are not uniform. Some bankers are extremely conservative, while others are more willing to accept some limited risks. If a small firm's loan application is neither obviously strong nor patently weak, its prospects for approval depend heavily on the bank's approach to small business accounts. Differences in willingness to lend have been clearly established by research studies, as well as by the practical experience of many business borrowers.

12-4d Negotiating the Loan

In negotiating a bank loan, a small business owner must consider the terms that will accompany the loan. Four key terms are included in all loan agreements: the interest rate, the loan maturity date, the repayment schedule, and the loan covenants.

INTEREST RATE The interest rate charged by banks to small companies is usually stated in terms of the prime rate or, occasionally, the LIBOR. The **prime rate**,

prime rate (base rate) The interest rate charged by commercial banks on loans to their most creditworthy customers.

or **base rate**, is the rate of interest charged by banks on loans to their most credit-worthy customers. The **LIBOR (London Interbank Offered Rate)** is the interest rate that London-based banks charge other banks in London, which is considerably lower than the prime rate.

If a banker quotes a rate of "prime plus 2" and the prime rate is 3 percent, the interest rate for the loan will be 5 percent (3% + 2%). Alternatively, a banker might state the rate as "prime plus 200 basis points." A **basis point** is 1/100th of one percent; thus, 200 basis points are the same as 2 percent.

The interest rate can be a floating rate that varies over the loan's life—that is, as the prime rate changes, the interest rate on the loan changes—or it can be fixed for the duration of the loan. A banker may also impose a floor on the interest rate so that it cannot go below a given rate. For instance the floor might be set at 3.5 percent, no matter the prime rate. If a banker does impose a floor, you might request a ceiling that the rate cannot go above. If the bank agrees to a ceiling of 6.5 percent, for example, you will know that your interest rate cannot go any higher than that.

Although a small firm should always seek a competitive interest rate, concern about the interest rate should not override consideration of the loan's maturity date, its repayment schedule, and any loan covenants.

LOAN MATURITY DATE As already noted, a loan's term should coincide with the use of the money—short-term needs require short-term financing, while long-term needs demand long-term financing. For example, since a line of credit is intended to help a firm with only its short-term needs, it is generally limited to one year. Some banks require that a firm "clean up" a line of credit one month each year. Because such a loan can be outstanding for only 11 months, the borrower can use the money to finance seasonal needs but cannot use it to provide permanent increases in working capital, such as accounts receivable and inventory.

REPAYMENT SCHEDULE With a term loan, the loan is set to be repaid over 5 to 10 years, depending on the type of assets used for collateral. However, the banker may have the option of imposing a **balloon payment** before the loan is fully repaid. A balloon payment allows the bank to require the borrower to pay off the balance of the loan in full at a specified time, rather than waiting the full term for the loan to be repaid. Assume, for example, that you borrow $50,000 at an interest rate of 6 percent, and the loan is to be repaid in equal monthly repayments over 84 months (seven years). The amount of each payment is determined to be $730 in order to pay off the loan in full by the end of the seven years.[9] However, the banker may include a term in the loan agreement giving the bank the right to "call" the loan at the end of three years, meaning that you would have to pay off what is still owed at that time ($31,100). The banker would have the choice of (1) requiring you to pay off the $31,100 at the end of the third year, or (2) allowing you to have the remaining four years to pay off the loan. This provision permits the banker to reassess the borrower's creditworthiness at the end of the third year if the business is not doing well.

LOAN COVENANTS In addition to setting the interest rate and specifying when and how the loan is to be repaid, a bank normally imposes other restrictions on the borrower. These restrictions, or **loan covenants**, require certain activities (positive covenants) and limit other activities (negative covenants) of the borrower to increase the chance that the borrower will be able to repay the loan. Some types of loan covenants that a borrower might encounter include the following:

1. The company must provide financial statements to the bank on a monthly basis or, at the very least, quarterly (positive covenant).

LIBOR (London InterBank Offered Rate)
The interest rate charged by London banks on loans to other London banks.

Basis point
1/100th of 1 percent when quoting an interest rate

balloon payment
A very large payment required about halfway through the term over which payments were calculated, repaying the loan balance in full.

loan covenants
Bank-imposed restrictions on a borrower that enhance the chance of timely repayment.

2. As a way to restrict a firm's management from siphoning cash out of the business, the bank may limit managers' salaries. It also may prohibit any personal loans from the business to the owners (negative covenant).

3. A bank may put limits on various financial ratios to make certain that a firm can handle its loan payments. For example, to ensure sufficient liquidity, the bank may require the firm's current assets to be at least twice its current liabilities—that is, the current ratio (current assets ÷ current liabilities) must be equal to or greater than 2. Or the bank might limit the amount of debt the firm can borrow in the future, as measured by the debt ratio (total debt ÷ total assets) (negative covenant).

4. The borrower will normally be required to personally guarantee the firm's loan. A banker wants the right to use both the firm's assets and the owner's personal assets as collateral. Even when a business is structured as a corporation and the owner can escape personal liability for the firm's debts—that is, the owner has *limited liability*—most banks still require the owner's personal guarantee (negative covenant).[10]

© Goodluz/Shutterstock.com

It is imperative that you pay close attention to the loan covenants being imposed by a banker. Ask for a list of the covenants before the closing date, and make certain that you can live with the terms. If you have an existing company, determine whether you could have complied with the covenants, especially key ratios, if the loan had been in place during the recent past. Then, if necessary, negotiate with your banker and suggest more realistic covenants. Bankers will negotiate, although they may sometimes try to convince you otherwise. After all, making loans is a primary source of profits for the bank.

You also need to be aware of what happens when you violate a loan covenant. Ultimately, the banker can make you repay the loan in full immediately. More often, the banker will increase the interest rate or require you to repay the loan in a shorter period of time. What happens will also depend on which covenant is violated. As one banker noted, "Some covenants are like yield signs, while others are stop signs."[11] In other words, bankers use covenants as warning lights to address any potential problems before they become fatal.

12-5 BUSINESS SUPPLIERS AND ASSET-BASED LENDERS

LO
12-5

Explain how business relationships can be used to finance a small firm.

Companies that have business dealings with a new firm are possible sources of funds for financing inventory and equipment. Both wholesalers and equipment manufacturers/suppliers may provide accounts payable (trade credit) or equipment loans and leases.

12-5a Accounts Payable (Trade Credit)

Credit extended by suppliers is very important to a startup. In fact, trade (or mercantile) credit is the source of short-term funds most widely used by small firms. As mentioned in Chapter 10, *accounts payable (trade credit)* is of short duration—30 days is the customary credit period. Most commonly, this type of credit involves an unsecured, open-book account. The supplier (seller) sends merchandise to the purchasing firm; the buyer then sets up an account payable for the amount of the purchase.

The amount of trade credit available to a new company depends on the type of business and the supplier's confidence in the firm. For example, wholesale distributors of sunglasses—a very seasonal product line—often provide trade credit to retailers by granting extended payment terms on sales made at the start of a season. Sunglass retailers, in turn, sell to their customers during the season and make the bulk of their payments to the wholesalers after they have sold and collected the cash for the sunglasses. Thus, the retailer obtains cash from sales before paying the supplier. More often, however, a firm has to pay its suppliers prior to receiving cash from its customers. In fact, this can be a serious problem for many small firms, particularly those that sell to large companies. (This issue will be addressed in a discussion of asset management in Chapter 22.)

12-5b Equipment Loans and Leases

Some small businesses, such as restaurants, use equipment that is purchased on an installment basis through an **equipment loan**. A down payment of 25 to 35 percent is usually required, and the contract period normally runs from three to five years. The equipment manufacturer or supplier typically extends credit on the basis of a conditional sales contract (or mortgage) on the equipment. During the loan period, the equipment cannot serve as collateral for another loan.

Instead of borrowing money from suppliers to purchase equipment, some small businesses choose to lease equipment, especially computers, photocopiers, and fax machines. Leases typically run for 36 to 60 months and cover 100 percent of the cost of the asset being leased, with a fixed rate of interest included in the lease payments. However, manufacturers of computers and industrial machinery, working hand in hand with banks or financing companies, are generally receptive to tailoring lease packages to the particular needs of customers.

It has been estimated that 80 percent of all firms lease some or all of their business equipment. Three reasons are commonly given for the popularity of leasing: (1) the firm's cash remains free for other purposes, (2) available lines of credit can be used for other purposes, and (3) leasing provides a hedge against equipment obsolescence. A business owner can make a good choice about leasing, however, only after carefully comparing the interest charged on a loan to the implied interest cost of a lease, calculating the tax consequences of leasing versus borrowing, and examining the significance of the obsolescence factor. Also, the owner must be careful about contracting for so much equipment that it becomes difficult to meet installment or lease payments.

12-5c Asset-Based Lending

As its name implies, an **asset-based loan** is a line of credit secured by assets, such as receivables, inventory, or both. The lender cushions its risk by advancing only a percentage of the value of a firm's assets—generally, 65 to 85 percent against receivables and up to 55 percent against inventory. Also, assets such as equipment (if not leased) and real estate can be used as collateral for an asset-based loan. Asset-based lending is a viable option for young, growing businesses.

Of the several categories of asset-based lending, the most frequently used is factoring. **Factoring** is an option that makes cash available to a business before accounts receivable payments are received from customers. Under this option, a factor (an entity often owned by a bank holding company) purchases the accounts receivable, advancing

equipment loan
An installment loan from a seller of machinery used by a business.

asset-based loan
A line of credit secured by working capital assets.

factoring
Obtaining cash by selling accounts receivable to another firm.

to the business 70 to 90 percent of the amount of an invoice. The factor, however, has the option of refusing to advance cash on any invoice it considers questionable. The factor charges a servicing fee, usually 2 percent of the value of the receivables, and an interest charge on the money advanced prior to collection of the receivables. The interest charge may range from 2 to 3 percent above the prime rate.

Another way to finance working capital is to sell purchase orders. With **purchase-order financing**, the lender advances the amount of the borrower's cost of goods sold for a specific customer order less a fee, typically somewhere between 3 and 8 percent. For instance, for a purchase order of $20,000, with the cost of goods sold being $12,000, the lender will advance the $12,000 less the fee charged. According to Jason Goldberg, vice president of marketing for Westgate Financial, this type of financing "attempts to address the issue of a company growing so rapidly that cash flow can't sustain growth." With a signed purchase order from a creditworthy customer, you can often get financing for almost the entire process, provided your gross profit margin (gross profit ÷ sales) is at least 35 percent. Although the fee is not insignificant, it makes sense when the entrepreneur would not otherwise be able to accept an order from a large customer. In times when credit is scarce, Goldberg says, it's an opportunity "to leverage the ability to sell product."[12]

12-6 PRIVATE EQUITY INVESTORS

LO 12-6

Describe the two types of private equity investors who offer financing to small firms.

Over the past two decades, private equity markets have been the fastest-growing source of financing for entrepreneurial ventures with the potential for becoming significant businesses. For an entrepreneur, these sources fall into two categories: business angels and venture capitalists.

12-6a Business Angels

Business angels are private individuals who invest in early-stage companies.[13] They are the oldest and largest source of early-stage equity capital for entrepreneurs. According to the Center for Venture Research at the University of New Hampshire, angel investments in 2011 amounted to $22.5 billion. A total of 66,230 businesses received funding from an estimated 318,480 angel investors.[14] The type of financing they provide has come to be known as **informal venture capital** because no established marketplace exists in which business angels regularly invest.

Business angels generally make investments in firms that are relatively small— over 80 percent of business angels invest in startup firms with fewer than 20 employees. They invest locally, usually no more than 50 miles from their homes. Some limit their investments to industries in which they have had experience, while others invest in a wide variety of business sectors.

Along with providing needed money, business angels frequently contribute know-how to new businesses. Because many of these individuals invest only in the types of businesses in which they have had experience, they can be very demanding. While they are generally more "friendly" as investors than some venture capitalists, their personal relationship with the entrepreneur has little impact on their decision to invest. Thus, the entrepreneur must be careful in structuring the terms of any such investors' involvement.

The traditional way to find informal investors is through contacts with business associates, accountants, and lawyers. Other entrepreneurs are also a primary source of help in identifying prospective investors. In addition, there are now a large number of formal angel networks and angel alliances in all major cities, both in the United

purchase-order financing
Obtaining cash from a lender who, for a fee, advances the amount of the borrower's cost of goods sold for a specific customer order.

business angels
Private individuals who invest in others' entrepreneurial ventures.

informal venture capital
Funds provided by wealthy private individuals to high-risk ventures.

States and abroad. Each angel group has its own process for evaluating deals. Some, for example, require entrepreneurs who are seeking funding to post their business plan on www.gust.com, a global platform for startup funding. The group screens the plans and selects those entrepreneurs who will be allowed to present to the group. In most cases, individual angels then make personal decisions about whether or not to invest, regardless of what the other angels do. If enough angels are interested, a detailed evaluation is undertaken before a final decision is made.[15]

Guy Kawasaki, the founder of Garage Technology Ventures, is now a venture capitalist and the author of *The Art of the Start* (a must-read for anyone wanting to start a new business). He offers the following suggestions about dealing with business angels:[16]

1. *Make sure the investors are accredited.* "Accredited" is legalese for "rich enough to never get back a penny." You can get into trouble for selling stock to those who aren't accredited—so don't.

2. *Make sure they're sophisticated.* Sophisticated angel investors have "been there and done that." You want angels' money, but you also want their knowledge and expertise.

3. *Don't underestimate them.* The idea that angel investors are easy marks is simply wrong. Angels care as much about how they will get their money back as venture capitalists do—maybe even more, because they're investing their personal, after-tax money.

4. *Understand their motivation.* Angel investors differ from venture capitalists in that business angels typically have a double bottom line. They've made it, so they want to pay back society by helping the next generation of entrepreneurs. Thus, they're often willing to invest in riskier deals to help entrepreneurs get to the next stage.

5. *Enable them to live vicariously.* One of the rewards of angel investing is the ability to live vicariously through an entrepreneur's efforts. Angels want to relive the thrills of entrepreneurship, while avoiding the firing line. They enjoy helping you, so seek their guidance frequently.

6. *Make your story comprehensible to the angel's spouse.* An angel's "decision-making committee" usually consists of one person: a spouse. So, if you've got a highly technical product, you must make it understandable for the angel's spouse when he or she asks, "What are we investing $100,000 in?"

7. *Sign up people the angel has heard of.* Angel investors are also motivated by the social aspect of investing with buddies in startups run by bright people who are changing the world. Once you've brought one angel on board, you're likely to attract a whole flock of other angels, too.

8. *Be nice.* Not infrequently, angel investors fall in love with entrepreneurs. An entrepreneur may remind an investor of a son or daughter, or even fill the position of the son or daughter the investor never had. Venture capitalists will sometimes invest in a schmuck as long as that schmuck is a proven moneymaker. If you're seeking angel capital, then you're probably not a proven moneymaker, so you can't get away with acting like a schmuck. Always be respectful to your investors.

12-6b Venture Capital Firms

In addition to business angels who provide informal venture capital, small businesses also may seek out **formal venture capitalists**, groups of individuals who form limited partnerships for the purpose of raising capital from large institutional investors, such

formal venture capitalists
Individuals who form limited partnerships for the purpose of raising venture capital from large institutional investors.

Living the Dream

"Shark Tank": Changing the Game of Angel Investing

"Shark Tank," the wildly successful television show, is quickly changing the angel investing landscape. The show features a variety of hopeful entrepreneurs with capital-hungry startups. They enter the "shark tank" one by one, with the hopes of securing an investment from one of the show's seasoned investors.

In many ways, the show accurately represents the process of obtaining capital from investors. The deals are structured like typical investments in which the entrepreneur exchanges a percentage of his or her company's equity for cash. The entrepreneurs must prepare a concise and compelling business plan and must be able to pitch it in a manner that demonstrates competency and keeps the investors' attention. This can often be a challenging process.

[T]he Sharks have a goal, too. They want a return on their investment and [to]own a piece of the next big business idea…. But if the pitch is poor, the Sharks will tear into the ill-prepared presenters and pass on the idea with a simple "I'm out!"

© cbpix/Shutterstock.com

Getting in front of an investor has traditionally been a lengthy and difficult process. Building a network and obtaining an introduction takes time. Since the show has aired, however, the gap is closing between entrepreneurs and potential investors.

More and more entrepreneurs are finding that angel investors are open to hearing their pitch if they present it in a quick, contest-style format. Sure, there are still plenty of angel connections happening from

networking and pitching individual investors. But the opportunities to get in front of an angel without an introduction at a competition are growing.

Small-scale angel investing competitions are becoming increasingly popular nationwide. One example is the Guppy Tank, southern California's own small-scale version of "Shark Tank." A group of angels with $500,000 dollars select 2 to 10 local startups in which to invest their money. FutureM also hosted a similar event at its 2012 marketing event in Boston.

Obtaining quick capital sounds like an entrepreneurial dream come true. However, it is important to realize that "Shark Tank" and competitions like it are just the starting point in entrepreneur-investor negotiations.

The contract for [Shark Tank] stipulates that "making an offer" on the show is definitely not a guarantee of investment. An offer on Shark Tank is an agreement to "negotiate in good faith" using the terms from the show as a starting point. This sounds unfair, but this is how it is done in the real world as well. "Shark Tank" is a reality show, but it is not a "game show." This is business. No one gets $100,000 from a 15-minute meeting.

Sources: Based on "Shark Tank: About the Show," ABC.com, http://abc.go.com/shows/shark-tank/about-the-show, accessed February 18, 2013; Carol Tice, "How Shark Tank is Changing Angel Investing," Entrepreneur.com, October 5, 2012, http://www.entrepreneur.com/blog/224597, accessed February 18, 2013; Nate Berkopec, "How exactly are the Investments On Shark Tank Executed? Do the Producers Get a Cut?" May 29, 2012, http://www.huffingtonpost.com/quora/how-exactly-are-the-inves_b_1554151.html, accessed February 18, 2013.

as pension plans and university endowments. Within the group, a venture capitalist serves as the general partner, with other investors constituting the limited partners. As limited partners, such investors have the benefit of limited liability.

A venture capitalist attempts to raise a predetermined amount of money, called a *fund*. Once the money has been committed by the investors, the venture capitalist evaluates investment opportunities in high-potential startups and existing firms. For example, the Sevin Rosen Funds raised $600 million for the Sevin Rosen Fund VIII. The money was then used to invest in a portfolio of companies.

For the investment, the venture capitalist receives the right to own a percentage of the entrepreneur's business. Reaching agreement on the exact percentage of ownership often involves considerable negotiation. The primary issues are the firm's expected profits in future years and the venture capitalist's required rate of return. Once an investment has been made, the venture capitalist carefully monitors the company, usually through a representative who serves on the firm's board.

Most often, investments by venture capitalists take the form of preferred stock that can be converted to common stock if the investor so desires. In this way, venture capitalists ensure that they have senior claim over the owners and other equity investors in the event the firm is liquidated but can convert to common stock and participate in the increased value of the business if it is successful. These investors generally try to limit the length of their investment to between 5 and 7 years, though it is frequently closer to 10 years before they are able to cash out.

Although venture capital as a source of financing receives significant coverage in the business media, *few small companies, especially startups, ever receive this kind of funding.* No more than 1 or 2 percent of the business plans received by any venture capitalist are eventually funded—not exactly an encouraging statistic. Failure to receive funding from a venture capitalist, however, does not indicate that the venture lacks potential. Often, the venture is simply not a good fit for the investor. So, before trying to compete for venture capital financing, an entrepreneur should assess whether the firm and its management team are suitable for a particular investor.

12-7 GOVERNMENT LOAN PROGRAMS

Several government programs provide financing to small businesses. Over the past decade, federal and state governments have allocated increasing, but still limited, amounts of money to financing new businesses. Local governments have likewise increased their involvement in providing financial support to startups in their areas. Though funds are available, they are not always easy to acquire. Time and patience on the part of the entrepreneur are required. Let's take a look at some of the more familiar government loan programs offered by various agencies.

LO
12-7

Distinguish among the different government loan programs available to small companies.

12-7a The Small Business Administration

The federal government has a long history of helping new businesses get started, primarily through the programs and agencies of the Small Business Administration (SBA). For the most part, the SBA does not loan money but serves as a guarantor of loans made by financial institutions. The five primary SBA programs are (1) the 7(a) Loan Guaranty Program, (2) the Certified Development Company (CDC) 504 Loan Program, (3) the 7(m) Microloan Program, (4) small business investment companies (SBICs), and (5) the Small Business Innovative Research (SBIR) Program.

7(A) LOAN GUARANTY PROGRAM The **7(a) Loan Guaranty Program** serves as the SBA's primary business loan program to help qualified small businesses obtain financing when they might not be eligible for business loans through normal lending channels. Guaranty loans are made by private lenders, usually commercial banks, and may be for as much as $750,000. The SBA guarantees 85 percent of loans not exceeding $150,000 and 75 percent up to $3.75 million. To obtain a guaranty loan, a small business must submit a loan application to a lender, such as a bank. After an initial review, the lender forwards the application to the SBA. Once the loan has been approved by the SBA, the lender disburses the funds. The loan proceeds can be used for working capital, machinery and equipment, furniture and fixtures, land and building, leasehold improvements, and debt refinancing (under special conditions). Loan maturity is up to 10 years for working capital and generally up to 25 years for fixed assets.

CERTIFIED DEVELOPMENT COMPANY (CDC) 504 LOAN PROGRAM The **Certified Development Company (CDC) 504 Loan Program** provides long-term, fixed-rate financing to small businesses to acquire real estate or machinery and equipment for expansion or modernization. The borrower must provide 10 percent of the cost of the property, with the remaining amount coming from a bank and a certified development company funded by the SBA.

7(M) MICROLOAN PROGRAM The **7(m) Microloan Program** grants short-term loans of up to $50,000 to small businesses and not-for-profit child-care centers for working capital or the purchase of inventory, supplies, furniture, fixtures, and machinery and equipment. The SBA makes or guarantees a loan to an intermediary, which in turn makes the microloan to the applicant. As an added benefit, the lender provides business training and support programs to its microloan borrowers.

Most banks regard microloans as too costly to administer directly to small business owners. Therefore, some nonprofit organizations, such as the Northeastern Pennsylvania Alliance and the Detroit Micro-Enterprise Fund, work with banks and foundations to make these microloans.[17]

SMALL BUSINESS INVESTMENT COMPANIES **Small business investment companies (SBICs)** are privately owned banks that provide long-term loans and/or equity capital to small businesses. SBICs are licensed and regulated by the SBA, from which they frequently obtain a substantial part of their capital at attractive rates of interest. SBICs invest in businesses with fewer than 500 employees, a net worth of no more than $18 million, and after-tax income not exceeding $6 million during the two most recent years.

SMALL BUSINESS INNOVATIVE RESEARCH (SBIR) PROGRAM The **Small Business Innovative Research (SBIR) Program** helps finance small firms that plan to transform laboratory research into marketable products. Eligibility for the program is based less on the potential profitability of a venture than on the likelihood that the firm will provide a product of interest to a particular federal agency.

12-7b State and Local Government Assistance

State and local governments have become more active in financing new businesses. The nature of the financing varies, but each program is generally geared to augment other sources of funding. Examples of such programs include the Golden Circle Loan Guarantee Fund, established by the city government of Des Moines, Iowa, to guarantee bank loans of up to $250,000 to small companies; and loans made to business

---

7(a) Loan Guaranty Program
A loan program that helps small companies obtain financing through a guaranty provided by the SBA.

Certified Development Company (CDC) 504 Loan Program
An SBA loan program that provides long-term financing for small businesses to acquire real estate or machinery and equipment.

7(m) Microloan Program
An SBA loan program that provides short-term loans of up to $50,000 to small businesses and not-for-profit child-care centers.

small business investment companies (SBICs)
Privately owned banks, regulated by the SBA, that provide long-term loans and/or equity capital to small businesses.

Small Business Innovative Research (SBIR) Program
An SBA program that helps to finance companies that plan to transform laboratory research into marketable products.

owners by the New Jersey Economic Development Authority at the U.S. Treasury rate, significantly lower than interest rates typically charged at banks.

Most of these loans are made in conjunction with a bank, which enables the bank to take on riskier loans for entrepreneurs who might not qualify for traditional financing. "And some loans have a lower down payment requirement," explains Donna Holmes, former director of the Penn State Small Business Development Center in University Park. "The bank may do 50 percent, the state program another 40 percent, and the borrower only has to come up with 10 percent; with a straight bank loan, the bank might be looking for 20 percent or 25 percent."[18]

While such government programs may be attractive to an entrepreneur, they are frequently designed to enhance specific industries or to facilitate certain community goals. Consequently, you need to determine that a program is in sync with your specific business objectives.

12-7c Community-Based Financial Institutions

Community-based financial institutions are lenders that serve low-income communities and receive funds from federal, state, and private sources. They are increasingly becoming a source of financing for small companies that otherwise would have little or no access to startup funding. Typically, community-based lenders provide capital to businesses that are unable to attract outside investors but do have the potential to make modest profits, serve the community, and create jobs. An example of a community-based financial institution is the Delaware Valley Community Reinvestment Fund, which provides financing for small companies in Philadelphia's inner-city area.

12-8 WHERE ELSE TO LOOK

The sources of financing that have been described thus far represent the primary avenues for obtaining money for small firms. The remaining sources are generally of less importance but should not be ignored by a small business owner in search of financing.

LO
12-8
Explain when large companies and public stock offerings can be sources of financing.

12-8a Large Corporations

Large corporations at times make funds available for investment in smaller firms when it is in their self-interest to maintain a close relationship with such a firm. For instance, some large high-tech firms, such as Intel and Microsoft, prefer to invest in smaller firms that are conducting research of interest, rather than conduct the research themselves.

12-8b Stock Sales

Another way to obtain capital is by selling stock to outside individual investors through either private placement or public sale. Finding outside stockholders can be difficult when a new firm is not known and has no ready market for its securities, however. In most cases, a business must have a history of profitability before its stock can be sold successfully.

Whether it is best to raise outside equity financing depends on the firm's long-range prospects. If there is opportunity for substantial expansion on a continuing

community-based financial institution A lender that uses funds from federal, state, and private sources to provide financing to small businesses in low-income communities.

basis and if other sources are inadequate, the owner may logically decide to bring in other owners. Owning part of a larger business may be more profitable than owning all of a smaller business.

PRIVATE PLACEMENT One way to sell common stock is through a **private placement**, in which the firm's stock is sold to select individuals—usually the firm's employees, the owner's acquaintances, members of the local community, customers, and suppliers. When a stock sale is restricted to private placement, an entrepreneur can avoid many of the demanding requirements of the securities laws.

PUBLIC SALE When small firms—typically, larger small firms—make their stock available to the general public, this is called going public, or making an **initial public offering (IPO)**. The reason often cited for a public sale is the need for additional working capital.

In undertaking a public sale of its stock, a small firm subjects itself to greater governmental regulation, which escalated dramatically following the rash of corporate scandals in publicly owned companies such as Enron, Tyco, and WorldCom. In response to such corporate malfeasance, the U.S. Congress passed legislation, including the Sarbanes-Oxley Act, to monitor public companies more carefully. This resulted in a significant increase in the cost of being a publicly traded company—especially for small firms. Then in 2010, Congress enacted the Dodd-Frank Act for the purpose of averting a financial crisis similar to the one experienced in 2008–2009. The legislation primarily relates to the financial sector but also includes strict regulations for all companies to ensure transparency and accountability, which again increases costs. Finally, publicly traded firms are required to report their financial results quarterly in 10Q reports and annually in 10K reports to the Securities and Exchange Commission (SEC). The SEC carefully scrutinizes these reports before they can be made available to the public. At times, SEC requirements can be very burdensome.

Common stock may also be sold to underwriters, which guarantee the sale of securities. Compensation and fees paid to underwriters typically make the sale of securities in this manner expensive. Fees frequently range from 20 to 25 percent (or higher) of the value of the total stock issued. The reasons for the high costs are, of course, the uncertainty and risk associated with public offerings of the stock of small, relatively unknown firms.

private placement
The sale of a firm's capital stock to select individuals.

initial public offering (IPO)
The issuance of stock to be traded in public financial markets.

crowdfunding
The process of raising very small investments from a large number of investors via the Internet.

Describe how crowdfunding can be used by some small businesses to raise capital.

12-9 CROWDFUNDING

Assume that you need $50,000 to fund a new business project and that you have tried the conventional sources of financing, but without success. You could always try crowdfunding.

Crowdfunding is the process of raising very small investments from a large number of investors online. It has mushroomed with the advent of crowdfunding websites, or *platforms* as they are frequently called. According to a study by Massolution, the dollar amount of crowdfunding increased from $530 million in 2009 to $1.3 billion in 2011, and was expected to be $2.8 billion in 2012.[19]

There are four basic approaches to crowdfunding: (1) donations, (2) rewards, (3) pre-purchases, and (4) equity investing. Individuals who *donate* make a contribution to support a given project without receiving anything tangible in return. This approach is more akin to a charitable contribution than an investment. Interestingly, there are people who enjoy helping an organization, even a business at times, without any promise of something in return.

In the second approach, *rewards*, supporters make a monetary contribution in return for a reward of some type. For example, BodBot, a startup providing exercise and nutrition recommendations on the Web, set a goal to raise $20,000 by crowdfunding. (It actually raised $43,210 from 795 participants.) In return for participating, the company offered different packages of workouts and other benefits, depending on the amount of the contribution, beginning at $20 and continuing up to $15,000! A similar approach to receiving a reward is a *pre-purchase*, in which the financial contribution is essentially the conditional pre-purchase of the entrepreneur's planned product. If the product launch is successful, contributors are sent the actual product (see the Living the Dream feature on page 340).

The foregoing approaches are not considered investments. The contributors are not loaning the firm money, nor are they receiving any equity ownership in the business. However, the *equity investing* approach does offer participants partial ownership (a very small percentage) in the business. *But they are investors*, and as a result, the company is subject to securities laws. As of the end of 2012, any participants in equity crowdfunding must be accredited investors, which requires them to have a net worth of at least $1 million, not including their primary residence.[20] For instance, Syntellia developed an app to assist visually impaired individuals with typing on a smartphone. The firm raised $900,000 with equity crowdfunding, along with funds provided by angel investors. But anyone participating had to be an accredited investor.

An entrepreneur who is considering crowdfunding as a way to raise money can use a large number of websites designed for this purpose. Two of the most popular websites are Kickstarter and Indiegogo. Both facilitate crowdfunding based on donations, rewards, and pre-purchases. As of late 2012, they did not provide equity crowdfunding. Kickstarter offers some basic guidelines on what it will accept:

> *Everything on Kickstarter must be a project. A project has a clear goal, like making an album, a book, or a work of art. A project will eventually be completed, and something will be produced by it.... Kickstarter does not allow charity, cause, or "fund my life" projects.*[21]

A website that does focus on equity crowdfunding is SeedInvest. But again, securities laws prohibit private companies from advertising or selling shares to investors who are not relatively wealthy—that is, "accredited," as defined by legislation.

Small businesses that raise equity through crowdfunding should be aware of potential problems that can arise. First, if crowdfunding investors receive voting rights, that fact may become a deterrent to raising money from angels and venture capitalists in the future. Such investors usually would not be interested in sharing voting rights with a large group of small investors. Second, a company should be wary about sharing detailed financial information and trade secrets with a multitude of crowdfunding investors.

In short, when it is a good fit, crowdfunding may be a viable option for small businesses that need to raise capital. And all signs suggest that this approach will become even more popular in the future.

We have now completed our discussion of what an entrepreneur needs to understand when seeking financing for a company, in terms of a firm's financial statements and forecasts (Chapters 10 and 11) and the different sources of financing typically used by small firms (Chapter 12). Our detailed explanations should help you avoid mistakes commonly made by small business owners when trying to get financing to grow a business.

Living the Dream

Parke New York: A Success at Crowdfunding

Solomon Liou is the founder of Parke New York, an online, luxury clothing brand based in downtown New York City. Liou describes his business concept as follows:

> Parke New York is a new vertically integrated, online denim brand, targeting a $13 billion market in the U.S. and $66 billion worldwide. Created with quality and aesthetics in mind, Parke combines premium fabrics and artisanal craftsmanship to provide the perfect fitting jeans. Additionally, by selling direct to consumers online, we can offer prices that are 50 percent less than traditional brands.

In 2012, Liou chose to use crowdfunding as a way to gauge consumer support for the brand and to raise capital. His plans were to launch the business in July 2013, based on the outcome of the crowdfunding effort.

As part of an effort to secure consumer support and demonstrate market demand, Parke New York hosted a rewards crowdfunding campaign on Kickstarter for 30 days (from December 19, 2012 to January 18, 2013). This campaign received an immense amount of support and revealed clear support within the fashion/denim niche.

To be more specific, the firm raised $90,535 from 634 individuals. Following this success, Liou and his team were prepared to expand manufacturing and distribution capabilities to sell Parke jeans to consumers across the United States.

Sources: Based on www.fundable.com/parke-new-york, accessed February 15, 2013; and www.parkenewyork.com/, accessed February 15, 2013.

12-1. Describe how a firm's characteristics affect its available financing sources.

- Four basic firm characteristics determine how a firm is financed: (1) the firm's economic potential, (2) the size and maturity of the company, (3) the nature of the firm's assets, and (4) the personal preferences of the owners with respect to the trade-offs between debt and equity.

- An entrepreneurial firm with high-growth potential has more possible sources of financing than does a firm that

provides a good lifestyle for its owner but little in the way of attractive returns to investors.

- Older and larger companies have more access to bank financing, while smaller firms tend to rely more on personal loans and credit cards.

- Tangible assets serve as great collateral when a business is requesting a bank loan, while intangible assets have little value as collateral for lenders.

12-2. Evaluate the choice between debt financing and equity financing.

- The choice between debt and equity financing involves trade-offs with regard to potential profitability, financial risk, and voting control.

- Borrowing money (debt) rather than issuing common stock (owners' equity) creates the potential for higher rates of return to the owners and allows them to retain voting control of the company, but it also exposes them to greater financial risk.

- Issuing common stock rather than borrowing money results in lower potential rates of return to the owners and the loss of some voting control, but it does reduce their financial risk.

12-3. **Identify the typical sources of financing used at the outset of a new venture.**

- The aspiring entrepreneur basically has three sources of early financing: (1) personal savings, (2) friends and family, and (3) credit cards.

- Personal savings is the primary source of equity financing used in starting a new business. A banker or other lender is unlikely to loan venture money if the entrepreneur does not have her or his own money at risk.

- Loans from friends and family may be the only available source of financing and are often easy and fast to obtain, although such borrowing can place the entrepreneur's most important personal relationships in jeopardy.

- Credit card financing provides easily accessible financing, but the high interest costs may become overwhelming at times.

12-4. **Discuss the basic process for acquiring and structuring a bank loan.**

- Bankers primarily make business loans in one of three forms: lines of credit, term loans, and mortgages.

- In making a loan decision, a banker always considers the "five C's of credit": (1) the borrower's *character*, (2) the borrower's *capacity* to repay the loan, (3) the *capital* being invested in the venture by the borrower, (4) the *collateral* available to secure the loan, and (5) the *conditions* of the industry and economy.

- Obtaining a bank loan requires a well-prepared loan request that addresses: (1) how much money is needed, (2) what the venture is going to do with the money, (3) when the money is needed, and (4) when and how the money will be paid back.

- A banker may request other detailed financial information, including three years of the firm's historical financial statements, the firm's pro forma financial statements, and personal financial statements showing the borrower's net worth and estimated annual income.

- An entrepreneur should carefully evaluate available banks before choosing one, basing the decision on factors such as the bank's location, the services provided, and the bank's lending policies.

- In negotiating a bank loan, the owner must consider the accompanying terms, which typically include the interest rate, the loan maturity date, the repayment schedule, and the loan covenants.

12-5. **Explain how business relationships can be used to finance a small firm.**

- Business suppliers can offer trade credit (accounts payable), which is the source of short-term funds most widely used by small firms.

- Suppliers also offer equipment loans and leases, which allow small businesses to use equipment purchased on an installment basis.

- An asset-based loan is financing secured by working capital assets, such as accounts receivable, inventory, or both.

12-6. **Describe the two types of private equity investors who offer financing to small firms.**

- Business angels are private individuals, generally with substantial business experience, who invest in early-stage ventures.

- Formal venture capitalists are groups of individuals who form limited partnerships for the purpose of raising capital from large institutional investors. The money is then invested in high-potential startups and existing firms for an ownership share.

12-7. **Distinguish among the different government loan programs available to small companies.**

- The federal government helps new businesses get started through the programs and agencies of the Small Business Administration (SBA), which include the 7(a) Loan Guaranty Program, the Certified Development Company (CDC) 504 Loan Program, the 7(m) Microloan Program, small business investment companies (SBICs), and the Small Business Innovative Research (SBIR) Program.

- State and local governments finance new businesses in various ways, with programs that are generally geared to augmenting other sources of funding.

- Community-based financial institutions are lenders that use funds from federal, state, and private sources to serve low-income communities and small companies that otherwise would have little or no access to startup funding.

12-8. **Explain when large companies and public stock offerings can be sources of financing.**

- Large companies may finance smaller businesses when it is in their self-interest to have a close relationship with the smaller company.

- Stock sales, in the form of either private placements or public sales, may provide a few high-potential ventures with equity capital.

12-9. **Describe how crowdfunding can be used by some small businesses to raise capital.**

- Crowdfunding is the process of raising very small investments from a large number of investors via the Internet.

- There are four basic approaches to crowdfunding: (1) donations, (2) rewards, (3) pre-purchases, and (4) equity investing.

Key Terms

7(a) Loan Guaranty Program p. 336
7(m) Microloan Program p. 336
asset-based loan p. 331
balloon payment p. 329
basis point p. 329
business angels p. 332
Certified Development Company (CDC) 504
   Loan Program p. 336
chattel mortgage p. 325
community-based financial institution p. 337

crowdfunding p. 337
equipment loan p. 331
factoring p. 331
formal venture capitalists p. 333
informal venture capital p. 332
initial public offering (IPO) p. 337
LIBOR (London InterBank Offered Rate) p. 329
line of credit p. 325
loan covenants p. 329

prime rate (base rate) p. 328
private placement p. 337
purchase-order financing p. 332
real estate mortgage p. 325
Small Business Innovative Research (SBIR)
   Program p. 336
small business investment companies
   (SBICs) p. 336
term loan p. 325

Discussion Questions

1. How does the nature of a business affect its sources of financing?

2. How is debt different from equity?

3. Explain the three trade-offs that guide the choice between debt financing and equity financing.

4. Assume that you are starting a business for the first time. What do you believe are the greatest personal obstacles to obtaining funds for the new venture? Why?

5. If you were starting a new business, where would you start looking for capital?

6. Explain how trade credit and equipment loans can provide initial capital funding.

7. a. Describe the different types of loans made by a commercial bank.

   b. What does a banker need to know in order to decide whether to make a loan?

8. Distinguish between informal venture capital and formal venture capital.

9. In what ways does the federal government help with initial financing for small businesses?

10. What advice would you give an entrepreneur who was trying to finance a startup?

You Make the Call

Situation 1

David Bernstein needs help financing his six-year-old, $3.5 million company, Access Direct, Inc. "We're ready to get to the next level," says Bernstein, "but we're not sure which way to go." Access Direct cleans and then sells used computer equipment for corporations. It is looking for up to $2 million in order to expand. "Venture capitalists, individual investors, or banks," says Bernstein, who owns the company with four partners, "we've thought about them all."

Question 1 What is your impression of Bernstein's perspective on raising capital to "get to the next level"?

Question 2 What advice would you offer Bernstein as to both appropriate and inappropriate sources of financing in his situation?

Situation 2

John Dalton is well on his way to starting a new venture—Max, Inc. He has projected a need for $350,000 in initial capital. He plans to invest $150,000 himself and either borrow the additional $200,000 or find a partner who will buy stock in the company. If Dalton borrows the money, the interest rate will be 6 percent. If, on the other hand, another equity investor is found, he expects to have to give up 60 percent of the company's stock. Dalton has forecasted earnings of about 16 percent in operating profits on the firm's total assets.

Question 1 Compare the two financing options in terms of projected return on the owner's equity investment. Ignore any effect from income taxes.

Question 2 What if Dalton is wrong, and the company earns only 4 percent in operating profits on total assets?

Question 3 What should Dalton consider in choosing a source of financing?

Situation 3

Mike Smith seeks your counsel about a problem that has grown out of a decision he made three years earlier to buy a warehouse. Up until then, he had rented three warehouses, where he stored containers and did pick-and-pack for retailers importing goods from abroad. Figuring it was time to consolidate, Smith found a building, negotiated a price of $3.5 million, put down $300,000, and borrowed $3.2 million from a bank at 7 percent interest.

It seemed like a good idea at the time. Then a recession hit. As his sales dropped, he struggled to make his monthly payment of $27,000. At present, he's behind in his payments and scared. Furthermore, the situation seems unlikely to improve anytime

soon. To make matters worse, he signed a personal guarantee on the loan and thinks he might lose his house. The bank is assessing the situation to decide what to do.

In a panic, Smith tells you, "I'm going to tell the bank I need eight months. It can take the money I'll owe for that time, plus what I owe now, and tack it onto the end of the mortgage. What do you think?"

"How do you know that's what the bank is looking for?" you ask.

"I have to offer them something," Smith says. "My wife and I could lose everything!"

"You aren't going to lose everything," you say, "and you're making a mistake to assume that you know what the bank wants."

Question 1 What guidance will you give Smith in negotiating with the bank?

Question 2 Why might you advise him not to go into a meeting with bank officers with a plan already in mind?

Experiential Exercises

1. Interview a local small business owner to determine how funds were obtained to start the business. Be sure you phrase questions so that they are not overly personal, and do not ask for specific dollar amounts. Write a brief report on your findings.

2. Interview a local banker about lending policies for small business loans. Ask the banker to comment on the importance of a business plan to the bank's decision to loan money to a small firm. Write a brief report on your findings.

3. Review recent issues of *Entrepreneur* and *Inc.*, and report to the class on the financing arrangements of firms featured in these magazines.

4. Interview a stockbroker or investment analyst on his or her views regarding the sale of common stock by a small business. Write a brief report on your findings.

Small Business & Entrepreneurship Resource Center

The Small Business & Entrepreneurship Resource Center offers complete small business management resources through a comprehensive database that covers all major areas of starting, operating, and maintaining a business from financing, management, marketing, accounting, taxes, and more. Go to www.cengagebrain.com and select the Longenecker text for more information on how to access this material.

1. Philanthropic sponsorship of science, in the form of expensive telescopes or expeditions to far-off places, has been around for centuries. But the Internet now permits microphilanthropy. Through crowdfunding, in which members of the public donate small sums, the possibility of scientific philanthropy has been extended. Ethan Perlstein, a pharmacologist at Princeton University, launched a bid on a site called RocketHub to collect $25,000 to study the

effect of drugs on the brain. Kristina Killgrove, an anthropologist at the University of West Florida, raised over $12,000 on RocketHub to examine the DNA of Roman skeletons. Donors receive no revenue if a crowdfunded science project is successful, but they will be kept up to date on its progress. After reading this article, why do you think people make donations that resemble a charitable contribution more than an investment? Would you invest in one of the scientific projects? If so, why?

2. An angel is a high-net-worth individual who invests capital in a company. Angel investors tend to inject startup capital into a company's seed round of investment. Ron Conway—an angel investor and founder of Angel Investors LP—made initial investments from personal funds in Ask Jeeves and Google. Loic Le Meur is a French angel investor

who also started a company that connects angel investors with startups through events in Paris and through an annual contest for European technology startups. Typically, angel investors are former entrepreneurs who have retired on profits earned from starting up successful businesses. According to this article, angel investment is declining. Since angels provide seed and startup capital, what would be the effect of this decline in investment on new venture formation and job creation?

Sources: "Many a Mickle Makes a Muckle; Crowdfunding Science (Crowdfunding Science Is All the Rage)," *The Economist*, Vol. 405, No. 8807 (October 20, 2012), p. 74; and "Angel Investors and Venture Capitalists," *Encyclopedia of Management*, 7th ed., Sonya D. Hill (ed.), (Detroit: Gale, 2012).

Video Case 12

Moonworks (P. 667)

Moonworks began installing Gutter Helmet® in Rhode Island, but soon the business began expanding further into the New England states and New York. Now it offers industry-leading home improvement products. Moonworks has had a long relationship with the Bank of Rhode Island, and this case tells the story of the company's financing and how it has changed along with the company over 15 years.

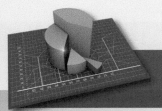

Business Plan

LAYING THE FOUNDATION

As part of laying the foundation for your own business plan, respond to the following questions regarding the financing of your venture:

1. What is the total financing required to start the business?

2. How much money do you plan to invest in the venture? What is the source of this money?

3. Will you need financing beyond what you personally plan to invest?

4. If additional financing is needed for the startup, how will you raise it? How will the financing be structured—debt or equity? What will the terms be for the investors?

5. According to your pro forma financial statements, will there be a need for additional financing within the first five years of the firm's life? If so, where will it come from?

6. How and when will you arrange for investors to cash out of their investment?

Endnotes

1. Mike Hofman, "The Big Picture," *Inc.*, Vol. 25, No. 12 (October 2003), p. 87.

2. Angel Capital Association, www.angelcapitalassociation.org, accessed September 30, 2012.

3. Quoted in Alison Stein Wellner, "Getting Started: Blood Money" *Inc.*, Vol. 25 (December 2003).

4. Ilan Mochari, "The Numbers Game," *Inc.*, Vol. 24, No. 12 (October 2002), pp. 65–66.

5. Asheesh Advani, "The Angel in Your Pocket," *Entrepreneur*, November 2009; and Steven Fischer, "The Perils of Using Personal Credit Cards to Fund Your Business," http://unintentionalentrepreneur.com/, accessed December 2010.

6. David Port, "But Where Is the Money?" www.entrepreneur.com/magazine /entrepreneur/2010/august/207500.html, accessed January 3, 2011.

7. *2012 Year-End Economic Report*, National Small Business Association, February 6, 2013, http://smallbusiness.foxbusiness.com

/entrepreneurs/2013/02/06/nsba-small-business-outlook-not-so-hot/#ixzz2LjjYlU74, accessed February 16, 2013.

8. Personal communication with Jack Griggs, board chair, Texas Heritage Banks, January 29, 2013.

9. To compute the $730 monthly payment, you can use a financial calculator or a computer spreadsheet:

   PV (present value) = 50,000 (current loan)

   N (number of payments) = 84 (7 years × 12 months = 84)

   I/yr (interest rate/month) = 0.5% (6% interest rate per year ÷ 12 months = 0.005 = 0.5%)

   FV (future value) = 0 (in 7 years)

   PMT (payment) = $730.43

10. Mochari, *op. cit.,* p. 64.

11. Comment by Jack Griggs, Chairman of Texas Heritage Bank, February 1, 2013.

12. C. J. Prince, "New Money," *Entrepreneur*, March 2008, www.entrepreneur.com/magazine/entrepreneur/2008/march/190066.html, accessed October 2, 2008.

13. For an excellent source on business angels, see Bill Payne, *The Definitive Guide to Raising Money from Angels*, http://billpayne.com/services/definitive-guide-raising-money-from-angel-investors, accessed January 5, 2013.

14. Jeffrey Sohl, "The Angel Investor Market in 2011: The Recovery Continues," Center for Venture Research, http://paulcollege.unh.edu/sites/default/files/2011_analysis_report.pdf, accessed January 16, 2013.

15. For a description of how angel networks function, see Aja Carmichael, "The Money Game: In Search of an Angel," *The Wall Street Journal*, January 30, 2006, p. R4. Also, visit the Angel Capital Association website at http://angelcapitalassociation.org.

16. Guy Kawasaki, "Garnering Angels," *Entrepreneur*, January 2008, www.entrepreneur.com/magazine/entrepreneur/2008/january/187614.html, accessed December 28, 2012.

17. Asheesh Advani, "Finally, Someone Wants to Give You Money," *Entrepreneur*, March 2010, www.entrepreneur.com/article/205058, accessed October 16, 2010.

18. C. J. Prince, "Alternate Financing Routes," *Entrepreneur*, March 2007, pp. 66–68.

19. "Crowdsourcing Industry Report," Massolution, February 2012.

20. In 2012, in order to make more capital available to small businesses, Congress passed the Jumpstart Our Business Startups, or JOBS, Act, which removes the requirement that investors have to be accredited in order to invest in private companies. However, as of January 2013, the Securities and Exchange Commission had not finalized the regulations for the act. It was expected that they would be completed in late 2013.

21. www.kickstarter.com/help/faq/kickstarter%20basics, accessed April 2013.

CHAPTER
13

Planning for the Harvest

© Watcharakun/Shutterstock.com

*After studying this chapter,
you should be able to...*

13-1. Explain the importance of having a harvest, or exit, plan.

13-2. Describe the options available for harvesting.

13-3. Explain the issues in valuing a firm that is being harvested and deciding on the method of payment.

13-4. Provide advice on developing an effective harvest plan.

**OPEN
LOOKING
AHEAD**

The following story of Tapestry Medical, Inc., is told by Robert Knorr, its founder and CEO. He discusses building the company and then "finishing well" by executing what proved to be a successful exit.

For as long as I can remember, I felt the entrepreneurial spirit burning within me. In the early part of my professional career, my desire was satisfied by creating new businesses for my employer, Johnson & Johnson. Within the security of a corporate environment, I had easy access to funding and talented people who helped me create several successful new businesses. Although in many ways I operated as an entrepreneur within a large corporation, ultimately Johnson & Johnson bore all the risks AND received all the rewards of each new business I created.

> **In the SPOTLIGHT**
> **Tapestry Medical**

After almost 20 years, I decided to leave Johnson & Johnson and venture out on my own. At that point in my career, I had the industry knowledge to start my own company in the healthcare field. I also had the confidence to use my own money to fund my company that began in my garage. By "bootstrapping" my company, I and a few members of the management team were able to maintain tight control of the

© gst/Shutterstock.com

company's ownership and control all decision making. Most importantly, this time I would bear the risks but also receive the rewards of my new business [Tapestry Medical]. Within a few years, Tapestry had established itself as the leading company in this small but growing field of remote patient monitoring. In fact, within four years Tapestry was among the fastest growing private healthcare companies in the U.S.

Although Tapestry's sales were growing rapidly, additional working capital was needed to sustain growth beyond what we could provide. Also, several competitors were interested in consolidating Tapestry's market share and best-in-class operations into their own companies. Following the financial crisis of late 2008, I decided that the time was right to sell Tapestry to a larger healthcare company with the resources to take the business to the next level. Potential acquirers included diversified healthcare companies interested in entering Tapestry's marketplace.

At the time, Tapestry was still a privately funded startup company competing against three large, well-funded publically traded companies. However, just prior to putting Tapestry up for sale, I signed an important co-marketing agreement with a leading healthcare software company that provided access to 500,000 potential new customers.

With impressive past results and a promising future, I engaged an investment banker who helped negotiate the best acquisition terms. After several months of intense negotiations, Tapestry was eventually acquired by its principal competitor, a leading healthcare company that had made several other acquisitions in this industry. I, along with key members of my management team, remained on board and were immediately given responsibility for merging Tapestry into the acquiring company's operations. The first year after the acquisition, sales of the new combined entity rose dramatically as a result of adopting best practices across both organizations and leveraging customer relationships.

Although Tapestry was founded and then sold within five years, there were periods of great uncertainty and risk. Looking back on the company sale, Knorr offers three pieces of advice:

- *Do whatever you can to detach yourself emotionally from selling your company.*
- *Establish a short list of "must haves" prior to beginning negotiations and remain flexible on all secondary points.*
- *Remember to thank (and when appropriate reward) everyone who helped you achieve your goals.*

Knorr's positive experience with selling Tapestry and then becoming an executive of the acquiring firm is not the norm, at least not without a lot of frustration. Being prepared for the harvest process and life after exiting your business is something that deserves your thoughtful attention.

Source: Written by Robert Knorr, founder and CEO, Tapestry Medical, Inc. February 28, 2013.

As you will learn in this chapter, exiting your business, or what we call the *harvest*, can be the best of times and the worst of times, depending in large part on how well you understand yourself, your business, and what is required to exit your business effectively. You may wonder why we address the issue of exiting a business so early in the text, choosing to delay instruction on managing a business to subsequent chapters. We do so because of our strong conviction that it is better for an entrepreneur to consider the exit sooner rather than later.

In previous chapters, we have talked about recognizing business opportunities and developing strategies for capturing these opportunities. Such activities represent the cornerstone for everything a company does. But, for entrepreneurs, that's not the end of the story. Experience suggests that an entrepreneur who is developing a company strategy should think about more than just starting (founding or acquiring) and growing a business. The entrepreneurial process is not complete until the owners and any other investors have exited the venture and captured the value created by the business. This final—but extremely important—phase can be enhanced through an effective harvest, or exit, plan. In other words, the goal is to create value during the entrepreneurial journey by making a difference and then *finishing well!*

LO 13-1

Explain the importance of having a harvest, or exit, plan.

13-1 THE IMPORTANCE OF THE HARVEST

Most small business owners do not like to think about the harvest, even though few events in the life of an entrepreneur, and of the firm itself, are more significant. Consequently, the decision to harvest is frequently the result of an unexpected event, possibly a financial crisis, rather than a well-conceived strategy.

Harvesting, or **exiting**, is the method that owners and investors use to get out of a business and, ideally, reap the value of their investment in the firm. Many entrepreneurs successfully grow their businesses but fail to develop effective harvest plans. As a result, they are unable to capture the full value of the business they have worked so hard to create.

An entrepreneur needs to understand that harvesting encompasses more than merely selling and leaving a business. It involves capturing value (cash flows), reducing risk, and creating future options—the reason we prefer the term *harvest* over *exit*. In addition, there are personal, nonfinancial considerations for entrepreneurs. Owners may receive a lot of money for their firms but still be disappointed with the harvest if they are not prepared for a change in lifestyle. Thus, carefully designing an intentional harvest strategy is as essential to an entrepreneur's personal success as it is to his or her financial success.

In this chapter, we offer suggestions for achieving a "successful" harvest. It is a mistake to define success only in terms of the harvest; the entrepreneurial journey should be successful as well. So, throughout the chapter, we encourage you to think about what success means to you. Arriving at the end of the journey only to discover that your ladder was leaning against the wrong wall is one of life's tragedies.

The harvest is vitally important to a firm's investors as well as to its founder. Investors who provide high-risk capital—particularly angels and venture capitalists—generally insist on a well-thought-out harvest strategy. They realize that it is easy to put money into a business, but difficult to get it out. As a result, a firm's appeal to investors is driven, in part, by the availability of harvest options. If investors are not convinced that opportunities will exist for harvesting their investment, they will be unlikely to invest.

START UP

ACTION

Planning for a Successful Harvest
The earlier you begin planning for a harvest, the more successful your eventual exit will most likely be. In fact, some of the steps involved in planning for the harvest, such as fine-tuning your company's strategies, focusing on internal growth, improving your financial systems, and creating an independent board, are the same as those required to build a successful company.

LO 13-2

Describe the options available for harvesting.

13-2 METHODS OF HARVESTING A BUSINESS

The four basic ways to harvest an investment in a privately owned company are (1) selling the firm, (2) distributing the cash flows generated by the business to its owners instead of reinvesting the cash, (3) offering stock to the public through an initial public offering (IPO), and (4) undertaking a private equity recapitalization. These options are shown graphically in Exhibit 13.1.

13-2a Selling the Firm

In any harvest strategy, the financial questions associated with the sale of a firm include how to value the firm and how to structure the payment for the business. Most frequently, an entrepreneur's motivation for selling a company relates to retirement and estate planning and a desire to diversify investments. Thus, in choosing a possible buyer, entrepreneurs should understand what they want to accomplish from the sale.

harvesting (exiting)
The process used by entrepreneurs and investors to reap the value of a business when they leave it.

13.1 Methods for Harvesting a Business

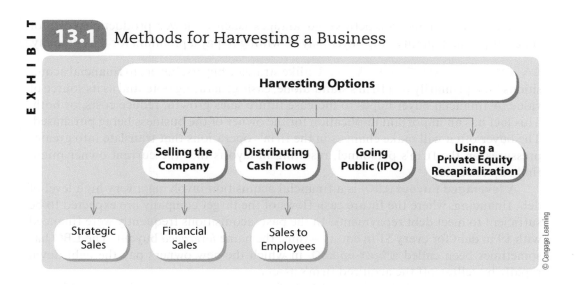

Potential buyers for a company can come from a number of places, including your customers, suppliers, employees, friends and family, or even a competitor. You may also want to use a business broker. A **business broker** is a professional who assists in the buying and selling of a business. In addition to finding possible buyers, a business broker can provide valuable guidance to the selling entrepreneur and help facilitate the negotiations. Brokers can, however, be relatively expensive, charging 5 to 10 percent of the selling price. Also, care has to be taken when selecting a broker. Not all brokers act professionally, and some make false claims regarding their qualifications. It is not unusual for an entrepreneur to be disappointed with a broker's contribution to the sale. For example, Robert Hall, the owner of Visador Corporation, hired a business broker to help sell his business. At one point in the negotiations, Hall gave the broker the firm's latest financial information that reported a downturn in sales in the previous month. Hall felt that ethics required that the buyer be given this information. The broker, as Hall learned later, chose not to give the information to the buyer so that the deal would not be adversely affected. After all, the broker received a fee only if the sale was consummated. (We will say more about Visador later in the chapter and in Appendix B. Go to www.cengagebrain.com and select the Longenecker text to access this appendix.)

In the search for potential buyers, it is essential that the selling entrepreneur understand the different types of buyers. In the sections that follow, we will look at three buyer groups in particular: (1) strategic buyers, (2) financial buyers, and (3) employees.

SALES TO STRATEGIC BUYERS Usually, a strategic buyer is a firm in a similar line of business in a different market or in need of new products and services to sell to existing customers. Another possibility is a buyer in an unrelated business that wants to acquire a seller's strengths to help the buyer's existing business. For example, IBM acquired a privately owned company, HealthLink, Inc., that provided information technology in the healthcare industry. Since IBM had not developed a presence in this niche area, acquiring HealthLink quickly gave it a way to compete in that space.

Strategic buyers value a business based on the synergies they think they can create by combining the acquired firm with another business. Since the value of a business to a buyer is derived from both its stand-alone characteristics and its synergies, strategic buyers may pay a higher price than would other buyers, who value the business only as a stand-alone entity. Thus, in strategic acquisitions, the critical issue is the degree of strategic fit between the firm to be harvested and the potential buyer's other business interests. If the prospective buyer is a current rival and if the acquisition would provide

business broker
A professional who assists in the buying and selling of a business.

long-term, sustainable competitive advantages (such as lower production costs or superior product quality), the buyer may be willing to pay a premium for the company.

SALES TO FINANCIAL BUYERS Unlike strategic buyers, buyers in financial acquisitions look primarily to a firm's stand-alone, cash-generating potential as its source of value. A financial buyer hopes to increase future sales growth, reduce costs, or both. This fact has an important implication for the owner of the business being purchased. The buyer often will make changes in the firm's operations that translate into greater pressures on the firm's personnel, resulting in layoffs that the current owner might find objectionable.

A **leveraged buyout (LBO)** is a financial acquisition involving a very high level of debt financing, where the future cash flows of the target company are expected to be sufficient to meet debt repayments. In the past, acquisitions frequently were financed with $9 in debt for every $1 in equity—thus, the name *leveraged* buyout. The LBO has sometimes been called a **bust-up LBO**, in which the new owners pay the debt down rapidly by selling off the acquired firm's assets.

Because buyers rely heavily on debt to finance the acquisition, the acquired company must have the following characteristics: (1) steady earnings over time, (2) attractive growth rates, (3) an effective management team already in place, and (4) assets that can be used as collateral on the debt. Otherwise, the risk is too great, and the transaction simply will not work.

Consider Visador Corporation, which was sold to a financial buyer for $67 million. The buyer financed the purchase as a leveraged buyout, incurring a lot of debt. The firm's total assets and debt and equity (as presented in the balance sheet) before and after the sale were as follows:

	Before the Sale	After the Sale
Total assets	$18,000,000	$67,000,000
Total debt	$ 5,000,000	$60,000,000
Equity	13,000,000	7,000,000
Total debt and equity	$18,000,000	$67,000,000

Visador's before-sale and after-sale numbers differ in two important respects. First, the total assets (and total debt and equity) increased from $18 million to $67 million. In other words, the founders of Visador had invested just over $18 million in the firm during their years of ownership, up to the point of the acquisition. However, the buyer was willing to pay $67 million for the business, based on future cash flows that were expected to be generated.

Second, before the sale, the assets were financed with 28 percent debt ($5 million total debt ÷ $18 million total assets) compared to 90 percent debt ($60 million total debt ÷ $67 million total assets) after the sale. Consequently, the firm was exposed to significantly more financial risk. If sales had decreased, the company may not have been able to service its debt. This is typical for bust-up leveraged buyouts.

More recently, the bust-up LBO has been replaced by the build-up LBO. As the name suggests, a **build-up LBO** involves pulling together a group of smaller firms to create a larger enterprise that might eventually be sold or taken public via an initial public offering.

The process of a build-up LBO begins with the acquisition of a company, which then acquires a number of smaller businesses that in some way complement it. These subsequent acquisitions may expand capacity in related or completely different businesses. The newly formed combination is operated privately for five years or so in order to establish a successful track record, and then it is sold or taken public. These acquisitions continue

leveraged buyout (LBO)
A purchase heavily financed with debt, where the future cash flows of the target company are expected to be sufficient to meet debt repayments.

bust-up LBO
A leveraged buyout involving the purchase of a company with the intent of selling off its assets.

build-up LBO
A leveraged buyout involving the purchase of a group of similar companies with the intent of making the firms into one larger company for eventual sale.

to rely heavily on debt financing, but to a lesser extent than bust-up LBOs. Build-up LBOs have occurred in a number of industries where smaller companies frequently operate, such as funeral services and automobile dealerships.

Sometimes, the selling firm's own management initiates an LBO to buy the business from the entrepreneur—in which case the arrangement is referred to as a **management buyout (MBO)**. An MBO can contribute significantly to a firm's operating performance by increasing management's focus and intensity. Thus, an MBO is a potentially viable means of transferring ownership from the founder to the management team. In many entrepreneurial businesses, managers have a strong incentive to become owners but lack the financial capacity to acquire the firm. An MBO can solve this problem through the use of debt financing, which is often underwritten in part by the selling entrepreneur.

SALES TO EMPLOYEES Established by Congress in 1974, **employee stock ownership plans (ESOPs)** have gradually been embraced by more than 10,000 companies. Once established, an ESOP uses employees' retirement contributions to buy company stock from the owner and holds it in trust. Over time, the stock is distributed to employees' retirement plans.

It is common for an owner to start an ESOP by selling only a portion of the company. But even if the owners sell all of their stock, they can still retain their management positions with the firm, thereby effectively maintaining control of the business. And an ESOP creates significant tax advantages for the seller. For instance, if the entrepreneur sells at least 30 percent of the company, taxes that may be owed as a result of the sale can frequently be deferred and not paid until a later date, in some cases indefinitely. For example, after the owner-managers of BFW Construction Company created an ESOP, they sold the business and rolled over the money from the shares into their personal retirement accounts. As a result, they have not paid taxes from the time the shares were put into the ESOP and will not have to pay them until they are required to begin distributing the money, when they are 70½ years old.[1]

A reason frequently given for selling to employees is to create an incentive for them to work harder—by giving them a piece of the profits. However, employee ownership is not a panacea. Although advocates maintain that employee ownership improves motivation, leading to greater effort and reduced waste, the value of increased employee effort resulting from improved motivation varies significantly from firm to firm. Selling all or part of a firm to employees works only if the company's employees have an owner's mentality—that is, they do not think in "9-to-5" terms. An ESOP may provide a way for the owner to sell the business, but if the employees lack the required mindset, it will not serve the business well in the future.

Employee education is necessary if an ESOP is to be effective. Consider the experience of Mick Slinger, chief financial officer of Van Meter Industrial, Inc., who thought his company's employee stock program was a great perk for employees. But at a company meeting, an employee said he didn't care at all about the stock fund, asking, "Why don't you just give me a couple hundred bucks for beer and cigarettes?" It was a wake-up call for Slinger, who says that many employees at the 100 percent employee-owned company "didn't know what stock was, didn't know what an [employee] owner was. I made the mistake of thinking that everyone thinks like me." So the company created an employee committee to raise awareness of stock ownership and how it

Consider Visador Corporation, designer/producer of residential staircases, which was sold to a financial buyer for $67 million. The buyer financed the purchase as a leveraged buyout.

management buyout (MBO)
A leveraged buyout in which the firm's top managers become significant shareholders in the acquired firm.

employee stock ownership plan (ESOP)
A method by which a firm is sold either in part or in total to its employees.

affects employees' net worth. Today, employees are much more engaged in the program, and the firm's management believes it has made a significant contribution to increasing its stock price and lowering employee turnover. But it required a lot of effort to make the plan work as desired.[2]

The approaches that have been described in this section for selling a company represent the primary ways in which small business owners exit their businesses. But the opportunity to sell a business can be affected by market conditions. For instance, during the recent recession, there were not many buyers—but neither were there many sellers. Entrepreneurs who had been considering an exit were holding back in the hope of an economic recovery when they would receive a better price for the business.

Michael Handelsman, general manager of BizBuySell, an online marketplace that lists companies for sale, offers these tips for selling a business in a difficult economy:[3]

- *Clean up the books.* Pay off small debts if you can, and make sure your records are ready for buyers' review.
- *Keep revenue strong.* Continue marketing and bringing in customers to show buyers that your business is still flourishing.
- *Consider your sector and market.* The downturn wasn't the same in every city or every industry. Research businesses sold in your sector or town to see if it's a good time to sell.

These tips are relevant at any time—recession or no recession—and even when you are not interested in selling.

The recession also affected the availability of financing from traditional sources. As a result, **seller financing**, in which a seller loans the buyer part of the purchase price of the business, became more prevalent. For instance, an entrepreneur purchased a business for $3.5 million and paid $2.7 million in cash, with the seller taking a note for the remaining $800,000, to be paid off over the next seven years. The $2.7 million in cash came from a bank loan of $2 million and $700,000 of the buyer's personal money. The loan from the seller was subordinated to the bank loan, so that if the buyer missed a payment to the bank, she could not make any payments to the seller until the bank loan was current.

13-2b Distributing the Firm's Cash Flows

A second harvest strategy involves the orderly withdrawal of the owners' investment in the form of the firm's cash flows. The withdrawal process could be immediate if the owners simply sold off the assets of the firm and liquidated the business. However, for a value-creating firm—one that earns attractive rates of return for its investors—this does not make economic sense. The mere fact that a firm is earning high rates of return on its assets indicates that the business is worth more as a going concern than a dead one. Instead, the owners might simply stop growing the business. By doing so, they would increase the cash flows that can be returned to investors.

In a firm's early years, all of its cash is usually devoted to growing the business. Thus, the company's inflow of cash during this period is zero—or, more likely, negative—requiring its owners to seek outside cash to finance its growth. As the firm matures and opportunities to grow the business decline, sizable cash flows frequently become available to its owners. Rather than reinvest all the cash in the business, the owners can begin to withdraw the cash, thus harvesting their investment. If they decide to adopt this approach, only the amount of cash necessary to maintain current markets is retained and reinvested. There is little, if any, effort to grow the present markets or expand into new markets.

seller financing
Financing in which the seller accepts a note from a buyer in lieu of cash in partial payment for a business.

Harvesting by slowly withdrawing a firm's cash from the business has two important advantages: The owners can retain control of the business while they harvest their investment, and they do not have to seek out a buyer or incur the expenses associated with consummating a sale. There are disadvantages, however. Reducing investment when the firm faces valuable growth opportunities could leave a firm unable to sustain its competitive advantage. The end result may be an unintended reduction in the value of the business. Also, there may be tax disadvantages to an orderly liquidation, compared with other harvest methods. For example, if a corporation distributes cash as dividends, both the company and the stockholders will be taxed on the income; this is known as **double taxation**. (However, there is no double taxation for a sole proprietorship, partnership, limited liability company, or S corporation.)

Finally, for the entrepreneur who is simply tired of day-to-day operations, siphoning off the cash flows over time may require too much patience. Unless other people in the firm are qualified to manage it, this strategy may be destined to fail.

double taxation
Taxation of income that occurs twice—first as corporate earnings and then as stockholder dividends.

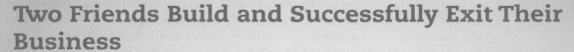

ENTREPRENEURIAL EXPERIENCES

Living the Dream

Two Friends Build and Successfully Exit Their Business

Jorge Fernandez and Bruce Goodhartz met 22 years ago, when both were working for a large commercial electrical contractor. Sharing a number of common goals, they decided to start their own business. Goodhartz describes building their company and their experience in finally exiting the business:

Experiencing early successes, we grew ESA Construction into one of the more recognizable names in dental construction in the [Dallas-Fort Worth] metroplex in less than three years. However, we knew that to stay competitive, we would need to strengthen our position. So we were the first of our competitors to build a website that showcased our previous dental projects; although at this early stage, it primarily served as a marketing tool and not for searches.

Jorge and I often wondered how we would ever "exit" from our business when the time came. Also, we had no idea as to the value of the business, other than what was on the books. So we hired an independent business valuation

© desert_fox99/view portfolio/iStockphoto.com

company and were shocked to learn that we indeed owned a company that had substantial value to others.

Based on recommendations for improving our value and becoming more marketable, we spent the next five years enhancing our brand recognition and removing the "Jorge and Bruce" from ESA Construction. We promoted our employees to key front-line positions with our customers and vendors; we aggressively increased our market share; we set up and maintained a Facebook page; and [we] reworked our website for maximum Google optimization.

[In 2011,] we had two confidential meetings over a six-month period with larger contractors and actually received a "Letter of Intent" from one of them, although it was an offer that we declined. Following these unsuccessful negotiations, we decided to take a break from marketing ESA and focus back on building our business and maintaining our market share—things that had started to slip as we were trying to sell the company. Then in fall 2012,

we approached our largest subcontractor, a younger, successful, and aggressive drywall contractor, about the idea of his buying a portion of our company. We saw it as a way to strengthen and grow the company into new markets. He would then be allowed to completely buy us out in five years.

While we agreed on terms, he could not get a bank to finance the deal. As it turned out, no bank would loan him the money unless he owned 100 percent of the company. Thus, he countered with an offer to buy the firm in total. We went through about four months of negotiations, bank appraisals, and valuations. To get the deal done, we had to reduce our asking price by about 8 percent, but we received the full amount in cash at the time of the sale.

We closed the sale on February 15, 2013, with Jorge and me receiving an employment agreement for one year at our former base salary, benefits, and the same job description as before, with the added role to help in the transition to the new ownership. The sale turned out to be good for Jorge and me as the former owners. But equally important, all of the ESA employees retained their positions and salaries, with new excitement and synergy at the office.

What's next for Jorge and me beyond our one-year employment is up in the air. We are having to learn how to work for someone else, which is different. Also, I want to take this time to do some special things with family—including being a new granddad. But I know that I would not be happy not working. So Jorge and I are open to the idea of continuing with the company and the new owner, whom we consider to be a good friend. In fact, we are in discussions about assisting ESA in opening offices in other Texas markets and possibly beyond. But where will we be in five years, only time will tell.

Source: Written by Bruce Goodhartz, co-founder and co-owner, ESA Construction, March 5, 2013. Reprinted with permission.

13-2c Initial Public Offering (IPO)

A third method of harvesting a firm is an initial public offering. As briefly discussed in Chapter 12, an **initial public offering (IPO)** occurs when a private firm sells its shares for the first time to the general public. This requires registering the stock issue with the Securities and Exchange Commission (SEC) and adhering to blue sky laws that govern the public offering at a state level. The purpose of these federal and state laws is to ensure adequate disclosure to investors and to prevent fraud. Businesses intending to conduct an IPO must file a detailed registration statement with the SEC, which includes in-depth financial, management, and operational information.

In the past, entrepreneurs frequently considered the prospect of an initial public offering to be the ultimate outcome for their efforts, bringing with it increased prestige in many business circles. However, that is rarely the case today, especially for smaller IPOs. In 2007, there were almost 300 IPOs in the United States. In the following year, the number of IPOs dropped from 80 to 57 percent. As shown in Exhibit 13.2, there were only 69 IPOs in 2009, increasing to 138 in 2012.

At the same time that the number of IPOs declined, the average size of IPOs increased; thus, offerings by smaller firms were not as prevalent. Also, the types of companies that investors prefer change from year to year. In the past, more-established firms financed with significant amounts of debt were in vogue. In 2012, most IPOs were financial companies, followed by firms in energy, consumer products, and technology.

THE COSTS OF MANAGING AN IPO An entrepreneur must consider more than just the initial costs of an IPO, which can be as much as 20 percent of the issue. He or she must also think hard about the costs of running a publicly traded company, which include significant ongoing costs associated with reporting its financial results to investors and to the SEC. These costs significantly increased in 2001, when the U.S. Congress passed the Sarbanes-Oxley Act. The act placed a much greater burden on companies to have good accounting practices and controls that will prevent egregious offenses by managers. In 2009, Congress passed the Dodd-Frank Act, which was primarily aimed at banks and other financial institutions to help avoid a repeat of the

initial public offering (IPO)
The first sale of shares of a company's stock to the public.

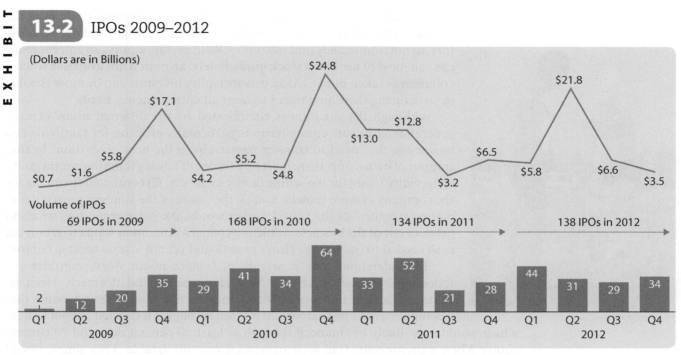

13.2 IPOs 2009–2012

(Dollars are in Billions)

$0.7 $1.6 $5.8 $17.1 $4.2 $5.2 $4.8 $24.8 $13.0 $12.8 $3.2 $6.5 $5.8 $21.8 $6.6 $3.5

Volume of IPOs

69 IPOs in 2009 → 168 IPOs in 2010 → 134 IPOs in 2011 → 138 IPOs in 2012 →

Q1	Q2	Q3	Q4	Q1	Q2	Q3	Q4	Q1	Q2	Q3	Q4	Q1	Q2	Q3	Q4
2	12	20	35	29	41	34	64	33	52	21	28	44	31	29	34
2009				2010				2011				2012			

Sources: Based on "IPO Watch," www.pwc.com/us/en/press-releases/2012/q3-ipo-watch-press-release.jhtml, accessed March 2, 2013; and Rob Starr, "PwC: 2012 IPO Market Surpasses 2011," www.big4.com/pricewaterhousecoopers/pwc-2012-ipo-market-surpasses-2011/. Both accessed March 2, 2013.

most recent financial crisis. However, it also added costly requirements for all publicly traded companies. Furthermore, these regulatory costs are disproportionate to a small firm and no small consideration in the decision to go public.

REASONS FOR GOING PUBLIC The purpose of the IPO process is to create a ready market for publicly trading the company's stock.

An IPO offers a number of benefits:[4]

1. It signals to investors that a firm is a quality business and will likely perform well in the future.

2. It has access to more investors when it needs to raise capital to grow the business.

3. Stock that is publicly traded helps to create an ongoing interest in the company and its continued development.

4. Publicly traded stock is more attractive to key personnel whose incentive pay includes the firm's stock.

While there are several reasons for going public, the primary reason is to raise capital. In most cases, money raised from selling a firm's stock to the public is used for expansion, paying down debt, and increasing the firm's liquidity (cash). In much fewer instances, initial public offerings result from entrepreneurs' desire to sell their stock. Thus, IPOs are seldom intended as an *immediate* exit strategy but rather as a way to raise capital for growth. Eventually, however, entrepreneurs can and frequently do sell their shares as a way to cash out of their companies.

13-2d Private Equity Recapitalization

A fourth method of harvesting is a **private equity recapitalization**, also called a *private equity recap*, where private equity investors provide a combination of debt and equity to the business, that allows the entrepreneur to cash out part of his or her investment

START UP

ACTION

Evaluate Your Business as a Buyer Would
Take time periodically to look at your company as if you were a prospective buyer. You'll notice things that you might otherwise overlook, such as improvements that you can make and best practices that you can adopt.

Private equity recapitalization
Private equity investors provide additional financing to a business that allows an entrepreneur the opportunity to cash out a portion of his or her investment, while possibly continuing to operate the business.

© Marcel Mooij/Shutterstock.com

in the company. The entrepreneur, most likely, will continue to manage the business. Private equity investors offer two key advantages that public investors do not: immediacy and flexibility. With private equity, an entrepreneur can sell most of her or his stock immediately, an option not available when a company is taken public. Also, private equity investors can be more flexible in structuring their investment to meet an entrepreneur's needs.

Although the situation is complicated by the different needs of each generation, a private equity recap is particularly effective for family-owned businesses that need to transfer ownership to the next generation. In that transfer of ownership, there must be a trade-off among three important goals: (1) liquidity (cash) for the selling family members, (2) continued financing for the company's future growth, and (3) the desire of the younger generation to maintain control of the firm. In other words, the older generation wants to get cash out of the business, while the younger generation wants to retain the cash needed to finance the firm's growth and yet not lose ownership control.

To understand how a private placement might work, consider the following approach taken by New Heritage Capital (formerly Heritage Partners), a firm that works with family-owned businesses:[5] Assume that a company could be sold for $20 million through a leveraged buyout (LBO), which would most likely be financed through at least 80 percent debt and 20 percent equity. Many entrepreneurs find such an arrangement intolerable. They simply would not want their company subjected to the risk associated with a large amount of debt financing. Also, with an LBO, the family generally loses control of the business.

As an alternative, the retiring generation might sell to New Heritage Capital for $18 million—10 percent less than the LBO price—of which $15 million would be paid to the retiring generation and $3 million reinvested in the business by the younger generation. For the $3 million investment, the younger generation would receive 51 percent of the equity. The remaining $15 million of the purchase price would be financed from two sources: $7 million in debt and $8 million from New Heritage Capital, consisting of $4 million in preferred stock and $4 million in common stock. The preferred stock would provide an annual dividend to the investors, while the common stock would give the new investor 49 percent of the firm's ownership (see Exhibit 13.3).

EXHIBIT 13.3 Private Placement–An illustration

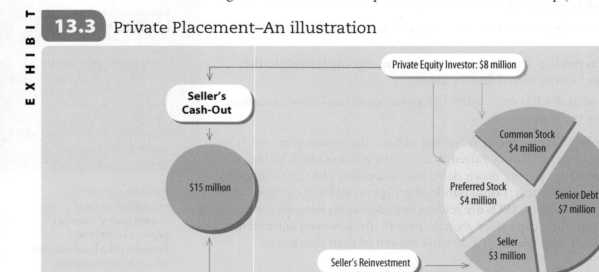

The differences between the two capital structures are clear. The debt ratio is much lower with the recapitalization than with the LBO, possibly allowing for a lower interest rate on the debt given less risk and permitting the firm's cash flows to be used to grow the firm, rather than to pay down debt. This arrangement allows the senior generation of owners to cash out, while the next generation retains control and the cash to grow the firm—a win-win situation. The younger generation also has the potential to realize significant economic gains in the future if the firm performs well after the sale.

13-3 FIRM VALUATION AND PAYMENT METHODS

As a firm moves toward the harvest, two issues are of primary importance: the harvest value (what the firm is worth) and the method of payment when a firm is sold.

LO
13-3

Explain the issues in valuing a firm that is being harvested and deciding on the method of payment.

13-3a The Harvest Value

Valuing a company may be necessary on numerous occasions during the life of the business—but it is never more important than at the time of the exit. Owners can harvest only what they have created. Value is created when a firm's return on invested capital is greater than the investors' opportunity cost of funds, which is the rate of return that could be earned on an investment of similar risk.

Growing a venture to the point of diminishing returns and then selling it to others who can carry it to the next level is a proven way to create value. How this incremental value is shared between the old and the new owners depends largely on the relative strengths of each party in the negotiations—that is, who wants the deal the most or who has the best negotiating skills.

Business valuation is part science and part art, so there is no precise formula for determining the price of a private company. Rather, the price is determined by a sometimes intricate process of negotiation between buyer and seller. Much is left to the negotiating skills of the respective parties. But one thing is certain: There must be a willing buyer. It doesn't matter what a firm's owner believes the business is worth; it is worth only what someone who has the cash is prepared to pay.

The specific approaches to and methods for valuing a company are described in Appendix B. (Go to www.cengagebrain.com and select the Longenecker text to access this appendix.) As described in the appendix, buyers and sellers frequently base the harvest value of a firm on a multiple of earnings. For instance, a company might be valued at five times its earnings. The experience of entrepreneur Robert Hall, who sold Visador Corporation for a multiple of earnings, provides the basis for the example used in Appendix B.

13-3b The Method of Payment

The actual value of a firm is only one issue; another is the method of payment. When selling a company, an entrepreneur has three basic choices: sell the firm's assets, sell its stock, or, if the buyer is another company, merge with the buyer by combining the two companies into one firm. The exiting entrepreneur may prefer to sell the firm's stock so that the gain on the sale will be a capital gain, resulting in lower taxes. The buyer, on the other hand, may prefer to purchase the firm's assets rather than buy the company's stock. Buying the assets relieves the buyer of responsibility for any of the selling firm's liabilities, known or unknown.

opportunity cost of funds
The rate of return that could be earned on another investment of similar risk.

Harvesting owners can be paid in cash or in the stock of the acquiring firm, with cash generally being preferred over stock. Entrepreneurs who accept stock in payment are frequently disappointed, as they are unable to affect the value of the stock once they have sold the firm. Only an entrepreneur who has great faith in the acquiring firm's management should accept stock in payment, and even then she or he is taking a big chance by not being well diversified. Having such a large investment in only one stock is risky, to say the least.

LO
13-4

Provide advice on developing an effective harvest plan.

13-4 DEVELOPING AN EFFECTIVE HARVEST PLAN

We have discussed why planning for the harvest is important and also described the methods for harvesting. However, understanding what the options are for exiting a company in no way guarantees a successful harvest. More times than not, owners who harvest their businesses are disappointed with the process and the outcome. In the sections that follow, we provide suggestions for crafting an effective exit strategy.[6]

13-4a Anticipate the Harvest

Entrepreneurs frequently do not appreciate the difficulty of harvesting a company. One investor commented that exiting a business is "like brain surgery—it's done a lot, but there are a lot of things that can go wrong." Harvesting, whether through a sale or a stock offering, takes a lot of time and energy on the part of the firm's management team and can be very distracting from day-to-day affairs. The result is often a loss of managerial focus and momentum, leading to poor performance.

Uncertainties accompanying an impending sale often lower employee morale. The stress can affect the whole organization, as employees become anxious about the prospect of a new owner. Len Baker, at Sutter Hill Ventures, offers this advice: "Don't start running the company for the liquidity event. Run the business for the long haul." There is also a risk of becoming so attentive to "playing the harvest game" that an entrepreneur may forget to keep first things first.

Investors are always concerned about how to exit, and entrepreneurs need to have a similar mindset. Peter Hermann, general partner at Heritage Partners, notes, "People generally stumble into the exit and don't plan for it." However, for Hermann, "The exit strategy begins when the money goes in." Similarly, Gordon Baty, managing partner of Zero Stage Capital and an angel investor, enters each investment with a clear understanding of its investment horizon and harvest plan: "We plan for an acquisition and hope for an IPO." Jack Kearney, at BDO Capital Advisors, LLC, indicates that an exit strategy should be formulated in advance, unless "the entrepreneur expects to die in the CEO chair. . . . The worst of all worlds is to realize, for health or other reasons, that you have to sell the company right now." Jim Knister, formerly with the Donnelly Corporation, advises entrepreneurs to start thinking two or three years ahead about how they are going to exit so that they can correctly position their companies.

This type of advice is particularly important when the entrepreneur is planning an IPO. Running a public company requires information disclosures to stockholders that are not required of a privately held firm. Specifically, this means (1) maintaining an accounting process that cleanly separates the business from the entrepreneur's personal life, (2) selecting a strong board of directors that can and will offer valuable business advice, and (3) managing the firm so as to produce a successful track record of performance.

Having a harvest plan in place is also very important because the window of opportunity can open and close quickly. Remember that the opportunity to exit is triggered by the arrival of a willing and able buyer, not just an interested seller. For an IPO, a hot market may offer a very attractive opportunity, and a seller must be ready to move when the opportunity arises.

In summary, an entrepreneur should always anticipate the harvest. In the words of Ed Cherney, an entrepreneur who has sold two companies, "Don't wait to put your package together until something dramatic happens. Begin thinking about the exit strategy and start going through the motions, so that if something major happens, you will have had time to think through your options."

13-4b Expect Conflict—Emotional and Cultural

Having purchased other companies does not prepare entrepreneurs for the sale of their own company. Entrepreneurs who have been involved in the acquisition of other firms are still ill-prepared for the stress associated with selling their own businesses. Jim Porter, who has been involved in a number of acquisitions, says, "It's definitely a lot more fun to buy something than it is to be bought." One very real difference between selling and buying comes from the entrepreneur's personal ties to the business that he or she helped create. A buyer can be quite unemotional and detached, while a seller is likely to be much more concerned about nonfinancial considerations.

For this reason and many others, entrepreneurs frequently do not make good employees. The very qualities that made them successful entrepreneurs can make it difficult for them to work under a new owner. In fact, an entrepreneur who plans to stay with the firm after a sale can become disillusioned quickly and end up leaving prematurely. As Len Baker observes, "There is a danger of culture conflict between the acquiring versus the acquired firm's management. The odds are overwhelming that somebody who's been an entrepreneur is not going to be happy in a corporate culture."

Conflicts occur to varying degrees whenever an entrepreneur remains with the company after the sale. Although the nature of the conflict varies, the intensity of the feelings does not. An entrepreneur who stays with the company should expect culture conflict and be pleasantly surprised if it does not occur.

13-4c Get Good Advice

Entrepreneurs learn to operate their businesses through experience gained in repeated day-to-day activities. However, they may engage in a harvest transaction only once in a lifetime. "It's an emotional roller-coaster ride," says Ben Buettell, who frequently represents sellers of small and mid-sized companies.[7] Thus, entrepreneurs have a real need for good advice, both from experienced professionals and from those who have personally been through a harvest. In seeking advice, be aware that the experts who helped you build and grow your business may not be the best ones to use when it's time to sell the company, as they may not have the experience needed in that area. So, choose your advisors carefully.

© Yuri Arcurs/Shutterstock.com

Jack Furst, at HM Capital Partners, believes that advisors can give entrepreneurs a reality check. He contends that, without independent advice, entrepreneurs frequently fall prey to thinking they want to sell unconditionally, when in fact they really want to sell only if an unrealistically high price is offered.

Professional advice is vital, but entrepreneurs stress the importance of talking to other entrepreneurs who have sold a firm or taken it public. No one can better describe what to expect—both in events and in emotions—than someone who has had the experience. This perspective nicely complements that of the professional advisor.

Perhaps the greatest misconception among entrepreneurs is that an IPO is the end of the line. They often feel that taking their firm public through an IPO means they have "made it." The fact is that going public is but one transition in the life of a firm. Many entrepreneurs are surprised to learn that a public offering is just the beginning, not an end.

An entrepreneur will not be able to cash out for some time after the completion of the IPO. In a sense, investors in the new stock offering have chosen to back the entrepreneur as the driving force behind the company—that is, they have invested in the entrepreneur, not the firm. While the daily stock price quotes will let the management team keep score, the business will have to reach another plateau before the founder can think about placing it in the hands of a new team and going fishing. Under these circumstances, getting good advice is a must.

13-4d Understand What Motivates You

For an entrepreneur, harvesting a business that has been an integral part of life for a long period of time can be a very emotional experience. When an entrepreneur has invested a substantial part of her or his working life in growing a business, a real sense of loss may accompany the harvest. Walking away from employees, clients, and one's identity as a small business owner may not be the wonderful ride into the sunset that was expected.

So, entrepreneurs should think very carefully about their motives for exiting and what they plan to do after the harvest. Frequently, entrepreneurs have great expectations about what life is going to be like with a lot of liquidity, something many of them have never known. The harvest does provide the long-sought liquidity, but some entrepreneurs find managing money—in contrast to operating their own company—less rewarding than they had expected.

Peter Hermann believes that "seller's remorse" is definitely a major issue for a number of entrepreneurs. His advice: "Search your soul and make a list of what you want to achieve with the exit. Is it dollars, health of the company, your management team or an heir apparent taking over?" The answers to these and similar questions determine to a significant extent whether the exit will prove successful in all dimensions of an entrepreneur's life.

Entrepreneurs are also well advised to be aware of potential problems that may arise after the exit. There are stories about people selling a firm or going public and then losing everything. Ed Cherney says, "It is more difficult to handle success than it is to handle struggling. People forget what got them the success—the work ethic, the commitment to family, whatever characteristics work for an entrepreneur. Once the money starts rolling in, people forget and begin having problems."

And for the entrepreneur who believes that it will be easy to adapt to change after the harvest, even possibly to start another company, William Unger, at the Mayfield Fund, quotes from Machiavelli's *The Prince:* "It should be remembered that nothing is more difficult than to establish a new order of things."

Living the Dream

Why My Exit Strategy Failed

Michael Flatt felt deep disappointment after selling his business, and his experience is not unusual for many entrepreneurs. His counsel: Get good advice before selling and understand that the money realized from the sale may not be of primary importance when compared to other considerations.

Exiting the company you founded is a natural part of entrepreneurship, and it can provide great financial rewards. It has great consequences for your successors in management and the employees you leave behind. And I made sure to attend to those. But the exit also has consequences for you. I took them too lightly.

In my case, everything pointed towards the wisdom of selling the natural disaster mitigation and reconstruction business I had founded 26 years earlier. I had built the company into a valuable, profitable power-house, but I felt I was burning out. My partners were aging. I sensed opportunities elsewhere, and my efforts to keep the staff together and engaged were wearing me out. I knew I could sell, which made all these headaches seem unnecessary.

Shortly after announcing the sale, we were contacted by three interested parties. Everything went smoothly. We even managed to miss the 2008 recession and, according to our consultants, we received an above-market price. As a businessman, I had done everything right. Inside, though, I was wracked by regret. What I forgot to consider were the things I enjoyed at work. I didn't ask myself the hard questions about why I was selling, what I wanted to gain—and most important, what I would miss if I sold.

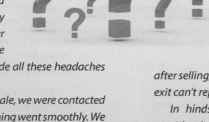

My advice to you—before you do what I did—is to stop and think. Go back to the fundamentals of your business, way back if you need to. You must first understand why you created your business. And I don't mean just the value proposition. I mean why are YOU there? What do you gain from continuing to stay with the company and what would you lose if you left? Be honest. If you can fully realize what you will be giving up, you will be able to envision the future.

Finally, go one step further and ask what else matters to you. What else do you want to accomplish in life, and will it be easier to do that with or without your company? This is by no means an easy question, but even success can't extinguish true passion: This is your chance to chase after your dreams. . . . [A]fter I sold the company, I soon realized that to be captain of my own ship was my dream. I missed leading my team, charting the company's course, and responding to challenges at a moment's notice. Today, four years after selling, I have learned that the riches of a successful exit can't replace the rewards of leadership.

In hindsight, I should have looked to someone outside the organization that could offer me perspective. A coach, perhaps, someone to ask me why I was selling, what I wanted to gain afterwards and most importantly, what I would be missing.

Source: Michael Flatt, "Why My Exit Strategy Failed," Inc.com, March 5, 2012, accessed January 17, 2013. Inc : the magazine for growing companies by Goldhirsh Group. Reproduced with permission of Goldhirsh Group via Copyright Clearance Center.

13-4e What's Next?

Entrepreneurs by their very nature are purpose-driven people. So, after the exit, an entrepreneur who has been driven to build a profitable business will need something to bring meaning to her or his life. Many entrepreneurs have a sense of gratitude for the benefits they have received from living in a capitalist system. As a result, they want to give back, with both their time and their money.

Judy Johnston is a great example of an entrepreneur who asked the question "What's next?" For Johnston, it will be a nonprofit venture. She used her life savings of $50,000 to found her first business, PrintPaks, which she sold to Mattel three years later for $26 million. Blue Lake Children's Publishing, Johnston's most recent startup, was founded in 2002—she hopes to sell it in the next five years. Her children's magazine, *Tessy & Tab*, will eventually need a video program, she says, but that's for a successor to figure out. "I know it has to be done, but somebody else needs to own the company when it happens," she says. "There's only so far I can take it, because I'm not motivated by just making more money. I'm not qualified or interested in running a really big company."

Blue Lake will likely be Johnston's last for-profit startup, but not her last startup endeavor. "I want to do something that doesn't involve having to return capital to investors," she says. Nonprofits are still fair game.[8]

The good news is that there is no limit to the number of worthy charitable causes, including universities, churches, and civic organizations. And it may be that, when all is said and done, the call to help others with a new venture may be too strong for an individual with an entrepreneurial mindset to resist. But whatever you decide to do, do it with passion and let your life benefit others in the process.

LOOKING BACK

13-1. Explain the importance of having a harvest, or exit, plan.

- Harvesting, or exiting, is the method entrepreneurs and investors use to get out of a business and, ideally, reap the value of their investment in the firm.
- Harvesting is about more than merely selling and leaving a business. It involves capturing value (cash flows), reducing risk, and creating future options.
- A firm's appeal to investors is driven, in part, by the availability of harvest options.

13-2. Describe the options available for harvesting.

- There are four basic ways to harvest an investment in a privately owned company: (1) selling the firm, (2) distributing the firm's cash flows to its owners, (3) offering stock to the public through an IPO, and (4) using a private equity recapitalization.
- In a sale to a strategic buyer, the value placed on a business depends on the synergies that the buyer believes can be created.

- Financial buyers look primarily to a firm's stand-alone, cash-generating potential as the source of its value.
- In leveraged buyouts (LBOs), high levels of debt financing are used to acquire firms.
- With bust-up LBOs, the assets of the acquired firm are sold to repay the debt. With build-up LBOs, a number of related businesses are acquired to create a larger enterprise, which may eventually be taken public via an initial public offering (IPO). A management buyout (MBO) is an LBO in which management is part of the group buying the company.
- In an employee stock ownership plan (ESOP), employees' retirement contributions are used to purchase shares in the company.
- The orderly withdrawal of an owner's investment in the form of the firm's cash flows can be achieved by simply stopping the firm's growth.
- An initial public offering (IPO) is used primarily as a way to raise additional equity capital to finance company growth, and only secondarily as a way to harvest the owner's investment.
- A private equity recapitalization is a form of outside financing that can allow the original owners to cash out part of their investment, but possibly continue to operate the business.
- Trying to finance liquidity and growth while retaining control is perhaps the most difficult task facing family firms.

13-3. Explain the issues in valuing a firm that is being harvested and deciding on the method of payment.

- Value is created when a firm's return on invested capital is greater than the investors' opportunity cost of funds.

- A firm will have greater value in the hands of new owners if the new owners can create more value than the current owners can.
- Often, buyers and sellers base the harvest value of a firm on a multiple of its earnings.
- Cash is generally preferred over stock and other forms of payment by those selling a firm.

13-4. Provide advice on developing an effective harvest plan.

- Investors are always concerned about exit strategy.
- Entrepreneurs frequently do not appreciate the difficulty of selling or exiting a company. Having purchased other companies does not prepare entrepreneurs for the sale of their own firm.
- Entrepreneurs who plan to stay with a business after a sale can become disillusioned quickly and end up leaving prematurely.
- Getting good advice is essential, from both experienced professionals and those who have personally been through a harvest.
- Entrepreneurs must carefully consider their motives for exiting and their plans for after the harvest.

Key Terms

harvesting (exiting) p. 348
business broker p. 349
leveraged buyout (LBO) p. 350
bust-up LBO p. 350

build-up LBO p. 350
management buyout (MBO) p. 351
employee stock ownership plan (ESOP) p. 351
seller financing p. 352

double taxation p. 353
initial public offering (IPO) p. 354
Private equity recapitalization p. 355
opportunity cost of funds p. 357

Discussion Questions

1. Explain what is meant by the term *harvesting*. What is involved in harvesting an investment in a privately held firm?

2. Why should an owner of a company plan for eventually harvesting his or her company?

3. Contrast a sale to a strategic buyer with one to a financial buyer.

4. Explain the term *leveraged buyout*. How is a leveraged buyout different from a management buyout?

5. Distinguish between bust-up LBOs and build-up LBOs.

6. What is the primary purpose of an initial public offering (IPO)? How does an IPO relate to a harvest?

7. Why might an entrepreneur find going public a frustrating process?

8. What determines whether a firm has value to a prospective purchaser?

9. What problems can occur when an entrepreneur sells a firm but continues in the management of the company?

10. How may harvesting a firm affect an entrepreneur's personal identity?

You Make the Call

Situation 1

After multiple conversations with investment bankers, 37-year-old David Sloan, co-owner of Li'l Guy Foods, a family-owned Mexican-food manufacturing business, realized that "there weren't a whole lot of people wanting to jump into this industry."

The 35-employee company was facing huge financial pressure from the rising costs of commodities like corn and plastic packaging. "We were under an assault on margins," Sloan says, something that made outside investors nervous. Still, the business enjoyed a strong base of customers that paid a premium for its products.

That was enough to attract the attention of a large, more sophisticated competitor, Tortilla King Inc., which had hedging policies in place that allowed it to lock in prices, guarding against increases. And since Tortilla King was already familiar with the industry and the company's customer base in the region, it was willing to take risks that outside investors were not. With costs high and consumer spending on the wane, Tortilla King president Juan Guardiola saw the acquisition of Li'l Guy Foods as a way to reduce competition and increase market share. "We were fighting in the market, cutting each other's margins," he says, "so it made a lot of sense to merge."

The two companies hammered out a deal, and a bank agreed to provide financing but backed out just as the deal was about to close—part of the broad pullback in business lending during 2008. So Sloan's company agreed to finance the purchase. Sloan says he would have preferred to walk away without being so invested in the combined company's future, but felt it would be too difficult to continue running the small business. So he went along with the deal. "It wasn't the most ideal transaction for us," he says.

Sources: Based on Arden Dale and Simona Covel, "Sellers Offer a Financial Hand to Their Buyers," *The Wall Street Journal*, November 13, 2008, p. B-1; www.lilguyfoods.com, accessed January 15, 2011; and Suzanna Stagemeyer, "Li'l Guy Sells to Tortilla King, Moves Manufacturing to Wichita," *Kansas City Business Journal*, September 14, 2008, www.bizjournals.com/kansascity/stories/2008/09/15/story2.html, accessed January 15, 2011.

Question 1 What would be the reasons for and against Sloan working for Tortilla King?

Question 2 What advice would you offer Sloan?

Situation 2

Ed and Barbara Bonneau started their wholesale sunglass distribution firm 30 years ago with $1,000 of their own money and $5,000 borrowed from a banker in Ed's hometown. The firm grew quickly, selling sunglasses and reading glasses to such companies as Walmart, Eckerd Drugs, and Phar-Mor.

Although the company had done well, the market had matured recently and profit margins narrowed significantly. Walmart, for example, was insisting on better terms, which meant significantly lower profits for the Bonneaus. Previously, Ed had set the prices that he needed to make a good return on his investment. Now, the buyers had consolidated, and they had the power. Ed didn't enjoy running the company as much as he had in the past, and he was finding greater pleasure in other activities, such as serving on a local hospital board and being actively involved in church activities.

Just as Ed and Barbara began to think about selling the company, they were contacted by a financial buyer, who wanted to use their firm as a platform and then buy up several sunglass companies. After negotiations, the Bonneaus sold their firm for about $20 million. In addition, Ed received a retainer fee for serving as a consultant to the buyer. Also, the Bonneaus' son-in-law, who was part of the company's management team, was named the new chief operating officer.

Question 1 Do you agree with the Bonneaus' decision to sell? Why or why not?

Question 2 Why did the buyers retain Ed as a consultant?

Question 3 Do you see any problem with having the Bonneaus' son-in-law become the new chief operating officer?

Situation 3

An entrepreneur addresses the difficult question of when to sell his business:

I started my telecommunications business when I was 18, and I'm going to be 47 this summer. It's a successful business and provides me with a good living.... Yet each day I feel more and more unfulfilled in what I'm doing.... I have a lot of business knowledge that I feel is being wasted here, just doing the same thing year after year. I've tried some side ventures.... I've also considered selling the business, but it's too large to be bought by a local competitor... and too small to attract the attention of large companies. Besides, I don't know what I'd do if I did sell it. And will whatever I do next allow me to earn as much money as I'm earning now? More important, will I like it, or will I regret letting go of the one thing I've had all my adult life?

Source: Norm Brodsky, Street Smarts: Ask Norm, *Inc.*, July 2008, pp. 69–70.

Question 1 Do you agree that the entrepreneur's company is not sellable?

Question 2 Are there any other options for the entrepreneur besides selling his business?

Question 3 What would you recommend the entrepreneur do? Why?

Experiential Exercises

1. Check your local newspaper to find a privately held company that has been sold recently. Try to determine the motivation for the sale. Did it have anything to do with the prior owners' desire to cash out of the business? If so, try to find out what happened.

2. Ask a local family business owner about future plans to harvest the business. Has the owner ever been involved in a harvest? If so, ask the owner to describe what happened and how it all worked out, as well as what she or he learned

from the experience. If not, ask whether the owner is aware of any company whose owners cashed out, and then visit that company owner to inquire about the exit event.

3. Visit a local CPA to learn about his or her involvement in helping entrepreneurs cash out of companies.

4. Search a business magazine to identify a firm that has successfully completed an initial public offering (IPO). See what you can find out about the event on the Internet.

Small Business & Entrepreneurship Resource Center

The Small Business & Entrepreneurship Resource Center offers complete small business management resources through a comprehensive database that covers all major areas of starting, operating, and maintaining a business from financing, management, marketing, accounting, taxes, and more. Go to www.cengagebrain.com and select the Longenecker text for more information on how to access this material.

1. *Question*: I run a home-based agency consisting of a part-time employee and myself, I would like to retire in the not-too-distant future. I have always assumed that my business could not be sold because it is so small and so dependent on me. Even if it could be sold, I have assumed that the price would be so small as to not be worth the effort. Am I correct?

   Answer: You are probably incorrect. If you run a profitable home-based agency, there is no reason why your agency could not be sold for a respectable price.

After reading this article, what specific advice would you give to this person about selling a business?

2. Owners who have been through the sale of a car dealership know the stresses associated with executing the transaction. From the seller's perspective, stresses can come from the thought of exiting the business, informing employees, negotiating the purchase agreement, tax implications of the sale, winding down operations, and the ability of the buyer to close the sale. The challenge for most dealers is not the ability to get good advice, it is the ability to recognize and take good advice. Do you agree with the author of this article that it is better for a seller to seek assistance from others and not negotiate every aspect of a transaction alone? Explain your answer.

Sources: Based on Mark Pestronk, "Home-Based Agent Wonders Whether Business Is Worth Selling," *Travel Weekly*, Vol. 71, No. 24 (June 11, 2012), p. 28; and Phil Villegas, "Recognize, Take Good Advice." *Ward's Dealer Business*, Vol. 43, No. 9 (September 1, 2009).

Case 13

Network Collie (P. 669)

In 2008, William Casey, along with three college friends, founded Network Collie. The company provided support for businesses wanting to use social networking at a time when this space was beginning to grow rapidly. While the founders had full-time jobs away from Network Collie, they were committing significant time to the new company. However, by late 2009, they knew something needed to happen if they were going to achieve the success in their original plans. At about the same time, two companies expressed interest in acquiring the firm, forcing the young owners to consider four options:

- quit their current jobs and commit to Network Collie on a full-time basis,
- hire someone to run the company,
- try and sell the company, or
- walk away and move on to the next idea.

Endnotes

1. Personal conversation with Bob Browder, former CEO, BFW Construction, Inc., April 10, 2011.

2. Simona Covel, "How to Get Workers to Think and Act Like Owners," *The Wall Street Journal*, February 7, 2008, p. B-1.

3. Carol Tice, "Is It Time to Sell?" *Entrepreneur*, January 2009, www.entrepreneur.com/magazine/entrepreneur/2009/january/199016.html, accessed February 5, 2012.

4. S. T. Certo, "Influencing Initial Public Offering Investors with Prestige: Signaling with Board Structure," *Academy of Management Review*, Vol. 28, No. 3 (2003), pp. 432–447.

5. This example was provided by Peter Hermann of Heritage Partners, a Boston venture capital firm, which obtained a registered trademark for the process it calls a Private IPO®.

6. The unattributed quotes in this part of the chapter are taken from personal interviews conducted as part of a research study on harvesting, sponsored by the Financial Executives Research Foundation and cited in J. William Petty, John D. Martin, and John Kensinger, *Harvesting the Value of a Privately Held Company* (Morristown, NJ: Financial Executives Research Foundation, 1999). For more information on Financial Executives Research Foundation, visit www.ferf.org or call (973) 765-1000.

7. Jeff Bailey, "Selling the Firm—and Letting Go of the Dream," *The Wall Street Journal*, December 10, 2002, p. B-6.

8. Jennifer Wang, "Confessions of Serial Entrepreneurs," *Entrepreneur*, January 8, 2009, www.entrepreneur.com/startingabusiness/successstories/article199436.html, accessed March 18, 2011.

© Majorosl/istockphoto.com

Building Customer Relationships

When it comes to developing and maintaining relationships with customers, Chris Zane is in a class by himself. Since getting into the bike shop business as a teenager, he has carefully applied everything he has learned about making connections to build that humble start into Zane's Cycles, which today is one of the largest retail bicycle stores in the United States. In his book, *Reinventing the Wheel*, Zane describes the secret to his success:

We're better than our competitors because we differentiate ourselves by offering more service than most customers consider reasonable. In other words, our goal is to blow them away with our attention to detail as soon as we meet them. The job of every Zane's employee is not just to sell stuff; it is to build relationships with our customers

In the SPOTLIGHT
Zane's Cycles
www.zanes.com

by servicing them in a manner they have rarely experienced before.

In other words, Zane isn't really in the business of selling bikes. Instead, he works to create relationships with customers that will leave them feeling good about the company, the products they buy from it, and the buying experience itself. For example, customers waiting for their bikes to be serviced are treated to free drinks at a beautiful mahogany coffee bar. And those who are unhappy with the service they receive (even the best of companies will come up short now and then) are invited back for follow-up attention and a few extras, like free toe clips and a handlebar light.

But excellent service doesn't always translate to great selling relationships, so Zane makes adjustments as needed. For example, at one time the shop offered free home pick-up and drop-off of bikes in need of repair, but this service discouraged the best customers from coming in to make connections and learn about new products hitting the market. So, Zane discontinued the service to create natural opportunities for personal interaction and relationship building inside the store. That refreshed many old connections—and sold a lot of bikes!

Zane's approach has been very carefully designed. He knows that a single lost customer will result in the loss of the $12,500 in sales that would have come in over the lifetime of that relationship. With this in mind, Zane teaches his employees to tend closely to each customer's experience in the store and to take every opportunity to build a lasting relationship. But that requires a deep understanding of buyers to guide one-on-one marketing efforts, a level of insight that is made possible by Zane's painstaking data collection practices.

Zane's passion for relationship building has led to an average annual growth rate of 23.5 percent, and now the company's revenues exceed $15 million a year. He's come a long way from his start as a teenager in the bike business, and there is no doubt that his attention to building strong customer relationships has paved the way for his company's prosperity— in addition to providing a very meaningful career for Zane as an entrepreneur.

Sources: Charles W. Lamb, Joseph F. Hair, and Carl McDaniel, *Marketing* (Mason, OH: South-Western Cengage Learning, 2013), p. 794; "Making Life Easier for His Customers," *Inc.*, May 9, 2011, www.inc.com/articles/201105/small-business-success -stories-zanes-cycles.html, accessed November 19, 2012; Chris Zane, *Reinventing the Wheel: The Science of Creating Lifetime Customers* (Dallas: BenBella Books, 2011); and "Zane's Philosophy," http://zanes.com/articles/zanes-philosophy-pg184.htm, accessed November 19, 2012.

Customers today are more powerful than ever. In this age of highly social and very mobile media, customers find it easier to sidestep traditional advertising by surveying social networks for advice on their purchases. They can make on-the-go price comparisons with laser-like precision and great convenience, thanks to the wealth of information online and simple technologies like barcode-scanning comparison apps. And if they don't like the way they have been treated by a brand or business, they can quickly report their displeasure to their Facebook friends and through online forums and user review websites like Yelp.com. Savvy small businesses are learning how to use the tools now available to establish strong and healthy customer relationships and build great companies.

Managing customer relationships pays enormous dividends. Long-term customers usually stay with a company because they trust it, and that trust naturally translates to increased sales. Loyal customers tend to buy a company's more expensive products, are less sensitive to price increases, and bring their friends in to do business, too.[1] If companies increase their customer retention by a mere 5 percent per year, they could see their net profits rise by as much as 80 percent.[2] Keeping customers is critical, so it's essential that firms do it effectively.

This chapter shows you how to create and maintain vital connections that will satisfy your customers, enhance the reputation of your business, and generate superior company performance. Chapters 15 through 18 discuss additional marketing topics essential to growth, based on the crucial customer focus that provides the foundation for this chapter.

14-1 WHAT IS CUSTOMER RELATIONSHIP MANAGEMENT?

Customer relationship management (CRM) means different things to different firms. To some, it means having employees simply smile and say "thank you" and "come again" to customers who have just made a purchase. For others, CRM is nothing short of complete customization of products and/or services to fit individual

Define *customer relationship management (CRM)*, and explain its importance to a small business.

customer needs. The goals of a CRM program for most small companies fall somewhere between these two perspectives.

Formally defined, **customer relationship management (CRM)** is a "company-wide business strategy designed to optimize profitability, revenue, and customer satisfaction by focusing on precisely defined customer groups."[3] It is a process or method that can be used to learn more about the needs and behaviors of customers with the specific purpose of building stronger relationships with them so that a firm can succeed. CRM involves treating customers the way the entrepreneur would want to be treated if he or she were a customer—the business version of the Golden Rule.[4]

Regardless of the level of a firm's commitment to customer relationship management, the central message of every CRM program is "Cultivate customers for more than a one-time sale." For decades, entrepreneurs have recognized the importance of treating customers well. "The customer is king" is, after all, an age-old mantra. What is new, however, is defining the concept more precisely and using the latest techniques and innovative technologies to implement effective customer relationship management practices.

14-1a Benefits of CRM to a Small Firm

Building relationships with customers is serious business for most small companies. This is underscored by a survey of entrepreneurs, who indicated that it is precisely because of the small size of their companies that they are able to respond quickly to customer-service issues. And being able to move quickly and effectively is enormously important. Indeed, of those surveyed, 84 percent said that this is one of the greatest advantages of running a small business.[5]

As depicted in Exhibit 14.1, a firm's next sale comes from one of two sources—a current customer or a new customer. Marketing efforts devoted to bringing in new customers sometimes leave current customers feeling taken for granted and neglected. But keeping existing customers happy should be a high priority. CRM programs address this.

Brian Vellmure, the founder and CEO of Initium Technology, a provider of CRM solutions to small firms, has identified five major economic benefits of maintaining relationships with current customers:[6]

1. It costs much more to acquire a new customer than to hold on to an old customer.

2. Long-time customers trust you and thus spend more money than new customers do.

3. Happy customers refer their friends and colleagues, leading to even more sales.

customer relationship management (CRM)
A company-wide business strategy designed to optimize profitability, revenue, and customer satisfaction by focusing on specific customer groups.

14.1 Sources of the Next Sale

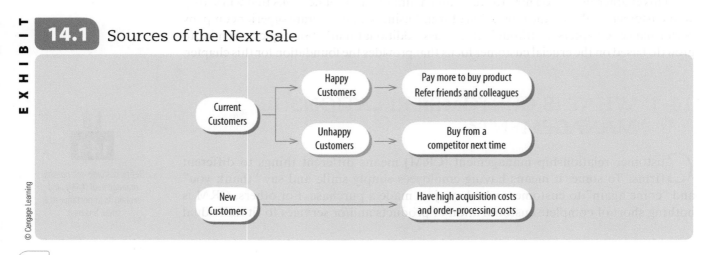

© Cengage Learning

EXHIBIT

14.2 Essential Materials of a Successful CRM Program

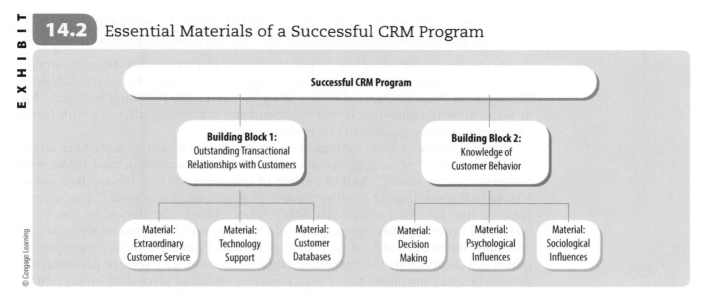

© Cengage Learning

4. It costs less to process orders for established customers, because they are already in the system and know how it works.

5. Current customers buy without discounts, so they are willing to pay more for products.

These factors contribute to profits and may explain why 47 percent of small firms report that they sell their products or services primarily to repeat customers.[7]

14-1b Essential Materials for a CRM Program

Assembling a CRM program requires an entrepreneur to know about and understand the basic foundations upon which a successful initiative can be established. In the remainder of this chapter, we consider the two crucial building blocks involved: (1) outstanding relationships with customers and (2) knowledge of consumer behavior. We will also examine the basic materials from which these building blocks can be constructed (see Exhibit 14.2).

14-2 OUTSTANDING CUSTOMER RELATIONSHIPS THROUGH EXTRAORDINARY SERVICE

To be successful in the long run, small companies need to concentrate on building positive transactional relationships with customers (see Building Block 1 in Exhibit 14.2). A **transactional relationship** is an association between a business and a customer that begins (or ends) with a purchase or a business exchange. Clearly, the nature of such relationships can vary greatly. But consumers who have positive interactions with a business are much more likely to become loyal customers. Four basic beliefs underlie our emphasis on providing exceptional customer service:

1. Small businesses possess greater potential for providing superior customer service than do large firms.

2. Superior customer service leads to customer satisfaction.

START UP

TOOLS

Customer Referrals Can Really Pay Off
It's not just current clients who make great customers. The friends that they refer are 18 percent more loyal and 16 percent more profitable. One company found that it earned a 60 percent return on the small referral incentive that it gave to its customers. To learn more, read Philipp Schmitt, Bernd Skiera, and Christophe Van den Bulte, "Why Customer Referrals Can Drive Stunning Profits," *Harvard Business Review*, Vol. 89, No. 6 (June 2011), p. 30.

LO 14-2

Discuss the significance of providing extraordinary customer service.

transactional relationship
An association between a business and a customer that begins (or ends) with a purchase or a business deal.

3. Customer satisfaction results in a positive transactional relationship.

4. Positive transactional relationships lead to increased firm profits.

As you can see, failure to emphasize customer service jeopardizes any effort to maintain a positive customer relationship. Edward Reilly, president and CEO of the American Management Association, said it best when he offered the following warning: "My message to small companies is that big companies are coming after you with better customer service, so you'd better be paying attention."[8]

There is plenty of room for improvement—for businesses of all sizes. One survey found that only 22 percent of customers describe their transaction experiences with companies as "excellent."[9] And 64 percent of customers say they have walked out of a store in the previous 12 months because of poor customer service.[10] This creates opportunities for entrepreneurs like Marx Acosta-Rubio, who started his toner cartridge and office supplies company, called OneStop, based on what he refers to as a "customer intimacy model." As part of its attentive service efforts, OneStop representatives call clients *before* they run out of supplies, maintaining a sense of personal connection by using the phone rather than expecting clients to place their orders online, which is the norm in the industry. As a result, OneStop has been able to generate tremendous sales with a limited sales staff, and its salespeople are nearly five times as productive as those working for its major competitors.[11]

14-2a Managing Customer Satisfaction

Why is customer satisfaction so important? Because happy customers are loyal customers, and that often leads them to cross-buy products with higher margins, react less to price increases, encourage their friends to buy the same products, and engage in other behaviors that tend to enhance the firm's profits. Research conducted by Ruth Bolton, professor of marketing at Arizona State University, has shown that, on average, a mere 10 percent increase in customer satisfaction leads to an 8 percent increase in the duration of customer relationships. This translates to an 8 percent increase in revenues generated over the long term.[12]

Companies control a number of factors that affect customer satisfaction. For example, customers have basic expectations regarding the benefits they should receive from any firm selling the product or service that your company provides. Your offering must meet these most basic expectations to satisfy customers and earn their repeat business. Beyond that, customers anticipate that your business will provide assistance to them at the time they make a purchase and again later if they should encounter problems. Keep in mind that those who buy prestige products, such as a Louis Vuitton purse or a Rolex watch, will expect more intensive assistance.

PERSONAL ATTENTION Personal attention is the "gold standard" against which the quality of customer service is judged. Firms that provide the best response to the needs of a specific buyer in a given situation are sure to have satisfied and loyal customers—and plenty of them. It follows, however, that personalized service will be an option only for those companies that listen intently to their customers and thus understand their precise needs.

Because small companies like flower shops, for example, have fewer customers and fewer layers of employees between the customer and the business owner, they are able to build stronger and closer relationships with those they serve and to hold on to them as customers. The following are some of the more common signposts on the road to extraordinary, and very personal, customer service:[13]

- *Doing business on a first-name basis.* Small ventures that know their customers by name and greet them as friends establish a bond that is powerful and encourages loyalty.

- *Keeping in touch.* Face-to-face and phone conversations are much more effective than e-mail messages or mass mailings. Asking for feedback during these interactions is helpful to your business and shows that you are committed to getting customers' approval. It also confirms that you care about more than selling.

- *Finding ways to help.* Helping customers doesn't always lead to an immediate sale, but it can be good for business, and at minimal cost. Send them articles and information of interest with a kind note attached, remind them of important dates (like birthdays and anniversaries), and so on.

- *Customizing your service to meet customer preferences.* By remembering your customers' personal preferences and adjusting your service to meet them, you increase the value of what you offer.

- *Addressing problems promptly.* When an issue arises, take steps to resolve it quickly. Doing so lets a customer know that he or she is important to you. Contact lost customers to find out why they went elsewhere and use that information to correct deficiencies.

Denny Fulk, a serial entrepreneur, emphasizes the importance of building and maintaining personal customer relationships to business success:

If you operate a business, no matter how small or large, customers like to feel there is a person who really cares about their needs. Whether the information shared is by telephone or e-mail, promptness and a personal approach are keys to the customer's having a good feeling about your company. Regardless of whether your business is a startup or a very established company, a customer who receives a prompt, accurate, and understanding response will be very likely to continue doing business with your company.[14]

Guy Kawasaki, author of *The Art of the Start*, is a convincing advocate of returning calls and e-mails promptly. To test Kawasaki's commitment, an entrepreneur e-mailed him at 10:00 p.m. one evening and received a reply in about 10 minutes![15]

CUSTOMER EXPERIENCE MANAGEMENT In recent years, some small business owners have begun to go beyond simple CRM, to **customer experience management (CEM)**. This approach recognizes that, with every interaction, customers learn something about a business that will either strengthen or weaken their satisfaction and desire to return, spend more, and recommend the company to others. One marketing expert summed it up: "You literally can't afford to ignore [CEM], because your customers take it personally every time they touch your products, your services, and your support."[16]

Having a positive experience with a business can actually become part of a firm's value equation—it's almost like money in the bank. Research has shown that 86 percent of customers would pay as much as 25 percent more for an excellent buying experience.[17] But stumble in this area and they will make you pay for it. A survey by Harris Interactive, a market research firm, found that 26 percent of respondents have posted negative comments online and 89 percent began doing business with a competitor after an unpleasant customer experience.[18]

customer experience management (CEM) An approach that recognizes that, with every interaction, customers learn something about a company that will affect their desire to do business there in the future.

Relationship-enhancing interactions can begin with very low-tech and inexpensive gestures that customers will perceive as "high touch." According to Spike Jones, senior vice president for digital experience at the public relations firm Fleishman-Hillard, getting started "can be as simple as having [customer-service] employees use photos of themselves as their online profile picture rather than the company logo" to add a personal touch.[19] Don't count on this alone to produce a good experience, but it can certainly help get the relationship off on the right foot.

One problem that jeopardizes the customer experience is long wait times. Because the public's tolerance for waiting has decreased significantly over the years, these are very likely to lead to serious frustration and lost sales—that is, unless you can find a way to shorten these delays or, better yet, turn them into an advantage. Many firms are experimenting with new strategies that will help them do exactly that.[20]

- Need to get your car's oil changed *and* wash the dog? An auto service shop in Plano, Texas, set up a dog wash station on the premises so that you can do both at the same time.
- Galpin Motors, Inc., a car dealership, put a Starbucks café in its waiting area to help customers pass the time more pleasantly.
- Surgeon Vishal Mehta launched MedWaitTime, a mobile app that lets patients know if the waiting room outlook is green (no wait), yellow (moderate wait), or red (long wait).
- Porter Airlines, a regional Canadian carrier, opened free business-style lounges so that all of its passengers can relax in comfort while waiting for their next flight to depart.

These strategies significantly improved customers' experience and boosted their loyalty to the products and services offered, with the results flowing to the bottom line of the companies involved.

ENTREPRENEURIAL EXPERIENCES

Living the Dream

Imitation Can Be the Sincerest Form of Flattery—and Just Plain Good Business

Small business owners often discover the best models for excellence in customer experience management (CEM) by taking a close look at big corporations that have programs that can be adapted, in some form, to the small company setting. When it comes to CEM, three service superstars—Starbucks, Apple, and Zappos—seem to be well ahead of the curve. John Moore, who was formerly in marketing at Starbucks Coffee and Whole Foods Market and now runs a marketing consultancy called Brand Autopsy

Marketing Practice, offers the following essence-capturing descriptions:

Immediately upon entering a Starbucks, your senses come alive. You smell the coffee. You hear the music. And you feel the warmth of the in-store décor. Your senses are further heightened as you order your grande, non-fat, no-foam, extra hot vanilla latte using language only spoken inside a Starbucks. The final touch point in the Starbucks buying experience occurs when you take the first sip of your drink. It's equal parts exhale and enjoyment. . . .

The retail buying experience at an Apple store is similar. No other retail store looks like or feels like an Apple store. Your senses are on perpetual overload as you see, hear, touch, and practically taste the delicious design of Apple's iPhones, iPads, and iMacs.

Zappos, an online shoe and apparel retailer, is the current darling of the retail world. . . . It's estimated that 75 percent of Zappos' total sales come from returning customers, and these repeat customers buy twice as much as new customers buy. . . . To foster the spirit of WOWing a customer, Zappos decided early on to divert much of its marketing budget to seemingly mundane customer service touch points.

A slow-loading website aggravates customers; that's why Zappos spends time and money to ensure its website loads faster than its retail competitors. Zappos promises to deliver orders to customers in two-to-five business days. However, the company, at its expense, over-delivers on its promise by shipping most orders for next-day delivery.

Customers are encouraged to buy multiple shoes, purses, and other apparel to see which fits best and ship back whatever doesn't fit at no cost for 365 days.

Tony Hsieh, Zappos CEO, makes the business case for [the company's CEM program] by explaining, "Over the years, the number one driver of our growth at Zappos has been repeat customers and word of mouth. Our philosophy has been to take most of the money we would have spent on paid advertising and invest it into customer service and the customer experience instead, letting our customers do the marketing for us through word of mouth."

Do you see any practices above that could fit nicely into a customer experience program for your business? It often pays to borrow best practices from other companies, adjust them to fit what you need, and then build an integrated program from that. If your results even begin to resemble those of Starbucks, Apple, or Zappos, your customers, your investors, and your bank account will be grateful.

Source: Excerpted from John Moore, "Becoming a Talkable Brand: How Customer Touch Points Lead to Customer Talking Points," *Baylor Business Review*, Spring 2012, pp. 22–23. Used with permission.

HONEST RELATIONSHIPS AND SERVICE AFTER THE SALE It's common for sales staff to work hard to cultivate a relationship with a client or customer to get them to buy and then quickly move on once they have earned their commission or sales reward, but this is very shortsighted. Research has shown that customers are significantly more satisfied and loyal to a company and tend to give it even more future business if they receive continued attention after a sale—and this is especially true if that contact is in-person or via the telephone.[21]

Most entrepreneurs truly care about their customers. The problem is that they often get so focused on building their businesses that their minds naturally move on to the next sale, and they may not even understand why following up is so important or know how to go about doing it. Fortunately, a number of helpful methods can help enhance customer relationships after a sale is completed. They include building value for a customer though post-sale follow-up; monitoring delivery and installation to make sure the customer is satisfied; checking in with a customer in person or via phone, e-mail, handwritten note, etc; and resolving any customer complaints to clear the way for future business.[22]

Keep in mind that it costs far more to replace a customer than to keep one. Providing exceptional customer service gives small firms a competitive edge, regardless of the nature of the business. They typically know their customers' needs better than larger firms do, and they can offer more personalized service. In addition, more tools are available than ever before to make this possible.

14-2b Evaluating a Firm's Customer Service Health

Establishing an effective customer service program begins with determining how well a firm is currently serving its customers (sometimes referred to a firm's *customer service quotient*). Strategies can then be developed to improve the effectiveness of customer service efforts. Exhibit 14.3 lists some popular approaches to creating customer service strategies and provides space for evaluating how well a small firm is currently performing in each area and what it can do to improve its customer service.

Although customer service issues may be identified through a formal review process within the small firm, they often surface via customer complaints in the course of normal daily business operations. Every firm strives to eliminate customer complaints. When they occur, however, they should be analyzed carefully to uncover possible weaknesses in product quality and/or customer service.

Small companies are *potentially* in a much better position than are large firms to respond to such grievances and to achieve greater customer satisfaction as a result.

EXHIBIT 14.3 Customer Service Strategies

Which of the following can be used to support your marketing objectives?	For each strategy, comment below on: 1. how well your company is doing. 2. improvements to pursue further.
Provide an exceptional experience throughout every transaction by ensuring that customers are acknowledged, appreciated, and find it easy to do business with you. Note that this requires you to (1) make a list of the typical chain of contacts between you and your customers—from when they first see your advertisement until you send them a customer survey after the sale—and (2) evaluate your company's performance on each contact point.	
Provide sales materials that are clear and easy to understand, including website, marketing materials, retail displays, and sales conversations.	
Respond promptly to customers' requests and concerns by acting with urgency and responsibility in customer inquiries, transactions, and complaints. Have a service recovery plan in place.	
Listen to customers and respond accordingly by soliciting feedback, encouraging interaction, staying engaged throughout transactions, and taking the appropriate action necessary to please the customer.	
Stand behind products/services by providing guarantees and warranties and ensuring customers that you deliver on your promises. Also, create products and deliver services that exceed expectations.	
Treat customers as family members and best friends by valuing them the same way you honor those you care most about.	
Stay in the hearts and minds of customers by not taking customers for granted and finding ways to let them know you have their best interests in mind.	
Other initiatives? List them here.	

Source: Adapted from "Exceptional Customer Experiences," Ewing Marion Kauffman Foundation, http://www.entrepreneurship.org/en/resource-center/exceptional-customer-experiences-worksheet.aspx, accessed on October 26, 2012.

Most problems can be solved simply by dealing with issues as they arise, thus giving customers more attention and respect. And showing respect is often easier for a small company because it has fewer employees and can give each of them the authority to act in customers' best interests. In contrast, large corporations often assign that responsibility to a single manager, who has limited contact with customers. John Stites, CEO and co-owner of a family-owned construction company explains that a small business owner "is closer to the customers and more likely to get accurate feedback, unfiltered by layers of management." He also points out that the owner of a company with only 100 customers will feel the loss of a single customer much more than the owner of a larger firm with 1,000 customers will.[23]

What do consumers do when they are displeased? As Exhibit 14.4 shows, these buyers have several options for dealing with their dissatisfaction, and most of these options threaten repeat sales. Small business owners can learn about customer service concerns through personal observation and other research techniques. By talking directly to customers or by playing the customer's role anonymously—for example, by making a telephone call to one's own business to see how customers are treated—an entrepreneur can evaluate service quality. Some restaurants and motels invite feedback on customer service by providing comment cards to those they serve.

Implementation of some forms of customer service can be inexpensive—or even free (customer-contact personnel may just need to be encouraged to smile and greet visitors warmly)—but offering a full program of superior customer service before, during, and after a sale can be a costly undertaking. These costs often can be passed along to the purchaser as part of the price of a product or service, or they can sometimes be recouped separately, based on the amount of service requested (through extended product warranties, for example). Many customers are willing to pay a premium price, as long as good service is part of the buying experience.

START UP

ACTION

Improving Your Serve
Offering excellent customer service may not come naturally to some small business owners. For an excellent primer to help you consider all the angles, take a look at "How to Deliver Great Customer Service," which can be found at www.inc.com/magazine/20100901/how-to-deliver-great-customer-service.html.

EXHIBIT

14.4 Consumer Options for Dealing with Product or Service Dissatisfaction

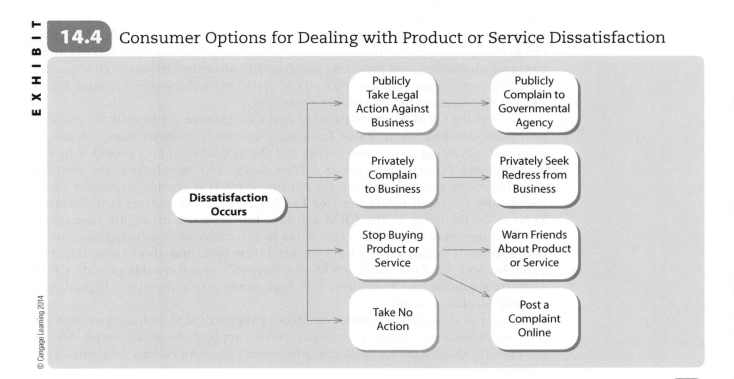

© Cengage Learning 2014

LO
14-3

Understand how technology can be used to improve customer relationships and the techniques used to create a customer database.

14-3 USING TECHNOLOGY TO SUPPORT CUSTOMER RELATIONSHIP MANAGEMENT

When it comes to analyzing and making use of customer data, a small business has options. A startup can easily manage the amount of data available, but this situation changes as the company grows and the contacts and accounts become more complex. For that reason, it's best to start thinking about available analytical technologies—from basic spreadsheets to very sophisticated CRM software packages—from the very beginning.

Many small companies keep track of their CRM numbers in a simple spreadsheet that can be expanded and updated as the business grows. The next step up would be to use a database management package like Microsoft Access. This offers greater utility and flexibility, as it can store large amounts of data and match data from multiple tables. Though not designed specifically for CRM programs, Access can certainly help you manage the data needed to guide customer care, basic advertising campaigns, and other marketing-related initiatives.

The most powerful tools available for customer relationship management are software programs designed specifically for CRM. According to recent research, 42 percent of small businesses have a CRM system already in place, and another 25 percent are planning to deploy such a program in the near future.[24] These packages allow companies to gather all customer contact information into a single data management program. Web-based marketers, in particular, are attracted to such technology, because it helps to make their complex job far more manageable. Most online shoppers expect to receive excellent customer service, and companies are much better positioned to give it if they use the options for interaction and personal attention that are designed into the software. Experts point out that customers typically appreciate the conveniences that are built into many company websites, but they can quickly become frustrated when the experience does not go exactly as planned. The burden of coordination is greatly eased when software can be used to help manage it.

Deciding which marketing activity should get initial CRM support is not always easy. However, the sales department is a popular place to start, because its personnel nearly always generate the most customer contact. CRM emphasizes such sales activities as filling orders promptly and accurately, managing follow-up contacts to ensure customer satisfaction, and providing user-friendly call centers to handle all inquiries, including complaints. It's a complex mix of tasks, but technologies are available to support all of these activities and many others.

To find the CRM software package that may provide the best fit for you and your firm, consider the included features, accessibility of buyer data, integrated sales and marketing tools, ease of use, and the help and support provided by the manufacturer. It might be wise to narrow down your search from the start by checking recommendations from the editors of *CRM* magazine, especially those specifically for small businesses (see Exhibit 14.5). These experts have declared Zoho to be the "king of the CRM software hill" because it's highly functional, cost-effective, easy to use, and expandable to accommodate a growing company.[25] Niche products that do exactly what you need them to do may also be available. For example, both CAR-Research XRM and Reynolds and Reynolds provide CRM software solutions for car dealers, with high-performance features designed specifically for that industry.

Concerns about having ample resources to support CRM technologies have led some small business owners to outsource certain applications. For example, hosted call centers, which handle e-mail and other online communications for clients, may

14.5 Highly Recommended CRM Software Packages for Small Businesses

CRM Package	Summary Description
Zoho CRM	Web-based, simple to set up and use, free for up to three users (small monthly charge for additional users), no long-term contracts, expandable to accommodate business growth, integrates seamlessly with Google applications and other Zoho programs.
Microsoft Dynamics	Very well supported, popular because of its overall functionality, hosted ("in the cloud") and on-premise options, interfaces with Microsoft Outlook and Web browser, monthly fee based on number of users.
NetSuite CRM+	Best for larger small businesses, excellent built-in e-commerce applications, more expensive than other options, additional charges for various add-ons.
Salesforce.com	A very popular package, considered a top innovator by CRM experts, many features and functions, expandable to accommodate business growth, some find it to be complicated to use.
SugarCRM	Good first CRM package, easy to set up and configure, tutorials available for assistance, basic package is free, charge for Professional Edition that offers access to many additional tools.

Sources: Based on Editors of *CRM*, "The 2012 CRM Market Leaders," www.destinationcrm.com/Articles/Editorial/Magazine-Features/The-2012-CRM-Market-Leaders-83897.aspx, accessed November 20, 2012; and Jenny Cathy, *San Diego News*, "The Five Best Small Business CRM Programs," May 24, 2012, http://sdnn.com/crm-software-reviews, accessed November 20, 2012.

be more cost effective than comparable in-house centers, a crucial consideration for many cash-strapped small businesses. In addition to cost, a lack of internal expertise can justify using these outside services.

Many companies have decided to control the cost of customer assistance by using alternatives like automated Web-based self-service systems, sometimes called *customer information management systems*. When a customer service rep handles a single telephone call, text chat, or e-mail, it can cost the company an average of $5 to $7, but self-service inquiries handled on the Internet cost less than 60 cents per contact. One popular self-service option is to post a list of Frequently Asked Questions (FAQs), and more than 40 percent of organizations have these on their websites. But even this simple tool is becoming more sophisticated. For example, a company can buy smart software that recognizes the questions its website visitors are most interested in and places those at the top of the list. Such systems can cut down the cost of serving customers while taking some of the repetition out of tending to their needs.[26]

The list of tools supporting CRM grows longer every day, and they are becoming much more user-friendly as time goes on. Executives and managers in large and small enterprises are tapping the power of the Internet to support the blogs, wikis, social networking sites, and other online communities that allow people to build social as well as business connections, to share information, and to collaborate on projects. The real power of these Web applications comes in the form of building relationships with customers.

> *A leading greeting-card and gift company . . . is one of many that have set up an online community—a site where it can talk to consumers and the consumers can talk to each other. The company solicits opinions on various aspects of greeting-card design and on ideas for gifts and their pricing. It also asks the consumers to talk about their lifestyles and even upload photos of themselves so that it can better understand its market.[27]*

Such online communities can provide a rich source of feedback and ideas for product development, and in a form that is much faster and cheaper to use than the focus groups and surveys that have been a staple of common marketing practices. But perhaps more important, Web tools can be used to give customers a sense of connection with the enterprise, an identity that results from their active participation in the company's business. For this, there is no substitute.

14-3a Creating a CRM Database

The best way to stay in touch with customers and to identify their needs is to talk to them. Such conversations lead to an understanding of each customer and provide a foundation on which to build a **customer database**. These databases are essential to a successful CRM program and typically include the following categories of information, with examples of specific data items provided:[28]

- *Personal information.* Name, address, phone number, e-mail address, clothing sizes, birthday, hobbies, memberships, etc.
- *Demographics.* Background information that can be used for market segmentation and other data analysis purposes, such as age, marital status, names and ages of family members, geographic location.
- *Lifestyle and psychographic data.* Homeowner versus renter status, car ownership (model and year), media preferences, payment methods of choice, recreational interests, etc.
- *Internet information.* Time spent on the Internet, frequency of visits to the company's website, and other online habits.
- *Transaction data.* Complete transaction history, including details such as prices paid, SKUs (which identifies specific products purchased), form of order (Web, phone, in-store, etc.), mode of payment, and delivery dates.
- *Profile of past responses.* Sales calls and service requests—including all customer- and company-initiated contacts—responses to past product or service promotions, and incentives redeemed.
- *Complaints.* Complete history of complaints regarding past purchases or service.

CRM data can almost always be collected at any **touch point**, which provides an occasion for contact between the business and its customers, whether in-person or online. Touch points can include interactions resulting from a phoned-in request for product information, completed and returned warranty cards, responses to online surveys, a visit from a salesperson, orders placed on the company's website—even a text message from a customer service representative. As indicated previously, some small companies prefer to collect data and feedback from customers using comment cards or questionnaires. While these can be effective, contact via the Internet is fast becoming the touch point of choice for companies as well as the customers they serve.

> *Instead of wasting time with phone numbers and mail surveys, companies are publicizing their Web sites as the first touch point for customer interactions. Web users can evaluate and purchase products, make reservations, indicate preferential data, and provide customer feedback on services and products. Data from these Web-based interactions are then captured, compiled, and used to segment customers, refine marketing efforts, develop new products, and deliver a high degree of individual customization to improve customer relationships.*[29]

In a CRM system, a customer's selection of a channel for interaction can be an important source of information in itself. For example, if the customer first contacts the company via e-mail, this provides an insight into his or her preferred method of communication, and the astute firm will consider that in all of its follow-up efforts.

customer database
A collection of information about a customer, including demographic data, attitudes, preferences, and other behavioral characteristics, as defined by CRM goals.

touch point
An interaction between a business and its customers.

14-3b Using a CRM Database

In a nutshell, an effective CRM program will (1) capture relevant customer data on interactions across important touch points, (2) analyze those data to better understand customers, and (3) use those insights to improve relationships with customers so that they are satisfied, loyal to the company and its products or services, and more willing to do business with it. The database for your company should include information on every customer you have ever had, as well as others whom you consider to be high-potential prospects. As time goes on and your database grows, you may want to further organize it according to region, economic status, customer focus, or any other variable that makes sense to your business and its marketing emphases.

© Helen King/Corbis

The Seattle Mariners baseball organization has used this process to "better understand the fans" and identify ways to boost attendance at games. The club launched a loyalty card program to collect data from as many touch points as possible. Now, every time a fan uses the card to snag a hotdog and a coke at a concession stand, buy a jersey from the online store, or purchase a bobblehead of a favorite player at a shop in the ballpark, the club is able to track the fan's attendance, as well as his or her activities and preferences. From collecting these data, the club knows to send an e-mail message if a fan is close to reaching "season ticketholder" status (which boosts sales). The loyalty program is also useful in monitoring complaints that can flag adjustments needed to boost fan satisfaction. As an example of how specific this can get, the CRM system found that one fan had complained about the smell of garlic fries. Knowing this, the organization was able to relocate him to a section "where there were no frequent consumers of garlic fries."[30] Such programs send a powerful message to customers, who are then inclined to do even more business with the company. But it takes a well-constructed database to get the process started.

On a more general level, you can use these data to set up a **customer segmentation strategy**, which involves a process of identifying customers that fit into smaller, more homogeneous groups. By focusing on those with similar demographic, psychographic, and lifestyle tendencies and sorting them by their previous purchases and payment histories, a marketing appeal can be crafted to meet their specific needs and generate greater sales. For example, a small real estate company could identify young, tech-comfortable customers and reach out to them with an online-intensive sales campaign, while trying to sell upscale homes to older, more affluent prospects using in-person appeals.

There are many other ways through which the data you gather can be used to form and strengthen relationships with customers and increase sales. One of these builds on the usefulness of the **80/20 principle**, which maintains that 80 percent of a company's sales will come from 20 percent of its customers. These percentages are not meant to be exact, but experience has shown that the idea generally holds true for most businesses. If a company has created a customer database and organized its data appropriately, it then becomes possible to identify the 20 percent who are the most loyal and who also deliver the greatest profitability to the company. Often, these "best customers" can be identified by running a **recency-frequency-monetary analysis**, which

customer segmentation strategy
A process of identifying customers that fit into smaller, more homogeneous groups.

80/20 principle
A principle that maintains that 80 percent of a company's sales will come from 20 percent of its customers.

recency-frequency-monetary analysis
An analysis that reveals customers most likely to buy from a firm in the future because they have made purchases recently, frequently, and in amounts that exceed some established minimum.

reveals those who are most likely to buy from you in the future because they have made purchases recently, frequently, and in amounts that exceed some appropriate minimum. Whatever method is used to identify them, you should go the extra mile with these customers to keep them happy and coming back to do more business. This might include anticipating their needs and tailoring product or service offerings to suit them, providing intensive customer service, or offering loyalty rewards to build long-term relationships. As for those who require intensive and costly effort but offer little to no potential to generate profits, it is best to find a way to reduce their cost to the company, perhaps by steering them to low-cost, self-service options online. Some businesses may even chose to end the relationship altogether.

As indicated in this chapter's Spotlight feature, Chris Zane knows that it is crucial to estimate the **Customer Lifetime Value (CLV)** for those who buy from his cycle shop if he is to create an effective CRM plan. The CLV is the total profit expected from all future sales to a customer and underscores the *long-term* value of each customer, which can then be communicated to others. Losing a sale today might not seem all that costly—until you factor in the likely loss of all future sales that can result from one interaction gone wrong. And since it can cost a lot more to acquire a new customer than to hold on to the ones you have, the loss can be greatly compounded. Everyone in the company needs to understand this so they will be more committed to treating customers well. The CLV can also give sales and service employees a better idea of how much they should spend to acquire and retain customers. Let's say you own a pizzaria and one of your loyal diners gets upset over a $12 meal. Before you decide how to handle the situation, keep in mind that his CLV could be as much as $8,000 (Pizza Hut's estimated CLV for its best customers). That's why having good data and knowing what to do with them can be so important.

14-3c Data Use and Privacy Concerns

Having so much data on customers puts considerable power in an entrepreneur's hands, and it is imperative that it be used responsibly. Customers may not be comfortable with everything required to gain the depth of insight necessary for successful CRM. For example, firms often watch customers' online shopping behavior very closely, taking note of the items they look at, for how long, and in what order. Some even analyze what customers say through social media, including comments left on blogs, frustrations expressed via Twitter, and more-private Facebook reflections. And this is just the start. The number of database-building options available to firms is great and growing.

There is no question that well-designed CRM systems provide value to customers (such as getting notices on sales that are both timely and relevant) and companies (such as predicting and planning for what customers will want next and generating higher response rates to e-mail offers), but there is still potential for abuse. To address privacy concerns, the process must be honest and transparent, the company must comply with applicable information-use laws, and permission to use personal data must be requested whenever appropriate. Because it can be very profitable to sell customer data to other companies or to

Customer Lifetime Value (CLV) The total profit expected from all future sales to a customer.

© SamBurt/iStockphoto.com

purchase data from third parties to fill gaps in any database being built, it can be quite tempting to misuse the data. But the trust of the customer is at stake, as well as the reputation of the company, and these must be protected. The long-term success of a CRM program depends on it.

Privacy concerns have grown tremendously with the rapidly expanding reach of computer applications and the mind-boggling growth of e-commerce, which make data collection easy and nearly cost-free. The risks to the customer are considerable, as some CRM experts have reported:

> *Online users have complained of being "spammed," and Web surfers, including children, are routinely asked to divulge personal information to access certain screens or purchase goods or services. Internet users are disturbed by the amount of information businesses collect on them as they visit various sites in cyberspace. Indeed, many users are unaware of how personal information is collected, used, and distributed.* [31]

Because of the sharp escalation in data collection and use, online and offline privacy practices are coming under increasing scrutiny. Though U.S. companies have, for the most part, been able to get away with self-policing, increased regulatory attention is coming. More than 50 nations now have or are in the process of enacting legislation designed to safeguard the handling of customer data in firms that do business internationally. Those that do business in the European Union or trade with a European company, for example, must comply with strict laws regulating these practices. Many countries are modeling their own systems after the European standard, so the burden of privacy protection is sure to rise. [32]

14-4 CUSTOMERS AS DECISION MAKERS

LO 14-4

Explain how consumers are decision makers and why this is important in understanding customer relationships.

Exhibit 14.2, on page 369, shows that the second primary building block supporting a successful CRM program involves knowledge of customer behavior. The three interrelated "materials" that combine to form that particular building block include the decision-making process, psychological influences, and sociological influences. Offering an expanded view, Exhibit 14.6 illustrates how consumer decision making flows through four stages: (1) need recognition, (2) information search and evaluation, (3) the purchase decision, and (4) post-purchase evaluation.

We'll use this widely accepted model to examine decision making among small business customers.

14-4a Need Recognition

Need recognition (stage 1) occurs when a consumer realizes that her or his current state of affairs differs significantly from some ideal state. Some needs are routine conditions of depletion, such as a lack of food when lunchtime arrives. Other needs arise less frequently and may evolve slowly. Recognition of the need to replace the family dining table, for example, may take years to develop.

A consumer must recognize a need before purchase behavior can begin; thus, the need-recognition stage cannot be overlooked. Many factors influence consumers' recognition of a need, either by changing the actual state of affairs or by affecting the desired state. Here are a few examples:

- A change in financial status (job promotion with a salary increase)
- A change in household characteristics (birth of a baby)

14.6 Simplified Model of Consumer Behavior

- Normal depletion (using up the last tube of toothpaste)
- Product or service performance (breakdown of a DVD player)
- Past decisions (poor repair service on a car)
- The availability of products (introduction of a new product)

An entrepreneur must understand the need-recognition stage in order to decide on the appropriate marketing strategy to use. In some situations, a small business owner will have to *influence* need recognition. In other situations, she or he may simply be able to *react* to needs that consumers have identified on their own.

14-4b Information Search and Evaluation

The second stage in consumer decision making involves the collection and evaluation of appropriate information. Internal sources of insight (usually from previous experiences with a product or brand) typically are considered first. However, prospective buyers usually turn to external sources (for example, input from friends and family, product-rating data from *Consumer Reports*, or feature descriptions from advertisements or salespeople) when their own past experience or knowledge is limited and the cost of gathering outside information is low.

To illustrate, suppose you are in the market for a big-screen television. If you work in the consumer electronics industry or have personal experience with some of the brands and models available (two *internal* sources of information), you probably know enough already to make a purchase decision. However, if you are like most people, you will need to gather information through *external* sources. You might ask for input from trusted friends, check out CNET's online reviews of big-screen models, and/or discuss model features with a salesperson at an electronics retailer. You'll need this information in order to make a sound decision when it's time to buy.

The search for information should help to clarify the purchase need and allow the consumer to establish **evaluative criteria** that will guide the decision process as it continues to unfold. That is, he or she will decide on the features or characteristics of the product or service that are to be used for comparison.

Small business owners should try to understand which evaluative criteria most consumers adopt, because these will be used to formulate their evoked set. An **evoked set**

evaluative criteria
The features or characteristics of a product or service that customers use for comparison.

evoked set
A group of brands that a consumer is both aware of and willing to consider as a solution to a purchase need.

is a group of brands that a consumer is both aware of and willing to consider as a solution to a purchase need. Thus, the initial challenge for a new company is to gain *market awareness* for its product or service. Only then will the brand have the opportunity to become part of consumers' evoked sets.

14-4c Purchase Decision

Once consumers have evaluated brands in their evoked set and made their choice, they must still decide how and where to make the purchase (stage 3). A substantial volume of retail sales now comes from nonstore settings, such as catalogs, TV shopping channels, and the Internet. These outlets have created a complex and challenging environment in which to develop marketing strategy. And consumers attribute many different advantages and disadvantages to various shopping outlets, making it difficult for the small firm to devise a single correct strategy. Sometimes, however, simple recognition of these factors can be helpful.

Of course, not every purchase decision is planned prior to entering a store or looking at a mail-order catalog. Studies show that most types of purchases from traditional retail outlets are not planned or intended prior to the customers' entering the store. This fact underscores the tremendous importance of such features as store layout, sales personnel, and point-of-purchase displays.[33]

14-4d Post-Purchase Evaluation

The consumer decision-making process does not end with a purchase. Small businesses desire repeat purchases from customers and thus need to understand post-purchase behavior (stage 4). Exhibit 14.7 illustrates several consumer activities that occur during post-purchase evaluation. Two of these activities—post-purchase dissonance and consumer complaints—are directly related to customer satisfaction.

Post-purchase dissonance is the psychological tension or anxiety that occurs immediately following a purchase decision when consumers have second thoughts as to the wisdom of their purchase. This dissonance can influence how a consumer evaluates a product and his or her ultimate level of satisfaction with it.

A consumer who is unhappy with the purchase process or the product during and after use may complain to the company, or even post a negative review on an online forum like Yelp.com. Despite the frustration or concern a complaint may cause, it creates an important opportunity for a business to make things right—a well-handled complaint may prevent the loss of a valuable customer. The outcome of the post-purchase process is a final level of customer satisfaction that affects customer loyalty and the likelihood of repeat purchases and product usage. It can also lead to brand switching and discontinued use of the product.

The best way to preserve customer satisfaction is to deal with issues and complaints as soon as possible and in the most effective way possible. This calls for a well-trained, informed, and cooperative work force. At The Angus Barn, owner Van Eure encourages employees to use the "20-Foot Rule"—that is, any restaurant employee within 20 feet of a problem should get involved in addressing it to make sure that all customers leave completely satisfied. For example, waiters might provide dessert to a diner free of charge or accommodate a customer's needs by altering the seating chart. Because they are so central to the success of the operation, Eure takes very good care of those who work for her, as reflected by a very low turnover rate. Her approach to resolving customer concerns may underlie the high satisfaction quotient of both her customers and her employees.[34]

post-purchase dissonance
The psychological tension or anxiety that occurs when a customer has second thoughts immediately following a purchase.

14.7 Post-Purchase Activities of Consumers

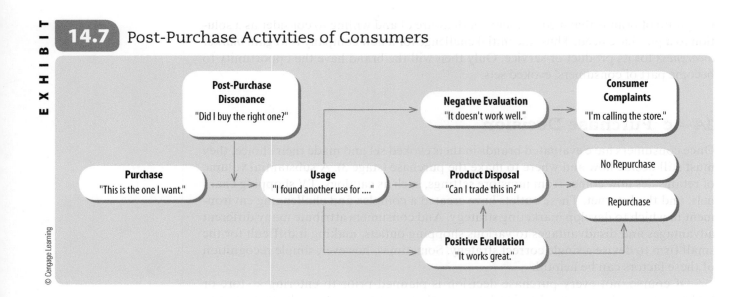

LO 14-5

Identify important psychological influences on consumer behavior.

14-5 UNDERSTANDING PSYCHOLOGICAL INFLUENCES ON CUSTOMERS

Another major component of the consumer behavior model, as presented in Exhibit 14.6 on page 382, is psychological influences. The four psychological influences that have the greatest relevance to small businesses are needs, perceptions, motivations, and attitudes.

14-5a Needs

Needs are often described as the starting point for all behavior. Without needs, there would be no behavior. Although consumer needs are innumerable, they can be identified as falling into four categories—physiological, social, psychological, and spiritual.

Consumers' needs are never completely satisfied, thereby ensuring the continued existence of business. One of the more complex characteristics of needs is the way in which they function together in shaping behavior. In other words, various needs operate simultaneously, making it difficult to determine which need is being satisfied by a specific product or service. Nevertheless, careful assessment of the needs-behavior connection can be very helpful in developing marketing strategy. But you should keep in mind that purchases of the same product can satisfy different needs. For example, consumers purchase food products in supermarkets to satisfy physiological needs, but they also purchase food in status restaurants to satisfy their social and/or psychological needs. Also, certain foods are demanded by specific market segments to satisfy religious or spiritual needs. A needs-based strategy would result in a different marketing approach in each of these situations.

needs
The starting point for all behavior.

perception
The individual processes that give meaning to the stimuli confronting consumers.

14-5b Perceptions

A second psychological factor, **perception**, encompasses those individual processes that ultimately give meaning to the stimuli consumers encounter. When this meaning is severely distorted or entirely blocked, consumer perception can cloud a small company's marketing effort and make it ineffective. For example, a retailer may mark its fashion clothing "on sale" to communicate a price reduction from usual levels, but customers' perceptions may be that "these clothes are out of style."

Perception depends on the characteristics of both the stimulus and the perceiver. Consumers attempt to manage huge quantities of incoming stimuli through **perceptual categorization**, a process by which things that are similar are perceived as belonging together. Therefore, if a small business wishes to position its product as being comparable to an existing brand, the marketing mix should reflect an awareness of perceptual categorization. For example, comparable quality can be communicated through similar prices or a package design with a color scheme bearing a resemblance to that of an existing brand. These techniques will help a consumer fit the new product into the desired product category.

Small businesses that attach an existing brand name to a new product are relying on perceptual categorization to pre-sell the new product. If, on the other hand, the new product is physically different or is of a different quality, a new brand name should be selected to create a distinctive perceptual categorization in the consumer's mind.

If a consumer has strong brand loyalty to a product, it will be difficult for other brands to penetrate his or her perceptual barriers. That individual is likely to have distorted images of competing brands because of a pre-existing attitude. Consumer perceptions thus present a unique communication challenge.

© Alexander Ivanov/Shutterstock.com

14-5c Motivations

Everyone is familiar with hunger pains, which are manifestations of the tension created by an unsatisfied physiological need. What directs a person to obtain food so that the hunger pains can be relieved? The answer is motivation. **Motivations** are goal-directed forces that organize and give direction to tension caused by unsatisfied needs. Marketers cannot create needs, but they can offer unique motivations to consumers. If an acceptable reason for purchasing a product or service is provided, it will probably be internalized by the consumer as a motivating force. The key for the marketer is to determine which motivations the consumer will perceive as acceptable in a given situation. The answer is found through an analysis of other consumer behavior variables.

Like physiological needs, the other three classes of needs—social, psychological, and spiritual—can be connected to behavior through motivations. For example, a campus clothing store might promote styles that communicate that the college student wearing those clothes has obtained membership in a social group, such as a fraternity or sorority.

Understanding motivations is not easy. Several motivations may be present in any situation, and they are often subconscious. However, they must be investigated if the marketing effort is to succeed.

14-5d Attitudes

Like the other psychological variables, attitudes cannot be observed, but everyone has them. Do attitudes imply knowledge? Do they imply feelings of good or bad, favorable or unfavorable? Does an attitude have a direct impact on behavior? The answer to each

perceptual categorization
The process of grouping things that are perceived as being similar.

motivations
Goal-directed forces that organize and give direction to the tension caused by unsatisfied needs.

of these questions is a resounding "Yes." An **attitude** is an enduring opinion, based on a combination of knowledge, feelings, and behavioral tendencies.

An attitude may act as an obstacle or a driver in bringing a customer to a product. For example, consumers with the belief that a local, family-run grocery store has higher prices than a national supermarket chain may avoid the local store. Armed with an understanding of the structure of a particular attitude, a marketer can approach the consumer more intelligently.

14-6

Recognize certain sociological influences on consumer behavior.

14-6 UNDERSTANDING SOCIOLOGICAL INFLUENCES ON CUSTOMERS

Sociological influences, as shown in Exhibit 14.6 on page 382, comprise the last component of the consumer behavior model. Among these influences are cultures, social classes, reference groups, and opinion leaders. Note that these influences represent different degrees of group aggregation: Culture involves large masses of people, social classes and reference groups represent smaller groups of people, and opinion leaders are individuals who exert influence.

14-6a Cultures

In marketing, **culture** refers to the behavioral patterns and values that characterize a group of customers in a target market. These patterns and beliefs have a tremendous impact on the purchase and use of products. Marketing managers often overlook the cultural variable because its influences are so subtly embedded within a society. International marketers who have experienced more than one culture, however, can readily attest to the impact of cultural influence.

The prescriptive nature of cultures should concern the entrepreneur. Cultural norms create a range of product-related acceptable behaviors that influence what consumers buy. However, because a culture changes by adapting slowly to new situations, what works well as a marketing strategy today may not work a few years from now.

An investigation of a culture within a narrower boundary—defined by age, religious preference, ethnic orientation, or geographical location—is called *subcultural analysis*. Here, too, unique patterns of behavior and social relationships must concern the marketing manager. For example, the needs and motivations of the youth subculture are far different from those of the senior citizen subculture. Small business managers who familiarize themselves with cultures and subcultures are able to create better marketing mixes.

14-6b Social Classes

Another sociological factor affecting consumer behavior is social class. **Social classes** are divisions within a society having different levels of social prestige. Occupation is probably the single most important determinant of social class. Other determinants include possessions, sources of income, and education. The social class system has important implications for marketing. Different lifestyles correlate with different levels of social prestige, and certain products often become symbols of a type of lifestyle. For products like grocery staples, social class analysis will probably not be very useful. For products like home furnishings, however, such analysis may help to explain variations in shopping and communication patterns.

attitude
An enduring opinion, based on a combination of knowledge, feelings, and behavioral tendencies.

culture
Behavioral patterns and values that characterize a group of consumers in a target market.

Social classes
Divisions within a society having different levels of social prestige.

14-6c Reference Groups

Technically, social class could be considered a reference group. However, marketers are generally more concerned with smaller groups such as families, work groups, neighborhood groups, and recreational groups. Reference groups are those small groups that an individual allows to influence his or her behavior.

The existence of group influence is well established. The challenge to the marketer is to understand why this influence occurs and how it can be used to promote the sale of a product or service. Individuals tend to accept group influence because of the benefits they perceive as resulting from it, and these perceived benefits give influencers various kinds of power. Five widely recognized forms of power—all of which are available to the marketer—are reward, coercive, referent, expert, and legitimate power.

Reward power and *coercive power* relate to a group's ability to give and to withhold rewards. Rewards may be material or psychological; recognition and praise are typical psychological rewards. A Pampered Chef in-home party is a good example of a marketing technique that takes advantage of reward power and coercive power. The ever-present possibility of pleasing or displeasing the hostess-friend encourages guests to buy.

Referent power and *expert power* involve neither rewards nor punishments. They exist because an individual attaches great importance to being part of a group or perceives the group as being knowledgeable. Referent power (based on one's admiration or respect for the power holder) influences consumers to conform to a group's behavior and to choose products selected by group members. Children are often affected by referent power, so marketers can create a desire for products by using cleverly designed advertisements or packages that appeal to this inclination. And a person perceived as an expert can be an effective spokesperson for a host of products because consumers trust his or her judgment.

Legitimate power involves authority and the approval of what an individual ought to do. We are most familiar with legitimate power at the societal level, but it can also be used in smaller groups. Social marketing efforts are an attempt to encourage a certain behavior as the right thing to do (for example, wear your seat belt, don't drink and drive).

14-6d Opinion Leaders

According to widely accepted communication principles, consumers receive a significant amount of information through individuals called opinion leaders, group members who play a key communications role.

Generally speaking, opinion leaders are knowledgeable, visible, and have exposure in the mass media. A small business firm can enhance its own image by identifying with such leaders. For example, a farm-supply dealer may promote its products in an agricultural community by holding demonstrations of these products on the farms of highly successful local farmers, who are typically the community's opinion leaders.

When Phil Knight established Nike, Inc., in the early 1970s, he used a marketing strategy that followed what he called the Five Cool Guys Principle. The idea was that if he could get five of the best and most popular athletes on a high school campus to wear his shoes, then others would want to buy the shoes for themselves. The "cool guys" would set the trend. Of course, the strategy can be applied at higher and more visible levels, which is why Nike has paid so much money over the years to get world-class

Don't Drink and Drive

© Becky Stares/Shutterstock.com

Efforts designed to encourage appropriate conduct are often based on appeals to legitimate power at the societal level, suggesting that some behaviors are simply the right thing to do.

reference groups
Small groups that an individual allows to influence his or her behavior.

opinion leaders
A group member who plays a key communications role.

athletes to don the company's products. Nike's tremendously successful marketing efforts are an illustration of the influence of opinion leaders.

In the modern era of social media, this effect can be magnified many times over to the benefit of small businesses. One mention of your company in a celebrity's "tweet" or even the briefest exposure of your product on a big hit YouTube video can push customer interest through the roof. In fact, some small businesses find that such occurrences can increase demand so much that they have a very difficult time coming up with enough product to satisfy it. This is a great problem to have, but it may be more challenging to deal with than you realize.

Customer relationship management will be at the heart of any business that is destined for success. A satisfied customer is likely to be a repeat customer who will tell others about your company. But establishing an effective CRM program is hard work—it requires a thorough knowledge of the major components of customer satisfaction, the development of a suitable customer database, wise handling of complaints, and an understanding of the customer decision-making process. Of course, it all starts with maintaining a helpful and positive attitude toward customers, but the more small business owners know about their customers, the better they will be able to meet their needs.

LOOKING BACK

14-1. Define *customer relationship management (CRM)*, and explain its importance to a small business.

- Customer relationship management (CRM) is a company-wide strategy that can be used to learn more about the needs and behaviors of customers with the specific purposes of building stronger relationships with them, thereby optimizing profitability.

- The central message of every CRM program is "Cultivate customers for more than a one-time sale."

- A CRM program recognizes the importance of keeping current customers satisfied to ensure their loyalty, given the high costs associated with attracting new customers.

- Being able to respond quickly to customer service issues is one of the greatest advantages of small firms.

- Two vital building blocks of any CRM program are outstanding transactional relationships with customers and knowledge of consumer behavior.

14-2. Discuss the significance of providing extraordinary customer service.

- To be successful in the long run, small firms must build positive transactional relationships in order to develop and maintain loyal customers.

- Providing exceptional customer service can give small firms a competitive edge, regardless of the nature of the business.

- Satisfied customers are loyal, which translates to increased revenue.

- Personal attention is the "gold standard" against which the quality of customer service is judged, and this can be strengthened by doing business on a first-name basis, keeping in touch with customers, findings ways to help them, customizing services offered, and addressing problems promptly.

- Customer experience management (CEM) recognizes that relationships with customers can be strengthened or weakened depending on the quality of the experience they have with a company.

- Providing excellent service after a sale (creating value by checking in, monitoring delivery and installation, resolving complaints, and so on) can give a small company a competitive edge.

- Establishing an effective customer service program begins with determining how well the firm is currently serving its customers, or its *customer service quotient*.

- Small business owners can learn about customer service problems through customer complaints, personal observation, and other research techniques.

- Although many types of customer service cost very little to offer, there are definite costs associated with superior levels of customer service.

14-3. Understand how technology can be used to improve customer relationships and the techniques used to create a customer database.

- It is best to start thinking about a small company's need for CRM technologies—from basic spreadsheets to sophisticated software packages—from the start.

- Forty-two percent of small businesses already use software to manage their CRM needs, and another 25 percent hope to adopt such programs in the near future.

- When selecting a CRM software package, consider factors such as included features, accessibility of data, integrated sales and marketing tools, ease of use, and support provided by the manufacturer.

- Concern about having ample support resources for CRM information technology has led some entrepreneurs to outsource certain applications.

- Tools for CRM management are growing in number and are becoming cheaper, more sophisticated, and easier to use.

- Blogs, wikis, social networking sites, and online communities offer ways of gathering customer feedback.

- Customer databases are essential to a successful CRM program, as they represent building material for the required knowledge of customers.

- Categories of useful customer information include personal information, demographics, lifestyle and psychographic data, Internet information, transaction data, profile of past responses, and a history of complaints.

- CRM data can be collected at any touch point (places where customer contact occurs) and used to guide customer segmentation strategies.

- According to the 80/20 principle, most of a company's sales will come from a relatively small number of its best customers, and a recency-frequency-monetary analysis can help to identify them.

- It is very important to think beyond any single transaction in order to focus on the customer lifetime value, representing all future expected sales from a customer.

- If a small company chooses to set up a customer database, then it is essential that all collected data be used ethically and responsibility to protect customer privacy.

14-4. Explain how consumers are decision makers and why this is important in understanding customer relationships.

- The four stages of consumer decision making are closely tied to ultimate customer satisfaction.

- Need recognition (stage 1) occurs when a consumer realizes that her or his current state of affairs differs significantly from some ideal state.

- Stage 2 in consumer decision making involves consumers' collection and evaluation of appropriate information from both internal and external sources.

- Once consumers have evaluated brands in their evoked set and made their choice, they must still decide how and where to make the purchase (stage 3).

- Post-purchase evaluation (stage 4) may lead to psychological dissonance or anxiety and complaint behavior, which can negatively influence customer satisfaction with the product or service and the business that provides it.

- The best way to preserve customer satisfaction is to deal with issues and complaints as soon as they come up.

14-5. Identify certain psychological influences on consumer behavior.

- The four psychological influences that have the greatest relevance to small businesses are needs, perceptions, motivations, and attitudes.

- Needs are often described as the starting point for all behavior.

- Perception encompasses those individual processes that ultimately give meaning to the stimuli confronting consumers.

- Motivations are goal-directed forces that organize and give direction to tension caused by unsatisfied needs.

- An attitude is an enduring opinion, based on a combination of knowledge, feelings, and behavioral tendencies.

14-6. Recognize certain sociological influences on consumer behavior.

- Among the sociological influences are cultures, social classes, reference groups, and opinion leaders.

- In marketing, the term *culture* refers to the behavioral patterns and values that characterize a group of customers in a target market.

- Social classes are divisions within a society having different levels of social prestige.

- Reference groups are those small groups that an individual allows to influence his or her behavior.

- Consumers receive a significant amount of information through opinion leaders, group members who play a key communications role.

Key Terms

Discussion Questions

1. Define *customer relationship management*. What is the central message of every CRM program?

2. Does CRM put more emphasis on current or potential customers? Why?

3. What are the two essential building blocks of a successful CRM program? What "materials" are used to construct these building blocks?

4. Why is a small business potentially in a better position to achieve customer satisfaction than a large firm?

5. What types of information should be part of a customer database?

6. How can a customer database be used to guide the marketing strategies of a small business?

7. In what ways can a small business use technology to support its customer relationship management efforts?

8. Briefly describe the four stages of the consumer decision-making process. Why is the first stage so vital to consumer behavior?

9. List the four psychological influences on consumers that were discussed in this chapter. What is their relevance to consumer behavior?

10. List the four sociological influences on consumers that were discussed in this chapter. What is their relevance to consumer behavior?

You Make the Call

Situation 1

Jeremy Shepherd is the founder and president of PearlParadise. com, in Los Angeles, California. His jewelry business recognizes the importance of ensuring that customers keep coming back. However, Shepherd is uncertain as to which customer retention techniques he should use to develop a strong foundation for repeat business. The firm's website has software capabilities to support customer interactions.

Question 1 What customer loyalty techniques would you recommend to Shepherd?

Question 2 What information would be appropriate to collect about customers in a database?

Question 3 What specific computer-based communication could be used to achieve Shepherd's goal?

Source: www.pearlparadise.com, accessed November 26, 2012.

Situation 2

Sometimes a creative twist on standard marketing research methods can improve their effectiveness. This was certainly true for Jason Belkin, owner of Hampton Coffee Company, with two coffee-house locations in New York and a mobile espresso van. At one time, Belkin used a mystery shopper service (which hires individuals to pose as real customers to evaluate a company's true service performance) to assess customer experiences, but he decided to turn to comment cards for the information he wanted. He now offers a free cup of coffee to customers who fill out a card. The card asks a number of questions, which you can see at http://hamptoncoffeecompany.com/assets/uploads/CommentCard-front.pdf.

Question 1 What are the advantages and disadvantages of the two approaches Belkin has used to assess customer experiences at his coffee shops? Which one would you recommend?

Question 2 Do you see any problems with offering a free cup of coffee as an incentive for filling out a comment card? Would you suggest any other options for encouraging customers to provide feedback?

Question 3 Take a look at the comment card that Belkin has posted online. What are the best features of the card? How might it be improved?

Sources: Hampton Coffee Company—Our Story, http://hamptoncoffeecompany.com /about-us/story, accessed October 31, 2012; Heather Larson, Coffee Talk, *MyBusiness*, www .nfib.com/mybusiness-magazine/article?cmsid=53793, accessed October 31, 2012; and Hampton Coffee Company—What's Your Opinion? http://hamptoncoffeecompany.com /assets/uploads/CommentCard-front.pdf, accessed November 26, 2012.

Situation 3

Jay Goltz owns a Chicago-based decorative frame company, Artists Frame Service, and three other businesses. And in his mind, customer service today is more important than ever. "Smiling and being pleasant is not enough," Goltz observes. He goes out of his way to hire great employees and trains them to handle even the most challenging questions and service requests. Then he goes a step or two further by making the following claims on his company's website:

- Our framing consultants have art backgrounds with an average of nine years of experience.
- We offer an extraordinary selection of picture frames sourced personally and passionately from around the world so you get the perfect frame.
- We take framing seriously. It's about details, higher standards and meeting our own expectations. You'll see and feel the difference.
- We frame your art in one week—with a huge inventory and a large staff of artisans, we can deliver on this commitment.

To ensure that all goes as planned, Goltz keeps extensive documentation on every job. If complaints arise, he can figure out what happened and deal with the problem quickly. Taking this approach, he can tell if a customer's dissatisfaction stems from, say, an employee's carelessness, inadequate equipment, or some other problem. If the cause is an employee's poor workmanship, Goltz will provide coaching to help improve that associate's performance. After that, if the problem still is not solved, the employee is fired. As Goltz sees it, "The company's first mission isn't having employees, it's staying in business. Customer service is the main advantage small businesses have over their big competitors, so you have to get that right—no matter what it takes."

Question 1 As a long-run strategy, will Goltz's approach to superior customer service quality be successful?

Question 2 Would you want to work for a company with such policies? What would be the pros and cons of working there?

Question 3 What suggestions would have you for Goltz? Can you see any ways to improve his system?

Sources: Artists Frame Service—Our Difference, www.artistsframe.com/services/our -difference.html, accessed November 26, 2012; and Megan Pacella, Strong Support, MyBusiness, www.nfib.com/mybusiness-magazine/article?cmsid=54314, accessed November 26, 2012.

Experiential Exercises

1. For several days, make notes on your own shopping experiences. Summarize what you consider to be the best customer service you received.

2. Interview a local entrepreneur about her or his company's consumer service efforts. Summarize your findings.

3. Interview a local entrepreneur about what types of customer complaints his or her business receives. Also ask how the entrepreneur deals with different complaints. Report your findings to the class.

4. Consider your most recent meaningful purchase. Compare the decision-making process you used to the four stages of decision making presented in this chapter. Report your conclusions.

Small Business & Entrepreneurship Resource Center

The Small Business & Entrepreneurship Resource Center offers complete small business management resources through a comprehensive database that covers all major areas of starting, operating, and maintaining a business from financing, management, marketing, accounting, taxes, and more. Go to www.cengagebrain.com and select the Longenecker text for more information on how to access this material.

1. Mobivity Holdings Corp. and the Bowling Proprietors' Association of America (BPAA) have formed a strategic relationship where the BPAA will provide Mobivity's mobile marketing solutions to their 4,000 members to enable bowling centers to reach customers on their mobile phones with promotional marketing, incentive, and loyalty programs. BPAA will integrate Mobivity's patented technology into its existing customer relationship management system. Over 5,000 local advertiser locations across America are already using Mobivity's technology. Do you think that bowlers will respond favorably to messages on their mobile phones or consider these messages intrusive? The central message of every CRM program is "Cultivate customers for more than a one-time sale." Does this technology cultivate customers? Explain.

2. Cooke Gallery in Seattle, Washington, strives to sell superior-quality, traditional artworks to tourists and local clients, while providing educational information, value, and excellent customer service. Ms. Cooke, who has seven years of experience as gallery manager, possesses excellent interpersonal and organizational skills and is committed to providing the highest-quality customer service. She trains the staff and educates her customers on the cultural aspects of each piece sold, and it is this level of customer service that is the basis of the business's success. At Cooke Gallery, customer service is based upon caring and respectful relationships. The staff's enjoyment for their work is passed on to customers, and there is always a positive atmosphere in the gallery. As well as discussing the artwork and the native culture, they willingly help tourists find their way around and give travel advice. How does exceptional customer service give a small firm like the Cooke Gallery a competitive edge?

Sources: "Mobivity to Help Deliver Mobile Marketing to More Than 3,500 US Bowling Centers," The Free Library—Internet Business News, December 6, 2012; and Gerald Rekve, "Art Gallery: COOKE GALLERY," in Lynn M. Pearce (ed.), Business Plans Handbook, Vol. 14 (Detroit: Gale, 2009).

Video Case 14

Numi Tea (P. 674)

Numi Tea was started in 1999 by the brother and sister team of Ahmed and Reem Rahim. Keeping it in the family is important at Numi. Every member of the Tea'm, as they call it, is committed to the company's core values of sustainability, creativity, and quality organics. This extends to their corporate customers and their producers as well. Like their teas, every relationship is carefully cultivated and maintained.

Alternative Case for Chapter 14

Video Case 2, PortionPac Chemicals, p. 646

Endnotes

1. "The Neglected Moneymaker: Customer Retention," April 25, 2007, http://knowledge.wpcarey.asu.edu/article.cfm?articleid=1408, accessed October 25, 2012.

2. Frederick Reichheld, The Loyalty Effect: The Hidden Force Behind Growth, Profits, and Lasting Value (Boston: Harvard Business School Press, 2008).

3. Charles W. Lamb, Joseph F. Hair, and Carl McDaniel, Marketing, 12th ed. (Cincinnati: Cengage Learning, 2013), p. 771.

4. Research has shown that the entrepreneur–customer relationship is actually reciprocal [see Dirk De Clercq and Deva Rangarajan, "The Role of Perceived Relational Support in Entrepreneur-Customer Dyads," Entrepreneurship Theory & Practice, Vol. 32, No. 4 (2008), pp. 659–683]. In other words, just as customers recognize that the way an entrepreneurial company treats them has an impact on their level of satisfaction with and commitment to the company, so does the customer's reputation and the reliability of the customer's exchanges with the company influence the entrepreneur's satisfaction with and commitment to that customer. One builds upon the other.

5. "Crunching the Numbers: Customer Service" Inc., Vol. 33, No. 4 (May 2011), p. 30.

6. Brian Vellmure, "Let's Start with Customer Retention," www.initiumtechnology .com/newsletter_120602.htm, accessed October 26, 2012.

7. National Federation of Independent Business, "Marketing Perspectives," http://411sbfacts.com/sbpoll-tables-res.php?POLLID=0054&QID=000000 01624&KT_back=1, accessed November 26, 2012.

8. Amy Barrett, "True Believers," www.businessweek.com/magazine /content/06_52/b4015401.htm?chan=smallbiz_smallbiz+index+page _sales+and+marketing, accessed January 12, 2011.

9. Lynne Meredith Schreiber, "CRM: You (Should) Love Your Customers, Now Work to Keep Them," www.startupnation.com/business-articles/1533/1 /crm-software-strategy.asp, accessed October 26, 2012.

10. "Crunching the Numbers" *op. cit.*, p. 24.

11. Lindsay Holloway, "Marx Acosta-Rubio," *Entrepreneur*, Vol. 36, No. 9 (September 2008), pp. 66–67.

12. "The Neglected Moneymaker," *op. cit.*

13. Some of these suggestions were adapted from Lesley Spencer Pyle, "Keep Your Customers from Straying," *Entrepreneur*, June 12, 2008, www .entrepreneur.com/article/194784, accessed October 26, 2012.

14. Personal communication with Denny Fulk, May 7, 2007.

15. John Greathouse, "Personal Pitch," www.infochachkie.com/personal-pitch, accessed October 26, 2012.

16. Harley Manning, "You Are in the Customer Experience Business, Whether You Know It or Not," *Forbes*, August, 28, 2012, www.forbes.com/sites /forrester/2012/08/28/you-are-in-the-customer-experience-business -whether-you-know-it-or-not, accessed October 29, 2012.

17. Oracle Corporation, "Seven Power Lessons for Customer Experience Leaders," February 2012, www.oracle.com/us/corporate/acquisitions/rightnow /seven-power-lessons-wp-1502937.pdf, accessed October 29, 2012.

18. *Ibid*.

19. Franci Rogers, ""Protecting Your Rep," *Baylor Business Review*, Spring 2012, pp. 42–45.

20. These examples were adapted from Alina Dizik, "Fun for the Whole Family: The Long Wait in Line," *Wall Street Journal*, August 10, 2011, pp. D1–D2.

21. Howard Stevens and Theodore Kinni, *Achieve Sales Excellence* (Avon, MA: Platinum Press, 2007).

22. Adapted from Thomas N. Ingram, Raymond W. LaForge, Ramon A. Avila, Charles H. Schwepker, and Michael R. Williams, *Sell* (Mason, OH: Cengage Learning, 2013).

23. Personal communication with John Stites, October 23, 2007.

24. Editors of *CRM Magazine*, "The 2012 CRM Market Leaders," www .destinationcrm.com/Articles/Editorial/Magazine-Features/The-2012 -CRM-Market-Leaders-83897.aspx, accessed November 16, 2012.

25. *Ibid*.

26. Darren Dahl, "What Seems to Be the Problem? Self Service Gets a Tune-Up," *Inc.*, Vol. 30, No. 2 (February 2008), pp. 43–44.

27. Salvatore Parise, Patricia J. Guinan, and Bruce D. Weinberg, "The Secrets of Marketing in a Web 2.0 World," *The Wall Street Journal*, December 15, 2008, p. R4.

28. Adapted from Dawn Iacobucci, *MM³* (Mason, OH: Cengage Learning, 2013), p. 192.

29. Lamb et al., *op. cit.*, p. 778.

30. *Ibid.*, pp. 774–775.

31. *Ibid.*, p. 793.

32. *Ibid*.

33. See, for example, Del I. Hawkings and David L. Mothersbaugh, *Consumer Behavior: Building Marketing Strategy*, 11th ed. (New York: McGraw-Hill Irwin, 2010), Chapter 17.

34. "Angus Barn—Our History," www.angusbarn.com/ohistory.htm, accessed November 20, 2012.

© Peshkova/Shutterstock.com

CHAPTER 15

Product Development and Supply Chain Management

OPEN LOOKING AHEAD

In his book *Animal Farm*, George Orwell quips, "All animals are created equal, but some animals are more equal than others." The quote applies to the world of business as well. In the past, large firms had easy access to the tools required to develop a new product quickly and cheaply, moving it from initial concept through final production with relative ease and little cost. Small businesses were not so lucky—most couldn't afford the equipment necessary to make that happen. Today, however, many new tools that radically reduce costs are available to entrepreneurs who want to bring a new product or service to market.

Suppose that you've created a mock-up, based on an idea for a product. You could then use a Cambridge University student's free program and a cheap webcam to turn it into a 3-D model (see http://mi.eng.cam.ac.uk/~qp202/

In the SPOTLIGHT
Tools that Are Powering Small Business Product Development

my_papers/BMVC09). Or you could try the free and easy-to-use Google SketchUp (http://google-sketchup.en.softonic.com) to create or revise your model.

© Subbotina/Dreamstime LLC

Once you've created a digital model, you could hire a company like Shapeways (www.shapeways.com) to build your creation using a variety of materials, including plastic (in various colors and grades of transparency), metal (silver, aluminum, and stainless steel), sandstone—even chocolate or sugar. You could also buy your own 3-D rapid-prototyping printer for only $2,199 (www.makerbot.com) and build it yourself.

Does your product need to be interactive? With the Arduino open-source electronics prototyping platform (www.arduino.cc), it has never been easier to embed a product with an electronic controller. This very inexpensive and easy-to-use control board allows your product to link to a variety of sensors to gauge its environment and then respond by controlling lights, motors, and other actuators.

Several workshops give entrepreneurs and do-it-yourselfers access to tools, equipment, instruction, and a community of like-minded individuals. Check out TechShop (http://techshop.ws) and WeWork Labs (http://weworklabs.com). And if you are not sure how to sell your first prototypes and build a customer base, why not try craft sites like Etsy (www.etsy.com) and tried-and-true auction sites like eBay (www.ebay.com). Want to build your own website and store? E-commerce platform providers like Volusion (www.volusion.com) and Shopify (www.shopify.com) can help you get started.

Perhaps you need capital to expand. The best known crowdfunding site in the world, Kickstarter (www.kickstarter.com), may be able to help. In the last four years, it has funded 79,314 projects with approximately $428 million. If you are further along, an innovation exchange like Innovatrs (www.innovatrs.net) can provide mentors, advisors, and investors to keep things moving forward. And if you need more information to protect your intellectual property as you are getting started, LegalZoom (www.legalzoom.com) may be just the ticket for you.

If you like the sound of all this but still need more assistance, companies such as Big Idea Group (www.bigideagroup.net) can walk you through the process from ideation to business incubation. Clearly, small businesses are no longer at a disadvantage when it comes to product development.

Sources: Based on the websites mentioned above, all accessed on December 3, 2012.

Everyone seems to be talking about the economy these days, and the conversations are often sprinkled with the terms *supply* and *demand*. These fundamental forces of the marketplace determine how high the prices of products and services are likely to be. *Supply* refers to the willingness of businesses to put a certain product or service up for sale, while *demand* represents the interest and ability of buyers to purchase it. If a product is in short supply, its price will almost always rise as demand takes over and motivated buyers scramble to purchase the limited goods available at that time.

Supply and demand also affect the operation of a small business, though in a slightly different way. Robert Kiyosaki, entrepreneur and celebrated author of the *Rich Dad Poor Dad* series of books, explains why these concepts are so important:

> *Think of demand as sales and marketing. It's your sales and marketing department's job to create demand by making sure that your customers know and buy what your company has to offer. Meanwhile, supply is represented by manufacturing, warehousing and distribution, aka the supply chain. It's your supply chain's job to be prepared to fulfill the demand created by the sales side.*[1]

This simplifies the formula but clearly explains the need for balance in these key areas of the company's operations.

In Chapter 14, you learned about customer decision making (demand) and the need for an entrepreneur to make a strong commitment to customer relationship management (CRM) to ensure that new customers are drawn to the company and connections to current customers are preserved. You also learned that marketing programs must reflect consumer behavior concepts if CRM efforts are to sustain the firm's competitive advantage. In this chapter, we discuss the demand side of the equation further, explaining how product innovation can lead to business growth (from increased demand), but you will also get a healthy dose of supply-side thinking. That is, we address product and supply chain management decisions, which together have a significant impact on the total bundle of satisfaction targeted to customers. Business growth can be a wonderful thing, but supply–demand balance is critical to enterprise success.

15-1 TO GROW OR NOT TO GROW

LO
15-1

Recognize the challenges associated with the growth of a small business.

Once a new venture has been launched, the newly created firm settles into day-to-day operations. Its marketing plan reflects current goals as well as any expansion or growth that will impact marketing activities.

Entrepreneurs differ in their desire for growth. Some want to grow rapidly, while others prefer a modest expansion rate. Many find that maintaining the status quo is challenge enough, and this becomes the driving force behind their marketing decisions. However, growth sometimes happens unexpectedly, and the entrepreneur is forced to concentrate all efforts on meeting demand. Consider what happened to an entrepreneur who showed a new line of flannel nightgowns to a large chain-store buyer, and the buyer immediately ordered 500 of them, with delivery expected in five days! The entrepreneur accepted the order, even though he had material on hand for only 50 gowns. He emptied his bank account to purchase the necessary material and frantically begged friends to join him in cutting and sewing the gowns. After several sleepless nights, he filled the order.[2]

As you can see, growing quickly can be a stressful proposition if you are not prepared. Many paths can lead a small business owner to similar situations. For example, a new entrepreneur may price a product too low, prompting some buyers to exploit the opportunity by placing large orders. This can be especially hard on a startup, because the final costs of production can exceed total revenues from sales. Also, if a small business is unable to deliver on time or with the level of quality promised, or if it must turn down an order because it can't handle the volume, its reputation can be damaged significantly.

Successful growth seldom happens on its own; it will occur only when a number of factors are carefully considered and well managed. When a business experiences rapid growth in sales volume, its income statements will generally reflect growing profits. However, rapid growth in sales and profits may be hazardous to the company's cash flows. A *growth trap* can occur, because growth tends to demand additional cash faster than it can be generated in the form of increased profits.

Inventory, for example, must be expanded as sales volume increases. Additional dollars must be spent on merchandise or raw materials to accommodate the higher level of sales. Similarly, accounts receivable must be expanded proportionately to meet the increased sales volume. A profitable business can quickly find itself in a financial bind, growing profitably while its bank accounts dwindle. (For more on forecasting financial requirements, including those related to raw materials and inventory, see Chapter 11. You can also refer to Chapter 22 to learn about effective methods for managing assets, such as accounts receivable, cash flows, and inventory.)

The growth problem is particularly acute for small companies. Increasing sales by 100 percent is easier for a small venture than for a Fortune 500 firm, but doubling sales volume makes an enterprise a much different business. Combined with difficulty in obtaining external funding, this may have unfavorable effects if cash is not managed carefully. In short, a high-growth firm's need for additional financing may exceed its available resources, even though the venture is profitable. Without additional resources, the company's cash balances may decline sharply, leaving it in an uncertain financial position.

Growth also places huge demands on a small company's personnel and the management style of its owners. When orders escalate rapidly—sometimes doubling, tripling, or more in one year's time—managerial and sales staff can become overwhelmed. At that point, major adjustments may be required immediately. But too many owners resist the idea that their "startup baby" is quickly morphing into a very different business—they may not be ready for the change or the new responsibilities. If they fail to adjust, they are likely to find that the increased demand will stretch their staff too thin, resulting in burnout, apathy, and poor overall performance.

Despite these and other challenges, the entrepreneurial spirit continues to carry small companies forward in pursuit of growth. Business expansion can occur in many ways. One common path to growth is paved by innovation.

15-2 INNOVATION: A PATH TO GROWTH

Studies have shown that small entrepreneurial firms produce twice as many innovations per employee as large firms. These innovations account for half of all those created and an amazing 95 percent of all *radical* innovations.[3] It could be said that innovation provides the soil in which a startup's competitive advantage can take root and grow, taking on a life of its own. Some widely recognized examples of small firm innovations are soft contact lenses, the zipper, overnight delivery services, the personal computer, and social media services like Facebook.

LO
15-2

Explain the role of innovation in a company's growth.

There is a certain glamour associated with innovation, but creating and then perfecting new products or services is often difficult to pull off. Clayton M. Christensen, a Harvard business school professor and the author of a number of books on innovation, points out that the road to new product development is rarely straight, and it is filled with potholes. His research bears this out. According to Christensen, "[Ninety-three percent] of all innovations that ultimately become successful started off in the wrong direction; the probability that you'll get it right the first time out of the gate is very low."[4] But remember, Christensen is talking about successful products and does not take into account tortured attempts to massage life into the 80 percent of all new products that end up failing or performing well below expectations.[5] Nobody said it would be easy.

15-2a Gaining a Competitive Advantage

From a menu of growth options, entrepreneurs generally choose the one they think will lead to the most favorable outcomes, such as superior profitability, increased market share, and improved customer satisfaction. These are some of the "fruits" of competitive advantage, and they all contribute to the value of the venture. However, when innovation is the goal, failure is always a risk. With that in mind, we offer a few "rules of thumb" that may help to reduce the risk in gaining a competitive advantage through innovation:

- *Base innovative efforts on your experience.* Innovative efforts are more likely to succeed when you know something about the product or service technology.

- *Focus on products or services that have been largely overlooked.* You are more likely to strike "pay dirt" in a vein that has not already been fully mined and in which competitors are few.

- *Be sure there is a market for the product or service you are hoping to create.* A new product or service is doomed to failure if the pool of potential customers is too shallow to generate enough sales for the company to recover its cost of innovation, along with a reasonable profit.

- *Pursue innovation that customers will perceive as adding value to their lives.* It is not enough to create a product or service that *you* believe in; people become customers when *they* believe your product or service will provide value they cannot find elsewhere.

- *Focus on new ideas that will lead to more than one product or service.* Success with an initial product or service is critical, of course, but investment in innovation packs even more of a punch when it also leads to other innovative products or services.

- *Raise sufficient capital to launch the new product or service.* Many formal investors will take on *market* risks, but they will not accept *product* risks. In other words, they want to see at least a working prototype, and preferably a developed product, before they invest in a new venture. To get to that point, the entrepreneur will most likely need to rely on more informal sources of capital, such as personal savings and investment from family and friends. This requires forward planning on investment.

Small companies that are "one-hit wonders" may find that the ride comes to an abrupt and unpleasant ending. While one innovation can provide a launch pad for a new and interesting business, continued innovation is critical to sustaining competitive advantage in the years to follow. One survey by *Inc.* magazine found that 13 of 30 company founders reported that their business turned out to be nothing like their original venture concept.[6]

15-2b Achieving Sustainability

The importance of a company's competitive advantage was underscored in Chapter 3, but this strength needs to be long-lasting to have great impact. A company can sustain its competitive advantage through the use of various strategies. For example, some entrepreneurs with sophisticated technologies obtain patents to protect them. Because obtaining a patent requires the disclosure of intellectual property to the public, they may choose instead to guard it by maintaining trade secrets (that is, taking steps to keep private a formula, a process, collected data, and more that give the company a competitive advantage). Others will try to operate "below the radar screen" of competitors, but unfortunately the effort to avoid attracting attention limits the growth potential of the enterprise. In some cases, businesses find protection through long-term contracts or alliances with larger and more powerful partners, which can lead to exclusive and secure deals as a distributor, vendor, or user of an important technology.[7] But regardless of the protective strategy selected, the goal is to develop the competitive muscle of the enterprise while establishing protective features as a safeguard against being swept aside by resource-rich rivals.

A business can take steps to block threats from competitors, but no competitive advantage lasts forever. Research has emphasized the importance of **sustainable competitive advantage**, a value-creating position that is likely to endure over time. To incorporate sustainability into strategy, an entrepreneur should use the firm's unique capabilities in a way that competitors will find difficult to imitate. However, since rivals will discover a way to copy any value-creating strategy sooner or later, it is important to plan for its transformation over the long run.

Exhibit 15.1 illustrates the competitive advantage life cycle, which has three stages: develop, deploy, and decline. Simply put, a firm must invest resources to *develop* a competitive advantage, which it can later *deploy* to boost its performance. But that position will eventually *decline* as rival firms build these advantages into their own strategies, new and better technologies emerge, customer preferences change, or other factors come into play.

sustainable competitive advantage
A value-creating position that is likely to endure over time.

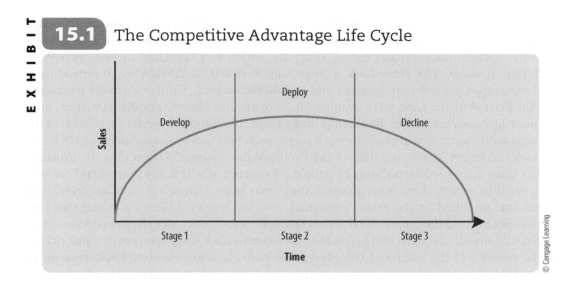

EXHIBIT **15.1** The Competitive Advantage Life Cycle

© Cengage Learning

To understand how this works, consider the Blue Buffalo Company, a maker of holistic pet food products. The company is small but growing, and it is unique in that only Blue Buffalo products contain LifeSource Bits, which provide "a precise blend of vitamins, minerals, and antioxidants."[8] But how long will the sales growth continue, given that the company's competitive advantage seems to be based mostly on its proprietary blends? When competitors come up with similar ingredients, Blue Buffalo's competitive advantage and the sales growth it generates may very well stabilize and eventually fall into decline. That's when it pays to be very forward-thinking.

In order to maintain performance over time, companies must continue to reinvent themselves—and it is very important that they do this *before* the business stalls. Research has shown that firms that wait until they hit a slump before making adjustments run a serious risk of failing to realize a complete recovery. In one study, only 7 percent were able to return to healthy levels of growth.[9]

So how can a small business maintain its performance? A firm is more likely to avoid a slump if it keeps a close eye on "hidden curves" related to its competition, its internal capabilities, and its people—and takes corrective measures before these hidden trends become apparent in the compa-

© hagit berkovich/Shutterstock.com

ny's financial results. Specifically, high performers have a way of (1) spotting changes in customer needs early on and adjusting to them ahead of their rivals, (2) upgrading capabilities to maintain marketplace advantages, and (3) developing and retaining people with "both the capabilities and the will to drive new business growth."[10] By taking these steps, a firm can extend its competitive advantage *before* the current strategy has run its course. So, small business owners can maintain their venture's performance and stay one step ahead of competitors if they keep an eye on the future and continuously improve their product and/or service offerings to meet the rising expectations of customers, all the while developing the capabilities and the people who make this possible.

Chapter 15 Product Development and Supply Chain Management

But staying ahead of competitors may require a small business owner to make some gutsy decisions. Jason Fried is co-founder and president of a Chicago-based Web applications company called 37signals, which was launched in 1999 as a Web design venture. The firm took a huge step forward in 2004 when it introduced Basecamp, a project-management and collaboration tool. Similar software packages that existed at the time were designed mostly around charts, graphs, statistics, and one-way communication. Basecamp broke from this standard model by providing its users with "a consistent place to work on projects and tools to swap ideas, share feedback, make revisions, and deliver the final product online." Given that the product has since been used by millions of people, 96 percent of whom say they would recommend it to others, there is no question that it has been a success. Users, however, had become attached to the existing product, making it very difficult to design in any changes beyond the incremental. Fried decided to start over, despite the costs and the risks involved. 37signals still offers the classic version for users who need or just prefer the security of the tried-and-true, but it has plans to launch a completely revamped product. It's the only way to keep it fresh and stave off the aggressive advances of innovative rivals.[11] A marketplace advantage is sustainable only for businesses that are already planning for the future and taking smart risks to beat all challengers to the competitive punch.

15-3 THE PRODUCT LIFE CYCLE AND NEW PRODUCT DEVELOPMENT

What creates the need for innovation in a specific business, and how can innovation be managed? We will examine these questions by looking at the product life cycle concept and a four-stage approach to new product development.

15-3a The Product Life Cycle

An important concept underlying sound product strategy is the product life cycle, which allows us to visualize the sales and profits of a product from the time it is introduced until it is no longer on the market. The **product life cycle** provides a detailed picture of what happens to the sales and profits of an *individual* product or service over time. (Although its shape is similar to that of the competitive advantage life cycle, shown in Exhibit 15.1 on page 399, the two models are very different in that the product life cycle reflects the sales and profit trend for a specific product or service, whereas the competitive advantage life cycle is based on the competitive edge of the company overall and can influence the sales of multiple products or services.) The product life cycle sales curve, shown in Exhibit 15.2, depicts slow and, ideally, upward movement in the initial stages. The stay at the top is exciting but relatively brief. Then, suddenly, the decline begins, and the downward movement can be rapid. Also note the shape of the typical profit curve. The introductory stage is dominated by losses, with profits peaking in the growth stage.

The product life cycle concept is important to a small business owner for three reasons. First, it helps the entrepreneur to understand that promotion, pricing, and distribution policies should all be adjusted to reflect a product's position on the curve. Second, it highlights the importance of revitalizing product lines, whenever possible, to extend their commercial potential. Third, it is a continuing reminder that the natural life cycle for most products rises and then falls; therefore, innovation is necessary for a firm's survival. Good business practice calls for forward-thinking product

product life cycle
A detailed picture of what happens to a specific product's sales and profits over time.

15.2 The Product Life Cycle

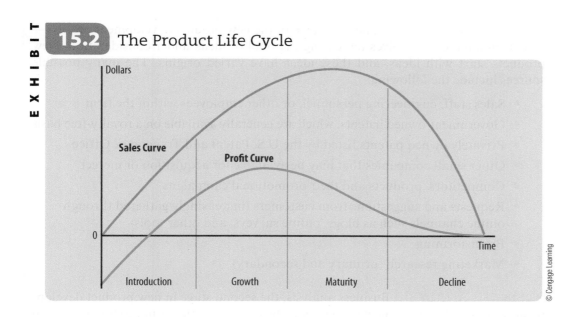

planning, which should begin before the curve of the existing life cycle peaks. This parallels the point made earlier about the need to extend the firm's competitive advantage *before* the current strategy has run its course.

Keep in mind that products and/or services and competitive advantages that are on the verge of decline can be reinvigorated using any number of different strategies. For example, companies may choose to modify a product or service by adding new features (such as "digital filters" on smartphones to allow users to alter photos) or proposing alternative uses (such as suggesting that baking soda placed in refrigerators can kill odors). Similarly, a competitive advantage can be refreshed through research and development that yields new patents (Palmetto Biomedical, Inc., for instance, is a nine-employee firm that has 60 patents or patents pending to protect the medical devices it invents), by expanding into complementary products (such as Oreck Corporation's addition of lightweight steam mops to its vacuum offerings), or by redefining the business (like The Walt Disney Company's shift from animation to a broader identity as an entertainment service provider). The point is that the downward trending sections of the life cycles presented in Exhibits 15.1 and 15.2 can be extended or reversed using the strategies mentioned above, among many others.

15-3b The New Product Development Process

It is usually up to the small business owner to find, evaluate, and introduce the new products that the company needs. This responsibility requires setting up a process for new product development. As in large businesses, where committees or entire departments are created for that purpose, new product development is best handled through a formalized process in small firms.

Entrepreneurs tend to view new product development as a monumental task—and it often is. Many find following the common four-stage, structured approach—idea accumulation, business analysis, development of the physical product, and product testing—to be the best way to tackle new product development. (Some of these stages may seem similar to those related to the launch of a new venture, as outlined in Chapter 3, but the focus here shifts to expanding an *existing* business through new product development.)

IDEA ACCUMULATION The first stage of the new product development process—idea accumulation—involves increasing the pool of ideas under consideration. New products start with ideas, and these ideas have varied origins. The many possible sources include the following:

- Sales staff, engineering personnel, or other employees within the firm
- Government-owned patents, which are generally available on a royalty-free basis
- Privately owned patents listed by the U.S. Patent and Trademark Office
- Other small companies that may be available for acquisition or merger
- Competitors' products and their promotional campaigns
- Requests and suggestions from customers (increasingly gathered through online channels such as blogs, online surveys, and other tools)
- Brainstorming
- Marketing research (primary and secondary)

BUSINESS ANALYSIS Business analysis, the second stage in new product development, requires that every new product idea be carefully studied in relation to several financial considerations. Costs and revenues are estimated and analyzed with techniques such as break-even analysis (a concept that is described in greater detail in Chapter 16). Any idea failing to show that it can be profitable is discarded during the business analysis stage. The following four key factors need to be considered in conducting a business analysis:

1. *The product's relationship to the existing product line.* Some firms intentionally add very different products to their product mix. In most cases, an added product item or line should be somehow related to the existing product mix. For example, a new product may be designed to fill a gap in a firm's product line or in the range of prices of the products it currently sells. If the product is completely new, it should have at least a family relationship to existing products to save on costs of manufacturing, distribution, promotion, and/or sales strategy.

2. *Cost of development and introduction.* Considerable capital outlays may be necessary when adding a new product. These include expenditures for design and development, marketing research to establish sales potential, advertising and sales promotion, patents, and additional equipment. One to three years may pass before profits are realized on the sale of a new product.

3. *Available personnel and facilities.* Obviously, having adequate skilled personnel and sufficient production capabilities is preferable to having to add employees and buy equipment. Thus, introducing new products is typically more appealing if the personnel and the required equipment are already available.

4. *Competition and market acceptance.* The potential competition facing a proposed product in its target market must not be too severe. Some studies suggest that a new product may be introduced successfully only if five percent of the total market can be secured. The ideal solution, of course, is to offer a product that is sufficiently different from existing products or that is in a price bracket where it avoids direct competition.

DEVELOPMENT OF THE PHYSICAL PRODUCT The next stage of new product development entails sketching out the plan for branding, packaging, and other supporting efforts, such as pricing and promotion. An actual prototype (usually a functioning model of the proposed new product) may be needed at this stage. After these components have been evaluated, the new product idea may be judged a misfit and discarded or it may be moved to the next stage for further consideration.

Many small business owners are intimidated by the thought of having to develop a prototype, but new technologies are changing all of that. As described in the Living the Dream feature on pages 403–404, Celestina Pugliese was able to bring her Ready Check Glo product to market in seven months and for a mere $11,800 in *total* costs, not just those related specifically to product development. This was possible because she used the Internet to locate the assistance she needed, and it paid off in a big way.

Brian Klock, owner of Klock Werks Kustom Cycles, makes one-of-a-kind motorcycles that are more like works of art than machines. Klock is able to build them quickly, thanks to an advanced technology called fused deposition modeling (FDM). This new rapid prototyping process, developed by a company called Stratasys, Inc., uses 3-D computer drawings to produce thermoplastic end-use parts that can be sanded, painted, drilled, coated, sealed, and bolted. The equipment manufactures parts by building up material layer upon layer, to very precise specifications. Selected to compete in the popular "Biker Build-Off" challenge, Klock's team had 10 days to build a bike. The FDM process cut fabrication time from three or four weeks to just a few days, while shaving project costs by about $15,000. After winning the challenge, Team Klock Werks raced the custom-made bike at Bonneville Salt Flats in Utah, where they were able to set a new land speed record![12]

PRODUCT TESTING The last step in the product development process, product testing, should determine whether the physical product is acceptable (safe, effective, durable, etc.). While the product can be evaluated in a laboratory setting, a limited test of market reaction should also be conducted.

While using a formalized process to handle new product development can be very helpful, it is much more likely to succeed if it is outwardly focused on customers. Inwardly focused firms—those that are only in it to please themselves or to beat rivals—are apt to fall short of the mark.[13] More than 80 percent of the high-performing companies in one recent study claimed to test and validate customer preferences periodically during the development process, compared with only 43 percent of the low performers. According to this analysis, the high performers were also twice as likely to research what, precisely, customers want.[14] Taking such steps provides the only reliable path to creating value for customers, which, in turn, can extend the company's performance.

Lighting the Way to Product Development

www.readycheckglo.com

In the summer of 2009, Celestina Pugliese of Melville, New York, and a friend were dining at a restaurant when the server dropped off the check, and then returned repeatedly to ask, "Are you ready to pay the check?" Each time, the diners said no and returned to their conversation, somewhat annoyed at the intrusion. After the fourth interruption, Pugliese started thinking out loud about the possibility of creating a check presenter with a light that would signal servers when diners were ready to pay the check.

She turned to the friend with whom she was dining and asked, "You have been in the restaurant business for over 25 years. Have you ever seen a guest check presenter with a light on it?" He answered, "No, I've never seen it before. I don't even think it exists." From that experience, Pugliese was inspired to start a new company to create and sell the Ready Check Glo Illuminating Guest Check Presenter.

Pugliese started looking for ways to make the most of the limited funds she could commit to her new venture. As a consequence of her lean startup mindset, she was able to get her business off the ground in just seven months and needed less than $12,000 to develop a market-ready product. She was able to do so because she arranged much of the required work through Internet sites that allowed her to find the talent she needed, from a patent attorney to a product manufacturer, for a fraction of the normal price. Because of the slow economy, thousands of professionals are flocking to the Web to search for work, which is also helping to drive down the cost of their services. This brew of macroeconomic developments suggests that there has never been a better time to start a new enterprise on a tight budget.

Small decisions on the road to new product development can make a huge difference in the final cost. For example, once you come up with an idea for a new product, the next step is to figure out if it is really unique. You can spend a good deal of money hiring a patent attorney to check this out for you, or you can do it yourself by visiting the website of the U.S. Patent and Trademark Office at www.uspto.gov (point your cursor to the "Patents" link at the top of the screen, and then click on the "Patent Search" link), by driving to one of the 80-plus Patent and Trademark Resource Centers around the country to get in-person assistance (see the PTO website for locations), or by doing a search through Google (www.google.com/patents) to see if anything resembling your idea has already been invented. Once Pugliese realized that her concept was truly unique, she decided to file for a one-year provisional patent, at minimal cost, to buy time to gauge market demand for the product and to position herself eventually to file a regular patent application.

Rather than spending upwards of $100,000 for the services of an engineer (which is not uncommon), Pugliese opted to use guru.com to hire a freelance engineer in Ohio who was willing to design her product for just $500. (She also used the site to find an attorney who filed a provisional patent application for her for a very reasonable $500 charge.) Pugliese found that joining a legitimate inventors' network can lead you to capable and reliable manufacturers, who will handle production at a reasonable cost. She resisted the temptation to sign with one of the countless invention development companies that advertise on television. While they may have saved her money and headaches, their services do not come cheap and many do not deliver results.

To be sure, developing a new product can be one of the most exciting features of the small business experience. But a heads-up approach can save a lot of money, which may mean the difference between a successful new line of business and one that does not get out of the starting gate. Pugliese's product has won numerous awards at trade shows around the world and is already in use by more than 1,000 high-prestige locations, with another 75,000 locations showing keen interest in it.

Sources: Personal conversation with Celestina Pugliese, January 7, 2013; "Ready Check Glo: Our Story," www.readycheckglo.com/our-story.html, accessed January 7, 2013; "First Look: 5 Cool New Hotel Gadgets," November 18, 2012, http://blog.overnightnewyork.com/first-look-5-cool-new-hotel-gadgets, accessed January 7, 2013; and Julie Bennett, "From Idea to Market," www.entrepreneur.com/article/217332, accessed January 7, 2013.

15-4 BUILDING THE TOTAL PRODUCT

LO 15-4

Describe the building of a firm's total product.

A major responsibility of marketing is to transform a basic product concept into a total product. Even when an idea for a unique new pen has been developed into physical reality in the form of the basic product, for example, it is still not ready for the marketplace. The total product offering must be more than the materials molded into the shape of the new pen. To be marketable, the basic product must be named, have a package, perhaps have a warranty, and be supported by other product features. Let's examine a few of the components of a total product offering: branding, packaging, labeling, and warranties.

15-4a Branding

An essential element of a total product offering is a **brand**, which is a means of identifying the product—verbally and/or symbolically. The most effective branding efforts are carefully designed and executed.

The brand identity of most small businesses will have the three components identified in Exhibit 15.3. The first of these features, the intangible **brand image** component—that is, people's overall perception of a brand—may be even more important to acceptance of a firm's bundle of satisfaction than the tangible brand-mark and brand name elements. Consumers tend to resist heavy-handed marketing appeals. They are far more likely to respond positively to businesses that craft and communicate interesting and consumer-relevant images that encourage an emotional connection to the firm.[15] A recent analysis found that the most effective American brands generate trust in the minds of buyers by conveying to them a sense of personal connection (Amazon), happiness (Coca-Cola), dependability (FedEx), and/or consistency (Ford). Being seen as cool (Apple), focused on the customer (Nordstrom), offering fantastic experiences (Target), or even a little quirky (Southwest Airlines) can also be powerful. But regardless of the emphasis or the story, branding is increasingly important because consumers will give their business to a company based more on the way they feel about it than on the facts and figures of the firm's selling proposition or its hard-hitting marketing campaigns.

The tangible components of brand identity are brand names and brandmarks. A **brand name** is a brand that can be spoken—like the name Dell. Since a product's brand name is so important to the image of the business and its products, careful attention should be given to its selection. In general, five rules apply in naming a product:

1. *Select a name that is easy to pronounce and remember.* You want customers to remember your product. Help them do so with a name that can be spoken easily—for example, Two Men and a Truck (the moving service mentioned in Chapter 5). Before choosing to use your own family name to identify a product, evaluate it carefully to ensure its acceptability.

brand
A verbal and/or symbolic means of identifying a product.

brand image
The overall perception of a brand.

brand name
A brand that can be spoken.

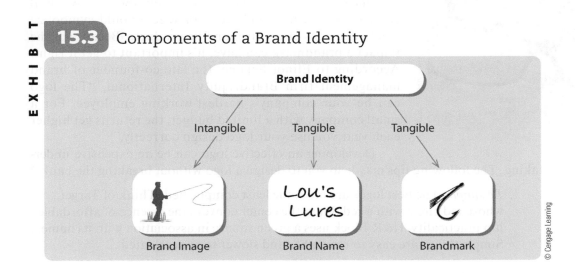

EXHIBIT 15.3 Components of a Brand Identity

Brand Identity

Intangible → Brand Image

Tangible → Lou's Lures → Brand Name

Tangible → Brandmark

© Cengage Learning

2. *Choose a descriptive name.* A name that is suggestive of the major benefit of the product can be extremely helpful. As a name for a sign shop, Sign Language correctly suggests a desirable benefit. But Rocky Road would be a poor name for a business selling mattresses or paving materials.

3. *Use a name that is eligible for legal protection.* Be careful to select a name that can be defended successfully. Do not risk litigation by copying or adapting someone else's brand name. For example, a new retailer named Wally-Mart would certainly be challenged by industry giant Walmart—even if the new store was actually started by someone named Wally.

4. *Select a name with promotional possibilities.* Long names are not compatible with good copy design on signs and billboards, where space is at a premium. A competitor of the McDonald's hamburger chain called Bob's has a name that will easily fit on any sign or billboard.

5. *Select a name that can be used on several product lines of a similar nature.* Customer understanding can be lost when a name doesn't fit a new line. The name Just Brakes is excellent for an auto service shop that repairs brakes, but the company had to help the car-owning public see past its name when it expanded into factory-scheduled maintenance services in 2011.

If you haven't already chosen a strong brand name, you might consider licensing one, especially if you have a product for which an appropriate name is available. Winston Wolfe, founder of Olympic Optical, a maker of industrial safety sunglasses for the shooting sports industry, harnessed the power of this approach for his business. By licensing the names Remington, Smith & Wesson, and Zebco, he was able to boost sales of his high-end sporting glasses dramatically by riding the wave of popular enthusiasm for these established brands. As he puts it, "Licensing the right name can be magic. It can separate you from the crowd and give you a great sales advantage. It can also allow you greater profit margins, since most consumers are willing to pay more for a brand name they know."[16]

© Lunamarina/Dreamstime LLC

A **brandmark** is the other tangible component of brand identity. It is a brand that *cannot* be verbalized–like the golden arches of McDonald's. A brandmark also has tremendous value. The Nike swoosh and the Chevy badge are marks widely associated with their owners. A small company's special "signature," or logo, should symbolize positive images of the firm and its products. Because of the impact a brandmark can have, it's important to get it right. According to Elinor Selame, the late co-founder of brand management firm BrandEquity International, "The logo can be your company's hardest-working employee. For a small company with a limited budget, the returns get higher each year you use your logo design correctly."[17]

Developing an effective logo can be an expensive undertaking. The following tips may help you to design a logo without breaking the bank:[18]

1. *Be simple.* The best logos are often the least complicated. Think of Target, whose red circle with a red dot in the center conveys the essence of affordable, hip practicality. H&R Block uses a green square in association with its name. Simple things are easy to remember and slower to appear dated.

brandmark
A brand that cannot be spoken.

2. *Design for visibility.* Nike paid Carolyn Davidson, a graphic design student, $35 to design the bold red swoosh that has been the firm's brandmark since its unveiling at the U.S. Track & Field Olympic Trials in 1972. One of its most positive qualities is that you simply cannot miss it wherever it is displayed.

3. *Leave it open to interpretation.* The logo should not explain, at a glance, the complete nature of your company. The best logos raise a question and are open to interpretation. One of the reasons the Nike swoosh is so effective is that it stands as an "empty vessel." Because it has no obvious meaning, Nike can build any image around it that serves the firm's purposes.

4. *Be relentlessly consistent.* Companies with strong graphic identities have built that recognition through years of use. Pick a typeface. Pick a color. Use them over and over again *on everything.* Eventually, you will be able to establish an identifiable look and feel.

5. *Recognize the importance of logo design.* Logos and colors are often considered "cosmetic," unimportant features of doing business. But most design-driven companies got to be that way through the efforts of highly placed advocates, such as Steve Jobs at Apple. Design programs work best when others know that they are championed by important people.

6. *Get good advice.* You can go pretty far with common sense. But sooner or later, you'll need the services of a professional graphic designer. The website of the American Institute of Graphic Arts (www.aiga.org), the largest professional organization for graphic designers, offers useful information about how to find and work with experienced professionals.

7. *Don't expect miracles.* Your company's image is the sum total of many factors. Make sure that your company looks, sounds, and feels smart in every way, every time it goes out in public.

Trademark and **service mark** are legal terms indicating the exclusive right to use a brand to represent products and services, respectively. Once an entrepreneur has found a name or symbol that is unique, easy to remember, and related to the product or service, it is time to run a name or symbol search and then to register the brand name or symbol. The protection of trademarks and service marks is discussed later in this chapter.

15-4b Packaging

In addition to protecting the basic product, packaging is a significant tool for increasing the value of the total product. Consider some of the products you purchase. How many do you buy mainly because of a preference for package design and/or color? The truth is that innovative packaging is often the deciding factor for consumers. If two products are otherwise similar, packaging may create the distinctive impression that makes the sale.

Adrian Bryce Diorio is the founder of BRYCE, an online organic skincare company that offers all-natural products that are infused with fresh vegetable and fruit purees. Despite the novelty and high quality, sales of BRYCE products were slow. When Diorio surveyed friends and customers to find out why, he discovered that packaging his products in cobalt blue bottles with clear labels, though attractive, didn't allow potential buyers to recognize the uniqueness of his skincare creations. They couldn't see the difference between his offerings and the slew of available lower-priced, generic creams.[19] He knew that he needed a solution to the problem.

trademark
A legal term indicating that a firm has exclusive rights to use a brand to promote a product.

service mark
A legal term indicating that a company has the exclusive right to use a brand to identify a service.

To make his lotions and cleansers pop off the page, Diorio switched to clear containers that showed off exactly how colourful and original [BRYCE] products are, made with "seeds, pulp, everything." He also incorporated each concoction's signature ingredient into the photography, such as a ripe pomegranate next to a jar of Mediterranean Pomegranate Exfoliating Polishing Scrub ... in an effort to "scream fresh, fresh, fresh!"[20]

Within six months of making these adjustments, sales of Diorio's products had increased 150 percent.[21] Nothing changed in the products themselves, but the look and design of the packaging and presentation increased consumer interest, showing just how important these features can be to a small business and its total product offering.

Financial constraints often prevent small businesses from pursuing creative packaging strategies that would boost sales. Entrepreneurs who can't afford the expensive equipment required for such packaging innovations can often work with "contract packagers," who are able to handle such orders at a low per-unit cost.[22] It certainly pays to consider what goes on the outside of your product, not just what's in it.

15-4c Labeling

Labeling serves several important purposes for manufacturers, which apply most labels. One purpose is to display the brand, particularly when branding the basic product would be undesirable. For example, a furniture brand is typically shown on a label and not on the basic product. On some products, brand visibility is highly desirable; Louis Vuitton handbags would probably not sell as well if the name label were only inside the purse.

A label is also an important informative tool for consumers. It often includes information on product care and use and may even provide instructions on how to dispose of the product.

warranty
A promise, written or unwritten, that a product will perform at a certain level or meet certain standards.

Laws concerning labeling requirements should be reviewed carefully. A number of government agencies issue regulations that must be followed to remain within the law, including the Food and Drug Administration (www.fda.gov/food/labelingnutrition/default.htm), the Federal Trade Commission (www.ftc.gov/os/statutes/fplajump.shtm), and the U.S. Department of Agriculture (www.fsis.usda.gov/regulations/Labeling_Guidance/index.asp). Very small businesses are exempt from many of these requirements, but it is wise to consider including information that goes beyond the specified minimum legal requirements if doing so would give an advantage to your company and the way your products are positioned in the marketplace.

15-4d Warranties

A **warranty** is simply a promise, written or unwritten, that a product will do certain things or meet certain standards. All sellers make an implied warranty that the seller's title to the product is good. A merchant seller, who deals in goods of a particular kind, makes the additional implied warranty that those goods are fit for the ordinary purposes for which they are sold. A written warranty on a product is not always necessary. In fact, many firms operate without written warranties, believing that offering one would likely confuse customers or make them suspicious.

© Astudio/Shutterstock

Warranties are important for products that are innovative, comparatively expensive, purchased infrequently, relatively complex to repair, and positioned as high-quality goods. A business should consider the following factors in rating the merits of a proposed warranty policy: cost, service capability, competitive practices, customer perceptions, and legal implications.

15-5 PRODUCT STRATEGY

Product strategy includes decisions about branding and other elements of the core component of the bundle of satisfaction, whether product or service. To be more specific, a **product strategy** describes the manner in which the product component of the marketing mix is used to achieve the objectives of a firm. This involves several supporting features:

- A **product item** is the lowest common denominator in a company's product mix. It refers to an individual item, such as one brand of bar soap.

- A **product line** is the sum of the related individual product items, but the relationship is usually defined generically. So, two brands of bar soap are two product items in one product line.

- A **product mix** is the collection of all product lines within a firm's ownership and control. A firm's product mix might consist of a line of bar soaps and a line of shoe polishes.

- **Product mix consistency** refers to the closeness, or similarity, of the product lines. The more items in a product line, the greater its depth; the more product lines in a product mix, the greater its breadth.

To illustrate how these features can come together, Exhibit 15.4 shows the product lines and product mix of the firm 180s, LLC, which makes innovative performance apparel and accessories.

15-5a Product Marketing versus Service Marketing

Traditionally, marketers have used the word *product* as a generic term to describe both goods and services. However, certain characteristics—tangibility, amount of time separating production and consumption, standardization, and perishability—lead to a number of differences between the strategies for marketing goods and those for marketing services (see Exhibit 15.5). Based on these characteristics, for example, the marketing of a pencil fits the pure goods end of the scale and the marketing of a haircut fits the pure services end.

Although marketing services obviously presents unique challenges that are not faced when marketing goods, space constraints prevent us from describing it separately. Therefore, from this point on in the chapter, a **product** will be considered to include the total bundle of satisfaction offered to customers in an exchange transaction, whether this involves a good, a service, or a combination of the two. In addition to the physical product or core service, a product also includes complementary components, such as its packaging or a warranty. The physical product or core service is usually the most important element in the total bundle of satisfaction, but that main feature is sometimes perceived by customers to be similar for a variety of products. In that case, complementary components become the most important features of the product. For example, a particular brand of cake mix may be preferred by consumers not because it is a better mix, but because of the unique toll-free telephone number on the package that can be called for baking hints. Or a certain dry cleaner may be chosen over others because it treats customers with respect, not because it cleans clothes exceptionally well.

product strategy
The way the product component of the marketing mix is used to achieve a firm's objectives.

product item
The lowest common denominator in the product mix—the individual item.

product line
The sum of related individual product items.

product mix
The collection of a firm's total product lines.

product mix consistency
The similarity of product lines in a product mix.

product
A total bundle of satisfaction—whether a service, a good, or both—offered to consumers in an exchange transaction.

15.4 Product Lines and Product Mix for 180s LLC

		BREADTH OF PRODUCT MIX					
		Ear Warmers	Gloves	Jackets	Booties	Hats/Masks	Scarves
DEPTH OF PRODUCT LINES	**Casual Wear**	13 Men's Styles, 19 Women's Styles	18 Men's Styles, 19 Women's Styles			5 Men's Styles, 4 Women's Styles	
	Training Gear			9 Men's Styles, 10 Women's Styles		7 Men's Styles, 11 Women's Styles	
	College Sports Apparel	30 Teams	31 Teams		11 Teams		20 Teams
	Outdoor Gear		1 Men's Style, 1 Women's Style			2 Men's Styles, 2 Women's Styles	
	Cause Gear	4 Women's Styles	4 Women's Styles				

Source: Compiled from www.180s.com, accessed December 8, 2012.

15.5 Services Marketing Versus Goods Marketing

© Cengage Learning

15-5b Product Strategy Options

Failure to clearly understand product strategy options will lead to ineffectiveness and conflict in the marketing effort. The major product strategy alternatives of a small business can be condensed into six categories, based on the nature of the firm's product offering and the number of target markets:

- One product/one market
- One product/multiple markets
- Modified product/one market
- Modified product/multiple markets
- Multiple products/one market
- Multiple products/multiple markets

Each alternative represents a distinct strategy, although two or more of these strategies can be attempted at the same time. However, a small company will usually pursue the alternatives in the order listed. Also, keep in mind that once a product strategy has been implemented, sales can be increased through certain additional growth tactics. For example, within any market, a small firm can try to increase sales of an existing product by (1) convincing nonusers in the targeted market to become customers, (2) persuading current customers to use more of the product, and/or (3) alerting current customers to new uses for the product.

When small businesses add products to their product mix, they generally select related products. But there are also strategies that involve unrelated products. For example, a local dealer selling Italian sewing machines might add a line of microwave ovens, an entirely unrelated product. This type of product strategy can be more difficult to pull off. However, it is occasionally used by small businesses, especially when the new product fits existing distribution and sales systems or requires similar marketing knowledge.

Adding an unrelated product to the mix to target a new market can be even more challenging to manage, as a business is attempting to market an unfamiliar product in an unfamiliar market. However, if well planned, this approach can offer significant advantages. For example, a company that sells both snow skis and surfboards expects that demand will be high in one market or the other at all times, smoothing the sales curve and maintaining a steady cash flow throughout the year. It is tempting to take on new product opportunities—sometimes to the point of becoming overextended— but staying manageably focused is critical.

15-6 THE LEGAL ENVIRONMENT

LO 15-6

Discuss how the legal environment affects product decisions.

Strategic decisions about growth, innovation, product development, and the total product offering are always made within the guidelines and constraints of the legal environment of the marketplace. Let's examine a few of the laws by which the government protects both the rights of consumers and the marketing assets of companies.

15-6a Consumer Protection

Federal regulations on such subjects as product safety and labeling have important implications for product strategy. For example, to protect the public against unreasonable risk of injury or death, the federal government enacted the Consumer Product Safety Act of 1972. This act created the Consumer Product Safety Commission to set safety standards for toys and other consumer products and to ban goods that are exceptionally hazardous, which ultimately increase the costs of doing business. This law was extended recently by the Consumer Product Safety Improvement Act of 2008, but its focus remains the same.[23] (To learn more about compliance requirements, consult the webpage of the U.S. Consumer Product Safety Commission that is specifically for small businesses at www.cpsc.gov/businfo/smbus.html.)

The Nutrition Labeling and Education Act of 1990 requires every food product covered by the law to have a standard nutrition label, listing the amounts of calories, fat, salt, and nutrients in the product. The law also addresses the accuracy of advertising claims such as "low salt" and "fiber prevents cancer." Although these legal requirements may seem to be a minor burden, some experts estimate that labeling costs can easily amount to thousands of dollars per product. The Food and Drug Administration provides a wealth of information regarding labeling requirements at www.fda.gov /food/labelingnutrition/default.htm, including guidelines for exemptions that apply to small businesses. These guidelines should be carefully followed to avoid problems.

15-6b Protection of Marketing Assets

The four primary means used by firms to protect certain marketing assets are trademarks, patents, copyrights, and trade dress.

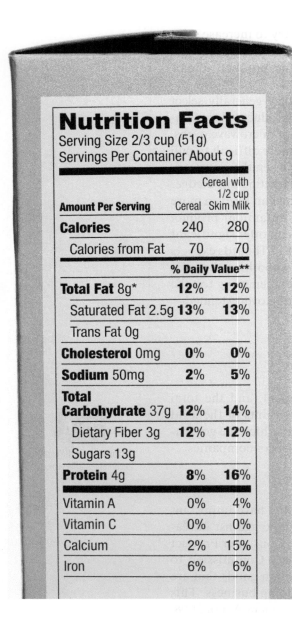

© Chris Sadowski/iStockphoto.com

TRADEMARKS Trademark or service mark protection is important, because it protects a company's distinctive use of a name, word, phrase, slogan, symbol, design, logo, picture, or any combination of these. In some cases, even a sound or scent (submitted for registration application in the form of a detailed written description) can be part of a trademark or service mark, but these *nontraditional marks* can be difficult to defend in court.[24] In essence, trademarks or service marks represent the way people identify your business.

Because names that refer to products or services are often registered, potential names should be investigated carefully to ensure that they are not already in use. Entrepreneurs can conduct their own searches online at www.uspto.gov or by using any of the more than 80 Patent and Trademark Resource Centers that can be found in nearly every U.S. state.[25] Small business owners often seek the advice of an attorney for assistance with trademark search and registration, but this may be necessary only if complications arise (for example, if the desired trademark is similar to one that is already registered). Applications for registration can be submitted online using the USPTO's Trademark Electronic Application System (www .uspto.gov/teas), but filing, search, and examination fees will be charged according to the schedule listed on the website.[26]

Common law recognizes a property right in the ownership of trademarks. However, reliance on common-law rights is not always adequate. For example, Microsoft Corporation claimed it had common-law rights to the trademark *Windows* because of the enormous industry recognition of the product. Nevertheless, the U.S. Patent and Trademark Office rejected Microsoft's trademark application, claiming the word was a generic term and, therefore, in the public domain.

Registration of trademarks is permitted under the federal Lanham Trademark Act, making protection easier if infringement is encountered. The act was revised in 1989 and now allows trademark rights to begin with merely an "intent to use," along with the filing of an application and payment of fees. Prior to this revision, a firm had to have already used the mark on goods shipped or sold. According to the USPTO, a company's federally registered trademark rights can last indefinitely, as long as the owner "continues to use the mark on or in connection with the goods and/or services in the registration and files all necessary documentation in the USPTO at the appropriate times."[27]

According to the law, a business must *use* a trademark in order to protect it, but it is also important to use it *properly*. Inform the public that your trademark is exactly that by labeling it with the symbol™ (℠ for a service mark). If that trademark or service mark is registered, the symbol® should be used.

PATENTS A **patent** is the registered, exclusive right of an inventor to make, use, or sell an invention. The two primary types of patents are utility patents and design patents. A **utility patent** covers the discovery or improvement of a new and useful process, machine, manufactured product, or "composition of matter." A **design patent** covers the appearance of a product and everything that is an inseparable part of the product. Utility patents are granted for a period of 20 years, while design patents are effective for 14 years.

patent
The registered, exclusive right of an inventor to make, use, or sell an invention.

utility patent
Registered protection for a new or improved process, machine, or product.

design patent
Registered protection for the appearance of a product and its inseparable parts.

Patent law also provides for **plant patents**, which cover the invention or discovery and reproduction of any distinct, new variety of living plant.[28]

To get answers to most of your patent-related questions, we suggest that you first visit the Patent and Trademark Office's "Patents for Inventors" webpage (www.uspto.gov/inventors/patents.jsp). But, because the process can be so complicated, it is advisable to retain a patent attorney to prepare a patent application. Even when a patent is secured, however, the protection it provides will not be perfect. If patent infringement can be proved, the court can require monetary damages and hand down injunctions to prevent further misuse, but the cost of getting to that point may be more than a small company can afford.

The patent-approval process has recently been overhauled in a way that may not be kind to small companies. Among other changes, the America Invents Act of 2011 has redefined what is and is not patentable and amends the procedure for challenging a patent during the review process. But more important to small firms, all patent applications are now prioritized according to a new "first-to-file" system that replaces the longstanding "first-to-invent" system. This new standard may allow big corporations with deep pockets and more familiarity with the process to "patent early and challenge often," potentially separating resource-strapped and less-connected small companies and garage tinkers from the inventions that they create.[29] So, inventors need to be very careful about discussing their ideas with others, including potential investors, who might be in a position to file quickly and secure patents on those inventions first.[30] The new system is clearly a game-changer.

COPYRIGHTS A **copyright** is the exclusive right of a creator (author, composer, designer, or artist) to reproduce, publish, perform, display, or sell work that is the product of that person's intelligence and skill. Works created on or after January 1, 1978, receive copyright protection for the duration of the creator's life plus 70 years. A "work made for hire" (work created by an employee for an employer) is protected for 95 years from its publication or 120 years from its creation, whichever is shorter.[31] Copyrights are registered in the U.S. Copyright Office of the Library of Congress, whose website (www.copyright.gov) provides an extensive supply of useful information about copyrights.

Under the Copyright Act of 1976, copyrightable works are automatically protected from the moment of their creation. However, any work distributed to the public should contain a copyright notice. This notice consists of three elements (all of which can be found on the copyright page in the front of this textbook): (1) the symbol©, (2) the year the work was published, and (3) the copyright owner's name.

The law provides that copyrighted work may not be reproduced by another person without authorization. Even photocopying such work is prohibited, although an individual may copy a limited amount of material for such purposes as research, criticism, comment, and scholarship. A copyright holder can sue a violator for damages.

TRADE DRESS The valuable intangible asset called **trade dress** describes those elements of a firm's distinctive operating image not specifically protected under a trademark, patent, or copyright. Trade dress is the "look" that a firm creates to establish its marketing advantage. For example, if the employees of a small pizza chain dress as prison guards and inmates, a "jailhouse" image could become uniquely associated with this business and, over time, become its trade dress. Trade dress can be protected under trademark law if it can be shown "that the average consumer would likely be confused as to product origin if another product had a similar appearance."[32] This is only one small part of the intellectual property rights picture, however. A small business needs to take measures to protect its legitimate claims to all such entitlements—that is, trademarks, service marks, patents, copyrights, and trade dress.

© timquo/shutterstock.com

plant patent
Registered protection for any distinct, new variety of living plant.

copyright
The exclusive right of a creator to reproduce, publish, perform, display, or sell his or her own works.

trade dress
Elements of a firm's distinctive image not protected by a trademark, patent, or copyright.

LO 15-7

Explain the importance of supply chain management and the major considerations in structuring a distribution channel.

15-7 SUPPLY CHAIN MANAGEMENT

The focus of this chapter so far has been on product development and total product strategy. However, a company's offerings are of use only to the extent that consumers have access to them. **Supply chain management** is a system of management that integrates and coordinates the ways in which a firm finds the raw materials and necessary components to produce a product, creates the actual product, and then delivers it to customers. It also coordinates the flow of payments between entities in the chain of transactions. Recent attention directed toward supply chain management has motivated both large and small firms to create a more competitive, customer-driven supply system. Effective supply chain management can potentially lower the costs of inventory, transportation, warehousing, and packaging, while increasing customer satisfaction.

Years ago, communication between parties in the supply chain was slow or nonexistent. But the Internet, with its simple, universally accepted communication standards, has brought suppliers and customers together in a way never before thought possible.

In this part of the chapter, we look briefly at some of the important features of supply chain management,[33] including the functions of intermediaries, the various distribution channels that can be folded into supply chain operations, and the basics of logistics.

15-7a Intermediaries

Intermediaries can often perform marketing functions better than the producer of a product can. A producer can perform its own distribution functions—including delivery—if the geographic area of the market is small, customers' needs are specialized, and risk levels are low. However, intermediaries generally provide more efficient means of distribution if customers are widely dispersed or if special packaging and storage are needed.

Some intermediaries, called **merchant middlemen**, take ownership of the goods they distribute, thereby helping a company to share or shift business risk. Other intermediaries, such as **agents** and **brokers**, do not take title to goods and, therefore, assume less market risk than do merchant middlemen.

15-7b Channels of Distribution

An effective distribution system is just as important as a unique package, a clever name, or a creative promotional campaign. In the context of supply chain operations, **distribution** encompasses both the physical transfer of products and the establishment of intermediary (middleman) relationships to achieve product movement. The system of relationships established to guide the movement of a product is called the **channel of distribution**, and the activities involved in physically moving a product through the channel of distribution are called **physical distribution (logistics)**. Distribution is essential for both goods (tangible products) and services (intangible products). However, since distribution activities are more visible for goods, our comments here will focus primarily on tangible products. Most services are delivered straight to the user—for example, an income tax preparer and a hairdresser serve their clients directly. Nonetheless, even the distribution of labor can involve channel intermediaries, such as when an employment agency provides a firm with temporary personnel.

A channel of distribution can be either direct or indirect. In a **direct channel**, there are no intermediaries—the product goes directly from producer to user. An **indirect channel** of distribution has one or more intermediaries between producer and user.

---

supply chain management
A system of management that integrates and coordinates the ways in which a firm finds the raw materials to make a product, creates the product, delivers it to customers, and receives payment for it.

merchant middlemen
Intermediaries that take ownership of the goods they distribute.

agents/brokers
Intermediaries that do not take ownership of the goods they distribute.

distribution
The physical movement of products and the establishment of intermediary relationships to support such movement.

channel of distribution
The system of relationships established to guide the movement of a product.

physical distribution (logistics)
The activities of distribution involved in the physical relocation of products.

direct channel
A distribution system without intermediaries.

indirect channel
A distribution system with one or more intermediaries.

15.6 Channels of Distribution

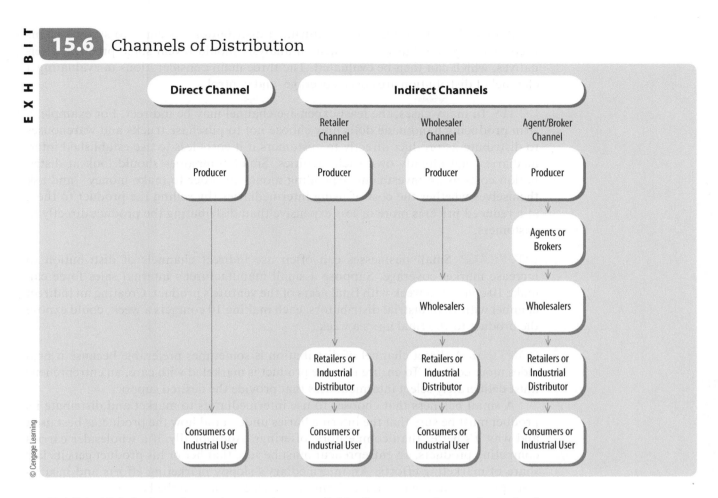

© Cengage Learning

Exhibit 15.6 depicts the various options available for structuring a channel of distribution. E-commerce (online merchandising) and mail-order marketing are direct channel systems for distributing consumer goods. Two cost-conscious airlines, Southwest Airlines and EasyJet, are examples of companies that use a direct channel to final consumers. Rather than sell tickets through travel agents and online travel service distributors, they sell flights directly to consumers through their own websites and in-airport ticket counters and self-service kiosks, which significantly reduces their operating costs.[34]

Indirect channels of distribution are shown on the right-hand side of Exhibit 15.6. Channels with two or three stages of intermediaries are probably the ones most typically used by small firms that produce products with geographically large markets. It is important to note that a small firm may use more than one channel of distribution, a practice called **dual distribution**.

Small businesses that successfully employ a single distribution channel may switch to dual distribution if they find that an additional channel will improve overall profitability. Alex Romanov, owner of Chagrin Shoe Leather & Luggage Repair, saw sales increase by 25 percent after the U.S. economy slowed in 2008 and Americans decided that it would be cheaper and wiser to repair their shoes than to buy new ones. His son, Ilya, had no interest in being a cobbler, so he launched American Heelers, an online business that receives by mail about 100 pairs of shoes for repair each week. These shoes are serviced in the elder Romanov's shop and returned to their owners. Establishing this father–son partnership has expanded the business by opening up two fronts for sales: a physical operation that takes orders directly from customers and an e-commerce operation that generates revenue from customers that live in other areas.[35]

dual distribution
A distribution system that involves more than one channel.

A logical starting point in structuring a distribution system is to study systems used by competing businesses. Such an analysis should reveal some practical alternatives, which can then be evaluated. The three main considerations in evaluating a channel of distribution are costs, coverage, and control.

COSTS In many cases, the least expensive channel may be indirect. For example, a firm producing handmade dolls may choose not to purchase trucks and warehouses to distribute its product directly to customers if it costs less to use established intermediaries that already own such facilities. Small companies should look at distribution costs as an investment—spending money in order to make money—and ask themselves whether the cost of using intermediaries (by selling the product to them at a reduced price) is more or less expensive than distributing the product directly to customers.

COVERAGE Small businesses can often use indirect channels of distribution to increase market coverage. Suppose a small manufacturer's internal sales force can make 10 contacts a week with final users of the venture's product. Creating an indirect channel with 10 industrial distributors, each making 10 contacts a week, could expose the product to 100 final users a week.

CONTROL A direct channel of distribution is sometimes preferable because it provides more control. To ensure that the product is marketed with care, an entrepreneur must deliberately select intermediaries that provide the desired support.

A small business that chooses to use intermediaries to market and distribute its product must be sure that the intermediaries understand how the product is best used and why it's better than competitors' offerings. Additionally, if a wholesaler carries competing products, an entrepreneur must be sure that her or his product gets its fair share of marketing efforts. An intermediary's sloppy marketing efforts and insufficient product knowledge can undermine the success of even the best product.

15-7c The Scope of Physical Distribution

In addition to the intermediary relationships that make up a channel of distribution, there must also be a system of **physical distribution (logistics),** which consists of the activities that physically move a product through a channel. The main component of physical distribution is transportation. Other components include storage and materials handling, delivery terms, and inventory management. (Inventory management is discussed in Chapter 21.)

TRANSPORTATION The major decision regarding physical transportation of a product is which method to use. Available modes of transportation are traditionally classified as airplanes, railroads, trucks, pipelines, and waterways. Each mode has unique advantages and disadvantages. For example, the train operator CSX Corporation runs radio ads that boldly announce, "Nature is spectacular, and we want to keep it that way. That's why CSX trains move a ton of freight nearly 500 miles on a single gallon of fuel."[36] The purpose of the ad campaign is twofold—to let potential customers know that the company offers inexpensive transportation services that also minimize environmental impact. But the choice of a specific mode of transportation is usually based on several criteria: relative cost, transit time, reliability, capability, accessibility, and traceability.

Transportation intermediaries are legally classified as common carriers, contract carriers, and private carriers. **Common carriers** are available for hire by the general public, without discrimination. Like common carriers, **contract carriers**, which engage in individual contracts with shippers, are subject to regulation by federal and/or state

common carriers
Transportation intermediaries available for hire to the general public.

contract carriers
Transportation intermediaries that contract with individual shippers.

agencies; however, they have the right to choose their clients at will. Transport lines owned by shippers are called **private carriers**.

STORAGE AND MATERIALS HANDLING

Lack of space is a common problem for small businesses. But when a channel system uses merchant middlemen or wholesalers, ownership of the goods is transferred, as is responsibility for the storage function. With other options, the small business must plan for its own warehousing. If a firm is too small to own a private warehouse, it can rent space in a public warehouse. When storage requirements are simple and do not involve much special handling equipment, a public warehouse can provide inexpensive storage.

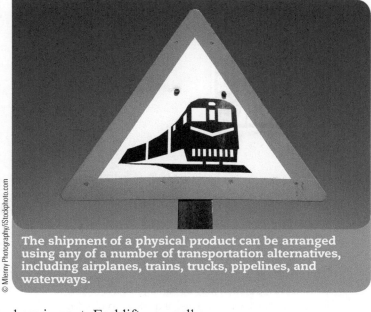

The shipment of a physical product can be arranged using any of a number of transportation alternatives, including airplanes, trains, trucks, pipelines, and waterways.

Even if it is in the right place at the right time, a damaged product is worth very little. Therefore, a physical distribution system must arrange for suitable materials-handling methods and equipment. Forklifts, as well as special containers and packaging, are part of a materials-handling system.

DELIVERY TERMS

A small but important part of a physical distribution system is the delivery terms, specifying which party is responsible for several aspects of the distribution. Delivery terms include paying the freight costs, selecting the carriers, bearing the risk of damage in transit, and selecting the modes of transport.

The simplest delivery terms—and the most advantageous to a small business as the seller—is F.O.B. (free on board) origin, freight collect. This shifts all of the responsibility for freight costs to the buyer. Ownership of the goods and risk of loss also pass to the buyer at the time the goods are shipped.

Logistics companies specialize in transportation and distribution services, providing trucking, packaging, and warehousing services for small and medium-size companies with limited in-house staff. Many small businesses believe that using **third-party logistics firms** (sometimes referred to as **3PLs**) is more cost effective than carrying out the same functions on their own. For example, one cosmetics company uses APL Logistics to handle the packaging and shipping of its health and beauty-aid products. Products produced in plants around the country go to the APL warehouse in Dallas, Texas, and are then shipped to distribution outlets nationwide.[37] More familiar firms offering 3PL services include household names such as FedEx and UPS, both of which offer customized assistance for small businesses that would prefer to focus on their primary operations and leave the transportation and distribution challenges to others.

As this chapter explains, innovation and growth are critical to competitive advantage and small business success. For this reason, the company's efforts to maintain existing products and develop new ones should be wisely managed according to a carefully devised product strategy. But it doesn't stop there. Thought must also be given to all facets of the physical flow of inputs and outputs. Managing the supply chain requires planning for how and where the firm will get components for the products it produces and how it will deliver the finished products to customers. Though many channels of distribution exist, each of these has benefits and drawbacks and must therefore be considered carefully. In the end, if all of these vitally important tasks are not managed effectively, the performance of the company is almost certain to decline.

private carriers
Lines of transport owned by shippers.

third-party logistics firm (3PL)
A company that provides transportation and distribution services to firms that prefer to focus their efforts on their primary operations.

15-1. Recognize the challenges associated with the growth of a small business.

- Some entrepreneurs find that maintaining the status quo is challenge enough.
- Growing a business too quickly can be stressful for a small firm's owners and personnel.
- A business's reputation may be damaged if it is unable to deliver on time or with the level of quality promised, or if it must turn down an order because it can't handle the volume.
- A growth trap may occur when a firm's growth soaks up cash faster than it can be generated.

15-2. Explain the role of innovation in a company's growth.

- Small entrepreneurial firms produce twice as many innovations per employee as large firms, accounting for half of all those created and an amazing 95 percent of all *radical* innovations
- The risk of failure increases when innovation is the goal.
- An entrepreneur can reduce the risk of innovation by basing innovative efforts on experience, targeting products or services that have been overlooked, ensuring a market for the product or service, emphasizing value creation for customers, pursuing new ideas that will lead to more than one product or service, and raising sufficient capital before launching a new product or service.
- Innovation is a means by which a firm can achieve and sustain a competitive advantage.
- The competitive advantage life cycle has three stages: develop, deploy, and decline.
- High-performing companies have an awareness of "hidden curves" related to their competitors, their internal capabilities, and the capabilities and motivations of their people.

15-3. Identify stages in the product life cycle and the new product development process.

- The product life cycle portrays a product from introduction through growth and maturity to sales decline.
- The new product development process has four stages: idea accumulation, business analysis, development of the physical product, and product testing.

- When conducting a business analysis on a new product, the following four factors should be considered: its fit with existing product lines, its development and introduction costs, the personnel and facilities available to get it started, and its competition and market acceptance potential.
- New technologies are making the creation of a working prototype for a new product much more manageable.
- Product testing determines whether a product is safe, effective, durable, etc.
- A new product development process is much more likely to succeed if it is focused on the firm's customers.

15-4. Describe the building of a firm's total product.

- Components of a total product offering include branding, packaging, labeling, and warranties.
- The intangible brand image component is important to consumers' acceptance of a firm's bundle of satisfaction.
- A brand name should be easy to pronounce and remember, descriptive, eligible for legal protection, full of promotional possibilities, and suitable for use on several product lines.
- In order to develop an effective but inexpensive logo, be simple, design for visibility, leave room for interpretation, emphasize consistency, recognize the importance of logo design, get good design advice, and don't expect miracles.
- Trademark and service mark are legal terms referring to a company's exclusive right to use a brand to represent products and services.
- Packaging is a significant tool for increasing total product value.
- A label is an important informative tool, providing brand visibility and instructions on product care and use.
- A warranty is important for products that are innovative, comparatively expensive, purchased infrequently, complex to repair, and positioned as high-quality goods.

15-5. Understand product strategy and the alternatives available to small businesses.

- Product strategy describes how a product is used to achieve a firm's goals and involves the product item, product line, product mix, and product mix consistency.
- Marketing services presents unique challenges not faced when marketing goods.
- There are six categories of major product strategy alternatives, which are based on the nature of the firm's product offering and the number of target markets.

15-6. Discuss how the legal environment affects product decisions.

- Federal legislation regarding labeling and product safety was designed to protect consumers.

- Meeting the legal requirements for labeling can cost thousands of dollars per product.
- The legal system provides protection for a firm's marketing assets through trademarks and service marks, patents, copyrights, and trade dress.
- According to the law, businesses must use a trademark or service mark in order to protect it, but they must also use it properly.
- Lawsuits concerning patent infringement can be costly.
- Copyrighted work may not be reproduced without authorization.
- A firm can use the law related to trade dress to protect its unique operating image.

15-7. Explain the importance of supply chain management and the major considerations in structuring a distribution channel.

- Effective supply chain management can potentially lower the costs of inventory, transportation, warehousing, and packaging, while increasing customer satisfaction.

- Intermediaries provide an efficient means of distribution if customers are widely dispersed or if special packaging and storage are needed.
- Distribution encompasses both the physical movement of products and the establishment of intermediary relationships to guide the movement of products from producer to user.
- A distribution channel can be either direct or indirect, and many firms successfully employ more than one channel of distribution.
- Costs, coverage, and control are the three main considerations in evaluating a channel of distribution.
- Transportation, storage and materials handling, delivery terms, and inventory management are the main components of a physical distribution system.
- Small companies with limited in-house staff sometimes find it helpful to use logistics firms for their transportation and distribution needs, as these vendors provide trucking, packaging, and warehouse services.

Key Terms

agents/brokers p. 414

brand p. 405

brand image p. 405

brand name p. 405

brandmark p. 406

channel of distribution p. 414

common carriers p. 416

contract carriers p. 416

copyright p. 413

design patent p. 412

direct channel p. 414

distribution p. 414

dual distribution p. 415

indirect channel p. 414

merchant middlemen p. 414

patent p. 412

physical distribution (logistics) p. 414

plant patent p. 413

private carriers p. 417

product p. 409

product item p. 409

product life cycle p. 400

product line p. 409

product mix p. 409

product mix consistency p. 409

product strategy p. 409

service mark p. 407

supply chain management p. 414

sustainable competitive advantage p. 398

third-party logistics firm (3 PLs) p. 417

trade dress p. 413

trademark p. 407

utility patent p. 412

warranty p. 408

Discussion Questions

1. What limitations on growth should a small business owner consider?

2. What can a small business do to reduce the risk associated with innovation efforts?

3. How could an understanding of the product life cycle concept help with the crafting of an effective product development strategy?

4. Can you identify and describe the stages that are involved in the product development process?

5. What are the primary components of a total product offering? Can you describe the importance of each of these components to the success of a new or existing product?

6. What are the five rules that apply generally to the selection of a good product name?

7. Define each of the following terms: product item, product line, product mix, and product mix consistency. How do these relate to a small company's product strategy options?

8. In what ways can a small company manage trademarks or service marks, copyrights, patents, and trade dress to protect its brand image? To protect the business itself?

9. Why should small businesses consider indirect channels of distribution for their products? Why involve intermediaries in distribution at all?

10. What major considerations should be factored into decisions regarding the structuring of a channel of distribution?

You Make the Call

Situation 1

The world's first elliptical bike, called the ElliptiGo, was invented by mechanical engineer and Ironman athlete Brent Teal and his friend and fellow cyclist and triathlete Bryan Pate, who had so much pain from knee and hip injuries that he was forced to narrow his exercise activity to low-impact options. Because Pate wanted to continue exercising but hated being locked away in a gym, he and Teal came up with a new product concept that would provide "a low-impact running device that [Pate] could ride on the street." The ElliptiGo is a mix between an elliptical trainer and a standard bicycle, but with 3- and 11-speed models that can make the ride as leisurely as a stroll or as aggressive as a full-out cycling workout. One observer describes it as having "the sleek curves of a high-end road bike, the clean lines of a Razor scooter, a pair of shiny carbon-fiber elliptical pedals, a smooth hub-and-crank stride mechanism and a steering column that collapses for easy storage." Check it out at www.elliptigo.com.

Question 1 Using the rules of thumb for reducing the risks related to introducing an innovative new product (see pages 397–398), how well are Teal and Pate likely to do with the ElliptiGo?

Question 2 What are the primary benefits and drawbacks of this innovation?

Question 3 What can Teal and Pate do to sustain or extend their competitive advantage with this new product?

Sources: Based on "ElliptiGo: Our Story," www.elliptigo.com/history.html, accessed December 17, 2012; John P., "The ElliptiGo Elliptical Training Bike," (September 10, 2012), http://geekbeat.tv /review-the-elliptigo-elliptical-training-bike-photos-video, accessed December 17, 2012; and Jennifer Wang, "On Your Left!" *Entrepreneur*, Vol. 38, No. 8 (August 2010), p. 17.

Situation 2

Tomboy Tools are just that—tools for women who want to do their own home improvement and repair projects. Friends Sue Wilson, Mary Tatum, and Janet Rickstrew, all of Denver, Colorado, were concerned that the tools they used for home repair projects were designed for men, not women. So they started Tomboy Tools to "empower women through hands-on education, quality tools, and … an internal culture that supports women and teaches them to feel confident using tools…." What is most interesting is how the products are sold—exclusively at in-home workshops led by Tomboy Tools' independent sales representatives. Instead of Tupperware or cosmetics, guests see basic home repair tools in action and learn simple home repair and improvement techniques. The company's founders chose the in-home approach to market their products because of its proven success with consumers, particularly women.

Question 1 What are the advantages and disadvantages of the in-home method of selling Tomboy Tools?

Question 2 What other channels of distribution might Tomboy Tools use?

Question 3 What do you think about the name "Tomboy Tools"?

Source: Based on "Tomboy Tools—About Us," www.tomboytools.com/about-us, accessed December 17, 2012.

Situation 3

Who hasn't heard of the energy drink Red Bull? It established a position as the 900-pound gorilla in the fast-growing energy drink market, the best seller in its product category. But Monster energy drink (an entrepreneurial rival that is owned by Monster Beverage Corporation but is bottled and distributed by the Coca-Cola Company) has been catching up over the last few years, hoping to challenge Red Bull's position at the top of the heap. While Red Bull still has a significant edge in market share measured by total sales (42 versus 35 percent), *Beverage Digest* reports that Monster actually sells more product in terms of physical volume. Monster reaches its core market of athletes and males aged 18 to 25 by flooding retailers with giant (16-ounce) cans of its various energy drink offerings, in essence super-sizing the much smaller cans sold by Red Bull. Its aggressive image, striking packaging, and oversized cans have helped Monster expand its position in the growing energy drink market.

Question 1 What is it about Monster's brand image and logo that makes it effective?

Question 2 How can good packaging help a product?

Question 3 Why is labeling an important part of the packaging for energy drinks like Monster?

Sources: Shelley DuBois, "How Hansen's Natural Created a Monster," *Fortune* (November 5, 2012), http://management.fortune.cnn.com/2012/11/05/how-hansens-natural-created -a-monster, accessed December 17, 2012; Bruce Horovitz, "Red Bull Targets Taste with Three New Flavors," *USAToday* (October 7, 2012), www.usatoday.com/story/money /business/2012/10/07/red-bull-energy-drinks-taste/1615351, accessed December 17, 2012; and Daniel Miller, Katie Oxendine, and Sarah Pedigo, Monster Beverage Corporation, *Krause Fund Research* (Spring 2012), accessed December 17, 2012.

Experiential Exercises

1. Interview the owner or owners of a local manufacturing business to find out how they view innovation in their market. Summarize your findings.

2. Ask some owners of small firms in your area to describe their new product development processes. Report your findings to the class.

3. Visit the website of an online retailer and take note of anything you can regarding brand names, package designs, labels, and warranties. Choose good and bad examples of each of these product components, and report back to the class.

4. Consider your most recent meaningful purchase. Compare the decision-making process you used to the four stages of the new product development process. Report your conclusions to the class.

5. Interview two different types of local retail merchants (for example, a boutique owner and a manager of a franchise) to determine how the merchandise in their stores is distributed to them. Contrast the channels of distribution used and write a brief report on your findings.

Small Business & Entrepreneurship Resource Center

The Small Business & Entrepreneurship Resource Center offers complete small business management resources through a comprehensive database that covers all major areas of starting, operating, and maintaining a business from financing, management, marketing, accounting, taxes, and more. Go to www.cengagebrain.com and select the Longenecker text for more information on how to access this material.

1. As a former bank underwriter, Anthony Colston, approved thousands of applications from business owners asking for credit to grow their companies. But when he struck out on his own as an entrepreneur, he found it difficult to get startup capital for his early childhood education center. After being turned down by commercial lenders, Colston applied for a microloan, a small short-term loan from $500 to $50,000 with interest rates from 3 percent to 18 percent. Accion Chicago, a microlender, started him off with an $8,000 loan that he used to pay contractors, buy toys and supplies, and develop a marketing campaign. If you need capital to expand your business or develop your innovation, how can securing a microloan be helpful?

2. The concept for Kelly House Inn revolves around several key words: *quality*, *innovation*, *value*, *freshness*, and *service*. Kelly House Inn will be a superior full-service restaurant, serving lunch and dinner and featuring responsible alcohol service. This new restaurant will give downtown Kimble, Michigan, the opportunity to offer residents, visitors, and businesspeople a unique and welcome alternative in casual dining. The need for such a quality establishment is well documented in a study commissioned by the Downtown Kimble Area Economic Enhancement Strategy Task Force. The study makes at least 50 references to the need for additional restaurants, with emphasis on excellent food, outdoor seating, and dining variety. Discuss ways that the Kelly House Inn can remain innovative and maintain a competitive advantage vis-à-vis other restaurants in downtown Kimble.

Sources: Emerald S. Morrow, "Closing the Capital Gap: Microloans Help Small Businesses with Much-Needed Seed Money," *Black Enterprise*, Vol. 43, No. 5 (December, 2012), p. 34; and "Restaurant: Kelly House Inn," *Business Plans Handbook*, Vol. 5, Kristin Kahrs and Paul Kahrs (eds.), (Detroit: Gale Research, 1998), pp. 327–337.

Video Case 15

Graeter's Ice Cream (P. 676)

This case demonstrates how one company expanded its business through its own growing chain of ice cream shops, distribution via partnerships with major supermarket and grocery store companies, and selective diversification into related ice cream products and baked goods.

Alternative Cases for Chapter 15

Endnotes

1. Robert Kiyosaki, "Even Steven," *Entrepreneur*, Vol. 36, No. 8 (August 2008), p. 36.

2. Debra Kahn Schofield, "Grow Your Business Slowly: A Cautionary Tale," www.gmarketing.com/articles/179-grow-your-business-slowly-a-cautionary-tale, accessed November 30, 2012.

3. Stephen Spinelli and Robert J. Adams, *New Venture Creation: Entrepreneurship for the 21st Century* (Boston: McGraw-Hill/Irwin, 2012), p. 14.

4. Reported in an interview with Martha E. Mangelsdorf, "Hard Times Can Drive Innovation," *The Wall Street Journal,* December 15, 2008, p. R2.

5. Neale Martin, "How Habits Undermine Marketing," *Financial Times*, July 1, 2008, www.ftpress.com/articles/article.aspx?p=1223844, accessed December 14, 2012.

6. Leigh Buchanan, *"Inc. 500,"* *Inc.*, Vol. 32, No. 7 (September 2010), p. 148.

7. Some of the strategies outlined here are mentioned in Anne Field, "Creating a Sustainable Competitive Advantage for Your Small Business," www.startupnation.com/business-articles/1522/1/competitive-advantage-small-business.asp, accessed December 4, 2012.

8. "The Blue Story," www.bluebuffalo.com/company-history, accessed December 14, 2012.

9. Matthew S. Olson and Derek van Bever, *Stall Points: Most Companies Stop Growing—Yours Doesn't Have To* (New Haven, CT: Yale University Press, 2008), p. 28.

10. Paul Nunes and Tim Breene, "Reinvent Your Business Before It's Too Late," *Harvard Business Review*, Vol. 89, No. 1/2 (January/February 2011), pp. 80–87.

11. Jason Fried, "Starting Over," *Inc.*, Vol. 34, No. 1 (February 2012), p. 40.

12. http://klockwerkcycles.com/about, accessed December 6, 2012; and "Biker Build Off," www.pddnet.com/article-biker-build-off, accessed December 6, 2012.

13. Jennifer Wang, "Be Disruptive," *Entrepreneur*, Vol. 39, No. 9 (January 2011), p. 20.

14. Mike Gordon, Chris Musso, Eric Rebentisch, and Nisheeth Gupta, "The Path to Developing Successful New Products," *The Wall Street Journal*, November 30, 2009, p. R5.

15. Paula Andruss, "Branding's Big Guns," *Entrepreneur*, Vol. 40, No. 4 (April 2012), pp. 50–55.

16. Personal communication with Winston Wolfe, February 8, 2011.

17. "Logo Design—Not Just a Pretty Typeface," www.logomojo.com/logo-design/logo-design-not-just-a-pretty-typeface, accessed December 6, 2012.

18. Adapted from Gwen Moran, "Best and Worst Marketing Ideas … Ever," *Entrepreneur*, Vol. 37, No. 1 (January 2009), p. 48; and "Logo Design," *op. cit.*

19. Jennifer Wang, "Skincare Startup's Lesson for Online Brands: Looks Matter" *Entrepreneur*, Vol. 40, No. 3 (March 2012), p. 48.

20. *Ibid.*

21. *Ibid.*

22. Laura Tiffany, "What Whole Package," *Entrepreneur*, Vol. 36, No. 2 (February 2008), p. 24.

23. "Public Law 110-314—August 14, 2008," www.cpsc.gov/cpsia.pdf, accessed December 11, 2012.

24. Eleni Mezulanik, "The Status of Scents as Trademarks: An International Perspective," *INTABulletin*, January 1, 2012, www.inta.org/INTABulletin/Pages/TheStatusofScentsasTrademarksAnInternationalPerspective.aspx, accessed December 21, 2012.

25. "Patent and Trademark Resource Center Opens at Western Illinois University," September 14, 2012, www.uspto.gov/news/pr/2012/12-58.jsp, accessed December 8, 2012.

26. "United States Patent and Trademark Office Fee Schedule," October 5, 2012, www.uspto.gov/web/offices/ac/qs/ope/fee100512.htm, accessed December 8, 2012.

27. "All About Trademarks," www.uspto.gov/smallbusiness/trademarks/faq.html#2, accessed December 8, 2012.

28. "All About Patents," www.uspto.gov/smallbusiness/patents/types.html, accessed December 11, 2012; and "Brown and Michaels, PC," www.bpmlegal.com/howtoterm.html, accessed December 11, 2012.

29. Jonathan Blum, "Protect Yourself," *Entrepreneur*, Vol. 39, No. 8 (August 2011), pp. 64–68.

30. Rachel Z. Arndt, "The Real Cost of Patent Reform," *FastCompany*, No. 162 (February 2012), p. 104.

31. "Copyright Basics," www.copyright.gov/circs/circ01.pdf, accessed December 11, 2012.

32. "Nolo's Plain-English Law Dictionary—Trade Dress," www.nolo.com/dictionary/trade-dress-term.html, accessed December 11, 2012.

33. A comprehensive discussion of supply chain management is beyond the scope of this book, but many excellent resources can provide helpful information on this subject. We recommend John J. Coyle, C. John Langley, Robert A. Novak, and Brian J. Gibson, *Supply Chain Management: A Logistics Perspective,* 9th ed. (Mason, OH: Cengage Learning, 2013); and Joel D. Wisner, Keah-Choon Tan, and G. Keong Leong, *Principles of Supply Chain Management: A Balanced Approach,* 3rd ed. (Mason, OH: Cengage Learning, 2012).

34. Vijay Verghese, "The End of the OTA-man Empire?" *Asian Conversations*, May 2011, www.asianconversations.com/OTAEmpire.php, accessed December 17, 2012.

35. Sarah E. Needleman, "In a Sole Revival, the Recession Gives Beleaguered Cobblers New Traction," *The Wall Street Journal,* February 2, 2009, pp. A1, A13.

36. "CSX—A Great Story to Tell: See Our Ads," www.csx.com/index.cfm/media/a-great-story-to-tell-see-our-ads, accessed December 12, 2012.

37. Personal communication with Dr. Pedro Reyes, associate professor of operations management, Baylor University, March 14, 2011.

CHAPTER 16

Pricing and Credit Decisions

Dyn began in a college apartment by offering a free service. The idea was to host a website on home computers or provide remote access back to a customer's PC. Initially, it was designed as a not-for-profit enterprise, but the founders became impatient with processing the paperwork necessary to get approval from the Internal Revenue Service. So they decided to form the company as an LLC. But how would they price their software after having offered it for free?

Dyn quickly moved to a donation-based service in an effort to stay afloat and add complementary services. According to CEO Jeremy Hitchcock, setting prices in those early days amounted to throwing darts at a dartboard. Over time, Dyn transitioned to a recurring revenue software-as-a-service (SaaS) model with a suite of IT services aimed at home and small and medium-size business markets. When the company

In the SPOTLIGHT
Dyn
http://dyn.com

switched from asking customers for a one-time donation to requiring an annual subscription, it experienced 80 percent growth in revenue. The owners learned that they were operating with a nearly fixed cost infrastructure, despite the increase in customers.

The one expense they had not thought through was the cost of acquiring a customer. Assessing the renewal rate for the firm's services and calculating the lifetime value of a customer led them to move from a B2C to a B2B business model. Given the low cost of the company's software applications, Dyn enjoyed considerably more profits from large business clients than from home consumers.

OPEN LOOKING AHEAD

After studying this chapter, you should be able to...

16-1. Discuss the role of cost and demand factors in setting a price.

16-2. Apply break-even analysis and markup pricing.

16-3. Identify specific pricing strategies.

16-4. Explain the benefits of credit, factors that affect credit extension, and types of credit.

16-5. Describe the activities involved in managing credit.

Despite low overhead costs, Dyn chooses to avoid discounting. A continuing issue is determining how to compensate salespeople in a highly competitive, rapidly changing environment. The owners have also recognized that they have a difficult time expressing the value their services offer. And they have learned that some customers are not worth obtaining or retaining, given the price they may be willing to pay.

As Hitchcock expresses it, "We prefer the gold standard for our customers. We find pricing to be a good way to find out where value is."

Sources: Dyn, http://dyn.com, accessed March 2, 2013; personal interviews with Jeremy Hitchcock, January 19, 2011 and February 13, 2013; and *Business NH Magazine*, "Dyn Makes 10 to Watch List Again," http://millyardcommunications.com/index.php?src=news&srctype=detail&category=News&refno=3381, accessed March 2, 2013.

I n this chapter, we introduce you to pricing and credit policies and practices for small firms. Economists develop price models, marketing experts write books about price negotiation, and psychologists study consumer behavior toward pricing. It would seem that pricing is as much an art as a science! The guidelines provided here can help you avoid mistakes, but owners must carefully evaluate daily the pricing decisions they make in their small businesses.

Very few business owners have any formal training in how to set the prices for the products and services they sell. Many times, their prices are based on what competitors are charging, some percentage above their costs, or just some instinctive feel. All too often, new business owners think their path to success is to undercut competitors' prices. Later in this chapter, we will explain why that can be dangerous. Keep in mind that pricing and credit decisions are vital to the success of a company because they influence the relationship between the business and its customers. These decisions also directly affect both revenue and cash flows. Of course, customers dislike price increases and restrictive credit policies. Therefore, the entrepreneur needs to set prices and design credit policies as carefully as possible, to avoid the need for frequent changes.

Like Jeremy Hitchcock, the CEO of Dyn (see the opening Spotlight), we believe that value should be at the heart of a pricing strategy. In marketing terms, **value** is "the extent to which a good or service is perceived by its customer to meet his or her needs or wants, measured by a customer's willingness to pay for it. It commonly depends more on the customer's perception of the worth of the product than on its intrinsic value."[1] The value of a product or service must be determined by the provider before its price can be set. Pricing decisions are critical in small business marketing. The **price** of a product or service specifies what the seller requires for giving up ownership or use of that product or service. Often, the seller must extend credit to the buyer in order to make the exchange happen. **Credit** is simply an agreement between a buyer and a seller that payment for a product or service will be received at some later date. This chapter examines both the pricing decisions and the credit decisions of small firms.

value
The extent to which a good or service is perceived by a customer as meeting his or her needs or wants, measured by the customer's willingness to pay for it.

price
A specification of what a seller requires in exchange for transferring ownership or use of a product or service.

credit
An agreement between a buyer and a seller that allows for delayed payment for a product or service.

16-1 SETTING A PRICE

LO 16-1

Discuss the role of cost and demand factors in setting a price.

I n setting a price, an entrepreneur decides on the most appropriate value for the product or service being offered for sale. The task seems easy, but it isn't. The first pricing lesson is to remember that total sales revenue depends on just two components, sales volume and price, and even a small change in price can drastically influence revenue. Consider the following situations, *assuming no change in demand*:

Situation A

Quantity sold	×	Price per unit	=	Gross revenue
250,000	×	$3.00	=	$750,000

Situation B

Quantity sold	×	Price per unit	=	Gross revenue
250,000	×	$2.80	=	$700,000

The price per unit is only $0.20 lower in Situation B than in Situation A. However, the total difference in revenue is $50,000! Clearly, a small business can lose significant revenue if a price is set too low.

Pricing is also important because it indirectly affects sales quantity. Setting a price too high for the value being offered may result in lower quantities sold, reducing total revenue. In the above example, quantity sold was assumed to be independent of price—and it very well may be for such a small price difference. However, a larger increase or decrease might substantially affect the quantity sold. It makes no sense to lower a price if you wind up selling the same number of products. On the other hand, it makes no sense to raise your price if the result is a big cut in sales. Pricing, therefore, has a dual influence on total sales revenue. It is important *directly* as part of the gross revenue equation and *indirectly* through its impact on demand.

Some Internet companies are discovering that frequent price changes can work in their favor. Mercent Corporation represents itself as the world's leading product advertising platform. Its website proclaims, "The rate of change in today's retail environment is accelerating."[2] The company responds by changing the prices of millions of products every hour. Eric Best, Mercent's CEO, stated, "The long-term implication is that a price is no longer a price."[3] A triggering factor for this behavior is that lower-priced products show up at the top of search results for shoppers who are making price comparisons.

Before beginning a more-detailed analysis of pricing, we should note that services are generally more difficult to price than products because of their intangible nature. However, the impact of price on revenue and profits is the same. Because estimating the cost of providing a service and the demand for that service is a more complex process than we can cover here, the following discussions will focus on product pricing.

RESOURCES

START UP

Service Pricing
For insights into the pricing of services, take a look at *The Marketing Plan Handbook* by Robert W. Bly, published by Entrepreneur Press in 2010.

16-1a Cost Determination for Pricing

For a business to be successful, its pricing must cover total cost plus an appropriate profit margin. Pricing, therefore, must be based on an understanding of the nature of costs.

Just as revenues can vary with the volume of products sold, so can costs react differently as the quantity produced or sold increases or decreases. Recall from Chapter 10 that the *cost of goods sold* increases as the quantity of products sold increases. Material costs and sales commissions are typical variable costs incurred as a product is made and sold. For instance, material costs may be $10 per unit. If the company sells 1,000 units, the total costs of goods sold would be $10,000, but that figure would change if the number of units increases or decreases. *Operating expenses* are those that remain constant at different levels of quantity sold, or fixed costs. For example, marketing expenses, factory equipment costs, and salaries of office personnel are operating expenses.

An understanding of the nature of different kinds of costs can help a seller minimize pricing mistakes. Although cost of goods sold and operating expenses do not behave in the same way, small businesses often treat them identically. An approach called **average pricing** exemplifies this high-risk practice. With average pricing, the total cost (cost of goods sold plus operating expenses) over a previous period is divided by the quantity sold in that period to arrive at an average cost, which is then used to

average pricing
An approach in which the total cost for a given period is divided by the quantity sold in that period to set a price.

set the current price. For example, consider the cost structure of a firm selling 25,000 units of a product in 2013 at a sales price of $8 each (see Exhibit 16.1). The average unit cost would be $5 (that is, $125,000 ($50,000 + $75,000) in total costs ÷ 25,000 units sold). The $3 markup provides a profit at this sales volume (25,000 units sold × $3 markup = $75,000).

However, Exhibit 16.2 shows that the impact on profit will be very negative if sales in 2014 reach only 10,000 units and the selling price has been set at the same $3 markup, based on the average cost in 2013. At the lower sales volume (10,000 units sold), the average unit cost increases to $9.50 (that is, $95,000 ÷ 10,000). This increase is, of course, attributable to the need to spread operating expenses over fewer units. *Average pricing overlooks the reality of higher average costs at lower sales levels.*

On rare occasions, pricing at less than total cost can be used as a special short-term strategy. Suppose some operating expenses are ongoing, even if part of the production facility is temporarily idle. In this situation, pricing should cover all marginal or incremental costs—that is, those costs incurred specifically to get additional business. Keep in mind the old business saying, "If you price below cost, you can't make it up in volume!" For example, you might bid on a contract that appears to offer a high price only to discover that you have to add personnel, equipment, or materials whose costs are more than that attractive price. Sometimes, business owners offer *loss leaders*, merchandise they intentionally sell below the direct product cost with the expectation that customers will buy more as they learn of other products and services the business has available. It can be unpleasant to discover that the loss leader was the only thing customers bought—no profit there. In the long run, all costs must be covered.

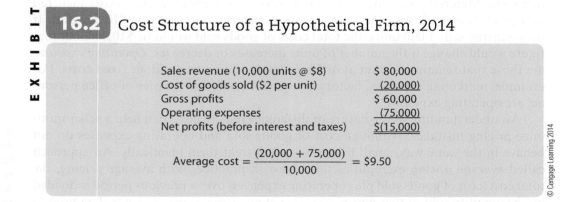

EXHIBIT 16.1 Cost Structure of a Hypothetical Firm, 2013

Sales revenue (25,000 units @ $8)	$200,000
Cost of goods sold ($2 per unit)	(50,000)
Gross profits	$150,000
Operating expenses	(75,000)
Net profits (before interest and taxes)	$ 75,000

$$\text{Average cost} = \frac{(50,000 + 75,000)}{25,000} = \$5$$

EXHIBIT 16.2 Cost Structure of a Hypothetical Firm, 2014

Sales revenue (10,000 units @ $8)	$ 80,000
Cost of goods sold ($2 per unit)	(20,000)
Gross profits	$ 60,000
Operating expenses	(75,000)
Net profits (before interest and taxes)	$(15,000)

$$\text{Average cost} = \frac{(20,000 + 75,000)}{10,000} = \$9.50$$

© Cengage Learning 2014

16-1b How Customer Demand Affects Pricing

Cost analysis can identify a level below which a price should not be set under normal circumstances. However, it does not show by how much the final price might exceed that minimum figure and still be acceptable to customers. Demand factors must be considered before making this determination.

ELASTICITY OF DEMAND Customer demand for a product or service is often sensitive to the price level. *Elasticity* is the term used to describe this sensitivity, and the effect of a change in price on the quantity demanded is called **elasticity of demand**. A product or service is said to have **elastic demand** if an increase in its price *lowers* demand for the product or service or a decrease in its price *raises* demand. A product or service is said to have **inelastic demand** if demand does not change significantly when there is a change in the price of the product or service.

In some markets, the demand for products or services is very elastic. With a lower price, the amount purchased increases sharply, thus providing higher revenue. For example, in the computer tablet industry, a decrease in price will frequently produce a more than proportionate increase in quantity sold, resulting in higher total revenues. For products such as salt, however, demand is highly inelastic. Regardless of price, the quantity purchased will not change significantly, because consumers use a fixed amount of salt.

The concept of elasticity of demand is important because the degree of elasticity sets limits on or provides opportunities for higher pricing. A small firm should seek to distinguish its product or service in such a way that small price increases will incur little resistance from customers and thereby yield increasing total revenue. Some business owners experiment beyond small price increases or decreases. Tony Sauer, owner of Urban Canine Doggy Day Spa, heard about a Chinese buffet restaurant that did not put prices on its meals; instead, it took a pay-what-you-want (PWYW) approach. Sauer decided to run a PWYW campaign for two months, allowing customers to determine the value of using his self-serve wash stations. It turned out that the average price paid was very close to what he had been charging. Sauer decided to use the PWYW approach once a year because of the new clients that it brought in.[4]

PRICING AND A FIRM'S COMPETITIVE ADVANTAGE Several factors affect the attractiveness of a product or service to customers. One factor is the firm's competitive advantage—a concept discussed in Chapter 3. If consumers perceive the product or service as an important solution to their unsatisfied needs, they are likely to demand more of it.

Companies want prospective buyers to see their products as special. But even if two products are physically similar, other factors typically differ. Speed of service, credit terms offered, delivery arrangements, personal attention from a salesperson, and warranties are but a few of the factors that can be used to distinguish one product from another. A unique and attractive combination of products and services may well justify a higher price.

A pricing tactic that often reflects a competitive advantage is **prestige pricing**, or setting a high price to convey an image of high quality or uniqueness. Erika Napoletano, professional business consultant and author of *The Power of Unpopular*, reported that one of the best pieces of advice she ever received was to raise the price of her entrepreneurial consulting sessions. She found the higher price also boosted her image. But she also learned that she had to back up the price by giving her market something special.[5] The influence of prestige pricing varies from market to market and from product to product. Because higher-income buyers are usually less sensitive to

elasticity of demand
The degree to which a change in price affects the quantity demanded.

elastic demand
Demand that changes significantly when there is a change in the price of a product or service.

inelastic demand
Demand that does not change significantly when there is a change in the price of a product or service.

prestige pricing
An approach based on setting a high price to convey an image of high quality or uniqueness.

ENTREPRENEURSHIP + INTEGRITY

Living the Dream

Asking Customers to Pay—What a Shock!

David Hauser made his customers mad . . . and lost a lot of them. His company, Chargify, had been providing basic customer billing software to small businesses for free with the expectation that they would eventually want to upgrade to a premium version that Chargify could bill for. The basic software must have been too good, though, because less than 1 percent became paying clients.

Angry Chargify users blasted Hauser for how he handled the price introduction. Chargify was not only flooded with angry e-mails, but it was also criticized in blogs, including Hacker News and TechCrunch. In a blog on the Chargify website, Hauser justified imposing a price on the product but acknowledged that he did a poor job of notifying customers. With no prior warning, Hauser had sent an e-mail to those using the software that after 45 days they would have to start paying or find a new provider. Businesses that had been early adopters of the software felt their efforts and feedback to Chargify should have been recognized by

being grandfathered into the new pricing arrangement in some way. Many were very small companies on whose budgets even small charges had an impact. In his apology on the Chargify blog, Hauser said,

> First, we didn't communicate often enough or early enough about our planned change. Second, we didn't show our appreciation to customers who had supported us early on by providing them a discount. Lastly, our new pricing structure left many authentic startup businesses unable to afford our services.

He was also honest in stating that the company's reputation had been damaged due to the error. The apology apparently resonated with customers. By 2012, the company was enjoying a comfortable profit.

Sources: Grasshopper, http://grasshopper.com/, accessed March 3, 2013; Chargify, https://chargify.com/, accessed March 3, 2013; Jason Del Rey, 2011, "Chargify's Clients Were Happy as Long as They Didn't Have to Pay. But When Prices Went Up, the Goodwill Went Away," *Inc.*, Vol. 33, No. 1, pp. 50–53.

price variations than those with lower incomes, prestige pricing typically works better in high-income markets.

Jeremy Hitchcock, introduced as the CEO of Dyn in the opening Spotlight, found that value-based pricing was difficult to explain to his customers. However, he discovered that if Dyn could gain a customer through one product, the quality of the software offered would enable the company to engage in platform pricing, providing upgrades for the customer at each level. The team at Dyn also discovered that being seen as a quality provider increased the company's ability to keep customers, thereby lowering costs.[6]

16-2 APPLYING A PRICING SYSTEM

LO 16-2

Apply break-even analysis and markup pricing.

In order to properly evaluate a pricing system, a small business owner must understand potential costs, revenue, and product demand for the venture. A key to that understanding is the ability to determine when enough products and services have been sold to cover the operating expenses of running your business–or, more simply, the ability to recognize the break-even point.

16-2a Break-Even Analysis

Break-even analysis has two phases: (1) examining cost–revenue relationships and (2) incorporating sales forecasts into the analysis. It allows the entrepreneur to compare alternative cost and revenue estimates in order to determine the acceptability of each price. Break-even analyses are usually represented by formulas and graphs, which help owners visualize how their businesses are functioning.

EXAMINING COST AND REVENUE RELATIONSHIPS The objective of the first phase of break-even analysis is to determine the sales volume level at which the product, at an assumed price, will generate enough revenue to start earning a profit. Exhibit 16.3(a) presents a simple break-even chart reflecting this comparison. *Fixed costs*, or operating expenses, as represented by a horizontal line in the bottom half of the graph, are $300,000. The section for the *variable costs* of making and selling the products, or cost of goods sold, is a triangle that slants upward, depicting the direct relationship of variable costs and expenses to output. In this example, variable costs are $5 per unit. The entire area below the upward-slanting total cost line represents the combination of fixed and variable costs and expenses. The distance between the sales and total cost lines reveals the profit or loss position of the company at any level of sales. The point of intersection of these two lines is called the **break-even point**, because sales revenue equals total costs and expenses at this sales volume. As shown in Exhibit 16.3(a), the break-even point is approximately 43,000 units sold, which means that the break-even point in dollar revenue is roughly $514,000.

break-even analysis
The examination of cost–revenue relationships and the incorporation of sales forecasts into the analysis.

break-even point
Sales volume at which total sales revenue equals total costs and expenses.

16.3 Break-Even Graphs for Pricing

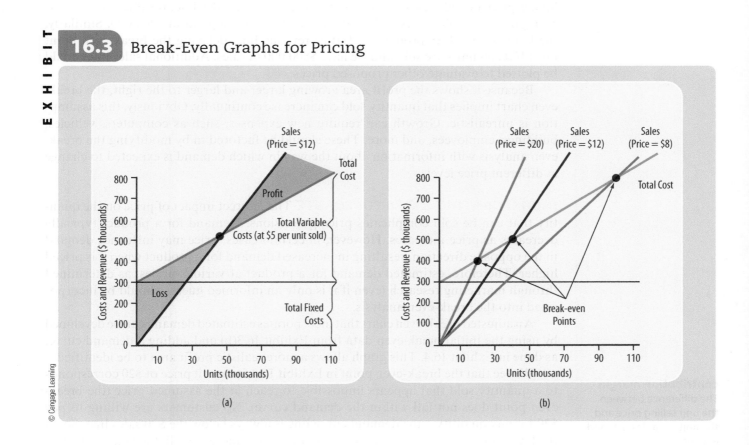

© Cengage Learning

(a)

(b)

Exhibit 16.3 (a) shows how you can visualize the break-even concept. Another way to think of it is as a simple math equation:

$$\text{Break-even point} = \frac{\text{Total fixed costs and expenses}}{\text{Unit selling price} - \text{Unit variable costs and expenses}}$$

$$\text{Break-even point} = \frac{\$300,000}{\$12 - \$5} = 42,857 \text{ units}$$

We can now see that the exact break-even point in units sold is 42,857. And given the $12 sales price, the dollar break-even point is $514,284 ($12 sales price per unit × 42,857 break-even units sold).

This example shows that the break-even point is a function of (1) the firm's fixed operating costs and expenses (numerator) and (2) the unit selling price less the unit variable costs and expenses (denominator). The higher the *fixed* costs, the more units we must sell to break even; the greater the difference between the unit selling price and the unit *variable* costs and expenses, the fewer units we must sell to break even. The difference between the unit selling price and the unit variable costs and expenses is the **contribution margin**; that is, for each unit sold, a contribution is made toward covering the company's fixed costs.

To evaluate other break-even points, the entrepreneur can plot additional sales lines for other prices on the chart. Don't be intimidated about drawing a graph or crunching the numbers to get a break-even point. The key issue is that calculating the break-even point helps you to determine whether you have a chance to make a profit by selling your products at certain prices. Every business owner must determine a way to represent these critical numbers so that she or he can understand them and run the business successfully. On the flexible break-even chart shown in Exhibit 16.3(b), the higher price of $20 yields a much more steeply sloped sales line, resulting in a break-even point of 20,000 units and a sales dollar break-even point of $400,000. Similarly, the lower price of $8 produces a flatter revenue line, delaying the break-even point until 100,000 units are sold and we have $800,000 in sales. Additional sales lines could be plotted to evaluate other proposed prices.

Because it shows the profit area growing larger and larger to the right, the break-even chart implies that quantity sold can increase continually. Obviously, this assumption is unrealistic. Growth can require new expenses, such as computers, vehicles, buildings, employees, and more. These should be factored in by modifying the break-even analysis with information about the way in which demand is expected to change at different price levels.

INCORPORATING SALES FORECASTS The indirect impact of price on the quantity that can be sold complicates pricing decisions. Demand for a product typically decreases as price increases. However, in certain cases, price may influence demand in the opposite direction, resulting in increased demand for a product when it is priced higher. Therefore, estimated demand for a product at various prices, as determined through marketing research (even if it is only an informed guess), should be incorporated into the break-even analysis.

An adjusted break-even chart that incorporates estimated demand can be developed by using the initial break-even data from Exhibit 16.3(b) and adding a demand curve, as done in Exhibit 16.4. This graph allows a more realistic profit area to be identified.

We see that the break-even point in Exhibit 16.4 for a unit price of $20 corresponds to a quantity sold that appears impossible to reach at the assumed price (the break-even point does not fall within the demand curve). No customers are willing to pay $20 for any quantity—the demand curve line is always below the $20 sales line. So, at the low price of $8, we would never break even—the more we sell, the greater the loss

contribution margin
The difference between the unit selling price and the unit variable costs and expenses.

16.4 A Break-Even Graph Adjusted for Estimated Demand

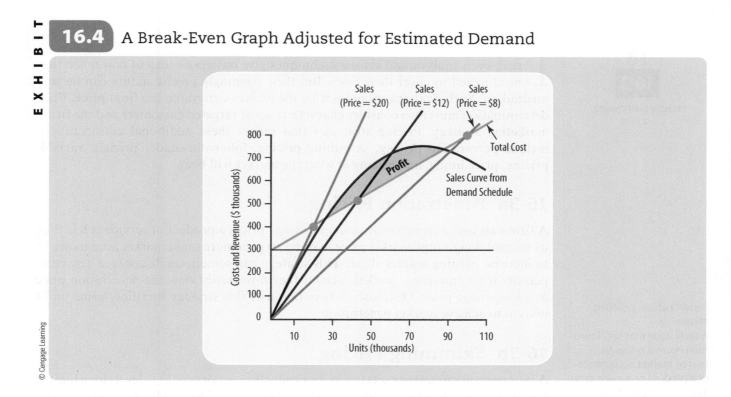

© Cengage Learning

would be. Only at $12 does the revenue from the demand curve rise above the total cost line. The potential for profit at this price is indicated by the shaded area in the graph.

16-2b Markup Pricing

Up to this point, we have made no distinction between pricing by manufacturers and pricing by intermediaries such as wholesalers and retailers since break-even concepts apply to all small businesses, regardless of their position in the distribution channel. Now, however, we briefly present some of the pricing formulas used by wholesalers and retailers in setting their prices. In the retailing industry, where businesses often carry many different products, **markup pricing** has emerged as a manageable pricing system. With this cost-plus approach to pricing, retailers are able to price hundreds of products much more quickly than they could by using individual break-even analyses. Manufacturers will often recommend a retail price for their products that retailers and wholesalers can use as guidelines. In calculating the selling price for a particular item, a retailer adds a markup percentage (sometimes referred to as a *markup rate*) to cover (1) operating expenses, (2) subsequent price reductions–for example, markdowns and employee discounts, and (3) the desired profit. It is important to have a clear understanding of markup pricing computations. Markups may be expressed as a percentage of either the *selling price* or the *cost*. For example, if an item costs $6 and sells for $10, the markup of $4 represents a 40 percent markup of the selling price [($4 markup ÷ $10 selling price) × 100] or a 66²/₃ percent markup of the cost [($4 markup ÷ $6 cost) × 100]. Two simple formulas are commonly used for markup calculations:

$$\frac{\text{Markup}}{\text{Selling price}} \times 100 = \text{Markup expressed as a percentage of selling price}$$

or

$$\frac{\text{Markup}}{\text{Cost}} \times 100 = \text{Markup expressed as a percentage of cost}$$

markup pricing
An approach based on applying a percentage to a product's cost to obtain its selling price.

16-3 SELECTING A PRICING STRATEGY

Break-even analysis and similar techniques give owners an idea of how much they need to sell to cover their costs. But their seemingly precise nature can be very misleading. Such analyses should not by themselves determine the final price. Price determination must also consider characteristics of targeted customers and the firm's marketing strategy. Pricing strategies that reflect these additional considerations include penetration pricing, skimming pricing, follow-the-leader pricing, variable pricing, price lining, and pricing at what the market will bear.[7]

16-3a Penetration Pricing

A firm that uses a **penetration pricing strategy** prices a product or service at less than its normal, long-range market price in order to gain more rapid market acceptance or to increase existing market share. This strategy can sometimes discourage new competitors from entering a market niche if they mistakenly view the penetration price as a long-range price. Obviously, a firm that uses this strategy sacrifices some profit margin to achieve market penetration.

16-3b Skimming Pricing

A **skimming price strategy** sets prices for products or services at high levels for a limited time period before reducing them to more competitive levels. This strategy assumes that certain customers will pay a higher price because they view a product or service as a prestige item. Use of a skimming price is most practical when there is little threat of short-term competition or when startup costs must be recovered rapidly. Another reason for using this strategy is the high cost of introducing a new product. The company may not have achieved economies of scale in production, so higher prices might be charged to customers that could be labeled *early adopters*. Some buyers like to be the first own or use new products or services, so they are willing to pay a premium price. To reach a larger market, however, the price usually needs to be reduced.

16-3c Follow-the-Leader Pricing

A **follow-the-leader pricing strategy** uses a particular competitor as a model in setting a price for a product or service. The probable reaction of competitors is a critical factor in determining whether to cut prices below a prevailing level. A small business in competition with larger firms is seldom in a position to consider itself the price leader. Different brands may have different characteristics, but customers often do not perceive sufficient differences to pay premium prices. Thus, small businesses selling commodities (products purchased primarily based on price) tend to be better off holding down costs so that they can price their merchandise in the same range as their larger competitors.

16-3d Variable Pricing

Some businesses use a **variable pricing strategy** to offer price concessions to certain customers, even though they may advertise a uniform price. Lower prices are offered for various reasons, including a customer's knowledge and bargaining strength. In some fields of business, therefore, firms make two-part pricing decisions: They set a standard list price but

penetration pricing strategy
A technique that sets lower than normal prices to hasten market acceptance of a product or service or to increase market share.

skimming price strategy
A technique that sets very high prices for a limited period before reducing them to more competitive levels.

follow-the-leader pricing strategy
A technique that uses a particular competitor as a model in setting prices.

variable pricing strategy
A technique that sets more than one price for a product or service in order to offer price concessions to certain customers.

© Ocean/Corbis

offer a range of price concessions to particular buyers—for example, those that purchase large quantities of their product. This chapter's Spotlight company, Dyn, sometimes negotiated pricing, trading off the services provided within an acceptable range.

16-3e Price Lining

A **price lining strategy** establishes distinct price categories at which similar items of retail merchandise are offered for sale. For example, men's suits (of differing quality) might be sold at $250, $450, and $800. The amount of inventory stocked at different quality levels would depend on the income levels and buying desires of a store's

price lining strategy
A technique that sets a range of several distinct merchandise price levels.

ENTREPRENEURIAL EXPERIENCES

Living the Dream

Commodity or Specialty?

Countless college students have begun their entrepreneurial careers with a T-shirt business. Some represent manufacturers and distributors and sell what others design. Others add their own touch—creative designs, color schemes, special event themes, and more. But the products are still T-shirts, items that many would consider commodities.

Brian Linton is a social entrepreneur. His first company sold sustainable jewelry and donated a percentage of its profits to ocean conservation initiatives. In 2010, he founded a T-shirt design business, United by Blue. Shirt colors are inspired by weathered buildings. The designs are meant to introduce people to what Linton calls "Hidden Gems," beautiful but forgotten objects and locales from around the world. United by Blue does not donate profits to charitable causes. Instead, it organizes cleanups, removing one pound of trash from oceans and waterways for each product sold.

United by Blue is a for-profit company that has to price its T-shirts at more than it costs to manufacture and distribute them. In the second year of operations, Linton learned that wholesale margins had dropped to 15 percent from the 60 percent level the company enjoyed when starting up. That did not leave much for covering operating expenses and certainly very little for its cleanup projects.

© YsaL/iStockphoto.com

United by Blue had been selling its products at the premium price of $29.50 each, because premium costs are associated with manufacturing and shipping the products. The company does not want to use materials or processes that could harm the environment. Shirts are made of slub cotton and packaged in banana-fiber bags, which are 50 times more expensive than plastic.

Linton calculated that fulfilling the company's mission would require a sales price to the consumer of $34.00 and feared that United By Blue might be pricing itself out of the market. In fact, two major chains did drop the brand. But some higher-end retailers saw an opportunity and picked it up. In short order, margins improved to 30 percent, and sales went up. United by Blue continues to seek ways of cutting costs but refuses to cut back on its environmental mission.

Sources: "United By Blue," www.unitedbyblue.com/, accessed March 14, 2013; Issie Lapowsky, 2012, "United By Blue's Eco-Friendly Values Sent Costs Soaring. Was It Time to Put Money before Mission?" *Inc.*, Vol. 34, No. 3, PP. 99–101; Susan Carpenter, "Fashion Focuses on Water Savings for World Water Day," http://latimesblogs.latimes.com/alltherage/2012/03/world-water-day.html, accessed March 14, 2013; Jane M. Von Bergen, "He's Hoping His Business Really Cleans Up," http://articles.philly.com/2012-12-26/business/36000141_1_ocean-conservation-ocean-city-trash, accessed March 14, 2013.

customers. A price lining strategy has the advantage of simplifying the selection process for the customer and reducing the necessary minimum inventory.

16-3f Pricing at What the Market Will Bear

The strategy of pricing on the basis of what the market will bear can be used only when the seller has little or no competition. Obviously, this strategy will work only for nonstandardized products. For example, a food store might offer egg roll wrappers that its competitors do not carry. Busy consumers who want to fix egg rolls but have neither the time nor the knowledge to prepare the wrappers themselves will buy them at any reasonable price.

Local, state, and federal laws must be considered in setting prices. For example, the Sherman Antitrust Act generally prohibits price fixing. Direct competitors cannot agree on the prices they will charge. Fixing prices can lead to prison sentences and fines or civil court lawsuits, resulting in significant legal expenses and possibly damage payments.[8] On the other hand, a recent Supreme Court decision gave manufacturers the authority to impose minimum prices at which retailers must sell their products. Large discount retailers objected, claiming that such policies are anticompetitive. But the Court concluded that smaller businesses might give better service to customers through the information they provide about products, only to see those customers then buy from a discounter that provides less service. Resale price maintenance is assumed to encourage stores to offer a better shopping experience.[9]

When a small business markets a line of products, some of which may compete with each other, pricing decisions must take into account the effects of a single product price on the rest of the line. Some companies engage in **adaptive pricing**, placing different values on a product or service for customers with different needs.[10] The next time you are shopping for shoes, check out the prices charged for various styles offered under the same brand. Why are different prices charged? Is it quality of materials or something else?

Continually adjusting a price to meet changing marketing conditions can be both costly to the seller and confusing to buyers. Thanks to the Internet, companies can monitor product sales in real time and determine immediately if dropping a price might lead to more sales or if raising it might make sense for a product in high demand product. Discounting can also be designed to meet a variety of needs. For example, a seller may offer a trade discount to a buyer (such as a wholesaler) that performs a certain marketing function for the seller (such as distribution). The stated, or list, price is unchanged, but the seller offers a lower actual price by means of a discount.

Small firms should not treat bad pricing decisions as uncorrectable mistakes. Remember, pricing is not an exact science. *If the initial price appears to be off target, make any necessary adjustments and keep on selling!*

adaptive pricing
A technique that places different values on a product or service for customers with different needs.

16-4 OFFERING CREDIT

In a credit sale, the seller provides products or services to the buyer in return for the buyer's promise to pay later. The major reason for granting credit is to make sales; credit encourages decisions to buy by providing an incentive for customers who can buy now but would prefer to pay later. But businesses want to make sure their customers will fully pay for what they are buying. An added bonus to the seller is that credit provides records containing customer information that can be used for sales promotions, such as direct-mail appeals to customers.

LO 16-4

Explain the benefits of credit, factors that affect credit extension, and types of credit.

16-4a Benefits of Credit

If credit buying and selling did not benefit both parties in a transaction, their use would cease. Buyers obviously enjoy the availability of credit, and small firms, in particular, benefit from being able to buy on credit from their suppliers. Credit provides small firms with working capital, often allowing marginal businesses to continue operations. Additional benefits of credit to buyers are (1) the ability to satisfy immediate needs and pay for them later, (2) better records of purchases on credit billing statements, (3) better service and greater convenience when exchanging purchased items, and (4) the ability to establish a credit history. Suppliers, on the other hand, extend credit to customers in order to facilitate increased sales volume and also to earn money on unpaid balances. They expect the increased revenue to more than offset the costs of extending credit, so that profits will increase. Other benefits of credit to sellers are (1) a closer association with customers because of implied trust, (2) easier selling through telephone- and mail-order systems and over the Internet, (3) smoother sales peaks and valleys, since purchasing power is always available, and (4) easy access to a tool with which to stay competitive.

16-4b Factors that Affect Selling on Credit

A business owner must decide whether to sell on credit or for cash only. In many cases, credit selling cannot be avoided, as it is standard trade practice in many types of businesses. It is important to note that in today's marketplace, credit-selling competitors will almost always outsell a cash-only firm.

Although a seller always hopes to increase profits by allowing credit sales, it is not a risk-free practice. Small firms frequently shift or at least share credit risk by accepting credit cards carried by customers rather than by offering their own credit. For example, the franchisee of a DoubleTree Hotel, part of the Hilton chain, may accept Hilton credit cards and other major credit cards, thereby avoiding the hassles of credit management. The business will pay a fee to the credit card company, but that cost may be less than the expense of managing its own independent credit system, especially when losses from bad debts are factored in. A retailer following this strategy must obtain merchant status with individual credit card companies. This is not an automatic process and can be problematic, particularly for home-based businesses.

Unfortunately, the cost of accepting major credit cards for payment over the Internet has increased. To deal with Internet fraud, small online retailers have turned to third-party firms (like PayPal, Charge.com, and Merchant Express) that specialize in handling Internet credit card payments. For example, PayPal offers a variety of plans with monthly fees at three levels: $0, $5, and $30, depending on level of services. Then there are transaction fees of 1.9 to 3.5 percent, depending on monthly sales volume, plus 15 to 30 cents.[11] Also, if a small firm makes credit sales online, it is subject to "chargebacks" whenever buyers dispute a transaction. Some credit card companies assess fines and threaten account termination if the number of chargebacks is excessive.

For a variety of reasons, a small business may or may not decide to sell on credit. There are five factors related to the entrepreneur's decision to extend credit: the type of business, credit policies of competitors, customers' ages and income levels, the availability of working capital, and economic conditions.

1. *Type of business.* Retailers of durable products typically grant more credit than do retailers that sell perishables or small service firms with primarily local customers. Most consumers find it necessary to buy big-ticket items on an installment basis, and the life span of such a product makes installment selling feasible.

2. *Credit policies of competitors.* Most firms in an industry offer comparable credit terms unless they have a competitive advantage that causes customers to be willing to pay cash. Wholesale hardware companies and retail furniture stores are examples of businesses that face stiff competition from credit sellers.

3. *Ages and income levels of customers.* Customers' ages and income levels are significant factors in determining credit policy. For example, a drugstore adjacent to a high school might not extend credit to high school students, who are typically undesirable credit customers because of their lack of both maturity and steady income.

4. *Availability of working capital.* Credit sales increase the amount of working capital needed by the business doing the selling. Open-credit and installment accounts tie up money that may be needed to pay business expenses.

5. *Economic conditions.* Business cycles are real. Owners sometimes have short memories when times are good, and they receive and extend credit without concern for an economic downturn. The recession of 2008 caused the bankruptcy of many that were overextended. But free enterprise systems are also characterized by recoveries and prosperity. Good credit management is critical to long-term success.

16-4c Types of Credit

There are two broad classes of credit: consumer credit and trade credit. **Consumer credit** is granted by retailers to final consumers who purchase for personal or family use. A small business owner sometimes uses his or her personal consumer credit to purchase supplies and equipment for the business. **Trade credit** is extended by nonfinancial firms, such as manufacturers and wholesalers, to business firms that are customers. Consumer credit and trade credit differ with respect to types of credit instruments, the paperwork, sources for financing receivables, and terms of sale. Another important distinction is that credit insurance is available only for trade credit.

CONSUMER CREDIT The three major kinds of consumer credit accounts are open charge accounts, installment accounts, and revolving charge accounts. Many variations of these credit accounts are also used. Credit cards (a type of revolving charge account) and debit cards (another alternative to cash for consumers) are discussed separately because of their widespread use.

Open charge accounts. When using an **open charge account**, a customer takes possession of products (or services) at the time of purchase, with payment due when billed. Customers typically have a month to pay their bills from the time their statements are sent. There is no finance charge for this kind of credit if the balance on the account is paid in full at the end of the billing period. Customers are not generally required to make a down payment or to pledge collateral. Small accounts at department stores are good examples of open charge accounts.

Installment accounts. An **installment account** is a vehicle for long-term consumer credit, useful for large purchases, such as a car, home appliance, or home renovation. A down payment is normally required, and annual finance charges can be a

consumer credit
Financing granted by retailers to individuals who purchase for personal or family use.

trade credit
Financing provided by suppliers to client companies.

open charge account
A line of credit that allows the customer to obtain a product or service at the time of purchase, with payment due when billed.

installment account
A line of credit that requires a down payment, with the balance paid over a specified period of time.

significant percentage of the purchase price. Payment periods are commonly from 12 to 36 months, although automobile dealers often offer an extended payment period of 60 months or even longer.

Revolving charge accounts. A revolving charge account is a variation of the installment account. A seller grants a customer a line of credit, and charged purchases may not exceed the credit limit. A specified percentage of the outstanding balance must be paid monthly, forcing the customer to budget and limiting the amount of debt that can be carried. Finance charges are computed on the unpaid balance at the end of the month.

CREDIT CARDS A credit card provides assurance to a seller that a buyer has a satisfactory credit rating and that the seller will receive payment from the financial institution that issued the card. Credit cards are usually based on a revolving charge account system. Depending on the issuer, we can distinguish three basic types of credit cards: bank credit cards, travel and entertainment credit cards, and retailer credit cards.

Bank credit cards. The best-known credit cards issued by banks or other financial institutions are MasterCard and Visa. Bank credit cards are widely accepted by retailers that want to offer credit but don't provide their own credit cards. Most small business retailers fit into this category. In return for a set fee (usually 2 to 5 percent of the purchase price) paid by the retailer, the bank takes the responsibility for making collections. Some banks charge annual membership fees to their cardholders. Also, cardholders are frequently able to obtain cash up to the credit limit of their card.

Travel and entertainment credit cards. Well-known examples of travel and entertainment credit cards are American Express and Diner's Club cards. Originally used for services, these cards are now widely accepted for sales of merchandise. As with bank credit cards, the collection of charges on an entertainment credit card is the responsibility of the sponsoring agency.

Retailer credit cards. Many companies—for example, department stores and oil companies—issue their own credit cards specifically for use in their outlets or for purchasing their products or services from other outlets. Customers are usually not charged annual fees or finance charges if the balance is paid each month.

DEBIT CARDS A variation on credit cards, and technically not a form of credit, is the debit card. A debit card is an alternative to cash in that its use immediately results in a withdrawal from the customer's bank account to pay for the product or service purchased. Some financial institutions arrange for extensions of credit, or grace periods, for delayed payments on a debit card.[12]

TRADE CREDIT Firms selling to other businesses may specify terms of sale, such as 2/10, net 30. This means that the seller is offering a 2 percent discount if the buyer pays within 10 days of the invoice date. Failure to take this discount makes the full amount of the invoice due in 30 days. For example, with these terms, a buyer paying for a $100,000 purchase within 10 days of the invoice date would save 2 percent, or $2,000.

Sales terms for trade credit depend on the product sold, as well as the buyer's and the seller's circumstances. The credit period often varies directly with the length of the buyer's inventory turnover period, which obviously depends on the type of product sold. The larger the order and the higher the credit rating of the buyer, the better the sales terms will be, assuming that individual terms are fixed

revolving charge account
A line of credit on which the customer may charge purchases at any time, up to a pre-established limit.

credit card
An alternative to cash whose use provides assurance to a seller that a buyer has a satisfactory credit rating and that payment will be received from the issuing financial institution.

debit card
An alternative to cash whose use results in an immediate withdrawal from the buyer's bank account to pay for products or services.

RESOURCES **Credit Research**
The Research Foundation of the National Federation of Independent Business (NFIB) regularly conducts studies on small business issues. One example is a 2012 survey of the NFIB's membership that addresses access to credit. It can be found at www.nfib.com /press-media/press-media -item?cmsid=59472.

for each buyer. The greater the financial strength and the more adequate and liquid the working capital of the seller, the more generous the seller's sales terms can be. Of course, no business can afford to allow competitors to outdo it in reasonable generosity of sales terms. In many types of businesses, terms are so firmly set by tradition that a unique policy is difficult, if not impossible, for a small firm to implement.

16-5 MANAGING THE CREDIT PROCESS

LO 16-5

Describe the activities involved in managing credit.

A small repair shop or clothing store that accepts Visa or MasterCard is transferring much of the credit risk to another party. In effect, the fee that the business pays the credit card company covers the credit management process. Banks and their business customers are often in conflict over the fees charged. A 2012 court case, for example, involved retailers' adding a surcharge to customers' bills for credit card use.[13] Many small business owners find that the fees cut their profits significantly. Those small firms that want to offer their own credit to customers need to understand the credit function. Let's take a look at some of the major considerations in developing and operating a comprehensive credit management program for a small business.

16-5a Evaluation of Credit Applicants

In most retail stores, the first step in credit investigation is having the customer complete an application form. The information obtained on this form is used as the basis for examining an applicant's creditworthiness. Since the most important factor in determining a customer's credit limit is her or his ability to pay the obligation when it becomes due, it is crucial to evaluate the customer's financial resources, debt position, and income or revenue level. The mobile content company, Amp'd Mobile, received $360 million from investors, then tried to save money by not running credit checks on customers. When it declared bankruptcy, 80,000 of its 175,000 customers were unable to pay their bills.[14]

The amount of credit requested also requires careful consideration. Drugstore customers usually need only small amounts of credit. On the other hand, business customers of wholesalers and manufacturers typically expect large credit lines. In the special case of installment selling, the amount of credit should not exceed the repossession value of the goods sold. Automobile dealers follow this rule as a general practice.

THE FOUR CREDIT QUESTIONS In evaluating the credit status of applicants, a seller must answer the following questions:

1. Can the buyer pay as promised?
2. Will the buyer pay?
3. If so, when will the buyer pay?
4. If not, can the buyer be forced to pay?

The answers to these questions have to be based in part on the seller's estimate of the buyer's ability and willingness to pay. Such an estimate constitutes a judgment of the buyer's creditworthiness. For credit to be approved, the answers to questions 1, 2, and 4 should be "yes," and the answer to question 3 should be "on schedule."

Every applicant is creditworthy to some degree. A decision to grant credit merely recognizes the buyer's credit standing. But the seller must consider the possibility that the buyer will be unable or unwilling to pay. When evaluating an applicant's credit status, therefore, the seller must decide how much risk of nonpayment to assume.

THE TRADITIONAL FIVE C'S OF CREDIT As explained in Chapter 12, the ability to repay a loan is frequently evaluated in terms of the five C's of credit: character, capacity, capital, conditions, and collateral. These factors are also indicators of a firm's ability to repay trade credit and deserve repeating:

- *Character* is the fundamental integrity and honesty that should underlie all human and business relationships. For business customers, character is embodied in the business policies and ethical practices of the firm.

- *Capacity* refers to the customer's ability to conserve assets, and to faithfully and efficiently follow a financial plan. A business customer should utilize its invested capital wisely and capitalize to the fullest extent on business opportunities.

- *Capital* consists of the cash and other liquid assets owned by the customer. A prospective business customer should have sufficient capital to underwrite planned operations, including an appropriate amount invested by the owner.

- *Collateral* consists of designated security given as a pledge for fulfillment of an obligation. It is a secondary source for loan repayment in case the borrower's cash flows are insufficient for repaying a loan.

- *Conditions* are such factors as business cycles and changes in price levels, which may be either favorable or unfavorable to the payment of debts. For example, an economic recession places a burden on both businesses' and consumers' abilities to pay their debts. Other adverse factors that might limit a business customer's ability to pay include strong new competition, labor problems, and fires and other natural disasters.

16-5b Sources of Credit Information

One of the most important, and most frequently neglected, sources of credit information is a customer's previous credit history. Properly analyzed, credit records show whether a business customer regularly takes cash discounts and, if not, whether the customer's account is typically slow.

Manufacturers and wholesalers can frequently use a firm's financial statements as an additional source of information. Obtaining maximum value from financial statements requires a careful ratio analysis, which will reveal a firm's working capital position, profit-making potential, and general financial health (as discussed in Chapter 10).

Pertinent data may also be obtained from outsiders. For example, arrangements may be made with other sellers to exchange credit data. Such credit information exchanges are quite useful for learning about the sales and payment experiences others have had with the seller's own customers or credit applicants.

Another source of credit information for the small firm, particularly about commercial accounts, is the customer's banker. Some bankers willingly supply credit information about their depositors, considering this to be a service that helps those firms or individuals obtain credit in amounts they can successfully handle. Other bankers believe that credit information is confidential and should not be disclosed.

Organizations that may be consulted regarding credit standings are trade-credit agencies and credit bureaus. **Trade-credit agencies** are privately owned organizations that collect credit information on businesses only, not individual consumers. After analyzing and evaluating the data, trade-credit agencies make credit ratings available to client companies for a fee. Dun & Bradstreet, Inc. (www.dnb.com), a nationwide trade-credit agency, offers a wide array of credit reports, including the Small

trade-credit agencies
Privately owned organizations that collect credit information on businesses.

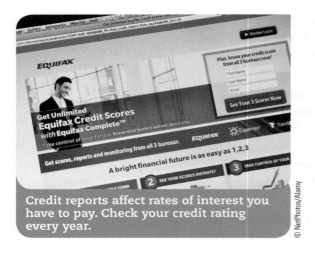

Credit reports affect rates of interest you have to pay. Check your credit rating every year.

Business Risk New Account Score and the Payment Analysis Report. Manufacturers and wholesalers are especially interested in Dun & Bradstreet's reference book and credit reports. Available to subscribers only, the reference book covers most U.S. businesses and provides a credit rating, an evaluation of financial strength, and other key credit information on each firm listed.

Credit bureaus are the most common type of consumer reporting agency. These private companies maintain credit histories on individuals, based on reports from banks, mortgage companies, department stores, and other creditors. These companies make possible the exchange of credit information on persons with previous credit activity. Some credit bureaus do not require a business firm to be a member in order to get a credit report. The fee charged to nonmembers, however, is considerably higher than that charged to members. The three primary online credit bureaus are Experian, Equifax, and TransUnion.[15]

16-5c Aging of Accounts Receivable

Many small businesses can benefit from an **aging schedule**, which categorizes accounts receivable based on the length of time they have been outstanding. Typically, some accounts are current and others are past due. Regular use of an aging schedule allows troublesome collection trends to be spotted so that appropriate actions can be taken.

Exhibit 16.5 presents a hypothetical aging schedule for accounts receivable. According to the schedule, four customers have overdue credit, totaling $200,000. Only customer 005 is current. Customer 003 has the largest amount overdue ($80,000). In fact, the schedule shows that customer 003 is overdue on all charges and has a past record of slow payment (indicated by a credit rating of C). Immediate attention must be given to collecting from this customer. Customer 002 should also be contacted, because, among overdue accounts, this customer has the second largest amount ($110,000) in the "Not due" classification. Customer 005, however, could quickly have the largest amount overdue and should be watched closely.

credit bureaus
Privately owned organizations that summarize a number of firms' credit experiences with particular individuals.

aging schedule
A categorization of accounts receivable based on the length of time they have been outstanding.

EXHIBIT 16.5 Hypothetical Aging Schedule for Accounts Receivable

	CUSTOMER ACCOUNT NUMBER					
Account Status (Days past due)	001	002	003	004	005	Total
120 days	—	—	$50,000	—	—	$ 50,000
90 days	—	$ 10,000	—	—	—	10,000
60 days	—	—	—	$40,000	—	40,000
30 days	—	20,000	20,000	—	—	40,000
15 days	$50,000	—	10,000	—	—	60,000
Total overdue	$50,000	$ 30,000	$80,000	$40,000	$ 0	$200,000
Not due (beyond discount period)	$30,000	$ 10,000	$ 0	$10,000	$130,000	$180,000
Not due (still in discount period)	$20,000	$100,000	$ 0	$90,000	$220,000	$430,000
Credit rating	A	B	C	A	A	—

© Cengage Learning

Customers 001 and 004 require a special kind of analysis. Customer 001 has $10,000 more overdue than customer 004. However, customer 004's overdue credit of $40,000, which is 60 days past due, may well have a serious impact on the $100,000 not yet due ($10,000 in the beyond-discount period plus $90,000 still in the discount period). On the other hand, even though customer 001 has $50,000 of overdue credit, this customer's payment is overdue by only 15 days. Also, customer 001 has only $50,000 not yet due ($30,000 in the beyond-discount period plus $20,000 still in the discount period), compared to the $100,000 not yet due from customer 004. Both customers have an A credit rating. In conclusion, customer 001 is a better potential source of cash. Therefore, collection efforts should be focused on customer 004 rather than on customer 001, who may simply need a reminder of the overdue amount of $50,000.

16-5d Billing and Collection Procedures

Timely notification to customers regarding the status of their accounts is essential for keeping credit accounts current. Most credit customers pay their bills on time if the creditor provides them with information verifying their credit balance. Failure on the seller's part to send invoices delays payments.

Overdue credit accounts tie up a seller's working capital, prevent further sales to the slow-paying customer, and lead to losses from bad debts. Even if a slow-paying customer is not lost, relations with this customer are strained for a time at least.

A firm extending credit must have adequate billing records and collection procedures if it expects prompt payments. Also, a personal relationship between seller and customer must not be allowed to tempt the seller into being less than businesslike in extending further credit and collecting overdue amounts. Given the seriousness of the problem, a small firm must decide whether to collect past-due accounts directly or turn the task over to an attorney or a collection agency.

Perhaps the most effective weapon in collecting past-due accounts is reminding the debtors that their credit standing may be in jeopardy. A lower credit rating is certain to happen if the account is turned over to a collection agency. Delinquent customers will typically attempt to avoid damage to their credit standing, particularly when it would be known to the business community. This concern underlies and strengthens the various collection efforts of the seller.

A small firm should deal compassionately with delinquent customers. There are people who will intentionally abuse a relationship and drag out or even refuse to make a payment. However, a collection technique that is too threatening not only may fail to work but also could cause the firm to lose the customer worth keeping or to become subject to legal action.

Effective collection practices usually consist of a series of steps, each somewhat more forceful than the preceding one. Historically, the process has started with a gentle written reminder; subsequent steps may include additional letters, telephone calls, registered letters, personal contacts, and referral to a collection agency or attorney. The timing of these steps should be carefully standardized so that each one automatically follows the preceding one in a specified number of days. More recently, some businesses have started to send text messages and e-mails as reminders, especially when they have a significant percentage of younger customers.

Various ratios can be used to monitor expenses associated with credit sales. The best known and most widely used expense ratio is the **bad-debt ratio**, which is computed by dividing the amount of bad debts by the total amount of credit sales.

bad-debt ratio
The ratio of bad debts to credit sales.

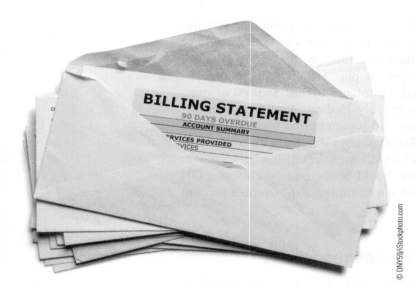

The bad-debt ratio reflects the efficiency of credit policies and procedures, and can help you to track how well you are managing the credit you have extended to customers. To compare the effectiveness of your firm's credit management with that of other firms, look for sources that provide industry financial ratios. (These are often available in university libraries.) Two examples are Dun & Bradstreet's *Industry Norms and Key Business Ratios* and the *Almanac of Business and Industrial Financial Ratios.* A relationship exists among the bad-debt ratio, profitability, and the size of the firm. Many times, small profitable retailers have a higher bad-debt ratio than large profitable retailers do.

16-5e Credit Regulation

The use of credit is regulated by a variety of federal laws, as well as state laws that vary considerably from state to state. The most significant piece of credit legislation is the federal Consumer Credit Protection Act, which includes the 1968 Truth-in-Lending Act. Its two primary purposes are to ensure that consumers are informed about the terms of a credit agreement and to require creditors to specify how finance charges are computed. The act requires that a finance charge be stated as an annual percentage rate and that creditors specify their procedures for correcting billing mistakes.

Other federal legislation related to credit management includes the following:

- The *Fair Credit Billing Act* provides protection to credit customers in cases involving incorrect billing. A reasonable time period is allowed for billing errors to be corrected. The act does not cover installment credit.

- The *Fair Credit Reporting Act* gives certain rights to credit applicants regarding reports prepared by credit bureaus. Amendments such as the Fair and Accurate Credit Transactions (FACT) Act, signed into law in December 2003, have strengthened privacy provisions and defined more clearly the responsibilities and liabilities of businesses that provide information to credit reporting agencies.

- The *Equal Credit Opportunity Act* ensures that all consumers are given an equal chance to obtain credit. For example, a person is not required to reveal his or her sex, race, national origin, or religion to obtain credit.

- The *Fair Debt Collection Practices Act* bans the use of intimidation and deception in collection, requiring debt collectors to treat debtors fairly.

It should be apparent by now that pricing and credit decisions are of prime importance to a small firm because of their direct impact on its financial health. But keep in mind that you are reading about pricing and credit in the section of this book entitled "Focusing on the Customer: Marketing Growth Strategies." Small business owners can fall into the trap of giving all their attention to costs of products, materials, and operations when setting prices. Be sure that your pricing decisions are driven by a customer focus: What is the customer willing and able to pay, and does that price enable you to make a profit? Providing value for your customers and putting them first is the way to move your business forward.

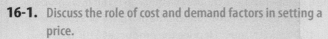

16-1. Discuss the role of cost and demand factors in setting a price.

- The total sales revenue of a firm is a direct reflection of two components: sales volume and price.
- The price must be sufficient to cover total cost plus some margin of profit.
- Pricing at less than total cost can be used as a special short-term strategy.
- A firm should examine elasticity of demand—the relationship of price and quantity demanded—when setting a price.
- A product's competitive advantage is a demand factor in setting price.

16-2. Apply break-even analysis and markup pricing.

- Analyzing costs and revenue under different price assumptions identifies the break-even point, the quantity sold at which total costs and expenses equal total sales revenue.
- The usefulness of break-even analysis is enhanced by incorporating sales forecasts.
- Markup pricing is a generalized cost-plus system of pricing used by intermediaries with many products.

16-3. Identify specific pricing strategies.

- Penetration pricing and skimming pricing are short-term strategies used when new products are first introduced into the market.
- Follow-the-leader and variable pricing are special strategies that reflect the nature of the competition's pricing and concessions to customers.

- A price lining strategy simplifies choices for customers by offering a range of several distinct prices.
- Pricing at what the market will bear should be used only when the seller has little or no competition.
- Local, state, and federal laws must be considered in setting prices, as well as any impact that a price may have on other product line items.

16-4. Explain the benefits of credit, factors that affect credit extension, and types of credit.

- Credit provides small firms with working capital. Its other benefits to borrowers are the ability to immediately satisfy needs and pay for it later, better records of purchases, convenience when exchanging purchased items, and the ability to establish a credit history.
- Benefits of credit to sellers include increased revenue from interest on unpaid balances, a closer association with customers, easier selling, smoother sales peaks and valleys, and easy access to a competitive tool.
- Type of business, credit policies of competitors, ages and income levels of customers, availability of adequate working capital, and economic conditions affect the decision to extend credit.
- The two broad classes of credit are consumer credit and trade credit.

16-5. Describe the activities involved in managing credit.

- Evaluating the credit status of applicants begins with the completion of an application form.
- A customer's ability to pay is evaluated through the five C's of credit: character, capacity, capital, conditions, and collateral.
- Pertinent credit data can be obtained from several outside sources, including formal trade-credit agencies such as Dun & Bradstreet.
- An accounts receivable aging schedule can be used to improve the credit collection process.
- A small firm should establish a formal procedure for billing and collecting from credit customers.
- It is important that a small firm follow all relevant credit regulations.

Key Terms

Discussion Questions

1. How does price relate to value in the eyes of a customer?

2. Give an example of a product for which there is elastic demand, and another example for inelastic demand.

3. Think of a brand that has been successful in using prestige pricing. How is the company able to use that strategy?

4. If a firm has fixed costs of $100,000 and variable costs per unit of $1, what is the break-even point in units, assuming a selling price of $5 per unit?

5. What is the difference between a variable pricing strategy and a price lining strategy? Under what circumstances would each be used?

6. If a small business conducts a break-even analysis properly and finds the break-even volume at a price of $10 to be 10,000 units, should it price the product at $10? Why or why not?

7. What are the major benefits of credit to buyers? What are its major benefits to sellers?

8. What does a company have to consider in establishing a credit policy?

9. What are four key questions in evaluating a credit applicant?

10. What are the five C's of credit? Why are they important?

You Make the Call

Situation 1

Frolic! is a membership-based indoor playground in Brooklyn, New York. Owners Carey Balogh and Julia Dawson see Frolic! as a community of families with babies and young children. They bill it as "the ultimate rock 'n' roll play space for the urban 'under six' crowd and their parents." When Frolic! opened, the owners considered what competitors were asking and charged a little less. But Frolic! offers more than space. Balogh and Dawson provide music lessons, organize birthday parties, and offer a coffee lounge and a boutique. In the early days of the business, the company lost money week after week.

Question 1 Are Balogh and Dawson offering too many services? What do you advise?

Question 2 Are Balogh and Dawson charging too low a price? What do you advise?

Question 3 If the owners raise their prices, how do you think their customers will react?

Sources: "Frolic!—About Us," http://frolicplayspace.com/about.html, accessed March 16, 2013; Norm Brodsky, "There's a Funny Thing about Entrepreneurs: They're Often Way too Optimistic about Sales and Way too Pessimistic about Prices," *Inc.*, Vol. 34, No. 5, (2012) p. 40.

Situation 2

Warren Keating is an artist in Los Angeles who was an early seller on eBay, following the pattern of many artists who

believe that auctioning their work is the way art should be sold. He has concluded that his market is made up of collectors, who would not want to see the value of what they are buying decline due to price cutting. Keating leans toward full retail pricing, and when he sells on eBay, it's through the "Buy It Now" listing or the more negotiable "Buy It Now or Make Offer." He thinks the biggest mistake an artist can make is inconsistent pricing that causes the buyer to lose confidence in the product's value. According to Keating, you should act with "courage and conviction."

Question 1 What do you think makes selling works of art different from selling other kinds of products? What makes it the same?

Question 2 Have you bought anything on eBay? If so, did you receive good value for the price you paid? If not, ask someone who has shopped successfully on eBay for advice on how to shop on that site, and report on what that person tells you.

Question 3 How would you price a work of art? What do you think the advantages and disadvantages of using an auction would be?

Sources: www.warrenkeating.com, accessed March 20, 2011; and Warren Keating, "Sell More Art Online with New Pricing Strategies," http://artistmarketingsalon.wordpress.com/2011/01/24/sell-more-art-online-with-new-pricing-strategies/, accessed March 20, 2011.

Situation 3

Giving customers time to pay their bill generates more sales. But when a recession hits, they may have trouble making payments. If you have businesses as clients, they may have slow-paying customers, which means that they'll be slow to pay you. That is what happened to Terry Croom's business, BizCon Group, a business services company, with a discount card as its primary product. Croom estimated that 50 percent of his customers–other small businesses–were behind in paying what they owed him. Croom needed those customers to keep his business operating, so he was hesitant to demand payment on past due accounts.

Question 1 Should a small business owner push customers to pay when times are tough? Why or why not?

Question 2 What problems do you think a business services company might have when its customers do not pay?

Source: Emily Maltby, "How Firms Cope with Slow Payers," *The Wall Street Journal*, November 14, 2011, p. R5.

Experiential Exercises

1. Pick a local retail business that also sells products on its website. Compare the prices listed online with those in the store. Are there any differences? Ask the owner to explain why or why not.

2. Many small companies regularly promote sales and other price changes on their websites. Track the changes that one such company makes for a week. Can you find any patterns in its actions? Why do you think the owners chose to make those changes?

3. Interview the credit manager of a retail store about the benefits and drawbacks of extending credit to customers. Report your findings to the class.

Small Business & Entrepreneurship Resource Center

The Small Business & Entrepreneurship Resource Center offers complete small business management resources through a comprehensive database that covers all major areas of starting, operating, and maintaining a business from financing, management, marketing, accounting, taxes, and more. Go to www.cengagebrain.com and select the Longenecker text for more information on how to access this material.

1. A new electronic point of purchase device, epop, offers retailers the ability to present easy-to-read pricing information with three-inch by four-inch LCD displays that require no power and can be updated often from a remote location. The displays replace individual item and shelf-edge labels. This technology may change the way North American retailers do business, because manual labeling is labor-intensive, costly, and too slow for managers to react to sales trends and competitive pressures. And epop reduces waste by automating sales prices for items that are approaching their expiration date. After reading this article, explain how epop helps retailers cut costs and gain a competitive advantage.

2. Due to the recession, you closed a restaurant within your hotel, but all leading periodicals have declared that the recession is over. You have to decide whether to reopen your restaurant. Given this scenario, some restaurants wait too long to be assured of breaking even, because they calculate their "full costs" should they reopen. Undue delay extends the agony of laid-off employees and the loss of market share. Rushing to reopen and book new business at prices that might not cover variable costs damages the health of the business. Do you agree with the author of this article that the middle ground is to reopen your restaurant at the marginal contribution break-even point? Explain your answer.

Sources: Michael Harnett, "Paperless Pricing: New LCD Device Offers Pricing, Product and Promotional Information with Automated Wireless Updates, *Frozen Food Age*, Vol. 55, No. 10 (May 2007), p. 32; and Clement Ojugo, "Knowing Your Break-Even Point Critical to Good Decision Making," *Nation's Restaurant News*, Vol. 43, No. 34 (September 14, 2009), p. 66.

Video Case 16

DYN (P. 678)

The story of Dyn is not unlike many tech startup stories. The difference is that it started during the dot.com boom, survived the bust, thrived after the dust settled, and surges ahead today. At the beginning of Dyn's history, pricing structure was evaluated monthly, but now that it's more established, forecasting is done depending on client needs.

Alternative Case for Chapter 16

Case 22, Pearson Air Conditioning & Service, p. 689

Endnotes

1. "Value," www.businessdictionary.com/definition/value.html, accessed March 2, 2013.

2. "Make Your Product Ads Work Harder," www.mercent.com /what-we-do/product-advertising?utm_expid=7859319-0&utm _referrer=http%3A%2F%2Fwww.mercent.com%2F, accessed March 2, 2013.

3. Julia Angwin and Dana Mattioli, "Don't Like This Price? Wait a Minute," *The Wall Street Journal*, September 5, 2012, pp. A1–A2.

4. http://urbancanine.com/, accessed March 2, 2013; and Jenna Schnuer, "The Honor System," *Entrepreneur*, Vol. 40, No. 7 (2012), pp. 85–89.

5. Erika Napoletano, "Because You're Worth It!" *Entrepreneur*, Vol. 41, No. 3 (2013), p. 25.

6. Personal interview with Jeremy Hitchcock, February 13, 2013.

7. For a comprehensive explanation of pricing strategies, see William M. Pride and O. C. Ferrell, *Marketing*, Chapter 21 (Mason, OH: Cengage Learning, 2014).

8. Ann C. Logue, "Sticker Shock," *Entrepreneur*, Vol. 40, No. 7 (2012), p. 64.

9. Matthew Bandyk, "Why Retailers May Not Have to Fear Price Fixing," http://money.usnews.com/money/blogs/risky-business/2008/08/18/why -retailers-may-not-have-to-fear-price-fixing, accessed March 16, 2013.

10. Mohammed Rafi, "Ditch the Discounts," *Harvard Business Review*, January–February 2011, pp. 23–25.

11. https://merchant.paypal.com/, accessed March 16, 2013.

12. http://usa.visa.com/personal/using_visa/personal_finance/debit.html, accessed March 16, 2013.

13. Tony Mecia, "Settlement Allows Retailers to Surcharge for Credit Card Use; Will They?" www.creditcards.com/credit-card-news /retailer-swipe-fee-consumers-settlement-surcharge-1282.php, accessed March 16, 2013; and Michelle Crouch and Fred O. Williams, "Credit Card Surcharges Now Allowed," www.creditcards.com/credit-card-news/credit -card-surcharges-allowed-1281.php, accessed March 16, 2013.

14. Inside CRM, "The 20 Worst Venture Capital Investments of All Time," www .insidecrm.com/articles/crm-blog/the-20-worst -venture-capital-investments-of-all-time-53532, accessed March 16, 2013.

15. Information regarding how to obtain free credit reports is available on the website of the Federal Trade Commission, www.consumer.ftc.gov /articles/0155-free-credit-reports, accessed July 9, 2013.

© Boston Globe/Getty Images.com

Promotional Planning

HubSpot, Inc.
www.hubspot.com

Business journalists regularly write about how marketing is changing. The founders of HubSpot, Inc., set out to be the cause of the change.

HubSpot was started in 2006 by Brian Halligan and Dharmesh Shah. Their idea was to provide what they describe as a "killer" marketing application—advising small businesses on how to leverage the Internet in order to "get found" by more prospects shopping in their niche and then to convert a high percentage of those prospects into customers.

Traditional marketing involves sending messages to customers, prospects, and sometimes the public in general, using a variety of media to project an image or encourage purchasing action. This is referred to as *outbound marketing*. Halligan is credited with coining the term *inbound*

marketing to refer to a company's ability to help itself get found by people already learning about and shopping in the firm's industry. This involves setting up a website that acts as a hub in the industry and attracts visitors naturally through search engines, through the blogosphere, and through social media sites.

Halligan and Shah argue that there has been a fundamental shift in marketing and that companies must transform themselves so that their marketing efforts are integrated with each other and with the rest of the organization. They believe that the old promotional formula, which involved compiling mail lists and e-mail lists, advertising, direct selling, attending trade shows, and other tactics for getting the attention of buyers allowed

OPEN
LOOKING
AHEAD

After studying this chapter,
you should be able to...

17-1. Describe the communication model and the factors that determine a promotional mix.

17-2. Explain methods of determining the appropriate level of promotional expenditures.

17-3. Explain how the Internet and social media are changing promotional practices.

17-4. Describe personal selling activities.

17-5. Identify advertising options for a small business.

17-6. Discuss the use of sales promotional tools.

people to block most messages. Their business model is to help their clients bring all their marketing activities together in a way that makes it easy for customers to find and do business with them.

According to Mike Volpe, chief marketing officer, HubSpot started small but grew quickly, following its own advice on sales and marketing. He believes the first key to its growth was a free tool that HubSpot offered, the Website Grader (http://websitegrader.com), which helps companies score their websites, determines if the websites have problems, and lets them know how popular their websites are. HubSpot's second initiative was to enter the blogosphere by introducing multiple blogs. One offers news about the company and its products, while another describes the launch of the HubSpot Marketing Library. A different blog provides marketing advice. The

company even invites guest bloggers, letting them know their work may be read by 145,000 subscribers who make 1,400,000 monthly visits to the site.

Volpe describes the culture of HubSpot as one that encourages experimentation, and he reports outsized returns on the new approaches that the firm has tried. But he says it also celebrates failures. Whether an experiment was well run is more important than the outcome it achieved. Through experimentation, HubSpot continues to adapt and grow.

Sources: Based on www.hubspot.com, accessed February 11, 2013; personal interviews with Mike Volpe, January 18, 2011, and January 25, 2013; Brian Halligan and Dharmesh Shah, *Inbound Marketing: Get Found Using Google, Social Media, and Blogs* (Hoboken, NJ: John Wiley & Sons, 2010); and Scott Denne, "HubSpots Revenue Shows a Glimpse of Marketing Tech Demand," http://blogs.wsj.com /venturecapital/2013/02/22/hubspots-revenue-shows-a-glimpse-of-marketing -tech-demand/?KEYWORDS=social+media, accessed February 23, 2013.

One of the first lessons that you quickly learn in running your own business is that everything you do affects everything else, that every part of your organization is connected. How you promote your products, your services, and your business itself have to be correlated with the skills of your staff, the layout of your facility, the reports from your sales force, and dozens of other resources and activities.

Today, search engines, social networks, blogs, and apps are changing how we get information and conduct business. So how does a customer know that you have something to sell? Does she or he randomly drive by your store and see your sign? Stumble across your website while surfing the Internet? Hear about your business from a friend or neighbor? If you want people to buy what you are selling, you need to let them know that you are open for business—and why they should buy from you. The way you get that message across is called *promotion*.

Promotion consists of marketing communications that inform potential consumers about a firm or its product or service and try to persuade them to buy it. Small businesses use promotion in varying degrees. In order to simplify our discussion of the promotional process, we group the techniques discussed in this chapter into four categories—Internet and social media, personal selling, advertising, and sales promotional tools.

A key decision in developing a promotional strategy is determining what you want to get out of it. Do you want to attract customers to your store or website? Are you asking them to buy a specific product or service? Or do you just want to plant the name of your business firmly in customers' minds so that they will think of you when they are ready to buy? This decision will drive what you choose to communicate to prospective customers and the means for getting your message out to them. From the perspective of inbound marketing, the decision will enable prospective customers to find your message.

First, let's look at the basic process of communication that characterizes promotion. An entrepreneur who understands that promotion is a special form of communication will be better able to grasp the entire process.

promotion
Marketing communications that inform and persuade consumers.

LO 17-1

Describe the communication model and the factors that determine a promotional mix.

17-1 PROMOTION IS COMMUNICATION

When you are promoting, you are communicating. As described in the Spotlight feature, communication technology is changing, but the basic process and purpose remain the same. Consider social media—Facebook, LinkedIn, Twitter, and so many others. According to Eve Mayer Orsburn, author of *The Social Media Business Equation*, "Social media is simply people communicating online."[1]

The basic communication model is simple—someone sends a message through a channel, and someone else receives it and understands it. Of course, in practice communication is much more complicated. Through your promotional activities, you seek to have a customer or prospective customer take action as a result of the message you send. So, has your message actually reached your target customer? Did the customer actually understand the message? Did he or she take the action you desired?

Adagio Teas sells a wide variety of teas online, as well as through brick-and-mortar locations. If you are shopping online, how can you assess the taste and aroma to make your buying decision? The owners of Adagio realized that the communication with customers could not go in only one direction. They wanted feedback from customers, and more. They found that social media provided ways for customers to communicate with each other. Adagio encourages customers to use Facebook, Twitter, and Google+ to post recommendations about its different products. Customer comments are presented as they come in—good and bad, no editing, and no deletions. The company reported a huge jump in sales after they opened the conversation.[2]

The promotional efforts of a small firm can encompass nonpersonal (advertising), personal (personal selling), combined (social media), and special (sales promotion) forms of communication. A term commonly used to describe how a business combines its promotional methods is **promotional mix**, a blend of nonpersonal, personal, combined, and special forms of communication aimed at a target market. The particular mix of the various promotional methods—advertising, personal selling, social media, and sales promotional tools—is determined by many factors, one of which is geography. A widely dispersed market generally requires mass coverage through advertising or social media, in contrast to the more costly individual contacts of personal selling. On the other hand, if the market is local or if the number of customers is relatively small, personal selling and point-of-display promotion may be more feasible.

Another factor is the size of the promotional budget. Small firms may not select certain forms of promotion, because the costs are just too high. Television advertising, for example, is generally more expensive than radio advertising. Pets.com has become the poster child for spending too much on advertising. Started in 1998 as an online business selling pet accessories and supplies, it shut down in 2000 after earning $619,000 in sales while spending $11,800,000 on advertising. The company spent $1,200,000 on a single Super Bowl ad.[3] The lower costs and more targeted nature of company websites have led many small firms to choose electronic media and inbound marketing strategies.

A third factor that heavily influences the promotional mix is a product's characteristics. If the product is of high unit value, such as manufacturing machinery, personal selling will be a vital ingredient in the mix. Personal selling is also an effective method for promoting highly technical products, such as a home security system, because a customer's knowledge about them is usually limited. On the other hand, nonpersonal advertising is more effective for a relatively inexpensive item, like potato chips.

Do not underestimate what you can learn from competitors. It is natural to want to stand out from the competition and try different tactics from those that established companies are using. You may discover, though, that your competitors have already tried your idea and found that it did not attract buyers. So, if everyone in your industry is using the same types of promotions, there may be a reason.

Finally, listen to your customers. Keep in mind that successful communication includes feedback. Find out whether your customers are posting negative comments about your company or your products online. Pay attention to the comments posted about other businesses to learn why customers are purchasing from them instead of from you. Consider meeting with a group of customers from time to time to get

promotional mix
A blend of nonpersonal, personal, combined, and special forms of communication aimed at a target market.

recommendations on how you can serve them better. No promotional activities will be successful day in and day out, for extended periods of time. You need to stay alert in order to make changes when tried-and-true techniques start wearing out.

Communicating with customers and prospects does not come without a price. Virtually every option you consider will have a cost. Think about all the promotional messages that come your way every day and all the sources from which they come. There are many stories about failed businesses that wasted money on marketing efforts. This is an area where you need to take budgeting seriously.

17-2 DETERMINING THE PROMOTIONAL BUDGET

LO
17-2

Explain methods of determining the appropriate level of promotional expenditures.

In Chapter 16, you learned that there is no magic formula for determining the right price for what you are selling. The same problem arises when figuring out how much a small business should spend on promotion. Four approaches that small business owners often use include the following:

1. Budgeting a fixed percentage of sales
2. Deciding how much is left over after other expenses are covered
3. Spending at the same level as competitors
4. Determining how much is needed to achieve objectives

17-2a Budgeting a Fixed Percentage of Sales

Many small businesses operate in stable markets with predictable revenue streams. In such cases, the simplest method of determining how much to budget for promotion is to earmark promotional dollars based on a percentage of sales. A firm's own past experiences should be evaluated to establish a promotion-to-sales ratio. If 2 percent of sales, for example, has historically been spent on promotion with good results, the firm can safely budget 2 percent of forecasted sales for future promotion. Secondary data on industry averages can also be used for comparison. Professional and industrial associations typically collect these data and report them to their members. A variation on the percentage-of-sales approach is to use a percentage of profits.

Budgeting Marketing Dollars
You can find a free template for compiling a marketing budget at www.score.org/resources/annual-marketing-budget-template.

A major shortcoming of allocating a percentage of sales is a tendency to spend more on promotion, when sales are increasing and less when they are declining. When the economy is booming, do you really need to spend more to attract customers? In a recession, however, using promotion to stimulate sales may be the most important way to let people know why they should be doing business with you. Of course, this strategy does not make sense for new firms with no historical sales figures on which to base their promotional budgets.

17-2b Deciding How Much Is Left Over After Other Expenses Are Covered

Spending whatever is left over when all other activities have been funded occurs all too often in small businesses. This is sometimes described as the "all you can afford" method. The decision about promotional spending might be made only when a media representative sells an owner on a special deal that the business can afford.

Small business owners should have objectives for the money that they spend. And they should be alert for new media opportunities.

17-2c Spending at the Same Level as Competitors

As mentioned earlier, sometimes competitors are doing things right. You should always ask yourself why competitors are using a particular ad media and spending money in a certain pattern throughout the year. The answer may be that they've learned something about people's shopping and buying habits. By duplicating the promotional efforts of close competitors, a business will be spending at least as much as the competition in the hope of reaching the same customers. If the competitor is a large business, this method is clearly not feasible. However, it can be used to react to short-run promotional tactics by small competitors.

Of course, this approach may result in copying competitors' mistakes as well as their successes. And the biggest pitfall can be that it makes you lazy. You don't want to ignore something that could really move your business forward. And if you design a new promotional strategy, competitors may try to copy it. They may increase their budgets to keep you from stealing their customers, and you may find yourself in an ad war.

17-2d Determining How Much Is Needed to Achieve Objectives

With your promotional budget, you may be trying to increase sales or profits, get more prospects to visit your website, gain better name or brand recognition for your company or your product, or simply increase the number of people reached by your message. Determining how much you need to accomplish your goals requires a comprehensive analysis of the market with a link to the firm's objectives. You should know how your target market is getting information. Is a new social medium becoming popular? Do your customers need to be introduced to your product, or are they looking for it? The options for spending promotional budgets are increasing every day.

Next, we consider specific options for promoting products and services, beginning with some of the newer ones. Advancements in communications technologies have led to new products and new methods for connecting businesses with their markets.

17-3 PROMOTION USING THE INTERNET AND SOCIAL MEDIA

The Pew Research Center through its Internet & American Life Project reports that social media users come from all demographics.[4] Companies that fail to recognize how the Internet and social media are changing how people communicate and process information are not likely to prosper. To gain a better understanding of what this means for small business owners, we look first at creating and managing websites, and then discuss the promotional opportunities offered by social media.

LO 17-3

Explain how the Internet and social media are changing promotional practices.

17-3a The Small Business Website

If you are not thinking about marketing when you set up and manage your company's website, you are missing opportunities and doing damage to your business. Numerous decisions must be made prior to launching a site. Three critical startup tasks are related to the likely promotional success of a corporate website: (1) creating and registering a site name, (2) building a user-friendly site, and (3) promoting the website.

CREATING AND REGISTERING A SITE NAME The Domain Name System (DNS) allows users to find their way around the Internet. Selecting the best domain name for a corporate website is an important promotional decision. Popular domain

© aabejon/iStockphoto.com

designations are .com, .net, .biz, .info, and .org. Domain names have a minimum of 3 and maximum of 63 characters preceding the domain designation. They must begin with a letter or number and end with a letter or number. They may not include a space. Follow the rules carefully to avoid problems when you register.[5]

Since a domain name gives a small business its online identity, it's desirable to select a descriptive and appealing name. Of course, some of the shorter, more creative names have already been taken, so most entrepreneurs choose to use the name of their business.[6] Like real estate, website names can be bought and sold. In 2013, the name Booker.com sold for $375,000.[7]

BUILDING A USER-FRIENDLY WEBSITE First impressions are important, and high-quality Web design gives a small e-commerce business the opportunity to make a good first impression on each visitor. Many technical specialists are available to help design and build a site. Our purpose here is simply to provide some useful ideas about website design (see Exhibit 17.1).

Websites fail to retain customers for many reasons. One of the most frequent problems is slow downloads. Online shoppers are impatient, and the slightest inconvenience sends them away. If your business is conducting a considerable amount of online business, a slow website translates into lost sales revenue. Lost revenue can be direct (for example, missed sales if you're selling online) or indirect (for example, loss of customer confidence if you're providing Web-based solutions to clients). The more important a website is to your business, the less you can afford to have it perform slowly or, worse, experience downtime.

EXHIBIT 17.1 Website Design Guidelines

- ○ **Select and register your domain name**. Comply with registration rules, and choose a descriptive and user-friendly name.
- ○ **Choose a Web host**. Determine the primary purpose of your website, and then locate the host that best fits that purpose, such as e-commerce, blogging, business, or some other option.
- ○ **Decide on the layout**. Design a site that balances attractiveness with the ability to interact.
- ○ **Provide easy navigation**. Do not overload a page. Enable users to access any content with as few clicks as possible.
- ○ **Stay consistent in style**. Inconsistency in headings, fonts, page layouts, color schemes, and terms only confuses visitors and appears amateurish.
- ○ **Make sure the website can be accessed by multiple devices**. Users may also search for your company from smartphones and tablets, as well as desktops and laptops.
- ○ **Engage in search engine optimization (SEO)**. Serious competitors are applying SEO strategies to improve their websites' visibility. Don't be left behind.
- ○ **Keep the website fresh**. Review your site frequently to remove outdated material, introduce new links, experiment with new formats, and make other changes.
- ○ **Include a call to action**. Think again about your purpose, and invite users to take the action you are seeking.
- ○ **Supply contact information**. Be sure that visitors know who you are and how to get in touch with you.

Sources: Based on www.webhostinggeeks.com, accessed February 10, 2013; www.register.com, accessed February 10, 2013; www.hostindex.com, accessed February 10, 2013; Sue Smith, "Website Design Guidelines," www.ehow.com/info_8160582_website-design-guidelines.html; and Anne Handley, "Sustainable Resources," *Entrepreneur*, Vol. 40, No. 5 (2012), p. 61.

Websites will also fail if they do not satisfy visitors' information needs. Frequently, this is because designers look inward to the business for Web design ideas, rather than outward to customer needs. Some experts recommend that firms integrate social networking into their websites from the beginning. Founder Joel Weingarten describes his company, StyleOwner, as the first true social selling platform. The company was launched in 2011 and enables branding retail partners to create online boutiques that they personalize for their social networks. The boutique owners are labeled "stylepreneurs," offering recommendations to friends and making a commission on each sale. Weingarten sees the consumer as benefiting from personalized service and supporting the store of someone the consumer trusts.[8]

PROMOTING THE WEBSITE A Web address can be promoted both to existing customers and to prospects by including the URL on print promotions, business cards, letterhead, and packaging. Special direct mail and radio campaigns can also be designed for this purpose. Additionally, a website can be promoted by placing banner advertisements on other websites, where a quick click will send users to the advertised site. When building HubSpot, Inc., Brian Halligan and Dharmesh Shah explained to clients that traditional promotion acts like a megaphone, broadcasting from one to many. Their idea for inbound marketing was for a firm's website to become a hub, enabling like-minded people to connect.[9]

Search engine optimization (SEO) is the process of increasing the volume and quality of traffic to a particular website. The higher your small business ranks in search engine results, the more visitors it will attract. An important goal is to make your website as search engine–friendly as possible.

Keep in mind, too, that there are many specialized search engines Your company might benefit from being registered with an engine, such as Go.com, a Disney property that represents itself as family friendly.[10] You can find guidelines for designing and submitting your website by visiting search engine websites.[11]

17-3b Social Media

Social media comprise social networking and microblogging websites, as well as other online means of communication, where users share personal messages, information, videos, and other content.That definition calls for us to define two more terms. Social networking refers to interacting online with other users who share common interests. Microblogging involves posting short messages or photos on a blog or social networking site, especially by using a cell phone or instant messaging. Smartphones, tablets, and other mobile devices are helping business owners find entirely new ways of reaching customers and prospects.

Among the many lessons for small business owners is that they cannot absolutely control how their businesses are viewed by consumers. Today's customers are often members of communities that are sharing real-time information about the products and services being offered. Entrepreneurs may find that they need qualified experts to guide them through the social media maze, just as many expect accountants to coach them through their financial statements.

Promoting businesses, products, and services through social media can be intimidating, if only because of the vast array of options available. But the same entrepreneurial attitude that helps an owner create and manage a small business can be applied in order to reach customers through online communication. Stay tuned for the rapid changes these technologies will continue to bring.

START UP

TRANSFORM

"One World, One Internet"

As you develop online promotional strategies, be sure to monitor the Internet Corporation for Assigned Names and Numbers (www.icann.org), which performs functions previously managed by the U.S. government. These include the Domain Name System, Internet Protocol addresses, space allocation, and other responsibilities. ICANN invites participation to fulfill its vision: "One World, One Internet."

social media
Social networking and microblogging websites, as well as other means of online communication, where users share personal messages, information, videos, and other content.

social networking
Interacting online with other users who share common interests.

microblogging
Posting short messages or photos on a blog or social networking site.

SOCIAL NETWORKING SITES Hundreds of social networks are available and accessible for small businesses to join communities, make contacts, introduce products and services, build customer relationships, and otherwise promote their ventures. Deciding which networks to use, learning how to use them, and staying active and involved by sharing information and monitoring what others are doing require resources that very few small businesses have.[12]

Which networks will connect you with current and prospective customers and help you discover what your competitors are doing, what new technologies may affect your business, and what social and cultural changes may affect your sales? Some networks are more general in nature, while others specialize. Look at the websites of your competitors to determine which networks they are encouraging visitors to click and join. Those are the ones your competitors think work best for them. A few examples can help you to see why you might or might not choose to select a particular site:

- *Facebook.* The 800-pound gorilla of social networking. Facebook links you with friends and others with whom you might be connected through work, study, or mutual interests. Businesses often set up fan pages in order to interact with customers.
- *Twitter.* A short-messaging service that businesses can use to provide real-time notifications to their followers.
- *LinkedIn.* A business-oriented network with the mission of connecting professionals and enabling companies to improve their competitiveness.
- *Viadeo.* An international business and professional networking site for developing relationships, solving problems, and recruiting executives.
- *StumbleUpon.* A website that helps visitors discover other websites they may not have known were available. Entirely new categories of networks and websites are constantly springing up.
- *Kaboodle.* A social shopping community. Users seek, recommend, and share information about products and services.

On the company website, Grey Sky Films posts photos of all 10 employees.[13] Co-founders Chris Vaglio and Mark Serao want to show off their work by using their team to spread the word. Employees are encouraged to tweet, to post on Facebook and MySpace, and to put videos on YouTube. Vaglio and Serao provide simple guidelines: simple, fun, interesting, but not negative or inappropriate.[14] If a business cannot afford a specialist in social media, opening up the opportunity for all employees may be an option. Businesses must be careful, however, not to compromise confidential information and to get permission when mentioning others on social networks.

DIRECT E-MAIL PROMOTION Before social networking sites became dominant, **e-mail promotion**, in which electronic mail is used to deliver a firm's message, provided and still provides a low-cost way to pinpoint customers and achieve high response rates. As more and more businesses began using e-mail for this purpose, however, customer inboxes become cluttered. And recipients are reluctant to open some e-mail messages, fearing they may contain computer viruses. Nevertheless, a number of surveys report that e-mail marketing is effective for many companies. According to an Econsultancy survey in 2012, 70 percent of business respondents reported good or excellent returns on investment in e-mail advertising.[15] Another study showed that retail businesses averaged returns of $44.25 for each dollar spent on e-mail marketing.[16]

Two obstacles to e-mail promotion have arisen. First, Congress passed the Can-Spam Act of 2003, which took effect on January 1, 2004, and established standards

e-mail promotion
Delivery of a firm's message by electronic mail.

regarding the use of commercial e-mail, enforceable by the Federal Trade Commission (FTC).[17] Second, anti-spam software, which sometimes also blocks legitimate e-mails, became popular. Before sending a promotional message by e-mail, marketers should consider testing their message by putting it through a preview tool. MailWasher and SpamButcher are examples of software packages that permit previews. Previewing allows you to see advertisements that may be delivered as e-mails without customers having to download them to their computers.

RECIPROCAL ADVERTISING AND HYPERLINKS A **hyperlink** is a word, phrase, or image that a user may click on to go to another part of a document or website or to a new document or website.[18] As promotional tools, hyperlinks are typically reciprocal. This enables readers to move from one website to another that may have information that relates to their original search or complements what the original website is offering. Companies, therefore, can give visitors more information by linking them to websites maintained by others. Hyperlinks may be free to the linked parties if those parties believe the connections are mutually beneficial. Otherwise, one company may have to pay a per-click charge to the other if it is seeking to obtain business from those using the primary website.

BLOGS The word *blog* is a contraction of the term *weblog*. **Blogs** are online journals that offer a writer's experiences, opinions, etc. (The term often refers to the website itself.) Bloggers often include hyperlinks to complement or supplement the ideas they have presented. The websites are generally intended to be interactive, allowing readers to leave comments. Many business owners have set up blogs related to their companies and products. This can be done for free on such websites as WordPress.com or Blogger .com. An owner can then comment on other blogs that may have related topics, each time including links back to his or her company blog.

Mike Volpe, of HubSpot, considers the introduction of a blog to have been a major breakthrough in the company's identity and a stimulus of its growth.[19] HubSpot founders Brian Halligan and Dharmesh Shah believe that a blog can establish a company as a thought leader in its market by keeping the company alive and fluid in the eyes of current and prospective customers. They point out that a blog can move a company higher in search engine rankings by providing additional pages on your site, additional keywords for searches, and the opportunity to add hyperlinks.[20]

MOBILE DEVICES Technological changes and consumer and commercial uses of mobile devices have exploded in recent years, along with the opportunities that these products offer to small firms. The Pew Research Center reported that the percentage of adults in the United States who owned computer tablets nearly doubled in one month, from December 2012 (10 percent) to January 2013 (19 percent).[21]

A **mobile device** is a generic term used to refer to a variety of wireless handheld computing devices that allow people to access information from wherever they are. When you are ready to promote your company and its products and services on mobile devices, keep in mind that your website may need to be reformatted to fit smaller portable screens. You want a clear layout with easy navigation. You may need a professional checkout service provider so that your customers don't have to worry about pulling out their credit cards and entering numbers in public locations.[22]

APPS **App** is shorthand for *application*, specifically a software application for business or entertainment. You may be well acquainted with apps for a variety of uses, including how to get along in a college community. With the spreading use of smartphones, individuals, businesses, nonprofit organizations, and even government agencies offer

hyperlink
A word, phrase, or image that a user may click on to go to another part of a document or website or to a new document or website.

blog
An online journal that offers a writer's experiences, opinions, etc.

mobile device
A generic term used to refer to a variety of wireless handheld computing devices that allow people to access information from wherever they are.

app
Abbreviation for a software application for business or entertainment.

apps to stay in contact and provide information to people on the go. For an example, take a look at the United States government's list of apps that can be downloaded at http://apps.usa.gov.

Large corporations use apps to make sure that their customers can reach them. Small business owners must take this method of communication seriously to compete and promote their companies. An app should not cost your business more than the revenue it brings in. While you don't have to invest in the most technologically advanced app, you should think about how people can have fun when they click on your app. For example, Flickr can be used to share photos, perhaps showing what a good time your customers are having with your products. And don't forget that when people use their mobile devices, they want responses and information *now*!

Small business owners avoid social media promotion at their risk. Exhibit 17.2 offers some do's and don'ts for social media marketing. Strategies and technologies are changing so fast, though, that you cannot assume what is working for you today will still work tomorrow. And keep in mind that until recently, an unsuccessful advertisement could be quickly pulled and forgotten. Now it lives on online, tarnishing the image of the company that spent good money to create it.

QUICK RESPONSE CODES Another tool for electronic communication that small business owners have been discovering is the **quick response (QR) code**. A QR code is a square barcode that connects to a website, a video, or some other web content. The barcode makes it easy for someone to access your site without typing in a URL. Prospective customers just scan the QR code with their phone camera or webcam. Business owners are finding lots of value in these codes. A code on a business card can be scanned to an address list. Codes can announce events or promotions for a company, giving days, times, locations, and other information. They may include an

quick response (QR) code
A square bar code that connects to a website, a video, or some other web content.

EXHIBIT 17.2 Do's and Don'ts of Social Media Marketing

Do's	Don'ts
• Do tell stories personalizing your brand and company. Post videos of customers using and enjoying your products.	• Don't overpromote. Provide more useful than promotional information.
• Do build relationships with opinion leaders, including journalists. Show an interest in what others are writing about. Bloggers and reporters often ask questions that you or someone in your company may be able to answer.	• Don't waste your time on the wrong network. Just because everyone seems to be on Facebook doesn't mean that your customer looks there for what you are selling. Make sure you know your target customers and where they get their information.
• Do ask your customers to review the products they buy from you. People trust the endorsements and recommendations of other customers more than those of someone who works for you.	• Don't expect your customers to be perfect. They will make spelling errors typing in keywords. Keep common misspellings associated with your product and business in your search engine list to help people find you.
• Do keep it quick and short. Even 140 characters can be too long at times.	• Don't use hype, slang, or abbreviations. They all look like spam and make your brand look cheap.
• Do take keywords seriously. Keywords bring people to your site. Emphasize the keywords your customers search for in your URL, in title tags, and in headings.	• Don't over-invest in social media at the expense of building content on your own website.

Sources: Based on Jenna Goudreau, "Five Social Media Tricks Every Entrepreneur Should Know," www.forbes.com/sites/jennagoudreau/2012/10/04/five-social-media-tricks-every-entrepreneur-should-know, accessed February 28, 2013; Daniel Lieberman, "Social Media Roundup—August 2012," http://www.franchising.com/articles/social_media_roundup__august_2012.html, accessed February 28, 2013; Heidi Cohen, "Customer Reviews: Social Media Content Supports Sales," http://heidicohen.com/customer-reviews-social-media-content-supports-sales-charts, accessed February 28, 2013; Emily Maltby, "Some Social-Media Tips for Business Owners," http://online.wsj.com/article/SB10001424127887323701904578274090683864964.html?KEYWORDS=social+media, accessed February 28, 2013; Caron Beesley, "Putting the 'Social' into Social Media Marketing: 3 Tips for Interacting with your Customers," http://www.sba.gov/community/blogs/community-blogs/small-business-matters/putting-social-social-media-marketing-3-tips-, accessed February 28, 2013; and Lisa Hoover, "Should Your Business Be on Facebook?" http://pcworld.about.net/od/webbasedapplications/Should-Your-Business-Be-on-Fac.htm, accessed February 28, 2013.

e-mail message that encourages a response. Connecting people to videos may generate the most attention. Mike Podlesny, owner of Mike the Gardener Enterprises, has a QR code on a bumper sticker that takes scanners to a YouTube video showing a "Seed of the Month" promotion that he developed.[23]

17-4 PERSONAL SELLING IN THE SMALL FIRM

LO 17-4
Describe personal selling activities.

As much as social media seem to be taking over the world, face-to-face contact still counts. Through personal selling, you can use body language to convey your message, answer questions and resolve problems immediately, and build confidence. When you are starting a new business, this may be your most important marketing tool. Small business owners should always think of themselves as personal sales representatives for their companies. Wherever you go as a business owner, you are the company to the people you meet. Your interpersonal skills may come into play in any number of ways. People you meet inside or outside of your business form judgments based on how they react to you. They also form judgments based on their interactions with any of your employees. So everyone working for you should know that he or she is making an impression that could lead to sales or could send a customer to someone else.

For many products, **personal selling**—a face-to-face meeting with a customer—is the best way to make a presentation and close a sale. Of course, with technology advances, the face you see may be on a computer screen or a smartphone or some other device. Personal selling includes the activities of both inside salespeople of retail, wholesale, and service establishments and outside sales representatives, who call on business customers and final consumers. In a small business, every person in the company is a salesperson. A customer who walks into a business or places a phone call or sends an e-mail to a business should not have to wait for hours or days to be taken care of by the owner or a certain employee—everyone must be ready to meet the customer's needs. The entrepreneur's responsibility is to make sure that all employees are prepared to do personal selling.

Before hiring a sales force for your company, calculate the costs and expected returns. This can be an expensive form of promotion per sale. For a small business, personal selling is labor intensive. It takes you and your employees away from the many other activities that may be critical to keeping your business alive.

17-4a The Importance of Product Knowledge

Effective selling is built on a foundation of product knowledge. A salesperson is expected to give individual attention to a prospect, perhaps being ready to negotiate and customize a product or service to fit a special need. With thorough knowledge, the salesperson can explain the product's or service's advantages, uses, and limitations, and can educate customers by answering questions and countering objections. Communication in this form of promotion should be interactive. Customers are seldom experts on the products they buy. However, they can immediately sense a salesperson's knowledge or ignorance. Personal selling degenerates into mere order-taking when a salesperson lacks product knowledge.

17-4b The Sales Presentation

The heart of personal selling is the sales presentation to a prospective customer. You should have a good idea of what you or your sales representatives will be ready to say. At this crucial point, an order is either secured or lost.

personal selling
A face-to-face meeting with a customer.

PROSPECTING A preliminary step leading to an effective sales presentation is **prospecting**, which has been thought of as the systematic process of continually looking for new customers. With expanding options and rapid changes in communication technology, it is better to think of prospecting as both looking for customers and making it easy for customers to find you. Prospecting also includes consideration of whether a potential customer can be well served by the company. This is especially important in screening true prospects from casual browsers when they initiate contact with you. Small business owners must use their limited resources wisely.

One of the most important skills a small business owner can have is the ability to network.[24] You will read more about *networking*, the process of developing and engaging in mutually beneficial relationships in Chapter 19. For now, we want to point out how building relationships through business and social interactions can lead to *personal referrals*. If you are able to demonstrate to friends, customers, and other business contacts that you deliver on your promises, that you have solutions to their problems and products and services that can make their lives better, those contacts may open other doors for you. They may let you use their names when introducing yourself to others. At a minimum, they can provide word-of-mouth endorsements, often the strongest recommendation you can get.

Another source of prospects is *impersonal referrals* from media publications, public records, and directories. Newspapers and magazines, particularly trade magazines, often identify prospects by reporting on new companies and new products. Engagement announcements in a newspaper can serve as impersonal referrals for a local bridal shop. Public records of property transactions and building permits can be impersonal referrals for a garbage pick-up service, which might find prospective customers among home buyers or those planning to build houses or apartment buildings.

A high-tech variation of impersonal referrals is taking place on various social websites like Facebook and Pinterest, where more and more subscribers are providing reviews of the establishments they patronize. With Google+, for example, you can target niche circles that users have created, finding prospects with special interests in welding or vacation home ownership or video gaming and more. Keep in mind that reviews posted on social networking websites can be positive or negative. Yelp.com now uses automated software to screen postings for suspicious reviews, such as criticisms of a company that might have been posted by a competitor.[25]

Prospects can also be identified without referrals through *marketer-initiated contacts*. Telephone calls or mail surveys, for example, help locate possible buyers. Finally, inquiries by a potential customer that do not lead to a sale can still create a "hot prospect." Small furniture stores often require their salespeople to fill out a card for each person visiting the store. These *customer-initiated contacts* can then be systematically followed up by telephone calls, and prospects can be notified of special sales. Some customers may become followers on your Twitter account and receive notification through Twitter of special offers. Contact information should be updated periodically. Firms with websites can similarly follow up with visitors who have made inquiries online.

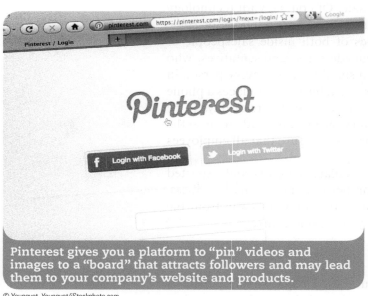

Pinterest gives you a platform to "pin" videos and images to a "board" that attracts followers and may lead them to your company's website and products.

© Youngvet Youngvet/iStockphoto.com

prospecting
A systematic process of continually looking for new customers.

17.3   Successful Sales Techniques

○ **Be honest**. Your prospect has to discover only one misrepresentation to lose all trust and confidence in you. You want customers who will come back to you and tell others how good you are.

○ **Know your audience**. Are you talking with the decision maker, or does this person need approval from someone else? How is your product or service used by this customer?

○ **Know how much time you have, and get to the point**. Many people recognize that time is their most valuable asset. Be sure to respect that. If you can't make clear in the first sentence or two why you're there, you'll lose your prospect's interest.

○ **Prepare an outline, and rehearse**. Be sure to cover all critical issues and logically order your presentation. Then test your ideas on others. Do they understand your message?

○ **Be relevant, and engage the customer**. Ask enough questions to know what is important to your prospective customer and how you can help him or her. Think of your presentation as a *conversation*. Be a better listener than a speaker.

○ **Believe in what you are selling, and be enthusiastic**. Be able to genuinely convey what makes your product or service better for the customer than anyone else's. But recognize that the world's best salespeople still hear *no* more than *yes*. Do not let that burn you out.

○ **Use visuals**. Size, technology requirements, safety and other issues might limit your ability to show your product. Nevertheless, visual representations help project customers into a situation where they better understand what the product will do for them.

○ **Get reactions from the prospect**. If the prospect does not ask questions, it is a sign that you have not communicated your message successfully. Be ready with questions of your own, questions that will solicit more than yes-or-no answers. You want to know what is preventing you from getting the results that you seek. You want to know how to make the prospect happy.

Sources: Based on Kelley Robertson, "Creating a Powerful Sales Presentation," www.businessknowhow.com/marketing/sales-presetnation.htm, accessed February 3, 2013; "Sales Presentation," www.m62.net/sales-presentation, accessed February 3, 2013; Kevin Davis, "10 Tips for Winning Sales Presentations," www.businessknowhow.com/marketing/winslspres .htm, accessed February 3, 2013; "The Keys to Great Sales Presentations," www.allbusiness.com/sales/selling-techniques/809-1.html#axzz2jtCKGWqf; accessed February 3, 2013.

PRACTICING THE SALES PRESENTATION Nothing substitutes for practice before making a sales presentation. Everything may be clear in your mind, but that does not guarantee that the right words will come out of your mouth. Successful salespersons recognize that style can count as much as content. One way to learn about your own style is to record the presentation in order to study it later and improve your delivery.

The best salespeople have done their homework. They have not only practiced their presentations, but they have also studied their prospective customers. They have thought about possible customer objections to the product and are prepared to handle them. Knowing something about customers' wants and needs will prepare you for most of their likely objections. Most objections can be categorized as relating to (1) price, (2) product, (3) timing, (4) source, (5) service, or (6) need. Training can be helpful in teaching salespeople how to deal with customers' objections.

Successful salespeople develop techniques, like those shown in Exhibit 17.3, for attracting a customer's attention, presenting reasons to buy, responding to objections, and closing a sale.

17-4c   Cost Control in Personal Selling

We have already explained that personal selling efforts can be expensive. You may not be spending as much on a salesperson as on an advertising campaign, but neither are you reaching as many people. Cost considerations are especially important for a new

Living the Dream

Know Your Audience

One trap that an entrepreneur can fall into is thinking everyone is just like her or him. If you were to see an old television advertisement for Sy Sperling's company, Hair Club, you would hear him say, "I'm not only the Hair Club president. I'm also a client." You might draw the conclusion that Sperling's venture idea happened only because of his personal experience.

Sperling did not limit his business model to his own worldview, though. He made a point of getting to know his clients and to shape his products to fill their needs. One example involves moving the physical locations of the hair restoration centers from typical retail locations to commercial office districts.

© Don Mason/Blend Images/Getty Images

Sperling learned that his clients felt that the treatments they were receiving were highly personal and didn't want to be in high-foot-traffic areas. Also, the external signage for the buildings announced "HCM," which also reflected that the business had begun to offer services to women.

As the company grew and prospered, it identified market niches that offered further opportunities for growth. In 2011, it partnered with a reality television series on the Discovery Channel, "American Chopper," drawing on the expert knowledge of the cast and crew. Two episodes of the series were devoted to the design and assembly of a motorcycle in honor of the 35th anniversary of the founding of the Hair Club.

Targeting bald motorcyclists may look like marketing segmentation in the extreme. For Sy Sperling and his team, however, it was a step to a broader market. They saw motorcycles representing power and freedom. That is what the Hair Club wants to offer its clients—to give them self-esteem, self-assurance, and freedom. It want clients to feel the wind in their hair.

Sources: Based on www.hairclub.com, accessed February 8, 2013; Andrew Adam Newman, "Hair Club Hitches Its Sidecar to a Biker Theme," www.nytimes.com/2011/03/28/business/media/29adco.html?_r=0, accessed February 8, 2013; and Erika Napoletano, "Putting Down Roots," *Entrepreneur*, Vol. 40, No.1 (2012), p. 22.

business that generally has very limited resources. While nothing can substitute for an entrepreneur's personal efforts to sell products and services and to represent the image and reputation of the firm, time spent selling is time away from other activities required for keeping the business open and operating.

Additionally, in the startup and early growth stages, a business may not have funds to support a full-time sales staff. The most cost-efficient mode of selling may be to use *sales or marketing representatives*, who are self-employed or work for a company whose purpose is to represent multiple businesses, thereby spreading out the costs of selling. They will not focus on your products alone, as your own employees would, but your company will have to compensate them only as merchandise is actually sold. Think of them as your partners. Provide any sales aids they may need to make their job easier. Keep communication channels open, and let them know that you are committed to making them successful.

17-4d The Compensation Program for Salespeople

Salespeople will not be motivated for the same reasons that an owner is. You may be in love with your product or service; you may be seeking to change the world. Your employees want to get paid. But they can be motivated by nonfinancial compensation as well as money. Research studies on small businesses have identified noncash incentives that relate to firm performance.[26]

NONFINANCIAL COMPENSATION Personal recognition and the satisfaction of reaching a sales quota are examples of nonfinancial rewards that motivate many salespeople. Small retail businesses sometimes post a photograph of the top salesperson of the week or month for all to see. Engraved plaques are also given as a more permanent record of sales achievements.

Nonfinancial compensation may also relate to personal and career advancement. Rewards for being a desired employee include opportunities for promotion, advanced education and training, and job security. Business owners should be aware that effective sales personnel are often competitive. They gain a sense of accomplishment by measuring their achievements against those of their peers. Some companies run internal competitions, which can be motivational. If the competition creates hostility among sales personnel, however, consider measuring performance against past achievements, or industry measures or competitions that may be conducted by professional associations.

FINANCIAL COMPENSATION As much as employees may believe in your vision for the firm, they have to take care of themselves and their families. Two basic plans used for financial compensation are commissions and straight salary. Each plan has specific advantages and limitations for the small firm.

Small businesses prefer to use commissions as compensation, because such an approach is simple and directly related to productivity. A certain percentage of the sales generated by a salesperson represents his or her commission. Revenue is generated for the firm, so the money is readily available to pay the salesperson. Such a plan incorporates a strong incentive for sales effort—no sale, no commission! On the negative side, a salesperson's job is always more than making the sale. Personnel on commission might be less likely to provide follow-up service or complete after-sale paperwork or other tasks that the business needs to have done.

The straight salary form of compensation provides salespeople with income security, regardless of sales made. However, working for a straight salary can potentially reduce a salesperson's motivation by providing income despite low performance or no sales at all.

Many businesses combine the salary and commission forms of compensation. Salary usually represents the larger part of compensation for a new salesperson. As the salesperson gains experience, the ratio is adjusted to provide more money from commissions and less from salary. And do not put a cap on what a salesperson can earn through commission. Many companies have lost their top producers by limiting incentives. Why would you stop rewarding someone who is making money for your business?

Whatever plan you choose should incorporate sales volume targets with a time frame for accomplishment, typically a month or a year. Additionally, the sales staff should know what the minimum expectations are for their performance. Beyond sales, these expectations can also include customer development, repeat sales, service efforts following sales, and other activities that contribute to the success of the company.

LO
17-5

Identify advertising options
for a small business.

17-5 ADVERTISING PRACTICES

Along with personal selling, advertising is likely to be part of the promotional strategy for your business. Ideas in advertising are communicated to businesses and consumers through media, such as television, radio, magazines, newspapers, direct mail, billboards, and the Internet.

17-5a Advertising Objectives

To use your money wisely, you should decide what your goals are when you advertise. **Advertising** is a strategy to sell by informing, persuading, and reminding customers of the availability or superiority of a firm's products or services. Without product or service strengths, such as quality and efficiency, advertising will not be enough to help your business survive and grow. Advertising must always be viewed as a complement to a good product and never as a replacement for a bad product.

The importance of honesty in advertising cannot be overstated. An entrepreneur should avoid creating misleading expectations with advertising, as such expectations are likely to leave customers dissatisfied. There is nothing wrong in speaking glowingly of a product or service that you believe in. But no false claims should be made.

advertising
A strategy to sell by informing, persuading, and reminding customers of the availability or superiority of a firm's products or services.

© PSL Images/Alamy

At times, advertising may seem to be a waste of money. It is expensive and adds little value to a product or service. As described in this chapter's Spotlight feature, other alternatives to advertising are emerging. Mike Hackley, founder and CEO of ShoppersChoice.com, wanted to promote his online entertainment and specialty products company on television, which is generally very expensive. He discovered that he could bid on airtime on national cable channels through Google TV Ads. As a result, his ads sponsored a show that reached his target market, exposing ShoppersChoice.com to 1.5 to 2 million viewers for about $3,000 per week.[27] Small business owners, like corporate executives, need to stay up to date with changes in technology and societal behavior.

17-5b Types of Advertising

product advertising
A presentation designed to make potential customers aware of a specific product or service and create a desire for it.

institutional advertising
A presentation of information about a particular firm, designed to enhance the firm's image in order to make its product advertising more credible and effective.

The two basic types of advertising are product advertising and institutional advertising. **Product advertising** is designed to make potential customers aware of a particular product or service and create a desire for it. **Institutional advertising**, on the other hand, conveys information about the business itself. It is intended to make the public aware of the company and enhance its image so that its product advertising will be more credible and effective.

Most small business advertising is of the product type. Small retailers' ads often stress products, such as weekend specials at a supermarket or sportswear sold exclusively in a women's clothing store. It is important to note, however, that the same advertisement can convey both product and institutional themes. With advertising, you are prospecting for customers who want your product, so the ideal solution is that they clearly understand that the best place to buy it is from your company. This may be approached in a variety of ways. A firm may stress its product in newspaper advertisements, for example, while using institutional advertising on websites. Decisions regarding the type of advertising to be used should be based on the nature of the business, industry practice, available media, and the objectives of the firm.

17-5c Advertising Specialists

An entrepreneur cannot be an expert in everything. Small business owners often contract with outside companies and individuals for accounting services, legal advice, transportation, and more. It is not unusual to rely on others' expertise to create promotional messages. Advertising agencies, suppliers, trade associations, and advertising media can provide his specialized assistance.

Advertising agencies provide many services, including the following:

- Graphic design, artwork, and even printing for specific advertisements and/or commercials
- Recommendations for media with the greatest "pulling power" for your product or service
- Copywriting for traditional ads, as well as for blogs, press releases, and other promotional materials
- Assistance with trade shows and merchandise displays
- Website design and social media management
- Mailing and e-mail list management

Since advertising agencies charge fees for their services, an entrepreneur must be sure that the return from those services will be greater than the fees paid. Of course, with the high level of computer technology currently available, creating print advertising in-house is becoming increasingly common among small firms. Some business owners are assisted by suppliers who furnish display aids and even entire advertising programs to their dealers. Trade associations also provide helpful assistance. In addition, advertising media themselves can provide some of the same services offered by an ad agency.

17-5d Frequency of Advertising

Determining how often to advertise is an important and highly complex issue for a small business. Obviously, advertising should be done regularly, and attempts to stimulate interest in a firm's products or services should be part of an ongoing promotional program. Continuity reinforces the presence of the company as the place for customers to buy when they are ready. One-shot advertisements that are not part of a well-planned promotional effort lose much of their effectiveness in a short period. Of course, some noncontinuous advertising may be justified, such as advertising to prepare consumers for the acceptance of a new product. Such an approach may also be used for holidays and seasonal events. Many products and services have some seasonal demand—landscaping services in warm months, snow removal in cold ones, costumes at Halloween, flowers on Valentine's Day. Deciding on the frequency of advertising involves a host of factors, both objective and subjective. This is another reason for entrepreneurs to seek professional advice.

17-5e Where to Advertise

Not everyone is a serious prospect for your business. You have to identify the market segment most likely to buy the products and services you offer and to buy them from you rather than other sources. This means restricting your advertising,

RESOURCES

Enchanting Customers and More
Through his books, website, social media and other means, Guy Kawasaki introduces countless ideas to entrepreneurs about starting and growing their ventures. Good places to look for promotional ideas include his books *The Art of the Start, Selling the Dream,* and *Enchantment.* More information is available on his website at www .guykawasaki.com.

perhaps by geography or customer type. From among the many media available, a small business owner must choose those that will provide the greatest return for the advertising dollar.

The most appropriate combination of advertising media depends on the type of business and its current circumstances. Furniture retailers and auto dealers use television and newspaper ads. Television keeps their name and products in front of the consumers, making them easy to remember when customers are ready to shop and buy. And when someone is ready to purchase a car or some furniture, she or he is likely to look in newspapers to compare products and prices. Hotels and restaurants near busy highways rely on billboards to attract patrons to their locations. Retirement communities and assisted-living facilities may obtain mailing lists from senior citizen centers and use direct mail to reach their target market. We are now at a stage of communication technology that demands the inclusion of a website in any combination of advertising media. Websites are the first step in identifying prospective sources of products and services by many consumers and businesses.

To make an informed selection, entrepreneurs should learn about the strengths and weaknesses of each medium, as shown in Exhibit 17.4. Study this information carefully, noting the particular advantages and disadvantages of each medium.

EXHIBIT 17.4 Advantages and Disadvantages of Major Advertising Media

Medium	Advantages	Disadvantages
Internet	Fastest-growing medium, including smartphones and tablets; ability to target demographics; easy to update; relatively short lead time required for creating Web-based advertising; natural fit with social networking	Possible difficulty in measuring ad effectiveness and return on investment; not all consumers have access; rapidly changing technologies may result in product obsolescence (smartphones/tablets); service issues
Newspapers	Geographic selectivity and flexibility; short-term advertiser commitments; news value and immediacy; year-round readership; high individual market coverage; co-op and local tie-in availability; short lead time	Little demographic selectivity; limited color capabilities; low pass-along rate; may be expensive
Magazines	Good reproduction, especially for color; demographic selectivity; regional selectivity; local market selectivity; relatively long advertising life; high pass-along rate	Long-term advertiser commitments; slow audience buildup; limited demonstration capabilities; lack of urgency; long lead time
Radio	Low cost; immediacy of message; can be scheduled on short notice; relatively no seasonal change in audience; highly portable; short-term advertiser commitments; entertainment carryover	No visual treatment; short advertising life of message; high frequency required to generate comprehension and retention; distractions from background sound; commercial clutter
Television	Ability to reach a wide, diverse audience; low cost per thousand viewers; creative opportunities for demonstration; immediacy of messages; entertainment carryover; demographic selectivity with cable stations	Short life of message; some consumer skepticism about claims; high campaign cost; little demographic selectivity with network stations; long-term advertiser commitments; long lead times required for production; commercial clutter
Direct Mail	Ability to target respondents; provides a detailed and personalized message	May be tossed out as "junk" mail; rising costs per qualified prospect
Outdoor Media	Repetition; moderate cost; flexibility; geographic selectivity	Short message; lack of demographic selectivity; high "noise" level distracting audience

© Cengage Learning

17-6 SALES PROMOTION

A more traditional marketing practice, which is also used on websites and mobile devices, is sales promotion. Generally, **sales promotion** includes any promotional technique, other than personal selling or advertising, that stimulates the purchase of a particular product or service. It typically offers a direct incentive to a purchaser to act by offering value above and beyond what the product provides at its normal price.[28]

For best results, sales promotion typically is used in combination with personal selling and advertising. Popular sales promotional tools include specialties, contests, premiums, trade show exhibits, point-of-purchase displays, free merchandise, publicity, sampling, and coupons. Social media companies enable small firms to compete head-on with their large competitors in cost-efficient ways through sales promotion. Many businesses make use of Foursquare, one of the social platforms highlighted at the Mobile World Congress, which enables businesses to introduce online loyalty programs. For example, the Nightingale Theater in Tulsa, Oklahoma, gives free popcorn and a beer on a customer's fifth check-in; Xoom in New York City offers a free smoothie to those who buy one and check-in with a friend.[29]

We briefly examine four of the most widely used promotional tools: specialties, trade show exhibits, coupons, and publicity.

17-6a Specialties

There are countless specialty items: calendars, pens, key chains, coffee mugs, and shirts. Almost anything can be used as a specialty promotion, as long as each item is imprinted with the firm's name or other identifying slogan. Contact information is also often included.

The distinguishing characteristics of specialties are their enduring nature and tangible value. The key to an effective specialty item is that it lasts—the customer or client has the tangible, visible item for months or years, keeping the name of your company or product in front of them. As functional products, they are worth something to recipients. Specialties can be used to promote a product directly or to create goodwill for a firm. They are excellent reminders of a firm's existence.

Finally, specialties are personal. They are distributed directly to the customer in a personal way, they can be used personally, and they have a personal message. A small business needs to retain its unique image, and owners often use specialties to achieve this objective. More information on specialties is available on the website of Promotional Products Association International at www.ppai.org.

17-6b Trade Show Exhibits

Advertising often cannot substitute for trial experiences with a product, and a customer's place of business is not always the best environment for product demonstrations. Trade show exhibits allow potential customers to get hands-on experience with a product.

Trade show exhibits are of particular value to manufacturers. The greatest benefit of these exhibits is the potential cost savings over personal selling. Trade show groups claim that the cost of an exhibit is less than one-fourth the cost of sales calls, and many small manufacturers agree that exhibits are more cost-effective than advertising.

LO 17-6

Discuss the use of sales promotional tools.

sales promotion An inclusive term for any promotional technique other than personal selling and advertising that stimulates the purchase of a particular product or service.

One website devoted to marketing tactics lists the following helpful tips regarding trade shows:[30]

- *Check out the trade show's history.* Does the show regularly attract large crowds? Will the show be adequately promoted to your potential customers?
- *Apply for a speaking opportunity.* Many shows have keynote speakers and breakout sessions on special topics. Also, having a customer speak on your behalf makes a great impression.
- *Pick a good location for the booth.* It will cost you extra, but a good location could be critical in a large show. Corner booths are best.
- *Prepare a professional-looking display.* You do not need to have the biggest, flashiest booth on the trade show floor to attract attendees. But signs, photographs of your products, and other business-related elements used in the display should appear to be professionally prepared.
- *Have a sufficient quantity of literature on hand.* Have plenty of professional–looking brochures or other handouts to distribute, and have them prepared well in advance of the show.
- *Bring the right staff.* You want someone who believes in the product and who enjoys talking with strangers.
- *Have the right giveaways.* Consider using the specialty promotion items just described. Don't waste money on novelty items that no one will use.
- *Follow up.* Have a plan for following up on leads as soon as you get home from the show.

17-6c Coupons

Coupons have been used as promotional tools for over a hundred years. Coca-Cola is credited with being the first company to use coupons. Asa Candler, a co-founder of the Coca-Cola Company, gave handwritten notes to customers that they could exchange for a free glass of Coke. The first official coupon was issued by C. W. Post, offering one cent off the price of a box of Grape-Nuts cereal. Consumers continue to cut coupons from newspapers and magazines, use coupons received through direct mail, and download them from the Internet.[31] Not only do they attract customers to purchase products, but coupons also have value even if they are not used. A study by University of Virginia professors found that consumers who received but did not redeem coupons actually increased their purchasing from the stores associated with the coupons.[32]

The world of couponing changed with Groupon. Groupon was launched in 2008, in response to the frustration that its founder, Andrew Mason, felt when trying to get a reply from a major corporation. Mason decided that collective action from large numbers of customers would get more attention and designed a platform that uses social media to gain commitment from individuals until a critical mass is reached. Groupon negotiates deals with businesses for reduced prices on merchandise and services that go into effect once the tipping point is reached—that is, when enough people have signed up for a coupon to obtain the discounted item.[33]

Groupon has spawned competitors, such as LivingSocial and SocialTwist. Many small businesses use these platforms to attract business in the hope of gaining returning customers. Some, however, have actually lost money, offering too large a discount and not retaining long-term customers. But others have taken actions to reduce their risks and build sales. The ice cream chain Gelato Spot invites coupon users to join their loyalty program, leading to more special offers. Gaffos.com, a designer eyewear business, follows up coupon orders with e-mails describing additional promotions. Both companies have gained repeat sales.[34] Entrepreneurs must sometimes go beyond the deal that is placed in front of them.

17-6d Publicity

Of particular importance to small firms is **publicity**, which provides visibility for a business at little or no cost. Publicity can be used to promote both a product and a firm's image. It is a vital part of public relations for the small business. A good publicity program requires regular contacts with the news media. As explained in Exhibit 17.2, journalists are opinion leaders. You can help them as much as they can help you if you and your business are the source of good stories.

Although publicity is not always free, the return on a relatively small investment can be substantial. HubSpot (see the Spotlight feature in this chapter) helps other companies attract customers with inbound marketing strategies rather than spending money on outbound promotion. And HubSpot follows its own teaching. In addition to channeling prospects to its website through search engine positioning and free services, it has relied on publicity. HubSpot's press releases and novel approach to doing business have caught the attention of print and broadcast media. The founders have been interviewed on public radio and cable news, and the exposure has helped build HubSpot's credibility and business.[35]

Other examples of publicity efforts that incur some expense include underwriting school yearbooks and sponsoring youth athletic programs. While the benefits are difficult to measure, publicity is nevertheless important to a small business and should be used at every opportunity.

publicity
A promotional strategy that provides visibility for a business at little or no cost.

ENTREPRENEURSHIP + INTEGRITY

Living the Dream

On a Mission

There is nothing new about business organizations engaging in corporate social responsibility, the intentional practice of having an overall positive impact on society. In the United States, corporations make donations to universities, hospitals, welfare agencies, and more. The name of a local company often appears on the uniforms of youth sports teams. Some enterprises that sell goods and services make it clear that they exist to do a social good. Ben & Jerry's sells ice cream, but the company has a core value of being involved in social and environmental

endeavors. The late actor Paul Newman created Newman's Own as a for-profit venture, but all profits are donated to charities. Muhammad Yunus, founder of Grameen Bank, received the Nobel Peace Prize in 2004 for organizing a bank that "provides credit to the poorest of the poor in rural Bangladesh, without any collateral."

Despite the precedents just described, a breakthrough seems to have occurred when Blake Mycoskie launched TOMS in 2006. He started the company shortly after visiting Argentina and seeing the hardships faced by children without shoes. TOMS is a for-profit company that gives a pair of shoes to a needy child every time a customer buys a pair from the firm. Later, it added eyewear, giving away glasses when someone buys a pair of TOMS eyewear. The company declares on its website that its actions have become a global movement.

There is evidence to support that contention. Lauren Walters and Will Hauser had a similar experience in Rwanda. They were shocked by the effects of malnutrition on children. Walters and Hauser formed Two Degrees, based on TOMS business model, to produce and sell healthy, natural, gluten free bars made with real fruit, nuts, seeds, and heritage grains like chia, quinoa, and millet. For every bar purchased, Two Degrees donates a nutrient-rich meal to a hungry child. Other companies that have adopted the approach initiated by TOMS include the One World Futbol

Project (soccer balls to developing countries), Roma Boots (kids' boots to Romania), and Warby Parker (eyeglasses to those in need in 25 countries).

Blake Mycoskie and other entrepreneurs are on a mission to make the world a better place. In doing so, they have received publicity that money cannot buy. The publicity introduces them to prospective customers, but it also helps gets the word out about the social goals they hope to achieve.

Sources: Based on "Corporate Social Responsibility—What Does It Mean?" www.mallenbaker.net/csr/definition.php, accessed March 1, 2013; "Social Mission FAQs," www.benjerry.com/company/frequently-asked-questions, accessed March 1, 2013; www.newmansown.com, accessed March 1, 2013; www.grameen.com/index.php?option=com_content&task=view&id=16&Itemid=112, accessed March 1, 2013; "Blake Mycoskie," www.toms.com/blakes-bio, accessed March 1, 2013; http://twodegreesfood.com, accessed March 1, 2013; Gwen Moran, "Nutrition Mission," *Entrepreneur*, Vol. 39, No. 6 (2011), p. 80; and Stephanie Schomer, "One Day Without Shoes," *Fast Company*, No. 154 (2011), p. 22.

17-6e When to Use Sales Promotion

A small firm can use sales promotion to accomplish various objectives. For example, small manufacturers can use it to stimulate channel members—retailers and wholesalers—to market their product. Wholesalers can use sales promotion to induce retailers to buy inventory earlier than they normally would, and retailers, with similar promotional tools, may be able to persuade customers to make a purchase.

Husband-and-wife team Robert Fishbone and Sarah Linquist were artists, not businesspeople. But when an exhibit of the work of Swedish artist Edvard Munch was coming to town (Munch's best-known work is called "The Scream"), Fishbone decided to design and produce inflatable "Screams." The product got photographed and written up in local newspapers, and eventually the *New York Times* published a story. Fishbone sent free inflatables to news and entertainment venues, where people were excited to see the product and wanted to tell others. Fishbone continues to promote creative ideas, using publicity as a key component of his marketing strategy.[36]

At its core, successful promotion is all about effective communication. The source (a small business) must have a message that intended recipients (in the target market) receive or find, understand, and act on. But this is not a simple exercise. Many decisions must be made along the way—decisions regarding the size of the promotional budget, the promotional mix, the nature and placement of advertising, the identification of high-potential prospects, participation in trade shows, and the list goes on. Rapid changes in technologies and in social behavior mean that companies of all sizes will make promotional errors along the way—and you will, too. Your job is to learn from those mistakes, keep your eyes and ears open for better ways to serve your customers and get the word out about why they should do business with you.

LOOKING BACK

17-1. Describe the communication process and the factors that determine a promotional mix.

- Every communication involves a source, a message, a channel, and a receiver.
- A promotional mix is a blend of nonpersonal, personal, combined, and special forms of communication aimed at a target market.
- A promotional mix is influenced primarily by three important factors: the geographical nature of the market, the size of the promotional budget, and the product's characteristics.

17-2. Explain methods of determining the appropriate level of promotional expenditures.

- Earmarking promotional dollars based on a percentage of sales is a simple method for determining expenditures.
- Spending only what can be spared is a widely used approach to promotional budgeting.
- Spending as much as the competition does is a way to react to short-run promotional tactics of competitors.
- The preferred approach to determining promotional expenditures is to decide what it will take to do the job, while factoring in elements used in the other methods.

17-3. Explain how the Internet and social media are changing promotional practices.

- Companies that fail to recognize how the Internet and social media are changing how people communicate and process information are not likely to prosper.
- Websites should have a descriptive and appealing name and be user-friendly.
- Efforts must be taken to promote websites.

- Search engine optimization is a necessary activity to attract visitors to a small business website.
- Through social networking and microblogging, customers share real-time information about products and services.
- There are many tools available for engaging in marketing and promotion through social media, such as e-mail, reciprocal advertising, hyperlinks, blogs, and apps.
- Small business owners must stay informed of developing and growing social media options, such as quick response (QR) codes.

17-4. Describe personal selling activities.

- Effective selling is based on a salesperson's knowledge of the product or service.
- A sales presentation is a process involving prospecting, practicing the presentation, and then making the presentation.
- Prospecting is the systematic process of continually looking for new customers.
- An entrepreneur is first and foremost a salesperson for the enterprise.
- The most attractive compensation plan for salespeople combines commissions and straight salary.

17-5. Identify advertising options for a small business.

- Common advertising media include television, radio, magazines, newspapers, billboards, and the Internet.
- Product advertising is designed to promote a product or service, while institutional advertising conveys information about the business itself.
- Sources for assistance with advertising include advertising agencies, suppliers, trade associations, and advertising media.
- A small firm must decide how often and where to advertise.

17-6. Discuss the use of sales promotional tools.

- Sales promotion includes any promotional technique, other than personal selling and advertising that stimulates the purchase of a particular product or service.
- Typically, sales promotional tools are used in combination with advertising and personal selling.
- Four widely used sales promotional tools are specialties, trade show exhibits, coupons, and publicity.

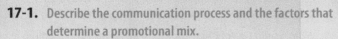

Key Terms

1. Discuss the advantages and disadvantages of each approach to budgeting funds for promotion.

2. What do you need to do to obtain a domain name?

3. What guidelines should you follow in designing your website?

4. If you were opening an office furniture store, how would you select a social networking site to introduce yourself to prospective customers?

5. Outline a system of prospecting that could be used by a health care spa. Incorporate all the techniques presented in this chapter.

6. Assume you have the opportunity to "sell" your course instructor on the idea of eliminating final examinations.

Prepare a sales presentation using the techniques in Exhibit 17.3.

7. What are some nonfinancial rewards that could be offered to salespeople?

8. What are the advantages and disadvantages of compensating salespeople by salary? By commissions? What do you think is an acceptable compromise?

9. What would be your first choice for an advertising medium if you owned a rental car agency? Why?

10. As a college student, what kind of app would be most useful to you—one for buying textbooks, studying socially, finding a place to live, or something else? If you were marketing that app, how could you get free publicity?

You Make the Call

Situation 1

How do you get retailers to stock your product when their shelves are already full? For Brian Levin, founder of Perky Jerky, it meant talking store managers into letting him give his product away. Perky Jerky is a meat snack with a caffeine kick, described on the company's website as "an all natural, ultra premium jerky that is unlike any other!" Perky Jerky "brand ambassadors" give out trinkets and offer customers tastes of the product in stores. They find that those who try the snack ask the stores to carry Perky Jerky. The company also contributes a portion of sales to two causes: Duchenne muscular dystrophy and Down syndrome.

Question 1 What do you think about giving away a product? Does it build sales, or does it suggest desperation?

Question 2 How would you budget for marketing expenses if you had hired sales representatives to give products away?

Question 3 Is it a good idea for businesses to donate to charities? If they do, should they publicize their contributions?

Sources: Based on www.perkyjerky.com, accessed March 2, 2013; and Jason Fell, "Building a (Nearly) Million-Dollar Brand on a Startup Budget," www.entrepreneur.com /article/219395#, accessed March 2, 2013.

Situation 2

Working in pet care and education, Michael Landa realized that he was seeing more and more overweight pets. He started Nulo, Inc., in an effort to turn things around. His strategy to break into the pet food industry, which is dominated by huge corporations, was to launch an online community, giving pet owners a chance

to share information on weight loss and nutrition. Nulo prides itself on offering fresh, simple recipes in small batches with nutritionally rich ingredients. The company stays active on Facebook, Twitter, and YouTube. It was the official pet food company for the 2012 Emmy Awards.

Question 1 If you were starting a company in an industry with large competitors, what steps would you take to prepare your advertising budget?

Question 2 If Lando had come to you for advice, what would you have told him about building an online community?

Question 3 Can Nulo's online community be sustained? What kinds of information should the company be sharing on its website?

Sources: Based on http://nulo.com/, accessed March 3, 2013; and Gwen Moran, "Build Up Your Pack," *Entrepreneur*, Vol. 39, No. 4 (2011), p. 48.

Situation 3

On the company website, Birchbox is labeled "the leading discovery commerce platform." Founded by Hayley Barna and Katia Beauchamp, the company is an e-commerce venture specializing in beauty, grooming, and lifestyle products, with a subscription-based marketing strategy. Each month, subscribers receive samples in a mix of categories, determined by a profile that subscribers complete. Birchbox lists their business partners on a brand page on their website. If subscribers like the products they sample, they can then purchase more through Birchbox. The company has a point system that enables subscribers to enjoy discounts and other benefits. As one subscriber expressed it,

"They send products I wouldn't necessarily spend money on, but once I get them, I realize I really like them."

Question 1 What risks are Barna and Beauchamp taking by giving away samples every month?

Question 2 If you owned a beauty product company, would you partner with Birchbox to market your products? Why or why not?

Question 3 What questions would you want to ask Birchbox before signing up to pay the subscription fee?

Sources: Based on www.birchbox.com, accessed March 2, 2013; and Suzy Evans, *Fast Company*, No. 152 (2011), p. 35.

Experiential Exercises

1. Interview the owners of one or more small businesses to determine how they develop their promotional budget. Classify the owners' methods as one or more of the four approaches described in this chapter. Report your findings to the class.

2. Evaluate the promotional effectiveness of the website for one of the companies described in this chapter.

3. Read one of the blog postings on HubSpot's website (www.hubspot.com). If you wanted customers to come to your website, would the blog make you want to know more about what HubSpot can do for you?

4. Plan a sales presentation. With a classmate role-playing a potential buyer, make the presentation in class. Ask the other students to critique your technique.

5. Interview a media representative about advertising options for small businesses. Summarize your findings for the class.

Small Business & Entrepreneurship Resource Center

The Small Business & Entrepreneurship Resource Center offers complete small business management resources through a comprehensive database that covers all major areas of starting, operating, and maintaining a business from financing, management, marketing, accounting, taxes, and more. Go to www.cengagebrain.com and select the Longenecker text for more information on how to access this material.

1. Can you convey the essence of your restaurant or a signature menu item in six seconds? That's a creative challenge posed by Vine, the free iPhone-based application, an offshoot of 500-million-member Twitter that adds sound and moving pictures to the microblogging experience. Big players already have jumped onto the social media platform, which Twitter recently debuted. Taco Bell used Vine for the introduction of its Cool Ranch Doritos Locos Tacos. How does this microblogging experience inspire creativity, express a brand's personality, and showcase product attributes? Is microblogging good for business-development? Why?

2. CareerConnections helps employment professionals find and hire qualified candidates by merging mobile technology and social media with traditional recruiting tactics such as print and radio ads. Virtual Job Fairs provide a low-cost, high-impact means of reaching the best prospects. Through the strategic combination of emerging and established techniques, CareerConnections mobilizes the attention of employed, experienced candidates and ignites the interest of passive job seekers. After reading this article, evaluate the use of mixing traditional recruitment tactics with social media. What are the pros and cons of a virtual job fair? Would you look for a job in this manner? Explain.

Sources: Based on Ron Ruggless, "Microblogging Gets Animated with Vine," *Nation's Restaurant News*, Vol. 47, No. 4 (February 25, 2013), p. 46; "Online Job Service: CareerConnections LLC," *Business Plans Handbook*, Michelle Lee (ed.), (Detroit: Gale, 2012).

Video Case 17

HUBSPOT, INC. (P. 680)

HubSpot is an Internet marketing company that caters to small businesses. It used to be that the size of your firm's sales force was the key to finding new customers, but that is not necessarily the case today, thanks to the Internet.

Alternative Case for Chapter 17

Video Case 14, Numi Tea, p. 674

Endnotes

1. Eve Mayer Orsburn, *The Social Media Business Equation* (Boston: Cengage Learning, 2012), p. 3.

2. Samuel Greengard, "Adagio Teas Steeps Its Product Development in Customer Feedback," *Entrepreneur*, Vol. 40, No. 6 (June 2012), p. 70.

3. Inside CRM, "The 20 Worst Venture Capital Investments of All Time," www.insidecrm.com/articles/crm-blog/the-20-worst-venture-capital-investments-of-all-time-53532, accessed February 3, 2012.

4. www.pewinternet.org, accessed February 23, 2013.

5. www.register.com, accessed February 9, 2013; www.domainnamesystems.com, accessed February 9, 2013; and www.101domain.com, accessed February 10, 2013.

6. http://wordpress.com, accessed February 10, 2013.

7. Ron Jackson, "Estate.com Changes Hands in the 2nd Biggest Sale of the New Year to Top This Week's Sales Chart," www.dnjournal.com/domainsles.htm, accessed February 10, 2013.

8. www.styleowner.com, accessed February 10, 2013; and Kara Ohngren "Personal Shopping," *Entrepreneur*, Vol. 40, No. 3 (2012), p. 80.

9. Brian Halligan and Dharmesh Shah, *Inbound Marketing: Get Found Using Google, Social Media, and Blogs* (Hoboken, NJ: John Wiley & Sons, 2009), pp. 12–13.

10. http://go.com, accessed February 10, 2013.

11. An extensive list of search engines with brief descriptions can be found at www.thesearchenginelist.com.

12. Intuit Websites, "How Small Businesses Use Social Media," www.intuit.com/websites/small-business-social-media-infographic, accessed February 24, 2013.

13. www.greyskyfilms.com/Meet-the-Team.htm, accessed February 24, 2013.

14. Gwen Moran, "The Risks of Oversharing," *Entrepreneur*, Vol. 39, No. 3 (2011), p. 60.

15. Econsultancy, "Email Marketing Census 2012," http://econsultancy.com/fi/reports/email-census, accessed February 24, 2013.

16. "Email Marketing Effectiveness," http://infographicsmania.com/email-marketing-is-alive-and-well, accessed February 24, 2013.

17. Federal Trade Commission, "CAN-Spam Act: A Compliance Guide for Business," http://business.ftc.gov/documents/bus61-can-spam-act-compliance-guide-business, accessed February 24, 2013.

18. www.techterms.com/definition/hyperlink, accessed February 24, 2013.

19. Personal interview with Mike Volpe, January 18, 2011.

20. Halligan and Shah, *op. cit.*, pp. 35–36.

21. Pew Research Center, "Tablet and E-book Reader Ownership Nearly Double over the Holiday Gift-Giving Period," http://libraries.pewinternet.org/2012/01/23/tablet-and-e-book-reader-ownership-nearly-double-over-the-holiday-gift-giving-period, accessed February 28, 2013.

22. Design Reviver, "8 Ways to Make Your Website Mobile Friendly," http://designreviver.com/tips/8-ways-to-make-your-website-mobile-friendly, accessed February 28, 2013; and Jennifer Kyrnin, "Writing a Mobile Friendly Website," http://webdesign.about.com/od/mobile/a/write-a-mobile-friendly-website.htm, accessed February 28, 2013.

23. Mike the Gardener Enterprises, https://averagepersongardening.com/seedsclub/step_2.php, accessed March 1, 2013; Gwen Moran, "Creative Code Concepts," *Entrepreneur*, Vol. 40, No. 3 (2013), p. 43; and "QR (Quick Response) Codes," www.prepressure.com/library/technology/qr-code, accessed March 1, 2013.

24. Esther Hormiga, Rosa M. Batista-Canino, and Agustín Sánchez-Medina, "The Impact of Relational Capital on the Success of New Business Start-Ups," *Journal of Small Business Management*, Vol. 49, No. 4 (2011), pp. 617–638; and Donna Marie De Carolis, Barrie E. Litzky, and Kimberly A. Eddleston, "Why Networks Enhance the Progress of New Venture Creation: The Influence of Social Capital and Cognition," *Entrepreneurship Theory and Practice*, Vol. 33, No. 2 (2009), pp. 527–545.

25. www.yelp.com/about, accessed February 8, 2013.

26. Dawn S. Carlson, Nancy Upton, and Samuel Seaman, "The Impact of Human Resource Practices and Compensation Design on Performance: An Analysis of Family-Owned SMEs," *Journal of Small Business Management*, Vol. 44, No. 4 (2006), pp. 531–543; and José L. Barbero, José C. Casillas, and Howard D. Feldman, "Managerial Capabilities and Paths to Growth as Determinants of High-Growth Small and Medium-Sized Enterprises," *International Small Business Journal*, Vol. 29, No. 6 (2011), pp. 671–694.

27. www.shopperschoice.com, accessed February 9, 2013; and Kasey Wehrum, "Run Cheap TV Commercials with Google TV Ads," www.inc.com/magazine/20090601/run-cheap-tv-commercials-with-google-tv-ads.html?nav=river. Accessed February 9, 2013.

28. "Definition of Sales Promotion," http://drypen.in/sales-promotion/definition-of-sales-promotion.html, accessed March 1, 2013.

29. Jack Aaronson, "Foursquare—Mixing Social Networks with Loyalty Programs," www.clickz.com/clickz/column/1711467/foursquare-mixing-social-networks-with-loyalty-programs, accessed April 2, 2011; and https://foursquare.com/about, accessed March 1, 2013.

30. Janet Attard, "Trade Show Dos and Don'ts," www.businessknow how.com, accessed March 1, 2013; and David Lavenda, "10 Ways to Make Sure Your Trade Show Isn't a Bust," www.fastcompany.com/1841035/10-ways-make-sure-your-trade-show-isnt-bust, accessed March 1, 2013.

31. www.couponcompany.co.za/About_Coupons_History.html, accessed March 1, 2013; and http://digsitevalue.net/k/history-of-coupons, accessed March 1, 2013.

32. Rajkumar Venkatesan and Paul Farris, "Unused Coupons Still Pay Off," *Harvard Business Review*, May 2012, p. 32.

33. www.groupon.com/about, accessed March 1, 2013; and Jolie O'Dell, "The History of Groupon," www.forbes.com/sites/mashable/2011/01/07/the-history-of-groupon/, accessed March 1, 2013.

34. Javier Espinoza, "Making the Most of Groupon," *The Wall Street Journal*, August 22, 2011, p. R6; and Gwen Moran, "Sealing the Deal-Seekers," *Entrepreneur*, Vol. 40, No. 6 (2012), p. 77.

35. www.hubspot.com/internet-marketing-company/press-room, accessed March 1, 2013.

36. Robert Fishbone, *Selling the Scream* (St. Louis, MO: On the Wall Publications, 2009); and www.robertfishbone.com/meet.html, accessed March 1, 2013.

© Alliance/Shutterstock.com

Global Opportunities for Small Businesses

As time goes on, more and more entrepreneurs are recognizing that going global—sometimes from the start—may be the best path for a new business.

That certainly has been true for Abe Fetterman and Lisa Qiu, inventors of a new cooking appliance for amateur chefs. Nomiku, an inversion circulator, can be used to cook *sous-vide*—that is, to cook meats and vegetables in sealed bags by submerging them in a water bath that is raised to a precisely controlled temperature. Gadget critics say the new product promises to deliver "perfectly

In the SPOTLIGHT
Nomiku.com
www.Nomiku.com

cooked meals, every time, with less fuss than you would expect."

For a long time, hardware-based startups like Nomiku had a hard time getting market traction, but that is definitely changing. In recent years, countless such companies have been launched. Opportunities to shift operations overseas have greatly reduced the cost of bringing products to market, which is enormously important to cash-strapped new ventures.

As some have observed, the new business plan is to "raise enough money to create prototypes in the U.S. that can be manufactured in Asia and sold online." Fetterman and Qiu raised more than $580,000 on Kickstarter and hope to snag additional seed funding soon.

© Nomiku

OPEN
LOOKING
AHEAD

After studying this chapter, you should be able to...

18-1. Describe the potential of small firms as global enterprises.

18-2. Identify the basic forces prompting small firms to engage in global expansion.

18-3. Understand and compare strategy options for global businesses.

18-4. Explain the challenges that global enterprises face.

18-5. Recognize the sources of assistance available to support international business efforts.

As mentioned in Chapter 15, the cost of developing prototypes has been dropping quickly, thanks to 3-D printers, and incubators are now providing more-than-affordable machine tools that can help to complete the process without breaking the bank. This is good news for hardware-based startups that have to squeeze all they can get from the limited investment funds they raise.

Offshoring production is crucial to cost-sensitive small companies, but getting set up overseas can be a challenge. Fortunately, assistance is available to match new firms with the manufacturing support they need in low-cost locations like China and Mexico. Selling products online, the final component of the new business model, is an activity in which small companies already shine. Internet selling allows even the tiniest of firms to reach markets in every corner of the world. From so many angles, the new venture picture is becoming an international one.

"We've thrown everything to the wind to commit to this," says Qiu. But the effort is paying off in the form of forward progress. The San Francisco couple invested $20,000 to develop a prototype of their innovative appliance, and they are already lining up production overseas. They are even taking advanced orders for anyone who wants to give Nomiku a try—as long as that person is willing to pay $359 for the privilege.

Sources: Pui-Wing Tam and Jessica A. Vascellaro, "Forget the Web, Start-Ups Get Real," *The Wall Street Journal*, August 18, 2012, p. B1; www.nomiku.com, accessed January 8, 2013; and http://uncrate.com/stuff/nomiku, accessed January 8, 2013.

For many small businesses, going global is essential to the long-term health and performance of the company. There was a time when national economies were isolated by trade and investment barriers, differences in language and culture, distinctive business practices, and various government regulations. However, these dissimilarities are fading over time as market preferences converge, trade barriers fall, and national economies integrate to form a global economic system. This process is the essence of **globalization**. Though the trend toward convergence tapered off during the recent economic slowdown, increasing globalization is still the norm, creating many new opportunities and competitors that did not exist even a few years ago. And with the astounding rate of economic growth in countries such as China and India, a small business owner would be unwise to ignore overseas opportunities.

As you read in the pages that follow about the challenges of international business and the many decisions that are involved in expanding abroad, you may become convinced that becoming a global entrepreneur is not for you. This is a normal reaction. But the opportunities are tremendously rewarding, and available resources can help you overcome any obstacles that may stand in your way. Later in this chapter, you will read about the numerous forms of assistance that can help you achieve your global ambitions. As you will see, many small businesses are showing that it can be done. You can do it, too!

LO 18-1

Describe the potential of small firms as global enterprises.

18-1 SMALL BUSINESSES AS GLOBAL ENTERPRISES

The potential of a global business is clear, but does that potential extend to small companies?[1] Research has shown that recent startups and even the smallest of businesses continue to expand overseas, despite the recent global economic slowdown.[2] In fact, many small companies, often called **born-global firms**,[3] are being launched with cross-border business activities in mind.[4] You are probably familiar with Skype, which was acquired by Microsoft in 2011. In 2003, the company was just a startup, and it was clearly an international business right from the beginning.

[Niklas] Zennstrom, who is Swedish, and his partner Janus Friis, a Dane, launched their Internet telephony company Skype in Luxembourg, with sales

globalization
The expansion of international business, encouraged by converging market preferences, falling trade barriers, and the integration of national economies.

born-global firms
Small companies launched with cross-border business activities in mind.

offices in London. But they outsourced product development to Estonia, the same fertile womb that had earlier gestated their music-sharing system, Kazaa.[5]

As illustrated in Exhibit 18.1, most of the firms on *Inc.* magazine's list of the 500 fastest-growing private companies have set up shop in various countries around the world, from Canada to New Zealand.

As global communication systems become more efficient and trade agreements pry open national markets to foreign competition, entrepreneurs are focusing more and more on international expansion opportunities. In some cases, they may be forced to enter foreign markets in order to compete with firms in their industry that have already done so.[6] But the research is clear: Size does not necessarily limit a firm's international activity. Small companies can build upon their unique resources to become global competitors.[7]

For some, the global option is practically unavoidable. For example, when Howard Pedolsky began to market his innovative, eco-friendly refrigeration technology, he found that European supermarkets were far more interested in it than were their American counterparts. It turned out that their attraction was the result of strict European standards, so Pedolsky realized that he would need to focus on developing a customer base in Europe first: "The European environment was just much stronger in our direction, and [supermarkets there] tend to spend more money on our products."[8]

The fact that many firms are going global does not mean that it is easy. The challenges that small businesses face in the international marketplace are considerable. First, a small business owner must decide whether the company is up to the task. To help entrepreneurs assess the impact of going global on

EXHIBIT

18.1   Where in the World Are Entrepreneurial Companies Doing Business?

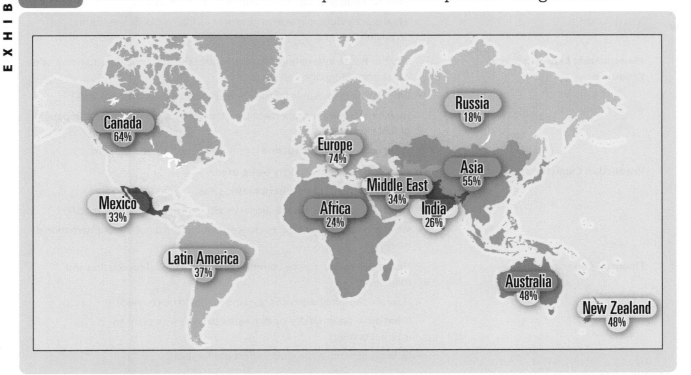

Source: Based on Issie Lapowsky, "Planting the Flag," *Inc.*, Vol. 33, No. 7 (September 2011), pp. 148–149.

their small business, the U.S. Department of Commerce publishes *A Basic Guide to Exporting.* This handbook outlines important questions entrepreneurs should consider when assessing their readiness for the challenges of global business (see Exhibit 18.2).

Once small business owners decide to expand internationally, they should study the social, technological, economic, and political forces in foreign markets to figure out how best to adapt their business practices, as well as their product or service, to local circumstances, and make other adjustments that are necessary to ensure smooth market entry. For example, doing business in the Middle East can require significant changes in what many small business owners would consider to be "standard business procedures."

> *In Saudi Arabia, the workweek begins on Saturday and ends on Wednesday, appointments are generally scheduled around five daily prayer times, and many businesses are closed in the afternoon. Most real business is conducted face to face, with far less reliance on documents and contracts than is typical in the Western world; therefore, the time it takes to do business is relative.*[9]

And that's just the beginning! When you consider that collecting or paying interest is forbidden in many Islamic states—along with a host of other fundamental differences—it becomes clear that navigating the unique hurdles of an international market like Saudi Arabia can be a serious challenge.

EXHIBIT 18.2 Questions to Consider Before Going Global

Management Objectives	• What are the company's reasons for going global? • How committed is top management to going global? • How quickly does management expect its international operations to pay off?
Management Experience and Resources	• What in-house international expertise does the firm have (international sales experience, language skills, etc.)? • Who will be responsible for the company's international operations? • How much senior management time should be allocated to the company's global efforts? • What organizational structure is required to ensure success abroad?
Production Capacity	• How is the present capacity being used? • Will international sales hurt domestic sales? • What will be the cost of additional production at home and abroad? • What product designs and packaging options are required for international markets?
Financial Capacity	• How much capital can be committed to international production and marketing? • How are the initial expenses of going global to be covered? • What other financial demands might compete with plans to internationalize? • By what date must the global effort pay for itself?

Source: Adapted from International Trade Administration, *A Basic Guide to Exporting: The Official Government Resource for Small- and Medium-Sized Businesses,* as cited in John B. Cullen and K. Praveen Parboteeah, *Multinational Management: A Strategic Approach,* 6th ed. (Cincinnati, OH: Cengage Learning, 2013), p. 256.

ENTREPRENEURIAL EXPERIENCES

Living the Dream

Going Global Has Its Downsides

As a partner in the Cambridge, Massachusetts–based, early-stage investment firm Atlas Capital, Ryan Moore has worked closely with entrepreneurs to help them shape their companies into promising ventures that reach some of the farthest corners of the world. He offers important words of caution to help entrepreneurs avoid some of the landmines they might encounter when they go abroad.

- When people from multiple continents work together to bring a project to fruition, they can't partake in the informal "water cooler" discussions that often build a team, making it stronger and able to push through some of the difficulties. Management has to find a way to pull these diverse teams together.
- There may be significant labor savings from going abroad, but they must be balanced against the management complexities of productivity and efficiency. The work ethics and practices of Asian countries are much different from those of North America and different still from those of the Europeans.
- The "28-hour day" (working across multiple time zones) is great, but holidays in all countries must be added to the operating schedule if a company is to avoid delays.
- The product is vitally important to startups. But when the design team is not aligned with the customer, culturally or otherwise, it increases the chances of disconnect, resulting in a product miss instead of a hit.
- Many countries have local labor retention challenges. Be aware of this before any sites are selected.

The location you choose will affect your ability to retain staff.
- An entrepreneur's sense of urgency in getting a business off the ground must be adjusted for the longer learning curve that is typical in international business. It can take more time to start making money.
- The ability to downsize can be costly, difficult, or seemingly impossible in some countries due to national or regional labor laws and regulations.

These and other pitfalls of going global are very real, and they can present serious headaches to the small business owner. But the good news is that the challenges are manageable, and the abundant opportunities are nearly out of this world.

© Tischenko Irina/Shutterstock.com

Source: Adapted from Darlene Flaig, "The Challenges and Opportunities of Going Global," *WPI Venture Forum Newsletter*, Vol. 20, No. 7 (March 2011), pp. 4–5.

18-2 THE FORCES DRIVING GLOBAL BUSINESSES

Given the difficulty of international business, why would any entrepreneur want to go global? Among the reasons are some that have motivated international trade for centuries. In 1271, Marco Polo traveled to China to explore the trading of Western goods for exotic Oriental silks and spices, which would then be sold in

LO
18-2

Identify the basic forces prompting small firms to engage in global expansion.

Chapter 18 Global Opportunities for Small Businesses

477

Europe. Clearly, the motivation to take domestic products to foreign markets and bring foreign products to domestic markets is as relevant today as it was in Marco Polo's day. Consider, for example, the clothing designer who sells Western wear in Tokyo or the independent rug dealer who scours the markets of Turkey to locate low-cost sources of high-quality products.

Complementing these traditional reasons for going global are motivations that epitomize the core of entrepreneurial drive. A writer for *Inc.* magazine describes the impulse to go global as follows: "Because it's what entrepreneurs do.... Globalization is risky. Entrepreneurs embrace risk. Therefore entrepreneurs embrace globalization.... [T]he chance to try new things in new places is like a jumper cable to the entrepreneurial engine."[10] In other words, many entrepreneurs are looking to do more than simply expand a profitable market. They also recognize that their enterprises are no longer insulated from global challengers and that they must consider the dynamics of the new competitive environment.[11]

One way to adjust to these emerging realities is through innovation, which is essential to competitiveness in many industries. Small businesses that invest heavily in research and development often can outperform their large competitors. But as R&D costs rise, they seldom can be recouped from domestic sales alone. Increasing sales in international markets may be the only viable way to recover a firm's investment. In some cases, this may require identifying dynamic markets that are beginning to open around the world and then locating in or near those markets.[12]

The basic forces behind global expansion can be divided into four general categories: expanding markets, gaining access to resources, cutting costs, and capitalizing on special features of location. Within each category fall some tried and true motivations, as well as some newer angles that have emerged with the global economy.

18-2a Expanding Markets

More than 95 percent of the world's population lives outside the United States, so it follows that globalization greatly increases the size of an American firm's potential market. One study of small companies found that their primary interest in internationalization was in accessing new markets and growing their business, as opposed to seeking resources abroad, gaining access to technologies, and avoiding regulatory pressures at home.[13] This study focused on the expansion of U.S. firms into Europe; the primary motivation for involvement in other parts of the world may be different. For example, it could very well be that most U.S. small companies doing business in Asia are seeking access to low-cost component sources or to relocate business processes via outsourcing.

COUNTRIES TARGETED Because the primary motivation for going global is to develop market opportunities outside the home country, the focus of globalization strategies tends to be on countries with the greatest commercial potential. In the past, these were the developed countries (those with high levels of widely distributed wealth). Today, companies are paying greater attention to emerging markets, where income and buying power are growing rapidly.

The term *BRICs* is often used to refer to the fast-growing economies of Brazil, Russia, India, and China. These markets have definitely captured the attention of many entrepreneurs. And that interest seems to be growing, as mainstay markets like Europe, Japan, and the United States continue to struggle with economic stagnation while China and India, in particular, continue to mount impressive recoveries (see Exhibit 18.3). The smaller BRIC countries, Russia and Brazil, have also been doing well (despite Brazil's downturn in 2012), but have not enjoyed the same level of growth and vigor as China and India.

18.3 BRIC Markets

Country	2011 Population (in millions)	2011 Wealth (GNI per capital)*	2011 Economic Growth (GDP growth, %)**
Brazil	196.7	10,720	2.7
China	1,334.1	4,940	9.3
India	1,241.5	1,410	6.9
Russia	141.9	10,400	4.3
World	**6,973.7**	**9,491**	**2.7**

*GNI = Gross National Income
**GDP = Gross Domestic Product

Source: From data provided by the World Bank Group, "WorlddataBank," http://databank.worldbank.org, accessed January 8, 2013.

Because of their immense populations and potential market demand, China and India have become the focus of many international firms. Combined, these two nations account for an astounding 40 percent of the world's six billion inhabitants, thus providing fertile ground for international expansion. And small companies are among the countless competitors battling for position in these emerging markets, with some maintaining a second office in those countries.

PRODUCTS PROMOTED International business authority Raymond Vernon observed in the mid-1960s that firms tended to introduce new products in the United States first and then sell them in less-advanced countries later, as demand in the home market declined.[14] In other words, they were using international expansion to extend a product's life cycle. Although this approach is effective under some circumstances, it has become less viable as customer preferences, income levels, and delivery systems have become more similar and product life cycles have contracted.

Today, products that sell at home are more likely to be introduced very quickly abroad, with little or no adaptation in many cases. Television programs, movies, print media, and the Internet are shaping cultural tastes throughout the world, and this is facilitating the entry of small businesses into international markets. American interests have long held a starring role in the cultural arena, inspiring widespread purchases of products such as blue jeans and fast food, and generating international interest in U.S. sports and celebrities. By informing consumers about the lifestyles of others, globalization is leading the world toward more common consumer preferences.

Highly specialized products are also well suited to international markets. As technology makes possible increasingly sophisticated goods, markets are demanding more differentiated products to satisfy their unique needs and interests. Expanded sales allow the makers of such products to recover the higher costs of product development. Many small companies follow focused business strategies, despite limited domestic market potential. For them, exploiting the advantage of specialized products across several international markets may be even more important than for their large corporate counterparts.[15]

MAKING THE MOST OF EXPERIENCE No matter which countries are targeted or products promoted, international expansion has the potential to provide benefits beyond the standard per-unit profits on additional items sold. As a venture expands and volume grows, it usually can find ways to work smarter or to generate efficiencies. Analysts first observed such **experience curve efficiencies** in the aircraft

experience curve efficiencies
Per-unit savings gained from the repeated production of the same product.

manufacturing industry. They noticed that each time a manufacturer doubled its total output, the production cost per aircraft dropped by 20 percent. In other words, per-unit costs declined by 20 percent when the firm manufactured four units instead of two, declined again by 20 percent when the firm made eight units instead of four, and so on.

What can explain this gain in efficiency? Most credit the outcome to learning effects and economies of scale. **Learning effects** occur when the insight an employee gains from experience leads to improved work performance. Learning effects can also take place at the level of the firm if the experiences of individual employees are shared, leading to improved practices and production routines across the organization. These gains from learning are greatest during the startup period and gradually decline over time. Efficiencies from **economies of scale**, on the other hand, continue to rise as the business grows and volume increases, because these savings derive from spreading investment costs across more units of output and acquiring more specialized (and thus more efficient) plants, equipment, and employees.

Though these also apply to purely domestic enterprises, small firms can accelerate gains from experience curve efficiencies by emphasizing international expansion, assuming they can manage the growth. The benefits of learning effects and economies of scale are especially apparent in startups based on complex technologies. The possibility of achieving experience curve efficiencies through accelerated globalization of emerging technologies is likely to stimulate the interest of startups and small companies in doing business abroad.

18-2b Gaining Access to Resources

Small firms today may leave the United States to gain access to essential raw materials and other factors of production. For example, the oil fields of Kuwait are tended not only by employees of global oil giants but also by hundreds of support personnel who work for small companies that have contracted to assist their large clients. These small players choose to locate operations in Kuwait (or Mexico, Nigeria, Saudi Arabia, etc.) for one simple reason: That's where the oil is! The same principle holds for manufacturers that require scarce inputs. For example, a number of aluminum producers have relocated to Iceland to tap the country's abundant and inexpensive hydroelectric and geothermal energy.[16]

Though small firms have traditionally pursued international ventures to obtain raw materials, increasingly the focus of their search is skilled labor.[17] For example, a rising number of technology companies are relocating their operations in Russia to get access to the people they need. Despite the fact that the installation of a telephone can take several months and crime bosses sometimes pay visits to demand protection money, these firms are lured to Russia by its highly educated human capital, a necessary resource that is in short supply in the United States. Of the 43 percent of Russians with university degrees, about a third are trained in science- or technology-related disciplines and thus are very well suited for highly skilled jobs. As something of a bonus for small firms, computer programmers and information technology professionals in Russia earn about 55 percent less than their American counterparts.[18]

There is no question that skilled labor around the world is within the reach of startups and other very small businesses. Consider Efrem Meretab, an Eritrean-born stock analyst who started his own investment research venture to offer PowerConnect, an investment research tool that can mine and compare information from thousands of company reports and pull it instantly into an analysis that can inform and guide investment decisions.[19] His company, MCAP Research LLC, has been able to harness the power of the Internet to find and hire employees around the globe. For example, when Meretab needed software developers to create PowerConnect, he linked back to

learning effects
Insights, gained from experience, that lead to improved work performance.

economies of scale
Efficiencies that result from expansion of production.

programmers with whom he had worked in the past, including talented coders living in far-off countries like Belarus, Ukraine, and Pakistan. These contract workers were able to get the job done, and at a very reasonable cost.[20] Of course, small businesses that take this approach don't do much for job creation in the United States, but they are still important new enterprises—and they are becoming more common as time goes on.

18-2c Cutting Costs

Many firms go global to reduce the costs of doing business. Among the costs that firms have traditionally reduced by venturing abroad are those related to raw materials, labor, and manufacturing overhead.

While some startups are launching as global enterprises, other small businesses are shifting their operations over time to international markets in order to exploit the same advantages. In fact, American businesses of all sizes have been slashing costs by contracting with independent providers overseas (an arrangement called **international outsourcing**) or by relocating their stateside operations abroad (which is sometimes referred to as **offshoring**). These initiatives have been especially popular in countries such as India and China, where high-skilled labor can be accessed at relatively little cost.[21]

Some of the most creative examples of international outsourcing have been spawned by entrepreneurial companies. Dorothy Clay Sims, a Florida attorney who often has to cross-examine medical experts, started a company called MD in a Box to provide access to highly qualified doctors who can serve as expert witnesses in legal proceedings. The creative twist in Sims's venture is that her experts offer their insights by long distance—*from India!* Here's how it works: An attorney in the United States deposes the opposing counsel's medical expert while a doctor in India listens in via Skype. The Indian doctor sends instant messages with suggested responses for the attorney, who can then refute the doctor being cross-examined, using correct medical terms in the process. Such expert advice would typically costs $500 to $1,000 per hour in the United States, but Sims hired a stable of Indian medical experts who get $20 to $35 an hour for their services. Indian doctors typically earn around $11,000 a year in their practices, so they are pleased with the extra income. MD in a Box charges $75 an hour ($200 per hour if the case is won), leaving Sims with a hefty profit.[22]

The business concept developed by Sims may be far from ordinary, but in a way it fits the common outsourcing pattern precisely. Most entrepreneurs who choose to outsource internationally, or relocate offshore, are seeking two things that are always important to the success of small companies: access to talented employees and/or reduced costs. MD in a Box provides both.

The advantages of globalization in reducing labor costs have long been recognized. However, in recent years a number of countries have formed regional free trade areas, within which commerce has been facilitated by reducing tariffs, simplifying commercial regulations, or even—in the case of the European Union—adopting a common currency. These cost-cutting measures can be a powerful inducement to small firms to move into the prescribed area. Since the enactment of the North American Free Trade Agreement (NAFTA), for instance, many foreign firms have chosen to locate production facilities in Mexico to take advantage of reduced tariffs on trade within that region and easy access to the American market.

international outsourcing
A strategy that involves accessing foreign business operations through contracts with independent providers.

offshoring
A strategy that involves relocating operations abroad.

18-2d Capitalizing on Special Features of Location

Some of the benefits of location are simply the result of unique features of a local environment. For example, Italian artisans have long been well known for their flair for design, and Japanese technicians have shown an ability to harness optical technologies for application in cameras, copiers, and other related products. Small companies that depend on a particular strength or resource often find that it makes sense to set up in a region that provides the best location for that type of business. This would explain why one Korean entrepreneur opened his chopstick-making company in Americus, Georgia (in the U.S.), where abundant supplies of wood allow him to shave 20 percent off his costs when compared to production in China.[23]

In some cases, there is no way to be authentic apart from being local. Josh Pollock, along with his Japanese wife and two of their American friends, found that the Western food in China was absolutely dreadful, but locals were still eating it up. So, in 2004, with $40,000 in investment money, they started Salvador's Food and Beverage Co., Ltd. In a coffee house in Kunming (a city of more than four million inhabitants), they now offer Western products—including ice cream, bagels and cream cheese, and Mexican food—to local customers.[24]

The way forward has not always been easy, and the team has had much to learn. Early on they ran into a bureaucratic brick wall, which required the outsiders to turn to a common practice in China—building their *guanxi*, or personal connections—to get the government approvals they needed.[25] Though still young, the enterprise has been wonderfully successful, which has led to yet other business opportunities, including consulting with local or international companies that want to establish a successful enterprise in China. For a reasonable fee, the Salvador's team will show you the ropes of doing business in China, a service that is based on first-hand experience and legitimate only as a result of being in-country.

Sometimes, the appeal of a location is a matter of cache or brand image. For example, while Chanel might like to manufacture its designer handbags in China to reduce costs, the company insists on producing them in Italy and France. These are both high-cost countries, but they have reputations that match Chanel's luxury image. These nations also have developed unique competencies, honed by hundreds of years of experience, that can accommodate the advanced designs and high quality that give the company its edge. Customers know that the high quality of the brand is scrupulously protected and thus are willing to pay a premium to buy Chanel's products, which covers the high manufacturing costs. But this is just one example. Other country settings provide their own location-specific strengths—including Colombia (high-quality coffee), Japan (anime-based video games), and Switzerland (precision watches)—and firms locate there to tap into those strengths.

Finally, small businesses are following large client firms to their new locations. As major corporations locate their operations abroad, their small suppliers find it necessary to go global with the client firms to ensure the continuation of important sourcing contracts. A small business owner may have no personal desire to expand internationally, but dependence on a major customer relocating abroad might leave the owner with no alternative.

So, some small companies moving into China are doing so with limited interest in the country's cheap labor and enormous market. Being there is necessary in order to provide corporate customers with ample delivery speed and efficiency.[26]

Small companies are sometimes pulled toward doing business abroad because of the unique advantages that are available in international locations.

© AIMSTOCK/iStockphoto.com

Traditional and emerging motivations for small businesses to go global are numerous, but the ultimate incentive is this: If you fail to seize an international market opportunity, someone else will. Under these conditions, the best defense is a good offense. Establishing a position outside of the domestic setting may preempt rivals from exploiting those opportunities and using them against you in the future.

18-3 STRATEGY OPTIONS FOR GLOBAL FIRMS

Once an entrepreneur has decided to go global, the next step is to plan a strategy that increases the potential of the firm. For most small businesses, the first step toward globalization is a decision to export a product to other countries or to import goods from abroad to sell in the market at home. These initial efforts are often followed by more sophisticated nonexport strategies, such as licensing, franchising, forming strategic alliances with international partners, or even locating facilities abroad.

LO 18-3
Understand and compare strategy options for global businesses.

18-3a Exporting

Exporting involves the sale of products produced in the home country to customers in another country. The U.S. Small Business Administration (SBA) recently announced that small firms represent more than 97 percent of American exporters, contributing 31 percent of the value of exported goods.[27] In some cases, this activity is a reflection of the reality of international competition. That is, some U.S. companies are steadily moving toward overseas markets because they recognize that foreign-owned companies are already competing against them in the United States. The SBA describes conditions in today's global marketplace as follows:

> *The division between domestic and international markets is becoming increasingly blurred. In a world of over 6 billion people, global communication networks, next-day airfreight deliveries worldwide and CNN, it no longer makes sense to limit your company's sales to the local or even to the national market. Your business cannot ignore these international realities if you intend to maintain your market share and keep pace with your competitors.*[28]

As the SBA statistics reveal, entrepreneurs are taking note and accepting the challenge. In fact, exporting is one of the most popular international strategies among small businesses because it provides a low-cost way to expand into the international arena. Taking this approach, small export companies can market and distribute their products in other countries without incurring the expense of supporting costly operations in those markets. If the financial benefits from international sales more than offset shipping costs and tariffs, exporting is a favorable option.

The Internet has fueled vigorous growth in export activity. Small firms now see the Web as a powerful tool for increasing their international visibility, allowing them to connect with customers who were previously beyond their reach. Entertainment Earth is an Internet retailer, started in 1995, that specializes in action figures, gifts, and other collectibles. It wasn't long before the founders decided to expand their reach by selling over the Internet, and the move has really paid off.[29] To date, Entertainment Earth has sold collectibles to hundreds of thousands of clients all around the world.

But you don't have to go it alone. Just ask Jeff Nipert, owner of CarAlarmsEtc. The venture specializes in mobile electronics—specifically, car alarms, keyless entry units, remote starters, and other related accessories. Although Nipert's company is just a small operation, the world is his sales floor. How did he manage to go global? In a word, eBay. The online marketplace giant can help the tiniest of businesses connect

exporting
Selling products produced in the home country to customers in another country.

with customers anywhere in the world, and getting started takes about as much time as it would to apply for a passport! And consider this: Of the sales revenue eBay generates, more than half comes from outside the United States—and that part of the business is growing much faster than the U.S. segment! Nipert concluded, "I felt if it wasn't costing me a dime extra for the [worldwide] exposure, I would be a fool not to take advantage of it."[30] To find out more about support services offered to eBay sellers, check out the firm's "Selling Internationally" tutorial.

Of course, exporting can be very challenging. Suddenly, you have to worry about communicating in a language other than English, translating payments into other currencies, and setting up international shipping. Products may have to be modified to meet government standards or the unique interests of buyers abroad, poor government connections may very well put your company at a great disadvantage in negotiations, and unfavorable exchange rates can make it difficult or even impossible to offer products at competitive prices and still make a profit. In some countries, the government may not allow a company to enter its market unless it is willing to reveal the specifics of its core technologies, which are often the bedrock of its competitive advantage.

Nonetheless, export success is within the reach of small companies. Given the nature of many of the specific measures adopted when the Obama administration set the goal of doubling exports over a five-year period, observers have concluded that small and medium-size businesses are likely to account disproportionately for the projected growth.[31] Indeed, the number of these firms that export has increased 20 percent since 2000, indicating that many small companies are already having considerable success selling their products and services abroad.[32] Typically, those that have excelled have done their homework in figuring out what products would sell in targeted markets—for example, what products local companies could not yet make for themselves. Then, they got close to the market and developed personal connections with influential decision makers, getting assistance wherever they could find it. A good place to start in your search for customers abroad is the U.S. Department of Commerce's Trade Information Center website (http://export.gov). Or get in touch with the foreign embassy community (http://embassy.org), select a country where you want to do business, and e-mail or call the country specialist for assistance. You may be surprised at the leads this can generate. Finally, you can check with officials from your state to see if they provide assistance. In many cases, an Internet search on "[insert name of your state here] foreign trade office" will lead you where you need to go.

USING TECHNOLOGY

Living the Dream

Spreading Gilt around the World

In the spring of 2007, Kevin Ryan introduced a fun and exciting form of e-commerce to shoppers in the United States. First mentioned in Chapter 9, his startup, New York City–based Gilt Groupe, is one of a handful of "flash sale websites" offering products from top designers on an invitation-only basis. To sweeten its deals, the company sells these products at insider prices. To add excitement to the shopping experience, the apparel, accessories, and lifestyle items that Gilt sells are truly unique—and, even more important, the selection changes every day.

Gilt's growth has been nothing short of amazing, with sales increasing at a healthy clip each year. But the secret of its success is the direct result of its dynamic sales model. By changing its product offerings daily, customers are drawn to the website often to see what's new, and the pages are changed in real time to keep up with shifts in consumer demand and product availability.

Because the business is so flexible, Ryan and his team decided that it was time to think about selling to markets around the world. They had hoped to offer brief specials "at a particular time of day, on a country-by-country basis, adjusted for time zones and hemispheres." It didn't take long for complications arising from different languages, confusing tax laws, a puzzling patchwork of postal regulations, and other unforeseen hitches to put a dent in the company's plans.

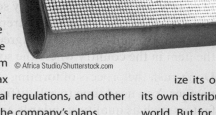
© Africa Studio/Shutterstock.com

Gilt Groupe decided to take a different approach. It signed on with an international shipping and logistics company called Borderfree, which allows its client firms to conduct business with 1.5 billion customers around the world. This relationship gave a huge lift to the retailer's global initiative, allowing it to extend its selling platform to 100 countries.

The integration took considerable effort to pull off, but the arrangement led to a number of powerful advantages and conveniences. For example, Borderfree's system allows Gilt to display its prices in each customer's local currency, and it automatically updates the firm's website to reflect the country-specific taxes and other costs that the customer will have to bear. And when an international order comes in, the company ships the product to one of Borderfree's warehouses in New Jersey or Ohio. Borderfree then handles everything else, receiving a small percentage of each sale for its trouble.

Gilt Groupe may choose to localize its operations even further some day, setting up its own distribution and customer-care facilities around the world. But for now, processing its sales through Borderfree seems to give Gilt Groupe the best of all worlds.

Sources: McKinsey & Company, "Gilt Groupe: Using Big Data, Mobile, and Social Media to Reinvent Shopping," November 2012, http://cmsoforum.mckinsey.com/article/gilt-groupe-using-big-data-mobile-and-social-media-to-reinvent-shopping, accessed January 8, 2013; www.fiftyone.com/solution, accessed January 8, 2013; and Dan O'Shea, "Think Global, Act Local," *Entrepreneur*, Vol. 40, No. 7 (July 2012), p. 47.

18-3b Importing

The flip side of exporting is **importing**, which involves selling products from abroad in the firm's home market. When a small company finds a product overseas that has market potential at home or identifies a product that would sell at home but cannot find a suitable domestic producer, an import strategy may be the best solution.

Linking up with vendors at international trade shows can also open the door to opportunity. Using imported products found at such shows, Holly Pennington sells fashion accessories through her 13 Compass Trading Company stores. Because of the depth of its merchandise, the company can accommodate both classic styles that create a professional look and cutting-edge designs featured in trendy fashion magazines, and many styles in between. Best of all, its products sell for a fraction of the prices charged for similar goods at high-end retailers. And customers like what they are getting, which is why this small company has been growing so fast.[33]

Regardless of the import strategy used, one of the most important factors for success is finding a good product vendor. This sounds easy enough to do, especially in this era of Internet-enabled matching services, online communication tools, and flexible and affordable travel. Though websites like Alibaba.com, MadeInChina.com, and GlobalSources.com seem to bring the goods you need right to your doorstep, finding and managing international suppliers for long-term relationships can be challenging. "I don't care if it's China or Timbuktu," says one entrepreneur with vast experience setting up international sourcing for small businesses. "The Internet does not suffice."[34]

START UP

RESOURCES

To Export or Not to Export?
Still not sure that your small business should be exporting? Watch the video at www.inc.com/exporting, and let small business owners and government experts help you see the global light.

importing
Selling products produced in another country to buyers in the home country.

© Charlie Edward/Shutterstock.com

In other words, it often takes an in-person visit to a prospective sourcing partner to know if it can meet the selection, quality, and quantity standards that can support your business.

This is not an easy option. However, it holds tremendous potential, especially if you follow a few simple guidelines:

- Learn as much as you can about the culture and business practices of the country from which you will be sourcing to avoid making deal-breaking mistakes.

- Do your research and be sure to select a source that is not a competitor or a company that hopes to learn from your operations so as to compete against you in the future.

- Protect your intellectual property so that your suppliers cannot easily take it from you. Some entrepreneurs require their sourcing partners to sign nondisclosure agreements so that they cannot patent the item in the country where the sourcing takes place.

- Don't rush the process of forming a relationship with a sourcing partner. You need time to ask difficult questions about important factors such as quality standards and capabilities, manufacturing flexibility, and time to order fulfillment.

- Work out transportation logistics ahead of time. A good freight forwarder can assist you with the mechanics of shipping, as well as help you with the confusing jumble of required documents. To get a sense of the process, review the rules and regulations on the U.S. Customs and Border Protection website at http://cbp.gov, and read the SBA's notes on importing at www.sba.gov/content /importing-goods.

At times, the process may seem so complicated that you may wonder if small companies should even be attempting to source from abroad. But it can be done, and with great benefit to your business.

18-3c Foreign Licensing

Importing and exporting are the most popular international strategies among small firms, but there are also other options. Because of limited resources, many small firms are hesitant to go global. One way to deal with this constraint is to follow a licensing strategy. **Foreign licensing** allows a company in another country to purchase the rights to manufacture and sell a firm's products in overseas markets. The firm buying these rights is called the **licensee**. The licensee makes payments to the **licensor**, or the firm selling those rights, normally in the form of **royalties**, which is a fee paid for each unit produced.

International licensing has its drawbacks. The foreign licensee makes all the production and marketing decisions, and the licensor must share returns from international sales with the licensee. However, foreign licensing is the least expensive way to go global, since the licensee bears all the costs and risks related to setting up a foreign operation.

Small companies tend to think of tangible products when they explore international licensing options, but licensing intangible assets such as proprietary technologies, copyrights, and trademarks may offer even greater returns. Just as Disney licenses its famous Mickey Mouse character to manufacturers around the world, a small branded apparel retailer called Peace Frogs used licensing when it introduced its copyrighted designs in Spain. As Peace Frogs' founder and president, Catesby Jones, has explained, the company exports its T-shirts directly into larger markets like Japan,

foreign licensing
Allowing a company in another country to purchase the rights to manufacture and sell a company's products in international markets.

licensee
The company buying licensing rights.

licensor
The company selling licensing rights.

royalties
Fees paid by the licensee to the licensor for each unit produced under a licensing contract.

but that strategy doesn't make as much sense in some countries. For example, Spain's lower per capita income, stronger domestic competition, and high tariffs made licensing a more attractive option. So Peace Frogs licensed the rights to manufacture its product to a Barcelona-based apparel maker.[35] From this agreement, Peace Frogs was able to generate additional revenue, but with almost no added expense.

Foreign licensing can also be used to protect against **counterfeit activity**, or the unauthorized use of intellectual property or manufacture of its products. If a firm in a foreign market is granted licensing rights, it can become a powerful local champion to help ensure that other firms do not use protected assets in an inappropriate way.

18-3d International Franchising

International franchising is a variation on the licensing theme. As outlined in Chapter 4, the franchisor offers a standard package of products, systems, and management services to the franchisee, which provides capital, market insight, and hands-on management. Although international franchising was not widely used before the 1970s, today it is the fastest-growing market-entry strategy of U.S. firms, with Canada as the dominant market, followed by Japan and the United Kingdom. This approach is especially popular with U.S. restaurant chains that want to establish a global presence. McDonald's, for example, has raised its famous golden arches in more than 119 countries around the world.[36] But small companies are being pulled toward international franchising as well, especially in countries where credit is readily available, financing barriers are weak, and demand for American goods and services is strong.[37]

Danny Benususan is the owner of Blue Note, a premier jazz club in Manhattan that opened its doors in 1981. Considered one of the top venues in the world for jazz and other forms of music, this club attracted the attention of international business-people who established four franchises in Japan and one in Italy. As a result, the club has successfully established itself as the world's only franchised jazz club network.[38] Blue Note has proved that there is more than one way for a small business to globalize.

18-3e International Strategic Alliances

Moving beyond licensing and franchising, some small businesses have expanded globally by joining forces with large corporations in cooperative efforts. An **international strategic alliance** allows firms to share risks and pool resources as they enter a new market, usually matching the local partner's understanding of the target market (culture, legal system, competitive conditions, etc.) or its access to low-cost labor with the technology or product knowledge of its alliance counterpart. One of the advantages of this strategy is that both partners take comfort in knowing that neither of them is "going it alone."

Strategic alliances can be used in many different ways by small companies to gain advantage internationally. At one time, Behlen Manufacturing Company, a maker of agricultural grain bins, drying systems, and metal-frame buildings, exported products to China. But co-president Tony Raimondo suspended shipments when he found out that Chinese copycats were making the same products, using local advantages such as cheaper labor to undercut Behlen on cost and sell at much lower prices. For a time, it looked as if the company would no longer be able to tap into this huge market. But then Raimondo hit on the idea of forming Behlen China, a 50/50 joint venture (a form of alliance in which two companies share equal ownership in a separate business) in Beijing. "In order for us to sustain market share," says Raimondo, "we had to be on the inside." Making product within China made

counterfeit activity The unauthorized use of a company's intellectual property or manufacture of its products.

international franchising Selling a standard package of products, systems, and management services to a company in another country.

international strategic alliance A combination of efforts and/or assets of companies in different countries for the sake of pooling resources and sharing risks.

RESOURCES

Worldwide Workforce
You may have decided that it would save money to produce your products in China. For some inside tips on finding a good manufacturing partner there, see www.inc.com/ss/6-tips -manufacturing-china#6.

it possible for Behlen to capitalize on the same advantages that Chinese factories had, and that has made all the difference. Behlen's success in China has spread to other international business initiatives, and the company still does a substantial share of its business overseas.[39]

18-3f Locating Facilities Abroad

A small business may choose to establish a foreign presence of its own in strategic markets, especially if the firm has already developed an international customer base. Most small companies start by locating a production facility or sales office overseas, often as a way to reduce the cost of operations. Amanda Knauer concluded that launching a new venture in the United States was too expensive, so she set her sights on Argentina. After doing some research, she went to Buenos Aires. A few months later, she was running her own business, Qara Argentina, a luxury leather goods manufacturer. It hasn't been easy. Knauer has had to learn the local Spanish dialect, negotiate a complicated and very different legal landscape, and master a new set of business practices. But the work has paid off, allowing her to establish her company in Buenos Aires, a city that is so interesting and beautiful that it is often called "the Paris of South America."[40]

Opening an overseas sales office can be a very effective strategy, but most small business owners should wait until sales in the local market are great enough to justify the move. An overseas office is costly to establish, staff, manage, and finance, so anticipated advantages are sometimes difficult to achieve. However, U.S. firms often locate their first international sales office in Canada, though European expansion is also common, with the English-speaking United Kingdom and Ireland being very popular locations. Still others have selected Asia, because of its economic dynamism and fast-growing consumer demand.

cross-border acquisition
The purchase by a business in one country of a company located in another country.

greenfield venture
A wholly owned subsidiary formed from scratch in another country.

Some small firms have grander ambitions and may purchase a foreign business from another firm through what is known as a **cross-border acquisition**, or even start a **greenfield venture**, by forming from scratch a new wholly owned subsidiary in another country. Either option is likely to be fraught with difficulties.

Go-it-alone strategies are complex and costly. They offer maximum control over foreign operations and eliminate the need to share generated revenues, but they also force companies to bear the entire risk of the undertaking. If the new subsidiary is a greenfield venture, the firm may have much to learn about running an enterprise in a foreign country, managing host-country nationals, and developing an effective marketing strategy. The commercial potential of a wholly owned international subsidiary may be great, but the hassles of managing it can be even greater. This option is not for the faint of heart.

LO
18-4
Explain the challenges that global enterprises face.

18-4 CHALLENGES TO GLOBAL BUSINESSES

Small businesses face challenges. *Global* small businesses face challenges on a much larger scale. However, the success of enterprising entrepreneurs in international markets proves that small firms can do better than survive—they can thrive! However, success requires careful preparation. Small business owners must recognize the unique complications facing global firms and adjust their plans accordingly. Beyond managing cultural differences, entrepreneurs need to pay attention to political risks, economic risks, and the relative ease of doing business in countries where they want to extend operations.

18-4a Political Risk

The potential for a country's political forces to negatively affect the performance of businesses operating within its borders is referred to as **political risk**. Often, this risk is related to the instability of a host nation's government. Potential problems range from threats as trivial as new regulations that restrict the content of television advertising to a government takeover of private assets. Political developments can threaten access to an export market, require a firm to reveal trade secrets, or even demand that work be completed in-country.

Many large corporations maintain a risk assessment office with staff trained to determine the risk profile of the individual countries for which they have planned projects. Because small firms cannot afford the cost of staffing such an office, some turn to inexpensive tools for risk assessment. One helpful resource is *Euromoney* magazine's "Country Risk Rankings," which is published once a year. These rankings provide a general sense of the political risks that companies will face when doing business abroad. Small businesses can develop international growth plans using these insights and make appropriate adjustments to their strategies. It's not a perfect method, but it is low cost and far better than planning a global strategy with no information at all.

18-4b Economic Risk

Economic risk is the probability that a country's government will mismanage its economy and affect the business environment in ways that hinder the performance of firms operating there. Economic risk and political risk are therefore related.[41] Two of the most serious problems resulting from economic mismanagement are inflation and fluctuations in exchange rates. While a full discussion of these factors is beyond the scope of this book, it is important to recognize that inflation reduces the value of a country's currency on the foreign exchange market, thereby decreasing the value of cash flows that the firm receives from its operations abroad.

Exchange rates represent the value of one country's currency relative to that of another country—for example, the number of Mexican pesos that can be purchased with one U.S. dollar. Sudden or unexpected changes in these rates can be a serious problem for small international businesses, whether they export to that market or have a local presence there.

Mary Ellen Mooney of Mooney Farms recognized the potential of exporting her sun-dried tomato products to France and came close to striking a deal with a local distributor a few years back, but the negotiations fell through when the exchange rate between the dollar and the euro changed.[42] To understand her dilemma, suppose the French distributor was willing to pay €5 (5 euros) for a package of sun-dried tomatoes. If the dollar and the euro were exchanged one to one, Mooney could convert €5 to $5. If $4.50 covered costs of production, transportation, insurance, and so on, then Mooney would earn a $.50 profit ($.5.00 − $4.50) per unit. But if the dollar were to *increase* in value relative to the euro, the situation would change drastically. Assume that the exchange rate changed to $.80 per €1. Then units selling for €5 would yield only $4 each (5 × .80), which would result in a $.50 loss on every sale.

Clearly, a good deal can quickly fall apart if exchange rates take a turn for the worse. This risk is especially serious for small companies that are just getting established in international markets. To protect against exchange rate shifts, many small firms choose to state their contracts in U.S. dollars, but this can give competitors an edge if they are willing to sell in the buyer's currency.

political risk
The potential for political forces in a country to negatively affect the performance of businesses operating within its borders.

economic risk
The probability that a country's government will mismanage its economy in ways that hinder the performance of firms operating there.

exchange rate
The value of one country's currency relative to that of another country.

© Lucia Pitter/Shutterstock.com

It can also lead to nonpayment if unfavorable shifts make goods or services too expensive for a foreign customer. The International Trade Administration of the U.S. Department of Commerce recommends that small firms use more sophisticated financial strategies and risk management tools, including forward contracts and options, which can be manageable (see http://www.trade.gov/publications/pdfs/tfg2008ch12 .pdf for details).

18-4c The Ease of Doing Business Index

Since 2003, the World Bank has been publishing the Ease of Doing Business Index to underscore to businesses and governments the large impact that regulatory conditions have on economic growth and development. The index is based on a survey of more than 9,600 local experts, including "lawyers, business consultants, accountants, freight forwarders, government officials, and other professionals routinely administering or advising on legal and regulatory requirements."[43] Following a very careful methodology, the process uses data related to 10 key sets of indicators—including the difficulty of starting a business, getting credit, and enforcing contracts—to create a ranking for 185 countries. This information can easily be used to shape the international expansion decisions of small businesses.

In Exhibit 18.4, countries are color-coded to indicate the relative ease of doing business in each—green represents "go" countries, which are relatively business-friendly; yellow signifies countries that are somewhat more challenging, where companies should "proceed with caution"; and red identifies "stop and think very carefully" countries, where small businesses are likely to have even more difficulty. While color coding is not a part of the index, the data provided are very helpful for planning. For specifics on the latest report, see www.doingbusiness.org/rankings.

Conducting business internationally will never be as easy as doing business at home—it is likely to stretch managerial skills and resources to the limit. Global

EXHIBIT

18.4 Ease of Doing Business

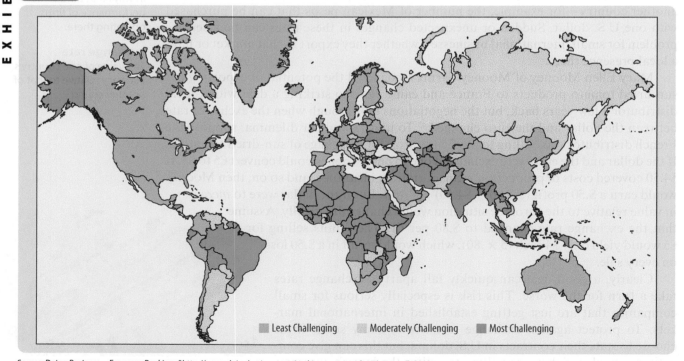

Least Challenging　　Moderately Challenging　　Most Challenging

Source: Doing Business—Economy Rankings," http://www.doingbusiness.org/rankings, accessed on January 7, 2013.

Part 4 Focusing on the Customer: Marketing Growth Strategies

commerce can complicate every task and raise difficult questions related to every function of the firm. However, the motivations to go global are sound, and others have already proved that it can be done. You can do it, too, if you plan carefully and take advantage of the resources available to help you achieve your global aspirations.

18-5 ASSISTANCE FOR GLOBAL ENTERPRISES

LO 18-5

Recognize the sources of assistance available to support international business efforts.

Help is available to small companies with international aspirations—you need only open your eyes to find it. Once you decide to enter the global marketplace, you will be amazed at how many resources there are to assist you.

18-5a Analyzing Markets and Planning Strategy

Among the many activities required to prepare a small firm for the challenges of going global, two are especially fundamental to success abroad: finding international markets that fit the company's unique potentials and putting together a game plan for entry into the target markets.

A small business should begin its research by exhausting secondary sources of information. The U.S. government offers a number of publications on how to identify and tap into global market opportunities. Also, the Small Business Administration stands ready to help small companies expand abroad. Many of the international programs and services of the SBA are delivered through U.S. Export Assistance Centers (USEACs).

One excellent source of information about global business for small companies is *Breaking into the Trade Game: A Small Business Guide to Exporting* (www.siue.edu/business/itc/pdf/Export_Guide_English.pdf). This nuts-and-bolts handbook from the SBA provides an overview of export strategy that is useful for both new and experienced exporters. It is designed to guide small firms through the complexities of going global, with chapters focused specifically on identifying markets, choosing an entry strategy, managing transactions, financing trade, arranging transportation, and forming strategic alliances.

Though not focused on small businesses alone, a website maintained by the International Trade Administration of the U.S. Department of Commerce (http://trade.gov) supplies helpful insights about international expansion. Publications such as *World Trade100* magazine (www.worldtradewt100.com) can also be useful, providing timely, in-depth analyses of world trade markets and business issues, especially as these are related to logistics. Beyond these resources, many state and private organizations supply trade information, trade leads, and company databases. One such source, TradePort (www.tradeport.org), offers information to promote international trade with California-based companies.

Talking with someone who has lived in or even visited a potential foreign market can be a valuable way to learn about it. For example, conversations with international students at a local university can be very helpful. However, the best way to study a foreign market is to visit the country personally. A representative of a small firm can do this either as an individual or as a member of a group that is organized for the purpose of exploring new international business possibilities.

18-5b Connecting with International Customers

Numerous resources are available to help a small company connect with customers in targeted international markets. They include trade leads, trade missions, and trade intermediaries.

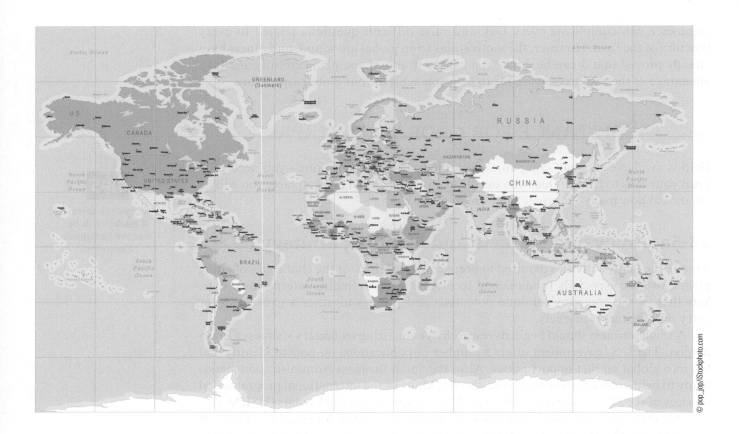

© pop_jop/iStockphoto.com

TRADE LEADS Trade leads are essential in identifying potential customers overseas. Accessed most often via the Internet, they offer an inexpensive way to establish vital links with buyers and suppliers in target markets. One good online source of trade leads is provided by the Center for International Business Education and Research at Michigan State University (see http://globaledge.msu.edu/Global-Resources /trade-leads). This website offers a wealth of international business resources, including leads that can direct a company to valuable partners in most of the world's markets. The website of the Federation of International Trade Associations (www.fita.org) will also help you identify trade leads. In addition, it provides news, announced events, and links to over 8,000 trade-related websites.

TRADE MISSIONS Joining a trade mission is another excellent way to evaluate a foreign market and connect with overseas customers. A **trade mission** is a planned visit to a potential international market, designed to introduce U.S. firms to prospective foreign buyers and to establish strategic alliances. These missions usually involve groups of five to ten business executives and are set up to promote international sales. Members of the group typically pay their own expenses and share in the operating costs of the mission. Foreign governments sometimes sponsor trade missions in order to promote business links with U.S. firms.

TRADE INTERMEDIARIES Perhaps the easiest way to break into international markets is to use a **trade intermediary**. Similar to the assistance wholesalers provide with domestic sales, trade intermediaries distribute products to international customers on a contract basis. These agencies tap their established web of contacts, as well as their local cultural and market expertise. In short, an intermediary can manage the entire export end of a business, taking care of everything except filling the orders— and the results can be outstanding. For example, American Cedar, Inc., wanted to

trade mission
A trip organized to help small business owners meet with potential foreign buyers and establish strategic alliances in an international market.

trade intermediary
An agency that distributes a company's products on a contract basis to customers in another country.

Confirming House (Buying Agent)	• Works for foreign firms that are interested in buying U.S. products. • "Shops" for lowest possible price for requested items. • Is paid a commission for its services. • Is sometimes a foreign government agency or quasi-governmental firm.
Export Management Company (EMC)	• Acts as the export department for one or several producers of products or services. • Solicits and transacts business in the names of the producers it represents or in its own name, in exchange for a commission, salary, or retainer plus commission. • May provide immediate payment for the products or services by arranging financing or directly purchasing products for resale. • Usually has well-established networks of foreign distributors already in place.
Export Trading Company (ETC)	• Acts as the export department for producers or takes title to the product and exports it under its own name. • May be set up and operated by producers. • Can be organized along multiple- or single-industry lines. • Can represent producers of competing products.
Export Agent, Merchant, or Remarketer	• Purchase products directly from the manufacturer, packing and marking the product according to its own specifications. • Sells the products overseas under its own name through contacts and assumes all risks. • Requires the producer to give up control of the marketing and promotion of its product.
Piggyback Marketer	• Is a manufacturer or service firm. • Distributes another firm's product or service.

Source: Adapted from *A Basic Guide to Exporting*, Chapter 5, "Methods and Channels," http://export.gov/basicguide/eg_main_038338.asp, accessed January 8, 2013.

expand the market for its cedar wood products overseas. With the assistance of a trade intermediary, the firm was able to generate 30 percent of its total sales from exporting. Then–company president Julian McKinney recalls how the story unfolded: "We displayed our products at a trade show, and an export management company found us. They helped alleviate the hassles of exporting directly. Our products [were] distributed throughout [Europe] from a distribution point in France."[44] An export management company is only one of the many types of trade intermediaries. Exhibit 18.5 describes the trade intermediaries that can best provide the assistance small businesses need.

18-5c Financing

The more information small firms have about direct and indirect sources of financing, the more favorably they tend to view foreign markets. Sources of this information include private banks and the Small Business Administration.

PRIVATE BANKS Commercial banks typically have a loan officer who is responsible for handling foreign transactions. Large banks may have an entire international department. Exporters use banks to issue commercial letters of credit and to perform other financial activities associated with exporting.

A **letter of credit** is an agreement to honor a draft or other demand for payment when specified conditions are met. It helps to ensure that a seller will receive prompt payment. A letter of credit may be revocable or irrevocable. An irrevocable letter of credit cannot be changed unless both the buyer and the seller agree to the change.

letter of credit
An agreement issued by a bank to honor a draft or other demand for payment when specified conditions are met.

The process of establishing a letter of credit is quite involved and can be very confusing. However, banks and other financial institutions that offer this service have expert staff who can explain how these documents work and will walk you through the process.

A guarantee from a reputable bank that the exporter will indeed be paid is critical to a small business that has stretched its resources to the limit just to enter the global game and thus cannot afford an uncollected payment. But what if the small business is on the import end of the exchange? How will its interests be protected? The letter of credit provides security for the receiving firm as well, because the exporter does not receive payment from the bank until it has released the title, or proof of ownership, of the delivered goods. Once the product has been shipped and the title transferred, the exporter receives a document called a **bill of lading** to confirm this. This document must be received before the bank will pay on the letter of credit. In brief, the letter of credit ensures that the exporter will receive payment only when the goods are delivered in-country, and it also guarantees that the exporter will be paid.

SMALL BUSINESS ADMINISTRATION The Small Business Administration (SBA) serves small U.S. firms primarily through its regional, district, and branch offices. Small businesses that are either already exporting or interested in doing so can receive valuable information from the SBA through conferences and seminars, instructional publications, and export counseling. An informative list of the financial assistance programs offered by the SBA to small firms is posted on the agency's website at www.sba.gov/content/financing-your-small-business-exports-foreign-investments-or-projects.

bill of lading
A document indicating that a product has been shipped and the title to that product has been transferred.

The reasons that a growing number of small firms are choosing to participate in international business include both time-honored motivations and those emerging in the new competitive landscape. Whatever your reasons are for entering the global arena, your company is certain to run up against serious challenges that purely domestic firms do not have to face. But assistance is available in abundance from a number of private and public agencies. With a little help and a lot of hard work, your company can succeed in the global marketplace.

LOOKING BACK

18-1. Describe the potential of small firms as global enterprises.

- Many startups and even the smallest of businesses continue to expand internationally, despite a slowed global economy.

- Some small companies called born-global firms are being launched with cross-border business activities in mind.

- Before going global, it is important for a small business owner to determine whether her or his company is up to the task.

- Small business owners who decide to go global must study the social, technological, economic, and political forces in a foreign market to determine how best to adapt products and ensure smooth entry.

18-2. Identify the basic forces prompting small firms to engage in global expansion.

- The basic forces behind global expansion are expanding markets, gaining access to resources, cutting costs, and capitalizing on special location features.

- Since more than 95 percent of the world's population lives outside the United States, globalization greatly expands the size of a firm's potential market.

- The fast-growing markets of the BRIC countries (Brazil, Russia, India, and China) are attracting small firms that wish to tap their enormous market potential.

- Because of converging preferences and delivery systems around the world, products that sell at home are more likely to be introduced very quickly abroad, often with little or no needed adaptation.

- Small businesses with a highly differentiated product may need an international market in order to increase sales enough to recover product development costs.

- Going global can accelerate gains from experience curve efficiencies (resulting from learning effects and economies of scale), especially for startups based on complex technologies.

- Sometimes, small businesses go global to gain access to resources, including raw materials and skilled labor.

- Another reason small firms enter foreign markets is to cut their costs in such areas as raw materials, labor, and manufacturing overhead.

- Businesses of all sizes have been slashing costs by contracting with independent providers overseas (*international outsourcing*) or relocating their stateside operations abroad (*offshoring*).

- Small businesses may want to capitalize on special features of an international location to create authenticity by being local, to enhance a brand's reputation, or to follow a large client firm.

18-3. Understand and compare strategy options for global businesses.

- Exporting can be facilitated by using the Internet to increase firms' international visibility.

- Importing should be used when products manufactured abroad have market potential at home.

- Other international strategies include foreign licensing, international franchising, international strategic alliances, and locating facilities abroad.

- Although they can be more complex than export strategies, some nonexport strategies (especially licensing) are actually the safest options for the small global business.

18-4. Explain the challenges that global enterprises face.

- Political risk is the potential for a country's political forces to negatively affect the performance of small businesses operating there. It varies greatly across nations.

- Economic risk is the probability that a government will mismanage its economy and affect the business environment in ways that hinder the performance of firms operating there (most notably through inflation and fluctuations in exchange rates).

- The World Bank's Ease of Doing Business Index can help a small company anticipate the overall level of difficulty of entering a specific country market.

18-5. Recognize the sources of assistance available to support international business efforts.

- Numerous public and private organizations provide assistance to small businesses in analyzing markets and planning an entry strategy.

- Small businesses can connect with international customers by reviewing sources of trade leads, joining trade missions, or using the services of trade intermediaries.

- For assistance in financing its entry into a foreign market, a small firm can turn to private banks (which can issue letters of credit) and programs initiated by the Small Business Administration.

Key Terms

bill of lading p. 494

born-global firms p. 474

counterfeit activity p. 487

cross-border acquisition p. 488

economic risk p. 489

economies of scale p. 480

exchange rate p. 489

experience curve efficiencies p. 479

exporting p. 483

foreign licensing p. 486

globalization p. 474

greenfield venture p. 488

importing p. 485

international franchising p. 487

international outsourcing p. 481

international strategic alliance p. 487

learning effects p. 480

letter of credit p. 493

licensee p. 486

licensor p. 486

offshoring p. 481

political risk p. 489

royalties p. 486

trade intermediary p. 492

trade mission p. 492

Discussion Questions

1. What is a "born-global" enterprise? What factors are encouraging the increase in the number of these companies?

2. How important is a careful cultural analysis to a small firm that wishes to enter an international market?

3. Do you believe that small companies should engage in international business? Why or why not?

4. What are the four basic forces driving small businesses to enter the global business arena? Which do you think is the most influential?

5. What are the emerging motivations persuading small business owners to go global? Do you think any of these motivations are likely to remain powerful forces ten years from now? Twenty years from now?

6. Why is exporting such a popular global strategy among small businesses? Do you think this should be the case?

7. What impact has the Internet had on the globalization of small firms? How do you think small companies will use the Internet for business in the future?

8. What nonexport strategies can small businesses adopt? In view of the unique needs and capabilities of small firms, what are the advantages and disadvantages of each of these strategies?

9. What are the three main challenges that small businesses face when they go global? What strategies can a small company use to deal with each of these challenges?

10. What forms of assistance are available to small global firms? Which is likely to be of greatest benefit to small companies? Why?

You make the Call

Situation 1

Jesse Acevas recognized the advantages of outsourcing software development work when he decided to start Victoris Consulting International, an information technology company. He has considered linking up with a service provider in Bangalore, India, because the wages are very low, the pool of well-trained employees is deep, and technical skills are strongly emphasized in the university system. But India is a long way from the company's home office in Phoenix, Arizona, which means greater travel costs, dealing with the hassle of working between times zones that are nearly opposite one another, and communication delays. There have also been reports of problems with infrastructure limitations (including poor or dropped Internet and phone connections), as well as the cost and quality of completed work. Finally, the cultural gap would be significant, even though most educated workers in India speak English.

Acevas has also been in touch with an operation in Guadalajara, Mexico. His contacts there tell him that the skilled workers he needs are available, the cultural gap is limited, turnover is very low, and technical staff will not need special visas to travel between Mexico and project sites in the United States. However, wages there are significantly higher than in Bangalore, university graduates in Mexico receive little practical training, and the law makes it very difficult to fire staff once they are hired.

The clock is ticking. Acevas needs to line up employees for three big contracts he is currently negotiating, and his potential clients all want to get their projects started within a month or so of a final decision. If he even closes two of the three deals, he will have much more work than his staff in the United States can handle. He will need additional employees—he's just not certain where to go for outsourcing support.

Question 1 What additional information would be helpful to Acevas as he ponders this decision?

Question 2 What additional advantages and disadvantages should Acevas consider when choosing between offshoring this work to India and "nearshoring" it to Mexico?

Question 3 Which location would you choose—India or Mexico? Build a case to support your final decision.

Situation 2

Frank Shipper and several other small business owners joined a trade mission to China to explore market opportunities there. The group learned that China has a population of over 1.3 billion and is one of the fastest-growing export markets for small and medium-size U.S. companies. Average annual income varies greatly across the country, but it is increasing rapidly. Annual per capita incomes ranges from a low of about $1,000 for rural workers to just under $3,500 in urban areas—even higher in Shanghai, Beijing, and other major cities. The World Bank estimates that the economy in China grows around 10 percent each year, and recent analyses indicate that the number of Internet users has been growing 11 percent year-over-year to reach 538 million. Furthermore, as the customer base in China continues to grow and quality-of-life expectations rise, the demand for various kinds of services increases greatly. Members of the group learned that 500 million people in China have cell phones, and nearly half of these people have mobile access to the Internet, with most of these being in large urban areas. On the downside, they found that counterfeit goods (from clothing and leather goods to software and DVDs) were readily available at a fraction of the cost of legitimate merchandise and that local merchants have expressed interest in doing business only with vendors with whom they have established relationships.

Question 1 What types of businesses would prosper in China? Why?

Question 2 What are the challenges and risks associated with doing business in China?

Question 3 What steps should Shipper take to address these challenges and risks in order to increase his chance of success in that market?

Sources: Bi Mingxin, "Income Gap Between China's Urban, Rural Residents Narrows in 2011," news.xinhuanet.com/english/china/2012-01/20/c_131371091.htm, accessed January 9, 2013; John Russell, "Internet Usage in China Surges 11 Percent," usatoday30.usatoday.com /tech/news/story/2012-07-19/china-internet-usage/56329450/1, accessed January 9, 2013; www.worldbank.org/en/country/china/overview, accessed January 8, 2013; and Michael Kanellos, "How Many New Cell Phone Accounts Are Opened in China a Day?" http://news .cnet.com/8301-10784_3-9724502-7.html, accessed January 9, 2013.

Situation 3

Steven Friedman is the founder of Brooklyn-based Holy Land Earth, which imports 16-ounce bags of soil from Israel for use at groundbreakings, burials, and other ceremonial events. The product holds special significance for people of various religious faiths, and each parcel of Holy Land Earth is certified to be genuine by a rabbi in Jerusalem. The company sells the soil for $39.95 per bag.

The obstacles the company has had to overcome are numerous. For example, import operations can be very difficult to set up, especially if they involve organic matter. Soil products cannot be imported without the permission of the U.S. Department of Agriculture, which requires getting them treated, tested, and formally approved. The new venture had to bear these costs on top of normal business expenses, such as obtaining the soil and then shipping, packaging, storing, marketing, and delivering it to buyers. Friedman worked with scientists to come up with a soil-cleaning process that satisfies U.S. import regulations, giving his startup a competitive advantage over would-be rivals.

Friedman is now considering ways to expand the market and potential of his young company. For example, he is thinking about marketing his soil product to Christian Evangelicals, and his website suggests a number of other applications, which include using the soil to feed potted plants, to promote good luck, or even to save as a keepsake. The future looks promising, but for now Friedman can take pleasure in knowing that his import operation is finally off the ground . . . in more ways than one.

Question 1 In your opinion, what new country markets would be likely to hold the greatest potential for additional sales for Friedman's company?

Question 2 Of the major strategy options mentioned in this chapter, which is Friedman currently following? Which of the other strategies would offer the safest path to further global expansion? the fastest path? the best path? Why?

Question 3 What are the greatest challenges Friedman is likely to face in the future? What sources of assistance would you suggest that he use as he takes on those challenges?

Sources: www.holylandearth.com, accessed February 21, 2011; Norm Brodsky, "You Do What?" www.inc.com/magazine/20080201/street-smarts-you-do-what.html, accessed January 9, 2013; and Martin Lindstrom, *Buyology: Truth and Lies About What We Buy* (New York: Random House, 2010), pp. 109–110.

Experiential Exercises

1. Conduct phone interviews with 10 local small business owners to see if they engage in international business. Discuss their reasons for going global or for choosing to do business only domestically.

2. Contact a local banker to discuss the bank's involvement with small firms participating in international business. Report your findings to the class.

3. Review recent issues of *Entrepreneur, Inc., MyBusiness*, and other small business publications, and be prepared to discuss several articles related to international business.

4. Do a Web search to find an article about a small business that first expanded internationally using an entry strategy other than exporting. From what you understand of the company's situation, suggest guidelines that could lead a firm to go global with nonexport strategies.

5. Consult online sources to develop a political/economic risk profile for a given country. Select a small company and explain what it would have to do to manage these risks if it were to enter the market of the profiled country.

6. Speak with the owner of a small international company. Which sources of assistance did that entrepreneur use when launching the global initiative? Which sources did the entrepreneur find most helpful? Which did the entrepreneur find least helpful?

Small Business & Entrepreneurship Resource Center

The Small Business & Entrepreneurship Resource Center offers complete small business management resources through a comprehensive database that covers all major areas of starting, operating, and maintaining a business from financing, management, marketing, accounting, taxes, and more. Go to www .cengagebrain.com and select the Longenecker text for more information on how to access this material.

1. Local dignitaries will gather for a ribbon-cutting ceremony in Whitsett, North Carolina, where America, not China, will make personal computers again. The new manufacturing facility is being built by a Chinese technology group. This move marks the latest twist in a globalization story. The original idea behind offshoring was that Western firms would save money by sending work to low-wage countries. However, this may not always be the case. Wages in China have been rising by 10 to 20 percent a year, whereas manufacturing pay in America has remained stable. There are also transport costs to consider. Although factory costs in North Carolina are substantially higher than those in China, the gap has narrowed considerably, making it reasonable for some companies to locate their manufacturing operations in the United States. After reading this article, discuss the advantages and disadvantages of offshoring.

2. From boats and planes to skyscrapers and shopping malls, size records are routinely broken. If the trend towards growing larger is clear, the economics of size are far murkier. If average costs fall as a firm grows, this suggests economies of scale exist, although results vary by industry. American dairy farms, for example, have been getting bigger, but studies suggest that there are still economies of scale to exploit, especially at farms with fewer than 200 cattle. By contrast, rail-industry studies show dwindling economies of scale over time as companies have grown. Do you think that overall, the limits of economies of scale have been reached for very large firms? Explain.

Sources: "Here, There and Everywhere," *The Economist*, Vol. 406, No. 8819 (January 19, 2013), p. 4; and "Land of the Corporate Giants; Free Exchange (Economies of Scale)(Essay)," *The Economist*, Vol. 405, No. 8809 (November 3, 2012), p. 76.

Case 18

Auntie Anne's Pretzels in China (P. 681)

This case describes the challenges that two first-time entrepreneurs encountered when taking the Auntie Anne's Pretzels franchise into China.

Alternative Case for Chapter 18

Case 5, The Avedis Zildjian Company Inc., p. 653

Endnotes

1. Data published by the SBA indicate that a large number of small and medium-size enterprises are already actively involved in exporting. The numbers become even more impressive when other forms of globalization are considered. (See "Frequently Asked Questions" http:// www.sba.gov/sites/default/files/FAQ_Sept_2012.pdf.)

2. This statement is consistent with a U.S. Commercial Service report mentioned in Emily Maltby, "Expanding Abroad? Avoid Cultural Gaffes," *The Wall Street Journal*, January 19, 2010, p. B5.

3. Terms other than *born global firms* are sometimes used. They include *born-international firms, global startups, international new ventures,* and *instant exporters*.

4. UN data indicate that the number of startups that are global from day one doubled between 1990 and 2006, from 30,000 to 60,000 [see Michael V. Copeland, "The Mighty Micro-Multinational," *Business 2.0*, Vol. 7, No. 6 (July 2006), pp. 107–114]. In many cases, the emphasis is not on simply selling products abroad; rather, it is on establishing operations wherever in the world it makes sense to do so. In other words, the strategy could be a way to locate near abundant resources or low-cost or highly trained labor to enhance the value proposition of the new venture.

5. Leigh Buchanan, "The Thinking Man's Outsourcing," *Inc.*, Vol. 28, No. 5 (May 2006), pp. 31–33.

6. See John A. Matthews and Ivo Zander, "The International Entrepreneurial Dynamics of Accelerated Internationalisation," *Journal of International Business Studies*, Vol. 38, No. 3 (May 2007), pp. 387–403.

7. Buchanan, *op. cit.*

8. Rich Sloan and Jeff Sloan, "Taking Your Startup to a Foreign Market," www.startupnation.com/articles/1471/1/startupforeign-market.asp, accessed December 19, 2012.

9. Shelby Scarbrough, "A Whole New World," *Entrepreneur*, Vol. 36, No. 6 (June 2008), p. 21.

10. Leigh Buchanan, "Gone Global," *Inc.*, Vol. 29, No. 4 (April 2007), pp. 88–91.

11. For more on this point, including a sophisticated analysis of internationalization drivers, see Stephanie A. Fernhaber, Patricia P. McDougall, and Benjamin M. Oviatt, "Exploring the Role of Industry Structure in New Venture Internationalization," *Entrepreneurship Theory and Practice*, Vol. 31, No. 4 (July 2007), pp. 517–542.

12. Svante Andersson, "Internationalization in Different Industrial Contexts," *Journal of Business Venturing*, Vol. 19, No. 6 (2004), pp. 851–875; "Don't Laugh at Gilded Butterflies," *The Economist*, Vol. 371, No. 8372 (April 22, 2004), pp. 71–73; and Oliver Burgel, Andreas Fier, Georg Licht, and Gordon C. Murray, "The Effect of Internationalization on Rate of Growth of High-Tech Start-Ups—Evidence for UK and Germany," in Paul D. Reynolds et al. (eds.), *Frontiers for Entrepreneurship Research*, proceedings of the 20th Annual Entrepreneurship Research Conference, Babson College, June 2002.

13. For an extended discussion of this study, see Edmund Prater and Soumen Ghosh, "Current Operational Practices of U.S. Small and Medium-Sized Enterprises in Europe," *Journal of Small Business Management*, Vol. 43, No. 2 (April 2005), pp. 155–169.

14. As described in Charles W. L. Hill, *Global Business Today* (New York: McGraw-Hill/Irwin, 2011), pp. 179–180.

15. Leslie E. Palich and D. Ray Bagby, "Trade Trends in Transatlantica: A Profile of SMEs in the United States and Europe," in Lester Lloyd-Reason and Leigh Sears (eds.), *Trading Places—SMEs in the Global Economy: A Critical Research Handbook* (Cheltenham, UK: Edward Elgar Publishing, 2007), pp. 64–65.

16. Henry Chu, "Iceland Divided over Aluminum's Role in Its Future," *Los Angeles Times*, March 26, 2011, http://articles.latimes.com/2011/mar/26/business/la-fi-iceland-economy-20110326, accessed on January 8, 2013.

17. In an attempt to prevent dangerous individuals from entering the country, the U.S. government has tightened visa and work permit restrictions, which has made it more difficult for companies to bring in the foreign talent they need. Also, many international students from countries like China and India train in the best universities in the United States and then return home, hoping to use their skills to get in on the ground floor of opportunities that are emerging in their rapidly developing home countries.

18. Robert Thornock and Wesley Whitaker, "Skolkovo: Russia's Emerging Silicon Valley," January 26, 2011, http://knowledge.wharton.upenn.edu/article.cfm?articleid=2699, accessed December 20, 2012.

19. http://mcapresearch.com/About.php, accessed January 2, 2013.

20. Mark Whitehouse, "Starting a Global Business, with No U.S. Employees," *The Wall Street Journal*, January 19, 2010, p. B8; and http://seanreadsthenews.typepad.com/seanreadsthenews/2010/11/wsj-how-to-start-a-business-with-no-us-employees.html, accessed January 3, 2013.

21. "China and the New Rules for Global Business," http://knowledge.wharton.upenn.edu/special_section.cfm?specialID=19, accessed January 8, 2013.

22. www.mdinabox.com/about_us.php, accessed January 2, 2013; and Francine Russo, "Doc in a Box," *Business 2.0*, Vol. 8, No. 5 (June 2007).

23. Rachel Z. Arndt, "Georgia Chopsticks," *Fast Company*, No. 165 (May 2012), p. 92.

24. Richard Wells, "Colin Flahive, Salvador's Café, Kunming," *Settling Magazine*, January 29, 2012, http://settlingmagazine.net/2012/qa-colin-flahive-salvadors-cafe-kunming, accessed January 3, 2013; and "Salvador's Coffee House, Kunming, China," www.salvadors.cn, accessed July 11, 2013.

25. *Ibid.*

26. Garry D. Bruton, David Ahlstrom, and Lu Yuan, "Before Heading to China …," *MIT Sloan Management Review*, November 30, 2009, http://sloanreview.mit.edu/executive-adviser/articles/2009/5/5154/before-heading-to-china, accessed January 3, 2013.

27. U.S. Small Business Administration Office of Advocacy, "Frequently Asked Questions," www.sba.gov/sites/default/files/FAQ_Sept_2012.pdf, accessed July 11, 2013.

28. U.S. Small Business Administration, *Breaking into the Trade Game: A Small Business Guide to Exporting*, Chapter 1, "Making the Export Decision," www.siue.edu/business/itc/pdf/Export_Guide_English.pdf, accessed January 3, 2013.

29. www.entertainmentearth.com/help/aboutee.asp, accessed January 3, 2013.

30. "Welcome to CarAlarmsEtc!" http://cgi3.ebay.com/ws/eBayISAPI.dll?ViewUserPage&userid=caralarmsetc, accessed January 3, 2013; Janelle Elms, "Go Global," *Entrepreneur*, Vol. 34, No. 9 (September 2006), pp.130–131; and Demitri Kalogeropoulos, "eBay Moves to Boost International Selling," *The Motley Fool*, October 4, 2012, http://beta.fool.com/sigmaswan/2012/10/04/ebay-moves-boost-international-selling/13481, accessed January 3, 2013.

31. The United States Office of Management and Budget, "Supporting Small Businesses and Creating Jobs," www.whitehouse.gov/omb/factsheet/supporting-small-businesses-and-creating-jobs, accessed January 3, 2013; and "Why Borders Still Matter," *Inc.*, Vol. 33, No. 4 (May 2011), pp. 120–121.

32. United States Trade Promotion Coordinating Committee, "2012 National Export Strategy," December 2012, www.trade.gov/publications/pdfs/nes2012.pdf, accessed January 3, 2013.

33. www.compasstradingco.com/compass-trading-co, accessed January 4, 2013; and personal communication with store management, February 8, 2008.

34. Christopher Hann, "Get the Goods Rolling," *Entrepreneur*, Vol. 40, No. 7 (July 2012), p. 25.

35. U.S. Small Business Administration, *Breaking into the Trade Game, op. cit.*, Chapter 8.

36. "McDonalds Worldwide," www.mcdonalds.ca/ca/en/our_story/mcdonalds_worldwide.html, accessed January 4, 2013.

37. Angus Loften, "Smaller Franchisers Expand Their Horizons," *The Wall Street Journal*, November 14, 2011, p. R7.

38. www.bluenotejazz.com/franchise/index.php, accessed January 4, 2013.

39. Elizabeth Wasserman, "Happy Birthday, WTO?" *Inc.*, Vol. 27, No. 1 (January 2005), pp. 21–23.

40. Karen E. Klein, "An American in South America's Paris," *Bloomberg Businessweek*, June 15, 2006, www.businessweek.com/smallbiz/content/jun2006/sb20060615_849958.htm, accessed February 17, 2011; and Nichole L. Torres, "Change of Scenery," *Entrepreneur*, Vol. 34, No. 8 (August 2006), p. 90.

41. One form of risk that is not within the control of a government but may have very serious effects on business performance is what some researchers call *environmental risk*. This suggests that climate change risks vary across global regions and should be a recognized decision-making factor [see Peter Romilly, "Business and Climate Change Risk: A Regional Time Series Analysis," *Journal of International Business Studies*, Vol. 38, No. 3 (May 2007), pp. 474–480].

42. Personal communication with Mary Ellen Mooney, April 18, 2011.

43. www.doingbusiness.org/methodology/methodology-note#Easeof DB, accessed January 7, 2013.

44. "Foreign Market Entry," www.foreign-trade.com/reference/trad8.htm, accessed January 8, 2013.

DashLocker

New York Businessman Trades Banking for Laundry StartUp

In 2010, corporate businessman Robert Hennessy traded his job as a research analyst at a New York hedge fund to start his own company, a high-tech laundry service on Manhattan's Upper East Side. Hennessy, who grew up in Atlanta and moved to New York in 2008, pursued banking for just two short years before starting his own company. What inspired the career change? Hennessy simply saw a need in the market and felt called to respond:

> It always baffled me that dry cleaners had the same hours as most hard-working New Yorkers and were closed on Sunday. Not many of us without laundry [service] in our apartments have three hours to spend washing our clothes.

The strength of the business idea that Hennessy identified lies in the inelasticity of demand for dry-cleaning services. As he explains, "You're going to breathe, you're going to get dirty, you're going to need to clean those clothes."

What initially began as a simple coin-operated laundromat grew into a business currently known as DashLocker, a round-the-clock dry-cleaning and wash-and-fold service. DashLocker operates as a kiosk system that enables customers to lock and unlock laundry bins with a credit card at any time of day. This allows them to drop off and retrieve laundry after traditional work hours have ended.

By simply registering a credit card online, customers are granted immediate access to the lockers. This type of access allows the storefront to be unstaffed throughout the day, minimizing operating expenses. The locker technology takes photographic inventory of the laundry so that no clothes are lost. Within 24 hours of drop-off, customers receive an e-mail or a text informing them that their laundry is ready for pick up.

The technology is powered by San Francisco–based laundry startup, Laundry Locker. Hennessy spent a year petitioning the company to allow him to license the software. His perseverance paid off. In the first month of operation,

the store generated almost $6,000 in sales and served over 100 customers. Within three months, monthly sales grew to $13,500. Since then, Hennessy has opened other locations.

The company targets "tech-savvy 20- to 40-year-olds with discretionary income." Prices for DashLocker services are at the upper end of dry-cleaning rates. Wash-and-fold services are priced at $1.25/pound, and dry-cleaning services are priced at $6 for pants and $2.25 for pressed shirts.

The business maintains strong growth potential, as lockers have the potential to be installed just about anywhere. Currently being considered are apartment buildings, gyms, and parking garages. Hennessy has also expanded services to include shoe shining and delivery.

DashLocker is committed to a social mission. It seeks to employ green, earth-friendly technology in its operations. The company's GreenEarth dry-cleaning machines use liquid silicone rather than perchloroethylene (perc). Hennessy describes liquid silicone as "liquefied sand that when broken down, deteriorates into sand, water, and carbon dioxide—natural elements whose exposure doesn't put anyone at risk." DashLocker not only seeks to transform the Manhattan laundry landscape but to shrink its carbon footprint globally.

Questions

1. How did Hennessy's background prepare him for starting a business? What entrepreneurial qualities does he embody?

2. What were Hennessy's entrepreneurial motivations for founding DashLocker?

3. What type of entrepreneurial opportunity did Hennessy identify, and how did he capitalize on those opportunities?

4. Describe DashLocker's growth potential.

5. Describe DashLocker's competitive advantage.

6. What impact does DashLocker have on society?

7. What do you think about DashLocker's social mission? What else could the company do to reduce its carbon footprint? Should businesses be concerned with social entrepreneurship?

8. Visit DashLocker's website at www.dashlocker.com and explore the process of signing up for its services. What recommendations would you give to Hennessy to make the process easier?

Sources: Based on Katherine Duncan. "A Fresh Spin on Clean Clothes." *Entrepreneur.* January 2013: p. 70; Nate Hindman, "DashLocker Formed As Banker Turned Entrepreneur Tries to Shake Up Dry-Cleaning World," *Huffington Post,* June 15, 2012, www.huffingtonpost.com /2012/06/15/dashlocker-dry-cleaning_n_1599767.html, accessed March 17, 2013; Matt Petronzio, "3 Ways to Simplify Your Offline Errands," *Mashable.* July 5, 2012, www.mashable .com/2012/07/05/tech-city-errands, accessed March 17, 2013; Alessia Pirolo, "The Latest in Laundry," *The Wall Street Journal,* July 23, 2012, http://online.wsj.com/article/SB100008723 96390443570904577543223512030502.html, accessed March 17, 2013; and Jason Shefiell, "New York Businessman's Start-Up Lets Customers Drop Off and Pick Up Laundry and Dry Cleaning at Conveniently-Placed Lockers," *NY Daily News,* January 17, 2013, www.nydailynews .com/life-style/real-estate/bizman-hopes-clean-laundry-start-article-1.1240764, accessed March 17, 2013.

PortionPac Chemicals
Integrity and Stakeholder Relationships

PortionPac® Chemicals was founded on social and environmental principles. Since 1964, sustainability led the business, their products, their relationships, and their success. Decades before it became a buzzword, PortionPac's founders, Syd Weisberg and Marvin Klein, believed in the value of sustainability and what it meant for the environment, the industry, and the people who lived and worked in both. Built on a foundation of environmental stewardship and social responsibility, PortionPac continues to strive toward creating the world's most sustainable solutions for clean buildings.

For PortionPac, being a leader in sustainability means considering the impact of everything they do, across all operations. Sustainable thinking permeates the entire company. This orientation shows up in the company's solutions, its facility, and its founding principles. PortionPac has always seen sustainability as an opportunity: a way to differentiate itself from the competition and a chance to do their part. This has never been viewed as a hindrance or an expense—it's just the way business is done. With premeasured packaging, safer product systems, and ongoing education, PortionPac's sustainable solutions help improve people's health, the environment, and the customers' bottom line.

PortionPac believes strongly in the critical work and tremendous effort of housekeepers, janitors, and food service professionals. The firm's goal is to make effective cleaning products that offer maximum safety for their employees to produce and for their clients to use. The company also holds itself accountable to the end-user and recognizes its role in health and safety.

In the early years, PortionPac had opportunities to enter lucrative markets where toxic cleaning products were commonplace. But rather than make standard dangerous germicides, the firm's founders opted for safer alternatives. In doing so, they demonstrated that less toxic options could actually be more effective at cleaning and disinfecting. It took years, but convincing the industry to make the switch became one of the company's founding principles and underscored the owners' commitment to worker safety.

PortionPac's commitment to the health and well-being of customers goes beyond manufacturing safer products—at the heart of the company's mission is education. PortionPac was the first chemical company in the cleaning industry to emphasize educational materials for the proper use of cleaning products as the most effective method to guarantee worker safety, boost productivity, and reduce error. By using international symbols and color-coding, simple to understand audiovisual materials, and interactive programming to teach customers and staff how to clean better, more safely, and with fewer chemicals, they've achieved this goal.

You won't find a separate "green" division within PortionPac because the entire company is committed to creating the world's most sustainable solutions for clean buildings. Its goal has always been to reduce the company's environmental footprint by decreasing the energy used in the production and distribution of its products, minimizing the adverse effect of its cleaning detergents on the environment, and avoiding the use of improper cleaning procedures that can turn out to be ineffective or even unsafe.

Caring about the environment and putting people first sounds like a pretty good way to do business, and PortionPac demonstrates every day that it's also great for a company's financial success. While growing the firm's operations, its owners have always considered the "triple bottom line" of social, environmental, and economic balance while growing operations. They made the conscientious decision before starting the company to continually improve environmental standards and the human condition—all while remaining profitable. That's why the company is recognized today as a leader in sustainability.

As more and more companies look for green products and consider the "3 P's" of people, the planet, and profit, it's clear—whether by regulation or recognition—that sustainability considerations are no longer just a smart way of looking at the world: it's becoming a practical way to run a profitable business. PortionPac helps organizations find sustainable solutions for their janitorial and sanitation needs. With over 40 years of experience connecting sustainability, accountability, and cleaning, they know the best solutions continually evolve, adapt, and improve. Because every company is different, they collaborate with clients one-on-one to create custom programs that work for them.

View the video and answer the questions that follow.

Questions

1. Based on what you have learned about PortionPac, what do you think the owners would claim to be the most important features of doing business with integrity? Do you agree? Why or why not?

2. Who are the most important stakeholders for PortionPac? What is the order of emphasis on the interests for these stakeholders—from most important and influential to least important and influential—on the company's decision-making processes? In your opinion, does this represent a wise ordering of stakeholder interests?

3. PortionPac is very concerned about the environment. Is the company's environmental focus good for the company? Why or why not?

4. Would you want to work for a company that operates according to the goals discussed in the case? What would be the pros and cons of working there?

Source: Compiled from interviews and information provided by PortionPac.
www.portionpaccorp.com. © 2012, Cengage Learning.

Brian Lovin is founder of The Kollection, a blog/website dedicated to emerging musicians and fans who want to know about the newest music available. He explains below, in his own words, how the site got started as a labor of love, with hopes of filling a gap in the marketplace. It wasn't long before The Kollection evolved into a popular online venue for music lovers around the world and a revenue-generating enterprise. Lovin's reflections about the business and his experiences with it provide instructive insights into a number of topics that are relevant to most startups. These topics include recognizing an opportunity, launching the business, dealing with growing pains from enterprise expansion, choosing a strategic direction, and adjusting business models in response to changing conditions.

It was June of 2010, during the year between my senior year of high school and freshman year of college. I was on vacation in Martha's Vineyard, without much in the way of entertainment. Back then, my music tastes largely originated from albums I had previously bought or heard online through services like Pandora. I had heard of music blogs, like Pitchfork, but had never really considered them to be anything worth following.

Around that time, mashups, a type of music combining two or more melodically similar songs into one new hybrid track, were becoming amazingly popular. I remembered how my high school friends always seemed to find the coolest mashups on the web. While relaxing in Martha's Vineyard that summer, I too found myself browsing online for mashups and other music and inadvertently stumbled upon blogs targeted to the college demographic. What immediately struck me about these blogs was their 90's-era visual design, their lack of organization, and their snail-paced downloads. It seemed painfully obvious that these blogs were set up and run by high school and college kids who had stumbled into the world of blogging and were struggling to find their way.

After checking out the blogs that were out there, I knew that I could do better. I was very confident of this because I had three years of web design and development experience under my belt from building blogs and websites for clients. I had learned how to drive traffic, improve search results, write content, etc.

Leaning on this expertise, I pulled up a domain name I had bought the previous year, thekollection.com, installed a quick blog, and began my search for new music online. I ended up finding some songs from lesser-known artists who had put their work online for free. I uploaded those songs to The Kollection, and began sharing them with my friends.

Those first few weeks were pretty slow. I was working hard to find sources of new music that would allow me to post at least one new song each day. Every time I posted a track, a trickle of visitors—just one or two at first—would stop by the site to listen and download. But word spread rather quickly and soon the trickle of hits was growing into a torrent of activity. By August of that year, The Kollection saw 2,800 visits. In September, 85,000 visitors stopped by to find new music. In October, the site had more than 200,000 hits. This rapid growth didn't continue forever, but by 2011 the site was tracking over 30,000 visits per day and nearly 1 million per month.

What had started out as a hobby and a personal project quickly became much more than that. Soon I was worried about being able to pay for our servers (only $200 per month at the time, but enough to be of concern for a college freshman). So in October of 2010, as traffic on the site was growing so fast, I printed my first line of Kollection tee shirts. The design was simple, and quite unremarkable—in fact, it was my first time ever designing for print, so I had to learn quite a lot—but that first batch of shirts sold faster than I had expected.

At that point I was confident that apparel would be a feasible option to make money on the site. We were still growing and gaining a lot of attention, and quickly. Artists begged to be on the site, fans praised the music selection, and people were sharing music across the web. It wasn't unusual for us to give a previously unknown artist tens of thousands of plays and downloads within a day.

In January of 2011, fans began to approach me and ask to write for the site. They saw The Kollection as a fun and worthwhile way to get a taste of the music industry. As a result of the interest, my team of authors grew quickly, peaking at around 15, but finally settling comfortably at around 6 writers in 2012 and into 2013. The team truly made The Kollection possible in 2011 and 2012—they helped me publish thousands of posts to the site in just a few years and upload several new songs per day. We were able to see from our tracking that fans visiting The Kollection were listening to and downloading millions of songs a month. We were revved up and running on a full tank of gas, and it didn't seem like things could possibly slow down.

But slow down they did. As 2011 turned into 2012, more and more college students and high schoolers were learning how easy it was to set up a blog and start sharing music for free online. Blogs began to pop up by the dozens, if not more, within a few months' time. Each of these tried hard to bring a unique essence to the game, but for a music blog with such a simple process, there really isn't much room to expand horizontally. In late 2011 I started to notice that more and more music blogs were consistently posting the same songs as every other site. This meant that the music blogging niche that I was in had become an easily replicable commodity that anybody could copy with very little effort.

So it was time to think more carefully about how to differentiate the site. Through 2011 we were able to make The Kollection stand out from the crowd with our emphasis on minimal design, structured organization, searchability, and speed. We always focused on making it as easy as possible for fans to quickly listen to and download new music. But as 2012 was approaching, other contenders had made headway with their website designs, and it became harder to separate them from The Kollection.

After giving it a lot of thought, I decided to take The Kollection in a few directions, which in hindsight probably caused me to spread the business too thin. First, I hired a company to develop an iOS and Android app so that fans could stream our music from their phones. Second, we spent over $4,000 on a run of tee shirts to expand our line of merchandise. Third, I redesigned and rebuilt the site with a functionality that allowed users to build their own playlists directly on the site, using songs we had posted.

Considered separately, these three avenues all performed very well. Our apps saw more than 30,000 downloads within two months, with fans listening to more than 1 million songs on their phones. Our apparel sold well, too, often with as much as several hundred dollars of merchandise being purchased a day. In fact, we broke even and started to make a profit on apparel within one month. The site redesign was also successful—pageviews continued to stay strong, and fans loved having the ability to build their own customized playlists with their favorite music.

But in early 2012, a few things came crashing down on The Kollection. You see, up until that point we had been using Soundcloud to upload and host all of our audio files. This allowed us to power mobile apps and make the most of the site redesign, while tracking the number of plays and downloads across the network. But, almost without warning, the plug was pulled on all of this due to a handful of copyright complaints. The Kollection has always focused on sharing music available for free from the artists themselves, but occasionally a song would slip through the cracks, one that really should not have been uploaded. As a result, in the first quarter of 2012 we lost our Soundcloud account, and because of that, our mobile apps no longer functioned and the playlist builder on the website could not operate.

We had spent thousands of dollars building The Kollection around Soundcloud, so this was a major disruption to the venture as a whole. We saw traffic stall, and fans became frustrated as a result of the loss of our differentiating features.

But we pushed on. My authors and I revived our core focus of sharing new music with fans around the world. We found failsafe ways to share music (legally) without worrying about copyright issues. We stripped the site down to its core features, removing the ability to build playlists, and we pulled our app from the app stores.

2012 also brought with it a host of new problems for The Kollection. Though services like Pandora had been around for a long time, that year the public's attention seemed to shift quickly toward online radio. Pandora, Spotify, Rdio, and other such services gained enormous traction in the music-discovery market, making it easier for friends to share with one another the music that they came across on the web. The Kollection and other blogs like it had the distinct advantage of being the first to share new music (for example, we could post a new song within minutes of its release), but as soon as these songs found their way into the libraries of big players like Spotify and Rdio, we lost the competitive advantage of having this new music.

Throughout 2012 our month-to-month costs remained relatively stable, but our income fluctuated wildly. We were running banner ads on a pay-per-click basis, earning us anywhere from $300 to $1,000 per month. But at the same time, merchandise sales slowed as inventory dwindled, and I had a hard time making a decision about the best way to move forward with the venture. On the one hand, I was in college and my time was limited, so I knew it was important to focus on one business model and revenue stream. While clothing ultimately made more money, it required a lot more work to design new lines, pack and ship every order, and support customers around the world who had problems with their orders. On the other hand, ads were a passive way to make money and didn't require any extra day-to-day effort. The downside of this option, however, is that the ads didn't generate as much profit as the merchandise, and earning $300 to $1,000 per month was just barely enough to maintain our server costs.

Ultimately, the biggest decision I had to make as the owner was to determine how much time and effort I was willing to invest in the website. It had grown to such a size that I couldn't run it on my own and had to have the help of my team of authors to make it work. At the same time, though, we weren't generating enough revenue to pay them as employees. So, I still needed to decide how to divide my time and effort between school and the venture, and I knew that it was unrealistic to expect The Kollection to continue growing without a new vision and drastic changes that would sufficiently differentiate the site from the competition.

The best road forward for The Kollection is not obvious to me at this point. Some things are non-negotiable. For example, we still want the site to drive a lot of traffic and remain a respected source in the music blog niche. Also, we definitely want to continue to promote new artists and their music and do this very well, pushing up pageviews and ad sales, but finding an ad platform that will allow us to make significant revenue from the traffic we generate has not been easy. Merchandise sales from The Kollection have been very helpful in the past, but they require a lot of time and attention, and I won't really have much extra bandwidth to give to this as long as I am a college student with a part-time job. This leaves me with some difficult decisions to make, but I am ready for the challenge and look forward to my future as an entrepreneur—no matter what direction it takes.

Questions

1. How did Lovin come to recognize the opportunity for his young venture? Of the three types of startups mentioned in Chapter 3, which one does The Kollection fit into? What was the source of this opportunity?

2. Complete a SWOT analysis for The Kollection. What does it say about the strengths that the startup can build on or the weaknesses that it must be particularly careful to protect itself against? Does this analysis reveal any promising future opportunities for Lovin and his venture? By your analysis, what threats put the enterprise most at risk?

3. What broad-based strategy is Lovin following at The Kollection? Is this the only and best way to position the company? Why or why not?

4. Conduct a feasibility analysis on the company, being sure to consider its market potential, industry attractiveness, and leadership. According to your assessment, how much promise does the venture offer?

5. What recommendations would you make to Lovin as he thinks about the company and its future?

Source: Story as told by Brian Lovin, founder and owner of The Kollection, March 26, 2013.

Two Men and a Truck®/ International, Inc.

Exceeding Customers' Expectations

Background

In 2007, TWO MEN AND A TRUCK®/INTERNA-TIONAL, Inc., was recognized on *Entrepreneur* magazine's list of Top 500 (it was ranked at number 171), named as one of America's top global franchises, listed on *Franchise Business Review*'s "Franchise 50," and selected as one of the top 25 franchises for Hispanics by the National Minority Franchising Initiative. According to the company's website (www.twomenandatruck.com), it is the first and largest local moving franchise system in the United States and offers a full range of home and business moving services.

History

TWO MEN AND A TRUCK started in the early 1980s as a way for two brothers to make extra money while they were in high school. Now, over 20 years later, the company has grown to more than 200 locations worldwide.

Brothers Brig Sorber and Jon Sorber started moving people in the Lansing, Michigan, area using an old pickup truck. They had their mom, Mary Ellen Sheets, develop a logo to put in a weekly community newspaper. That stick men logo still rests on every truck, sign, and advertisement for the company. After the brothers left for college, Sheets continued to field calls for moving services while she also worked a full-time data-processing job with the state of Michigan. In 1985, she decided to make things official by purchasing a 14-foot truck for $350 and hiring a pair of movers. That $350 is the only capital Sheets has ever invested in the company. Her experience with data analysis, combined with her commitment to customer service, earned her a spot on a 1988 graduate business panel at Michigan State University. When a fellow panelist suggested she franchise her little company, Sheets decided to consult with an attorney.

In 1989, Sheets awarded the first location outside of Michigan to her daughter, Melanie Bergeron. The office was in Atlanta, Georgia. When the company reached 39 franchises, Sheets asked Bergeron to assume the role of company president while she pursued a seat in the Michigan State Senate. Bergeron is now chair of the board. TWO MEN AND A TRUCK's long track record of aggressive growth continues under Bergeron's progressive leadership and keen business strategies. Her accomplishments have been showcased on the cover of *Franchising World* magazine and in numerous other publications, including *Franchise Times*. Brig and Jon Sorber returned to their Lansing roots in the mid-1990s to team up with their mom and older sister. Brig is now the president and chief executive officer, while Jon serves as executive vice president. The first truck that Sheets bought in 1985 has now multiplied into a fleet of more than 1,200 trucks.

Customers benefit from having trained, uniformed movers who are insured and bonded to handle any home move and business moving tasks. The company has come a long way—and logged a lot of miles—since Sheets sketched the first "stick men." TWO MEN AND A TRUCK continues to pave the way for future growth and innovation, while remaining focused on exceeding customers' expectations.

The firm now has more than 200 locations operating worldwide, including 32 U.S. states, Canada, and Ireland. In 2010 alone, with 1,300 trucks currently on the road, the system completed 317,841 moves. The company reached the milestone of 2,000,000 moves in 2005.

Franchising

Franchise territories are based on population, generally between 250,000 and 420,000 people per marketing area. The initial franchise fee is $45,000, or $85,000 if the franchisee has previously operated in the area. Total startup costs (including facility, trucks, equipment, and other expenses) range from $158,000 to $460,910. Franchisees pay a royalty of 6 percent of gross revenue, plus 1 percent for advertising.

TWO MEN AND A TRUCK has always focused on training its employees with the latest techniques and the best equipment available—and on treating everyone as they would want their grandmother treated, otherwise known as THE GRANDMA RULE®. Before a new franchisee can open a location, he or she must attend a two-week training course in Lansing, Michigan, conducted by home office staff at STICK MEN UNIVERSITY®. There, franchisees are taught by subject-matter experts about the computer systems, how to market their new business, and how to hire, manage, and lead their teams. (Throughout the year, STICK MEN UNIVERSITY offers online classes that cover everything from marketing tactics to leadership to making accurate estimates. Several instructor-led courses are also available online.)

Franchisees also work in a two-story home built inside the TWO MEN AND A TRUCK headquarters. During this portion of the training, students are taught how to maneuver, wrap, pack, and load items such as a grand piano, a china cabinet filled with breakables, glass tables, a washer and dryer, and a flat-screen television. Students are expected to be able to recognize obstacles and empty the house as quickly and efficiently as possible. A truck box, built to scale, is also located in the training facility. Students must be able to fully pack the back of the truck with the items from the home.

Many other tools are available to franchisees, including detailed monthly reports, newsletters, extranet, a system-wide annual meeting, a toll-free support line, a tradeshow booth, a complete line of TWO MEN AND A TRUCK branded clothing and professional marketing materials, and a system-wide purchasing system.

Before answering the following questions, reread Chapter 4 and watch the TWO MEN AND A TRUCK video for this chapter.

View the video and answer the questions that follow.

Questions

1. Limiting sales territories is one of the common restrictions that franchise contracts impose on franchisees. Do an Internet search for TWO MEN AND A TRUCK franchises in your immediate area. How many are there? Does this number reflect the company's population requirements?

2. Which moving companies compete with TWO MEN AND A TRUCK in your area? Are there differences in their rates of success? How could you measure those differences? Are there differences in their advertising? In their rates for items such as boxes and packing supplies? Which companies have an advantage, and why?

3. Suppose that after owning a TWO MEN AND A TRUCK franchise for five years, you decided to go out on your own with a new moving company called Four Movers. What kinds of legal issues would you face?

Source: Compiled from interviews and information provided by TWO MEN AND A TRUCK. www.twomenandatruck.com. © 2012, Cengage Learning.

The Avedis Zildjian Company, Inc.
Innovation Through the Generations

In 1999, Armand Zildjian broke with family tradition when he promoted his daughter Craigie to the position of chief executive officer of the Avedis Zildjian Company. She was the first woman to carry that responsibility in the company, which had survived for almost 400 years. He finished breaking the glass ceiling by appointing his younger daughter, Debbie, as vice president of human resources.

The Avedis Zildjian Company, headquartered in Norwell, Massachusetts, is the world's largest manufacturer of cymbals and drumsticks. Estimates of the firm's global market share range from 50 to 65 percent. On the company website, http://zildjian.com, there is a list of world-famous artists who use the firm's cymbals and drumsticks. These artists cover all musical genres: rock, punk, metal, hip hop, jazz, Latin, country, gospel, orchestral, marching, and more.

History

The Avedis Zildjian Company is the oldest family business in the United States. Incorporated in Quincy, Massachusetts, in 1929, the venture was actually established centuries earlier in Constantinople (now Istanbul), Turkey. The founder of the company, Avedis, was an Armenian alchemist, searching for means to convert base metals to gold. In the process, he discovered a new way of treating alloys, primarily copper and tin, that enabled him to produce cymbals that had clarity and strength beyond anything previously seen. Cymbals had been around for a long time, having been found in ancient Egyptian tombs.

Avedis's work was recognized by Sultan Osman II of Turkey, who adopted the cymbals for bands playing for royal weddings, religious feasts, calls to prayer, and the Ottoman army. The sultan gave Avedis the name "Zildjian," which has been translated from Turkish and Armenian to mean "cymbal-maker" or "cymbal smith."

The Zildjian family documents the origin of the company in 1623, when the sultan granted Avedis permission to leave the palace and start his business. For the next three centuries, the secret process for casting cymbals was passed from generation to generation to the oldest male next in line. In the 1920s, the leader of the family enterprise, Aram, had no children. He contacted his nephew, Avedis III, who had emigrated to the United States, asking him to take over the business. Avedis III agreed, on the condition that the firm would relocate to North America. By then, the United States had become the dominant market in the world for musical instruments. He guided the business through the Great Depression of the 1930s and through World War II.

When Avedis III died in 1979, his sons, Armand and Robert, were senior executives in the company. They had a parting of the ways, with Robert leaving to create a competing cymbal manufacturer, Sabian Cymbals, in New Brunswick, Canada. Armand grew the Avedis Zildjian Company through sales and new product lines before handing over the leadership to his daughters.

Innovation from Generation to Generation

The Zildjian family has been producing cymbals for more than 390 years. Can this be described as an innovative company? Hundreds of years ago, businesses were not faced with the global competitive environment that exists today. The company did, however, begin selling products internationally very early in its history. And there were competitors in Turkey, which became known for cymbals much in the way that the production of gongs is associated with China. So the firm had to be sensitive to the needs and demands of its customers, as well as pay attention to international political and economic conditions.

Originally, cymbals needed to be heavy and sturdy. They were used by armies in ways similar to the use of bugles by the modern U.S. military. Then in the late 1600s, German musician Nicolaus Strungk called for Turkish cymbals in his opera "Esther." However, it was not until the 19th century that composers like Berlioz and Wagner began featuring cymbals in their works. Furthermore, they demanded that only Zildjian cymbals be used. This represented a new market for the company.

Avedis Zildjian II, who headed the business at that time, initiated an entirely new promotional campaign. Zildjian cymbals had always carried a signature, but those wore off quickly. So Avedis II starting stamping each cymbal with the company's trademark in both Turkish and French. Then he went on the road or, more accurately, on the water. Having built a ship, he took the company's products to international exhibitions and trade shows in Paris, London, and other major cities, introducing customers to the high quality of Zildjian cymbals.

Other changes occurred when the firm relocated to the United States and Avedis III took charge. Carefully listening to customers, he began introducing new product lines, the first being cymbals for drum sets. Famous performers, including Gene Krupa, Chick Webb, and Papa Jo Jones, encouraged Avedis III to make thinner cymbals for dance bands. When World War II began, the firm was downsized to three employees but survived by refocusing on military bands.

Following the war, Avedis III's son, Armand, carried on his father's initiatives by developing personal relationships with top drummers and percussionists, ensuring that the company would continue to provide what customers were looking for. He also invested in the latest manufacturing processes and equipment and in 1988 opened a drumstick manufacturing facility.

Today, experimentation continues under Craigie's leadership as the latest CEO, with such advances as cymbals made of titanium, new lathing patterns, and a coated cymbal series.

Family Values

The mission statement for the Avedis Zildjian Company is as follows:

> *To expand the Company's global leadership as the only serious choice in cymbals, drumsticks, and selected specialty percussion instruments by providing superior quality, product innovation, and outstanding customer service. To strive for continuous improvement through professional management and employee participation, while building the Company's value, preserving its family character, and enhancing its rich heritage.*

The company has a firm commitment to its employees. It provides incentive pay for working faster, producing more, and for doing jobs right the first time. Under Craigie's leadership, there has been no overseas outsourcing of jobs.

Craigie and Debbie know they will face challenges in the future. Economic conditions change, competitors can be creative and aggressive, and technology is continually moving forward. To make sure they are ready for the challenges, family members must prove themselves before joining the company. To qualify for a job at the family firm, a family member must do all of the following:

- Intern while in high school or college to gain an appreciation for the company's standards.
- Graduate from college, preferably with a business degree.
- Obtain work experience outside the family firm.

When they accept a position in the company, the new employees cannot report to one of their relatives.

Cady Zildjian Bickford met all of those qualifications when she joined the Avedis Zildjian Company as the first member from the 15th generation. When Craigie was being interviewed by a reporter from NBC's *TODAY* program, she turned to Cady's 4-year-old daughter, asking her, "Do you want to work for the company, Emilia?" Emilia did not hesitate. Her emphatic answer was "Yes!"

Questions

1. What do you think has been more important to the survival of the Avedis Zildjian Company, its trade secrets for manufacturing cymbals or the commitment of the family?

2. If you were a consultant to the Avedis Zildjian Company, what advice would you offer to prepare it for the following:
   a. A global economic recession?
   b. Technology advances in electronic music?
   c. Increased global competition?

3. What rules would you recommend that a family-owned firm have for hiring family members?

4. As a family member, what might be some advantages to working in a family business? What might be some disadvantages?

5. Which kind of business is more likely to be innovative—a family-owned business or non-family-owned business? Why?

Sources: Based on "The Avedis Zildjian Company," http://zildjian.com, accessed March 30, 2013; Thomas R. Navin, "World's Leading Cymbal Maker: Avedis Zildjian Company," *Bulletin of the Business Historical Society*, Vol. 23, No. 4 (December 1949), pp. 196–206; Bob Dotson, "American Story: How a 390-Year-Old Family Business Avoids Layoffs," http://todaynews.today.com/_news/2013/03/06/17087359-american-story-how-a-390-year-old-family-business-avoids-layoffs?lite&type=photo, accessed March 29, 2013; Stephanie Becker, "Producer's Notebook: Taking a Crash Course in Cymbals," http://todaynews.today.com/_news/2013/03/06/17181249-producers-notebook-taking-a-crash-course-in-cymbals?lite, accessed March 29, 2013; "About Zildjian," www.x8drums.com/Zildjian-Cymbals-s/284.htm accessed March 29, 2013; "Zildjian History," www.activemusician.com/Zildjian-History--t2i193; "The History of Zildjian Cymbals," www.flacche.com/index.php?option=com_content&view=article&id=77&Itemid=97; and Kim Gittleson, "Trade Secrets of Oldest Family Firm in US," www.bbc.co.uk/news/business-18261045, accessed March 29, 2013.

Hyper Wear, Inc.

Writing an Executive Summary for a Business Plan

CASE
6

Hyper Wear was founded in 2008 to participate in the functional fitness market, along with such recognized brands as CrossFit and Zumba. The company first designed a men's weight vest called a Hyper Vest®, followed by the SandBell® and SteelBell®, which were designed to be used as free weights. In 2011, the firm raised money from outside investors and hired Denver Fredenburg as its CEO. By 2012, sales were approximately $1 million, and the firm needed more money to fund its growth. Fredenburg has written a business plan to be used in raising the needed money. The Hyper Wear, Inc., Executive Summary is presented on the text's website, which can be accessed by going to www.cengagebrain.com and selecting the Longenecker text.

Questions

1. Is Hyper Wear's executive summary more of a synopsis or a narrative?

2. If you were an investor, would the executive summary spark your interest in the opportunity? In other words, would you continue reading the business plan for more details?

3. What do you like about this executive summary? What do you dislike?

4. Would you suggest that Fredenburg make any changes or additions to the executive summary? If so, what do you suggest?

ReadyMade Magazine

Focus and Segmentation

ReadyMade markets itself as a magazine catering to GenNesters, the group of consumers ages 25 to 35 who are just settling down after college. These young consumers are buying their first houses and taking on domestic and decorating roles for the first time. They are interested in being stylish, while at the same time maintaining their own unique personalities.

But the magazine appeals to a wide variety of readers other than just GenNesters. *ReadyMade* has subscribers in all age groups—from teens looking to update their rooms to retirees looking for projects to enliven their homes. This diversity offers a unique challenge to *ReadyMade* as it tries to promote itself to advertisers who need to know what sort of people will be reached through advertisements appearing in the publication.

ReadyMade is named after the term that Marcel Duchamp coined in 1915 for a series of sculptures that playfully rethought the relationship between people and mass-produced objects, everyday items, and art. *Ready-Made* magazine is about people who make things and the culture of making, so it consists mostly of do-it-yourself projects and both short and long articles. Subscribers are invited to submit projects, recipes, and story ideas relating to the culture of making, inventive practices and people, of-the-moment cultural trends and products, and food trends.

Before answering the questions below, reread Chapter 7 and watch the *ReadyMade* video for this chapter.

View the video and answer the questions that follow.

Questions

1. How does *ReadyMade* communicate the demographics of its reader base to advertisers who want to see specific statistics about *ReadyMade*'s target market?

2. What sort of segmentation does *ReadyMade* use when it markets to businesses and investors?

3. What ideas do you have that would help *ReadyMade* reach out to new subscribers without alienating its loyal base?

Source: From Lamb/Hair/McDaniel, *Essentials of Marketing, 7e.*
© 2012 Cengage Learning.

Couchsurfing International
A Story of Startup, Growth, and Transformation

In ancient civilizations, it was a common practice to open one's home to travelers who needed a place to sleep. This prompted the sharing of news, stories, and information. Couchsurfing International, a travel-oriented social networking site based in San Francisco, is dedicated to reviving the ancient practice and the social exchange that goes along with it.

Chapter One: The Founders

THE CONCEPTIONIST After graduating from college in 1997 with a degree in computer science, Casey Fenton decided to see some of the world before settling down. When he came across a relatively inexpensive flight from Boston to Reykjavik, Iceland, he decided to buy it but had no idea where he would stay or what he should see while there. He knew that he did not want to be a garden-variety tourist, staying in a hotel and traveling to the typical sights. Rather, he wanted to immerse himself in the Icelandic way of life—this, he believed, was what traveling should be all about.

To zero in on definite travel plans, Fenton called and e-mailed almost 2,000 students from the University of Iceland, asking if they had a couch or spare room that he could stay in for a night or two. He received more than 50 offers for possible accommodations not only in Reykjavik, where the university is situated, but also in other towns located nearby. Using these leads, he made connections, set up specific travel plans, and left for his Icelandic adventure.

The trip ended up being a truly unforgettable experience. The locals showed him things he could never have found on his own, and he built great friendships along the way. Fenton decided that he wanted to help others see the world as he was able to, through the eyes of native hosts. On the flight home, he came up with the idea that would become the foundation of "The Couchsurfing Project." Fenton spent the next couple of years programming and setting up the website for Couchsurfing.org. He also took a position with a startup called Fuxito Worldwide, but he continued working on the code that would lead to the eventual launch of his slowly blossoming website project.

THE ENTREPRENEUR Daniel Hoffer had three well-defined passions that developed at a young age: a love for traveling, helping others, and computer programming. An avid traveler since he was a boy, he gained a

sense of purpose and perspective from learning about different cultures. With this confidence and direction, he figured out how to use his computer science skills to fulfill his desire to help others. The first online community that Hoffer launched grew into what would become a nonprofit educational program in Massachusetts and an online bulletin board that allowed physically disabled patients to connect with high school students.

Prior to getting his MBA from Columbia Business School and working for numerous computer technology companies, Hoffer studied philosophy at Harvard University. Apparently, his studies weren't enough to keep him busy, because he remained actively engaged in the computer science world during that time and helped launch multiple startups. One of these companies, founded in 1999 as a venture-backed operation, was an international soccer website called Fuxito Worldwide. Although this endeavor was only one of hundreds of projects with which Hoffer would become involved, Fuxito was the venture that would lead Hoffer to his true calling.

THE VISIONARY Sebastian Le Tuan was born to help cultivate a world of cultural acceptance through travel. A native of France, Le Tuan eventually followed his heart and his love for technology to Silicon Valley in California. But while he was still a teenager, he spent time with a host family in Catalan, Spain, which helped him to understand that experiencing cultures on a personal level is paramount to releasing judgment and embracing differences. Though he had an undergraduate degree in cognitive science from the University of California at Berkley, Le Tuan managed to harness his passion for software development, as well, through various research initiatives. He worked for several companies as a software designer, with a focus on user experience. Eventually, he landed a position at a Web-based company called Fuxito Worldwide, where he would come to find his broad span of interests and experience perfectly matched for an innovative endeavor that was just waiting to come together.

Chapter Two: Birth of a Business

Fenton, Hoffer, and Le Tuan brought their own unique backgrounds, interests, and talents when they joined Fuxito Worldwide and ended up making important contributions to the venture. Though they worked on different aspects of the company, the three formed a close friendship based on a shared love for innovation, exploration, and serving those in need. They realized that their diverse specialties, together with a unified purpose and vision, could help them develop a website that would revolutionize the way people travel. Thus began The Couchsurfing Project.

THE PATH TO 501(C)(3) STATUS After spending a number of years forming their ideas into a concrete plan, Fenton, Hoffer, and Le Tuan all agreed steadfastly on many aspects of their startup concept, the most important of which was that it would be launched as a nonprofit organization. In March 2003, the three co-founders filed in New Hampshire to incorporate Couchsurfing as a 501(c)(3), but it was not added to the official list of registered charities in the state until November 14, 2007. (See Chapter 8 for more information about 501(c)(3) status.) Why the delay? By taking their time to register the organization as a nonprofit with the state attorney general (which is required by law in the state of New Hampshire), Couchsurfing sidestepped certain recordkeeping and reporting responsibilities. This move led the Department of Justice in New Hampshire to investigate the organization at the end of 2007. With the pressure to comply growing, the company eventually sent the required documents for 2003 to 2006 to the attorney general, and the organization was officially added to the registered charities list.

WEBSITE LAUNCH After filing for 501(c)(3) status in 2003, the three co-founders finally launched a beta version of the website. Because he had been so involved with the development of the basic idea and the coding that was needed, Fenton naturally accepted the role of executive director. Hoffer had experience managing small startup companies, so he gravitated toward strategic development–related responsibilities. LeTuan had a solid grasp of the connection between human experience and both technology and cultural acceptance, so he headed the development of the website's overall purpose and mission. This provided the budding venture with a vision that could support and sustain the dedication and commitment of its members. A year after its beta testing was initiated, the website went public, and the founders were confident that users would come to discover and appreciate the power of relationship-based, reduced-cost travel.

Chapter Three: Riding the Wave of a ".org"

The founders fully believed that their venture would touch the lives of millions of people, but in the year following the website's launch, only 6,000 members joined the community. The founders continued to follow the same strategy for the next year, which saw membership jump to nearly 50,000. And with the continued growth came other new opportunities—that is, until 2006 rolled around.

In June 2006, the venture hit a serious snag: As a result of numerous technical errors within Couchsurfing's databases, the profiles of all of its members were lost. Because so much information had vanished and the future of the venture seemed to be so in doubt, Fenton sent out an e-mail to the masses, reporting, "It is with a heavy heart that I face the truth of this situation. Couchsurfing as we knew it doesn't exist anymore."

Immediately upon sending out this message, Fenton started receiving a great deal of criticism. But at the same time, many members were very supportive, which inspired the Couchsurfing team to design a new website (called CS2.0) within a couple of weeks after the technical failures. The team also created a new slogan for the venture, "Participate in Creating a Better World, One Couch at a Time," which fit the new culture of the rehabilitated enterprise. With the continued support of past and current members, in addition to the international media attention that the new website received, Couchsurfing's membership exploded from around 50,000 to over 3.5 million individuals by the beginning of 2012. During this period, nearly 5.5 million travel-related connections were formed using this one-of-a-kind community website.

Chapter Four: What to Do When Growing Too Fast

Up to this point, the only revenues that Couchsurfing had received were from donations and its identification verification service (highly recommended, but not required), which could be used to confirm that a member was who he or she claimed to be. Fenton and Hoffer were strongly committed to providing an online source of help to travelers looking for free places to stay and to offering that service without the advertisements and expenses that other travel websites featured. But with the explosion of growth Couchsurfing had experienced, the management team needed to decide if remaining a nonprofit was best for the future of the company. To complicate matters further, Couchsurfing applied to receive 501(c)(3) status in November of 2007, only to see its application be formally rejected by the IRS in early 2011. From this setback, Hoffer came to realize that the nonprofit structure can blunt organizational innovation and flexibility as a result of increased regulatory oversight and various auditing requirements stipulated by law.

In their search for guidance, they sought the advice of four people who were members of the venture's board of directors: Tony Espinoza, Matt Cohler, Jonathan Teo, and Todor Tashev. These seasoned executives brought a wealth of experience to discussions about the company and its future. Espinoza had worked at Apple and had served as vice president and general manager for MTV

Networks, vice president and co-founder of When.com, vice president of AOL, and CEO of SuperSecret.com. Cohler was one of the founding members of LinkedIn, where he served as vice president and general manager. He was also one of the first five employees hired at Facebook and is currently a general partner at Benchmark, a venture capital firm. Teo was a member of the strategy team at Google and a principal at Benchmark, where he helped initiate the original investments in companies like Twitter and Instagram. Tashev had worked as a venture capital analyst for JP Morgan and later became a partner at investment firm Omidyar Network, where he directed consumer Internet and mobile initiatives.

These board members suggested using a new organizational form specifically designed to use the power of business to solve a social or environmental problem. As a B Corporation (or benefit corporation), performance and accountability standards are demanding, sustainability must be a primary thrust, and transparency is forced through B Impact Reports that have to be filed. But the team quickly realized that converting to this form would allow them to accept investments, and be nimble and flexible while remaining true to their original and continuing social mission. Responding to this advice, the team decided to change its status officially to a B corporation in late 2011.

This new organizational form brought new opportunities, but also greater challenges. On the opportunity side, it led to $15 million in investments to fuel the expansion of the company so that it could keep up with escalating market interest. This funding was led by investment heavyweights like Benchmark, General Catalyst Partners, Menlo Ventures, and Omidyar Network. It also allowed the firm to begin to earn profits from its nearly 3.5 million users, but the founders maintained that Couchsurfing would continue to offer its services free of charge to its users. They added, however, that the change would also allow them to explore "alternative revenue streams."

While the change in status at Couchsurfing opened the door to greater opportunity, it also presented its share of risk. Change can erode confidence and will almost always generate at least some resistance. It certainly created significant backlash for Couchsurfing. About 3,000 members of the company's online community actually formed a group under the title "We are against CS becoming a for-profit corporation." This group voiced their reactions, which were varied and included statements such as "The structure of CS belongs to the community," "Members are no longer part of a true community, they are customers/consumers of a service sold by Couchsurfing International Inc.," and "The worst part is that the assets of a non-profit should not be allowed to change into a for-profit." These reactions indicate that the struggles at Couchsurfing International—following its conversion from a nonprofit organization to a for-profit entity that continues to provide benefits to society—are probably far from over.

Questions

1. How would you describe the founding team of Fenton, Hoffer, and Le Tuan? Is it a balanced team? What does each member bring to the business? Can you see gaps in their skill sets and capabilities that should be adjusted for in some way?

2. What is the form of organization that Fenton, Hoffer, and Le Tuan first chose for Couchsurfing International? Assess the advantages and disadvantages of the major organizational forms mentioned in Chapter 8. Which of these would have been best for the company when it was founded? Why?

3. Identify and describe the organizational form to which the team most recently transitioned the firm. Was it a good decision to make this change? In your opinion, how well was the transition handled? In what ways might it have been managed better?

4. Assess the fit of the board of directors with Couchsurfing based on the profiles of those members mentioned in the case (the company has additional directors). What are the strengths and weaknesses of these board members, including potential gaps in their knowledge? Do you see any ways in which their advice to the entrepreneurial team may not have been in the best interests of the company?

Sources: Case contributed by Garad Soderman; www.opencouchsurfing.org/tag/legal, accessed April 5, 2013; Nicole Perlroth, "Non-Profit Couchsurfing Raises Millions in Funding," *Forbes*, August 24, 2011, www.forbes.com/sites/nicoleperlroth/2011/08/24/non-profit -couchsurfing-raises-millions-in-funding, accessed April 4, 2013; Bobbie Johnson, "After Going For-Profit, Couchsurfing Faces Revolt," http://gigaom.com/2011/09/01/after-going -for-profit-couchsurfing-faces-user-revolt, accessed April 3, 2013; and Michael del Castillo, "Global Traveler Raises $15 Million to Put Strangers in Your Living Room," *Upstart Business Journal*, August 22, 2012, http://upstart.bizjournals.com/money/loot/2012/08/22 /couchsurfing-raises-15m-for-mobile-apps.html?page=all, accessed April 4, 2013.

Cookies-N-Cream
A Moveable Location

Cookies-N-Cream is an independent brand that sells its products from a truck that provides a moveable location and low overhead. Based in Brooklyn, New York, the company's owners, Scrills, P Loc and DJ Jon Blak, are preparing a second truck, which they're renovating and planning to move into Los Angeles sometime in the next year.

The Cookies-N-Cream brand is one that encompasses two creative outlets—clothing and designer toys—neither of which are cookies or cream. In an era of "me-too" clothing brands and toys, the owners set out to create a culture brand that draws on different influences—New York City lifestyle/culture, art, street couture, designer toys, high fashion, music, and pop/underground culture, just to name a few—all with a distinct personality and attitude of their own. Designer toys refer to toys and other collectibles created in limited quantities by artists and designers, and collected mostly by adults. Some of the toys/art pieces include the Puma SneakerHead, Hapiko, Dumny, and Shoot sculptures.

Based on their belief in being "true to yourself," the owners called their brand Cookies-N-Cream and built a grassroots company that's authentic and fun. With their attention to detail and focus on creating "playful luxury" products, they've developed a cult following that enjoys the experience that is Cookies-N-Cream. The owners represent the independent and avant-garde attitude that embodies their roots and today's youth.

View the video and answer the questions that follow.

Questions

1. What are some location advantages that Cookies-N-Cream has that a brick-and-mortar retailer doesn't have? Are there any drawbacks to a mobile vendor's choice of location?

2. Discuss site costs, retailing and office equipment, and other financial considerations of a mobile vendor such as Cookies-N-Cream.

3. What legal considerations affect Cookies-N-Cream's choice of location? How do those compare with the legal considerations of brick-and-mortar and home-based businesses?

Source: Compiled from interviews and information provided by Cookies-N-Cream. http://www.bakedinny.com. © 2012, Cengage Learning.

Harper & Reiman, LLC

Understanding a Firm's Financial Statements

Harper & Reiman, LLC, is a consulting firm that caters to nonprofit organizations. The company is headquartered in Dallas, Texas, and has recently expanded to include an office in Amarillo, Texas, Harper's home town.

The business was founded in 2000 by Brett Harper and Anna Reiman, who met in an entrepreneurship class in college and discovered that they shared a passion for serving and developing the nonprofit sphere. Following graduation, they both were employed by J.P. Morgan. They frequently worked together on common assignments. On a number of occasions, they worked with nonprofit organizations whose innovative processes allowed them to "do more with less." The not-for-profits simply were not able to throw a lot of cash at problems, as many large business organizations do, and had to think and act like entrepreneurs if they were to achieve their missions. Harper and Reiman soon came to believe that for-profit businesses could learn from the really good nonprofits.

After eight years at JP Morgan, Harper and Reiman decided to start their own consulting firm, Harper & Reiman, LLC. At first, they limited their work to financial advisory services, knowing that many nonprofits needed help in managing their financial operations. The company developed financial management software that centers on liquidity analytics and enables nonprofits to shorten cash conversion cycles and strengthen liquidity. They gradually expanded into other services, including sustainable business solutions, infrastructure consulting, risk management, and innovation services.

The company has experienced significant growth, with sales approaching $29 million in 2013—far beyond anything the owners could have imagined. For one thing, the company distinguished itself in the industry by designing a payment system that allows nonprofits to make payments for Harper & Reiman services in seasons when donations are the highest. However, it also required Harper & Reiman to diversify its client base so that receivables are consistently being collected. Essentially, the company has applied the advice it gives to clients to itself.

While the majority of consulting clients are located near the two regional offices, the firm's software has been sold nationwide on a limited basis. Wanting to enter new geographical markets, Harper and Reiman are considering a marketing strategy to increase the firm's national visibility. However, before beginning a major expansion, they want to evaluate the firm's financial health.

Harper & Reiman, LLC

Balance Sheets for years ending 2012 and 2013

	2012	2013	Changes
Assets			
Current assets:			
Cash	$ 15,500	$ 218,500	$ 203,000
Accounts receivable	3,989,000	4,428,000	439,000
Inventory	4,155,000	4,678,000	523,000
Prepaid expenses and deposits	138,500	144,000	5,500
Other current assets	105,500	105,500	—
Total current assets	$ 8,403,500	$ 9,574,000	$1,170,500
Fixed assets:			
Gross fixed assets	$ 7,541,000	$ 8,519,000	$ 978,000
Accumulated depreciation	(3,822,500)	(4,377,000)	(554,500)
Net fixed assets	3,718,500	4,142,000	423,500

(Continued)

Harper & Reiman, LLC (continued)

	2012	2013	Changes
Other assets	11,500	1,000	(10,500)
TOTAL ASSETS	$ 12,133,500	$ 13,717,000	$ 1,583,500
Debt (Liabilities) and Equity			
Current liabilities:			
Notes payable to bank	$ 1,100,000	$ 1,192,000	$ 92,000
Accounts payable	1,931,000	2,238,500	307,500
Accrued expenses	920,500	884,000	(36,500)
Total current liabilities	$ 3,951,500	$ 4,314,500	$ 363,000
Long-term debt	3,614,000	4,257,000	643,000
Total debt	$ 7,565,500	$ 8,571,500	$ 1,006,000
Stockholders' equity:			
Common stock	$ 356,000	$ 391,500	$ 35,500
Additional paid-in capital	498,000	649,000	151,000
Retained earnings	3,714,000	4,105,000	391,000
Total stockholders' equity	$ 4,568,000	$ 5,145,500	$ 577,500
TOTAL DEBT AND EQUITY	$ 12,133,500	$ 13,717,000	$ 1,583,500

Income Statements for Years Ending 2012 and 2013

	2012	2013
Net sales	$ 27,069,000	$ 28,911,500
Cost of goods sold	(18,880,500)	(20,524,500)
Gross profits	$ 8,188,500	$ 8,387,000
Selling and general and administrative expenses	(6,805,500)	(6,953,000)
Operating profits	$ 1,383,000	$ 1,434,000
Interest expense	(481,500)	(535,500)
Interest income	5,500	10,000
Profits before tax	$ 907,000	$ 908,500
Income taxes	(385,000)	(377,000)
Net profits	$ 522,000	$ 531,500

Statement of Retained Earnings for years ending 2012 and 2013

	2012	2013
Beginning retained earnings	$ 3,298,000	$ 3,714,000
Net profits	522,000	531,500
Dividends	(106,000)	(140,500)
Ending retained earnings	$ 3,714,000	$ 4,105,000

Harper & Reiman, LLC (continued)

Statement of Cash Flows for years ending 2012 and 2013

	2012	2013
Operating activities:		
Net profits	$ 522,000	$ 531,500
Depreciation	564,500	554,500
Profits before depreciation	$ 1,086,500	$ 1,086,000
Increase in accounts receivable	$ (464,000)	$ (439,000)
Payments for inventory:		
Increase in inventory	(572,000)	(523,000)
Increase in accounts payable	68,500	307,500
Total payment for inventory	(503,500)	(215,500)
Increase in prepaid expenses	(19,000)	(5,500)
Increase (decrease) in accrued expenses	87,500	(36,500)
Cash flows from operations	$ 187,500	$ 389,500
Investing activities:		
Increase in gross fixed assets	$ (861,500)	$ (978,000)
Decrease (increase) in other assets	—	10,500
Cash flows from investing activities	$ (861,500)	$ (967,500)
Financing activities:		
Increase in notes payable	$ 625,000	$ 92,000
Increase (decrease) in long-term debt	(112,500)	643,000
Issued common stock	77,500	186,500
Cash dividends paid	(81,000)	(140,500)
Cash flows from financing activities	$ 509,000	$ 781,000
Net change in cash	$ (165,000)	$ 203,000
Beginning cash	180,500	15,500
Ending cash	$ 15,500	$ 218,500
Industry norms:		
Current ratio	2.2	
Return on assets	12.6%	
Operating profit margin	6.3%	
Total asset turnover	2.00	
Debt ratio	40.0%	
Return on common equity	15.0%	

Question

1. Harper and Reiman are interested in examining four specific issues: liquidity, profitability, the risk occurring from debt financing, and the rate of return the business is providing to them as owners. They also want to have a good sense of the sources and uses of cash flows in the business. Given the firm's recent financial results, as shown above, evaluate the company's financial situation as it relates to the owners' concerns. What advice would you give to Harper and Reiman?

Source: This case was prepared by Lauren Houser, April 2013.

Ashley Palmer Clothing, Inc.

Financial Forecasting

Ashley Palmer Clothing, Inc., produces dresses for women. The firm was launched in June 2009 by Ashley Jantz and Amanda Palmer, both graduates of Boston College. Ashley Palmer designs apparel for the modern woman's shape rather than using the traditional standard sizing.

History of Sizing Clothing

In 1939, the National Bureau of Home Economics of the U.S. Department of Agriculture was charged with standardizing sizing for women's clothing. Over a two-year period, some 15,000 women were given full-body measurements. This system created the sizing system that is still in use today.

Studies have found that the average body proportions of American women when the sizing charts were created are different from the body proportions of today's women. Specifically, American women in 1939 were markedly more slender and shorter. The result is that it is difficult for some women to find clothing that fits well. In the September 2009 issue of *Fashionista Magazine*, Jantz, who stands six feet tall, said,

[W]e were tired of not finding the clothes that were the right fit so we decided it would be a good venture to create products for today's women based on bust measurement, cup size and torso length.

The Opportunity

For Jantz and Palmer, this problem represented an opportunity. After considerable research, they decided to start a business that produced fitted clothing for today's young women. They recruited a young up-and-coming fashion designer, Joy Lee, who had experience in apparel design for several major women's clothing brands. Seven months after starting the business, they offered their first dresses for sale online.

Then, in early 2010, the firm began supplying clothes to two well-known high-end retailers. Within a year after becoming a supplier to these exclusive retail outlets, the company's production orders had more than doubled. In order to keep up, the firm added five more team members in October 2010.

Sales continued to increase over the next three years, reaching $4.7 million in 2013. During this same time, the number of employees grew from 7 to 16. The company also moved into a 4,000-square-foot facility and added additional sewing equipment and presses.

Planning for Growth

In August 2013, Ashley Palmer ventured into creating professional attire for young women. The products received rave reviews. Within three months, the retail outlets had sold over 90 percent of their inventories, quickly placing orders for more products.

The founders, while excited about the prospect of sales growth, began to worry. Based on their estimates, the company would most probably experience a 50 percent growth rate, compared to the 25 percent they had experienced over the past two years. They knew that if they were to avoid cash flow problems from the anticipated growth, they needed to anticipate the asset requirements and additional financing that would be required to sustain their business.

The owners believed they would need to purchase state-of-the-art industrial sewing machines, cutting tables, and pressing machines at a cost of $280,000. The new equipment would be depreciated over 14 years, using straight-line depreciation. Jantz also thought that the following assumptions were appropriate:

1. Cash, accounts receivable, and inventory would follow their same relationships to sales as in the past two years; that is, each asset would maintain the average asset-to-sales percentages experienced in 2012 and 2013.

2. Both cost of goods sold and marketing expenses are variable and would approximate the same percentage of sales as in 2012 and 2013.

3. General and administrative costs are fixed in nature but should increase to $130,000 in the next year.

4. The interest rates on the already outstanding debt would be renegotiated, which would reduce the interest on this debt to $45,000.

5. The firm's tax rate should be about 40 percent.

To meet the firm's financing needs, Palmer has negotiated a line of credit (short-term debt) with Amway Bank for up to $100,000. The bank has also agreed to loan the firm $150,000 for purchasing new equipment; this is to be repaid over five years. The principal on the latter loan is to be repaid in $30,000 annual payments, with interest payments being made on the remaining balance of the note. Both notes will carry a 5 percent interest rate. The short-term notes payable and long-term debt owed in 2013 will be reduced by $50,000 and $30,000, respectively.

Accounts payable and other current liabilities should increase proportionally with sales increases.

Finally, Jantz and Palmer are willing to provide more of their own money in the form of equity up to a total of $100,000 in equity if needed. They will also lower the amount of dividends they have been paying themselves (about 40 percent of earnings over the past two years). They both have decided to limit their dividends individually to $15,000, or a total of $30,000.

Ashley Palmer Clothing, Inc.
Income Statements or the Years Ending December 31, 2011, 2012, and 2013

	2011		2012		2013	
Sales	$3,000,000	100.0%	$3,760,000	100.0%	$4,700,000	100.0%
Cost of goods sold	(2,400,000)	80.0%	(3,045,600)	81.0%	(3,877,500)	82.5%
Gross profits	$ 600,000	20.0%	$ 714,400	19.0%	$ 822,500	17.5%
Marketing expenses	(215,000)	7.2%	(250,000)	6.6%	(275,000)	5.9%
General & administrative expenses	(90,000)	3.0%	(100,000)	2.7%	(110,000)	2.3%
Depreciation expense	(25,000)	0.8%	(25,000)	0.7%	(25,000)	0.5%
Operating profits	$ 270,000	9.0%	$ 339,400	9.0%	$ 412,500	8.8%
Interest expense	(66,000)	2.2%	(66,000)	1.8%	(66,000)	1.4%
Profits before taxes	$ 204,000	6.8%	$ 273,400	7.3%	$ 346,500	7.4%
Taxes @ 40%	(81,600)	2.7%	(109,360)	2.9%	(138,600)	2.9%
Net profits	$ 122,400	4.1%	$ 164,040	4.4%	$ 207,900	4.4%
Dividends paid	$ (48,960)		$ (65,616)		$ (83,160)	
Addition to retained earnings retained earnings	$ 73,440		$ 98,424		$ 124,740	

Ashley Palmer Clothing, Inc.
Balance Sheets for the Years Ending December 31, 2011, 2012, and 2013

	2011	2012	2013
Assets			
Cash	$ 48,000	$ 95,424	$ 60,000
Accounts receivable	150,000	175,000	246,816
Inventory	335,000	390,000	511,500
Total current assets	$ 533,000	$ 660,424	$ 818,316
Plant & equipment	$ 560,000	$ 560,000	$ 560,000
Accumulated depreciation	(125,000)	(150,000)	(175,000)
Net plant & equipment	$ 435,000	$ 410,000	$ 385,000
TOTAL ASSETS	$ 968,000	$1,070,424	$1,203,316

(Continued)

Balance Sheets for the Years Ending December 31, 2011, 2012, and 2013 (continued)

	2011	2012	2013
Debt (Liabilities) and Equity			
Accounts payable	$ 128,000	$ 153,000	$ 135,000
Short-term notes payable	250,000	275,000	275,000
Other current liabilities	46,000	50,000	51,152
Total current liabilities	$ 424,000	$ 478,000	$ 461,152
Long-term debt	300,000	250,000	275,000
Total debt	$ 724,000	$ 728,000	$ 736,152
Owner's capital	$ 155,560	$ 155,560	$ 155,560
Retained earnings	88,440	186,864	311,604
Total equity	$ 244,000	$ 342,424	$ 467,164
TOTAL DEBT AND EQUITY	$ 968,000	$1,070,424	$1,203,316

Questions

1. Given the assumptions that Jantz and Palmer have made, prepare a pro forma income statement and balance sheet for 2014. Assume that the line of credit provided by the bank will be needed for the full year.

2. Using the financial ratios presented in Chapter 10, compare Ashley Palmer's ratios over time, including the pro forma ratios for 2014. If the bank requires a current ratio of at least 1.5 and a debt ratio not to exceed 55 percent, can the owners expect to be able to honor these covenants?

3. Prepare a statement of cash flows for 2013 and the 2014 projections. What did you learn from these statements?

Source: Written by Thomas Totoe, April 2013.

Moonworks

From Gutters to Home Remodeling

Not only is financing a startup business a challenge, but sometimes remaining fiscally fit for survival is itself a difficult hurdle to overcome. The first three years of starting a business can be the toughest, but how does a company that has been operating for several years continue to find sources of financing? Economic conditions, products, and customer bases can change, sometimes leaving a once-sustainable company in jeopardy of not meeting the day-to-day expenses of operation.

Managing cash flows invariably takes more than just matching payables with receivables, covering payroll, and paying taxes and insurance. As business conditions change, so can the money coming into a company. Even after startup loans have been retired, a line of credit or loan from a good funding provider is essential to keep a business moving forward.

Moonworks, a Rhode Island–based remodeling business founded as Moon Associates in 1993, enjoyed a modest rise to financial success by selling a product called GutterHelmet. Backed by the financial resources of BankRI, president and CEO Jim Moon turned GutterHelmet into a household name in New England by marketing it with help from local celebrities. Between 1993 and 2005, Moon Associates grew to $14 million in revenue by selling the product throughout New England, New York, and southwest Florida, while working out of a 10,000-square-foot building the company owns in Woonsocket, Rhode Island. During that time, the company installed more gutters in the New England states and New York than all other gutter companies combined.

As business boomed, Moon assembled a top-notch management team and started offering other products like garage organizing systems and hurricane shutters, but GutterHelmet remained the company's largest cash generator. To set the stage for future growth, the company's management began implementing industry-leading business systems.

The tide started to change in 2006. The market for gutter protection and remodeling showed signs of weakening in a slowing housing market, and the competition started putting a dent in GutterHelmet. There was no seasonal uptick in fall orders, and Moon Associates began exploring other means of generating operating cash, including the sale of their Florida operation. About the same time, Andersen Company's full-service window replacement division, Renewal by Andersen, had entered the Rhode Island home improvement market and was seeking a partner. After months of negotiation, Moon Associates struck a deal to be the sole southern New England partner, and Renewal by Andersen of Rhode Island soon debuted. With this partnership, Moon Associates was positioned to serve its existing customer base with Andersen's stylish, energy-efficient windows.

Yet the partnership didn't provide Moon Associates with the necessary boost. In 2007, GutterHelmet sales dropped 50 percent, to $6 million. Despite efforts to advertise on the Internet, new business leads were hard to generate. Renewal by Andersen of Rhode Island endured the normal financial hardships of starting up, and Moon Associates' bottom line went in the red after total company revenues plummeted 30 percent. Moon Associates needed something more than a new product line or division to return the company to profitability.

New England winters can be hard, and the winter of 2007/2008 was even tougher for Moon Associates. For the first time, the company's management team had to figure out how to turn around a negative bottom line at a time when business in general was changing. Moon went back to the drawing board to look for top-level talent. Local celebrities weren't the answer, so he recruited industry veteran Paul Thibeault, formerly Home Depot's Home Services northeast manager, to inject muscle into the company's sales force. But building sales would take time, and the company needed new capital to move forward. Moon Associates called on an old friend, the company's long-term financial partner, BankRI. Banker Matt Weiner and BankRI believed in Moon Associates' business plan and increased the company's credit line to keep Moon Associates on track.

The capital enabled Moon Associates' management team to play a hunch that Renewal by Andersen of Rhode Island could make a dent in the Cape Cod, Massachusetts, market. Further, the company diversified its product line to include general exterior home replacement products like roofing and siding, as well as insulation and hot water heaters. Moon Associates changed its name to Moonworks and shifted its focus to being a leading regional home improvement company and began to emphasize repeat customer business instead of new customer generation.

By the end of 2008, the company had emerged from the red and had a solid black bottom line. Revenues had grown 39 percent, and cash flows were positive.

Moonworks was named the "Best of the Best, Smaller Market," an award that goes to the best-performing Renewal by Andersen dealer in the country.

Moonworks continued to grow over the next two years, again receiving top recognition from Renewal by Andersen, while expanding its window-remodeling territory into Hartford and northern Connecticut. In 2010, the company posted revenues of $12.7 million, more than twice that in 2007. A crowning achievement was the company's receipt of the "Big 50 Award," *Remodeling Magazine's* annual award recognizing exceptional performance in the remodeling and replacement contracting industry.

View the video and answer the questions that follow.

Questions

1. Describe what a line of credit involves, and explain the legal obligation of a bank to provide capital with a line of credit.

2. On what three priorities might BankRI representative Matt Weiner have based the decision to extend Moon Associates' line of credit or offer additional financing? What are the "five C's of credit"?

3. Even as the remodeling market weakened and taking on extra financing became risky, what are some things that Moon Associates' president and CEO Jim Moon did to sustain the company's long-term profitability?

4. Could Moon Associates have obtained the needed capital to not only keep the company running but expand its Renewal by Andersen line through a mortgage loan? If so, how long could such a loan be financed?

Network Collie

In June 2010, William Casey had just finished his last day at a national conference for IT and software companies. He was attending on behalf of his current employer but was also there to promote Network Collie, a data management company he had started a little more than two years earlier with three college friends. Launching the new company had been hard work but also exciting for Casey and his three co-founders: Dallena Nguyen, Cody Rose, and John Dalton. Today was no different. Throughout the conference, they had received positive feedback from potential customers about their new service. However, Casey was still questioning whether Network Collie would be a long-term success. He definitely had a passion to be an entrepreneur and believed that Network Collie had potential for success. However, the team was having difficulty closing larger sales orders, and he questioned the commitment from the founding team, including his own. He knew that these two areas needed to be addressed and a firm direction for the company needed to be established before he would begin to feel comfortable with the company's future.

After dinner, the team began to share stories about conversations they had had with potential customers during the conference. The discussion quickly turned to how they should move forward. They talked about continuing down the same path, but everyone agreed that something

different needed to happen if they were going to achieve success. Their conversation focused on the long-term prospects and the potential value of Network Collie, as well as the individual needs and circumstances of the founders. Each of the founders had different ideas about how to move forward, but the final choices were to (1) quit their jobs and commit to Network Collie on a full-time basis, (2) hire someone to run the company, (3) try to sell the company, or (4) walk away.

The team debated the pros and cons of each idea. They still believed their service was the best among their competition. At the same time, all of them were concerned about the risk of leaving their current jobs. Another concern was that the first two options would require the company to obtain capital from outside investors, which was something they had never attempted before. Casey knew that the time for a decision about the future of Network Collie was now. He just wasn't sure which choice was the right choice.

Background

If ever there was a fast-rising and potentially sustainable growth market, social networking certainly was in 2009. Its foreseeable future is truly exciting based on long-term projections. As shown in Exhibit C13.1, the social

C13.1 U.S. Social Network Users and Penetration, 2009–2013

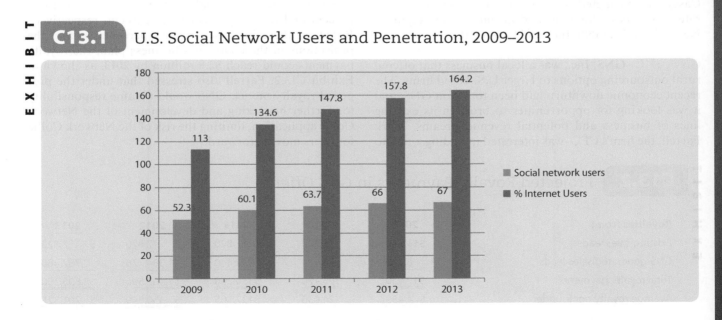

network phenomenon was projected to grow to over 164 million users and to comprise over 67 percent of the online population by 2013.

When Network Collie was started, social networking was beginning to find a solid niche in the business world for connecting with customers and promoting products and services. Thus, the challenge of tracking information across a vast array of sites and capturing the data in a useful format for business utilization had the potential to open a whole new area of business information management. Participating in this new industry and developing a sustainable business model that allowed businesses to monitor and utilize the potential marketing benefits seemed like a logical path to follow.

In spring 2009, in an effort to refine the service's value proposition and their ability to communicate the firm's potential value as an investment opportunity, the Network Collie team entered and won a business plan competition at the local university. They were then recognized at an awards banquet where potential investors were also in attendance. At the dinner, Rose had a conversation with a local entrepreneur who was very impressed with the Network Collie concept. During their conversation, the entrepreneur commented that Rose and his team could easily develop the software application, prove its viability, and sell it to someone for around $1 million. Their work was beginning to pay off, and the future looked amazingly bright. They had never thought that it would be so easy to build and grow the idea into such a valuable enterprise so quickly.

Opportunities to Exit

Within a week of winning the business plan competition, Casey was contacted by representatives from two separate companies who expressed an interest in acquiring Network Collie: GNS, Inc., and Groovy ID.

GNS, INC. GNS, Inc., was a local business that offered rural outsourcing options to larger U.S.-based firms. The recent economic downturn had been tough on GNS, and it was looking for opportunities to broaden its existing lines of business and potential revenue streams. Mark Farrell, the firm's CEO, was interested in finding a way to bring Network Collie into the GNS product line, possibly through an acquisition. Following their initial meeting, Farrell began to make inquiries with his board members and significant investors to gauge their willingness to pursue Network Collie as a potential partner or acquisition. The Network Collie team was hopeful that GNS could help Network Collie get to market and capture a broader customer base more quickly.

Casey and Rose attended a lunch meeting with Farrell in May 2009, hoping that the terms of a potential deal would be discussed. After that meeting, it became clear that Farrell was also interested in bringing Casey on board as a full-time employee at GNS. This added another layer of uncertainty and anxiety for Casey and the rest of the team. Casey now had to consider leaving his current employer to work for a different company across town. It also raised concerns that GNS might attempt to include more value in Casey's employment offer, which would not benefit the rest of the team. Casey decided to have a separate meeting with Farrell to discuss his possible employment with GNS in the hopes that he could keep it a separate issue from the acquisition.

On July 1, 2009, Farrell delivered an official offer from GNS. While the team was hoping for a cash offer, GNS presented a royalty model that would pay the Network Collie founders 12 percent of gross proceeds for existing sales leads and 7 percent of gross proceeds for those generated by GNS. The founders would also be entitled to 12 percent of the proceeds from any sale of the intellectual property behind the Network Collie application.

Approximately two weeks later, Farrell presented a spreadsheet showing the potential royalty payments to the Network Collie founders. He had increased the percentages in his original offer from 12 percent to 15 percent and from 7 percent to 10 percent, respectively. Based on these increased royalty percentages and the projections in the company's business plan, the royalty payments could reach $2.8 million by 2013, as shown in Exhibit C13.2. Farrell also stressed that under the proposed royalty model, GNS would assume responsibility for further marketing and development of the Network Collie application, limiting the risk of the Network Collie founders moving forward.

EXHIBIT C13.2 Projected Royalty Payments in GNS Offer

Royalties from:	2009	2010	2011	2012	2013
Existing sales leads	$11,340	$16,200	$ 17,820	$ 17,820	$ 17,820
GNS-generated sales leads	6,480	79,920	532,440	1,384,776	2,787,480
Total royalty payments	$17,820	$96,120	$550,260	$1,402,596	$2,805,300
Average royalty per founder	$ 4,455	$24,030	$137,565	$ 350,649	$ 701,325

GROOVY ID Groovy ID, the second firm expressing an interest in Network Collie, provided a service for consumers to organize, track, and analyze their social networks. Groovy ID had approached the Network Collie team earlier, expressing an interest in providing their research service as a bundled feature included in its paid accounts. Casey thought the most likely arrangement would be a fixed pricing schedule for each contact researched by Network Collie over the next 6–12 months. However, the Groovy ID representatives introduced the idea of acquiring Network Collie. This was a surprise to Casey and the rest of the team.

It was almost two months later before Casey heard from Groovy ID again. Its management team was struggling with the integration of another technology and an investor relationship that had turned sour. Casey had a handful of conversations regarding the integration of Network Collie's service into Groovy ID's paid accounts. In one of those conversations, the Groovy ID team brought up the possibility of acquiring Network Collie again, but this time they seemed more serious.

Several conversations about a potential acquisition moved quickly. Eventually, Groovy ID made an offer splitting the total compensation paid to Network Collie into three distinct pieces, based on Network Collie's intellectual property, potential revenue from existing sales leads, and Casey's joining Groovy ID (primarily to integrate the Network Collie service into the acquiring company). This again created the potential for Casey's interest in any potential transaction to differ from the rest of the Network Collie team. Casey decided he would negotiate his employment once they reached an agreement on the other two pieces of the potential deal.

Groovy ID was willing to make cash payment for the intellectual property. Its team would need to conduct due diligence, but it mentioned a price range of $150,000–$250,000. The potential revenue issue was more difficult for the two sides to agree upon. Groovy ID's senior management was intent on maintaining as much cash as possible, given that it was still in the early stages of development and could experience a lack of cash flow in the next 6 to 18 months without further investment. As a result, Groovy ID's offer did not include upfront or subsequent cash payments for the potential revenue. Instead, Groovy ID would credit the Network Collie founders with additional equity in Groovy ID based on the revenue generated from the existing sales leads.

Casey learned during the negotiations that Groovy ID was motivated to close the deal in the next four to six weeks. It was in the process of finishing a patent application and wanted to include Network Collie's intellectual property in the application before the deadline. Given their desire to close the deal quickly, the team responded to the initial offer by asking for $350,000 for the intellectual property, an additional $150,000 upfront for the potential revenue, plus a potential equity position depending on the success of Network Collie's existing sales leads. However, Casey

received no response to the counteroffer from Groovy ID's management.

Waiting for a Better Deal

While Casey and the rest of the team were excited to have two companies interested in purchasing Network Collie, they were disappointed in how each offer was structured. With respect to the GNS royalty model, they did not feel comfortable exiting the company without a guaranteed payment and giving up control of the product development and marketing efforts that would determine the long-term value of the royalties. While the potential for annual payments in excess of $1 million was tempting, the team believed it could find another deal that would include a cash component or an equity position in an attractive acquirer. Because the Groovy ID offer would provide some cash and an equity position in a new, emerging company that could be more attractive in the future, the team was more interested in that offer. However, the cash component of Groovy ID's offer was still well below the team's target price of at least $750,000.

Casey and the other founders ultimately decided to turn down both offers because they would be giving up the company for too little and assuming too much risk. Casey and Rose still felt strongly that they should be able to secure close to $1 million or more for selling the company. They also were confident that Network Collie's application and existing sales leads would deliver significant success in the future. In fact, they estimated that the company had the potential to achieve almost $28 million in annual sales by 2013 (see Exhibit C13.3).

Progress Slows

Casey was beginning to get frustrated with the lack of progress Network Collie was making. During the past six months, he and the rest of the team continued to have the same experience over and over again with potential customers. Everyone acknowledged the growing use of social networking and seemed interested in the data Network Collie could provide. However, the sales consultants the team hired were not delivering substantial leads and orders. Overall, the potential revenue in the company's sales pipeline was not materializing as quickly as Casey wanted, with only $30,000 in orders to that point.

Even though Casey and the rest of the team believed in the potential of Network Collie, the lack of progress over the past six months had begun to wear on the four co-founders. Each of them was busy with a full-time job and a personal life, and finding time to focus on Network Collie was becoming more difficult. Regardless of how much business was coming in, a significant amount of time was required to update and maintain the software application

	2009	2010	2011	2012	2013
Revenues	$ 140,400	$ 907,200	$5,443,200	$13,996,800	$27,993,600
Operating expenses:					
Travel	$ 25,000	$ 51,500	$ 106,090	$ 163,909	$ 225,102
Marketing expenses	750,000	772,500	795,675	800,000	800,000
Office rent	9,750	9,270	9,548	9,835	10,130
Office utilities	2,400	2,472	2,546	2,623	2,701
Internet and server costs	1,200	3,708	3,819	3,934	4,052
Computers	12,000				
Technology improvements	10,000	10,300	10,609	10,927	11,255
Total operating expenses	$ 810,350	$ 849,750	$ 928,287	$ 991,228	$ 1,053,240
General & administrative expenses:					
Salaries	$ 280,000	$ 394,400	$ 869,664	$ 1,585,844	$ 2,702,994
Benefits	60,000	89,654	119,531	149,643	180,006
Furniture	5,000	5,000	5,000	5,000	5,000
Office improvements	3,000	8,240	8,487	8,742	9,004
Office supplies	6,000				
Total G&A expenses	$ 354,000	$ 497,294	$1,002,682	$ 1,749,229	$ 2,897,004
Earnings before depreciation and amortization (EBITDA)	$ (1,023,950)	$ (439,844)	$3,512,231	$11,256,343	$24,043,356
Depreciation expenses:					
Depreciation on computers	$ 2,400	$ 1,920	$ 2,458	$ 1,003	$ 486
Depreciation on furniture	715	612	900	485	286
Total depreciation expenses	$ 3,115	$ 2,532	$ 3,358	$ 1,488	$ 772
Total expenses	$ 1,167,465	$ 1,349,576	$1,934,327	$ 2,741,945	$ 3,951,016
Earnings before taxes	$ (1,027,065)	$ (442,376)	$3,508,873	$11,254,855	$24,042,584
Income tax	0	0	1,228,106	3,939,200	8,414,904
Net income	$ (1,027,065)	$ (442,376)	$2,280,767	$ 7,315,655	$15,627,680

and website for all of the changes taking place on each of the social networks. This became more of a problem in 2010 as a number of the social networks, including Facebook and Twitter, were making changes to their sites that required significant changes to the Network Collie application. The team was also receiving requests from some of its customers to perform research on certain smaller, niche social networks. The team felt it needed to meet these requests in order to develop a reputation for customer service and to keep existing customers coming back for more.

DECISION TIME It was time for Casey and the rest of the Network Collie team to make a decision. Where was the company headed, and did they want to commit 100 percent to the business? Were the team members ready to leave their jobs? Could they find investors? They had worked so hard over the past two years and believed they had created a valuable service, but the question remained whether it would translate into actual sales and the scalable company they were seeking. The team also began to question whether they should relent on their $1 million price tag and emphasis on an upfront cash payment, and instead actively shop the company. After talking through all of the different options a number of times, the team sat in silence for a few moments. Casey knew it was time to make a decision. He just hoped it was the right one.

Source: The case, as presented here, has been adapted from the original case, written by Professor Jim Litton in the College of Business Administration at Abilene Christian University. This case is based on an actual company; however, the names and places have been altered for confidentiality, per the entrepreneur's request.

Questions

1. Given the early stage of the business, should the Network Collie management team even be considering an exit at this time? Why or why not?

2. If a company acquires Network Collie, what are they buying? What are they not buying?

3. What criteria should the Network Collie management team use in making a decision on what they should do?

4. In your opinion, is Network Collie really worth $1 million?

5. What do you see as the advantages and disadvantages of the two offers the Network Collie founders have received?

6. What would you advise the Network Collie team to do?

Numi Tea
Cultivating Customer Relationships

Numi Tea was started in 1999 by brother and sister team Ahmed and Reem Rahim. Keeping it in the family is important at Numi. Reem's artwork adorns every box of tea. The Rahims' childhood friend, Hammad Atassi, is director of food service. Every member of the Tea'm, as they call it, is committed to the company's core values of sustainability, creativity, and quality organics. This extends to their corporate customers and their producers, as well. Like their teas, every relationship is carefully cultivated and maintained.

In recent years, demand for organic and ethically produced products has exploded. At the same time, economic influences have driven affluent and natural foods consumers to large discounters, grocery chains, warehouse clubs, and online shops. "In the positioning of our brand, we wanted to target a certain type of customer base, from natural health food stores to fine dining and hotels to universities and coffee shops," says Ahmed, Numi's CEO. "But what I've been most surprised about in our growth is the mass market consumer."

According to Jennifer Mullin, vice president of marketing for Numi, the average Numi consumer is college educated, female, and buys two to three boxes of tea per month—usually green tea. She also buys organic products whenever possible. Until Mullin joined the team, Numi had assumed its customers fit the same profile as its young staff. Mullin's findings proved that the company needed to focus additional energy on reaching older customers and moms, as well as its target college market.

To reach younger consumers, Numi boosts product awareness on college campuses, where people are more inclined to be interested in issues of sustainability, fair trade, and organics. The big hurdle with these potential customers is price. Because Numi teas are a premium product, they have a higher price point than conventionally produced teas. Numi prices range from $15.99 for 1.6 ounces and up, depending on the tea variety and size of package. Because college students have limited cash, Numi determined that it could access college customers best by getting university food service departments to serve tea as part of prepaid meal plans. The strategy has been a success. Not only do these food service contracts represent huge accounts for Numi, but they also encourage trial by students. Sampling is Numi's most successful marketing activity for attracting new users, and now students can drink Numi teas essentially for free.

For many organics consumers, the most compelling reason for drinking Numi tea is its health benefits. But while Numi is organic, the company rarely advertises this aspect of its business. Some analysts think that if *organic* and *natural* become mere marketing buzzwords, a lack of trust may arise among consumers, as some products will inevitably fail to live up to marketers' claims. With this in mind, Numi believes it is best to educate consumers about its products. "We have an in-house PR team that works with editors of women's magazines to educate consumers on tea and make sure they understand the healthy properties of tea," says Mullin. The team always follows up by samplings at Whole Foods stores or at events targeted toward environmentally conscious customers.

Numi has been fortunate to be the tea of choice in high-end restaurants, hotel chains, and cruise lines. The food service industry in total makes up about 40 percent of their business. Along with that comes added pressure to deliver on price, quality, and customer service. While the company clearly leads in quality, it is hard for any small business to compete with giant food service companies on price.

An important part of Numi Tea is its story. To tell that story, the management team needs to forge very hands-on, personal relationships with restaurant food and beverage managers, giving them a natural competitive advantage. A regular teabag may be cheaper, but there's not much else to say about it. When Atassi can conduct a private cupping (tea tasting) for the kitchen staff and explain all the different exotic teas, as well as talk about the farms and farmers that grow the tea all over the world and the company's commitment to sustainability, it's pretty much a slam dunk before the tea is even steeped. Turnover is notoriously high in the food service industry, so there's always a chance that a new chef or buyer will go another direction. Luckily for Numi, this hasn't been the case. Due in part to excellent customer relationships, it is more common for the company to keep the old client *and* follow the chef or buyer to his or her new restaurant.

Numi's success in the food service industry has driven retail business. While there are countless testimonials about customers' experiencing Numi tea at a friend's house for the first time, a surprising number of Numi converts come from restaurants. As the requests from consumers wanting to know where to get Numi in their local area have rolled in, the company has expanded to reach retail customers. Once available only at natural food stores and cafes, Numi teas can now be found in such stores as Target, large grocery store chains, and even some warehouse club stores. While good for the consumer, this poses a potential threat to the Rahims' carefully maintained fine-dining customer relationships. A problem could arise if the same premium tea served at a restaurant is also available at the local Target. So far the two channels have co-existed peacefully.

As the company grows, one of the biggest challenges to its marketing model will be to maintain the family feel on a global scale. Jennifer Mullin and her team have begun tailoring e-mail communications to newsletter subscribers to inform them about local events and are hoping to add some regional sales and marketing teams in the near future. They've also added Numi fan sites on Facebook and Twitter. The sites are monitored by a staffer to address any questions or concerns about the products. Most importantly, no matter how busy they may get, founders Ahmed and Reem will always be there, lending a personal touch through their art, personal stories, and

experiences. While Numi is still fairly new, the company is expanding rapidly in the United States and enjoying success overseas, as well. Whatever the marketing and PR teams do to promote the tea products—store samplings, environmental events, or partnerships with like-minded companies—they always keep an eye on the demographic and psychographic profiles of their consumers.

View the video and answer the questions that follow.

Questions

1. Do you consider Numi's relationships with its producers as important to its marketing as the relationships with its customers?

2. How does Numi use technology to enhance its customer relationships? Can you suggest other ways in which the management team can use technology to reach consumers of Numi teas?

3. What methods would you suggest that Numi use to collect customer data?

Source: From *BOONE/KURTZ, Contemporary Marketing, 14e*. 2010 Cengage Learning.

Graeter's Ice Cream
Product Innovation and Long-Term Success

Graeter's Ice Cream has been a Cincinnati tradition for generations. Since the days before refrigeration, the family-owned business, with its Fresh Pot process of making frosty treats, has been a popular choice among Ohioans. Since generating a loyal following in 1870, soon after the company's forefathers began selling fresh ice cream made two gallons at a time from an open-air street market, Graeter's has become synonymous with ice cream.

Ice cream was a novelty when Louis Charles Graeter and his wife, Regina, began making ice cream daily in the back room of a storefront on East McMillan Street. The couple sold their ice cream along with chocolate confections out front and lived upstairs. Since there were no mechanized freezers at the time, ice cream was a rare treat, and the Graeters had to make small batches using rock salt and ice.

As commercial refrigeration became widespread, Graeter's Ice Cream was able to produce and store more products while still servicing consumers from the McMillan street building. The business, however, took a blow when "Charlie" was killed in 1919 in a streetcar accident. In the 1920s, Regina realized that the company could reach more customers by expanding to other locations. She took a gamble and opened a satellite store across town—what would become the first of several neighborhood stores to open as the company positioned itself as a maker of quality ice cream available just about anywhere in town.

Following Regina's death in 1955, sons Wilmer and Paul took over the business, before ushering in a third generation of family leadership with Wilmer's four children. Over the next 30 years, the face of the ice cream business changed. As more ice cream makers entered the market and grocery stores became a viable outlet, selling ice cream entered a new realm. Most competitors built business on volume, and quality suffered, despite lower prices. Graeter's, meanwhile, stayed the course and continued with its time-consuming Fresh Pot process of spinning the recipe along a chilled container. Although Graeter's followed the trend and offered its ice cream in grocery stores, its retail outlets remained to offer consumers a distinctive buying experience.

Over the years, Graeter's developed a line of candy and bakery goods, but ice cream has been the company's staple, enabling the small business to gain a national reputation. In recent years, the company has appeared on the Food Network, Fine Living Channel, Travel Channel, and History Channel. A crowning achievement occurred when Oprah Winfrey gave her personal endorsement to Graeter's, calling it the best ice cream she'd ever tasted. Mail-order sales substantially increased.

Growth has come in leaps and bounds for Graeter's. With an aggressive marketing effort and a strong alliance with the Kroger chain, the company more than doubled its number of grocery store outlets in 2009. Today, the ice cream, now available in 22 flavors, can be found at 1,700 supermarkets and grocery stores, as well as company-owned retail stores in Ohio, Missouri, Kentucky, and nearby states. Graeter's also expanded its distribution network to include restaurants and country clubs, and it operates an online store that offers overnight shipping in 48 states, including California, its largest market. Also, the company has diversified its portfolio by offering a line of ice cream cakes and pies, travel packs, and sundaes, in addition to baked goods and candies.

But the company is committed to further expansion. Graeter's recently boosted its production capacity from one factory to three, aiming for distribution to even more supermarkets and grocery stores throughout the country. Additional retail stores as far away as Los Angeles and New York are planned.

While competition continues to stiffen, Graeter's remains one of the priciest ice creams on the market, even without the shipping costs associated with online ordering. At the retail level, the ice cream is considered a premium product and commands a higher price than other brands. With Kroger as its largest distribution partner, the company has been able to build strong brand loyalty, as evidenced by a recent trial in the Denver area. Graeter's marketed 12 flavors in 30 King Sooper stores in Denver with hopes of selling two or three gallons per store per week. Within a few weeks, stores were selling an average of five gallons.

The company continues to focus on making its product available at the country's largest food stores, but its leaders are cognizant that new products, including established brands in a new market, have a high failure rate. Challenges ahead are the company's ability to establish relationships with new consumers and build brand awareness.

View the video and answer the questions that follow.

Questions

1. What distinguishes Graeter's Ice Cream from other ice cream makers and makes its products desirable to consumers?

2. While its ice cream was a success from the start, what innovations has the company made to sustain its competitive advantage?

3. Cite examples of Graeter's Ice Cream's supply chain management. Explain how the company uses direct channel and indirect channel distribution.

Source: Compiled from interviews and information provided by Graeter's. http://www .graeters.com. Written by Tim Blackwell, Freelance Reporter. © 2012, Cengage Learning.

Dynamic Network Services, Inc.
Finding the Right Price

The Story

The Dynamic Network Services (Dyn) story is not unlike those of many tech startups. The difference is that Dyn started during the dot-com boom, survived the bust, thrived after the dust settled, and surges ahead today. Deeply rooted as an Internet infrastructure company, it began with a focus on the domain name system (DNS) and continues to expand by offering a wider range of infrastructure services.

Since 1998, Dyn has served 4,000,000 homes, small businesses, and enterprise users with a suite of DNS, e-mail, domain registration, and virtual servers. It provides customers—from the hobbyist to the *Fortune* 500 enterprise—with reliable and scalable IT services at competitive and predictable prices, through easy-to-use and secure interfaces. Individuals and companies partner with Dyn to manage their website traffic, e-mail delivery, and uptime, and to harden their internal and external network connectivity.

It has built a rock-solid Global IP Anycast network using only top-level providers and equipment and has provided it at an affordable price. "Uptime is the bottom line" for them and for companies like 37 signals, Zappos, HomeAway, Twitter, Audience-Science, and more who depend on Dyn to keep their Web presence and e-mail delivery at peak performance for their users.

Like many of its Web 2.0 customers looking to monetize, Dyn Inc. has been there, done that. It started as a free service based out of a college apartment—a couple of guys with a big idea. That service, then operating as DynDNS.org, was a dynamic DNS service for a home user to host a website on a home computer or remote access back to a PC. Over time, as the user base grew and became more demanding, Dyn turned to a donation-based service in an effort to stay afloat and add complementary services. Later, Dyn transitioned to a recurring revenue software-as-a-service (SaaS) model with a suite of IT services aimed at the home/SMB market.

Fast-forward to 2005, and its story of maturation continues. Dyn initiated a customer audit and mining exercise of the over 2,000,000 active DynDNS.com users at the time. From this, the company realized that many high-profile corporations were using its consumer-grade service. This revelation, coupled with the simple fact that the premium, externally managed DNS industry lacked options, encouraged Dyn to unveil a new brand, the Dynect Platform. Dynect was introduced to the outsourced DNS market in the fall of 2007.

Today

Today, Dyn Inc. has served over 14,000,000 home/SMB users on the DynDNS.com brand and has over 1,000 corporate/enterprise customers on its globally deployed Dynect Platform. The company has moved beyond offering DNS exclusively and now offers e-mail delivery services through its SendLabs brand. The days of simple word-of-mouth growth are long gone, and Dyn has become a much more proactive player.

Not only does it provide services to consumers and corporations, it also provides services to the government. All federal government agencies that have the .gov designation were given until December 2009 to deploy DNS Security Extensions (DNSSEC) for their domains. DNSSEC adds a layer of security to DNS so that computers can verify that they have been directed to the proper server, preventing the most dangerous types of DNS attacks and cyber-hacking. Implementing DNSSEC is especially critical for high-risk government sites because they are often targeted by cyberattackers and are expected by users to be safe.

DNS is the backbone of the Internet's infrastructure. Without it, websites won't work, period. Once hackers have control over a DNS server, they have free reign to mislead and redirect Web users to unsafe territory. Due to the increase of companies reporting attacks of this nature, it has now become more critical than ever to implement this additional layer of security at the DNS level. Government and other critical industries such as banking, online retail, healthcare, and education are also prime candidates for DNSSEC, as they may be a larger target for potential attackers.

Pricing and Credit Decisions

Because technology changes rapidly from day to day, Dyn experiences shorter product cycles than do companies that deal with tangible products. In a noncommoditized scenario, the company finds it easier to be flexible with pricing. As a result, each customer requires different pricing strategies. Outliers—those who are not the average customer—can be more demanding of services, but are not more costly to the company because Dyn's costs are fixed. Customers, however, are willing to pay a different rate when traffic and consistency are different. When demand goes up, prices go up.

The company does expense analyses to determine pricing. In the beginning, pricing structure was evaluated monthly, but now that Dyn is more established, forecasting is done quarterly or semi-annually, depending on client needs. Its invoice structure is annual—one year in advance—so the greatest risk to Dyn is credit card fraud.

Before answering the questions below, reread Chapter 16, and watch the Dyn Inc. video for this chapter.

Questions

1. Explain the importance of fixed and variable costs to Dyn's pricing decisions.
2. Basing your answer on the discussion of prestige pricing in Chapter 16 and on the Dyn Inc. video, how does the concept of elasticity of demand relate to Dyn's pricing structure? Or does it?
3. Do you think Dyn would benefit from offering credit to its customers?

Source: Compiled from interviews and information provided by Dyn Inc. http://dyn.com.
© 2012, Cengage Learning.

Brian Halligan and Dharmesh Shah, the founders of HubSpot®, met at MIT in 2004. The company is based in Cambridge, Massachusetts, directly across from the campus where it was first envisioned. Both Halligan and Shah were interested in the transformative impact of the Internet on small businesses and were early students of Web 2.0 concepts. After two years of discussions and early work, in June of 2006 the company was officially founded and funded.

The most interesting aspect of the Internet's impact on business from HubSpot's perspective is how it has changed the nature of shopping and subsequently the shape of every vendor's sales funnel. Ten years ago, if a company was interested in buying a new product or service, it started by attending trade shows, reading industry journals, and going to seminars to learn more. Early in the process, it would engage directly with key vendors' salespeople who would provide product information.

Today, that same process looks very different. The potential customer starts by googling relevant keywords. The prospect spends time on each vendor's site, subscribing to the most interesting vendor blogs, perhaps joining an industry discussion forum, etc. Relatively late in the decision cycle, the prospect engages the vendor's salespeople directly. That first vendor conversation today is much different from the one a decade ago because the prospect often knows as much about the vendor's product as the sales rep does and the prospect is already much more "qualified."

The Internet has tended to make every marketplace more efficient. Just as eBay makes the niche market for Pez dispensers, WWI shovels, and 1975 World Series ticket stubs more efficient, the Internet as a whole is making niche markets for intellectual property law, system dynamics consulting, and food brokerage more efficient. It used to be that the size of a firm's sales force was the key to finding the most new customers, but that is not necessarily the case today. The good news for small businesses is that on the Internet, no one can tell if you are a sole proprietorship or a large consultancy.

The Internet disproportionately favors small businesses since it enables them to position their niche products so that they are available to everyone who is shopping for them, regardless of the prospective customer's location. HubSpot Inbound Marketing Software helps over 4,000 customers to generate traffic and leads through their websites, and to convert more of those leads into customers. Its vision has been to provide a killer marketing application and provide great advice to small businesses, enabling those companies to leverage the disruptive effects of the Internet and "get found" by more prospects.

Most small businesses have a website that behaves like their old paper-based brochures, but just sits online. It is rarely updated, is not given significant visibility by search engines, has low traffic levels, does not encourage return visits, does not enable/track conversions, etc. What HubSpot does is transform that relatively static website into a modern marketing machine that produces the right leads and helps convert a higher percentage of them into qualified opportunities.

HubSpot focuses on tools to help the small business owner create, optimize, and promote content; capture, manage, and nurture leads to win more customers; and learn to make smart marketing investments that get results. Some of the tools it provides include social media, blogging, search engine optimization, and content management.

View the video and answer the questions that follow.

Questions

1. How has the salesperson's role changed because of Internet marketing? Consider differences in prospecting and presentation.

2. Do you agree with HubSpot that a prospect is more "qualified" to make purchasing decisions when it uses information found on the Internet?

3. How might the salesperson's compensation be different or the same with Internet sales versus traditional sales methods?

4. Should a new small business rely solely on Internet promotion? What other methods should it use?

Source: Compiled from interviews and information provided by HubSpot, Inc. www.hubspot.com. © 2012, Cengage Learning.

Auntie Anne's Pretzels in China

The news was something to celebrate. It was 2007, and Wen-Szu Lin and his partner, Joseph Sze, had just learned that they had been approved to be the first franchisees to take Auntie Anne's Pretzels into China. This promised to be the opportunity of a lifetime! With more than 1.3 billion potential customers and a fast-expanding economy, how could they miss?

Lin was very well prepared for this foray into entrepreneurship. After all, he had been born in neighboring Taiwan and lived there until the age of seven, so he was fluent in Mandarin Chinese. He also had completed an MBA in entrepreneurial management from the prestigious Wharton School of Business. Sze, who also had a Wharton MBA and was similarly prepared, shared Lin's assessment of the opportunity and his excitement for the chance to introduce Auntie Anne's to the Chinese market. With franchise agreement in hand, and after a great deal of planning and preparation, they opened their first store around the time of the Beijing Olympics in 2008. But it didn't take long for the new small business owners to realize that they might have bitten off more than they could comfortably chew.

Every Auntie Anne's pretzel sold around the world is made from the same secret recipe, and the expansion into China would use it as well. Lin's plan was very simple: Import the pretzel mix, along with other key ingredients, and start making pretzels fast enough to satisfy the fast-growing appetites of Chinese consumers. It seemed to be a foolproof strategy—that is, until the Chinese government decided to get involved. A key delivery of pretzel mix passed through customs quickly and without a hitch, but this probably makes sense, since that office cares mostly about collecting required taxes. But serious problems surfaced just after that, when the China Entry-Exit Inspection and Quarantine Bureau (CIQ), which is the agency that is responsible for determining whether imported food products are safe to eat, announced that it had tested the shipment and had to declare it unfit for human consumption.

When he got word of the decision, Lin immediately recognized that it had the power to ruin the new venture before it could get out of the starting block. How can you make Auntie Anne's pretzels if you can't use the exact mix of ingredients in the company's formula? But the CIQ office in China was warning Lin and his partner that they might have to dump about 5,000 bags (equal to an entire 40-foot shipping container) of the franchisor's proprietary mix down the drain. The agent assigned to their case, Mr. Zeng, delivered the ultimatum, contingent on his department's test of a second sample of the mix.

The loss would be devastating, effectively shutting down their operations—but even the challenge of disposal would take some work. They would have to open each bag of mix and pour it into a drain large enough to handle the load, being certain to wash it down slowly and with enough care to avoid clogs. Lin and his partner knew the drill all too well. The CIQ had already forced them to dispose of more than 1,300 pounds of caramel for having "dangerously high" levels of the preservative sorbic acid (five times the allowable limit), contrary to U.S. test results showing that the shipment was very safe.

So here they were . . . again! The situation would have been humorous if it had not been so tragic for the business. The official report claimed that the pretzel mix contained dangerous levels of a kind of bacteria that is found only in dairy products. What made these findings so interesting is that the mix contained no dairy products, only common ingredients such as flour, salt, and sugar. Challenging the report led nowhere; in fact, Mr. Zeng made it very clear that he would condemn the shipment outright if Lin continued his protests. The company's entire future was staked on its ability to get a second sample to pass tests performed by a CIQ lab that provided results that apparently were less than accurate or honest.

At one point, Lin was called to the CIQ headquarters to figure out what to do with a condemned shipment. What he found there was revealing, to say the least, and it gave him an up-close sense of how government offices can work in other countries. When he showed up to meet with the company's assigned inspector, he noticed that Mr. Zeng was focused intently on the computer screen in front of him, squinting as if he were trying to read fine print. Lin reports being "thoroughly impressed by his concentration, unexpected for a government employee." Mr. Zeng realized that he was waiting by the door and responded, "Please wait a few minutes as I finish up my work." Wanting to start this crucial relationship off on the right foot, Lin cheerfully indicated that he would. While he waited, Lin looked around the office and sized up the operation. What he noticed there was very eye-opening.

The shelves and table were filled with packaged food items, from wine bottles to canned foods to candies. They must receive many samples, I thought. . . . Empty cookie and chocolate candy wrappers littered each inspector's desk, all from the same company called Crai, an Italian firm that wanted to launch a group of restaurants and grocery stores in China at that time. A good friend of mine who headed up Crai's importing had been complaining to me about the lengthy process at CIQ for months. Specifically, she mentioned several items that had been rejected and "destroyed" by CIQ: cookies and chocolate candies. What a coincidence, I thought, as I looked at the crumb-covered desks. I sure hope that these customs agents did not hurt their stomachs during the "destruction" process.

When he turned his attention back to Mr. Zeng, he found him still hard at work with his razor-sharp focus on the computer monitor unbroken. But by then it was clear that he was using one hand to type and the other to move the mouse wildly. The action he used was so frenzied that Lin couldn't help but wonder what in the world the inspector was doing. He concluded that Mr. Zeng must have been working with some kind of advanced Excel spreadsheet model or perhaps proprietary customs software. But it was neither, and that became obvious from what he heard next.

Faint sounds crackled and exploded from his computer. I leaned in and listened carefully. Shhuuuu . . . boom! Boom. Boom. Crack, pop, pop, pop. Boom!!! That was not music. It was the sounds of guns and bombs going off! I realized. Mr. Zeng continued wriggling the mouse, clicking on its buttons while his left hand tapped the space bar and several letter keys with lightning speed. I envied his focus. I could see his screen reflected in the window behind him. His computer monitor was full of monsters trying to kill each other. Warcraft! Well, a Chinese version of it. Mr. Zeng was not working tirelessly to clear as many customs forms as possible before the Olympics—he was playing computer games.

And Mr. Zeng was really getting into it, with beads of sweat forming on his forehead after about five minutes of intense action. About ten minutes after that, the beads had gathered into streams that were starting to roll down the side of his face.

This was serious commitment, but Mr. Zeng was not alone in his extracurricular engagement. Based on the reflections in the window, Lin could see the computer monitors of other inspectors, too, and realized that very little work was actually being done in that office. Lin described the scene as follows:

One inspector preferred red blouses to green ones, and seemed like an adept shopper from the many windows she had opened to compare similar products across several websites. The next inspector had true, raw talent as well as commendable organization skills. He had ten small Instant Messenger windows placed evenly and symmetrically from the top left of his screen to bottom right. Conversations flowed smoothly and quickly across all ten. I could type nearly 100 words per minute, but I was no match for this inspector. I silently applauded his talent in keeping up with so many screens, and making it seem effortless.

From these observations and the interactions Lin had during his visit with Mr. Zeng later that day, it seemed clear that the agency's work and the reports its employees were handing down were not very trustworthy.

As time went on and the hassles from CIQ mounted, Lin's frustrations continued to build. The inspection process was hardly serious or accurate, and yet it was destroying his new company, one rejected shipment at a time. And to add insult to injury, the Chinese government routinely gives wide berth to domestic producers, allowing them to get away with all manner of unsafe practices. At one point, Lin purchased a product from a local vendor that caused half of his employees to lose their sight, and no one seemed to care—it was simply par for the course in China. (These workers later recovered their eyesight, thanks to changes in health care practices that were just being made.) But when it came to his imported supplies, suddenly health concerns were paramount. It seemed to be a rigged system.

Lin eventually managed to save the pretzel mix from destruction, but only after he called in favors "from friends and friends of friends"—anyone who might have pull with the Chinese government. He finally received word that a second sample of the mix passed all tests—but this was nothing short of miraculous, since Lin had never provided one to the CIQ or to Mr. Zeng! This made the whole affair even more bizarre.

Perhaps Lin and his partner's situation could only be explained by something they learned from a conversation with the wife of the U.S. Ambassador. She revealed that their hassles with customs probably had nothing to do with the safety of the shipments. In the wake of a scandal that exposed melamine-tainted milk products in China, many countries—the United States included—put a hold on food and agricultural products from China. So Mr. Zeng's regulatory decisions may have been political tit for tat and nothing more, but this is scant comfort for the entrepreneur whose business fails as a result of political gamesmanship.

Lin has concluded that he and his business partner were always at a disadvantage when it came to doing business in China. "You really need to have that prior experience and those prior relationships," he says. "When we showed up, we didn't really have any prior relationships." This, among other shortcomings, led ultimately to the closing of the partners' Auntie Anne's Pretzel stores in 2012, and they have each moved on to greener pastures of opportunity. But their experiences abroad illustrate the stark differences that can exist between doing business in the United States and operating in other countries. These naturally ramp up the potential complications for small business owners who willingly accept the adventure of global expansion, with its inherent hazards and potential rewards.

Questions

1. What were the primary motivations that led Lin and his partner to start a new business in China? Given their experiences there, do you think they should have considered launching in another country instead? Where? Why?

2. Of the global strategies mentioned in Chapter 18, which option did Lin and Sze choose for their move into China? Did they choose the right strategy for them and their enterprise?

3. What do you think Lin and his partner did right when they attempted to start their business? What do you think they did wrong? What recommendations would you have for them?

4. Given the details of this case and other key facts that you know about China, assess the opportunities for U.S. small companies that may want to do business there. What features of the country should be particularly attractive to entrepreneurs who are seeking to expand internationally by going into China?

5. What challenges to doing business in China did Lin and Sze experience? List any issues that may present distinct problems for other U.S. small companies that may want to do business there.

Sources: Based on Kevin Hardy, "The Problem with China," *QSR* (October 2012), http://www.qsrmagazine.com/exclusives/problem-china, accessed April 8, 2013; Knowledge@ Wharton, "Food for Thought: Why Auntie Anne's Pretzels Failed in China," (March 6, 2013), http://knowledge.wharton.upenn.edu/article.cfm?articleid=3203, accessed April 8, 2013; Frank Langfitt, "Auntie Anne's Pretzels in Beijing: Why the Chinese Didn't Bite," NPR Books, (February 11, 2013), http://www.npr.org/books/authors/171079606/wen-szu-lin, accessed April 8, 2013; Wen-Szu Lin, *The China Twist* (BC Publishing, 2012).

Andrew Mason and the Rise and Fall of Groupon

After four and a half intense and wonderful years as CEO of Groupon, I've decided that I'd like to spend more time with my family. Just kidding—I was fired today.

With these words, predictably flippant in their tone, Andrew Mason stepped down from his position at the helm of Groupon, the deal-of-the-day company that sells coupons for deeply discounted goods and services to customers who must get others to buy them, too, before they all can use them. Mason will always enjoy the distinction of having founded what became the "Fastest Growing Company Ever," to quote *Forbes* magazine. But Isaac Newton could have directed his words as aptly to Groupon as he did to gravity: What goes up apparently must come down.

So how did things go so horribly wrong? It may have been Mason's playful behavior that established the culture at the company that seemed to serve it so well for so long. He clearly had a reputation for being something of a goofball, often coming off more like a big kid than the leader of a major new firm with a multi-billion-dollar market value. These antics might have been seen as cheap entertainment while the company was growing, but when sales began to decline and the firm's stock price retreated, Mason's offbeat style and the company's fun-focused atmosphere suddenly became less than amusing.

It also didn't help that Mason had no significant business experience prior to starting Groupon. The music-major-turned-software-developer stumbled upon the idea for the company and became its CEO almost by default. And it showed. With his often-rumpled appearance and strong leaning toward all things wacky, he seemed more intent on promoting the company's comical vibe than on actually making the business work. Mason fashioned Groupon into a lively place to work, where the dress code and vacation policy were loose, and comedians wrote ad copy and served in customer support roles. But this was just the tip of the iceberg. Making the fun last at Groupon was very serious business.

And then there were the problems with the company's business model. Consumers didn't like the forward planning required to take advantage of its offers—that is, the need to buy a deal in advance, print it out, redeem it in time, etc. Participating vendors also had complaints. If a deal ended up being a smash hit with subscribers, the merchant could very well be flooded with more customer demand than it could handle. And because the deals featured steep discounts in order to get new customers to bite, they could be expensive to offer. Many vendors quickly noticed that they were getting a lot of bargain hunters coming through their doors but few continuing customers, so as a result, they started to cool to the idea of signing up for more offers.

The extraordinary pace of change at the company was also creating serious headaches for Mason. The tempo of innovation was so fast and so furious that management struggled to keep up, which generated its share of conflict. One observer described the situation this way: "The size and complexity of Groupon grew so quickly that it outpaced the rate of maturity of the organizational culture—much like a gangly, pimply teenager [who] grows to 6 feet tall."

Finally, there were concerns about Mason's struggle to relate to some of the employees. Many respected his grasp of Web technology and keen product development prowess but recognized that he wasn't much of a people person and often failed to appreciate employees in roles that were vital to the company and its success, most notably sales. For example, there were at least five layers of bureaucracy between Mason and the company's sales staff, causing a disconnect between the two and leading some to believe that he probably would have preferred to have had fewer salespeople and the headaches that naturally go along with them.

Despite the problems, the firm did have something going for it; at least Google thought so. The online-search giant reportedly made an offer to buy the business for about $6 billion in November 2010. The two sides negotiated for weeks, but Mason, figuring the deal wasn't sweet enough, decided to walk away. It was at this point that observers seriously began to question his business judgment and his ability to lead such a large enterprise. But Mason stood by his decision:

> Life is not about money. . . . The reason that we made a decision to be an independent company is we quite simply wanted control of our destiny. We wanted the ability to make big bets and take smart risks and go after what we saw as a big opportunity.

The shortsightedness of Mason's decision is now very apparent, but life offers very few "do-overs."

Mason's rejection of Google's offer was only the beginning of his slide at Groupon. The chorus of questions about his ability to lead such a large and growing business were about to grow much louder. In June 2011, Groupon filed for an IPO (an initial public offering, allowing shares of the company to be sold to the general public) and raised $700 million in the process. But this focused an intense spotlight on the firm and how it was being managed. Suddenly Mason's "incessant jokiness" was no laughing matter for government regulators and investors. His college-kid-like demeanor raised doubts about his suitability to lead a publicly traded firm. One business writer recounts an episode that occurred during a series of presentations given to raise interest in the IPO that certainly lifted more than a few eyebrows:

> *Between meetings with bankers, Mason, a self-professed video game junkie, played a game called Whale Trail on his iPhone. In the game, the player navigates a cheerful flying whale named Willow through a psychedelic sky while trying to gobble rainbow-colored bubbles and avoid black clouds that do the bidding of the evil Baron Von Barry.*

Mason explained his behavior by saying that the game was great "for just tuning out," adding with a laugh that iTunes had just listed it as "one of the best games for four- to six-year-olds." That's not exactly what investors want to see in the CEO who is running their business.

In the wake of the IPO, Groupon's financial difficulties escalated. After the company posted a new loss of $67 million, the firm's stock took a tumble, from a peak of around $31 to a low of $2.63 in November 2012. It eventually settled at $5 per share, but by that point, the company had lost around 75 percent of its IPO value. And as a telling sign of investor sentiment, the price bounced up by nearly 12 percent when the news of Mason's firing was finally announced.

Before being forced out as CEO, Mason was already moving the company away from the daily-deal business and toward the creation of what he was calling an "operating system for local commerce." This software platform would allow customers to turn to Groupon as a source of information to guide their search for products, services, and the lowest prices for both. Merchants could use the system to advertise their offerings, as well as using it as a touchpoint for the sales they made and as a hook for pulling customers back for more business. It was an ambitious project, leading some investors to

further question Mason's wisdom and business acumen—even *after* his departure from the firm. They came to think of Groupon as a public company that was in desperate search of a business that just might pull it out of its sticky situation. Also, there was a concern that existing competitors would challenge the company on its planned path for recovery. These included powerhouses like OpenTable (which dominates online restaurant reservations), customer loyalty program providers (such as American Express, Visa, Citibank, and Amazon), Google and PayPal (with recently expanded offerings for local merchants), and Square (with its suite of software that reduces the transaction costs and hassles for small businesses). Finding a competitive opening in such a crowded marketplace would not be easy.

While the Groupon story did not have a happy ending for Mason, it provides important lessons about entrepreneurial leadership. As one writer put it,

> *Andrew Mason has his own kind of panache. Not the epic, Steve Jobs panache. Or the eclectic, Barry Diller panache. Or even the oafish, Steve Ballmer panache. But as CEO of one of the fastest-growing startups in history, he had the small-scale, misfit quirkiness of an indie movie. Panache-ette.*

Without a doubt, the story is unique. But to be fair, Mason's distinctive leadership style and the company culture that it engendered may have been both Groupon's greatest advantage and the very anchor that eventually pulled it nearly under. The playful and giddy style that Mason personified spawned the company's meteoric rise to greatness, but did not endear it to the Wall Street players who laid a heavy hand to the rudder of this publicly traded company. That's the way the game is played, and some entrepreneurs are simply not suited to be a part of it. Perhaps Andrew Mason was one of them.

Questions

1. How would you describe the leadership skills of Andrew Mason? How would you rate his leadership style? In what ways does he fit the profile of the typical business founder? In what ways is he different?

2. Assess the organizational culture at Groupon. What are its strengths and its weaknesses? What changes would you make to the culture to improve the performance of the company?

3. Do you think that it was because of Mason that Groupon was unable to transition smoothly through its growth and development stages, or can you identify other possible causes?

4. What kind of leader do you think would be best suited to run Groupon? Create a profile of its ideal leader. Then create a profile of the ideal leader of a technology startup, and compare the two. What would you recommend as a plan for developing leaders of startups into leaders who are well equipped to manage large but still-entrepreneurial firms?

5. In your opinion, what are some of the other problems at Groupon?

Sources: David Streitfeld, "Groupon Dismisses Chief After a Dismal Quarter," *The New York Times*, March 1, 2013, p. B1; John Kotter, "Andrew Mason's Departure Reflected His Leadership Style," http://www.forbes.com/sites/johnkotter/2013/03/02/andrew-masons-departure-reflected-his-leadership-style, accessed March 23, 2013; Lauren Etter and Douglas MacMillan, "The Education of Groupon CEO Andrew Mason," www.businessweek.com/articles/2012-07-12/the-education-of-groupon-ceo-andrew-mason, accessed March 23, 2013; Kevin Kelleher, "The Defenestration of Andrew Mason," http://pandodaily.com/2013/02/28/the-defenestration-of-andrew-mason, accessed March 26, 2013; Eric Jackson, "Source of Groupon Problems: Managing People," www.forbes.com/sites/ericjackson/2012/08/14/source-of-groupon-problems-managing-people, accessed March 24, 2013; Joan Lappin, "Don't Cry for Groupon's Andrew Mason," http://www.forbes.com/sites/joanlappin/2013/03/05/dont-cry-for-groupons-andrew-mason, accessed March 23, 2013; Herb Greenberg, "Worst CEO in 2012," www.cnbc.com/id/100320782, accessed March 26, 2013; and "Hey Groupon, Can You Spare Some Culture Change?" http://chicagobrander.com/tag/groupon-culture, accessed March 25, 2013.

Jason Fried and Hiring Practices at 37signals

Intentional Selection

It takes excellent people to build a great company.

Since launching Chicago-based Web applications company 37signals in 1999, Jason Fried, its co-founder and president, has developed a careful and deliberate approach to finding and managing people for his company. Why is he so intentional in his hiring? This is how Fried answers that question:

Hiring people is like making friends. Pick good ones, and they'll enrich your life. Make bad choices, and they'll bring you down. Who you work with is even more important than who you hang out with, because you spend a lot more time with your workmates than with your friends.

The company has a deliberately small staff of 20, and it works hard to keep them happy. After 11 years in business, only two people have left to pursue opportunities elsewhere—and one of those returned after working at another company for seven years.

Fried's hiring method has served 37signals well, but it is unusual in some ways. For example, he hires late (only "after it hurts") and never before a new employee is needed. He won't even hire "the perfect catch" if he doesn't have "the perfect job" open for that person. Invent a position to keep a talented person from getting away? Never! And Fried won't hire for a job he has never performed himself. In his mind, there is no way to find the right person for a job if you don't understand the position on a deep level.

Fried's approach to evaluating job candidates is also a little out of the ordinary. Résumés are ignored ("they're full of exaggerations, half-truths, embellishments—even outright lies"). Cover letters are given extra weight, because they reveal who wants the specific job being offered (and not just any job), and they also show who can write well. ("When in doubt, always hire the better writer," Fried suggests.) And during interviews, Fried listens carefully for signs of self-initiative. He reasons that

candidates who ask, "How do I do that?" or "How can I find out this or that?" often are not used to figuring things out for themselves and thus would be a drain on others. On the other hand, Fried likes it when a candidate asks, "Why?" He interprets this as "a sign of deep interest in a subject" and "a healthy dose of curiosity." Details can make a huge difference.

Even if all indications are positive, Fried still chooses to go slow. "We . . . try to test-drive people before hiring them full time. We give designers a one-week design project to see how they approach the problem," paying them $1,500 for their time. Fried sometimes extends the project into a month-long contract "to see how we feel about the person and how the person feels about us." The point is to avoid hiring mistakes that would be bad for the company and unfair to the candidate.

As the economy continues to struggle, many small businesses are finding that they have to hire very carefully—as Fried is doing—or even get by with fewer workers. Some are turning to flexible management practices, like cross-training employees, hiring temporary workers on an as-needed basis, or forming outsourcing partnerships to adjust to fluctuations in market demand. But one way or another, the small business show must go on—and that means having the right people on board when you need them.

Questions

1. Do you think Fried's hiring methods are reasonable? Will they lead to good hires for his growing company? What are the best features of his approach (if you believe there are any)?

2. Do you think it is a good idea for Fried to take a pass on "perfect" candidates because he doesn't have an attractive job open for them at the moment? Is it smart for Fried to let talented candidates get away by refusing to create more suitable positions to keep them?

3. If Fried were to use the behavioral interview format, what kinds of questions might be especially helpful, given what you know of the types of people he prefers to hire?

4. What recommendations would you have for Fried regarding his hiring practices?

Sources: Based on Jason Fried, "The Importance of Hiring Late," BigThink.com, http://bigthink.com/users/jasonfried, accessed April 11, 2013; Jason Fried, "Never Read Another Resume," *Inc.*, Vol. 32, No. 5 (June 2010), pp. 36–37; Jason Fried and David Heinemeier Hansson, *Rework* (New York: Crown Publishing, 2010); Sarah E. Needleman, "Entrepreneurs Prefer to Keep Staffs Lean," *The Wall Street Journal*, March 2, 2010, p. B5; Heesun Wee, "Slow Crawl to Prosperity as Small Business Hiring Dives," CNBC.com, April 4, 2013, http://www.cnbc.com/id/100613971, accessed April 11, 2013; and "37signals: Our Story," http://37signals.com/about, accessed April 10, 2013.

VIDEO CASE 21

River Pools & Spas
Managing Operations in a Challenging Economy

In 2001, 23-year-old Jason Hughes was working part-time on a construction crew for Jim Spiess, owner of Prestige Builders of Lancaster, Virginia. Impressed with Hughes's work ethic and capacity to learn, Spiess asked him to consider taking a full-time position with his firm. Hughes had been building homes every summer since his teens. But he told Speiss that what he really wanted to do was to start his own swimming pool construction company, and that he would do exactly that if he had the financial backing. This sparked Spiess's interest, and he asked Hughes to put some numbers together. What quickly followed was River Pools & Spas' first business plan.

The plan was just enough to give Spiess and Hughes the necessary enthusiasm and vision to start what today has become one of the premier pool and spa companies in the Maryland/Virginia area. During their first year, they installed a handful of pools, and 2002 was a year of solid growth, during which they installed about 40 pools. Despite record rainfall in 2003 and 2004, River Pools still grew in leaps and bounds, and by the end of 2004 the business model changed focus. They decided to move away from installing vinyl-liner above-ground and inground pools. Although they would still offer above-ground pools and spas, there was now an understanding within the company that, based on industry surveys, customers wanted a pool with low maintenance, longevity and exceptional warranties, and aesthetic appeal.

The only pool with these qualities is fiberglass/composite, and so the change was made. The renewed focus brought about more record years from 2005 throughout 2007. Such growth put River Pools & Spas in the top 5 percent of all inground pool companies in the country. It has also established the most popular and informative educational blog and video library in the swimming pool industry, showing the owners' commitment to excellence. Both of the owners are very family-oriented and believe they owe their success to moral values, great employees, dedicated customers, quality, service, and integrity.

Beating the Odds and the Economy

In 2005, River Pools & Spas had over 75 inground pool installations, 20 full-time employees, and a beautiful new 10,000-square-foot showroom/warehouse in Tappahannock, Virginia. Despite being a down-year for many companies, 2006 continued to show great promise for the future of the company, with another 80 inground pools being installed in the area. The following year was River Pools & Spas' greatest accomplishment to date. In an industry that had started to decline in most states due to the slow housing market, River Pools & Spas continued to demonstrate strong growth. Its final results in 2007 were 88 fiberglass pool installations.

Spiess and Hughes had a good system until the economy crashed. They were making plenty of money but had far too many employees and started to lose ground. They're now down to six employees: a bookkeeper, an office manager, two production managers—one of whom doubles as the service manager—and two installation crews.

They had been renting space at a retail location at $8,000 per month, so they bought their own building and closed up the retail space, which was break-even at best. Their current office is a big metal building with a warehouse and five offices, and an empty showroom. After the brick-and-mortar plan was deemed too expensive, they moved everything to the Web, and this became their new storefront. They now have the world-leading website for fiberglass pools and get requests from Utah to Costa Rica.

Such growth has put River Pools & Spas in the top 5 percent of all inground pool companies in the country. One might assume that this growth has hurt quality, but that is clearly not the case when every potential customer receives a reference list with every inground pool customer (over 550) the company has ever installed a pool for, including the homeowner's name, address, and telephone number.

View the video and answer the questions that follow.

Questions

1. Review the history of the operations of River Pools & Spas, from start to success to scaling back. How was the company affected by scaling back? What changes made it more competitive?

2. Describe how River Pools & Spas' customer focus affects the business. What can the owners do to ensure that the quality of their products and services remains high?

3. Does this company use a synchronous management approach?

Source: Compiled from interviews and information provided by River Pools & Spas. http://www.riverpoolsandspas.com. © 2012, Cengage Learning.

Pearson Air Conditioning & Service

Managing a Firm's Working Capital

CASE

22

Bob and Scott Pearson, father and son, are the owners of Pearson Air Conditioning & Service, based in Dallas, Texas. Bob serves as president, and Scott as general manager. The firm sells General Electric, Carrier, and York air-conditioning and heating systems to both commercial and residential customers and services these and other types of systems. Although the business has operated successfully since the Pearsons purchased it in 2002, it continues to experience working capital problems.

Pearson's Financial Performance

The firm has been profitable under the Pearsons' ownership. In fact, profits for 2011 were the highest for any year to date. Exhibit C22.1 shows the income statement for the year ending December 31, 2011.

The balance sheet as of December 31, 2011, is presented in Exhibit C22.2. Note that the firm's total debt now exceeds the owners' equity. However, $10,737 of the firm's liabilities was a long-term note payable to a stockholder. This note was issued at the time the Pearsons purchased the business, with payments going to the former owner.

Pearson's Cash Balance

Pearson Air Conditioning & Service currently has a cash balance in excess of $28,000. The owners have a policy of maintaining a minimum cash balance of $15,000, which allows them to "sleep well at night." Recently, Bob

has thought that they would still be able to "breathe comfortably" as long as they kept a minimum balance of $10,000.

Pearson's Accounts Receivable

The accounts receivable at the end of 2011 were $56,753, but at times during the year, receivables could be twice this amount. These accounts receivable were not aged, so the firm had no specific knowledge of the number of overdue accounts. However, the firm had never experienced any significant loss from bad debts. The accounts receivable were thought, therefore, to be good accounts of a relatively recent nature.

Customers were given 30 days from the date of the invoice to pay the net amount. No cash discounts were offered. If payment was not received during the first 30 days, a second statement was mailed to the customer and monthly carrying charges of 1/10 of 1 percent were added.

On small residential jobs, the firm tried to collect from customers when the work was completed. When a service representative finished repairing an air-conditioning system, for example, he or she presented a bill to the customer and attempted to obtain payment at that time. However, this was not always possible. On major items, such as unit changeouts—which often ran as high as $2,500—billing was almost always necessary.

On new construction projects, the firm sometimes received partial payments prior to completion, which helped to minimize the amount tied up in receivables.

EXHIBIT C22.1 Pearson Air Conditioning & Service Income Statement for the Year Ending December 31, 2011

Sales revenue	$727,679
Cost of goods sold	466,562
Gross profit	$261,117
Selling, general, and administrative expenses (including interest expense)	189,031
Profits before tax	$ 72,086
Income tax	17,546
Net profits	$ 54,540

Source: William J. Petty. © 2011, Cengage Learning.

Case 22 Pearson Air Conditioning & Service

689

Assets

Current assets:

Cash	$ 28,789
Accounts receivable	56,753
Inventory	89,562
Prepaid expenses	4,415
Total current assets	$179,519
Loans to stockholders	41,832
Autos, trucks, and equipment, at cost, less accumulated depreciation of $36,841	24,985
Other assets	16,500
Total assets	$262,836

Debt (Liabilities) and Equity

Current debt:

Current maturities of long-term notes payable*	$ 26,403
Accounts payable	38,585
Accrued payroll taxes	2,173
Income tax payable	13,818
Other accrued expenses	4,001
Total current debt	$ 84,980
Long-term notes payable*	51,231
Total stockholders' equity	126,625
Total debt and equity	$262,836

*Current and long-term portions of notes payable:

	Current	Long-Term	Total
• 10% note payable, secured by pickup, due in monthly installments of $200, including interest	$ 1,827	$ 1,367	$ 3,194
• 10% note payable, secured by equipment, due in monthly installments of $180, including interest	584	0	584
• 6% note payable, secured by inventory and equipment, due in monthly installments of $678, including interest	6,392	39,127	45,519
• 9% note payable to stockholder	0	10,737	10,737
• 12% note payable to bank in 30 days	17,600	0	17,600
	$26,403	$51,231	$77,634

Pearson's Inventory

Inventory accounted for a substantial portion of the firm's working capital. It consisted of the various heating and air-conditioning units, parts, and supplies used in the business.

The Pearsons had no guidelines or industry standards to use in evaluating their overall inventory levels.

They believed that there *might* be some excessive inventory, but, in the absence of a standard, this was basically an opinion. When pressed to estimate the amount that might be eliminated by careful control, Scott pegged it at 15 percent.

The firm used an annual physical inventory that coincided with the end of its fiscal year. Since the inventory level was known for only one time in the year, the income statement could be prepared only on an annual basis. There was no way of knowing how much of the inventory had been used at other points and, thus, no way to calculate profits. As a result, the Pearsons lacked quarterly or monthly income statements to assist them in managing the business.

Scott and Bob had been considering changing from a physical inventory to a perpetual inventory system, which would enable them to know the inventory levels of all items at all times. An inventory total could easily be computed for use in preparing statements. Shifting to a perpetual inventory system would require that they purchase new computer software. However, the cost of such a system would not constitute a major barrier. A greater expense would be involved in the maintenance of the system—entering all incoming materials and all withdrawals. The Pearsons estimated that this task would require the work of one person on a less than full-time (possibly half-time) basis.

Pearson's Note Payable to the Bank

Bank borrowing was the most costly form of credit. The firm paid the going rate, slightly above prime, and owed $17,600 on a 90-day renewable note. Usually, some of the principal was paid when the note was renewed. The total borrowing could probably be increased if necessary. There was no obvious pressure from the bank to reduce borrowing to zero. The amount borrowed during the year typically ranged from $10,000 to $25,000.

The Pearsons had never explored the limits the bank might impose on borrowing, and there was no clearly specified line of credit. When additional funds were required, Scott simply dropped by the bank, spoke with a bank officer (who also happened to be a friend), and signed a note for the appropriate amount.

Pearson's Accounts Payable

A significant amount of Pearson's working capital came from its trade accounts payable. Although accounts payable at the end of 2011 were $38,585, payables varied over time and might be double this amount at another point in the year. Pearson obtained from various dealers such supplies as expansion valves, copper tubing, sheet metal, electrical wire, and electrical conduit. Some suppliers offered a discount for cash (2/10, net 30), but Bob felt that establishing credit was more important than saving a few dollars by taking a cash discount. By giving up

the cash discount, the firm obtained the use of the money for 30 days. Although the Pearsons could stretch the payment dates to 45 or even 60 days before being "put on C.O.D.," they found it unpleasant to delay payment more than 45 days because suppliers would begin calling and applying pressure for payment.

Their major suppliers (Carrier, General Electric, and York) used different terms of payment. Some large products could be obtained from Carrier on an arrangement known as "floor planning," meaning that the manufacturer would ship the products without requiring immediate payment. The Pearsons made payment only when the product was sold. If still unsold after 90 days, the product had to be returned or paid for. (It was shipped back on a company truck, so no expense was incurred in returning unsold items.) On items that were not floor-planned but were purchased from Carrier, Pearson paid the net amount by the 10th of the month or was charged 18 percent interest on late payments.

Shipments from General Electric required payment at the bank soon after receipt of the products. If cash was not available at the time, further borrowing from the bank became necessary. Purchases from York required net payment without discount within 30 days. However, if payment was not made within 30 days, interest at 18 percent per annum was added.

Can Good Profits Become Better?

Although Pearson Air Conditioning & Service had earned a good profit in 2011, the Pearsons wondered whether they were realizing the *greatest possible* profit. The slowdown in the construction industry during 2011 was currently affecting their business. They wanted to be sure they were meeting the challenging times as prudently as possible.

Questions

1. Evaluate the overall performance and financial structure of Pearson Air Conditioning & Service.

2. What are the strengths and weaknesses in this firm's management of accounts receivable and inventory?

3. Should the firm reduce or expand the amount of its bank borrowing?

4. Evaluate Pearson's management of accounts payable.

5. Calculate Pearson's cash conversion period. Interpret your computation.

6. How could Pearson Air Conditioning & Service improve its working capital situation?

Source: Personal communication with Scott Pearson, president, Pearson Construction and Pearson Air Conditioning & Service, July 2012.

Jack's Restaurant
Intellectual Property Rights

Jack, a successful restaurant owner whose upscale establishment offers signature dishes, is selling his business to two of his employees—Sophia, his sous chef, and Hal, the maître d'. Jack's Place is a trendy neighborhood restaurant and bar that has a loyal customer base built from a frozen food line created by Jack and Sophia over the years from the restaurant's fresh menu.

Sophia and Hal are eager to purchase the restaurant and operate it under the same name, featuring the same dishes, frozen food line, and level of service that Jack's Place customers have come to expect. Sophia is a long-time employee who helped develop some of the signature dishes that made Jack's Place a popular destination in the neighborhood. A favorite dish is her Scaloppine al Marsala, which is based on a Sicilian family recipe.

As contract negotiations begin, Jack tells Sophia and Hal that he wishes to retain the intellectual property rights to the frozen food items as he enters into retirement. While he has no plans to open another restaurant, Jack believes that at some point he may want to market those dishes during his retirement for some residual income. Therefore, he suggests that a confidentiality agreement be drawn before the sale is final.

Sophia and Hal, who wish to continue operating Jack's Place under its existing business plan, feel that if Jack keeps the rights to the frozen food items the future success of the restaurant could be compromised. If Jack's Place can't offer the same food items that have enabled the business to succeed in years past, then the restaurant could lose its customer base. And if Jack would use the recipes—including Sophia's Scaloppine al Marsala—to open another restaurant, then Jack's Place would surely fail.

Ten years ago, when Sophia began working for Jack, the restaurant didn't offer the frozen food line. Over the years, she worked closely with Jack to develop the dishes, offering her own blends of spices and herbs. Therefore, she believes that she shares some intellectual property rights to the recipes. Jack, however, contends that Sophia

doesn't have any rights because, as an employer, he paid her to help develop that product line. The recipes, Jack says, are his trade secrets.

While Jack insists that he isn't going to open another restaurant, Sophia and Hal believe they need protection if they agree to let Jack retain the rights to the recipes. On the advice of his brother-in-law, who is a lawyer, Hal suggests that a noncompete agreement be drawn up to protect the new buyers against competition from their former employer. The agreement would prohibit Jack from opening a restaurant within a 10-mile radius for five years. Should Jack default on the agreement, then Hal and Sophia would have grounds for legal action.

Jack contends that signing a noncompete agreement would be foolish on his part, because he doesn't know what the next five years will bring. Sophia and Hal believe it would be equally crazy on their part to buy the restaurant without its frozen food line and allow Jack to have the signature dishes and possibly to compete against them.

The seller and buyers are at an impasse. The deal is in jeopardy unless an amicable agreement is reached.

View the video and answer the questions that follow.

Questions

1. Do Sophia and Hal have valid grounds for asking Jack to sign a noncompete agreement?

2. Assume Jack signs the noncompete agreement. Two years later, he opens a restaurant five miles away. If Hal then sues for breach of the noncompete, what arguments might Jack raise?

3. Are Hal and Sophia's demands reasonable? Do you think the recipes constitute trade secrets?

4. What compromise might be met that would be legal, ethical, and fair? Can you think of a business solution that would help Jack, Hal, and Sophia resolve their differences?

Source: Based on Business Law Digital Video Library, Real World Legal series, video #77.
Written by Tim Blackwell, Freelance Reporter. © 2004–2010, Cengage Learning.

Index

Business Plan
January 2013

BlueAvocado CONFIDENTIAL

Source: BlueAvocado, Co. Reprinted with permission.

Table of Contents

1.0 BLUEAVOCADO OVERVIEW

A women-led C-corporation headquartered in Austin, Texas, BlueAvocado's vision is to inspire consumers to reduce their ecological footprint with eco-chic products for life and home. Tapping the $10B sustainable living segment, BlueAvocado's product portfolio includes reusable shopping kits, lunch kits, washable Ziploc replacements, recycling bins, eco-travel, and eco-beauty items. In 2011 (name not provided), a multi-million dollar brand, author, and celebrity, joined the company as an investor and lead designer to tap the 18–25 millennial segment. Currently all BlueAvocado–branded products are made with certified 50%–100% post-consumer PET water bottle fabric from REPREVE® and an impact label on each product showing the waste avoided or bottles upcycled, and its carbon footprint. In April 2012, the company launched its technology service with a green rewards iPhone application with Whole Foods and the Whole Planet Foundation, rewarding shoppers who make daily green actions with coupons that can be used or donated to mirco-enterpreneurs. The app received a *Wired* magazine award for one of the best green apps for 2012. BlueAvocado has a distribution partnership with 100-year old distributor (name not provided), who has secured placement in more than 5,000 flagship retail outlets including: The Container Store, Whole Foods, BedBath & Beyond, Meijer, JCPenney, Target, and Safeway. BlueAvocado has been featured in major media outlets including *People, RealSimple, InStyle, CNN* and more. To capitalize on the growth opportunity, BlueAvocado is raising $3–4M in equity capital to hire key sales and marketing executives, build inventory, launch national marketing programs, create a Made-in-the-USA line and expand its green rewards technology ecosystem.

2.0 THE COMPANY

2.1 Sustainability Vision

BlueAvocado Co™ (the "Company") is a women-led, C-corporation located in Austin, Texas. It is not only *what* BlueAvocado makes that counts, but *how we operate* that sets us apart as a leading sustainable brand and business. The company's vision outlines our triple-bottom line goals that include the economic, social and environmental impact metrics. We measure ourselves against these goals quarterly, and share our results with our key stakeholders. Underpinning this vision is a "One Planet" stakeholder-driven business model that aligns all of our key stakeholders around the vision that we must cherish and preserve the finite resources of our planet. In addition, our mission—"Do good. Get it done." reminds our team members of the job we have to do every day. Our corporate values reinforce a culture aligned to create joy and impact.

BlueAvocado endorses CERES principles, a ten-point environmental code of conduct that reinforces a company's commitment to environmental awareness, stewardship and accountability. Four key codes of the CERES principles that underscore many of our decisions include: protection of the biosphere, reducing use of natural resources, reducing the disposal of wastes, and inspiring energy conservation. To measure and share its environmental and economic performance, BlueAvocado publishes an annual sustainability report, following the international standards set by the Global Reporting Initiative (GRI). As a privately-held company, this is a unique and significant initiative, underscoring the commitment to a triple-bottom-line.

> **BlueAvocado Vision & Metrics**
> - Deliver a strong ROI for shareholders
> - Create an impact that makes a ripple—where the acts of one affect the lives of many.
> - Empower millions of people to reduce their carbon footprint— because they can
> - Take a stand for the planet and leave it billions of pounds lighter in CO_2 emissions
> - Invest in the dreams and journeys of other women entrepreneurs

For BlueAvocado, sustainability is a platform for innovation. From product development to marketing, BlueAvocado has sought to reduce our environmental impact and make a ripple. Our product development roadmap is guided by consumer behavior and how millions are greening their lives. Working with leading market research firm BBMG, we work to stay on the cutting edge of green trends, while seeking the input of our BlueAvocado fans and retail customers. In addition to creating products that reduce our impact, BlueAvocado has created a supply chain to back-up its green products. The company forged a partnership with (name not provided), using their (name not provided)™ recycled polyester fabric, made from recycled bottles and waste yarn. (Name not provided) offers a level of certification at the fiber level that ensures the percentage of recycled content. In addition, BlueAvocado partnered with (name not provided) to audit its own energy use throughout its supply chain. In addition, BlueAvocado conducted its own audit of its manufacturer to ensure the company's was meeting environmental, health, safety and labor standards.

BlueAvocado takes this vision of behavior change to the consumer, providing a carbon footprint label (a nutrition label for the planet) on every product, reminding the shopper of the plastic bags and carbon avoided with each trip, and annualized over the course of a year. As part of its mission-driven marketing campaign,

BlueAvocado created the Billion Bag Pledge, inviting 1 million to pledge to avoid 1 billion plastic bags. To inspire participation in the Billion Bag Pledge, BlueAvocado created "Schlumpy," an 8-foot ball covered in 1,000 plastic bags (the number an average family uses in a year) to be its mascot. As a tangible symbol for environmental problems too big to ignore, Schlumpy has "rolled" around the country, from Los Angeles to New York, music festivals to rallies and races, raising awareness about the damaging environmental effects of plastic bags and inviting Americans to kick their habit of more than 100 billion plastic bags each year, as a first step on a journey to awareness and understanding about what living a greener life means. At the end of 2009, BlueAvocado had gathered the support of thousands pledging to avoid 1.4 million plastic bags, was a social media celebrity and had been featured on CNN at the National Mall for Earth Day.

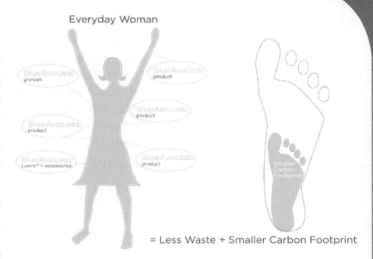

Everyday Woman

= Less Waste + Smaller Carbon Footprint

BlueAvocado founding management team members—Amy George, Paige Davis, and Melissa Nathan—are committed to and steeped in the field of sustainability. In addition, they have tapped the expertise of management team members, leading sustainability consultants, investors, and Board Members who have played key leadership roles in product development, organizational development and green sourcing with leading companies like Whole Foods, Helen of Troy, MPower Labs, Levi's and Patagonia. As a company, BlueAvocado has tapped the expertise of market leaders, to create a fresh green brand that resonates with the needs of a new generation of consumers, and whose mission is *sincere*, and the opportunity for potential environmental impact—*significant*.

2.2 Key Differentiators

1. Green Business Model from Inception

   - Offers retailers confidence in their backing of a green brand and potential partners an authentic, traceable and transparent commitment to sustainability
   - Recycled materials used on product, packaging and in promotional materials; processes to reduce waste
   - Carbon footprint label on every product, audited by Green Mountain Energy, shows the customer the impact they make—plastic bags reduced and CO_2 avoided, every time they shop
   - Stakeholder Model
   - Invites supply chain partners to green processes and practices through education and opportunity
   - Follows CERES Principles (see "Company" Section 8.2)
   - Follows the BSR Sustainable Consumption model which works to close the loop on the supply chain, and reduce resource consumption throughout the process (see below)

2. Retail in Mass Distribution Channels

- Placement in mass retail outlets, breaking through the niche green retail segments, BlueAvocado is securing shelf space and creating success in 9 key retail channels with a focus on mass retailers: Grocery, Mass, Department Store, Home, Catalog, Online Retailer, Direct TV, BA.com.

- Distribution by (name not provided), 100-year old distributor with access to most home retailers today as a result of the success of their launch of the Keurig single-serve coffee maker, which has made retailers millions of dollars.

3. Key Strategic Partnerships

- BlueAvocado forged a partnership with (name not provided), a manufacturer of textiles based in North Carolina. The company offers a unique recycled polyester fabric made from recycled plastic bottles and yarn that is certified using proprietary thumb printing technology. The company has forged a partnership with BlueAvocado, underwriting media and public relations initiatives, partnering on sales efforts with key national accounts (i.e., Target), and investing in private label merchandise powered by BlueAvocado.

- (Name not provided), the longest serving green power provider in the U.S. BlueAvocado partnered with (name not provided) to create a first of its kind "carbon label," which is a CO_2 emissions footprint for the production and factory shipment. In addition, (name not provided) worked with BlueAvocado to offset 100% of its CO_2 emissions associated with producing and shipping their bags. With this purchase, Blue Avocado helped to avoid over 30 metric tons of CO_2, a harmful greenhouse gas that contributes to global warming. This has the same environmental impact as: driving a car over 75,000 miles, planting over 4,000 trees annually and recycling over 27,000 pounds of newspaper.

- (Name not provided) is a celebrity partner and designer at BlueAvocado. This partnership provides tremendous brand awareness, market validation, and access to design talent that helps create better products for the fashionable consumer. (Name not provided) participation in our business has also drawn the attention of other top designers, who are eager to design green products that tap our supply chain and green vision.

- Collegiate Licensing Company—The Collegiate Licensing Company (CLC) is the nation's leading collegiate trademark licensing and marketing company, assisting collegiate institutions in protecting, managing and developing their brands. Founded in 1981, CLC is the oldest and largest collegiate licensing agency in the nation and currently represents nearly 200 colleges, universities, bowl games, athletic conferences, The Heisman Trophy, and the NCAA (including the Men's and Women's Final Four, the College World Series, and all NCAA Championships). In 2009, BlueAvocado's reusable shopping system (including all 6 items) was approved as reusable shopping tote option. CLC's mission is to select only high-quality brands. This provides competitive advantage and differentiation to our retailers.

4. Commitment to Shifting Consumer Behavior

- Design, positioning and services to increase use of system and educate consumers about their environmental impact, including a carbon label that describes the company and products carbon footprint.

- Use of packaging to help remember your bag as targeted communications to empower customers to remember their bags
- Implementation of technology services

5. Technology Service that underscores role as the consumer brand of the future

- Provides tighter relationship with our customer, rewarding them for green steps on their journey
- Provides weekly insights to our customers behavior which fuels product development, marketing, and potential for the greening of America
- Platform to inspire retailers to understand their shoppers' green needs and provide products that cater to that lifestyle and customer
- Technology service that allows for incremental retailer service revenue, daily visibility with the retailer customer, and puts us in the hands of thousands daily

3.0 WORLDWIDE SUSTAINABILITY MARKET OPPORTUNITY

3.1 The Economic Market

In the May issue of *Harvard Business Review*, sustainability was identified as a "megatrend" of our time, like the information technology generation, sustainability would define the next 60 years. The companies that would capitalize on this opportunity as market "Winners" would be those companies that transformed their business, not just through risk mitigation, but investing in innovation of their products and business model to deliver significant environmental impact. BlueAvocado is in a unique position to catapult its sincere commitment to sustainability and become a market "winner" and leader in the category, creating a platform for growth for the next 30+ years.

The U.S. market for green products that nurture a healthy, sustainable lifestyle (often referred to as LOHAS) is estimated at a $208 billion market in the U.S., and is fast-growing annually (Lohas.org). Globally it is estimated at $600 billion. According to a National Geographic Society/GlobeScan survey of 17,000 people in 17 countries, environmentally friendly behavior among consumers in 10 out of 17 countries has increased over the past year, with consumers in Brazil, India, and China scoring the highest. In addition, GlobeScan's analysis reveals that "consumers are sending a message that they want 'less talk and more action' from business (and government), or at least action before talk."

According to the Natural Marketing Institute, the LOHAS market can be classified into the following segments with the estimated market opportunity in the U.S. alone:

- **Natural Lifestyles ($10.3B U.S. Market)** (Apparel and accessories, indoor & outdoor furnishings, organic cleaning supplies, compact fluorescent lights, social change philanthropy)
- **Personal Health ($117.41B U.S. Market)** (Natural organic products, nutritional products dietary health supplements, integrative health care)
- **Alternative Energy ($700B U.S. Market)** (Renewable energy, carbon credits/off-sets)
- **Alternative Transportation ($20B U.S. Market)** (Hybrid vehicles, biodiesel fuel, car sharing programs)
- **Eco Tourism ($42B U.S. Market)** (Eco-tourism travel and adventure travel)

3.2 The Reusable Tote Category

BlueAvocado's mission has been to design lifestyle products that make it easy to "do good and get it done" targeting the $10B (U.S.) natural lifestyles market segment. BlueAvocado introduced its first product—the reusable shopping kit intentionally. Market data and advocacy groups often cited "buying a reusable bag" as an "easy first step" on the journey for consumers going green. The company estimates the U.S. reusable bag market, at $1.9 billion. Growing regulatory pressure and retailer support for "bring your own bags" to provide alternatives to the plastic bags, is fueling growth in the category. In 2008, Swedish Furniture Company IKEA and organic grocery Whole Foods market banished plastic bags. China and Australia have banned plastic bags and numerous cities around the world have joined them. Earlier this year Wal-Mart Stores Inc., the world's largest grocery and retail chain, pledged to cut its plastic shopping bag waste by 33 percent—or 9 billion bags a year—by 2013 and began a bag-free trial in California, eliminating plastic bags at three stores. Target Corp. in April handed out 1.5 million reusable tote bags in honor of Earth Day. In addition, Target's 5-cent rebate program for every time a shopper uses their own bags instead of a new plastic one is shifting behavior in America. In August 2010, Mexico City banned plastic bags.

In August 2010, California considered statewide legislation (Bill AB 1998) that would eliminate the distribution of 19 billion plastic bags in California, making them the first state in the U.S. to ban plastic bags. While the bill did not pass it set standards for manufacturers in the reusable bag industry, focusing on the following key attributes:

- Durability = Defined as a bag that must last 100 uses, to be classified as truly reusable and environmentally better than the disposable plastic bag alternative
- Washability = Must be able to be washed or wiped clean to remove or eliminate harmful bacteria
- % Post-consumer waste used in material = While the legislation did not require a certain amount, it set the standard for some % of post-consumer waste to be used in the manufacture of the product, providing transparency to allow the consumer to decide

BlueAvocado bags meet or exceed the California standard for durability, washability, and % of post-consumer waste. While California did not succeed, cities are adopting the legislation at the local level and retailers are studying options to leapfrog the marketplace and comply with these standards. As of September, more than 30 cities including LA (the largest city to date) and the state of Hawaii has banned or taxed plastic bags.

Appendix A BlueAvocado Business Plan

3.3 The "Conscious Consumer"

According to market research studies in the U.S., the target "conscious consumers" possess the following key traits:

- Busy women (35–45) working hard inside and out of the home, with an average of 2 children
- Controlling discretionary spending for the household
- Focusing on convenience, style and value
- Makes an average of 94 trips to the grocery store annually and spend 2 hours a week shopping
- Naturally wants to do the right thing, aligning purchasing decisions with social values

The company expanded its market to include millennials age 18–25 years of age, who will represent the #1 segment of consumer spending by 2015 and 87% of whom expect businesses and brands to act and offer green. BlueAvocado's unique focus on women customers makes the case for tapping this growing marketplace.

Market Opportunity: $10B Sustainable Living Products
Growing Faster Than Other Consumer Goods Sectors

More Women Buy Green	Reduce & Reuse	Millennials Inspired by Green	Convenience + Price Key

Likely to Buy Green? 45% Women 36% Men 70M Women	Top Ways to Reduce Footprint 28%= Reduce 17% = Reuse	18-34 yr olds are 2X inspired by green vs. GenerationX	40% buy green if readily available for modest price premium

Sources: Cohn & Wolfe Sustainable Brands Report – April 2012, BBMG Conscious Consumer

Confidential © 2012 BlueAvocado Co.

3.4 The Socially Responsible Investor

The exponential growth of Socially Responsible Investing (SRI) over the past 20 years is the best evidence that investors and the market will reward companies that make positive contributions to society. Between 1995 and 2007, total dollars under professional management in SRI grew from $639 billion to $2.71 trillion (www.sri.org), outpacing the overall market. SRI investments may include enterprises with good employer-employee relations, strong environmental practices, products that are safe and useful, and operations that respect human rights around the world. Community investing, investing in businesses, organizations and individuals overlooked by traditional lenders, is the fastest growing area of SRI. Over the past decade, community investing has grown over 540 percent, from $4 billion to $25.8 billion in assets. The bottom line is that more and more investors adopt and use SRI strategies not only because such investments allow a focus beyond the bottom line, but also because returns are comparable to those of more conventional investments.

3.5 The Environmental Opportunity

REUSABLE BAGS

In June 2009, the United Nations called on every country to ban plastic bags since there was no justification, and they were killing marine life. Plastic bags are a significant environmental problem, the primary component of urban litter pollution and marine litter pollution worldwide. Single-use plastic bags are light, aerodynamic and are littered at a high rate. Once littered, plastic bags travel through the environment, ultimately ending up in the ocean where they join giant "garbage patches" of plastic litter circulating in ocean vortices. In the North Pacific Gyre North of Hawaii, for example, plastic litter originating from California and elsewhere in the North Pacific Rim, ends up in the vortex. In February, scientists discovered another giant "garbage patch" in the Atlantic. In the U.S., Oprah has featured the "garbage patch" island on Earth Day issue for the past two years, challenging consumers to stop using plastic bags. As a result, consumers are more aware of the degradation of our oceans, and the urgency to invite personal and global change. In the U.S., we consume more than 100 billion plastic bags each year.

SUSTAINABLE CONSUMPTION

With population growth, increasing per capita consumption, and tremendous technological capacity leading to ever greater levels of production and consumption, we have begun to reach planetary limits, threatening the health and function of ecological systems that support all activity on Earth. Consider these facts: [i]

- Marine biodiversity loss is increasingly impairing the ocean's capacity to provide food, maintain water quality, and recover from disturbances.
- More than 386,000 square miles (1 million square kilometers) of forest were lost around the world between 2000 and 2005, representing a 3.1 percent loss of total forest as estimated from 2000.
- In 60 percent of European cities with more than 100,000 people, groundwater is being used at a faster rate than it can be replenished.
- By recent estimates, our global footprint now exceeds the world's capacity to regenerate by about 30 percent, and if our current demands continue, by 2030 we will need the equivalent of two planets to maintain our lifestyles.

As a result, new consumer products companies have to be faced with a new paradigm. Business for Social Responsibility (BSR) has the most holistic view of a "closed-loop" business model designed

TOP TEN MARINE DEBRIS ITEMS

RANK	DEBRIS ITEM	NUMBER OF DEBRIS ITEMS	PERCENTAGE OF TOTAL DEBRIS ITEMS
1	CIGARETTES/CIGARETTE FILTERS	2,189,252	21%
2	BAGS (PLASTIC)	1,126,774	11%
3	FOOD WRAPPERS/CONTAINERS	943,233	9%
4	CAPS, LIDS	912,246	9%
5	BEVERAGE BOTTLES (PLASTIC)	883,737	9%
6	CUPS, PLATES, FORKS, KNIVES, SPOONS	512,517	5%
7	BEVERAGE BOTTLES (GLASS)	459,531	4%
8	BEVERAGE CANS	457,631	4%
9	STRAWS, STIRRERS	412,940	4%
10	BAGS (PAPER)	331,476	3%
	TOP TEN TOTAL DEBRIS ITEMS	8,229,337	80%
	TOTAL DEBRIS ITEMS WORLDWIDE	10,239,538	100%

SOURCE: OCEAN CONSERVANCY/INTERNATIONAL COASTAL CLEANUP 2009

to support sustainability consumption (see below). The BSR model offers a framework for action in three key areas:

- **Product Design:** Enable sustainability from the start with design that delivers value without taxing natural resources—or people—in the process.
- **Consumer Engagement and Behavior:** Influence sustainable consumer choices and behavior through actionable information.
- **End-of-Use:** Use closed loop models that extend the productive life of materials and energy, and avoid waste.

3.6 Retailers' Focus on Sustainability

Sustainability initiatives for retailers are divided into two views: what the consumer sees (i.e., products), and the initiatives the retailer embraces to increase impact and reduce waste (i.e., energy conservation, green buildings, community activism, labor policies). Publicly traded retailers are under pressure by shareholder groups to enact environmental and social initiatives and disclose environmental and social information through Sustainability Reports. These communication tools have spawned new strategies and initiatives but are largely reactionary and focused on risk mitigation and cost reduction. As one of the largest retailers in the world, Walmart's Sustainability initiatives are elevating the topic of sustainability and forcing action among retailers around the world. In less than a decade, Walmart has migrated from the status of underlord among environmentalists, to being one of the most talked-about/innovative companies at sustainability conferences. While one could argue the initiatives are designed to reduce costs in the supply chain, and not drive product or business innovation, no one can deny the impact. Since 2009, Walmart has launched Supplier Sustainability Assessments to 100,000 suppliers to track environmental footprint and resource use. In 2010, Walmart announced the Sustainability Index designed to rate the sustainability of products and companies, and ultimately share the rating with customers. In 2011, Walmart partnered with Patagonia via the Sustainable Apparel Consortium to create an Index for apparel manufacturers to follow. Despite growing awareness around the importance of sustainability, the retail segment is lagging other industry segments in their sustainability leadership.

Newsweek conducts the only comprehensive study of companies "GREEN RANKINGS" across industries that focus on the 500 largest companies in the U.S. and around the world. The rankings do not assess the "customer experience" (i.e., products), but they do assesses the companies' environmental footprint (including greenhouse-gas emissions and water use); management (including environmental policies, programs, and initiatives); and disclosure (including company reporting and involvement in transparency initiatives). In their 2011 survey, only 8 retailers were in the top 100 companies nationwide. The top 5 by ranking are heralded as Office Depot—#1, Staples—#2, Best Buy—#3, Walmart—#4, and Kohl's—#5. BlueAvocado analyzes the sustainability profile of each retailer, targeting those with a sustainability mission and with stated objectives to increase the number of green products.

While the grocery channel has pursued organic and all-natural product growth, the mass retail channel has not pursued the introduction of "non-food" sustainable products. However, evidence suggests the consumer and the marketplace is ripe for green products. This has been the fasted growing segment at the Natural Products Expo (ExpoWest) in recent years, doubling or tripling in number of vendors and far outpacing the food industry for growth. In addition to Walmart, three other retailers have a corporate goal to increase the number of green products and greener companies on their shelves: Target, Kohl's and Safeway. All of these initiatives have been launched in the last 6–12 months. Each retailer has a different method to vet these products to verify green claims (as an example Target has a green claim team). However, the charter is clear that mass retailers want to inspire their customers with more sustainable products, but this is a new field for many mass retailers.

4.0 PRODUCT OVERVIEW

4.1 At the "Pit" of the BlueAvocado

At the "pit," or center, of BlueAvocado's Brand and Product Innovation lies a simple core philosophy: We make it EASY for our target customer to Do Good and Get It Done™. The Company founders and employees hold true to the belief that change is about being mindful, not militant—and about finding some joy in the process. The Company's brand and product innovation is driven by its commitment to using the following questions as our roadmap for all that we do. When answered in the affirmative, the results are products and processes built not only to last—but built to make a difference:

1. **ENVIRONMENT:** Are our products creating solutions that allow people to reduce their impact on the environment?
2. **INNOVATION:** Are we going the distance to make our products unique—providing greater functionality to make it EASY to be green?
3. **INSPIRATION:** Do our products inspire customers to make change in a way that is joyful?

SUSTAINABLE LIVING
made simple and delightful.

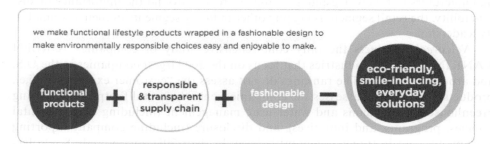

we make functional lifestyle products wrapped in a fashionable design to make environmentally responsible choices easy and enjoyable to make.

functional products + responsible & transparent supply chain + fashionable design = eco-friendly, smile-inducing, everyday solutions

4.2 Brand Overview & Channel Stratification

As a company, BlueAvocado's brand stands for certified, eco-friendly, smile inducing everyday solutions you can trust. We want our brand to be one customers and retailers can turn to for greener and more innovative options. We work to stratify our brand in market with a "good, better, best" strategy. This evolves to meet the changes and opportunities in the marketplace.

Good Channel: $9.99 & Under Eco-collection—Primarily Grocery & Drug Channel

- Brand: BlueAvocado Eco-collection
- Retailer-specific Brand: BlueAvocado for Target, BlueAvocado for Whole Foods

Better Channel: Home, Department Stores, Specialty Grocery, Direct TV, Catalog

- BlueAvocado
- XO(eco) by BlueAvocado

Best Channel: Specialty Retail

- BlueAvocado Made in the USA (in development)
- BlueAvocado 100 – 100% Post-consumer

4.3 Category Overview and Growth

BlueAvocado continues to look at category expansion in three ways: Can we green our customers lifestyle in this area or offer green options? Does the retailer see growth in this area? Is there a core need not being addressed in our customers lives? In addition, we evaluate if there is incremental growth tangential to the categories we are currently in within a traditional "buyer footprint," and incremental product development expansion based on manufacturing strength (i.e., eco-cosmetic bags). For many retailers, BlueAvocado is offering a first-to-market "Eco-Collection," helping them bolster their green offerings, while addressing growing market segments. The company continues to study trends in consumer behavior and mass retail in the growth in green categories and look to offer innovation that matches with the company's product development strength. Three new categories identified for incremental growth this year are recycling storage bins, back-to-class and lightweight travel.

Food-on-the-go category is a fast growing segment. There are two segments of growth in lunch: adults (primarily women) that are carrying their lunch to work and kid's back-to-school lunch accessories. Adult consumers are eating healthier and looking for ways to reduce costs from their budget. Retailers from Bed Bath & Beyond to TJMaxx to Belk have introduced "lunch" as new categories of expansion in the last 12 months and realized tremendous growth. The fashionable alternatives are the categories that are experiencing the fastest growth, versus traditional "cooler" options. BlueAvocado has been instrumental partnering with retailers to pioneer this category, from (name not provided) to (name not provided), offering both the first lunch option and the only "eco-option" for many of the retailers.

- Washable Food Storage: The second segment of growth is the light weight food storage. The primary goal is to eliminate the Ziploc for disposable solutions and reserve it for heavy-duty applications, thus reducing packaging waste in lunches, diaper bags, and for everyday storage. As highlighted in a recent New York Times article, "The Plastic Sandwich Bag Flunks" there is tremendous pressure to move away from disposable items in the traditional lunch bag (i.e., Ziplocs, throw-away drinks) to environmentally friendly back-to-school products that reduce waste. Retailers like The Container Store are seeing significant growth in the category. Certain schools in the United States and entire provinces in Canada support "boomerang lunch" programs where everything that goes to school must come back with the child. These trends are driving options that are washable, lightweight, and durable. BlueAvocado leverages its strength to offer great innovation, and in many cases the only eco-option made from recycled materials for consumers on the retail shelf.

- Reusable shopping category is seeing a resurgence from its peak in 2008 and 2009, driven by growing city and state bans and regulatory requirements to ensure durability, washability and recycled fiber certification. Grocery continues to be the destination for these products, but mass retailers are looking to add "market totes" into their assortment. In addition to grocery, drug and convenience store retailers are seeking to meet the regulatory requirements, we anticipate an upgrade for many retailers. BlueAvocado is working to offer greener lower-price point solutions, and marry these with our technology options.

- Recycling Segment: Recycling is often a "first-step" for many consumers, who want to adopt a greener lifestyle. Americans have doubled their waste in the last 5 years. However, they are recycling 40% more than they were 5 years ago. While many cities offer "free" curbside recycling bins, there is inconsistency in the offerings nationwide. In addition, there are single-stream waste feeds and waste streams that need to be sorted. Retailers are seeing a demand in this category. BlueAvocado is offering recycling/storage bins for home, school, or office that allow consumers to have more fashionable options, while offering staging/collecting receptacles that can be dumped into municipal bins.

- Eco-Cosmetic/Travel: There are two trends that are driving growth in this category: regulations at airports that charge for luggage thus demanding more lightweight/carry-on options and the demand from retailers to offer "eco-friendly" alternatives.

Sustainable products for home and life are at their infancy for many mass retailers. BlueAvocado wants to be the destination brand for eco-products for mass retailers. The company will evaluate expansion into other home and garden products in 2013 but looks for pilot support for retailers to justify the investment and expansion.

4.4 Competitive Overview

BlueAvocado's goal is to be the greenest home brand available in mass retail at the right price. The company has successfully gained a beach head in mass channels from big-box to grocery and department stores, while maintaining its market capture in specialty channels. Many of BlueAvocado's competitors are strong only in grocery but have not crossed over to leaders like BedBath & Beyond or Bloomingdale's. In addition, the company offers a range of prices and products in the good, better, best strategies allowing the company to invite value and luxury consumers to participate in greening their lives.

BlueAvocado also analyzes the competition at the individual product category, feature/function, and retailer level to ensure we understand our value differentiators. Below is a quick summary of what makes BlueAvocado great.

4.5 Proprietary Position

BlueAvocado has invested in an intellectual property portfolio to include brand, trademarks, and patentable designs and innovations. The company has a utility patent application filed for the "shopping bagsystem" focusing on the attributes and interchangeable features of the shopping system.

- Registered brand marks: BlueAvocado®, nuBLU®, XO(eco)®, gro-pak® shopping system
- URLs: blueavocado.com, xoeco.com, schlumpy.com

- Copyright: Carbon label
- Patent filed: Shopping Bag System

We have identified a number of additional IP investment opportunities for 2013 to reinforce our market position:

- Brandmarks: Green rewards app (TBD), Clever Bag name (TBD)
- Copyright: Key BlueAvocado custom prints
- Patents: (re)zips, technology reward, green point exchange, clever bag
- Design Patent: 1–2 unique silhouettes

5.0 TECHNOLOGY SERVICES OVERVIEW

5.7 Launch Timeline

BlueAvocado will leverage its technology pilot and customer relationship with Whole Foods to create a 2.0 framework. The company plans to hire a business leader and a technology team to create the universal framework for a national green rewards loyalty program. The company expects initial phase of development to be around $500K; this may be offset by investment from Whole Foods and its supplier partners. If the team recruitment occurs in November, the beta will launch in February/March with Whole Foods with a full debut on Earth Day (April 2013). The company will also recruit additional customers of different sizes to be part of the full-scale launch in Fall 2013. By Fall 2013, the company will have recruited sales and customer service personnel to market, recruit and manage additional customer requirements.

6.0 SUPPLY CHAIN

6.1 Description of Supply Chain

Our goal is to minimize the complexity of the supply chain by sourcing materials, printing and manufacturing in one location. After receiving cost proposals from three factories—Taiwan, Indiana, and China, we elected the low cost provider in China to meet our margin objectives. We identified a manufacturing facility in China, as a result of an in-depth search for the best quality facility and ultimately the one that allowed us to produce the most competitive product. As a company, we are committed to maintain a highly transparent supply chain and have obtained factory audits on all factories as well as personally visiting the factories throughout the year.

BlueAvocado is currently working with (name not provided) as its manufacturing partner who manages factory

SUPPLY CHAIN

MILL

(sources the Repreve recycled polyester yarn) (blends with virgin polyester yarn)

(weaves fabric)

(dyes fabric, prints patterns with special tooling)

BA CUSTOM DESIGNS

(BA designs custom patterns)

FACTORY

(holds fabric, packaging, raw goods)

(cut-n-sew patterns)

(Quality Control)

(Assemble / Packaging)

relationships with J.B. Bags, our mill, printer and UNIFI Repreve China. (Name not provided) has vast experience bringing products to major retailers in the U.S. including Costco, Target, Meijer, and Sam's Club as well as specialty retailers including REI and BassPro. Specific services included in the partnership include costing, program planning, quality control, factory audit and compliance.

Since 2010, BlueAvocado has partnered with (name not provided), a 100-year old supplier of end-to-end supply chain solutions. (Name not provided) has over 1 million in warehouse space, the latest state of the art J.D. Edwards system, and EDI set-up via Commerce Hub with most retailers in America today. The company operates three main warehouses that provide geographic distribution throughout the U.S., including: Redlands, CA, Chicago, IL, and Knoxville, TN. (Name not provided) will expand into Canada in 2013, and BlueAvocado will leverage this expansion to tap this new market. Given their efficiencies, (name not provided) is able to ship to store and offer drop ship programs that make market expansion possible.

American Shipping is currently BlueAvocado's shipping supplier from China to U.S. They offer LCL, 20 foot container and 40 foot container services. In addition, they offer a warehouse for Point-of-Entry programs. The company evaluated transferring business to a new supplier to take advantage of a better pricing structure and reduce gross margin.

6.2 Production Timeline

The BlueAvocado supply chain, estimated time and key vendors are as follows:

- Materials Sourcing–Find & Print Fabric (30–60 days)
- Manufacturing (Cut-n-Sew) in China (4–12 weeks)
- Transferred product to port of export is Ningbo, China (2–3 days)
- American Shipping Company will handle the shipping via container between China to the U.S. warehouse (14–17 days on water).
- Port of import is LAX (1–4 days on to achieve import clearance)
- American Shipping will ship on to Planet E by rail in Dallas (1–2 weeks days)
- PlanetE offers full warehousing, shipping, and electronic data interchange (EDI) for online sales support

6.3 Factory Audit

BlueAvocado's primary factory has undergone a number of audits, initiated with BlueAvocado's own audit in 2009 to evaluate quality, environmental and social indices. The factory initially scored 87% from Bureau Veritas, and the company implemented a corrective action plan (CAP) and continues to monitor. In addition, BlueAvocado has worked with JCP, Tupperware and Princess House to conduct a number of audits in the last 3 years, providing a similar score of 83%, and identifying areas of improvement related to quality.

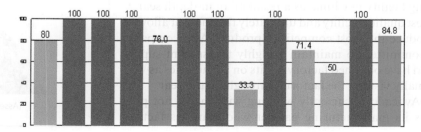

Appendix A BlueAvocado Business Plan

6.4 Material Sourcing

BlueAvocado recognizes price is the greatest driving factor for market adoption. However, we have explored using materials that were sustainable (i.e., bamboo, corn resin) or reused (i.e., recycled plastic, nylon, etc.) in all cases. BlueAvocado elected recycled polyester textile for the primary material of the premium product. In cases where hardware (grommets, zippers) are used, we have requested recycled materials. The final is made of approximately 50% recycled material (list of materials per product is above next to each product picture).

BlueAvocado recently partnered with a leader in U.S. textiles—(name not provided), which produces (name not provided) recycled polyester yarns. (Name not provided) yarns are traceable, using both post-consumer (PET bottles) and post-industrial fiber wasted. The yarns are made in Asia. Each production run is audited by (name not provide) using a thumbprinting technology in order to carry the (name not provided) label, guaranteeing the produces are made of certified recycled materials. (Name not provided) and BlueAvocado are partnering on several sales and marketing initiatives to forge the relationship and expand both brands amongst consumer media audiences.

BlueAvocado is partnering with (name not provided) to take advantage of its Textile Takeback program and recycling center, allowing customers to upcycle existing polyester products or old BlueAvocado products. This innovative program allows the company to "close-the-loop" on its supply chain. The company continues to evaluate how to increase the percentage of (name not provided) in its product line. In 2012, it introduced its first 100% (name not provided) product, via the green mesh produce bags. Additional sustainable fabrics will also be explored to provide greater depth to our core product offerings.

6.5 Made-in-the-USA Initiative

BlueAvocado is evaluating partners with whom to launch the BlueAvocado Made-in-the-USA product line, offering the company to create job opportunities, reduce international risk, and provide product stratification. Retailers like JCPenney, Target, and Whole Foods have articulated an interest in Made-in-the-USA products. The company is evaluating 4–6 plants in Q4, with a goal to launch this product line in March 2012 at the International Home & Housewares show.

7.0 SALES & MARKETING

7.1 Sales Team

BlueAvocado is the green brand leader for home retailers today, capturing shelf space and online space in 11 key retail channels with the market leader in the category. BlueAvocado partners with (name not provided) who serves as the national distributor and sales team to top-tier retailers. Their national sales team of 8 key account managers, each with an average of 30 years of experience works in the field with BlueAvocado to secure placement on the shelve of national retailers. (Name not provided) is a 100-year old company, and the #1 distributor for home retailers today with brands like Keurig, Sensio, Starbucks, and Procter and Gamble in their portfolio they have access to the executive leadership for home, general merchandise, food storage, electrics, and executive leadership in the buying chain. With pre-established vendor set-up via EDI with most retailers, (Name not provided) leadership has enabled BlueAvocado to grow from their beachhead of 1,000 stores to 5,000 stores in 18 months.

Building on this strong position and the growth potential, BlueAvocado will build out its sales team to support (name not provided) and target key segments not part of (name not provided) core focus area. Key hires include Director of Sales & Marketing, National Account Manager, and Sales Coordinator. BlueAvocado will forge additional distribution opportunities to support growth in the Canadian market, personal beauty care, specialty grocery, and specialty boutiques.

7.2 2013 Sales Goals

Key sales goals for 2013 include:

- Ensuring success in key (name not provided) accounts that will drive majority of revenue growth for 2013 (JCP, Target, Safeway, BedBath & Beyond, Amazon.com)
- Secure adoption at new key accounts–COSTCO, Office Max, Fred Meyer/Kroger, 7-Eleven
- Secure pilot program at Kohl's with the (name not provided) collection
- Secure support for the (name not provided) xo(eco) collection in market with the 2013 line
- Continued growth of Princess House from $800K to $1.2M
- Leveraging success in department stores with premium line (Celebrity, Made in the USA)
- Leverage national mobile app partnership with Whole Foods to build placement in front-end, grocery and Whole Body
- Forge distribution opportunities and partnerships in key areas:
  - Canada
  - Beauty
  - Specialty grocery
  - Specialty boutiques
- Working with BA-Digital team to secure pilots and adoption of the "green games app"

7.3 Sales Channels & Key Accounts

BlueAvocado is currently available in 10 different channels—all providing access to the multi-bag, female shopper:

- Mass Retailers
- Niche Housewares/Retail
- Online Retailers
- Catalog
- Specialty/Natural Grocery Stores
- Mass Grocery Stores
- Direct TV to Consumer
- Grocery Stores
- Company Website (blueavocado.com)
- Discounters
- Private label partners

Appendix A BlueAvocado Business Plan

Mass Retailers: BlueAvocado will continue to target national retailers, as a key part of their strategy and differentiation. The company is in stock at more than 900 BedBath&Beyond stores, and will be on Target and JCPenney shelves (900–2100 stores) by March 2013. Additional retailers in this segment which are forecasted for 2013 include OfficeMax, COSTCO, and 7-eleven. For 2013, most of the growth is forecasted in this channel.

Niche/Specialty Retailers: BlueAvocado has been adopted by The Container Store who is a category leader for home organization and is on the shelf at the first Greenhouse, eco-products focused home improvement superstore.

Boutiques & Ace Hardware: Upon launch, BA established strong portfolio of small boutiques. With limited sales resources, the company not focused on this segment for the last few years. In 2013, BA will recruit sales reps in target regional areas, with a focus in cities that have plastic bag bans that help drive adoption. Key regions include Northeast (NY), Northwest (Seattle, Portland), and California.

Online Retailers: The company is currently a vendor on Staples.com, Amazon.com, Cooking.com, Drugstore.com, and Reuseit.com. The company will look continue to grow this channel, leveraging (name not provided)'s established vendor set-up via Commerce Hub with most major retailer.com's. Potential strategic partners include: (names not provided). In addition, BlueAvocado is in discussions with UNFI's Honest Green back-end portal providing online distribution and marketing of "green products" to specialty grocers nationwide.

Catalog: Catalogs offer BlueAvocado the opportunity to explain the story of our brand, our impact and our product impact. In addition, the primary catalog shopper is a direct profile of the BA customer. The company is currently distributed via Amway Global catalog. The company is in conversations with QCI Direct and Miles Kimball. Additional targets include Garnet Hill, Viva Terra, Acacia, Serena & Lily, Chefs Catalog, Napa Style, Travelsmith, Magellan's, Territory Ahead, Sundance, Soft Surroundings, Sahalie, Herringtons, Cambria Cove, Femail Creations, Northstyle, Restoration Hardware-Baby & Child, Pottery Barn.

Company Website: To generate online sales via the company's website, the company will continue to invest in public relations, online advertising, strategic partnerships with green and fashion ad networks, niche newsletter sponsorship, and targeted Search Engine Optimization campaigns.

Grocery & Natural Food Stores: The company has secured adoption in grocery store chains taking a leadership role in the plastic bag alternatives and seeking fashionable and green alternatives for their food-on-the-go category. BlueAvocado has key accounts with Whole Foods in 5 regions with the front-end-buying team. Given this is the most competitive environment, the company has not focused on this segment. However, the company has had early success Sprouts, GreenLife Grocery, Draeger's, Metropolitan Market and Bristol Farms and will seek distribution partners in 2013 that tap and can support the sales demands of this channel. Leveraging the national partnership with Whole Planet Foundation and the mobile green rewards application, the company will push to seek additional store penetration within Whole Foods of its everyday, and is looking at bringing the Made in the USA line into this segment.

Direct to Consumer: BlueAvocado has offered its products for sale on television to the home shopper community. The direct-to-shopper environment offers unique opportunity to describe the brand, how it works, and its functionality and fashionability "live." BlueAvocado will look to tap HSN and QVC, leveraging unique function, value and celebrity-endorsed offerings.

Discount Retailers: Discount retailers offer BA an effective channel to reduce slow-moving inventory and obsolete items and patterns. The company forged partnerships with key retailers in 2009 including (name not provided) (800 stores), (name not provided) (220 stores), (name not provided), (name not provided)—Canada (80 stores), (name not provided) and (website not provided).com. The company will selectively partner with these retailers so as not to compromise the value created in the main channels.

Private Label: BlueAvocado does partner with companies and brands to offer co-branded or private label programs. Forecasted at between 5 and 10 percent of 2013 revenue, BA will build on its partnership with (name not provided) to help them provide soft goods for food-on-the-go and travel to their Latina market in Texas and California. The company will continue to look for opportunities to partner with (name not provided) to bring greener products to worldwide customers. In addition, the company partners with brands like (names not provided) to create private label and co-branded pieces that support marketing strategies.

7.4 Marketing Mix

BlueAvocado is one of the top green brands in our categories and has been featured in national home and fashion magazines—from *RealSimple* and *Better Housekeeping* to *Glamour* and *People*. From inception, the company invested in creating an authentic green brand and ensuring we used our packaging and product labels to share our vision and our impact at the product-level. BlueAvocado has accomplished a tremendous market momentum, despite having invested little in marketing relative to sales (since inception—average 5–7%). The company plans to invest 10–15% of its revenue on marketing initiatives in 2013 to support its 3x growth goals. The company will build on its marketing team led by Chief Inspiration Officer Paige Davis and supported by a Marketing Assistant. The company plans to hire a Marketing Manager with green consumer brand experience to build and implement a plan. With market validation of the digital technology service, the company will also hire a Marketing Manager to manage the digital services implementation.

Key marketing efforts to date include:

1. Building customer demand and brand awareness via public relations efforts in key national media, blogs, and trades,
2. Supporting tradeshows to drive retailer demand and awareness,
3. Supporting retailer-specific marketing initiatives (i.e., Amazon Vine) to drive sell-through within the store environment,
4. Developing product-level brand strategy to reinforce vision and create a coherent story,
5. Creating sales tools, catalogs and collateral to support the sales team,
6. Creating packaging and point-of-sales tools in the retail environment to drive sell through, and
7. Maintaining and driving sales on the company's online store (blueavocado .com) which provide strong gross margin.

BlueAvocado will make a significant investment in marketing this year to support the company's 3x growth and environmental goals. 2013 new marketing objectives include:

- Driving sell-through inside stores (physical and virtual)
- Leveraging (name not provided)'s role as a BlueAvocado ambassador and spokesperson to drive awareness and placement of BlueAvocado and XO(eco)
- Launch the Ross Bennett men's collection

- Increasing blueavocado.com sales potential with a store re-launch, online advertising plan
- Securing placement of BlueAvocado's premium line in department stores (XO(eco), Made in the USA)
- Re-launching BlueAvocado into the specialty grocery segment and green boutiques
- Refine brand strategy with celebrity to articulate a "American Designer" series
- Partnering with the BlueAvocado digital team to brand, secure adoption, and use of BlueAvocado's "green game" platform
- Leveraging the Make Change Not Waste Whole Foods customer base, and insights to inform 2014 product development and invite them to be BlueAvocado fans
- Launching BlueAvocado into the Canadian market
- Tapping the BlueAvocado/clever bag launch

BlueAvocado's marketing mix includes:

BRAND DEVELOPMENT

As a consumer brand, BlueAvocado puts an emphasis on its brand, sub-brand and overall brand management strategies. In 2012, the company developed a sub-brand XO(eco) to reflect the collection designed by (name not provided). The company will refresh its brand strategy to include additional celebrities in a universal framework. In addition, BlueAvocado will continue to evaluate its brand strategy to ensure it is reinforcing its differentiators, environmental impact, and channel strategy.

PUBLIC RELATIONS

Since inception, BlueAvocado has partnered with leading PR firms to secure placement in key media trades and gift guides. (Name not provided) PR firm (pro-bono) and (name not provided) publicist at UTA are currently partnering with BlueAvocado to secure placement, leveraging (name not provided)'s role as designer and investor. (Name not provided) has been featured on the cover of Glamour featuring her BlueAvocado XO (eco) line (May 2012), cover of ALLURE (November 2012) and cover of Lucky Magazine (March 2012). In addition, we have secured placement in dozens of print and online magazines, and TV including *People, InStyle, MTV.com, ecoturre, Good Afternoon America*, and *Larry King Live*. BlueAvocado sponsors key events with giveaway items both locally via partnerships with like-minded customers like Sustainable Food Center fundraisers and nationally with events like the Lucky FABB fashion blogger event, featuring LC as the keynote. The company plans to hire a PR firm who specializes in green consumer brands to manage and expand opportunities on a more consistent basis, and employing innovative initiatives to both inspire environmental action and realize brand exposure in traditional and online media.

SOCIAL MEDIA

BlueAvocado continues to use social media platforms to build community, create brand awareness, and drive retailer success (partners and online store).
Here are ways we engage with our community.

- BlueAvocado has a customer database of more than 5,000 online customers. With the launch of the Whole Planet iPhone app, BlueAvocado has access to a larger community of 5,000 customers (12% detailed customer information). In addition, BlueAvocado is tapping (name not provided)'s audience to build its Facebook page and Twitter fans. To date, BlueAvocado has 2,586 Facebook fans, and 1,983 Twitter followers.

- BlueAvocado leverages existing social networking applications to build brand loyalty and word of mouth (i.e., Facebook, MySpace, YouTube, twitter, Pinterest), BlueAvocado seeks feedback from customers, educates and provides deals via these mediums. BlueAvocado provides giveaways and promotions via partnership offers to run on various social networks and SEO campaigns. Examples of key successful strategic partnerships include: Ecorazzi Twitter Thursday: Through a 3 hour giveaway period with popular celebrity green blog Ecorazzi, BlueAvocado nearly doubled its Twitter base and gained additional customers and Facebook followers who are now loyal customers. Currently BlueAvocado engages monthly (and bi-weekly) via (website not provided).com's 500,000 Facebook fans and 2 million Twitter fans.

- Community

- Deal of the Day Promotions: Through ships with group couponing sites like (name not provided) and (name not provided), we were able to extend our brand into new geographic regions and gain additional viral buzz to customers who are now part of the BlueAvocado database. BlueAvocado proved to be a top performer on both of these programs exceeding number of coupons purchased and google alert postings.

- The company launched BlueAvocado's Billion Bag Pledge campaign to create awareness for "problems too big to ignore" led by Schumply, the 8 foot plastic bag ball. The point of the campaign was to secure pledges of people willing to kick their plastic bag habit. Our goal was to get 1 million pledges and avoid 1 billion plastic bags. The online viral video was so successful, stores and schools wanted him to come for openings, Earth Day and education. Schlumpy has traveled from Austin to Tennessee to California to Washington DC, creating a platform for more environmental change. There is an ability to use him as an educational tool in schools around the world, it has the ability to create education, while increasing brand awareness in a positive way. In BlueAvocado's estimate, the Billion Bag Pledge campaign with grassroots and viral media efforts has reached 6x the individuals of its traditional marketing efforts. In addition, Schlumpy has the added benefit of inspiring adults through the power of kids. The company will evaluate the potential of this brand asset in its 2013 planning.

- The company has evaluated partnering with (name not provided) to create a video series that creates environmental awareness leveraging (name not provided)'s passion for oceans and sense of humor. The goal would be to drive online success at Amazon.com and other online retailers, while raising money for Ocean Recovery Alliance and Oceana to support reclamation and preservation of oceans.

ADVERTISING

BlueAvocado has not historically invested in traditional advertising, with the exception of spot placement related to local events or tradeshows. The company has invested in online merchandising initiatives via Amazon.com that "boost" the company's brand placement in the category, including A+ pages, brand store, and the VINE. The company will evaluate 2013 investment in traditional, mobile and online advertising initiatives that drive sell through at key retail partners to include but not limited to:

- Support of (name not provided) partnership providing visibility nationwide inside Whole Foods stores annually, with concentration in February

- Print ads in National fashion magazines driving shoppers to adopt (name not provided)'s line

- Online Google advertising with targeted fashion and green online properties
- Catalog listing in national "green" pages
- Co-operative sponsorships that target core audience in key regions
- Mobile advertising/coupons directed at key retailers

7.5 Market & Competitive Research

BlueAvocado believes it is important to understand trends of consumers, retailers and competitors. The company takes steps to conducts and invests in primary research, and takes advantage of secondary research. The company was a pioneer sponsor of BBM G's The Collective, providing a platform for BlueAvocado to conduct primary research among green consumers. In addition, BlueAvocado taps BBMG and Cohn & Wolfe's conscious consumer and green brand reports. The company surveys its customers online, via Facebook, and via focus groups to both evaluate consumer lifestyle trends and receptivity for new products and prints. In addition, BlueAvocado continually researches industry reports and trends available through trade magazines and associations.

7.6 Pricing Strategy

BlueAvocado's pricing model is designed to achieve a target of 35–55% gross margin, and 10–25% net margin. Margins for retailers typically range between 40–60%. Margins for grocery stores on private label/co-brands range between 30–50%. Our pricing model accommodates these needs while still providing solid profit margin to BlueAvocado. We do offer FOB China and POE programs and work with our retailers on volume purchases.

8.0 FINANCIAL OVERVIEW

8.1 2012 Financial Performance

BlueAvocado has consistently achieved strong top-line growth and is forecasting profitability for the year 2012. In 2011 the company achieved $885K in revenue and in 2012 the company more than doubled with revenues of approximately $2M. The company grew its retail stores from 1000 in 2011 to more than 3,500 stores by the end of 2012. The Princess House private label direct-import program produced strong growth for 2012, comprising 45% of revenue for 2012, but impacted overall company gross margin. For 2013 Princess House will remain an important customer with an improved gross margin and will represent less than 10% of sales thereby further improving company-wide gross margin. Below are summaries of 2012 financial results in addition to customer level detail for 2013 sales that are already committed so are now in various stages of discussion on delivery terms.

8.2 2013 Cash Cycles

BlueAvocado has focused on securing strong terms with key suppliers to improve cash cycles, a key to success for a growing business. Key terms are indicated below:

- **Manufacturer**—Net 45 Days from shipment (flexibility to extend to Net 60 on larger orders); 30% down payment on private label and large scale programs ($100K wholesale value). BlueAvocado is not responsible for working goods inventory, packaging or raw material fibers unless dormant for 6 months. The broker and factory take full responsibility for these investments.

- **Fulfillment Facility**—(Name not provided) will bill BlueAvocado Net 30 for shipments, with the cost between 12–15% of sale.
- **Accounts Receivables**—BlueAvocado has worked to negotiate favorable terms from key suppliers. As they seek additional margin or fast timelines, BlueAvocado has negotiated more favorable than normal terms. Average A/R is Net 30, they range from Net 15 to Net 60. (Name not provided) will manage invoicing and collection of most BlueAvocado receivables, maintaining the Net 30–40 day average. The company will continue to manage direct the few accounts that it handles, like private label programs (Princess House) and Whole Foods.

BlueAvocado does not have a current working capital bank line so has financed inventory and receivables with equity capital and some purchase order-backed loans from shareholders. With further growth in inventory and receivables in 2013, coupled with marketing, webstore and technology platform enhancements, the company will seek the placement of additional equity in 2013 which will enable it to bring on another bank partner to facilitate working capital needs.

8.3 2013 Forecast

For 2013 the company is forecasting more than a 3x growth to achieve over $8M in revenue and $800K in operating profitability. A majority of this revenue is based on established accounts: Whole Foods, JCP, Target, BedBath&Beyond, Safeway, plus 3 growth accounts whose commitments are expected soon: OfficeMax, COSTCO, and 7-Eleven. The company has not included material revenue from the technology business unit in this forecast. However, the company is working to ensure there is revenue from customers to fuel its technology initiatives. The company expects to be available in more than 8,000 stores and Canada by the end of 2013.

8.4 Five-Year Forecast

Key to BlueAvocado's growth will be the adoption of our brand and products by major retailers, expansion of the product line, and success of major retail partners (including Target, JCP, Bed Bath Beyond). BlueAvocado has the opportunity to deliver significant top-line growth and significant incremental EBITDA by 2015.

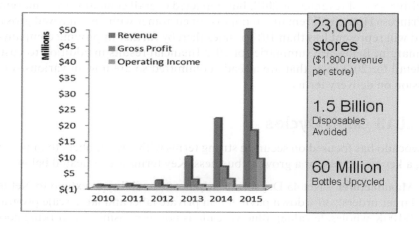

Appendix A BlueAvocado Business Plan

9.0 TEAM

The BlueAvocado management team is committed to the company's growth, and playing key roles in the evolution. The company continually looks for ways to bring experts into the company as management team members, consultants and advisors to help it grow.

9.1 Management Team

BlueAvocado's team includes 7 full-time employees in Austin, accounting and legal consultants, and more than 12 manufacturing rep team members nationwide. Blue Avocado's management team represents more than 100 years of expertise in general management, retail, strategy, marketing/sales, product development e-commerce and sustainability. The management team is strengthened by their mutual respect, commitment to teamwork, and passion for success. As needed, BlueAvocado also contracts with additional consultants to manage product design from pattern development, to color forecasting to sample development and merchandising. BlueAvocado plans to recruit team members in 2013 to facilitate our growth.

Amy George: Co-Founder and CEO, Amy George brings 19 years of experience in business, marketing and sustainability to the role of "Chief Ozone Officer." In her role at BlueAvocado, George has created a business model built on sustainable practices and processes, managed a national sales team to achieve 300% growth, and cultivated relationships with more than 700 retailers and key accounts including Whole Foods, Nieman Marcus, Sur La Table, The Container Store, Drugstore.com and Cooking.com. In addition, George has managed the investor and Advisory Board for BlueAvocado, recruiting individuals from PeopleAdmin, Whole Foods, Dell, The Container Store, MPower Labs and Patagonia to invest in the start-up venture. George also helped pioneer unique sustainability initiatives and was responsible for the company's first 2010 sustainability report entitled—One Planet™. Prior to joining BlueAvocado, George helped privately-held Pavilion Technologies to market software that allowed manufacturing giants Chevron-Phillips, Cemex and Nestle to increase productivity, reduce their energy use (and carbon footprint), and track real-time emissions. The company achieved 30% year over year growth and was acquired in October 2007 by Rockwell Automation. George has pioneered new initiatives with a number of non-profit and social responsible organizations including Calvert Social Investment Foundation, Sustainable Food Center, The CSR Group, People's Community Clinic and PeopleFund. As a Board member with the Sustainable Food Center, George was instrumental in founding the Austin Farmer's Market, recently ranked one of the top 10 markets in the country. Nominated for Austin Under 40 and Barbara B. Jordan award for community service, George holds an MBA from The University of Texas at Austin and a Bachelor of Arts in English from The University of Florida. George lives in Austin, Texas and is a reusable bag shopper for her husband and two boys.

Paige Davis: As Co-Founder and "Chief Inspiration Officer" of BlueAvocado, Paige Davis brings her strategic perspective and background as a sustainability consultant and social media entrepreneur. Through collaborative partnerships, Paige assures the BlueAvocado business model inspires engagement marketing and sustainability awareness into all aspects of the business and communication efforts. Paige is responsible for the creation and management of the BlueAvocado website and social media strategy including the success of the popular social media "Billion Bag Pledge" campaign featured nationally through MSNBC, *USA Today*, CNN. Within 1.5 years in market Paige created and managed the PR and marketing campaigns for all product launches and sustainability initiatives securing placement in the top national media publications including *Shape*, *InStyle*, *RealSimple*, *Healthy*, *Better Homes and Gardens*, and multiple online communities. In addition, Paige managed all online sales and strategic partnerships with key online retailers including Amazon.com, Cooking.com, and Soap.com as well as being responsible for the private label sales channel resulting in key relationships with Microsoft, O.N.E Water and Hello Kitty. Paige also forged key strategic partnerships with partners including Green Mountain Energy and Kiva.org. Prior to joining BlueAvocado, Paige worked in the Bay Area for Organic Inc. working with clients including Wells Fargo, Chrysler, and Barnes and Noble to develop first generation web commerce capabilities. Paige then consulted independently with top consumer brands conducting market research, analyzing industry trends, and developing strategic recommendations within the emerging online environment. Following her passion for integrative health and sustainable living, she founded Pilates360, a wellness and Pilates studio based in Austin, Texas while simultaneously working with several start-ups in the green category, advising on social media, branding and strategic partnership development. Paige received her B.A. in Journalism and Environmental Science from Indiana University at Bloomington and was recently selected as a U.S. Fellow for the British American Project's Sustainability Conference.

Felix Chavez: As Vice President of Operations, Felix Chavez brings more than 20 years of experience in retail sales, operations, inventory management and production to his role as VP, Operations. Formerly he served as VP of Sales Operations with Helen of Troy, an El Paso, Texas headquartered developer, manufacturer and distributor of personal care and housewares and consumer products. Under his leadership in various management positions, Felix contributed to the successful growth of the company's sales from $36 million in 1984 to over $500 million in 2005. Under his leadership at BlueAvocado, he oversees profitably and COGS reduction, management of fulfillment facility, production, and sales operations to meet market demands, and improve customer service through on time delivery, production quality and compliance.

Melissa Nathan: Product Visionary and Co-Founder, Melissa Nathan brings to BlueAvocado, over 19 years of business, marketing and public relations experience to BlueAvocado's management team. As Chief Innovation Officer, Melissa led the creation and execution of BlueAvocado's award-winning brand and product portfolio, achieving recognition from industry insiders including International Housewares Design, New York Gift Show, Fast Company, REAL SIMPLE, Sustainable Life Media and Austin ADDY's. In the company's first two years in market, Nathan oversaw the launch of over 200 products, including the gro-pak™—the country's first reusable grocery shopping system. From inception, Melissa served as brand steward, overseeing the design criteria and philosophy that made BlueAvocado's messaging and product portfolio inviting, engaging and impactful. Melissa's additional responsibilities include managing the company's overseas manufacturing relationships as well as its domestic "direct to consumer" channel including the launch at Home Shopping Network where she represented BlueAvocado in its on-air debut. Prior to BlueAvocado, Melissa worked in a number of sectors including international business, politics, government, finance and not-for-profit. Melissa's business acumen is derived in part from her time spent on Wall Street at Solomon Smith Barney in the cosmetics and household products industry as well as from her experience helping to launch the international division for Warnaco, Inc., a Fortune 500 company. Melissa's background in international and public relations includes time spent as Chief of Protocol for the United States Embassy in Mexico City. She began her public relations career as a press advance person in presidential politics and spent a brief period working in the Scheduling and Advance office at the White House. During her time in Austin, Nathan worked as the first Development Director for the Austin Film Society, helping to launch the first Texas Film Hall of Fame. Most recently, she spent three years as the Director of Marketing and Development for LifeWorks helping to raise and sustain an $8 million operating budget. Melissa received her BA from Duke University and holds an MBA from The University of Texas at Austin. Nathan currently resides in Austin, Texas and is wife and proud mother of two.

9.2 Board of Directors

The BlueAvocado Board of Directors is composed of the following five individuals:

Amy George – Chair of the Board, Founder

Jack Long – Investor Representative

Lee Valkenaar – Investor (Retail Representative)

Paige Davis – Founder

Melissa Nathan – Founder

9.3 Advisory Board

The BlueAvocado Strategic Advisory Board is a network of experts who have agreed to give BlueAvocado Co. meaningful help on a regular basis in many different areas, including retail sales, sustainable design/sourcing, manufacturing, law, organizational development, and product development. Their abilities, experience, and knowledge were selected for how they complement BlueAvocado's needs or the organization as a whole.

10.0 CAPITAL PLAN

10.1 Exit Potential

BlueAvocado believes the demand for green consumer products will continue to grow. The company imagines exit potential in as little as 2 to 4 years, with attainment of key revenue growth and profitability. Financial market research demonstrates that transactions in the sustainability sector have exceeded those of the overall market.

11.0 SUMMARY

BlueAvocado has a vision of making life better for women and the planet. Consumers are concerned about climate change, industrial pollution, food safety and natural resource depletion. BlueAvocado is creating a vision, where products can help reduce our impact on the planet, empower more women entrepreneurs, and deliver economic value for its shareholders.

For more information, please contact:

Amy George
amy.george@blueavocado.com